Social
Scientific
Studies
of Religion

Social
Scientific
Studies
of Religion: A Bibliography

by
Morris I. Berkowitz
and
J. Edmund Johnson

University of Pittsburgh Press

Acknowledgment

The acknowledgment of all the aid and assistance that has made the appearance of this volume possible is almost as enormous a task as the preparation of the volume itself. We owe a primary debt to the libraries of the University of Pittsburgh, Duquesne University, and Pittsburgh Theological Seminary, and to the Carnegie Library of Pittsburgh, the Jewish Theological Seminary Library of New York City, and the Library of Congress, Washington, D. C. Our trips to the latter two libraries were financed by the Pittsburgh Pastoral Institute, whose members also offered wise and useful suggestions.

Richard L. Park, Dean, Division of the Social Sciences, University of Pittsburgh, made substantial funds available for the typing of the final manuscript; and Professor Jiri Nehnevajsa, Chairman of the Department of Sociology, provided financial aid and encouragement in the form of time released from other activities.

Mrs. Charles Whitman typed the entire final draft, working with exceptional dedication on difficult material. Mrs. Barbara Jameson and Mr. Pui-Leung Lee jointly assembled the author index, and Miss Devra Lee Davis compiled and typed the list of journals and abbreviations with the aid of Miss Karen Creighton. Mrs. Paul Enscoe typed much of the rough materials.

The authors discovered early that this was not a scholarly book as much as it was a mass of clerical and stenographic problems: Miss Josephine Stagno solved them all. Towards the end she devoted several months of full-time activity to unravelling the mess which the authors had made, and she became the *ex officio* director of the project. We were delighted to work with her. She was aided in these tasks by the senior author's wife Janice, who supplemented her household activities with proofreading, typing, and other efforts.

M. I. B.
J. E. J.

Table of Contents

ix

Introduction

The beginning of any bibliographical effort is perilous due to the necessity of making judgments concerning the organization of the materials to be presented. Assuming that the compilers are reasonably competent in the gathering of items, the utility of the bibliography will depend largely on its organization. Technically it is simple to reject the first three organizational alternatives that come to mind: (1) list the items in the order in which they are gathered, (2) list the items alphabetically, and (3) list the items alphabetically after first dividing them into articles and books. Bibliographies ordered in these ways are of little use unless they are short enough to be scanned in their entirety and the titles lucid enough to allow the interested reader to select relevant items. It is not at all clear, however, that the last two kinds of organization (although neater and more traditional) are more useful than the completely unassorted list, except that they allow the user of the bibliography to look for the names of authors already known to him.

When dealing with more sophisticated classification schemes, the design selected will make the bibliography more useful to some people and correspondingly less useful to others. In developing a particular categorical scheme there is an implicit assumption that certain theoretically or empirically justifiable categories are more valuable than others. This represents, if not a theoretical position, at least a "stance" toward the content of the field. Those users of the bibliography who share that stance will find fault with the work only insofar as there are errors of omission and commission; those who reject the stance as theoretically untenable will find it difficult to make use of the bibliography since the category scheme will not have cognitive meaning for them. The bibliography will represent to them a useful collection of items, the utility of which is interfered with by a scheme of seemingly obtuse categories.

Thus, cautious bibliographers may tend to avoid substantively meaningful categories in order to orient their work towards the widest possible audience. This strategy, however, produces bibliographies with category titles that sound very much like the chapter titles found in an introductory textbook. These bibliographies offer no help in the ordering of significant new data about subject matters which have not been extensively researched, and therefore they do not indicate where work needs to be

done. They are rapidly outdated, particularly in areas of knowledge in which the orientation is towards substantive problems rather than more fundamental theoretical concerns. (This assumes, of course, that the basic theoretical structures of the field of study change more slowly than the field's contemporary substantive organization.)

The selection of a classification scheme is especially difficult for a multidisciplinary bibliography. In the social-scientific study of religion, for example, multiple traditions are derived from each discipline which has used religion either as a classificatory or an analytic variable. For those social scientists who are concerned with problems in which a major classification is by geographical area (for example, many anthropologists), any bibliography not organized geographically immediately loses some of its usefulness. Similarly, students of a particular religion or historical period who do not find material classified by such headings will be disappointed.

The authors do not feel that any of these countless specific classifications serve a useful purpose for the majority of analytically oriented social scientists. We feel that people interested in the functions of the ministry in western culture (for example) have a great deal to learn from the functions of the religious practitioner in many faiths and in many geographical areas. To restrict the literature search to a specific religious tradition or a certain geographical area is to ignore the potential theoretical fruitfulness implicit in comparing the role of the shaman and the role of the magician with the role of the Presbyterian minister. This bibliography is organized in a fashion which will juxtapose studies of all three of these religious functionaries as well, of course, as others.

Assumptions about Religion

This bibliography begins with the fundamental assumption that religion is a universal phenomenon and that, as such, religions perform similar functions, if not universally, in at least a sufficient number of cultures to make cross-cultural comparisons meaningful. Similarly, the authors make a second assumption, that cultures are institutionally more or less integrated and therefore one can study the interrelations between religion and economic institutions in any culture and compare this relationship across culture and time. We do not, however, make the assumption, as

Max Weber seems to, that religion holds the central analytic key to the understanding of culture.[1]

Our search, then, was to develop classificatory categories which stressed the fundamental wholeness of the cultural experience of man, covering as much of religious experience as social scientists can study (even if they have not), and allowing for functional cross-cultural classifications.

Procedures for Obtaining Items

This bibliography began with a systematic perusal of approximately eighty journals in the social sciences which, according to our own judgment (and that of many helpful colleagues), include the most important social science periodicals available in English, French, and German. These journals were inspected from their first date of publication through the year 1965, and every item bearing directly upon religion was annotated for classification.[2]

Our plans were soon subjected to significant modification. The great number of articles on religion which we amassed from German and French sources led us to conclude that the cost in time and effort of compiling a multilingual bibliography would not justify the return. Although the literature we reviewed is multilingual, it is derived from the same basic social science tradition, and this tradition is well represented in English.[3] We therefore decided to concentrate on English language sources. Our knowledge of the foreign sources leads us to argue that the primary result of their inclusion would be a repetition of similar types of studies, not an increase in the scope of material studied.

A major problem of this bibliography is similar to that of most multi-lingual bibliographies—the emphasis is on the work of European and American scholars. We have tried to be multicultural in our collection of items, but much valuable material from non-Western cultures is not available to us. We feel the need for Russian and Slavic sources, not to mention Japanese, Chinese and Arabic, which we do not have the linguistic competence to include. It is from scholars studying these other cultures that new issues and new perspectives are most likely to be found.[4]

[1]Although it is difficult to demonstrate in one place where Weber makes this assumption explicit, the bulk of his later work (*The Protestant Ethic and the Spirit of Capitalism, Ancient Judaism, The Religion of China*, etc.) could certainly lead one to this conclusion.

[2]Those journals which were completely covered are marked with an asterisk in the list of journals appended to this bibliography. We counted as "completely covered" journals which were available to us in slightly broken series; that is, when one or a few issues were missing from available library collections.

[3]For proof, see the ample references under 8a6.

[4]In Japan, there are over a dozen journals dealing specifically with Buddhism and Shintoism (e.g., *Bukkyogaku Kenkyu*, "Studies in Buddhism"; *Kikan Shinto Shigaku*, "Shinto History Quarterly"; *Osaki Gakuho*, "Journal of Nichiren and Buddhism Studies"; *Zengaku Kenkyu*, "Studies in Zen Buddhism"), all entirely in Japanese.

A further modification was the decision to survey only samples from the wealth of anthropological literature. Our initial survey in the *American Anthropologist* and *Anthropos* (to mention two) yielded several hundred sources which would have overwhelmed our already burgeoning categories 2 and 3 ("Descriptions of Religion" and "History of Religion"). When we examined some outstanding anthropological bibliographies we found their coverage so complete that we discarded several hundred citations from the anthropological literature, leaving only enough in the bibliography to indicate the breadth and depth of the coverage of these journals. We retained those items which stressed materials of the greatest interest to us, notably those on religious practitioners and the impact of religion on other social institutions.

Much the same rationale was used when we discovered how much social science content can be found in nominally religious journals like the *Journal of Religion, Lumen Vitae*, and the *Mennonite Quarterly Review*. We selected enough material from religious sources to show, in every section where they are relevant, the journals which traditionally contain a great many articles on the specific subject matter. Scholars may use this, at least in part, as a guide to useful journals in their fields as well as a bibliography.

We also reviewed standard bibliographic reference sources and sought to trace the reference notes from those articles which we had systematically surveyed.[5]

We searched through the various International Bibliographies compiled by the International Committee for Social Science Documentation (on Economics, Political Science, Social and Cultural Anthropology, and Sociology), *Psychological Abstracts, Sociological Abstracts, Index Medicus*, etc. We also included as many of the existent bibliographies in religion as we could find and examine. This was done for two reasons: (1) in order to make available to the users of our bibliography other, more specific source material, and (2) so that we would not duplicate previous investigations.[6]

When we had some idea of the bulk of material at hand, we decided that it had grown beyond reasonable bounds for either the writers or the potential users, and we arbitrarily decided to include no books published prior

[5]Some of the major sources we used for the initial verification of our items were the various catalogues of the New York Public Library Reference Department; the *National Union Catalogs* of the Library of Congress; the Pan American Union's *Index to Latin American Periodical Literature*; and the *Library Catalogue* of the University of London's School of Oriental and African Studies.

[6]See section 9 "Bibliographies of Religion and Encyclopedias and Dictionaries" as well as other more specific subject headings, such as: H. L. Roberts, *Foreign Affairs Bibliography: A Selected and Annotated List of Books on International Affairs, 1952–1962* in Section 4a; and Stroupe, H. S., *The Religious Press in the South Atlantic States, 1802–1865: An Annotated Bibliography with Historical Introduction*, in 4g3. Both are cross-referenced to category 9.

to 1945 and not reprinted since that date. We were aware of the great mass of reprintings in the post-war years and felt that this was a reasonable criterion. We simultaneously decided to retain journal publications from earlier dates, because many of them are extremely important and are generally unavailable except in their original form.[7]

By this time we had a good idea of the range of materials available and those publications most likely to contain a significant number of important materials. We proceeded to sample extensively many of the journals which we could not completely survey. We went to issues of journals in which we had already (through one of our earlier operations) discovered that items existed, and looked not only at those items but at issues of the journal which were bound in the same volume. When this controlled browsing proved fruitful, we proceeded to survey the other volumes of the journal, taking references which seemed central to our analytic persuasion. Our work was continually stymied by incomplete sets of journals and the usual problems of finding critical issues which were at the bindery, temporarily housed in a colleague's office, or had disappeared. We kept notes on our failures and late in 1965 took two trips, one to the Library of Congress in Washington and one to the library of the Jewish Theological Seminary in New York,[8] to complete our journal coverage.

From the beginning we had maintained the selection criterion of availability, thereby rejecting any book-length items available only in mimeographed form or which had appeared as doctoral dissertations or masters' theses.[9] Our application of the same criterion to journals resulted in the elimination of items appearing in journals not generally available to English-speaking scholars. Where there was doubt about availability we retained the references.

Our final criterion was that of completeness of the reference in question. Frequently bibliographies list journals without volume numbers, books without publishers, and both without dates. We eliminated any item whose completeness we could not verify. For journal articles we defined completeness as author, title, journal name, volume, and pages; for books, author, title, place of publication, publisher, and date.[10] At the end of our efforts, after reasonable attempts to determine the missing information, we reluctantly discarded incomplete references. The present bibliography of more than six thousand items is a distillation from over twice that number of original citations. The most painful day of our collaboration was April 15, 1966, when we reluctantly decided that we could add no more items and put aside approximately five hundred sources which we had tried but failed to verify.

This, then, is not a *complete* bibliography, but a *working-survey* bibliography of more than six thousand available, published, verified English language items, spread over more than 130 classifications.

Criteria for Classification

Every item included in the bibliography has been classified into one of the 132 classifications through the procedure of matching the content of the item with definitions of our categories. Samples of these definitions appear following this section. The major thrust of item collection had been to identify studies which related religion to other social-behavioral variables. As a result, over three-quarters of our items were easily placed in obvious categories. The other quarter, however, were categorized only with difficulty, due primarily to a difference in the orientation of the writer of the work in question from that of the compilers of the bibliography. This most frequently occurred in sources drawn from nominally religious, philosophical, and historical sources. When confronted with these items we used criteria of placement which, insofar as possible, forced classification into categories of relationship rather than categories of description of history; secondly, we attempted specifically to put items into categories 4 and 5 (Religion as Related to Other Social Institutions and Behavior, and Religon and Social Issues), in order to bring them into relevance for current research. However, we attempted not to corrupt the author's intent by these procedures and liberally cross-referenced such items.[11]

No problematic items were classified by either compiler alone. Classifications were frequently attempted independently and then discussed when differences occurred.

Many empirical studies reported so much data about so many variables that it was difficult to maintain our limit of only two cross-references and still represent each item in those places where potential users would be most likely to look for it. More significant than this problem, however, was the difficulty of overlapping, not mutually exclusive, categories. Here we faced contradictory criteria: we

[7]See for example: Goldenweiser, A. A., "Religion and Society: A Critique of Durkheim's Theory of the Origin and Nature of Totemism," in the *Journal of Philosophy, Psychology and Scientific Method* (listed in category 1), and the series of articles on the sociology of religion by H. H. Maurer in the *American Journal of Sociology* (listed in category 3a1).

[8]These trips were financed by the Pittsburgh Pastoral Institute, whose members also provided much needed advice and encouragement.

[9]We did include, however, bibliographies that contain many such theses and dissertations. See: Little, L. C., *Researches in Personality, Character and Religious Education: A Bibliography of American Doctoral Dissertations, 1885–1959.* Pittsburgh: Univ. of Pittsburgh Press, 1962, 215p.; Menges, R. J. and Dittes, J. E., *Psychological Studies of Clergymen: Abstracts of Research.* N.Y.: Thomas Nelson & Sons, 1965, 202p.; and others.

[10]Where possible we have noted the number of pages of the books. We added this information to aid the scholar in assessing the dimension of the task involved in using such works. We did not, however, make a point of searching out and recording this data.

[11]Frequently this resulted in the separation of items by the same author about the same religion or people. The author index can be used to pull together the works of one author on a specific society.

deemed it highly desirable to have sufficient categories of fine enough dimension that no one would have an overwhelming number of references but in dividing these large categories to make their size more manageable we continually faced the danger of losing discrimination between categories and subverting our own initial efforts to describe as well as list. The compromise left us with categories containing too many items in a few cases (e.g., 4a1 and 4g), and in a few other cases with categories with significant overlap of content (e.g., 4h and 5b1; 4j and 5c). In a final proofreading we re-examined classified items in each category, moved some, added many cross-references, and listed in each major category those categories to which it is most closely related. The "see also" sections frequently begin with a reference to several other total categories.

The general structure of the classification system itself follows a consistent pattern throughout the bibliography. Immediately following the main heading are the most general materials in the area. Under some of these main headings are found un-numbered subheadings indicating that the general literature can be conveniently subdivided (e.g., category 3 has an un-numbered subheading, "Precursors of Modern Religion"). The main subheading (second level of classification) then specifies a particular aspect of the main heading and reports these sources. Within this secondary breakdown often there is an additional series of categories in which even more detailed sources are listed. Finally, on a few occasions, there is an alphabetical listing within the third level of classification.

This can be illustrated as follows: Category 5 contains general items which relate religion to social issues. Categories 5a through g specify certain major issues on which there have been substantial amounts of scholarly work. For example, 5a emphasizes "Relations Between Religious Groups," and is so entitled. Directly following 5a are the most general pieces dealing with this area. Category 5a1 is even further specialized and deals only with ecumenical movements. Category 5a2 deals with "Conflict Between Religious Groups" and, since there is a great deal of literature in this area, is further subdivided into a general section (immediately following the heading of the major category) and two alphabetical divisions, "Anti-Semitism" and "Christian Divisions." These final alphabetical headings were derived empirically. Where there are enough sources (we considered six a sufficient number) a subheading was added. A numbered subheading such as 5a2 was added in those cases where approximately 12 sources were available, and a second order subheading (such as 5a) where 20 or more sources were available.[12] These empirical criteria do not apply to the primary headings, but they do explain some lack of parallelism between categories. Category 5d ("Religion and Peace and War") is not further subdivided because there were not a sufficient number of studies.

[12]There are several breaches of these numerical rules, based on decisions made when they conflicted with other desiderata.

Category 5e, on the contrary, has four subdivisions due to the amount of concern about "Religion and Missions." (One would wish that the priorities had been reversed in this case.) This also explains why "Shintoism" and "Secularism, Humanism, and Atheism" are accorded secondary classification as categories 2f and 2g, while in category 3 the very few sources on Shintoism are in the general listings under "Other Religions" (3f) and "Secularism, Humanism, and Atheism" appears as 3f4.

Category 1—Definitions of Religion

The first category of this classification deals with the relationship between religious activity and academic disciplines, as well as basic definitions of religion. Here will be found general statements of definition, followed by statements of the relationship or interaction between "Religion and Magic" (1a), "Religion and Social Work" (1g), and so on. Generally speaking this major category contains few substantive pieces, only theoretical and, even more frequently, philosophical treatises. There is one exception, and that is in category 1a, "Religion and Magic," in which there are basic definitional efforts, of course, but an occasional narrative report of the transition between the two types of belief systems is also included.

Category 1 itself is devoted to definitional efforts of the subject matter of religion. The nature of the literature is such that few monographic studies or theoretical volumes can be considered as having a basic definitional thrust; rather, the definitional efforts are secondary to the primary purposes of the work. Where this is the case, the work is listed under the classification most relevant to its subject matter. Where definition is regarded as a major effort, the work is also cross-classified here. The majority of the entries to be found in Category 1, then, are short articles, most frequently in essay form, whose burden is definitional.

Category 2—Descriptions of Religion and
Category 3—History and Development of Religion

We have generally eschewed descriptive materials except in Categories 2 and 3. In these categories we have organized the materials according to major religious groupings (Judaism, Hinduism, etc.). Included in these two categories are descriptions of specific religions in specific societies.[13] If the item in question was written after 1945, we considered it to be a contemporary description and put it into Category 2. If produced prior to 1945 or produced subsequent to that date but relating to events prior to 1945, it was put into Category 3. The two criteria operative, then, are the date of the production of the item and its content. If a description does not state that it is

[13]Attal, R., Tunisian Jewry During the Last Twenty Years. *Jew. J. Sociol.*, 2/1, 1960, p.4–15—is included under the subheading Judaism, 2b; Allo, I. E., From Sect to Denomination in English Quakerism. *Brit. J. Sociol.*, 15/3, 1964, p.207–21—is under Christianity: Protestants, 3a1, etc.

based on older materials, it is assumed contemporaneous. Had we combined these two categories, the number of entries would have been burdensome. Scholars concerned with the status of Islam in India in the recent past should search under Islam in Category 2d. There they will find: Ikram, S. M. and Embree, A. T., *Muslim Civilization in India.* N.Y.: Columbia Univ. Press, 1964, 325p. Scholars interested in how Islam in India came to its present form should look under Category 3 and will find among others: Nabi, M. N., *Development of Muslim Religious Thought in India from 1200 A.D. to 1450 A.D.* Aligarh, India: The Aligarh Muslim Univ. Press 1962, 210p.

Like all bibliographers we were faced with problems of definition which had to be resolved before classification could begin. This was an immediate difficulty in Categories 2 and 3. For example, numerous divisions from the central positions of Christianity have occurred during 2,000 years of development. Some of these can appropriately be called "sects" (such as Jehovah's Witnesses), and they are listed with the rest of the "Protestant" listings. This will be offensive to some members of religious groups (Mormons, for example, cannot be happy with classification as "Protestant"). We tried to avoid continually expanding our list of religions by dividing Christianity into three major divisions. Roman Catholics are easily identifiable and are viewed separately (2a2), as are the divisions within the Catholic tradition that have split into various national and rite-oriented churches, such as the Greek and Russian Orthodox, which is our second classification (2a3). Our third group of Christians is nominally entitled "Protestant" but includes those churches and sectarian groups which, although they do not trace their origin to the period of the Protestant Reformation, can be considered as having sprung from a central Christian tradition and are neither Orthodox nor Roman Catholics (2a1). The title "Other Religions" in Categories 2 and 3 does not refer to religions which have as their base one of the major religious movements separately listed as a sub-class of Categories 2 and 3, but rather to religions which are not normally identified with those traditions. To do otherwise would be chaotic. Within American Protestantism, for example, there exists a bewildering array of sectarian movements.[14] To try to sub-classify each of these without reference to their point of departure would be to unnecessarily confuse the issue. There are, however, confusions. How, for example, does one classify the sectarian and cultic movements described by Lanternari, which are the result of syncretistic movements?[15] Where these seem, in the judgment of the authors, to be striking new departures and the effect of the indigenous religion remains strong even after the arrival

of the missionary, we have classified them as "Other Religions" (2h and 3f).

In these two classifications our bibliography is weakest in representation of the materials drawn from anthropological field work. The extraordinary scholar George Peter Murdock is compiling data on well over 400 cultures in the World Ethnographic Atlas. His bibliographies are available, as is his analytic work on these cultures.[16] The Human Relations Area Files should also be used as a significant bibliographical (and textual) asset to anyone with interests primarily related to field materials. For us to have attempted to include the materials compiled by so many years of assiduous work would have been both futile and pretentious.[17]

We included under "Other Religions" works on "Confucianism and Taoism," although we recognize the reluctance of some scholars to count Confucianism as other than an ethical system. We are guided by the basic consideration that a body of literature exists dealing with Confucianism as if it were a religion, and scholarly prudence dictates its inclusion for this, if no other, reason.

Category 4—Religion as Related to Other Social Institutions and Behavior

In this category are studies and theoretical statements that relate aspects of religion to other social activities. Two major kinds of studies are included here: (1) those that relate a religious organization to some other institution or socially patterned behavior system and (2) those that relate how people who are religious behave in other social arenas, presumably as a function of their religious belief.

This category is poorly titled because there are subcategories that cannot be considered "institutional" in any reasonable sense. In essence, we derived the sub-categories from what is in the literature, rather than attempting to compress the literature into some predetermined theoretical mold. So, for example, it would have been theoretically more correct to have included "Religion and Child-Rearing Practices" (4c) as a subcategory of "Religion and Marriage and the Family" (4e). But the literature abounds with studies of the former as well as the latter, and it seemed good sense to separate them in order to make the utilization of this volume simpler for individuals with specialized needs. Category 4 and its subdivisions demonstrate the strength of various theoretical positions in the social sciences. "Religion and Sexual Behavior" (4i) is dominated by the contributions of psychiatrists in much the same way that the subsection "Church-State Relationships" (4a1), under "Religion and Political Behavior"

---

[14]See: Landis, B. Y. (ed.), *Yearbook of American Churches: Information on All Faiths in the U.S.A.* N.Y.: National Council of Churches of Christ in the U.S.A., 1965; Rosen, L. (ed.), *Religions in America.* N.Y.: Simon and Schuster, 1963.

[15]Lanternari, V., *The Religions of the Oppressed: A Study of Modern Messianic Cults* (Trans. L. Sergio). N.Y.: New American Library, 1965.

[16]Each issue of *Ethnology*, published at the University of Pittsburgh, contains installments on additional societies in the Ethnographic Atlas.

[17]Murdock, G. P., *Outline of World Cultures.* New Haven: Human Relations Area Files, 1958; Ibid., *Outline of South American Cultures.* New Haven: Human Relations Area Files, 1951; Ibid., *Ethnographic Bibliography of North America.* New Haven: Human Relations Area Files, 1960, and others.

(4a), is dominated by political scientists. Along with Category 5, this category contains the great majority of non-historical studies.

Category 5—Religion and Social Issues

In the early history of this bibliography, Category 5 was a series of additional subheadings under Category 4. It was separated in response to the growing awareness that many of the authors writing about the "social issues" included in this category regarded them as emotionally laden and/or as posing a great challenge to contemporary religion. There is little else than this emotional tone to justify the division between Categories 4 and 5. In separating them we have gained the advantage of keeping both categories within reasonable size dimensions, although we have undoubtedly suffered the consequences of establishing a "time-bound" category that in future years will seem less and less controversial. But any bibliography of this sort must be at least in part an interim report on the state of the field.

In the contemporary social scientific study of religion the major issues are defined by religious practitioners of the field as much as by social scientists. Notice, for example, that "Religion and Health" (5b) concerns both "Mental Illness" (5b1) and "Population Growth and Control" (5b2); the latter is a dominant concern of contemporary Catholicism. Similarly, 5c, "Religion and Civil Rights/ Human Rights," reflects the concern of the fifties and sixties with the Negro revolution and the role of religion in regard to it. We were somewhat surprised to discover that "Religion and Missions" (5e) is still a controversial subject, as is, to many writers, the role of religion in regard to problems of adolescence and old-age, "Religion and Age" (5f).

Category 6—Religion and Social Change

Category 6 reflects a continuing concern of social scientists with the relationship between religion and the process of change. There are only five subheadings within this category, and two of them represent basically different assumptions about the nature of religion. Category 6a, "Religion and the Maintenance of Social Order," contains many items which implicitly assume the correctness of the Marxian proposition that religion functions to maintain the *status quo*, and consequently social order. Contrarily, 6b, "Religion as a Change Agent," contains the writings of authors who look to religion as a source of social change and who accept the fundamental hypotheses usually related to the works of Max Weber. The third Category, 6c, includes works concerned with "Changes in Religion Itself," 6d separates from the general-change literature that literature which refers to "Messiahs and Prophets of Religion," and 6e stresses the "Effects of Social Change on the Church."

One would assume that in the years since Marx's declarations about the functions of religion much would have been done in this basic examination. Such is not the case. The number of entries in the first two subcategories of this classification are relatively few, compared with how much has been written in other areas of investigation; and even fewer of them are, even by rough criteria, empirical. This is an area apparently reserved for polemics rather than research.

Category 7—The Impact of Religious Belief on Behavior

Category 7 contains two major sections: 7a, "The Religious Leader and His Roles" and 7b, "The Parishioner." In these categories we attempted to view the two major classes of religious members in terms of the writings about them. We defined "The Religious Leader" as anyone who, during the practice of a religious, cultic, or magical ritual, either occupies a formal position distinct from that of laity, or has the responsibility for certain performances of a different order of influence or worth than the average participant. We thus included in this category magicians, shamans, ministers, rabbis, and priests. In 7a4 are included those studies of the social-psychological background of leaders, their training, and so forth. In both 7a3 and 7b3, "Beliefs Related to Religion," we included for leaders and parishioners those practices, beliefs, and values which do not fall adequately under the headings of Categories 4 and 5. When in doubt about appropriate categorization, we cross-referenced these sources to both Categories 4 and 5. The only other sub-classification which needs explanation here is 7d, "Conversion and Assimilation," in which we placed studies of behavior which relate to converted or assimilated individuals or to their backgrounds.

Category 8—Religion, Textbooks, Analytic Articles, and Readers

In this classification we are frequently dealing with products designed for a society oriented to the college student. With the exception of analytic articles, most of the listings in Section 8 are designed for the use of classroom teachers faced with teaching a course in the "psychology of/sociology of/ philosophy of/ or something else of/ religion." The number of textbooks is legion, both in the form of textbooks and collections of readings. We list some of them here not for the edification of scholars, as much as a service for scholars who are frequently teachers and who occasionally want to search for new teaching materials. Wherever possible, we have taken analytic work and classified it primarily under its subject matter of analysis, rather than in this section. This has been true of all but the broadest gauge statements, which we have felt constrained to include here rather than elsewhere. Of special interest to researchers should be 8a1, "Emphasis Analysis of Contemporary Religion," which includes methodological statements about the study of religion. Also of interest is 8a4, which contains a listing of those items which contain "Description or Review of Programs" in the study of religion.

Here we have tried to include position papers, statements by members of institutes and statements about the state of affairs in various countries relative to the study of religion. We have also included a representative number of reviews of various meetings, institutes, etc. from the journals we have sampled. These sources hopefully will acquaint the user of the bibliography with the type and contents of such gatherings.

Category 8a6 represents a belated acknowledgment of reality on the part of the compilers. We resisted a section entitled "Classics and the Commentators" as long as we could. The resistance was predicated on the completely theoretical nature of this kind of category, as well as the all too predictable differences of opinion about what represents a classic. When we were finally faced with more than a dozen discourses on Max Weber, as well as on Ernst Troeltsch, it became obvious that not to include a section with such a subheading would make it difficult for users of the bibliography to find the major works and commentaries of such men. Faced with the necessity of the category, we decided that we would include no one in it who was still living at the time of this writing. We then used the number of items of comment about the work of a particular man as a basis for inclusion in or exclusion from this category. We did not feel competent to judge who were the classic authors in disciplines of which we are not members, and we could not justify spending the time to do an opinion survey of social scientists. Still, since we as soci-

ologists found numerous sources by and on three generally recognized "experts" in three differing fields (S. Freud—psychology/psychiatry, E. Troeltsch—history of religion, and M. Weber—sociology), we placed these men in separate subcategories. Works by other well-recognized scholars (J. Wach, E. Durkheim, etc.) were, given our limiting criteria, placed in the more general 8a6 category.

Category 9—Bibliographies of Religion and Encyclopedias and Dictionaries

In this final category are included items of two basic kinds, primarily those items identifying themselves as bibliographies, encyclopedias, and dictionaries of religion; and secondarily, those works which, although having a primary listing elsewhere, also include a substantial bibliographic effort on the part of the author.[18] This category, as in the case of Category 8, represents a formal rather than an analytic category, and should be useful for those who need basic data concerning the history of religious events, the definition of terms, the biographies of religious leaders, and bibliographies relevant to specialized areas of knowledge.

[18]Since many of the reviews of literature, the longer monographs, and most of the book-length works contain rather extensive documentation, we could only begin to note a few of these sources. In addition, we have noted a few of the types of journals which periodically review the literature in their areas of special interest, as: the *American Jewish Historical Quarterly*, *Pastoral Psychology*, etc.

1. Definitions of Religion

Bernard, L. L.   The Sociological Interpretation of Religion. *J. Rel.*, 18/1, 1938, p.1–18.

Caillois, R.   *Man and the Sacred* (Trans. M. Barash). Glencoe: Free Press, 1959.

Clark, W. H.   Religion as a Response to the Search for Meaning: Its Relation to Scepticism and Creativity. *J. Soc. Psychol.*, 60, 1963, p.127–38.

Dimock, H. S.   Trends in the Redefinition of Religion. *J. Rel.*, 8, 1928, p.434–52.

Eliade, M.   *The Sacred and the Profane: The Nature of Religion.* N.Y.: Harper, 1961, 256p.

Goldenweiser, A. A.   Religion and Society: A Critique of Durkheim's Theory of the Origin and Nature of Religion.   *J. Philos. Psychol. Scientific Meth.*, 4, 1917, p.113–24.

Horton, R.   Definition of Religion, and Its Uses. *J. Roy. Anthropol. Inst.*, 90/2, 1960, p.201–26.

Huxley, J., *et al.*   Living Religions and Their Life Purpose. *Sociol. R.*, 17/4, 1925, p.255–93.

King, I.   The Evolution of Religion From the Psychological Point of View.   *Amer. J. Sociol.*, 14/4, 1909, p.433–50.

Kishimoto, H.   An Operational Definition of Religion. *Numen*, 8/3, 1961, p.236–40.

Kring, W. D.   *Religion is the Search for Meaning.* Boston: Starr King Press, 1963, 63p.

Kristensen, W. B.   *The Meaning of Religion: Lectures in the Phenomenology of Religion* (Trans. J. B. Carman).   The Hague: Martinus Nijhoff, 1960, 532p.

Lesser, A.   Superstition. *J. Philos.*, 28, 1931, p.617–28.

Leuba, J. H.   The Meaning of "Religion" and the Place of Mysticism in Religious Life. *J. Philos.*, 18, 1921, p.57–67.

Mackintosh, H. R.   *Types of Modern Theology.* London: Nisbet, 1954.

Marty, M. E.   Sects and Cults. *Ann. Amer. Acad. Polit. Soc. Sci.*, 332, 1960, p.125–34.

Morrow, E. B.   *Scientific Views of Religion.*   N.Y.: Philosophical Library, 1957, 348p.

Mukerjee, R.   Social Conception of Religion. *Sociol. Soc. Res.*, 13/6, 1929, p.517–25.

Nida, E. A.   Religion: Communication With the Supernatural. *Pract. Anthropol.*, 7/3, 1960, p.97–112.

Pettazzoni, R.   On the Attributes of God. *Numen*, 2/1–2, 1955, p.1–27.

Rank, O. and Sachs, H.   Theory of Religion (Trans. C. R. Parpie).   *Amer. Imago*, 21/1–2, 1964, p.73–84.   See also: Investigation of Myths and Legends, p.33–72.

Schmidt, P. F.   *Religious Knowledge.*   Glencoe, Illinois: Free Press of Glencoe, 1961, 147p.

Smith, J. E.   The Experiential Foundations of Religion. *J. Philos.*, 55/13, 1958, p.538–46.

Spalding, H. N.   *The Divine Universe: A Study of Religions and Religion.*   Oxford: Blackwell, 1958, 354p.

Thornman, D. J.   The Sociological Concept of Religion. *Amer. Cath. Sociol. R.*, 12/3, 1951, p.148–53.

Watt, W. M.   *Truth in Religions: A Sociological and Psychological Approach.*   Chicago: Aldine Publishing Co., 1963.

Wax, R. and Wax, M.   The Magical World View. *J. Sci. Stud. Rel.*, 1/2, 1962, p.179–88.

Wells, A. R.   Is Supernatural Belief Essential in a Definition of Religion. *J. Philos.*, 18, 1921, p.269–75.

1a. Religion and Magic

Ames, M. M. Buddha and the Dancing Goblins: A Theory of Magic and Religion. *Amer. Anthropol.*, 66, 1964, p.75–82.

Blumberg, P. Magic in the Modern World. *Sociol. Soc. Res.*, 47/2, 1963, p.147–60.

Bouisson, M. *Magic: Its Rites and History.* London: Rider, 1960, 319p.

De Vries, J. Magic and Religion. *Hist. Rel.*, 1/2, 1962, p.214–21.

Eliade, M. *Myths, Dreams and Mysteries* (Trans. P. Mairet). N. Y.: Harper, 1961.

Frazer, J. G., *et al.* Religion and Magic. In T. Parsons, *et al.* (eds.)—*Theories of Society.* N. Y.: Free Press, 1961, p.1077–161.

Gardner, G. B. *The Meaning of Witchcraft.* London: Aquarian Press, 1959, 288p.

Goode, W. J. Magic and Religion: A Continuum. *Ethnos*, 2–4, 1949.

Goody, J. Religion and Ritual: The Definitional Problem. *Brit. J. Sociol.*, 12/2, 1961, p.142–64.

Gotesky, R. The Nature of Myth and Society. *Amer. Anthropol.*, 54, 1952, p.523–31.

Hymes, D. H. and Wasserman, I. On the Nature of Myth: An Analysis of Some Recent Criticism. *Amer. Anthropol.*, 55, 1953, p.455–60.

Jevons, P. The Definition of Magic. *Sociol. R.*, 1/2, 1908, p.105–17.

Jung, C. G. *Essays on a Science of Mythology.* N.Y.: Pantheon Books, 1949.

Kapelrud, A. S. The Interrelationship Between Religion and Magic in Hittite Religion. *Numen*, 6/1, 1959, p.32–50.

Leuba, J. H. Magic and Religion. *Sociol. R.*, 2/1, 1909, p.20–35.

Lissner, I. *Man, God, and Magic.* N.Y.: Putnam's Sons, 1961, 344p.

Long, C. H. Religion and Mythology: A Critical Review of Some Recent Discussions. *Hist. Rel.*, 1, 1962, p.322–31.

Mukerjee, R. Sociology and Mysticism. *Sociol. Soc. Res.*, 15/4, 1931, p.303–10.

Rosenthal, T. and Siegel, B. J. Magic and Witchcraft: An Interpretation from Dissonance Theory. *Southw. J. Anthropol.*, 1/2, 1959, p.143–67.

Titieu, M. A Fresh Approach to the Problem of Magic and Religion. *Southw. J. Anthropol.*, 16/3, 1960, p.292–8.

Vetter, G. B. *Magic and Religion.* N.Y.: Philosophical Library, 1958, 555p.

Webster, H. *Magic: A Sociological Study.* Stanford: Stanford Univ. Press, 1948, 524p.

Woods, F. J. *Cultural Values of American Ethnic Groups.* N. Y.: Harper, 1956.

See Also: 2h6, 3, 3f, 7

Bascom, W. 8a2
Demos, R. 8a2
George, G. 8a2
Hyman, S. E. 8a2
James, E. O. 8a2
Kluckhohn, C. 8a2
Lewis, L. S. 8a2
Malinowski, B. 8a6
Monro, D. H. 8a2
Reik, T. 3b
Sebeok, T. A. 7e
Severn, W. 7a1

1b. Religion and Science

Bryson, L., *et al.* (eds.) *Perspectives on a Troubled Decade: Science, Philosophy and Religion, 1939–49.* N.Y.: Harper, 1950.

Compton, J. J. Some Contributions of the History of Science to Selfclarity in Religion. *J. Sci. Stud. Rel.*, 3/2, 1964, p.147–57.

Cooley, W. F. Can Science Speak the Decisive Word in Theology? *J. Philos.*, 10, 1913, p.296–301. See also: J. H. Leuba—A Rejoinder, p.411–4.

Coulson, C. A. *Science and Christian Belief.* Chapel Hill: Univ. of North Carolina Press, 1955, 127p.

Coulson, C. A. *Science and Religion: A Changing Relationship.* London: Cambridge Univ. Press, 1955, 35p.

DeRopp, R. S. *Science and Salvation: A Scientific Appraisal of Religion's Central Theme.* N.Y.: St. Martin's Press, 1962, 308p.

DeWolf, L. H. Religion in an Age of Science. *J. Bib. Rel.*, 16, 1948, p.201–4.

Dillenberger, J. *Protestant Thought and Natural Science.* Garden City: Doubleday, 1960.

Dinsmore, C. A. The Influence of Science on Modern Religious Thought. *Soc. Forces,* 2/2, 1924, p.239–44.

Fothergill, P. G. *Evolution and Christians.* London: Longmans, 1961, 395p.

Fuse, T. M. The Relevance of Religion in an Age of Science: A Case for Dialectical Theology. *J. Hum. Relat.,* 12/2, 1964, p.230–41.

Gregory, R. A. *Gods and Men: A Testimony of Science and Religion.* London: Stuart and Richards, 1949, 214p.

Heim, K. *Christian Faith and Natural Science* (Trans. N. H. Smith). N.Y.: Harper, 1953, 256p.

Holmer, P. L. Scientific Language and the Language of Religion. *J. Sci. Stud. Rel.,* 1/1, 1961, p.42–55. See also: H. Holcomb—Comment, p.55–60.

Holmer, P. L. *Theology and the Scientific Study of Religion.* Minneapolis: T. S. Denison, 1961.

Hornberger, T. Puritanism and Science: The Relationship Revealed in the Writings of John Cotton. *New England Quart.,* 10, 1937, p.503–15.

Hsu, F. L. K. *Religion, Science and Human Crisis.* London: Routledge & Kegan Paul, 1952.

Jeanine, M. The Catholic Sociologist and the Catholic Mind. *Amer. Cath. Sociol. R.,* 17/1, 1956, p.2–9.

Kennedy, G. (ed.) *Evolution and Religion: The Conflict Between Science and Theology in Modern America.* Boston: Heath, 1957, 114p.

Long, E. Le R. *Religious Beliefs of American Scientists.* Phila.: Westminster, 1954.

Maybury, R. H. What Has Science Done to Religion? *Numen,* 8/1, 1961, p.151–8.

Merton, R. K. Puritanism, Pietism and Science. In R. K. Merton—*Social Theory and Social Structure.* N.Y.: Free Press, 1963.

Moraczewski, A. The Contribution of Science to Religion. *Bull. Atomic Sci.,* 13/1, 1957, p.27–31.

Mowrer, O. H. Religion as Thesis and Science as Antithesis. *Hanover Forum,* 5/1, 1959, p.37–46.

Ong, W. J. (ed.) *Darwin's Vision and Christian Perspectives.* N.Y.: Macmillan, 1960, 154p.

Oxnam, G. B. Religion and Science in Accord. *Ann. Amer. Acad. Polit. Soc. Sci.,* 256, 1948, p.141–7.

Ramsey, I. T. *Religion and Science: Conflict and Synthesis, Some Philosophical Reflections.* London: SPCK, 1964, 98p.

Reiser, O. L. and Davies, B. Religion and Science in Conflict. *Ann. Amer. Acad. Polit. Soc. Sci.,* 256, 1948, p.132–40.

Richardson, A. *The Bible in the Age of Science.* Phila.: Westminster Press, 1961, 192p.

Russel, B. *Religion and Science.* N.Y.: Oxford Univ. Press, 1961, 256p.

Sayili, A. Islam and the Rise of Seventeenth Century Science. *Belleten,* 22/87, 1958, p.343–69.

Schilling, H. K. *Science and Religion: An Interpretation of Two Communities.* N.Y.: Scribners, 1962, 272p.

Stark, R. On the Incompatibility of Religion and Science: A Survey of American Graduate Students. *J. Sci. Stud. Rel.,* 3/1, 1963, p. 3–20. See also: A. M. Greeley, *et al.*—Comment; R. Stark—Reply, 3/2, 1964, p.239–43.

Stark, W. The Socio-Religious Origins of Modern Science. *R. Int. Sociol.,* 20/79, 1962, p.323–31.

Stuermann, W. E. *Logic and Faith: A Study of the Relations Between Science and Religion* (Westminster Studies in Christian Communication). Phila.: Westminster Press, 1962, 192p.

van de Wetering, J. E. God, Science and the Puritan Dilemma. *New England Quart.,* 38, 1965, p.494–507.

Westfall, R. S. *Science and Religion in 17th Century England.* New Haven: Yale Univ. Press, 1953.

See Also: 8, 7a3, 7b3

Gillispie, C. C.   6e
Grebstein, S. N.   4a1
Hiltner, S.   8a6
Schwantes, R. S.   4b
Stark, W.   8a6
White, E. A.   6e

1c.   Religion and Philosophy/Law

Alston, W. P. (ed.) *Religious Belief and Philosophical Thought.* N.Y.: Harcourt, Brace and World, 1963, 626p.

Aubrey, E. E. Naturalism and Religious Thought. *J. Philos.,* 48, 1951, p.57–66. See also: H. W. Schneider—Natural Thought and the World of Religion, p.66–

74; and, E. E. Aubrey—Reply to Professor Schneider, p.74–7.

Beckwith, B. P. *Religion, Philosophy, and Science: An Introduction to Logical Positivism.* N.Y.: Philosophical Library, 1957, 241p.

Bleeker, C. J. The Phenomenological Method. *Numen*, 6/2, 1959, p.96–111.

Bochenski, J. M. *The Logic of Religion*. N.Y.: New York Univ. Press, 1965, 179p.

Brightman, E. S. Goals of Philosophy and Religion. *Philos. East West*, 1/4, 1952, p.6–17.

Bronstein, D. J. and Schulweis, H. M. (eds.) *Approaches to the Philosophy of Religion*. N.Y.: Prentice-Hall, 1954, 532p.

Buber, M. *Eclipse of God: Studies in the Relation Between Religion and Philosophy*. N.Y.: Harper, 1957, 152p.

Buber, M. *The Knowledge of Man: Selected Essays* (Trans. M. Friedman and R. G. Smith). N.Y.: Harper, 1965, 208p.

Carmichael, P. A. Limits of Religious Knowledge. *Philosoph. Phenom. Res.*, 10/1, 1949, p.53–64.

Cassirer, E. *Language and Myth* (Trans. S. K. Langer). N. Y.: Dover, 1946.

Chan, W. T. *A Source Book in Chinese Philosophy*. Princeton: Princeton Univ. Press, 1963, 856p.

Cholos, A. G. What is Natural Law? *Mod. Law R.*, 21/6, 1958, p.570–90.

Christian, W. A. Philosophical Analysis and Philosophy of Religion. *J. Rel.*, 39/2, 1959, p.77–87.

Christian, W. A. *Meaning and Truth in Religion*. Princeton: Princeton Univ. Press, 1964, 269p.

Cochrane, A. C. *The Existentialists and God*. Phila.: Westminster Press, 1956, 174p.

Cornford, F. M. *From Religion to Philosophy: A Study in the Origins of Western Speculation*. N.Y.: Harper, 1957, 275p.

Coulson, N. J. *A History of Islamic Law*. Edinburg: The University Press, 1964, 264p.

Dandekar, R. N. Religion and Philosophy in the Age of the Guptas (Circa 200–700). *Rocznik Oriental*, 21, 1957, p.85–108.

Daube, D. Texts and Interpretation in Roman and Jewish Law. *Jew. J. Sociol.*, 11/1, 1961, p. 3–28.

Demos, R. and Ducasse, C. J. Symposium: Are Religious Dogmas Cognitive and Meaningful? *J. Philos.*, 51, 1954, p.145–72.

Ducasse, C. J. *A Philosophical Scrutiny of Religion*. N.Y.: Ronald Press, 1953.

Dumery, H. *The Problem of God in Philosophy of Religion* (Trans. C. Courtney). Evanston: Northwestern Univ. Press, 1964, 135p.

Edman, I. Religion and the Philosophical Imagination. *J. Philos.*, 25, 1928, p.673–85.

Emmet, D. Reason in Recent Theological Discussion. *Polit. Quart.*, 26/3, 1955, p.276–85.

French, F. C. The Relation of Psychology to the Philosophy of Religion. *J. Philos.*, 2, 1905, p.701–7.

Ghoraba, H. The Dilemma of Religion and Philosophy in Islam. *Islamic Quart.*, 2/4, 1955, p.214–51.

Gill, J. H. Wittgenstein and Religious Language. *Theol. Today*, 21/1, 1964, p.59–72.

Gurvitch, G. Magic and Law. *Soc. Res.*, 9/1, 1942, p. 104–22.

Hardy, M. L. J. *Blood Feuds and the Payment of Blood Money in the Middle East*. Leiden: E. J. Brill, 1963, 106p.

Hayward, J. F. *Existentialism and Religious Liberalism*. Boston: Beacon Press, 1962.

Hick, J. *Philosophy of Religion*. Englewood Cliffs: Prentice-Hall, 1963, 111p.

Hick, J. (ed.) *Faith and Philosophers*. N.Y.: St. Martin's Press, 1964, 256p.

Horowitz, I. L. Averroism and the Politics of Philosophy. *J. Rel.*, 22/4, 1960, p. 698–727.

Hutchinson, J. A. *Faith, Reason and Existence: An Introduction to Contemporary Philosophy of Religion*. N.Y.: Oxford Univ. Press, 1956, 306p.

James, E. O. *The Beginnings of Religion*. London: Hutchinson's Univ. Library, 1948.

James, E. O. *The Concept of Deity*. London: Hutchinson's Univ. Library, 1950.

Jurji, E. J. *Phenomenology of Religion*. Phila.: Westminster Press, 1963.

Kaufman, G. D. Philosophy of Religion: Subjective or Objective? *J. Philos.*, 55/2, 1958, p.57–70.

Kaufmann, W. *Critique of Religion and Philosophy*. N.Y.: Harper, 1958, 325p.

Khadduri, M. Nature and Sources of Islamic Law. *George Washington Law R.*, 22, 1953, p.3–23.

Kimpel, B. F. *Language and Religion*. N.Y.: Philosophical Library, 1957.

Klamke, E. D. Are Religious Statements Meaningful? *J. Rel.*, 40, 1960, p.27–39.

Konvitz, M. R. (ed.) *First Amendment Freedoms: Selected Cases on Freedom of Religion, Speech, Press, Assembly*. Ithaca, N.Y.: Cornell Univ. Press, 1963, 933p.

Kroner, R. *Speculation and Revelation in Modern Philosophy*. Phila.: Westminster Press, 1961, 269p.

Lowrie, W. About Justification by Faith Alone. *J. Rel.*, 32, 1952, p.231–41.

MacKinnon, F. B. The Effect of Religious Principles on Lawyers' Ethical Problems. *Christ. Scholar*, 40, 1957, p.238–44.

McPherson, T. Positivism and Religion. *Philosoph. Phenom. Res.*, 15/3, 1954, p.319–30.

Michalson, C. (ed.) *Christianity and the Existentialists.* N.Y.: Scribners, 1965, 228p.

Moore, C. A. Philosophy as Distinct From Religion in India. *Philos. East West*, 11/1-2, 1961, p.3–26.

Myers, G. E. (ed.) *Self, Religion and Metaphysics.* N.Y.: Macmillan, 1961, 241p.

Nader, L. Choices in Legal Procedure: Shia Moslem and Mexican Zapotec. *Amer. Anthropol.*, 67/2, 1965, p.394–400.

Parsons, H. L. A Reformulation of the Philosophical Presuppositions of Religion. *J. Rel.*, 42/2, 1962, p.119–32.

Philosophie de la Religion. *Bibliography of Philosophy* (Bibliographie de la Philosophie), 12/4, 1965, p.317–26; see other issues.

Radhakrishnan, S. *Religion and Society.* London: Allen and Unwin, 1959.

Ramadan, S. *Islamic Law: Its Scope and Equality.* London: Macmillan, 1961, 171p.

Rescher, N. *Studies in the History of Arabic Logic.* Pittsburgh: Univ. of Pittsburgh Press, 1963, 103p.

Rogers, A. K. The Relation of the Science of Religion to the Truth of Religious Belief. *J. Philos.*, 1, 1904, p.113–8.

Royce, J. E. *Man and His Nature: A Philosophical Psychology.* N.Y.: McGraw-Hill, 1961, 398p.

Sahakian, W. S. *Philosophies of Religion.* Cambridge: Schenkman Publishing Co., 1965, 476p.

Schulweis, H. M. Myth and Existentialism. *Judaism*, 6, 1957, p.303–10.

Scott, N. A., Jr. Religious Implications in the Humanities. *J. Hum. Relat.*, 2/2, 1954, p.16–24.

Shideler, E. W. Logical Treatment of Religious Propositions. *J. Bib. Rel.*, 23, 1955, p.278–85.

Sikes, W. W., *et al.* The Theologian and the Philosopher: A Dialogue. *Rel. Life*, 33/3, 1964, p.334–450.

Singer, M. and Ammerman, R. R. (eds.) *Introductory Readings in Philosophy.* N.Y.: Scribners, 1962.

Smart, N. (ed.) *Historical Selections in the Philosophy of Religion.* N.Y.: Harper and Row, 1962, 510p.

Smith, J. E. *Reason and God: Encounters of Philosophy and Religion.* New Haven, Connecticut: Yale Univ. Press, 1961, 274p.

Smith, R. V. Analytical Philosophy and Religious Theological Language. *J. Bib. Rel.*, 30/2, 1962, p.101–8.

Smith, Wilf. C. *The Meaning and End of Religion: A New Approach to the Religious Traditions of Mankind.* N.Y.: Macmillan, 1963, 340p.

Thomas, G. F. *Christian Ethics and Moral Philosophy.* N.Y.: Scribners, 1955, 539p.

Whitfield, G. J. N. *Philosophy and Religion: An Introduction to Some Questions of Beliefs.* Wallington, Surrey: Religious Education Press, 1955, 128p.

Wild, J. Plato and Christianity: A Philosophical Comparison. *J. Bib. Rel.*, 17, 1949, p.3–16.

Williams, B. C. Religion in Philosophy Textbooks. *J. Bib. Rel.*, 25, 1957, p.206–10.

Williams, J. R. *Contemporary Existentialism and Christian Faith.* Englewood Cliffs, New Jersey: Prentice-Hall, 1965, 180p.

Zimmer, H. R. *Philosophies of India.* N.Y.: Meridian Books, 1956, 687p.

Zuurdeeg, W. F. The Implications of Analytical Philosophy for Theology. *J. Bib. Rel.*, 29/3, 1961, p.204–10.

See Also: 2, 3, 4a, 4d, 4e, 5c, 6a

Albert, E. M.   9
Bryson, L. (ed.)   1b
Chan, W. T.   9
Collins, J.   9
Coltrera, J. T.   9
Cornford, F. M.   3
Coulson, N. J.   6a
Farran, D. D'O.   4e2
Heim, K.   1b
Hutchinson, J.   7f
Jaspan, M. A.   6a
Lyons, J.   9
Maududi, A.   2d
McGrath, J. J.   4a1
Monson, C. H., Jr.   8b
Royce, J. R.   1e
Schmidt, P. F.   8a2
Silberman, B.   9
Von Elbe, J.   5d
Zuurdeeg, W. F.   8a2

1d.   Religion and History

Albright, W. F.   *History, Archaeology and Christian Humanism.* N.Y.: McGraw-Hill Co., 1964, 388p.

Alilunas, L. J.   Ethnocentrism in Public and Parochial School American History Textbooks. *Rel. Educ.,* 60/2, 1965, p.83–9.

Bleeker, C. J.   The Future Task of the History of Religion. *Numen,* 7/2–3, 1960, p.221–34.

Case, S. J.   The Historical Study of Religion. *J. Rel.,* 29/1, 1949, p.5–14.

Connolly, J. M.   *Human History and the Word of God: The Meaning of History in Contemporary Thought.* Macmillan Co., 1960, 352p.

Eliade, M.   The History of Religions in Retrospect: 1912–1962. *J. Bib. Rel.,* 31/2, 1963, p.98–109.

Eliade, M. and Kitagawa, J. M.   *The History of Religions: Essays in Methodology.* Chicago: Univ. of Chicago Press, 1959.

Friedrich, C. J.   Religion and History. *Confluence,* 4/1, 1955, p.105–15.

Garstang, J.   History of the Bible. *Amer. J. Econ. Sociol.,* 3/3, 1943, p.371–85.

Goodenough, E. R.   Religionswissenschaft. *Numen,* 6/2, 1959, p.77–95.

James, E. O.   The Influence of Folklore on the History of Religion. *Numen,* 9/1, 1962, p.1–16.

Krug, M. M.   Young Israelis and Jews Abroad: A Study of Selected History Textbooks. *Comp. Educ. R.,* 7/2, 1963, p.142–7.

Landis, C.   Psychotherapy and Religion. *R. Rel.,* 10, 1946, p.413–24.

Latourette, K. S.   The Christian Understanding of History. *Amer. Hist. R.,* 54, 1949, p.259–76.

Nichols, J. H.   Church History and Secular History. *Church Hist.,* 13/2, 1944, p.87–99.

Toynbee, A. J.   *An Historian's Approach to Religion.* N.Y.: Oxford Univ. Press, 1956.

Wach, J.   The Place of the History of Religions in the Study of Theology. *J. Rel.,* 27/3, 1947, p.157–77.

Werblowsky, R. J. Z.   Marburg and After? *Numen,* 7/2–3, 1960, p.215–20.

White, L., Jr.   Christian Myth and Christian History. *J. Hist. Ideas,* 3/2, 1942, p.147–58.

See Also: 3, 6

Alilunas, L. J.   4g
Buck, H. M.   8a5
Eliade, M.   6
Marcus, J. F.   8a5
Pettazzoni, V.   3
Werblowsky, R. J. Z.   8a4

1e.   Religion and Psychiatry, Medicine, Psychology

Alcorn, D. E.   New Testament Psychology. *Brit. J. Med. Psychol.,* 16, 1937, p.270–80.

Angers, W. P.   Clarifications Toward the Reapproachment Between Religion and Psychology. *J. Individ. Psychol.,* 16, 1960, p.73–6.

Appel, K. E.   The Concept of Responsibility in Psychiatric Thought. *J. Rel. Health,* 2/1, 1962, p.30–41.

Becker, R. J.   Links Between Psychology and Religion. *Amer. Psychol.,* 13, 1958, p.566–8.

Bentley, M.   Mind, Body, and Soul in Medical Psychology. *Amer. J. Psychol.,* 45, 1933, p.577–91.

Berger, E. M.   Zen Buddhism, General Psychology and Counseling Psychology. *J. Counseling Psychol.,* 9/2, 1962, p.122–7.

Bergman, P.   The Role of Faith in Psychotherapy. *Bull. Menninger Clin.,* 22, 1958, p.92–103.

Biddle, W. E.   *Integration of Religion and Psychiatry.* N.Y.: Macmillan, 1955, 171p.

Boisen, A. T.   The Psychiatric Approach to the Study of Religion. *Rel. Educ.,* 23, 1928, p.201–7.

Bowers, M. K.   Protestantism and Its Therapeutic Implications. *Ann. Psychother.,* 1/2, 1959, p.6–14.

Braceland, F. J. (ed.)   *Faith, Reason and Modern Psychiatry.* N.Y.: Kenedy, 1955.

Braceland, F. J. and Stuck, M.   *Modern Psychiatry: A Handbook for Believers A Comprehensive Survey of Every Aspect of Modern Psychiatry—Its Background, Theories, Techniques, Future and Relation to Religion.* Garden City, N.Y.: Doubleday, 1963, 346p.

Bronner, A.   Psychotherapy With Religious Patients. *Amer. J. Psychoth.,* 18/3, 1964, p.475–87.

Butler, P.   Church History and Psychology of Religion. *Amer. J. Psychol.,* 32, 1921, p.543–51.

Carrington, W. L.   *Psychology, Religion, and Human Need: A Guide for Ministers, Doctors, Teachers, and Social Workers.* Great Neck, N.Y.: Channel Press, 1957, 315p.

Casey, R. P. The Psychoanalytic Study of Religion. *J. Abnorm. Soc. Psychol.*, 33, 1938, p.437–53.

Casey, R. P. Religion and Psychoanalysis. *Psychiatry*, 6, 1943, p. 291–30.

Cattell, R. B. *Psychology and the Religious Quest.* N.Y.: Nelson, 1948.

Cedarleaf, J. L. The Clinical Use of the Initial Religious Interview. *J. Past. Care*, 11, 1957, p.156–61.

Clark, W. H. *The Psychology of Religion.* N.Y.: Macmillan, 1958.

Conrad, P. Responsibilities of a Christian Medical Worker. *J. Christ. Med. Assoc. India*, 35, 1960, p. 225–8.

Cox, D. *Jung and St. Paul: A Study of the Doctrine of Justification by Faith and Its Relation to the Concept of Individuation.* N.Y.: Association Press, 1959, 361p.

Cromwell, H. Religion in Nursing Practice. *Amer. J. Nursing*, 49, 1949, p.768–70.

Curran, C. A. Religious Factors and Values in Counseling. *Cath. Counselor*, 3, 1958, p.3–5.

Daneman, E. A. and Smith, J. I. Post-Graduate Pastoral Counseling Seminars. *Dis. Nerv. Syst.*, 20, 1959, p. 575–81.

Doniger, S. (ed.) *The Nature of Man, In Theological and Psychological Perspective.* N.Y.: Harper, 1962, 264p.

Draper, E. *Psychiatry and Pastoral Care.* Englewood Cliffs, New Jersey: Prentice-Hall, 1965, 144p.

Eckstein, R. A Clinical Note on the Therapeutic Use of a Quasi-Religious Experience. *J. Amer. Psychoanal. Assoc.*, 4/2, 1956, p.304–13.

Eckstein, R. Faith and Reason in Psychotherapy. *Bull. Menninger Clin.*, 22, 1958, p.104–8.

Emery, E. Van N. Co-Operation Between Clergyman, Psychiatrist and Social Worker. *Rel. Educ.*, 1929, p. 624–30.

Farrell, B. A. Psychological Theory and the Belief in God. *Int. J. Psychoanal.*, 36, 1955, p.1–18.

Ferm, V. The Psychology of Religion. In A. A. Roback (ed.)—*Present Day Psychology.* N.Y.: Philosophical Library, 1955, p.961–72.

Fletcher, J. Psychiatry and Religion: Conflict or Synthesis. *J. Past. Care*, 6, 1952, p.12–8.

Fromm, E. *Psychoanalysis and Religion.* New Haven: Yale Univ. Press, 1950, 119p.

Fromm, E. Psychoanalysis and Zen Buddhism. *Psychologia*, 2, 1959, p.79–99.

Fromm, E., *et al. Zen Buddhism and Psychoanalysis.* N.Y.: Harper, 1960, 180p.

Fromm, E. *The Dogma of Christ and Other Essays on Religion, Psychology and Culture.* N.Y.: Holt, Rinehart and Winston, 1963, 212p.

Gassert, R. G. and Hall, B. H. *Psychiatry and Religious Faith.* N.Y.: Viking, 1964, 171p.

Gibson, R. R. Religion and Psychiatry: What Kind of Friendship? *J. Rel. Health*, 2/2, 1963, p.143–9.

Ginsburg, S. W. Concerning Religion and Psychiatry. *Child Study*, 30, 1953, p.1–20.

Godin, A. Recent Publications in the Psychology of Religions. *Lumen Vitae*, 19/2, 1964, p.351–76.

Goldman, A. Psychiatry and Religion. *Rel. Educ.*, 52, p.355–60.

Griffin, M. Value Judgements in Psychiatry and Religion. *J. Rel. Health*, 4/2, 1965, p.180–7.

Group for the Advancement of Psychiatry, Psychology, and Religion. *Some Steps Toward Mutual Understanding and Usefulness.* N. Y.: Group for the Advancement of Psychiatry Publications, 1960.

Guntrip, H. *Psychotherapy and Religion.* N. Y.: Harper, 1957.

Hacker, F. J. Scientific Fact, Religious Values and Psychoanalytic Experience. *Bull. Menninger Clin.*, 19, 1955, p.229–39.

Jacobs, H. *Western Psychotherapy and Hindu-Sadhânâ: A Contribution to Comparative Studies in Psychology and Metaphysics.* N.Y.: International Universities Press, 1961, 232p.

Jelliffe, S. E. The Christian Formulation and Medicine. *Psychiat. Quart.*, 13, 1939, p.705–10.

Johnson, G. B., Jr. The Development of Pastoral Counseling Programs in Protestantism: A Sociological Perspective. *Pac. Sociol. R.*, 1/2, 1958, p.59–63.

Johnson, F. E. *Psychology of Religion.* N.Y.: Abingdon, 1945.

Johnson, P. E. The Contribution of Psychology to the Teacher of Religion. *J. Rib. Rel.*, 24, 1956, p.167–72.

Johnson, P. E. The Clinical Approach to Religion. *J. Past. Care*, 15, 1961, p.7–12.

Jones, E. E. *Essays In Applied Psycho-analysis: Vol. 2; Essays in Folklore, Anthropology and Religion.* London: Hogarth Press, 1951.

Jung, C. G. *Psychological Reflections* (Ed. J. Jacobi). N.Y.: Pantheon Books, 1953, 342p.

Jung, C. G. *Psychology and Religion: West and East.* N.Y.: Pantheon Books, 1958.

King, S. H. and Funkenstein, D. H. Religious Practice and Cardio-Vascular Reactions During Stress. *J. Abnorm. Soc. Psychol.*, 53, 1957, p.135–7.

Klausner, S. *Psychiatry and Religion: A Sociological Study*. N.Y.: Free Press, 1964.

Klausner, S. The Religio-Psychiatric Movement. *R. Rel. Res.*, 5/2, 1964, p. 63–74; see also 6/1, p.7–22.

Knight, J. A. Calvinism and Psychoanalysis: A Comparative Study. *Past. Psychol.*, 14, 1963, p.10–7.

Knight, J. A. *A Psychiatrist Looks at Religion and Health*. N.Y.: Abingdon Press, 1964.

Kora, T. Psychotherapy, Existence, and Religion. *Psychoanal. Psychoanal. R.*, 46, 1959, p.91–8.

Lehrman, N. S. The Normality of the Sexual Feelings in Pastoral Counseling. *Past. Psychol.*, 11, 1960, p.49–52.

Leonard, A. Religious Psychology of Today. *Lumen Vitae*, 12, 1957, p.233–43.

Liebman, J. L. (ed.) *Psychiatry and Religion*. Boston: Beacon Press, 1948.

Linn, L. and Schwarz, L. W. *Psychiatry and Religious Experience*. N.Y.: Random House, 1958.

Loomis, E. A., Jr. Child Psychiatry and Religion. *Past. Psychol.*, 7, 1956, p.27–8, 30, 32–3.

Lorand, S. Psycho-Analytic Therapy of Religious Devotees: A Theoretical and Technical Contribution. *Int. J. Psychoanal.*, 43/1, 1962, p.50–5.

Mairet, P. (ed.) *Christian Essays in Psychiatry*. N.Y.: Philosophical Library, 1956, 187p.

McDonnell, K. Psychiatry and Pastoral Psychology. *Lumen Vitae*, 12, 1957, p.253–9.

Meyer, A. E. *Mind, Matter, and Morals: The Impact of the Revolutionary New Findings in Neurophysiology and Psychology Upon the Problems of Religion, Ethics, and Human Behavior*. N.Y.: American Press, 1957, 192p.

Misiak, H. and Staudt, V. M. *Catholics in Psychology: A Historical Survey*. N.Y.: McGraw-Hill, 1954, 309p.

Mowrer, O. H. *The Crisis in Psychiatry and Religion*. Princeton, New Jersey: Van Nostrand, 1961.

Nand, D. S. The Study of Religion and Culture Through the Total Psychoanalysis of the Individuals. *Psychologia*, 3, 1960, p.119–30.

Novey, S. Considerations on Religion in Relation to Psychoanalysis and Psychotherapy. *J. Nervous Ment. Disease*, 130, 1960, p.315–24.

Oates, W. E. *What Psychology Says About Religion*. N.Y.: Association Press, 1958, 128p.

Oden, T. C. Revelation and Psychotherapy. *Continuum*, 2/2, 1964, p.239–64. See also: A. Godin, 2/4, 1965, p.672–9; T. C. Oden, 3/1, p.91–5; A. Godin, 3/2, p.215–9.

Oetting, E. R. The Treatment of Interpersonal Relationships in Psychotherapy as a Function of Religious Socialization. *J. Sci. Stud. Rel.*, 4/1, 1964, p.100–1.

Outler A. C. *Psychotherapy and the Christian Message*. N.Y.: Harper, 1954.

Paddock, F. A Philosophical Investigation of the Relation Between Psychoanalysis and Theology. *J. Past. Care*, 13, 1959, p.38–41.

Papanek, H. Ethical Values in Psychotherapy. *J. Individual Psychol.*, 14, 1958, p.160–6.

Pius XII. *Applied Psychology: Address of His Holiness Pope Pius XII to the Congress of the International Association of Applied Psychology, April 10, 1958*. Washington, D.C.: National Catholic Welfare Conference, 1958.

Preston, R. A. Landmarks in the Relations of Psychiatry and Religion. *Bull. Menninger Clin.*, 19, 1953, p.191–8.

Pruyser, P. W. Religion and Psychiatry. *Menninger Quart.*, 11/3, 1957, p.2–5.

Religious Organizations Engaged in Hospitals and Nursing Education Activities. *Hosp. Progr.*, 41/2, 1960, p.261–86.

Riley, H. J. The Common Grounds Between Psychiatry and Religion. *Ment. Hyg.*, 48/3, 1964, p.351–5.

Roberts, D. E. *Psychotherapy and a Christian View of Man*. N.Y.: Scribners, 1950.

Rolo, C. (ed.) *Psychiatry in American Life: Its Effect on Medicine, Writing, Religion, Art, Children, Morals*. Boston: Little, Brown, 1963, 246p.

Ross, N. Psychoanalysis and Religion. *Amer. J. Psychoanal. Assoc.*, 6/3, 1958, p.519–39.

Royce, J. R. Psychology, Existentialism, and Religion. *J. Genet. Psychol.*, 66, 1962, p.3–16.

Runestam, A. *Psychoanalysis and Christianity* (Trans. O. Winfield). Rock Island, Illinois: Augustana Press, 1958, 194p.

Sato, K. Psychotherapeutic Implications of Zen. *Psychologia*, 1, 1958, p.213–8.

Schroeder, T. The Psychoanalytic Approach to Religious Experience. *Psychoanal. R.*, 16, 1929, p.361-76.

Scott, E. M. "Will" and Religion as Useful Adjuncts in Psychotherapy. *Psychol. Rep.*, 1/4, 1955, p.379–81.

Sherman, M. H. Values, Religion and the Psycho-Analyst. *J. Soc. Psychol.*, 45, 1957, p.261–9.

Sierksma, F. *The Gods As We Shape Them*. London: Routledge, 1960, 195p.

Spinks, S. *Psychology and Religion: An Introduction to Contemporary Views*. London: Methuen & Co., 1963, 221p.

Stedman, R. E.   Anthropocentrism in Religion and Theology. *London Quart. R.*, 159, 1934, p.345–53.

Stern, K.   *The Third Revolution: A Study of Psychiatry and Religion*. N.Y.: Harcourt, Brace and Co., 1954, 306p.

Stevenson, I.   Assumptions of Religon and Psychiatry. *Bull. Menninger Clin.*, 19, 1955, p.195–209.

Stoops, J. D.   The Psychology of Religion. *J. Philos.*, 2, 1905, p.512–9.

Strunk, O., Jr.   Psychology, Religion, and C. G. Jung: A Review of Periodical Literature. *J. Bib. Rel.*, 24, 1956, p.106–13.

Strunk, O., Jr.   A Redefinition of the Psychology of Religion. *Psychol. Rep.*, 3/1, 1957, p.138.

Sullivan, J. J.   Two Psychologies and the Study of Religion. *J. Sci. Stud. Rel.*, 1/2, 1962, p.155–64.

Tweedie, D. F.   *Legotheraphy and the Christian Faith*. Grand Rapids: Baker Book House, 1961.

Vanderveldt, J. and Odenwald, R.   *Psychiatry and Catholicism*. N.Y.: McGraw-Hill, 1957.

Vaughan, R. P.   Religions and Psychotherapy. *R. Rel.*, 17, 1958, p.73–81.

Watson, G.   Moral Issues in Psychotherapy. *Amer. Psychol.*, 13, 1958, p.574–6.

Wheeler, W. F. and di Nardo, R.   Psychoanalysis and Pastoral Psychology. *Homil. Pastoral R.*, 58, 1958, p.469–75.

White, V.   *Soul and Psyche: An Enquiry Into the Relationship Between Psychotherapy and Religion*. N.Y.: Harper & Brothers, 1960.

Wile, I. S.   Psychoanalysis and Religion. *Ment. Hyg.*, 16/4, 1932, p.529–63.

Woodward, L. H. and Kluge, W.   The Relationship Between Religion and Psychotherapy in the Adjustment of the Individual. *J. Psychiat. Soc. Work*, 18/2, 1948, p.59–80.

Wolf, A. J.   Psychoanalysis and Religious Experience. *J. Rel. Health*, 2/1, 1962, p.74–80.

Zilboorg, G.   *Psychoanalysis and Religion*. N.Y.: Farrar, Strauss & Cudahy, 1962, 243p.

See Also: 4h, 4i, 5b, 5g

Bartemeir, L. H.   8a6
Bier, W. C.   8b
Birmingham, W.   4d
Boverman, M.   7a1
Bruder, E. E.   7a1
Burchard, E. M. L.   8a6
Cole, W. G.   4i
Coltrera, J. T.   9
Drakeford, J. W.   8a4
Dunbar, H. F.   5b
Edgar, G. W.   7a1
Erikson, E. H.   4h
French, F. C.   1c
Freud, S.   8a6
Gladstone, I.   5b
Godin, A.   7a1
Gregory, W. E.   8a4
Gross, G. A.   7a1
Havens, J.   8a
Hostie, R.   8a2
Jordan, G. R., Jr.   5b
Kiell, N.   9
Kiev, A.   5b1
Klausner, S.   7a1
Klink, T. W.   7a
LaBarre, W.   5b1
Larson, R. F.   7a3
LeBras, G.   9
Naegele, K. D.   7a4
Noveck, S. (ed.)   5b1
Parrinder, E. G.   8a5
Philip, H. L.   8a6
Rubenstein, R. L.   8a4
Schaer, H.   8a6
Scholefield, H. B.   7a
Siegman, A. W.   8a2
Smith, W. J.   7a1
Strunk, O., Jr.   8a4
Tufari, P.   8a2
Weatherhead, L. D.   5b1
Wedel, T. O.   1g

1f.   *Religion and Social Sciences*

Allport, G. W.   Behavioral Science, Religion, and Mental Health. *J. Rel. Health*, 2/3, 1963, p.187–97.

Augustine, D.   The Scientific Catholic Sociologist. *Amer. Cath. Sociol. R.*, 18/1, 1957, p.2–9.

Becker, H.   Supreme Values and the Sociologists. *Amer. Sociol. R.*, 6, 1941, p.155–72.

Clark, W. H.   How do Social Scientists Define Religion? *J. Soc. Psychol.*, 47, 1958, p.143–7.

Clemmens, A. H.   The Catholic Sociologist Faces a New Social Order. *Amer. Cath. Sociol. R.*, 4/3, 1943, p.158–64.

Curtis, J. H.   The Uncertain Sound of the Trumpet:

Catholic Values and Medical Sociology. *Amer. Cath. Sociol. R.*, 22/4, 1961, p.291–8.

Donovan, J. D. American Catholic Sociologists and the Sociology of Religion. *Amer. Cath. Sociol. R.*, 15/2, 1954, p.104–14.

Ellwood, C. A., *et al.* Roman Catholic Sociology: Symposium. *Sociol. Soc. Res.*, 26, 1941, p.114–20.

Evans—Pritchard, E. E. Religion and the Anthropologists. *Blackfriars*, 41/480, 1960, p.104–18.

Fitzpatrick, J. P. Catholic Responsibilities in Sociology. *Thought*, 26/102, 1951, p.384–96.

Fitzpatrick, J. P. Catholics and the Scientific Knowledge of Society. *Amer. Cath. Sociol. R.*, 15/1, 1954, p.2–5.

Francke, M. The Socio-Economic Interpretation of Mythology. *Folklore*, 54/4, 1943, p.369–77.

Fukuyama, Y. The Uses of Sociology By Religious Bodies. *J. Sci. Stud. Rel.*, 2/2, 1963, p.195–203.

Furfey, P. H. Why a Supernatural Sociology? *Amer. Cath. Sociol. R.*, 1/4, 1940, p.167–71.

Givens, R. and Garza, J. The Treatment of Religion in Introductory Sociology Texts. *J. Sci. Stud. Rel.*, 5/1, 1965, p.59–63.

Goodwin, L. Religion and the Behavioral Sciences. *Rel. Educ.*, 55, 1960, p.253–6.

Grafton, T. H. Religious Origins and Sociological Theory. *Amer. Sociol. R.*, 10/6, 1945, p.726–39.

Harte, T. J. Catholics as Sociologists. *Amer. Cath. Sociol. R.*, 13/1, 1952, p.2–9.

Honigsheim, P. Sociology of Religion. In H. Becker and A. Boskoff (eds.)—*Modern Sociological Theory*. N.Y.: Dryden Press, 1957, p.450–81.

Hughes, J. E. Catholic Scientist and Sociologist: A Question of Identity. *Amer. Cath. Sociol. R.*, 24/4, 1963, p.285–301.

Hunt, C. L. The Sociology of Religion. In J. S. Roucek (ed.)—*Readings in Contemporary American Sociology*. Paterson, New Jersey: Littlefield, Adams & Co., 1961.

Hunter, D. Theology and the Behavioral Sciences. *Rel. Educ.*, 55, 1960, p.248–64.

Huppeler, V. K. The Introductory Course in Sociology in the Catholic Colleges and Universities. *J. Educ. Sociol.*, 7/1, 1933, p.26–9.

Jones, W. R. Sociology and the Church of England. *Sociol. R.*, 17/2, 1925, p.131–5.

Kane, J. J. Are Catholic Sociologists a Minority Group? *Amer. Cath. Sociol. R.*, 14/1, 1953, p.2–12.

Kolb, W. L. Images of Man and the Sociology of Religion. *J. Sci. Stud. Rel.*, 1/1, 1961, p.5–22. See also: T. Parsons—Comment, p.22–9; W. L. Kolb—Rejoinder, 1/2, 1962, p.214–7.

Kolb, W. L. Values, Positivism and the Functional Theory of Religion: The Growth of a Moral Dilemma. *Soc. Forces*, 31/4, 1953, p.305–11.

Kraemer, H. and Abrecht, P. Can Sociology Help the Church? *Ecumen. R.*, 3/4, 1951, p.388–93.

Lipset, S. M. Jewish Sociologists and Sociologists of the Jews. *Jew. Soc. Stud.*, 17, 1955, p.177–8.

Means, R. L. Protestantism in American Sociology. *Christ. Cent.*, 81/51, 1964, p.1554–6.

Mueller, F. H. The Possibility and Scope of a Supernatural Sociology. *Amer. Cath. Sociol. R.*, 1/3, 1940, p.141–6.

Mueller, F. H. What Constitutes a Sociology of Religion. *Amer. Cath. Sociol. R.*, 2/3, 1941, p.147–51.

Muensterberger, W. and Axelrod, S. (eds.) *Psychoanalysis and the Social Sciences*. N.Y.: International Universities Press, 1958, 297p., vol. 5.

Mulvaney, B. G. The Department of Sociology of the Catholic University of America, 1894–1955. *Amer. Cath. Sociol. R.*, 16/4, 1955.

Muntsch, A. A Catholic Approach to Anthropology. *Amer. Cath. Sociol. R.*, 2/3, 1941, p.159–65.

Nida, E. A. The Role of Cultural Anthropology in Christian Missions. *Pract. Anthropol.*, 6/3, 1959, p.110–6.

Repke, A. Religion in Sociology Texts. *Sociol. Soc. Res.*, 20/3, 1936, p.255–9.

Report of the Committee on the Teaching of Sociology in High Schools, Seminaries, Colleges, and Universities. *Amer. Cath. Sociol. R.*, 17/1, 1956, p.37–43.

Rosenstiel, A. Anthropology and the Missionary. *J. Roy. Anthropol. Inst.*, 89/1, 1959, p.107–15.

Ross, E. J. Sociology and the Catholic. *Amer. Cath. Sociol. R.*, 1/1, 1940, p.6–9.

Ross, E. J. Christian Social Concepts and the Sociologist. *Amer. Cath. Sociol. R.*, 2/2, 1944, p.90–6.

Rowell, T. The Teaching of Religion in Relation to Sociology. *J. Bib. Rel.*, 7, 1939, p.69–74; 106.

Salisbury, W. and Scholfield, F. Teaching Sociological Concepts by Learning About Religion. *Rel. Educ.*, 52/6, 1957.

Salomon, A. Prophets, Priests, and Social Scientists: Sociology of Religion and the Religion of Sociology. *Commentary*, 7, 1949, p.594–600.

Schelsky, H. Can Continual Reflection be Institutionalized? Some Thoughts on a Modern Sociology of Religion. *Crosscurrents*, 15/2, 1965, p.171–89.

Schroeder, W. W. Cognitive Structures and Religious Research. *R. Rel. Res.*, 3/2, 1961, p.72–81.

Seifort, H. J. Theology and Social Science en Rapport. *R. Rel. Res.*, 2/2, 1960, p.62–9.

Shippey, F. A. The Relations of Theology and the Social Sciences According to Gabriel Le Bras. *Archiv. Sociol. Rel.*, 10/20, 1965, p.79–93.

Solomon, A. Hugo Grotius and the Social Sciences. *Polit. Sci. Quart.*, 62, 1947, p.62–81.

Stroup, H. Theological Implications in Anthropology. *Encounter*, 21, 1960, p.464–8.

Sturzo, L. A Sociology of the Supernatural. *Amer. Cath. Sociol. R.*, 3/4, 1942, p.204–14.

Taubes, J. Theology and Political Theory. *Soc. Res.*, 22/1, 1955, p.57–68.

Thomas, J. L. The Sociological Implications of Catholic Thought. *Amer. Cath. Sociol. R.*, 22/1, 1961, p.3–10.

Tufari, P. Functional Analysis in the Sociology of Religion. *Soc. Compass*, 7/1, 1960, p.9–20; see also 7/2, p.121–37.

Von Wiese, L. The Social, Spiritual and Cultural Elements of the Interhuman Life. *Sociol. R.*, 29/2, 1937, p.136–53.

Woods, F. J. The Image of the American Catholic Sociologist. *Amer. Cath. Soc. R.*, 23/3, 1962, p.195–206.

Yinger, J. M. Some Consequences of the Scientific Study of Religion. *Rel. Educ.*, 52, 1957, p.350–4.

See Also: 4a, 4b, 8

Berndt, C. H. 5e3
Carrier, H. 9
Cuthbert, M. 7a4
Edmonson, M. S. 6
Firth, R. 8a2
Goddijn, W. 8a4
Kirkpatrick, C. 4g5
Lee, D. D. 4g
Parsons, T. 4g, 8a2
Schneider, L. 8a2
Smith, R. 8a4
van der Meyer, A. 8a2
Wertheim, W. F. 8a4
Yinger, M. 8a2

1g. *Religion and Social Work*

Abts, D. M. *Some Religious and Ethical Problems in the Practice of Catholic Social Workers.* Washington: Catholic Univ. Press, 1945, 125p.

Baldwin, R. M. The Minister and the Social Worker. *Family*, 26/4, 1945, p.149–54.

Banerjee, G. R. Concepts of Social Work in the Gita. *Ind. J. Soc. Work*, 25/1, 1964, p.29–34.

Banerjee, G. R. Karma Yoga and Social Case Work in India. *Ind. J. Soc. Work*, 24/4, 1964, p.229–234.

Bowman, H. L. Mental Hygiene in Relation to Religion. *Ment. Hyg.*, 20/2, 1936, p.177–88.

Chakerian, C. G. (ed.) *The Churches and Social Welfare.* Hartford: 1955, 1965, 2 vols.

Chakerian, C. G. Religious Sponsorship. In H. L. Lurie (ed.)—*Encyclopedia of Social Work.* N.Y.: National Association of Social Workers, 1965, p.654–9, vol. 15; see other issues.

Coughlin, B. J. A Growing Issue in Church and State. *Soc. Work*, 10/4, 1965, p.77–84.

Durnall, E. J., Jr., *et al.* Symposium: The Counselor and His Religion. *Personnel Guid. J.*, 36, 1958, p.326–34.

Evans, D. The Social Work of the Church in a Factory Town. *Ann. Amer. Acad. Polit. Soc. Sci.*, 30/3, 1907, p.75–80.

Evans, T. S. The Christian Settlement. *Ann. Amer. Acad. Polit. Soc. Sci.*, 30/3, 1907, p.55–61.

Farwell, P. T. The Social Work of a Suburban Church. *Ann. Amer. Acad. Polit. Soc. Sci.*, 30/3, 1907, p.68–74.

Goldstein, S. E. *The Synagogue and Social Welfare: A Unique Experiment 1907–1953.* N.Y.: Published for Stephen Wise Free Synagogue and Hebrew Union College, Jewish Institute of Religion, By Bloch, 1955, 376p.

Hall, M. P. and Howes, I. V. *The Church in Social Welfare Work.* London: Routledge and Kegan Paul, 1965, 272p.

Johnson, F. E. (ed.) *Religion and Social Work.* N.Y.: Institute for Religious and Social Studies, 1956.

Kerby, W. J. Social Work of the Catholic Church in America. *Ann. Amer. Acad. Polit. Soc. Sci.*, 30/3, 1907, p.45–54.

Kobak, D. A Religio-Psychiatric Clinic. *Insight*, 4/2, 1965, p.29–33.

Lauerman, L. L. *Catholic Education for Social Work.* Washington: Catholic Univ. Press, 1945, 124p.

Lifton, W. M. Counseling and the Religious View of Man. *Personnel Guid. J.*, 31, 1953, p.366–7.

Lynn, R. L. *The National Catholic Community Service in World War II*. Washington: Catholic Univ. Press, 1952, 290p.

Mahmassani, S. Social Work Based on Religious Concepts in Islam. *Islamic Lit.*, 6, 1954, p.605–13.

McCabe, A. R. Pastoral Counseling and Case Work. *Family*, 24/7, 1943, p.256–61.

McCabe, P. C. and Turner, F. J. (eds.) *Catholic Social Work: A Contemporary Overview*. Ottowa: Catholic Charities Council of Canada, 1965, 137p.

McCormick, M. U. *Thomistic Philosophy in Social Casework*. N.Y.: Columbia Univ. Press, 1948, 148p.

Pins, A. M. What Kind of Jewish Communal Worker Do We Need? *J. Jew. Commun. Serv.*, 42/1, 1965, p.60–72.

Scheller, A. H. Catholic Social Service and Professional Training. *Amer. Cath. Sociol. R.*, 4/4, 1943, p.205–9.

Shapiro, M. S. The Dilemmas of Jewish Agencies—Real and Unreal (In the Light of Jewish Needs, Social Change and Government Programs). *J. Jew. Commun. Serv.*, 42/1, 1965, p.18–26.

Siedenburg, F. The Religious Value of Social Work. *Amer. J. Sociol.*, 27/5, 1922, p.637–45.

Silver, H. Jewish Communal Service: Historical Perspectives. *J. Jew. Commun. Serv.*, 39/1, 1962, p.7–19.

Spencer, S. W. Religion and Social Work. *Soc. Work*, 1/3, 1956, p.19–26.

Spencer, S. W. Religious and Spiritual Values in Social Casework Practice. *Soc. Casework*, 38, 1957, p.519–26; see also: Discussion, 39, 1958, p.236–40.

Spencer, S. W. and McLarnan, G. The Religious Component in Social Work Practice. *Luth. Soc. Welf. Quart.*, 4/2, 1964, p.3–14.

Stroup, H. The Common Predicament of Religion and Social Work. *Soc. Work*, 7/2, 1962, p.89–93.

Villenauve, R. *Catholic Social Work*. Montreal: Grand Seminary of Montreal, 1955, 146p.

Wedel, T. O. The Group Dynamics Movement and the Church. *Theol. Today*, 10, 1954, p.511–24.

Wright, R. R., Jr. Social Work and the Influence of the Negro Church. *Ann. Amer. Acad. Polit. Soc. Sci.*, 30/3, 1907, p.81–93.

Zeff, D. and Greenberg, I. The Jewish Casework Agency: Problems and Prospects in a Time of Paradox. *J. Jew. Commun. Serv.*, 42/1, 1965, p.49–56.

See Also: 4e, 5, 5b, 5g, 7a

Cossette, J.   7b3
Coughlin B. J.   4a1
Emery, E. Van N.   1e
Levy, C. S.   4f1, 4g4
Wynn, J.   7a1

1h. Religion and Education

Bennett, J. C., *et al.* Religion and Public Education: A Symposium. *Rel. Educ.*, 55, 1960, p.265–96.

Blanshard, P. *Religion and the Schools: The Great Controversy*. Boston: Beacon Press, 1963, 265p.

Bridston, K. R. and Culver, D. W. *Pre-Seminary Education*. Minneapolis: Augsburg Publishing House, 257p.

Buckley, W. F., Jr. *God and Man at Yale*. Chicago: Henry Regnery, 1951.

Commission on Religion in the Public Schools, American Association of School Administrators. *Religion in the Public Schools*. Washington, D.C.: American Association of School Administrators, 1964.

Delrey, M. Attitude of Parents Toward Lay Teachers. *Cath. Educ. R.*, 54/8, 1956, p.459–66.

Dierenfield, R. H. *Religion in American Public Schools*. Washington, D.C.: Public Affairs Press, 1963.

Donovan, J. D. *The Academic Man in the Catholic College*. N.Y.: Sheed & Ward, 1964.

Fineberg, S. A. Christmas and Hanukkah in the Public Schools. *J. Intergr. Relat.*, 1/3, 1960, p.47–53.

Gluck, H. Lay Teacher Morale in Catholic Schools. *Cath. Educ. R.*, 52/9, 1954, p.537–41.

Johnson, E. V. (ed.) *American Education and Religion: The Problem of Religion in the Schools*. N.Y.: Harper, 1952, 414p.

Knight, F. H. Theology and Education. *Amer. J. Sociol.*, 44/5, 1939, p.649–83.

LaNoue, G. R. Religious Schools and "Secular" Subjects. *Harvard Educ. R.*, 32/3, 1962, p.255–91.

Lines of Communication in a Parochial School. *Bull. Nat. Cath. Educ. Assoc.*, 54/1, 1957, p.214–20.

McCluskey, N. G. *Catholic Viewpoint on Education*. N.Y.: Hanover House, 1959, 192p.

Nuesse, C. J. Sociology in Catholic Education: Prospect for Capital Development. *Amer. Cath. Sociol. R.*, 16/1, 1955, p.1–11.

Politella, J. *Religion in Education: An Annotated Bibliography.* Oneonta, N.Y.: Amer. Association of Colleges for Teacher Education, 1956.

Price-Jones, A. Religion and Literature. *Confluence,* 4/2, 1955, p. 194–201.

Walter, E. A. (ed.) *Religion and the State University.* Ann Arbor: Michigan Press, 1964.

Wells, C. D. The Motion Picture Versus the Church. *Sociol. Soc. Res.,* 16/6, 1932, p. 540–6.

2.   Descriptions of Religion

Adams, C. J. *A Reader's Guide to the Great Religions.*
N.Y.: Free Press, 1965, 364p.

Anesaki, M. *Religious Life of the Japanese People* (Rev.
H. Kishimoto). Tokyo: Kokusai Bunka Shinkokai,
1961, 105p.

Baeta, C. *Prophetism in Ghana: A Study of Some "Spiritual" Churches.* London: S.C.M. Press, 1962, 169p.

Bellah, R. N. The Religious Situation in the Far East.
Contemp. Rel. Japan, 4, 1963, p.95–117.

Benignus, E. L. Current Religious Trends in China. *J.
Bib. Rel.,* 15, 1947, p.199–205.

Berry, G. L. *Religions of the World.* N. Y.: Barnes
and Noble, Inc., 1952.

Bolshakoff, S. *Russian Nonconformity: The Story of 'Unofficial' Religion in Russia.* Phila.: Westminster Press,
1950, 192p.

Braden, C. H. *These Also Believe: A Study of Modern
American Cults and Minority Religious Movements.*
N.Y.: Macmillan 1949, 491p.

Bunce, W. K. *Religions in Japan: Buddhism, Shinto,
Christianity.* Rutland, Vermont: C. E. Tuttle, 1955,
194p.

Burr, N.R. A *Critical Bibliography of Religion in
America.* Princeton: Princeton Univ. Press, 1961,
2 vols.

Burrell, S. A. (ed.) *The Role of Religion in Modern
European History.* N. Y.: Macmillan Co., 1964.

Carrison, W. Characteristics of American Organized Religions. *Ann. Amer. Acad. Polit. Soc. Sci.,* 256, 1948,
p.14–24.

Centre for African Studies. *Religion in Africa: Proceedings of a Seminar.* Edinburgh: University Press, 1964,
130p.

Chakravarti, T. N. *Some Aspects of Religious Life in
Bengal.* Calcutta: Univ. of Calcutta, Dept. of Ancient Indian History and Culture, 1957, 53p.

Chan, W. T. *Religious Trends in Modern China.*
N.Y.: Columbia Univ. Press, 1953.

Chêng, T. K. *The Religious Outlook of the Chinese.*
London: China Society, 1956, 8p.

Church and Society in Japan Today. *Ecumen R.,* 8/2,
1956, p.143–53.

Creel, H. G. *Chinese Thought From Confusius to Mao
Tse-Tung.* London: Eyre & Spottiswoode, 1954,
301p.

Danielou, J., *et al.* *Introduction to the Great Religions*
(Trans. A. J. LaMothe, Jr.). Notre Dame: Fides,
1964, 142p.

Devanandan, P. D. The Religious and Spiritual Climate
of India Today. *Ecumen. R.,* 8/3, 1956, p.307–24.

Dinistheimer, G. G. H. Two Studies on the Religions of
China. *Archiv. Sociol. Rel.,* 1/4, 1957, p.133–42.

Edwards, E. D. Religion in Modern China. *Pac. Aff.,*
28/1, 1955, p.79–81.

Ferm, V. (ed.) *Religion in the Twentieth Century.* N.Y.:
Philosophical Library, 1948, 470p.

Frazier, E. F. *The Negro Church in America.* N.Y.:
Schocken Books, 1964.

Gard, R. A. (ed.) *Great Religions of Modern Man.*
N. Y.: George Braziller, 1961, 5 Vols.

Garrison, W. E. Characteristics of American Organized Religion. *Ann. Amer. Acad. Polit. Soc. Sci.,* 256,
1948, p.14–24.

Gurian, W. (ed.) *The Soviet Union, Background, Ideology, Reality: A Symposium.* Notre Dame: Univ.
of Notre Dame, 1951, 216 p.

Harper, E. B. (ed.) *Religion in South Asia: Papers.* Seattle: Univ. of Washington Press, 1964, 199p.

Herberg, W. Religious Communities in Present-Day
America. *R. Polit.,* 16/2, 1954, p.155–74.

Hertzler, J. O. Religious Institutions. *Ann. Amer. Acad.
Polit. Soc. Sci.,* 256, 1948, p.1–13.

Hoffman, H. *The Religions of Tibet.* London: Allen &
Unwin, 1961.

Hudson, W. S. *Religion in America.* N.Y.: Scribners,
1965, 448p.

Hughes, E. R. and Hughes, K. *Religion in China.* London: Hutchinson's Univ. Library, 1950.

Irving, K. Religion in the Middle East. *Curr. Hist.,* 32,
1957, p.327–31.

Johnston, R. F. *The Development of Negro Religion.* N. Y.: Philosophical Library, 1954.

Jurji, E. J. *The Middle East: Its Religion and Culture.* Phila.: Westminster Press, 1956.

Kidder-Smith, G. E. *New Churches of Europe.* N.Y.: Holt, Rinehart & Winston, 1964.

Kim, K. W. The Meaning of Negativism in Oriental Religions. *J. Bib. Rel.*, 18, 1950, p.29–33.

Kitagawa, J. M. *Religions of the East.* Phila.: Westminster Press, 1960, 319p.

Kolarz, W. *Religion in the Soviet Union.* N.Y.: St. Martin's Press, 1961.

Landis, B. Y. *World Religions.* N.Y.: Dutton, 1957.

Lee, J. O. Religion Among Ethnic and Racial Minorities. *Ann. Amer. Acad. Polit. Soc. Sci.*, 332, 1960, p.112–24.

Macquarrie, J. *Twentieth Century Religious Thought.* N. Y.: Harper & Row, 1963.

Mahadevan, T.M.P. Religion in India. *Indo-Asian Cult.*, 10/2, 1961, p.179–82.

Mamoria, C. B. Religious Composition of Population in India. *Mod. R.*, 100/3, 1956, p.189–98.

Mann, W. E. *Sect, Cult and Church in Alberta.* Toronto: Univ. of Toronto Press, 1955.

Mathison, R. *Faiths, Cults and Sects of America, From Atheism to Zen.* Indianapolis: Bobbs-Merrill Co., 1960, 384p.

Mayer, F. E. *The Religious Bodies of America.* St. Louis: Concordia, 1954.

Melish, W. H. *Religion Today in the U. S. S. R.* N.Y.: National Council of American-Soviet Friendship, 1945, 46p.

Nanzig, D. The New Status of Religious Groups. *J. Intergr. Relat.*, 2/1, 1961, p.18–26.

Noss, J. B. *Man's Religions.* N.Y.: The Macmillan Co., 1949.

Olmstead, C. E. *Religion in America:Past and Present.* Englewood Cliffs: Prentice-Hall Co., 1961.

Parrinder, E. G. *An Introduction to Asian Religion.* London: S. P. C. K., 1957, 138p.

Parrinder, E. G. The Religious Situation in West Africa. *Afr. Aff.*, 59/234, 1960, p.38–42.

Parrinder, E. G. *Religion in an African City.* N.Y.: Oxford Univ. Press, 1953.

Parsons, T. The Pattern of Religious Organization in the United States. *Daedalus*, 88/3, 1959, p.65–85.

Radhakrishnan, S. Indian Religious Thought and Modern Civilization. *Indo-Asian Cult.*, 7/1, 1958, p.5–30.

Rakoczi, B. I. Religious Faiths and Practice Among the Gypsies of France. *J. Gypsy Lore Society*, 37/1-2, 1958, p.31–40.

Ring, G. C. *Religions of the Far East.* Milwaukee: Brace, 1950.

Roggendorf, J. The Place of Religion in Modern Japan. *Japan Quart.*, 5/1, 1958, p.452–63.

Salisbury, W. S. *Religion in American Culture: A Sociological Interpretation.* Homewood, Illinois: Dorsey Press, 1961.

Schneider, H. W. *Religion in Twentieth Century America.* Cambridge: Harvard Univ. Press, 1952.

Shuster, G. N. *Religion Behind the Iron Curtain.* N. Y.: Macmillan, 1954, 281p.

Smith, H. W. *Man and His Gods.* Boston: Little, Brown, and Co., 1952.

Smith, J. W. and Jamison, A. L. (eds.) *Religion in American Life.* Princeton: Princeton Univ. Press, 1961, 4 vols.

Speigelberg, F. *Living Religions of the World.* London: Thames & Hudson, 1957, 511p.

Sperry, W. L. *Religion in America.* N.Y.: Macmillan Co., 1946.

Sweet, W. W. *The American Churches: An Interpretation.* N.Y.: Abingdon-Cokesbury Press, 1948, 153p.

Sweet, W. W. *American Culture and Religion: Six Essays.* Dallas: Southern Methodist Univ. Press, 1951, 114p.

Thomas, G. F. *Religious Philosophies of the West.* N. Y.: Scribners, 1965, 454p.

Thomas, J. L. Religion in American Society. *Soc. Order*, 6, 1956, p.241–6, 312–8.

Thomas, J. L. *Religion and the American People.* Westminster, Maryland: Newman Press, 1963.

Tully, R. Religious Organizations. *Ann. Amer. Acad. Polit. Soc. Sci.*, 313, 1957, p.76–8.

Ullendorf, E. *The Ethiopians: An Introduction to Country and People.* London: Oxford Univ. Press, 1960, 232p.

Underhill, R. M. Religion Among American Indians. *Ann. Amer. Acad. Polit. Soc. Sci.*, 311, 1957, p.127–36.

Vogt, V. O. *Cult and Culture: A Study of Religion and American Society.* N. Y.: Macmillan, 1951, 263p.

Weigel, G. *Churches in North America.* Baltimore: Helicon Press, 1961.

Wells, C. D. Religious Institutional Types. *Sociol. Soc. Res.*, 17/6, 1933, p.551–9.

Wendland, H. D. Church and Society in Japan Today. *Ecumen. R.*, 8/2, 1956, p.143–53.

Zahn, J. C. (ed.) *Religion and the Face of America.* Berkeley: Univ. of California Press, 1958.

See Also: 3,6

Anderson, P. B.   4a1
Burstein, S. R.   9
Cogley, L. (ed.)   8a1
Day, C. B.   3
Donovan, J. D.   7a4
Erskine, H. G.   4f
Gausted, E. S.   3

Goddijn, H.P.M.   8a2
Hertzberg, A.   5a
Hunter, E. A.   4f2
Kruitj, J. P.   5a3
Lambert, R.   6c
Leeson, I.   9
Moberg, D. O.   8a1
Offner, C. B.   5b
Parsons, T.   8a2
Patterson, R. L.   7b3
Potter, K. H.   8a1
Robbins, R. H.   9
Solomon, V.   7d
Yang, C. K.   3

2a. Christianity

Allen, E. L. Religious Thought in Great Britain (1900–1950). *Rel. Life*, 20, 1951, p.203–13.

Assunta, M. (ed.) *The Church in the World: A Bibliography. Reading For Teachers and Students in Undergraduate and Graduate Courses of Study on the Church.* Cincinnati, Ohio: CSMC Press, 1963, 129p.

Attwater, D. *The Christian Churches of the East.* Milwaukee: Bruce, 1947–48, 2 Vols.

Bastide, R. Religion and the Church in Brazil. In T. Smith and A. Marchant (eds.)—*Brazil: Portrait of Half a Continent.* N. Y.: Dryden Press, 1951, p.334–55.

Berdyaev, N. *Christian Existentialism.* N.Y.: Harper, 1965, 333p.

Berger, P. L. *The Noise of Solemn Assemblies.* Garden City: Doubleday & Co., 1961.

Bertrams, W. *The Papacy, The Episcopacy and Collegiality* (Trans. P. T. Brannon). Westminster, Maryland: Newman Press, 1964, 151p.

Brunner, H. E. *Christianity and Civilization.* N.Y.: Scribners, 1948–49, vol. 2.

Bushee, F. A. The Church in a Small City. *Amer. J. Sociol.*, 49/3, 1943, p.223–32.

Carpenter, G. W. The Role of Christianity and Islam in Contemporary Africa. *Afr. Today*, 1959, p.90–113.

Chittick, H. N. The Last Christian Stronghold in the Sudan. *Kush*, 11, 1963, p.264–72.

Cross, F. L. (ed.) *The Oxford Dictionary of the Christian Church.* London: Oxford Univ. Press, 1958, 1492p.

Fichter, J. H. and Maddox, G. L. Religion in the South, Old and New. In J. McKinney, and E. Thompson (eds.) *The South in Continuity and Change.* Durham, North Carolina: Univ. of North Carolina Press, 1965.

Gerrish, B. A. (ed.) *The Faith of Christendom: A Sourcebook of Creeds and Confessions.* Cleveland: Meridian Books, 1963, 371p.

Highet, J. *The Churches in Scotland Today: A Survey of Their Principles, Strength, Work and Statements.* Glascow: Jackson Son & Co., 1950, 257p.

Hope, N. V. Church and Religion in Present-Day Scotland. *Theology To-Day*, 9, 1953, p.494–501.

Hunter, L. S. (ed.) *Scandinavian Churches: A Picture of the Development and Life of the Churches of Denmark, Finland, Iceland, Norway, and Sweden.* London: Faber, 1965, 200p.

Littell, F. H. *The German Phoenix: Men and Movements in the Church in Germany.* Garden City: Doubleday & Co., 1960.

Maillart, E. The Christian Fishermen of Malabar. *Geogr. Mag.*, 30/8, 1957, p.315–25.

Mead, F. S. *Handbook of Denominations in the United States.* N. Y.: Abingdon, 1965, 272p.

Obenhaus, V. *The Church and Faith in Mid-America.* Phila.: Westminster Press, 1963, 174p.

Peel, R. *Christian Science: Its Encounter with American Culture.* Garden City: Doubleday and Co., 1965, 224p.

Warner, W. L. and Srole, L. *The Social Systems of American Ethnic Groups.* New Haven: Yale Univ. Press, 1945.

See Also: 3a, 6

Barnett, J. H.   5a1
Callaway, T. N.   2e
Carrier, H.   9
Christian Periodical Index   9

2a1. Protestants

Ady, C. H. *The English Church and How it Works.* London: Faber, 1944, 300p.

Andrews, E. D. *The People Called Shakers: A Search for the Perfect Society.* N.Y.: Oxford Univ. Press, 1953, 309p.

Andrews, T. *The Polish National Catholic Church in America and Poland.* London: S. P. C. K., 1953, 117p.

Armytage, W. H. G. The Moravian Communities in Britain. *Church Quart. R.*, 158, 1957, p.141–52.

Banton, M. An Independent African Church in Sierra Leone. *Hibbert J.*, 55/216, 1956, p.57–63.

Barnes, W. W. *The Southern Baptist Convention, 1845–1953.* Nashville: Broadman Press, 1954, 329p.

Barnett, H. G. *Indian Shakers: A Messianic Cult of the Pacific Northwest.* Carbondale, Illinois: Southern Illinois Univ. Press, 1957, 378p.

Beecher, L. J. African Separatist Church in Kenya. *World Domin.*, 31, 1953, p.5–12.

Bloch-Hoell, N. *The Pentocostal Movement.* London: Allen & Unwin, 1964, 256p.

Braden, C. S. The Sects. *Ann. Amer. Acad. Polit. Soc. Sci.*, 256, 1948, p.53–62.

Braden, C. S. *Christian Science Today: Power, Policy, Practice.* Dallas: Southern Methodist Univ. Press, 1958.

Bram, J. Jehovah's Witnesses and the Values of American Culture. *Trans. New York Acad. Sci.*, 19/1, 1956, p.47–54.

Calley, M. J. C. Pentecostal Sects Among West Indian Migrants. *Race*, 3/2, 1962, p.55–64.

Calley, M. J. C. *God's People: West Indian Pentacostal Sects in England.* N.Y.: Oxford Univ. Press, 1965, 182p.

Cameron, R. M. *Methodism and Society in Historical Perspective.* N. Y.: Abingdon Press, 1961.

Carstems, C. G. The Salvation Army: A Criticism. *Ann. Amer. Acad. Polit. Soc. Sci.*, 30/3, 1907, p.117–28.

Carter, P. *The Decline and Revival of the Social Gospel.* Ithaca: Cornell Univ., 1954.

Clark, E. T. *The Small Sects in America.* N.Y.: Abingdon Press, 1949, 256p.

Clear, V. The Church of God: A Study in Social Adaptation. *R. Rel. Res.*, 2/3, 1961, p.129–33.

Cobb, J. B., Jr. *Varieties of Protestantism.* Phila.: Westminster Press, 1960, 271p.

Conkin, P. K. *Two Paths to Utopia: The Hutterites and the Llano Colony.* Lincoln: Univ. of Nebraska Press, 1964.

Dall, E. E. Social and Economic Organization in Two Pennsylvania German Religious Communities. *Amer. J. Sociol.*, 57, 1951, p.168–77.

Davies, H. *The English Free Churches.* London: Oxford Univ. Press, 1963, 208p.

Davis, J. A Study of Protestant Church Boards of Control. *Amer. J. Sociol.*, 38/3, 1932, p.418–31.

Dohi, A. and Drummond, R. The Non-Church Movement in Japan. *J. Ecumen. Stud.*, 2/3, 1965, p.448–68.

Dohrman, H. T. *California Cult: The Story of Mankind United.* Boston: Beacon Press, 1958, 163p.

Drake, T. W. *Quakers and Slavery in America.* New Haven: Yale Univ. Press, 1950, 245p.

Dunstan, J. L. (ed.) *Protestantism.* N.Y.: G. Braziller, 1961, 255p.

Eddy, C. N. Store-Front Religion. *Rel. Life*, 28, 1958–59, p. 68–85.

England, R. W. Some Aspects of Christian Science as Reflected in Letters of Testimony. *Amer. J. Sociol.*, 59/5, 1954, p.448–53.

Ferm, V. *A Protestant Dictionary.* N. Y.: Philosophical Library, 1951, 283p.

Ferm, V. (ed.) *The American Church of Protestant Heritage.* N. Y.: Philosophical Library, 1953, 280p.

Francis, E. K. *In Search of Utopia: The Mennonites in Manitoba.* Glencoe: Free Press, 1955.

Goen, C. C. Fundamentalism in America. *Southw. J. Theol.*, 2, 1959, p.52–62.

Griswold, A. W. New Thought: A Cult of Success. *Amer. J. Sociol.*, 40/3, 1934, p.309–18.

Halverson, M. and Cohen, A. (eds.) *A Handbook of Christian Theology: Definitive Essays on Concepts and Movements of Thought in Contemporary Protestantism.* N. Y.: World, 1958.

Harmon, N. B. *Understanding the Methodist Church.* Nashville: Methodist Publishing House, 191p.

Harrison, P. M. *Authority and Power in the Free Church Tradition: A Social Case Study of the American Baptist Convention.* Princeton: Princeton Univ. Press, 1959, 248p.

Harrison, P. M. Church and Laity Among Protestants. *Ann. Amer. Acad. Polit. Soc. Sci.*, 332, 1960, p.37–49.

Hawley, F. The Keresan Holy Rollers: An Adaptation to American Individualism. *Soc. Forces*, 26/3, 1948, p.272–80.

Hawthorn, H. B. *The Doukhobors of British Columbia.* Vancouver: Univ. of British Columbia and J. M. Dent & Sons, 1955, 342p.

Haynes, L. L., Jr. *The Negro Community Within American Protestantism.* Boston: Christopher Publishing House, 1953.

Hayward, V. E. W. African Independent Church Movement. *Int. R. Missions*, 52/206, 1963, p.163–72.

Hewson, L. A. *An Introduction to South African Methodists.* Cape Town: Standard Press, 1951, 114p.

Highet, J. The Protestant Churches of Scotland: A Review of Membership, Evangelistic Activities and Other Aspects. *Archiv. Sociol. Rel.*, 8, 1959, p.97–104.

Highet, J. *The Scottish Churches: A Review of Their State 400 Years After the Reformation.* London: Sheffington & Son, 1960, 224p.

Hine, L. Are American Baptists Declining: Chicago Baptists, 1931–1955. *Foundations*, 3, 1960, p.114–56.

Hodge, W. H. Navaho Pentecostalism. *Anthropol. Quart.*, 37/3, 1964, p.73–93.

Hoekema, A. *The Four Major Cults: Christian Science, Jehovah's Witnesses, Mormonism, Seventh Day Adventism.* Grand Rapids, Michigan: W. B. Eerdmans Publishing Co., 1963, 447p.

Holt, I. L. and Clark, E. T. *The World Methodist Movement.* Nashville: The Upper Room, 1956, 148p.

Homer, D. G. Administrative Organization of the Mormon Church. *Polit. Sci. Quart.*, 57/1, 1942, p.51–71.

Hook, W. F. The Lutheran Church in the Carolinas Sociologically Interpreted. *Luth. Quart.*, 11, 1959, p.60–7.

Hostetler, J. A. *Amish Life.* Scottdale, Pennsylvania: Herald Press, 1959, 39p.

Hostetler, J. A. *Mennonite Life.* Scottdale, Pennsylvania: Herald Press, 1959, 39p.

Hostetler, J. A. *Amish Society.* Baltimore: John Hopkins Press, 1963, 347p.

Iglehart, C. W. *A Century of Protestant Christianity in Japan.* Tokyo: C. E. Tuttle, Co., 1959.

Isichei, E. A. Organization and Power in the Society of Friends. *Archiv. Sociol. Rel.*, 10/19, 1965, p.31–47.

Johnston, R. F. *The Religion of Negro Protestants.* N.Y.: Philosophical Library, 1956.

Kennedy, G. H. *The Methodist Way of Life.* Englewood Cliffs: Prentice Hall, 1958, 216p.

Kohler, W. Protestantism in Japan. *Swiss R. World Aff.*, 5/7, 1955, p.14–6.

Lee, R. The Organizational Dilemma in American Protestantism. *Union Sem. Quart. R.*, 16, 1960, p.9–19.

Lloyd, R. *The Church of England in the Twentieth Century.* London: Longmans, 1946/50, 2 Vol.

Lookes, H. *The Quaker Contribution.* N.Y.: Macmillan, 1965, 128p.

Louden, S. *The True Face of the Kirk: An Examination of the Ethos and Tradition of the Church in Scotland.* N.Y.: Oxford Univ. Press, 1963.

Mackie, R. C. Impressions of the Church of South India. *Ecumen. R.*, 9/1, 1956, p.27–32.

Makler, H. M. Centralization/Decentralization in Formal Organizations: A Case Study of American Protestant Denominations. *R. Rel. Res.*, 5/1, 1963, p.5–11.

Maston, T. B. Baptists, Social Christianity, and Culture. *Rel. Educ.*, 61, 1964, p.521–31.

Mayfield, G. *The Church of England.* N.Y.: Oxford Univ. Press, 1958, 213p.

Meade, S. E. American Protestantism Since the Civil War. *J. Rel.*, 36, 1956, p. 1–15; see also p.67–89.

Molnar, A. *Czechoslovak Protestantism Today.* Prague: Central Church Publishing House, 1954, 41p.

Muelder, W. G. *Methodism and Society in the Twentieth Century.* N.Y.: Abingdon, 1961.

O'Dea, T. F. *The Mormons.* Chicago: Univ. of Chicago Press, 1957.

Payne, E. A. *The Free Church Tradition in the Life of England.* London: S. C. M. 1951, 192p.

Peel, R. V.   The Wackacobi: Extremists of Our Own Times. *West. Polit. Quart.*, 16/3, 1963, p.569–97.

Pelt, O. D. and Smith, R. L.   *The Story of National Baptists.* N.Y.: Vantage Press, 1960, 272p.

Pfautz, H. W.   A Case Study of an Urban Religious Movement: Christian Science. In E. W. Burgess and D. J. Bogue (eds.)   *Contributions to Urban Sociology.* Chicago: Univ. of Chicago Press, 1964, p.284–303.

Phillips, J. M.   The Formation of a Japanese Protestant Tradition. *Japan. Christ. Quart.*, 29, 1963, p.260–9.

Piercy, C. B.   *The Valley of God's Pleasure.* N.Y.: Stanford House, 1961.

Pike, R.   *Jehovah's Witnesses: Who They are, What They Teach, What They Do.* N.Y.: Philosophical Library, 1954, 140p.

Poblete, R. and O'Dea, T. D.   Anomie and "The Quest for Community:" The Formation of Sects Among the Puerto Ricans of New York. *Amer. Cath. Sociol. R.*, 21/1, 1960, p.18–36.

Pollard, F. E., *et al. Democracy and the Quaker Method.* N.Y.: Philosophical Library, 1950, 160p.

Redekop, C.   Decision-Making in a Sect. *R. Rel. Res.*, 2/2, 1960, p.79–86.

Rice, C. S. and Steinmetz, R. C.   *The Amish Year.* New Brunswick, New Jersey: Rutgers Univ. Press, 1956, 224p.

Roberts, T. E.   *Baptists and Disciples of Christ.* London: Carey, Kingsgate Press, 1951.

Schilling, S. P.   *Methodism and Society in Theological Perspective.* N.Y.: Abingdon, 1960, 318p.

Schreiber, W. I.   *Our Amish Neighbors.* Chicago: Univ. of Chicago Press, 1962, 226p.

Simey, T.   The Church of England and English Society. *Soc. Compass*, 11/3–4, 1964, p.5–11.

Slosser, G. J. (ed.)   *They Seek a Country: The American Presbyterians, Some Aspects.* N.Y.: Macmillan, 1955, 330p.

Smith, E. L.   *The Amish People: 17th Century Tradition in Modern America.* N.Y.: Exposition, 1958, 258p.

Stroup, H.   *The Jehovah's Witnesses.* N.Y.: Columbia Univ. Press, 1945, 180p.

Sweet, W. W.   The Protestant Churches. *Ann. Amer. Acad. Polit. Soc. Sci.*, 256, 1948, p.43–52.

Tillyard, F.   The Distribution of Free Churches in England. *Sociol. R.*, 27/1, 1935, p.1–18.

Toews, A. P.   *American Mennonite Worship: Its Roots, Development and Application.* N.Y.: Exposition Press, 1960, 193p.

Walker, W.   *The Creeds and Platforms of Congregationalism.* Boston: The Pilgrim Press, 1960, 604p.

Watson, B.   *A Hundred Years War: The Salvation Army 1865–1965.* London: Hodder and Stoughton, 1965, 318p.

Weatherford, W. D. and Brewer, E. E. C.   *Life and Religion in Southern Appalachia.* N.Y.: Friendship Press, 1962.

Webster, D.   *Pentecostalism and Speaking with Tongues.* London: Highway Press, 1965.

Welbourn, F. B.   Independency in East Africa. *Ecumen. R.*, 11/4, 1959, p.430–6.

Whalen, W. J.   *Armageddon Around the Corner: A Report of Jehovah's Witnesses.* N.Y.: John Day Co., 1962.

Whalen, W. J.   *Latter-Day Saints in the Modern Day World: An Account of Contemporary Mormonism.* N.Y.: John Day Co., 1964, 319p.

Willms, A. M.   The Brethren Known as Hutterites. *Canad. J. Econ. Polit. Sci.*, 24/3, 1958, p.391–405.

Wilson, B. R.   *Sects and Society: A Sociological Study of Elim Tabernacle, Christian Science, and Christadelphians.* Berkeley: Univ. of Calitornia Press, 1961.

Wishlade, R. L.   *Sectarianism in Southern Nyasaland.* London: Oxford Univ. Press, 1965, 170p.

Yamada, H. and Bethel, D. M.   The Spirit of Jesus Church. *Japan. Christ. Quart.*, 30/3, 1964, p.220–4.

Yarnall, H.   An Example of the Psychopathology of Religion: The Seventh-Day Adventist Denomination. *J. Nervous Ment. Disease*, 125, 1957, p.202–12.

Young, K.   *Isn't One Wife Enough: The Story of Mormon Polygamy.* N.Y.: H. Holt & Co., 1954, 476p.

See Also:

Pfautz, H. W. 6c
Schlegel, S. A. 6c
Scott, W. H. 6c
Smith, T. L. 6c
Sundkler, V. G. M. 5a1

Walzer, M. 6b
Wearmouth, R. F. 4
Weisberger, B. A. 6c
Whitley, O. R. 6c
Wilkens, E. 6b

2a2. Catholics

Addis, W. E. and Arnold, T. *A Catholic Dictionary* (Rev. T. B. Scannell, Further Rev. P. E. Hallet). London: Routledge and Kegan Paul, 1951, 843p.

Alexander, R. J. The Church. In R. J. Alexander—*Today's Latin America*. Garden City: Doubleday & Co., 1962, p.217–36.

Barry, C. J. *The Catholic Church and German Americans*. Milwaukee: Bruce, 1953.

Blanchard, J. *The Church in Contemporary Ireland*. Dublin: Clonmore & Reynolds, Ltd., 1963, 124p.

Brantl, G. (ed.) *Catholicism*. N.Y.: G. Braziller, 1961, 256p.

Calvez, J. Y. *The Social Thought of John XXIII* (Trans. G. J. M. McKenzie). Chicago: Henry Regnery Co., 1965, 121p.

Caporale, R. *Vatican II: Last of the Councils*. Baltimore: Helicon Press, 1964, 192p.

Carthy, M. P. *Catholicism in English-Speaking Lands*. N.Y.: Hawthorne Books, 1964, 141p.

Considine, J. J. (ed.) *The Church in the New Latin America*. Notre Dame: Fides Publishers, 1964, 240p.

Corbishley, T. *Roman Catholicism*. N.Y.: Harper, 1964, 160p.

Cross, R. D. *The Emergence of Liberal Catholicism in America*. Cambridge: Harvard Univ. Press, 1958.

Deazevedo, T. Catholicism in Brazil: A Personal Evaluation. *Thought*, 109, 1953, p.253–74.

DeGuibert, J. *The Jesuits: Their Spiritual Doctrine and Practice*. Chicago: Institute of Jesuit Sources, 1964, 694p.

Ellis, J. T. *American Catholicism*. Chicago: Univ. of Chicago Press, 1956.

Etteldorf, R. *The Catholic Church in the Middle East*. N.Y.: Macmillan, 1958.

Fichter, J. H. *Southern Parish: Dynamics of a City Church*. Chicago: Univ. of Chicago Press, 1951.

Fichter, J. H. The Profile of Catholic Religious Life. *Amer. J. Sociol.*, 58/2, 1952, p.145–9.

Glanzman, G. S. and Fitzmyer, J. A. *An Introductory Bibliography for the Study of Scripture*. Westminster, Maryland: Newman Press, 1961, 135p.

Greeley, A. M. Some Information on the Present Situation of American Catholics. *Soc. Order*, 13, 1963, p. 9–24.

Kacorowski, S. *History of Social Catholicism in Poland*. Washington: National Committee for a Free Europe, Mid-European Studies Center, Research Doc., No. 15, 1953, 82p.

Kane, J. J. The Social Structure of American Catholics. *Amer. Cath. Sociol R.*, 16/1, 1955, p.23–30.

Kane, J. J. Church and Laity Among Catholics. *Ann. Amer. Acad. Polit. Soc. Sci.*, 332, 1960, p.50–9.

Kennedy, J. J. Dichotomies in the Church. *Ann. Amer. Acad. Polit. Soc. Sci.*, 334, 1961, p.54–62.

Lynskey, E. M. *The Government of the Catholic Church*. N.Y.: J. P. Kenedy & Sons, 1952, 99p.

Madsen, W. *The Virgin's Children: Life in An Aztec Village Today*. Austin: Univ. of Texas Press, 1960, 248p.

Marino, A. I. *The Catholics in America*. N.Y.: Vantage Press, 1960, 300p.

Mathew, D. *Catholicism in England: The Portrait of a Minority-Its Culture and Tradition*. London: Eyre & Spottiswoode, 1955.

McCarthy, T. P. (ed.) *Guide to the Catholic Sisterhoods in the United States*. Washington: Catholic Univ. Press, 1964, 404p.

McKnight, J. P. *The Papacy: A New Appraisal*. N.Y.: Rinehart, 1953.

Murray, J. C. The Roman Catholic Church. *Ann. Amer. Acad. Polit. Soc. Sci.*, 256, 1948, p.36–42.

Neville, R. *The World of the Vatican*. N.Y.: Harper & Row, 1962, 256p.

North, R. G. *Sociology of the Biblical Jubilee*. Rome: Pontifical Biblical Institute, 1954, 245p.

O'Brien, K. R. *Nature of Support of Diocesan Priests in the United States of America*. Washington: Catholic Univ. Press, 1949, 162p.

O'Dea, T. F. *The American Catholic Dilemma*. N.Y.: Sheed & Ward, 1958, 144p.

Ong, W. J. *Frontiers in American Catholicism*. N.Y.: Macmillan, 1957.

Pelikan, J. *Riddle of Roman Catholicism.* Nashville: Abingdon Press, 1959.

Pike, F. B. The Catholic Church in Central America. *R. Polit.*, 21/1, 1959, p.83–113.

Putz, L. J. (ed.) *The Catholic Church, U. S. A.* Notre Dame: Fides, 1956.

Reynoldine, M. (ed.) *The Catholic Booklist 1964.* Haverford, Pennsylvania: Catholic Library Assoc., 1964, 70p.; see other issues.

Scharper, P. (ed.) *American Catholics: A Protestant-Jewish View.* N.Y.: Sheed & Ward, 1959.

Sheppard, L. C. (ed.) *Twentieth Century Catholicism.* N.Y.: Hawthorn Books, 1965, 286p.

Skydsgaard, K. E. (ed.) *The Papal Council and the Gospel: Protestant-Theologians Evaluate the Coming Vatican Council.* Minneapolis: Augsburg Publishing House, 1961.

Spitzer, A. Aspects of Religious Life in Tepoztlan. *Anthropol. Quart.*, 30/1, 1957, p.1–17.

The Twentieth Century Encyclopedia of Catholicism (H. Daniel-Rops, Editor-in-Chief). N.Y.: Hawthorne Books, 1964, 144 Vols.

Valkenier, E. The Catholic Church in Communist Poland, 1945–1955. *R. Polit.*, 18/3, 1956, p.305–26.

Ward, C. K. Some Aspects of the Social Structure of a Roman Catholic Parish. *Sociol. R.*, 6/1, 1958, p.75–93.

Ward, L. R. *Catholic Life U. S. A.: Contemporary Lay Movements.* St. Louis: B. Herder Book Co., 1959, 263p.

Watter, M. The Present Status of the Church in Venezuela. *Hisp. Amer. Hist. R.*, 1933, p.23–45.

Williams, M. *The Catholic Church in Action.* N.Y.: P. J. Kenedy & Sons, 1958.

Williams, M. J. *Catholic Social Thought.* N.Y.: Ronald Press, 1950.

Zajaczkowski, W., *et. al.* (eds.) *The Catholic Periodical Index: A Cumulative Author and Subject Index to a Selected List of Catholic Periodicals, January 1963– December, 1964.* Haverford, Pennsylvania: The Catholic Library Assoc., 1965, 717p.; see other issues.

Zubek, T. J. *The Church of Silence in Slovakia.* Whiting, Indiana: J. Lach, 1956, 310p.

See Also:

Attwater, D. 9
Barnes, S. H. 6
Bosworth, W. 4a1
Brown, W. E. 3a2
Cronin, J. F. 4b
Curran, C. A. 6c
Cutler, A. 5e1
Davies, H. 6c
Devolder, P. N. 7b
Evans, I. 9a
Foley, A. S. 7a
Giles, E. 7a1
Gurian, W. 4
Hales, E. E. Y. 6c
Harte, T. J. 4
Houtart, F. 4f
Howes, R. G. 6
Hughes, E. C. 3a2
Kapsner, O. L. 9(2)
Lavaud, B. 7a
McManus, W. E. 4g4
Mehok, W. J. 2a2, 4j
Melady, P. 6e
National Catholic Welfare Conf. 4g4
O'Connor, D. A. 4
Petrie, J. 7a
Poage, G. 7a
Powers, F. J. 4a
Rafton, H. P. 7a3
Saint Joseph's Seminary 9
Schmideler, E. 4j4
Schuyler, J. B. 4
Shuster, G. M. 5b2
Thorman, D. J. 7b
Watkin, E. 4g4
Watkin, E. I. 6c
Weima, J. 5a2
Young, B. 8a2

2a3. Orthodox

Abramstov, D. F. *Complete Directory of Orthodox Catholic Churches in the United States.* Phila.: Orthodox Catholic Literature Association, 1953, 48p.

Anderson, P. B. The Orthodox Church in Soviet Russia. *Foreign Aff.*, 39/2, 1961, p.299–311.

Bolshakoff, S. *The Foreign Missions of the Russian Orthodox Church.* London: Society for Promoting Christian Knowledge, 1943, 120p.

Casey, R. P. *Religion in Russia.* N.Y.: Harper & Brothers, 1946, 198p.

Filipovic, M. S. Folk Religion Among the Orthodox Population in Eastern Yugoslavia. *Harvard Slavic Stud.*, 1954, p.359–74.

French, R. M. *The Eastern Orthodox Church.* London: Hutchinson's Univ. Library, 1951, 186p.

Guillou, M. J. *The Spirit of Eastern Orthodox* (Trans. D. Attwater). Glen Rock, New Jersey: Paulist Press, 1964, 121p.

Hardy, E. R. *Christian Egypt, Church and People: Christianity and Nationalism in the Patriarchate of Alexandria.* N.Y.: Oxford Univ. Press, 1952, 242p.

Levada, Y. A. The Social Position of Russian Orthodoxy (Trans. R. Pickering). *J. World Hist.*, 8/1, 1964, p.123–45.

Meyendorff, J. *The Orthodox Church: Its Past, and Its Role in the World Today.* N.Y.: Pantheon Books, 1963, 244p.

Phillippou, A. J. (ed.) *The Orthodox Ethos: Studies in Orthodoxy.* Oxford: Holywell Press, 1964, 288p.

Schlesinger, R. The Orthodox Church in the Ukraine. *Soviet Stud.*, 6/1, 1954, p.64–74.

Spinka, M. *The Church in Soviet Russia.* N.Y.: Oxford Univ. Press, 1956, 179p.

Waddams, H. The Church in Soviet Russia. *Soviet Stud.*, 5/1, 1953, p.8–17.

See Also:

Andrews, T.   9
Curtiss, J. S.   4a1
Levada, Y. A.   4a1
London, I. D.   7b
Martinos, A.   9
Minihan, J.   8a4
Schmemann, A.   3a3
United States   9

2b. Judaism

American Jewish Committee: *American Jewish Yearbook.* Phila.: Jewish Publication Society, 66, 1965, 652p.; see preceding volumes.

Attal, R. Tunisian Jewry During the Last Twenty Years. *Jew. J. Sociol.*, 2/1, 1960, p.4–15.

Attal, R. The Statistics of North African Jewry. *Jew. J. Sociol.*, 5/1, 1963, p.27–34.

Austri, D. Y. The Jewish Community of Mexico. *In Dispersion*, 2, 1962, p.51–73.

Bentwich, N. *The Jews in Our Time.* Baltimore: Penguin Books, 1960, 175p.

Berkovits, E. *Judaism: Fossil or Ferment?* N. Y.: Philosophical Library, 1956, 176p.

Birnbaum, P. *A Book of Jewish Concepts.* N. Y.: Hebrew Publishing Co., 1964, 719p.

Bloch, J. *Of Making Many Books: An Annotated List of the Books Issued by the Jewish Publication Society.* Philadelphia: Jewish Publication Society of America, 1953, 329p.

Brotz, H. Negro "Jews" in the United States. *Phylon*, 13/4, 1952, p.324–37.

Brotz, H. *The Black Jews of Harlem.* London: Collier-Macmillan, 1964.

Carlebach, J. *The Jews of Nairobi, 1904–1962.* The Nairobi Hebrew Congregation, 1962, 90p.

Chiel, A. A. *The Jews in Manitoba.* Toronto: Univ. of Toronto Press, 1961.

Chouraqui, A. North African Jewry Today. *Jew. J. Sociol.*, 1/1, 1959, p.58–68.

Clark, K. B. Jews in Contemporary America. *Jew. Soc. Serv. Quart.*, 31, 1954, p.12–22.

Cohen, E. E. (ed.) *Commentary on the American Scene: Portraits of Jewish Life in America.* N.Y.: A. Knopf, 1953.

Cohen, P. S. Alignments and Allegiances in the Community of SHAARAYIM in Israel. *Jew. J. Sociol.*, 4/1, 1962, p.14–38.

Cohon, S. S. The Contemporary Mood in Reform Judaism. *J. Bib. Rel.*, 18, 1950, p.155–9.

Dawidowicz, L. S. What Future for Judaism in Russia? *Commentary*, 22/5, 1956, p.401–7.

Dicker, H. *Wanderers and Settlers in the Far East: A Century of Jewish Life in China and Japan.* N.Y.: Twayne, 1962.

Dresner, S. H. *The Jew in American Life.* N.Y.: Crown Publishers, 1963, 319p.

Duker, A. G. Notes on the Culture of American Jews. *Jew. J. Sociol.*, 2, 1960, p.98–102.

Ehrman, A. The Commandment Keepers: A Negro "Jewish" Cult in America Today. *Judaism*, 8/3, 1959, p.266–70.

Engelman, U. Z. The Jewish Synagogue in the United States. *Amer. J. Sociol.*, 41, 1935, p.44–51.

Feitelson, D. Aspects of the Social Life of Kurdish Jews. *Jew. J. Sociol.*, 1/2, 1959, p.201–16.

Feldman, A. J. *The American Jew: A Study of Backgrounds.* N. Y.: Bloch Publishing Co., 1959, 52p.

Freedman, M. The Jewish Population of Great Britain. *Jew. J. Sociol.,* 4/1, 1962, p.92–100.

Freedman, M. (ed.) *A Minority in Britain: Social Studies of the Anglo-Jewish Community.* London: Vallentine, Mitchell & Co., 1964, 296p.

Friedman, T. and Gordis, R. *Jewish Life in America.* N.Y.: Horizon Press, 1955, 352p.

Gans, H. J. American Jewry: Present and Future. *Commentary,* 21, 1956, p.422–30; see also p.555–63.

Gans, M., *et al. Index to Jewish Periodicals June 1963— May 1964: An Author and Subject Index to Selected American and Anglo-Jewish Journals of General and Scholarly Interest.* Cleveland, Ohio, 1964, 465p.

Gerwirtz, L. B. *The Authentic Jew and His Judaism: An Analysis of the Basic Concepts of the Jewish Religion.* N.Y.: Bloch Publishing Co., 1961, 306p.

Ginsberg, M. A Review of the European Jewish Communities Today and Some Questions for Tomorrow. *Jew. J. Sociol.,* 6/1, 1964, p.118–31.

Gittelsohn, R. B. *Modern Jewish Problems.* N.Y.: Union of American Hebrew Congregations, 1964, 239p.

Glazer, N. What Sociology Knows About American Jews. *Commentary,* 9, 1950, p.275–84.

Glazer, N. *American Judaism.* Chicago: Univ. of Chicago Press, 1957.

Goldfarb, S. D. *Ready-Reference Jewish Encyclopedia.* N.Y.: Shilo, 1963, 248p.

Goldstein, I. *The American-Jewish Community: Trends, Potentials, Leadership, and Organization.* N.Y.: Bloch Publishing Co., 1960, 40p.

Gordon, A. I. *Jews in Transition.* Minneapolis: Univ of Minnesota, 1949.

Gordon, J. (ed.) *The Jews in the Soviet Satellite Countries.* Syracuse: Syracuse Univ. Press, 1953, 500p.

Gordon, W. H. *A Community in Stress.* N.Y.: Living Books, 1964, 269p.

Gould, J. American Jewry: Some Social Trends. *Jew. J. Sociol.,* 3/1, 1961, p.55–75.

Gutman, I. The Jews of Poland After World War II. *In Dispersion,* 2, 1962, p.81–92.

Halpern, B. *The American Jew: A Zionist Analysis.* N.Y.: Theodor Herzl Foundation, 1956, 174p.

Handlin, O. *Adventure in Freedom: Three Hundred Years of Jewish Life in America.* N.Y.: McGraw-Hill, 1954.

Handlin, O. The American Jewish Pattern After 300 Years. *Commentary,* 18/4, 1954, p.296–307.

Harrison, B. Judaism. *Ann. Amer. Acad. Polit. Soc. Sci.,* 256, 1948, p.25–35.

Herberg, W. *Judaism and Modern Man: An Interpretation of Jewish Religion.* Phila.: Jewish Publication Society of America, 1951, 314p.

Hertzberg, A. (ed.) *Judaism.* N. Y.: G. Braziller, 1961, 256p.

Hirschberg, H. Z. The Problem of the Judaized Berbers. *J. Afr. Hist.,* 4/3, 1963, p.313–9.

Horowitz, I. L. The Jewish Community of Buenos Aires. *Jew. J. Sociol.,* 4/2, 1962, p.147–71.

Institute of Jewish Affairs. *European Jewry Ten Years After the War: An Account of the Development and Present Status of the Jewish Communities of Europe.* N.Y.: Institute of Jewish Affairs, 1956, 293p.

Jacobs, L. *Principles of the Jewish Faith.* N.Y.: Basic Books, 1964, 473p.

Jacobson, D. The Jews of South Africa. *Commentary,* 23/1, 1957, p.39–45.

Kallen, H. M. American Jews: What Now? *Jew. Soc. Serv. Quart.,* 32/1, 1955, p.12–9.

Kertzer, M. N. *What is a Jew?* N.Y.: World, 1953.

Krausz, E. An Anglo-Jewish Community: Leeds. *Jew. J. Sociol.,* 3/1, 1961, p.88–106.

Learsi, R. *The Jews in America.* Cleveland: World Publishing Co., 1954.

Lebeson, A. L. *Pilgrim People.* N.Y.: Harper & Brothers, 1950, 624p.

Lehmann, R. P. *Nova Bibliotheca Anglo-Judaica: A Bibliographical Guide to Anglo-Jewish History, 1937– 1960.* London: Jewish Historical Society of England, 1961, 232p.

Lerner, R. N. A Note on Argentina Jewry Today. *Jew. J. Sociol.,* 6/1, 1964, p.75–80.

Leventman, S. and Kramer, J. R. *Children of the Gilded Ghetto: Conflict Resolutions of Three Generations of American Jews.* New Haven: Yale Univ. Press, 1961, 228p.

Levitte, G. Impressions of French Jewry Today. *Jew. J. Sociol.,* 2/2, 1960, p. 172–84.

Lipman, V. D. Synagogal Organization in Anglo-Jewry. *Jew. J. Sociol.,* 1/1, 1959, p.80–93.

Loewe, R. Defining Judaism: Some Ground Breaking. *Jew. J. Sociol.,* 7/2, 1965, p.153–75.

Lowi, T. Southern Jews: The Two Communities. *Jew. J. Sociol.,* 6/1, 1964, p.103–17.

Lurie, H. L. *A Heritage Affirmed: The Jewish Federation Movement in America.* Phila.: Jewish Publication Society of America, 1961, 481p.

Margolis, I. and Markowitz, S. L. *Jewish Holidays and Festivals.* N.Y.: Citadel Press, 1962, 123p.

Massarik, F. The Jewish Community. In M. B. Sussman (ed.)—*Community Structure and Analysis.* N.Y.: Thomas Y. Crowell Co., 1959, p.237–52.

Mattuck, I. I. *The Essentials of Liberal Judaism.* London: Routledge, 1948, 184p.

Monet, D. The Jewish Community of Egypt. *New Outlook,* 1/1, 1957, p.25–8.

Nathan, N. Notes on the Jews of Turkey. *Jew. J. Sociol.,* 6/2, 1964, p.172–89.

Nove, A. Jews in the Soviet Union. *Jew. J. Sociol.,* 3/1, 1961, p.108–20.

Plotnik, L. The Sephardin in New Lots. *Commentary,* 25/1, 1958, p. 28–35.

Poll, S. *The Hasidic Community of Williamsburg.* Glencoe: Free Press, 1962.

Pollack, A. Jews in Sweden. *In Dispersion,* 1, 1962, p.54–70.

Pool, D. de S. and Pool, T. de S. *An Old Faith in the New World: Portrait of Shearith Israel, 1654–1954.* N.Y.: Columbia Univ. Press, 1955, 595p.

Rabinowitz, I. L. South African Jewry Today. *In Dispersion,* 2, 1963, p.137–46.

Roth, C. (ed.) *The Standard Jewish Encyclopedia.* N.Y.: Doubleday, Garden City, 1959.

Roth, C. The Zealots: A Jewish Religious Sect. *Judaism,* 8/1, 1959, p.33–40.

Roth, L. *Judaism: A Portrait.* N.Y.: Viking Press, 1961, 240p.

Sanua, V. D. A Review of Social Science Studies on Jews and Jewish Life in the United States. *J. Sci. Stud. Rel.,* 4/1, 1964, p.71–83.

Sapolinsky, A. The Jewry of Uruguay. *In Dispersion,* 2, 1963, p.74–88.

Scholem, G. G. *Major Trends in Jewish Mysticism.* N.Y.: Schocken, 1954.

Schwarz, S. M. *The Jews in the Soviet Union.* Syracuse: Syracuse Univ. Press, 1951, 380p.

Sherman, C. B. *The Jew Within American Society.* Detroit: Wayne State Univ. Press, 1965, 260p.

Silver, A. H. *Where Judaism Differed: An Inquiry into the Distinctiveness of Judaism.* N.Y.: Macmillan, 1956, 318p.

Sklare, M. Church and Laity Among Jews. *Ann. Amer. Acad. Polit. Soc. Sci.,* 332, 1960, p.61–9.

Smythe, H. H. and Gershuny, T. Jewish Castes of Cochin, India. *Sociol. Soc. Res.,* 41/2, 1956, p.108–11.

Smythe, H. H. and Pine, J. J. Jews in America Since World War II. *Phylon,* 16/1, 1955, p.65–70.

Spector, S. I. Jewish Survival: A Cultural Paradox. *J. Educ. Sociol.,* 30/4, 1956, p.200–8.

Steinbach, A. D. (ed.) *Jewish Book Annual, Volume 20.* N.Y.: Martin Press, Jewish Book Council of America, 1963, 235p.; see other years.

Strizower, S. *Erotic Jewish Communities.* London: Thomas Yoseloff, 1962.

Tint, H. The Jews of France. *Jew. J. Sociol.,* 1/1, 1959, p.127–31.

Umen, S. *The Nature of Judaism.* N.Y.: Philosophical Library, 1961, 152p.

Weiss, J. G. (ed.) *Papers of the Institute of Jewish Studies.* London: Oxford Univ. Press, Vol. 1, 1964, 210p.

Wilson, E. *The Scrolls From the Dead Sea.* N.Y.: Oxford Univ. Press, 1955.

Winsberg, M. D. *Colonia Baron Hirsch: A Jewish Agricultural Colony in Argentina.* Gainesville: Univ. of Florida Monograph, No. 19, 1963, 71p.

See Also: 3b, 5a

Runes, D. B. 9
Schiper, L. 8a6
Schmidt, N. J. 4f1
Schwab, H. 4f2
Shunami, S. 9

Steinbach, A. D. 9
Steinberg, S. 6c
Vlavianos, B. J. 4a
Yetiv, I. 6c
Zeitlin, J. 7a2

2c. *Hinduism*

Berreman, G. D. *Hindus of the Himalayas.* Berkeley: Univ. of California Press, 1963, 430p.

Bhattacharya, T. P. The Cult of Brahma. *J. Bihar Res. Society*, 40/4, 1954, p.365–94; see also 41/1, p.13–58.

Carstairs, G. M. *The Twice-Born: A Study of a Community of High-Caste Hindus.* London: Hogarth Press, 1957.

Chakravarti, C. The Hindu Rituals. *Bull. Ramakrishna Mission Inst. Cult.*, 8/9, 1958, p.212-7.

Chakravarty, A. Hinduism: A Reevaluation. *Civilisations*, 7/4, 1957, p.500-6.

Danielou, A. *Hindu Polytheism.* N.Y.: Bollingen Foundation, 1964, 537p.

Devanandan, P. D. *A Bibliography on Hinduism.* Bangalore: Christian Institute for the Study of Religion and Society, 1961, 14p.

Dumont, P. E. The Animal Sacrifice in the Taittiriya-Brahmana. *Proc. Amer. Philos. Society*, 106/3, 1962, p.246–63; see also 107/2, 1963, p.177–82.

Fuchs, S. *The Children of Hari.* Vienna: Verlag Herold, 1950, 463p.

Gervis, P. *Naked as They Pray.* London: Cassell, 1956, 217p.

Harper, E. B. A Hindu Village Pantheon. *Southw. J. Anthropol.*, 15/3, 1959, p.227–34.

Hermanns, M. *Hinduism and Tribal Culture.* Bombay: K. L. Fernandes, 1957, 59p.

Ingalls, D. The Brahman Tradition. *J. Amer. Folklore*, 71/281, 1958, p.209–15.

Karve, I. K. *Hindu Society: An Interpretation.* Poona: Deccan College, 1961, 171p.

Katiresu, S. A. *Handbook of Saiva Religion.* Madras: Natesan, 1950.

Mahadevan, T. M. P. *Outlines of Hinduism.* Bombay: Chetana, 1956, 312p.

Mahar, P. M. A Ritual Pollution Scale for Ranking Hindu Castes. *Sociometry*, 23, 1960, p.292–306.

Monier-Williams, M. *Hinduism.* Calcutta: Susil Gupta, 1951.

Morgan, K. W. (ed.) *The Religion of the Hindus.* N.Y.: Ronald Press, 1953, 434p.

Nandimath, S. C. *A Handbook of Virasaivism.* Dharwar, South India: Lingayat Education Association, 1953, 269p.

Patterson, M. L. P. and Inden, R. B. (eds.) *Introduction to the Civilization of India, South Asia: An Introductory Bibliography.* Chicago: Syllabus Division, Univ. of Chicago Press, 1962, 412p.

Prabhu, P. H. *Hindu Social Organization: A Study in Socio-Psychological and Ideological Foundations.* Bombay: Popular Book Depot, 1958, 387p.

Ramaswami, A. C. P. *Fundamentals of Hindu Faith and Culture: A Collection of Essays and Addresses.* Hollywood, California: Vedanta Press, 1959, 160p.

Renou, L. (ed.) *Hinduism.* N.Y.: G. Braziller, 1961, 255p.

Sakena, S. K. Hinduism. *Stud. Gen.*, 15/10, 1962, p.625–32.

Singer, M. The Radha-Krishna Bhajans of Madras City. *Hist. Rel.*, 2/1, 1963, p.183–226.

Wilson, H. H. *Religious Sects of the Hindus.* Calcutta: Susil Gupta, 1958, 221p.

Zaehner, R. C. *Hindu and Muslim Mysticism.* London: Athlone Press, 1960, 234p.

Zaehner, R. C. *Hinduism.* London: Oxford Univ. Press, 1962, 272p.

See Also: 3c, 4j1

Coomaraswamy, A. K. 4j4
Cormack, M. L. 4j4
Derrett, J. D. M. 4a1
Devanandan, P. D. 8a4
Dimock, E. C., Jr. 7b2
Ghurye, G. S. 4j1
Heimsath, C. H. 4a
Hutton, J. H. 4j1
Kolenda, P. M. 8a2
Kulkarni, C. M. 4a
Leach, E. R. 8a1
Natarajan, S. 6c
Panikkar, K. M. 6c
Parrinder, E. G. S. 8a2
Srinivas, M. 4j1 (2)
Stroup, H. 4j1
Vidyarthi, L. P. 7b2

2d. Mohammedanism

Abdulmaliki, A. Muslims in Nigeria. *Islamic R.*, 45/9, 1957, p.24–7.

Abel, A. Islam, Religion of Salvation. *Ann. Cent. Rel.*, 2, 1962, p.99–112.

Ad-Din, A. B. S. The Origins of Sufism. *Islamic Quart.*, 3/1, 1956, p.53–64.

Ahmad, A. *Studies in Islamic Culture in the Indian Environment.* London: Oxford Univ. Press, 1964, 312p.

Ansari, G. Muslim Caste in India. *East. Anthropol.*, 9/2, 1955–56, p.104–11.

Arberry, A. J. *Revelation and Reason in Islam.* London: Allen & Unwin, 1957, 122p.

Baljon, J. M. S. *Modern Muslim Koran Interpretation (1880–1960).* Leiden: E. J. Brill, 1961, 135p.

Braden, C. S. Islam in America. *Int. R. Missions*, 48/191, 1959, p.309–17.

Brelvi, M. *Islam in Africa.* Lahore: Institute of Islamic Culture, 1964, 657p.

Burckhardt, T. *An Introduction to Sufi Doctrine* (Trans. D. M. Matheson). Lahore: S. M. Ashraf, 1960, 155p.

Calverley, E. E. Negro Muslims in Hartford. *Muslim World*, 55/4, 1965, p.340–5.

Carrere D'Encausse, H. Islam in the U S S R. *Cent. Asian R.*, 9/4, 1961, p.335–51.

Courtois, V. The Ahmadiyya Anjuman. *Notes Islam*, 6, 1953, p.50–61, 100–9, 134–8.

Cragg, K. *The Call of the Minaret.* N.Y.: Oxford Univ. Press, 1964, 380p.

Cragg, K. *The Dome and the Rock: Jerusalem Studies in Islam.* London: SPCK, 1964, 262p.

Crowder, M. Islam in Northern Nigeria. *Geogr. Mag.*, 1958, p.304–16.

Crowder, M. Islam on the Upper Niger. *Geogr. Mag.*, 1958, p.222–35.

DePlanhol, X. *The World of Islam.* Ithaca: Cornell Univ. Press, 1959.

Dorman, H. G. *Toward Understanding Islam.* N.Y.: Teachers College: Columbia Univ. Press, 1948.

Dubler, C. E. Islam. *Asiat. Stud.*, 1/4, 1960, p.32–54.

Eberhard, W. Modern Tendencies in Islam in Pakistan. *Sociologus*, 10/2, 1960, p.139–52.

Eister, A. W. Perspective on the Functions of Religion in a Developing Country: Islam in Pakistan. *J. Sci. Stud. Rel.*, 3/2, 1964, p.227–38.

Essien-Udom, E. The Nationalist Movements of Harlem. In J. H. Clarke (ed.)—*Harlem: A Community in Transition.* N.Y.: The Citadel Press, 1963.

Fisher, H. J. *Ahmadiyyah: A Study in Contemporary Islam on the West African Coast.* London: Oxford Univ. Press, 1963, 206p.

Fyzee, A. A. A. *A Modern Approach to Islam.* Bombay: Asia Publishing House, 1963, 127p.

Gibb, H. A. R. *Modern Trends in Islam.* Chicago: Univ. of Chicago Press, 1947.

Gibb, H. A. R. *Mohammedanism.* London: Oxford Univ. Press, 1949, 205p.

Gibb, H. A. R. and Kramers, J. H. (eds.) *Shorter Encyclopaedia of Islam.* Leiden: E. J. Brill, 1953, 671p.

Gibb, H. A. R., *et al.*, (eds.)—*The Encyclopedia of Islam.* (Not yet complete.) Leiden: E. J. Brill, 1960, FF.

Gowing, P. G. *Mosque and Moro: A Study of Muslims in the Philippines.* Manila: Philippine Federation of Christian Churches, 1964, 120p.

Granqvist, H. Muslim Death and Burial Customs in a Bethlehem Village. *Muslim World*, 49/4, 1959, p.287–95.

Guillaume, A. *Islam.* London: Cassell and Co., 1963, 210p.

Hagopian, E. C. Islam and Society: Formation in Morocco Past and Present. *J. Sci. Stud. Rel.*, 3/1, 1963, p.70–80.

Halls, C. Muslims in Western Australia. *Islamic R.*, 49/3, 1961, p.17–8.

Hansen, H. H. *The Kurdish Woman's Life: Field Research in a Muslim Society, Iraq.* Copenhagen: National Museum, 1961, 213p.

Hassan, Y. F. The Penetration of Islam in the Eastern Sudan. *Sudan Notes*, 44, 1963, p.1–8.

Hatchett, J. F. The Moslem Influence Among American Negroes. *J. Hum. Relat.*, 10/4, 1962, p.375–82.

Heyd, U. (ed.) *Studies in Islamic History and Civilization.* Jerusalem: Magnes Press, Hebrew Univ., 1961.

Hobhom, A. Islam in Germany. *India R.* 39, 1951, p.11–7.

Hodgkin, T. L. Muslims South of the Sahara. *Curr. Hist.*, 32, 1957, p.345–50.

Hodgkin, T. L. The Fact of African History: Islam in West Africa. *Afr. South*, 2/3, 1958, p.89–99.

Ikram, S. M. and Embree, A. T. *Muslim Civilization in India.* N. Y.: Columbia Univ. Press, 1964, 325p.

Islam in England. *Islamic R.*, 51/4-5-6, 1963, p.34-6; see also 51/7-8-9, p.32-3.

Johns, A. H. Malay Sufism as Illustrated in an Anonymous Collection of Seventeenth Century Tracts. *J. Malayan Branch Roy. Asiat. Society*, 30/2, 1959, p.5-111.

Johns, A. H. Sufism in Indonesia. *J. Southw. Asian Hist.*, 2/2, 1961, p.10-23.

Kabir, H. Indian Muslims. *Indo-Iranica*, 8/3, 1955, p.1-14.

Kamali, S. A. The Moral Basis of Faith: An Islamic Interpretation. *Muslim World*, 55/1, 1965, p.9-18; see also 55/2, p.112-6.

Kesby, J. D. Muslims of Senegal. *West Afr. R.*, 33/417, 1962, p.37-43.

Kesby, J. D. Islam in Senegal. *Islamic Quart.*, 7/1-2, 1963, p.40-50.

Khan, M. H. *Islam*. N. Y.: Harper & Row, 1962.

Khan, M. R. *Islam in China*. Delphi, India: National Academy, 1963, 144p.

Kotb, S. *Social Justice in Islam* (Trans. J. B. Hardie). Washington: American Council of Learned Societies, 1953, 298p.

Kritzeck, J. and Winder, R. B. (eds.) *The World of Islam*. N.Y.: St. Martin's Press, 1959, 234p.

Levy, R. *The Social Structure of Islam*. N.Y.: Cambridge Univ. Press, 1962, 536p.

Lincoln, C. E. *The Black Muslims in America*. Boston: Beacon Press, 1960.

Lomax, L. E. *When the Word is Given: A Report on Elijah Muhammad, Malcolm X and the Black Muslim World*. N.Y.: New American Library, 1964.

MacCreery, R. Moslems and Pagans of the Anglo-Egyptian Sudan. *Moslem World*, 1946, p.252-60.

Makien, M. The Huis-A Muslim People. *China Reconstructs*, 7/6, 1958, p.20-2.

Maududi, A. *Islamic Law and Constitution* (Trans. and ed. K. Ahmad). Lahore: Islamic Publications, 1960, 350p.

Montgomery, W. W. The Conception of the Charismatic Community in Islam. *Numen*, 7/1, 1960, p.77-90.

Morgan, K. W. (ed.) *Islam-The Straight Path: Islam Interpreted by Muslims*. N.Y.: Ronald Press, 1958, 453p.

Moyal, M. A. Religious Life of the Tziganes. *Muslim World*, 43, 1953, p.130-4.

Nasr, S. H. *An Introduction to Islamic Cosmological Doctrine*. Cambridge: Harvard Univ. Press, 1964, 312p.

Okah, J. Islamic Civilization in West Africa. *Latitude*, 1960, p.33-42.

Padwick, C. *Muslim Devotions*. London: SPCK, 1961.

Palmier, L. H. Modern Islam in Indonesia: The Muhammadiyah After Independence. *Pac. Aff.*, 27/3, 1954, p.255-63.

Pearson, J. D. *Index Islamicus Supplement 1956-1960: A Catalogue of Articles on Islamic Subjects in Periodicals and Other Collective Publications*. Cambridge: W. Heffer and Sons, 1962, 316p.

Pearson, J. D. and Ashton, J. F. *Index Islamicus 1906-1955: A Catalogue of Articles on Islamic Subjects in Periodicals and Other Collective Publications*. Cambridge: W. Heffer & Sons, 1959, 897p.

Plessis, D. Muslims in South Africa: The Cape Malays. *Islamic R.*, 3, 1952, p.17-8.

Rahman, F. Internal Religious Developments in the Present Century Islam. *J. World Hist.*, 2/4, 1955, p.862-79.

Rosenthal, F. The "Muslim Brothers" in Egypt. *Muslim World*, 37, 1947, p.278-91.

Schacht, J. Islam in Northern Nigeria. *Stud. Islam.*, 8, 1957, p.123-46.

Schimmel, A. *The Spiritual Aspects of Islam*. Venezia-Roma: Instito per la Collaborazione Culturale, 1963, 91p.

Schuon, F. *Understanding Islam*. London: Allen & Unwin, 1963, 159p.

Seale, M. S. *Muslim Theology: A Study of Origins With Reference to the Church Fathers*. London: Luzac and Co., 1964.

Shack, W. A. Black Muslims: A Nativistic Religious Movement Among Negro Americans. *Race*, 3/1, 1961, p.57-68.

Shah, I. *The Sufis*. London: W. H. Allen, 1964, 430p.

Sheikh, M. S. *Studies in Muslim Philosophy*. Lahore: Pakistan Philosophical Congress, 1962, 235p.

Shustery, A. M. A. *Outlines of Islamic Culture*. Bangalore: Bangalore Press, 1955.

Smith, Wilf. C. *Modern Islam in India*. London: V. Gollancz, 1946, 344p.

Sourdel, D. *Islam*. N.Y.: Walker & Co., 1962.

Stankievich, J. *The White Ruthenian Mohammedans of Brooklyn*. Washington: National Committee for a Free Europe, Mid-European Studies Center, Research Documents, no. 35, 1953, 11p.

Stevenson, R. C. Some Aspects of the Spread of Islam in the Nuba Mountains. *Sudan Notes*, 44, 1963, p.9-20.

Thomas, L. V. Recent Developments in Turkish Islam. *Mid. East J.*, 6/1, 1952, p.22–40.

Thompson, W. The Sects and Islam. *Muslim World*, 39, 1949, p.208–22.

Tibawi, A. L. Islam and Secularism in Turkey Today. *Quart. R.*, 1956, p.325–37.

Trimingham, J. S. *Islam in the Sudan.* N.Y.: Oxford Univ. Press, 1949, 280p.

Trimingham, J. S. *Islam in Ethiopia.* London: Oxford Univ. Press, 1952, 299p.

Trimingham, J. S. *Islam in West Africa.* Oxford, England: Clarendon Press, 1959.

Trimingham, J. S. *Islam in East Africa.* London: Edinburgh House Press, 1962.

Tritton, A. S. *Islam: Belief and Practice.* London: Hutchinson's Univ. Library, 1951, 200p.

Veccia, V. L. *An Interpretation of Islam.* (Trans. A. Caselli). Washington: American Fazl Mosque, 1957, 87p.

Von Grunebaum, G. E. *Muhammadan Festivals.* London: Abelard-Schuman, 1958, 107p.

Von Nieuwenhuijze, C. A. O. *Aspects of Islam in Post-Colonial Indonesia: Five Essays.* The Hague: W. Van Hoeve, 1958, 248p.

Vucinich, W. S. Moslems of the Soviet Union. *Curr. Hist.*, 24/137, 1953, p.6–11.

Wadud, K. A. The Mussulmans of Bengal. *Visva-Bharati Quart.*, 14, 1948, p.17–32.

Weekes, R. V. *Pakistan: Birth and Growth of a Muslim Nation.* Princeton: D. Van Nostrand Co., 1964, 278p.

Wilber, D. N. The Structure and Position of Islam in Afghanistan. *Mid. East J.*, 6/1, 1952, p.41–8.

Williams, J. A. (ed.) *Islam.* N.Y.: G. Braziller, 1961, 256p.

Wolf, C. U. Muslims in the American Mid-West. *Muslim World*, 50/1, 1960, p.39–48.

(The) World of Islam. *Curr. Hist.*, 32/190, 1957, p.321–63.

Worthy, W. The Nation of Islam: Impact and Prospects. *Midstream*, 1962, p.26–44.

Ziadeh, N. A. *Sanusiyah: A Study of a Revivalist Movement in Islam.* Leiden: E. J. Brill, 1958, 148p.

See Also: 3d, 6

A'la Maududi, S. A.   6c
Alatas, S. S.   8a6
Al⁰ Karmi, H.   7b2
Anderson, J. N. D.   6a
Awad, B. A.   4j4
Badeau, J. S.   6c
Barclay, H. B.   6d
Berkes, N.   6c
Carpenter, G. W.   2a
Creswell, K. A. C.   9
Donaldson, D. M.   4d
Draz, M. A.   4g3
El-Saaty, H.   4b
Faris, N. A.   6e
Faruki, K. A.   4a1
Frankino, S. P.   5g
Hitti, P. K.   3d
Jeffery, A.   6c, 8b
Kedourie, E.   8a1
Kerekes, T.   6
Khadduri, M.   6c
Latif, S. A.   6
Laue, J. H.   6b
Lichtenstadter, I.   4j4, 6
Lincoln, C. E.   7a4
Loewenthal, R.   9
Parenti, M.   6c
Pipes, R.   6c
Rahbar, D.   4d
Rahman, F.   6d
Ramadan, S.   1c
Rosenthal, E. I.   4a
Sharabi, H.   6c
Sheikh, N. A.   4b
Smith, W. C.   4a1, 6c
Von Grunebaum, G. E.   5b
Wach, J.   7b2
Watt, W. M.   6a, 7b3
Zaehner, R. C.   2c

2e. *Buddhism*

Appleton, G. *Buddhism in Burma.* London: Longmans Green, 1944, 49p.

Bapat, P. V. A Glimpse of Buddhist China Today. *Maha. Bodhi*, 64/8, 1956, p.388–92.

Basak, R. *Lectures on Buddha and Buddhism.* Calcutta: Sambodhi Publications, 1961, 130p.

Bibliography on Buddhism (Edited by the Commemoration Committee for Professor Hanayama's Sixty-First Birthday). Tokyo: Hokuseido, 1960, 884p.

Buddhism in Ceylon and Its Influences on the People. *Ceylon Today*, 12/4, 1963, p.36–43.

Callaway, T. N. *Japanese Buddhism and Christianity: A*

Comparison of the Christian Doctrine of Salvation With That of Some Major Sects of Japanese Buddhism. Tokyo: Shinkyo, Shuppansha, 1957, 320p.

Clauson, G. L. M., *et al. Bibliographie Bouddhique, XXI–XXIII.* Paris: Libraire d'Amerique et d'Orient Adrien-Maissonneuve, 1952, 211p.; see other issues.

Conze, E. *Buddhist Thought in India: Three Phases of Buddhist Philosophy.* London: Allen and Unwin, 1962, 302p.

Coomaraswamy, A. K. *Buddha and the Gospel of Buddhism* (Rev. D. L. Coomaraswamy). N.Y.: Harper, 1964, 320p.

Coughlin, R. J. Some Social Features of Siamese Buddhism. *Asia,* 2/7, 1952, p.403–8.

Dasgupta, S. *Obscure Religious Cults.* Calcutta: Firma K. L. Mukhopadhyay, 1962, 436p.

David-Neel, A. *The Secret Oral Teachings in the Tibetan Buddhist Sects.* Calcutta: Maha-Bodhi Society, 1956.

David-Neel, A. *Magic and Mystery in Tibet.* N.Y.: University Books, 1958, 320p.

de Nebesky-Wojkowitz, R. *Oracles and Demons of Tibet: The Cult and Iconography of the Tibetan Protective Dieties.* London: G. Cumberledge, Oxford Univ. Press, 1956, 666p.

Ekvall, R. B. *Religious Observance in Tibet: Patterns and Functions.* Chicago: Univ. of Chicago Press, 1964, 313p.

Eliade, M. *Yoga: Immortality and Freedom* (Trans. Wm. R. Trask). N.Y.: Pantheon Books, 1958.

Eliot, N. E. *Japanese Buddhism.* N.Y.: Barnes & Noble, 1959, 449p.

Ellegriers, D. The Notion of Salvation in Chinese Buddhism. *A. Cent. Rel.,* 2, 1962, p.203–18.

Factor, D. *The Doctrine of Buddha.* N.Y.: Philosophical Library, 1965, 132p.

Fussell, R. *The Buddha and His Path to Self-Enlightenment: A First Introduction to Buddhism.* London: Buddhist Society, 1955, 173p.

Gard, R. A. *A Select Bibliography for the Study of Buddhism in Thailand in Western Languages.* Compiled at the request of the Mahamakut Library, Mahamakut Univ., 1957, 17p.

Gard, R. A.(ed.) *Buddhism.* N.Y.: G. Braziller, 1961, 256p.

Ghosh, M. India's Living Buddhism. *Indo-Asian Cult.,* 5/1, 1956, p.82–5.

Gonze, E. *Buddhism: Its Essense and Development.* Oxford: B. Cassirer, 1951, 224p.

Govinda, A. B. *Foundations of Tibetan Mysticism: According to the Esoteric Teachings of the Great Mantra, Om Mani Padne Huṁ.* N.Y.: Dutton, 1960, 310p.

Guenther, H. V. The Levels of Understanding in Buddhism. *J. Amer. Orient. Society,* 78/1, 1958, p. 19–28.

Heimann, B. Within the Framework of Indian Religion: The Main Dogma of Buddhism. *Numen,* 8, 1961, p. 1–11.

Holsten, W. Buddhism in Germany. *Int. R. Missions,* 48/192, 1959, p.409–20.

Hooykaas, C. Buddha Brahmins in Bali. *Bull. School Orient. Afr. Stud.,* 26/3, 1963, p.544–50.

Humphreys, C. *Buddhism.* London: Penguin Books, 1951, 256p.

Humphreys, C. *Zen Buddhism.* London: George Allen and Unwin, 1957, 242p.

Humphreys, C. *Zen Comes West: The Present and Future of Zen Buddhism in Britain.* N.Y.: Macmillan, 1960.

Humphreys, C. *A Popular Dictionary of Buddhism.* London: Arco Publications, 1962, 233p.

Humphreys, C. *Zen: A Way of Life.* N.Y.: Emerson Books, 1965, 199p.

Jacobson, N. P. *Buddhism: The Religion of Analysis.* London: Allen & Unwin, 1965.

King, W. L. Myth in Buddhism: Essential or Peripheral? *J. Bib. Rel.,* 29/3, 1961, p.211–8.

King, W. L. *A Thousand Lives Away: Buddhism in Contemporary Burma.* Cambridge: Harvard Univ. Press, 1964, 238p.

Kitagawa, J. M. Unitive and Divisive Factors in Contemporary Buddhism. *Civilisations,* 7/4, 1957, p.515–28.

Kitagawa, J. M. Buddhism in Taiwan Today. *France-Asie,* 18/174, 1962, p.439–44.

Kottar, B. K. Zen Buddhism. *Quart. J. Mythic Society,* 49/2, 1958, p.119–34.

Ling, T. O. *Buddhism and the Mythology of Evil: A Study in Theravada Buddhism.* London: Allen & Unwin, 1962, 179p.

Ling, T. O. The Dimension of Theravada Buddhism in Burma. *Hibbert J.,* 60, 1962, p.314–22.

Marlow, A. N. Zen Buddhism. *Hibbert J.,* 57/228, 1959, p.20–9.

Maupin, E. W. Zen Buddhism: A Psychological Review. *J. Consult. Psychol.,* 26, 1962, p.362–78.

McDougall, C. *Buddhism in Malaya.* Singapore: D. Moore, 1956, 61p.

Mendelson, E. M. A Messianic Buddhist Association in Upper Burma. *Bull. School Orient. Afr. Stud.*, 24/4, 1961, p.560–80.

Mitra, S. K. Buddhism in South-East Asia. *Indo-Asian Cult.*, 6/4, 1958, p.377–86.

Murti, T. R. V. *Central Philosophy of Buddhism.* London: Allen and Unwin, 1955.

Nakamura, H. The Concept of Man in Buddhist Philosophy. *Stud. Gen.*, 15/10, 1962, p.632–46.

Nash, M. Burmese Buddhism in Everyday Life. *Amer. Anthropol.*, 65/2, 1963, p.285–95.

Niles, D. T. Buddhist Ceylon. *World Domin.*, 29, 1951, p.211–22.

Obeyesekere, G. The Great Tradition and the Little in the Perspective of Sinhalese Buddhism. *J. Asian Stud.*, 22/2, 1963, p.139–53.

Organ, T. W. Reason and Experience in Mahāyāna Buddhism. *J. Bib. Rel.*, 20, 1952, p.77–83.

Phillips, B. (ed.) *The Essentials of Zen Buddhism: An Anthology of the Writings of Daisetz Suzuki.* N.Y.: E. P. Dutton, 1962.

Pulley, W. Is a New Image for Buddhism in the Making? *Calcutta R.*, 174/2, 1965, p.111–22.

Rao, S. K. R. Buddhism in Burma. *Quart. J. Mythic Society*, 49/3, 1958, p.195–201.

Richardson, H. E. The Karma-pa Sect. *J. Roy. Asiat. Society*, 3/4, 1958, p.139–64.

Richardson, H. E. The Karma-pa Sect: A Historical Note. *J. Roy. Asiat. Society*, 1/2, 1959, p.1–18.

Ross, N. W. (ed.) *The World of Zen: An East-West Anthology.* N.Y.: Random House, 1965, 362p.

Senzaki, N. and McCandless, R. S. *Buddhism and Zen.* N.Y.: Philosophical Library, 1953, 85p.

Shōjun, B., *et al.* (eds.) *A Bibliography of Japanese Buddhism.* Tokyo: CIIB Press, 1958, 180p.

Spencer, R. F. Social Structure of a Contemporary Japanese-American Buddhist Church. *Soc. Forces*, 26/3, 1948, p.281–7.

Stcherbatsky, T. *The Conception of Buddhist Nirvana.* The Hague: Mouton and Co., 1965, 250p.

Suriyabongs, L. *Buddhism in Thailand.* Bangkok: Prae Bhittaya, 1955, 88p.

Suzuki, D. T. *Zen and Japanese Culture.* N.Y.: Pantheon Books, 1959.

Suzuki, D. T. *Outlines of Mahayana Buddhism.* N.Y.: Schocken Books, 1963, 383p.

Tim, P. M. *Buddhist Devotion and Meditation.* London: SPCK, 1964, 104p.

Tsukamoto, Z. Japanese and Chinese Buddhism in the Twentieth Century. *J. World Hist.*, 6/3, 1961, p.572–602.

Von Fürer-Haimendorf, C. *The Sherpas of Nepal: Buddhist Highlanders.* London: John Murray, 1964, 298p.

Waddell, L. A. *The Buddhism of Tibet: Lamaism With Its Mystic Cults, Symbolism and Mythology, and in Its Relation to Indian Buddhism.* Cambridge: Heffer, 1958, 598p.

Wayman, A. Totemic Beliefs in the Buddhist Tantras. *Hist. Rel.*, 1, 1961, p.81–94.

Welch, H. H. The Re-Interpretation of Chinese Buddhism. *China Quart.*, 22, 1965, p.143–53.

Wienpahl, P. *The Matter of Zen: A Brief Account of Zazen.* N.Y.: N.Y. Univ. Press, 1964, 162p.

Wright, A. F. Buddhism and Chinese Culture. *J. Asian Stud.*, 17/1, 1957, p.17–42.

Yang, I. F. *Buddhism in China.* Kowloon, Hong Kong: Union Press, 1956, 98p.

See Also: 2f, 2h2, 3e, 3f1

Aung, H.   5a1
Benedict, R.   2h
Conze, E.   3e
Embree, J. F.   4f2
Fromm, E.   1e
Hori, I.   7a1
Horner, I. B.   4j4
Lobsang, R. T.   7a
Mendelson, E. M.   4a1
Miller, B. D.   7b1
Murphy, R. F.   7b3
Nivolon, F.   4a
Peiris, W.   4j4
Slater, R. L.   7b3
Von Glasenapp, H.   8a5
Welch, H.   6e
Wood, E.   9

2f. Shintoism

Anesaki, M. *History of Japanese Religion: With Special Reference to the Social and Moral Life of the Nation.* Rutland, Vermont: Charles E. Tuttle Co., 1963.

Bellah, R. N. *Tokugawa Religion.* Glencoe: Free Press, 1957.

Braden, C. S.   Religion in Postwar Japan. *J. Bib. Rel.*, 21/3, 1953, p.147–53.

Fujisawa, C.   *Concrete Universality of the Japanese Way of Thinking: A New Interpretation of Shintoism.* Tokyo: Hokuseido Press, 1958, 160p.

Fujisawa, C.   Shinto Influence on Japanese Life. *Contemp. Japan*, 25/2, 1958, p.241–9.

Ono, S. and Woodward, W. P.   *Shinto: The Kami Way.* Tokyo: Bridgeway Press, 1962, 116p.

Ross, R. H.   *Shinto: The Way of Japan.* Boston: Beacon Press, 1965, 176p.

See Also: 2e, 2h2, 3fl

Benedict, R.   2h
Embree, J. F.   4f2
Holtom, D. C.   4a
Schuon, F.   8a4

2g.   *Secularism, Humanism, and Atheism*

Acquaviva, S. S.   The Psychology of Dechristianization in the Dynamics of the Industrial Society. *Soc. Compass*, 7/3, 1960, p.209–25.

Blackham, H. J.   Guide to Humanist Books in English. *Plain View*, supplement no. 1, 1962, 84p.

Blackham, H. J.   Modern Humanism. *J. World Hist.*, 8/1, 1964, p.100–22.

Borne, E.   *Atheism* (Trans. S. J. Tester). N.Y.: Hawthorne Books, 1961, 156p.

Bryson, G.   Early English Positivists and the Religion of Humanity. *Amer. Sociol. R.*, 1, 1936, p.343–62.

Campbell, C. B.   Research Note: Membership Composition of the British Humanist Association. *Sociol. R.*, 13/3, 1965, p.327–37.

Charlton, D. G.   *Secular Religions in France, 1815–1870.* London: Oxford Univ. Press, 1963, 250p.

Church of England, National Assembly, Social and Industrial Council. *Moral Re-Armament: A Study of the Movement.* Westminster: Church Information Board of the Church Assembly, 1955, 47p.

Crocker, L. G.   Recent Interpretations of the French Enlightenment. *J. World Hist.*, 8/3, 1964, p.426–56.

Driberg, T.   *The Mystery of Moral Re-Armament.* London: Secker and Warburg, 1964.

Eliade, M.   History of Religions and a New Humanism. *Hist. Rel.*, 1, 1961, p.1–8.

Flint, J. T.   The Secularization of Norwegian Society. *Comp. Stud. Society Hist.*, 6, 1963–64, p.325–44.

Frumkin, R. M.   Scientific Millenialism as the Coming World Ideology. *J. Hum. Rel.*, 10, 1962, p.145–62.

Galanter, M., *et al.*   Debate: Secularism East and West. *Comp. Stud. Society Hist.*, 7/2, 1965, p.133–72.

Gerth, H. H.   Midwestern Sectarian Community. *Soc. Res.*, 2/3, 1944, p.354–62.

Guyua, M.   *The Non-Religion of the Future: A Sociological Study.* N.Y.: Schocken Books, 1962, 538p.

Hans, N.   Two Aspects of Humanism in England and America. *Comp. Educ. R.*, 7/2, 1963, p.113–8.

Harkness, G. E.   *The Modern Rival of the Christian Faith: An Analysis of Secularism.* N.Y.: Abingdon-Cokesbury, 1952.

Hayes, C. J. H.   *Nationalism: A Religion.* N.Y.: Macmillan, 1960, 187p.

Hong, H.   *This World and the Church: Studies in Secularism.* Minneapolis: Augsburg Publishing House, 1954, 143p.

Houf, H. T.   Is Humanism Religion? *J. Bib. Rel.*, 14, 1946, p.101–6.

Kallen, H. M.   Secularism as the Common Religion of a Free Society. *J. Sci. Stud. Rel.*, 4/2, 1965, p.145–51.

Lacroix, J.   *The Meaning of Modern Atheism* (Trans. G. Barden). N.Y.: Macmillan, 1965, 115p.

Lamont, C.   *The Philosophy of Humanism.* N.Y.: Philosophical Library, 1957, 243p.

Leppe, I.   *Atheism in our Time* (Trans. B. Murchland). N.Y.: Macmillan, 1963, 195p.

Maritain, J.   The Meaning of Contemporary Atheism. *Curr. Rel. Thought*, 10/4, 1950, p.22–9.

Persons, S.   *Free Religion: An American Faith:* New Haven: Yale Univ. Press, 1947, 168p.

Spitz, L.   *The Religious Renaissance of the German Humanists.* Cambridge, Massachusetts: Harvard Univ. Press, 1963.

Symposium on Humanism. *Soc. Order*, 3, 1953, 96p.

Ten Hoor, M.   Humanism As a Religion. *Philosoph. Phenom. Res.*, 15/1, 1954, p.82–97.

Wilbur, E. M.   *A History of Unitarianism.* Cambridge: Harvard Univ. Press, 1946, 1952, 2 Vols.

Williams, P. (ed.)   Secularism in Japan. *Japan. Christ. Quart.*, 31/4, 1965, p.215–61.

Wilson, J. B.   Darwin and the Transcendentalist. *J. Hist. Ideas*, 26/2, 1965, p.286–90.

Xenakis, J. Desupernaturalization. *J. Sci. Stud. Rel.,* 1964, 3/2, p.181–8. See also: H. R. Holcomb-Comment, p.189–92.

See Also: 3f4, 4d, 7c, 7d

Cox, H. 4f1
Marty, M. E. 7c
Rumke, H. C. 7c
Spann, J. 5

2h. Other Religions

Aochi, S. Tenriko-Its Origin and Creed. *Contemp. Japan,* 26/4, 1960, p.762–6.

Archer, J. C. *The Sikhs: A Study in Comparative Religion.* Princeton: Princeton Univ. Press, 1946, 353p.

Arnst, W. The Nargorkun-Narlinji Cult. *Oceania,* 32/4, 1962, p.298–320.

Bach, M. *Strange Sects and Curious Cults.* N.Y.: Dodd, Mead & Co., 1963.

Barton, R. F. *The Mythology of the Ifuagos.* Phila.: American Folklore Society, 1955.

Beattie, J.H.M. The Ghost Cult in Bunyoro. *Ethnology,* 3/2, 1964, p.127–51.

Beattie, J. H. M. Group Aspects of the Nyoro Spirit Mediumship Cult. *Hum. Prob. Brit. Centr. Afr.,* 30, 1961, p.11–38.

Beier, U. The Egungun Cult. *Nigeria,* 51, 1956, p.380–92.

Beier, U. Shango Shrine. *Black Orpheus,* 4, 1958, p.30–5.

Benedict, R. *The Chrysanthemum and the Sword.* Boston: Houghton Mifflin Co., 1946.

Best, E. *Some Aspects of Maori Myth and Religion.* Wellington: R. E. Owen, 1954, 43p.

Bhattacharyya, A. The Cult of the Village Gods of West Bengal. *Man India,* 1955, p.19–30.

Bhattacharyya, A. Cult of the Tree-Deities of Bengal. *Ind. Folklore,* 3/4, 1958, p.26–46.

Bhattacharyya, A. Popular Nature Worship in Bengal. *Ind. Folklore,* 2/2, 1959, p.129–43.

Blacker, C. New Religious Cults of Japan. *Hibbert J.,* 60, 1962, p.369–80.

Bode, D. F. A. Iran and Its Ancient Religion. *Bull. Ramakrisna Mission Inst. Cult.,* 14/11, 1963, p.426–32.

Boeke, J. H. Talist Development in Indonesia and in Uganda: A Contrast. *Int. Soc. Sci. Bull.,* 6/3, 1954, p.424–33.

Borhegyi, S. F. The Cult of Our Lord of Esquipulas in Middle America. *Palacio,* 61/12, 1954, p.387–401.

Braden, C. S. *These Also Believe: A Study of Modern American Cults and Minority Religious Movements.* N.Y.: Macmillan Co., 1949.

Brewster, P. G. Snake-Handling Religious Cults in the United States. *Int. Archiv. Ethnogr.,* 48/2, 1958, p.227–37.

Bunzel, R. L. Introduction to Zuni Ceremonialism. *Bur. Amer. Ethnol. Ann. Rep.,* 47, 1932, p.467–544.

Burridge, K. O. Social Implications of Some Tangul Myths. *Southw. J. Anthropol.,* 12/4, 1956, p.415–31.

Burridge, K. O. The Cargo Cult. *Discovery,* 23/2, 1962, p.22–7.

Campbell, J. Renewal Myths and Rites of the Primitive Hunters and Planters. *Eranos Jahrbuch,* 28, 1959, p.407–58.

Carrasco, P. Pagan Rituals and Beliefs Among the Chontal Indians of Oaxaca, Mexico. *Anthropol. Rec. Univ. Calif.,* 20/3, 1960, p.87–117.

Carrasco, P. Tarascan Folk Religion. In M. S. Edmonson, *et al.—Synoptic Studies of Mexican Culture.* New Orleans: Middle American Research Institute, Tulane Univ., 1957.

Cato, A. C. A New Religious Cult in Fiji. *Oceania,* 1947, p.146–56.

Christensen, J. B. The Tigari Cult of West Africa. *Pap. Michigan Acad. Sci. Arts Letters,* 39, 1953, p.389–98.

Colson, E. *The Plateau Tonga of Northern Rhodesia: Social and Religious Studies.* Manchester: Manchester Univ. Press, 1962, 237p.

Craig, E. Religious Life of the Auckland Maori. *Te Ao Hou,* 7/3, 1959, p.56–7.

Dale-Green, P. *Cult of the Cat.* Boston: Houghton Mifflin, 1963, 189p.

Davenport, W. H. The Religion of Pre-European Hawaii. *Soc. Proc. Hawaii,* 16, 1952, p.20–9.

de Beauclair, L. The Religion of the Yami on Botel Tabago. *Sociologus,* 9/1, 1959, p.12–23.

de Heusch, L. Possession Cults and Initiatory Religions of Salvation in Africa. *A.Cent. Rel.,* 2, 1962, p.127–68.

Dole, G. Endo Cannibalism Among the Amahuaca Indians. *Trans. New York Acad. Sci.,* 24/5, 1962, p.567–73.

Downs, J. F. *Washo Religion.* Berkeley: Univ. of California Press, 1961.

Dusenberry, V. *Montana Cree: A Study in Religious Persistence.* Stockholm: Almqvist, 1962, 277p.

Ekvall, R. B. Some Aspects of Divination in Tibetan Society. *Ethnology,* 2/1, 1963, p.31–9.

Elliott, A. J. A. *Chinese Spirit-Medium Cults in Singapore.* London: London School of Economics and Political Science, Dept. of Anthropology, Monographs on Social Anthropology, New Series, #14, 1953.

Evans-Pritchard, E. E. Zande Clans and Totems. *Man,* 61, 1961, p.116–21.

Ewers, J. C. The Bear Cult Among the Assiniboin and Their Neighbors of the Northern Plains. *Southw. J. Anthropol.,* 11/1, 1955, p.1–14.

Ewers, J. C. The Assiniboin Horse Medicine Cult. *Anthropol. Quart.,* 29/3, 1956, p.57–68.

Fauset, A. H. *Black Gods of the Metropolis: Negro Religious Cults of the Urban North.* Phila.: Univ. of Pennsylvania Press, 1945, 126p.

Feracca, S. E. The Yuwipi Cult of the Oglala and Sicangu Teton Sioux. *Plains Anthropol.,* 6/13, 1961, p.155–63.

Ferreira, J. V. The Problems of Maratha Totemism. *Ind. J. Soc. Work,* 25/2, 1964, p.135–51.

Festinger, L., *et al. When Prophecy Fails.* N.Y.: Harper & Row, 1964.

Flornoy, B. *Jivaro: Among the Headshrinkers of the Amazon.* London: Elek, 1953, 224p.

Forde, D., *et al. African Worlds: Studies in the Cosmological Ideas and Social Values of African Peoples.* London: Oxford Univ. Press, 1954, 243p.

Fortune, R. F. *Manus Religion: An Ethnological Study of the Manus Natives of the Admiralty Islands.* Lincoln: Univ. of Nebraska Press, 1965, 391p.

Geertz, C. *The Religion of Java.* Glencoe: Free Press, 1960.

Gelfand, M. The Religion of the Mashona. *Nada,* 33, 1956, p.27–31.

Gelfand, M. The Mhondoro-Chaminuku. *Nada,* 36, 1959, p.6–10.

Gelfand, M. *Shona Ritual, With Special Reference to the Chiminuka Cult.* Cape Town: Juta & Co., 1959, 217p.

Gelfand, M. *Shona Religion With Special Reference to Makorekore.* Cape Town: Juta, 1962, 184p.

Gildea, R. Y. Religion in the Ashanti Province of Ghana. *Soc. Sci.,* 38/4, 1963, p.209–12.

Gough, E. K. Cults of the Dead Among the Nayars. *J. Amer. Folklore,* 71/281, 1958, p.446–78.

Graham, D. C. *The Customs and Religion of the Ch'iang.* Washington: Smithsonian Institution, 1958, 114p.

Graham, D. C. *Folk Religion in Southwest China.* Washington: Smithsonian Institution, 1961, 246p.

Griaule, M. *Conversations with Ogstemmèli: An Introduction to Dogon Religion.* London: Oxford Univ. Press, 1965, 230p.

Haitz, L. *Juju Gods of West Africa.* St. Louis: Concordia Publishing House, 1961, 113p.

Hammond-Tooke, W. D. Some Bhaca Religious Categories. *Afr. Stud.,* 19/1, 1960, p.1–13.

Harner, M. J. Jivaro Souls. *Amer. Anthropol.,* 64/2, 1962, p.258–72.

Harrison, J. E. *Prolegomena to the Study of Greek Religion.* N.Y.: Meridian Books, 1955, 682p.

Hermanns, M. Contribution to the Study of Kadar Religion. *Man,* 55/161, 1955, p.145–51.

Herskovits, M. J. and Herskovits, F. S. An Outline of Dahomean Religious Belief. *Amer. Anthropol. Assoc. Mem.,* 41, 1933.

Hine, R. V. Cult and Occult in California. *Pac. Spect.,* 8/3, 1954, p.196–203.

Hogbin, H. I. Pagan Religion in a New Guinea Village. *Oceania,* 1947, p.120–45.

Holley, H. *Religion for Mankind.* London: Ronald, 1956, 248p.

Horowitz, M. M. The Martiniquan East Indian Cult of Moldevidan. *Soc. Econ. Stud.,* 10/1, 1961, p.93–100.

Horton, R. *The Gods as Guests: An Aspect of Kalabari Religious Life.* Lagos, Nigeria: Magazine Publications, 1960, 71p.

Horton, R. The Kalabari World-View: An Outline and Interpretation. *Africa,* 32/3, 1962, p.197–220.

Howard, J. H. The Tree Dweller Cults of the Dakota. *J. Amer. Folklore,* 68/268, 1955, p.169–74.

Howelis, W. *The Heathens: Primitive Man and His Religions.* N.Y.: Doubleday, 1948, 306p.

Huber, H. *The Krobo: Traditional Social and Religious Life of a West African People* (Studia Instituti Anthropos, Vol. 16). St. Augustine:The Anthropos Institute, 1963, 306p.

Hultkrantz, A. Configurations of Religious Belief Among the Wind River Shoshoni. *Ethnos,* 21/3–4, 1956, p.194–215.

International Institute For the Study of Religions. Soka Gakkai—Its Origin and Philosophy. *Contemp. Japan,* 26/3, 1960, p.530–4.

Jeffreys, M. D. W. The Cult of Twins Among Some African Tribes. *S. Afr. J. Sci.*, 59/4, 1963, p.97–107.

Jenness, D. Canadian Indian Religion. *Anthropologica*, 1, 1955, p.1–17.

Jest, M. C. Religious Beliefs of the Lepchas in the Kalimpong District (West Bengal). *J. Roy. Asiat. Society*, 3/4, 1960, p.124–34.

Kaut, C. R. Notes on Western Apache Religious and Social Organization. *Amer. Anthropol.*, 61/1, 1959, p.99–102.

Krader, L. Buryat Religion and Society. *Southw. J. Anthropol.*, 10/3, 1954, p.322–51.

Kroeber, A. L. and Gifford, E. W. *World Renewal: A Cult System of Native Northwest California.* Berkeley: Univ. of California Press, 1949.

Kronenberg, A. Some Notes on the Niam Religion of the Nyimang. *Kush*, 7, 1959, p.197–213.

Langton, E. *Essentials of Demonology.* London: Epworth Press, 1949, 231p.

Leacock, S. Fun-Loving Deities in an Afro-Brazilian Cult. *Anthropol. Quart.*, 37/3, 1964, p.94–110.

Lessa, W. A. Sorcery on Ifaluk. *Amer. Anthropol.*, 63/4, 1961, p.817–20. See also: M. E. Spiro—Sorcery, Evil Spirits and Functional Analysis: A Rejoinder, p.820–4.

Lewis, F. B. Modern Spiritualism. *Interpretation*, 11, 1957, p.438–54.

Li, Y. Y. The Structure of the I Fugao Religion. *Bull. Inst. Ethnol. Acad. Sinica*, 9, 1960, p.387–409.

Lopatin, I. A. *Social Life and Religion of the Indians in Kitimat, British Columbia.* Los Angeles: Univ. of California Press, 1945, 118p.

Lopatin, I. A. *The Cult of the Dead Among the Natives of the Amur Basin.* The Hague: Mouton, 1960, 211p.

Lucas, J. O. The Religion of the Yorubas, Being an Account of the Yoruba Peoples of Southern Nigeria, Especially in Relation to the Religion of Ancient Egypt. Lagos, Nigeria: C. M. S. Bookshop, 1948, 420p.

Lucier, C. Noatagmint Eskimo Myths. *Anthropol. Pap. Univ. Alaska*, 6, 1958, p.89–117.

Lunhardt, G. *Divinity and Experience: The Religion of the Dinka.* N.Y.: Oxford Univ. Press, 1961, 328p.

Macauliffe, M., *et al.* (eds.) *The Sikh Religion: A Symposium.* Calcutta: Susil Gupta Private, 1958, 155p.

Marshall, L. Kung Bushman Religious Beliefs. *Africa*, 32/3, 1962, p.221–52.

May, L. C. The Dancing Religion: A Japanese Messianic Sect. *Southw. J. Anthropol.*, 10, 1954, p.119–37.

Mayne, F. B. Beliefs and Practices of the Cult of Father Divine. *J. Educ. Sociol.*, 9/3, 1935, p.296–306.

Middleton, J. The Yakan Cult Among the Lugbara. *Man*, 58, 1958, p.112.

Middleton, J. *Lugbara Religion: Ritual and Authority Among an East African People.* London: Oxford Univ. Press, 1960, 276p.

Middleton, J. The Yakanor Allah Water Cult Among the Lugbara. *J. Roy. Anthropol. Inst.*, 93/1, 1963, p.80–108.

Millroth, B. *Lyuba: Traditional Religion of the Sukuma.* Uppsala: Almquist and Wikell, 1965, 217p.

Morton-Williams, P. The Yoruba Ogboni Cult in Oyo. *Africa*, 30/4, 1960, p.362–74.

Morton-Williams, P. An Outline of the Cosmology and Cult Organizations of the Oyo Yoruba. *Africa*, 34/3, 1964, p.243–61.

Mountford, C. P. *The Tiwi: Their Art, Myth and Ceremony.* London: Phoenix, 1958, 185p.

Munro, N. G. *Ainu Creed and Cult.* N.Y.: Columbia Univ. Press, 1963, 182p.

Murphy, R. F. *Mundurucú Religion.* Berkeley: Univ. of California Press, 1958, 146p.

Nadel, S. F. *Nupe Religion.* London: Routledge & Kegan Paul, 1954.

Needham, R. Blood, Thunder, and Mockery of Animals. *Sociologus*, 14/2, 1964, p.136–49.

Nida, E. A. and Smalley, W. A. *Introducing Animism.* N.Y.: Friendship Press, 1959, 64p.

Nilles, J. The Kuman of the Chimbu Region, Central Highlands, New Guinea. *Oceania*, 21/1, 1950, p.64–5.

Oberg, K. Afro-Brazilian Religious Cults. *Sociologica*, 21/2, 1959, p.134–41.

Opler, M. K. Two Japanese Religious Sects. *Southw. J. Anthropol.*, 6, 1950, p.69–78.

Ouwehand, C. *Namazu-e and Their Themes. An Interpretive Approach to Some Aspects of Japanese Folk Religion.* Leiden: E. J. Brill, 1964, 276p.

Pal, M. K. An Obscure Folk-Cult of Lower Bengal. *Ind. Folklore*, 3/1, 1958, p.11–3.

Parrinder, E. G. *African Traditional Religion.* N.Y.: Hutchinson's Univ. Library, 1954.

Parrinder, E. G. Indigenous Churches in Nigeria. *West Afr. R.*, 31/394, 1960, p.87–93.

Parsons, R. T. Religion in Kono Village Life. *Sierra Leone Bull. Rel.*, 1/2, 1959, p.36–47.

Parsons, R. T. *Religion in African Society: A Study of the Kono People of Sierra Leone and Its Social Environment, With Special Reference to the Function of Religion in That Society.* Leiden: E. J. Brill, 1964, 246p.

Paul, H. G. B. A Prehistoric Cult Still Practiced in Muslim Darfur. *J. Roy. Anthropol. Inst.,* 86/1, 1956, p.77–86.

Pauw, B. A. *Religion in a Tswana Chiefdom.* London: Oxford Univ. Press for the International African Inst., 1960, 258p.

Pettersson, O. *Jabmek and Mabmeaimo: A Comparative Study of the Dead and the Realm of the Dead in Lappish Religion.* Lund: Gleerup, 1957, 253p.

Pillai, K. K. Popular Religion Among the Ceylon Tamils. *Tamil Cult.,* 8/1, 1959, p.26–31.

Rassers, W. H. *Pañji, The Culture Hero: A Structural Study of Religion in Java.* The Hague: M. Nijhoff, 1959, 304p.

Reay, M. *The Kuma: Freedom and Conformity in the New Guinea Highlands.* London: Cambridge Univ. Press, 1959, 222p.

Reichard, G. A. *Navaho Religion.* N.Y.: Pantheon Books, 1950, 2 vols.

Riordan, J. The Wrath of the Ancestral Spirits. *Afr. Stud.,* 20/1, 1961, p.53–60.

Ross, A. Chain Symbolism in Pagan Celtic Religion. *Speculum,* 34, 1959, p.39–59.

Ruel, M. J. Religion and Society Among the Kuria of East Africa. *Africa,* 35/3, 1965, p.295–306.

Ruud, J. *Taboo: A Study of the Malagasy Fady.* London: Allen and Unwin, 1960, 313p.

Schärer, H. *Ngaju Religion: The Conception of God Among a South Borneo People.* The Hague: Martinus Nijhoff, 1963, 229p.

Schneider, D. B. *Konkokyo, A Japanese Religion: A Study in the Continuities of Native Faiths.* Tokyo: The International Institute for the Study of Religions, 1962, 166p.

Schram, L. *The Monguors of the Kansu-Tibetan Border: Their Religious Life.* Phila.: American Philosophical Society, 1957.

Scott, W. H. Social and Religious Culture of the Kalingas of Mapukayan. *Southw. J. Anthropol.,* 16/2, 1960, p.174–90.

Seneviratne, H. L. Some Aspects of the Negative Cult Among the Sinhalese. *Ceylon J. Hist. Soc. Stud.,* 4/2, 1961, p.149–56.

Simpson, G. E. The Shango Cult in Nigeria and Trinidad. *Amer. Anthropol.,* 64/6, 1962, p.1204–19.

Singh, K. *The Sikhs.* London: Allen & Unwin, 1953.

Spittler, R. P. *Cults and Isms.* Grand Rapids: Baker Book House, 1962.

Stark, F. The Yezidi Devil-Worshippers. *Geogr. Mag.,* 31/4, 1958, p.527–37.

Stone, D. Cult Traits in Southeastern Costa Rica and Their Significance. *Amer. Antiq.,* 28/3, 1963, p.339–59.

Stonor, C. R. Notes on Religion and Ritual Among the Dafla Tribes of the Assam Himalayas. *Anthropos,* 52/1–2, 1957, p.1–23.

Tanner, R. E. S. An Introduction to the Northern Basukuma's Idea of the Supreme Being. *Anthropol. Quart.,* 29/2, 1956, p.45–56.

Tanner, R. E. S. An Introduction to the Spirit Beings of the Northern Basukuma. *Anthropol. Quart.,* 29/3, 1956, p.69–81.

Tanner, R. E. S. The Spirits of the Dead: An Introduction to the Ancestor Worship of the Sukuma of Tanganyika. *Anthropol. Quart.,* 32/2, 1959, p.108–24.

Thompson, J. B. Some Notes on African Ritual Sacrifice. *Nada,* 34, 1957, p.123–9.

Thomsen, H. Japan's New Religions. *Int. R. Missions,* 48, 1959, p.283–93.

Thomsen, H. *The New Religions of Japan.* Rutland, Vermont: Charles E. Tuttle Co., 1963.

Topley, M. Chinese Religion and Religious Institutions in Singapore. *J. Malayan Branch Roy. Asiat. Soc.,* 29/1, 1956, p.70–118.

Topley, M. The Great Way of Former Heaven: A Group of Chinese Secret Religious Sects. *Bull. School Orient. Afr. Stud.,* 26/2, 1963, p.362–92.

Tyler, H. A. *Pueblo Gods and Myths.* Norman, Oklahoma: Univ. of Oklahoma Press, 1964.

Underhill, R. M. *Papago Indian Religion.* N.Y.: Columbia Univ. Press, 1946.

Van Baal, J. The Cult of the Bullroarer in Australia and Southern New Guinea. *Bijdrag. Taal-Land-Volkenk.,* 119/2, 1963, p.201–14.

Van Sicard, H. The Free Cult in the Zimbawe Culture. *Afr. Stud.,* 5/4, 1946, p.257–67.

Voegelin, C. F. The Shawnee Female Deity. *Yale Univ. Pub. Anthropol.,* 10, 1946, 21p.

Vogt, E. Z. Ceremonial Organization in Zinacantan. *Ethnology,* 4/1, 1965, p.39–52.

Ward, B. E. Some Observations on Religious Cults in Ashanti. *Africa,* 26/1, 1956, p.47–61.

Welbourn, F. B. Some Aspects of Kiganda Religion. *Uganda J.,* 26/2, 1962, p.171–82.

Widengren, G. Researches in Syrian Mysticism: Mystical Experiences and Spiritual Exercises. *Numen*, 8/3, 1961, p.161–98.

See Also: 3f, 5e, 8a3

Brannan, N.   7b3
Clark, S. D.   4a
Falkenberg, J.   4e

Fall, B. B.   4a
Goode, W. J.   8a3
Hadfield, L. P.   4a1
Lanternari, V.   6d
Pettersson, O.   4a1
Rattray, R. S.   4g1
Rhoades, H. T. F.   7i
Schmitz, C. A.   4g1
Turner, H. W.   6c

2h1.   Cargo Cults

Berndt, R. M.   A Cargo Movement in the Eastern Central Highlands of New Guinea. *Oceania*, 23/1, 1952, p.40–65; see also: 23/2, p.137–58; 23/3, 1953, p.202–34.

Burridge, K. O.   Cargo Activity in Tangu. *Oceania*, 24/4, 1954, p.241–54.

Lawrence, P.   Cargo Cult and Religious Beliefs Among the Garia. *Int. Archiv. Ethnogr.*, 47, 1955, p.1–20.

Lawrence, P.   The Madang District Cargo Cult. *S. Pacific*, 8/1, 1955, p.6–13.

Lawrence, P.   *Road Belong Cargo: A Study of the Cargo Movement in the Southern Madang District, New Guinea.* N.Y.: Humanities Press, 1965, 291p.

Oosterwal, G.   A Cargo Cult in the Mamberamo Area. *Ethnology*, 2/1, 1963, p.1–14.

Read, K. A.   A "Cargo" Situation in the Markham Valley, New Guinea. *Southw. J. Anthropol.*, 14/3, 1958, p.273–94.

Stanner, W. E. H.   On the Interpretation of Cargo-Cults. *Oceania*, 29/1, 1958, p.1–25.

Worsley, P. M.   *The Trumpet Shall Sound: A Study of "Cargo" Cults in Melanesia.* London: MacGibbon & Kee, 1957, 290p.

Worsley, P. M.   Cargo Cults. *Sci. Amer.*, 200/5, 1959, p.117–28.

See Also:

Alagoma, D.   6
Firth, R.   8a3
Guiart, J.   4a
Inglis, J.   8a1
Jarvie, I. C.   8a3
Julius, C.   8a5
Leeson, I.   9

2h2.   Confucianism and Taoism

Chang, C. Y.   An Introduction to Taoist Yoga. *R. Rel.*, 3/4, 1956, p.131–48.

Chang, C. Y.   *Creativity and Taoism: A Study of Chinese Philosophy, Art and Poetry.* N.Y.: Julian Press, 1963, 241p.

Cheng, F. T.   Confucianism and Chinese Civilization. *Civilisations*, 1/3, 1951, p.13–23.

Creel, H. G.   What is Taoism? *J. Amer. Orient. Society*, 76/3, 1956, p.139–52.

Creel, H. G.   *Confucius and the Chinese Way.* N.Y.: Harper, 1960, 363p.

Koo, Y. C.   The Revival of Confucianism. *Chinese Cult.*, 4/4, 1963, p.1–11.

Nivison, D. S. and Wright, A. F. (eds.) *Confucianism in Action.* Stanford: Stanford Univ. Press, 1959.

Shigeki, K.   Confucianism in Japanese Life. *Japan Quart.*, 11/2, 1964.

Weber, M.   *The Religion of China: Confucianism and Taoism* (Trans. H. H. Gerth). Glencoe: Free Press, 1951.

Wright, A. F. (ed.)   *The Confucian Persuasion.* Stanford: Stanford Univ. Press, 1960.

Wu-Chi, L.   *A Short History of Confucian Philosophy.* N.Y.: Dell Publishing Co., 1964, 226p.

See Also;

Boles, D. E.   4a1
Callis, H. G.   4a1
Chang, C.   3fl
Levenson, J. R.   4a1, 6c
Smith, W.   6a

Collier, J.   The Peyote Cult. *Science*, 115, 1952, p.503–4.

Dittmann, A. T. and Moore, H. C.   Disturbance in Dreams as Related to Peyotism Among the Navaho. *Amer. Anthropol.*, 59, 1957, p.642–9.

Howard, J. H.   The Mescal-Bean Cult of the Central and Southern Plains: An Ancestor of the Peyote Cult? *Amer. Anthropol.*, 59, 1957, p.75–87.

LaBarre, W., *et al.*   Statement on Peyote. *Science*, 114, 1951, p.582–3.

Malouf, C.   Gosiute Peyotism. *Amer. Anthropol.*, 44, 1942, p.93–103.

Newberne, R. E. L.   *Peyote.* Lawrence: Univ. of Kansas Press, 1955.

Radin, P.   A Sketch of the Peyote Cult of the Winnebago. *J. Rel. Psychol.*, 7, 1914, p.1–22.

Stewart, O. C.   Ute Peyotism: A Study of a Cultural Complex. *Univ. Colorado Stud. Series Anthropol. No. 1*, 1948, 42p.

See Also;

Barber, B.   8a3
Gorton, B. E.   4al
LaBarre, W.   8a4
Merriam, A. P.   4g1

2h4.   Shamanism

Coe, M.   Shamanism in the Bunún Tribe, Central Formosa. *Ethnos*, 20/4, 1955, p.181–98.

Dioszegi, V.   Problems of Mongolian Shamanism. *Acta Ethnographica*, 10/1–2, 1961, p.195–206.

Dioszegi, V.   Tuva Shamanism. *Acta Ethnographica*, 11, 1962, p.143–90.

Fairchild, W. P.   Shamanism in Japan. *Folklore Stud.*, 21, 1962, p.1–122.

Madsen, W.   Shamanism in Mexico. *Southw. J. Anthropol.*, 11, 1955, p.48–57.

Murdock, G. P.   Tenino Shamanism. *Ethnology*, 4/2, 1965, p.165–71.

Nadel, S. F.   A Study of Shamanism in the Nuba Mountains. *J. Roy. Anthropol. Inst.*, 76/ pt. 1, 1946, p.25–37.

Posinsky, S. H.   Yoruk Shamanism. *Psychiatric Quart.*, 39/2, 1965, p.227–43.

Rahmann, R.   Shamanistic and Related Phenomena in Northern and Middle India. *Anthropos*, 54, 1959, p.681–760.

Rock, J. F.   Contributions to the Shamanism of the Tibetan Chinese Borderland. *Anthropos*, 54, 1959, p.796–818.

See Also:

Devereux, G.   5bl
Eliade, M.   8a4
Harper, E. B.   7al
Loeb, E. M.   7a
Smith, M.   7a
Winstedt, R. O.   7a

2h5.   Voodoo

Anderson, J. Q.   The New Orleans Voodoo Ritual Dance and Its Twentieth-Century Survivals. *S. Folklore Quart.*, 24/2, 1960, p.135–43.

Beynon, E. D.   The Voodoo Cult Among Negro Migrants in Detroit. *Amer. J. Sociol.*, 43/6, 1938, p.894–907.

Bourguignon, E.   The Persistence of Folk Belief: Some Notes on Cannibalism and Zombis in Haiti. *J. Amer. Folklore*, 72/ 283, 1959, p.36–46.

Cannon, W. B.   "Voodoo" Death. *Amer. Anthropol.*, 44, 1942, p.169–81.

Christopher, R. A.   The Sacred Waters of Oxalia, An Eerie Predawn Visit to a Brazilian Voodoo Ceremony. *Americas* (OAS), 7/1, 1955, p.23–6.

Deren, M.   *Divine Horsemen: The Living Gods of Haiti.* London: Thames & Hudson, 1953.

Metraux, A.   *Voodoo in Haiti* (Trans. H. Charteris). N.Y.: Oxford Univ. Press, 1959, 400p.

Metraux, A.   *Haiti: Black Peasants and Their Religion.* London: Harrap., 1960, 110p.

Simpson, G. E.   The Vodun Service in Northern Haiti. *Amer. Anthropol.*, 42, 1940, p.236–55.

Simpson, G. E.   The Belief System of the Haitian Vodun. *Amer. Anthropol.*, 47, 1945, p.35–59.

Simpson, G. E.   Magical Practices in Northern Haiti. *J. Amer. Folklore*, 67/266, 1954, p.395–403.

See Also:

Brewster, P. G.   8a5
Kiev, A.   5b

Alland, A., Jr. Abron Witchcraft and Social Structure. *Cah. Et. Afr.*, 5, 1965, p.495–502.

An-Che, L. Bon: The Magico-Religious Belief of the Tibetan-Speaking Peoples. *Southw. J. Anthropol.*, 4/1, 1948, p.31–41.

Baroja, C. J. *The World of Witches* (Trans. O. N. V. Glendinning). Chicago: Univ. of Chicago Press, 1964, 313p.

Berndt, R. M. A 'Devastating Disease Syndrome': Kuru Sorcery in the Eastern Central Highlands of New Guinea. *Sociologus*, 8/1, 1958, p.4–28.

Bristow, K. S. *Moro Magic in Mindanao.* Fresno, California: Academy Library Guild, 1958, 94p.

Burton W. F. P. *Luba Religion and Magic in Custom and Belief.* Tervuren: Musee Royal de l'Afrique Centrale, 1962, 198p.

Debrunner, B. *Witchcraft in Ghana: A Study on the Belief in Destructive Witches and Its Effect on the Akan Tribes.* Kumasi: Presbyterian Books Depot, 1959, 210p.

Evers, H. D. Magic and Religion in Sinhalese Society. *Amer. Anthropol.*, 67/1, 1965, p.97–9.

Hughes, P. *Witchcraft.* London: Longmans Green, 1952, 220p.

Maple, E. The Witches of Dengie. *Folk Lore* (London), 73, 1962, p.178–84.

Middleton, J. and Winter, E. H. (eds.) *Witchcraft and Sorcery in East Africa.* N.Y.: F. A. Praeger, 1963, 302p.

Munday, J. T. *Witchcraft in Central Africa and Europe.* London: United Society for Christian Literature, Lutterworth Press, 1956, 100p.

Parrinder, E. G. *Witchcraft: European and African.* N.Y.: Barnes and Noble, 1963, 215p.

Reay, M. The Sweet Witchcraft of Kuma Dream Experience. *Mankind*, 5/11, 1962, p.459–63.

Reynolds, B. *Magic, Divination and Witchcraft Among the Barotse of Northern Rhodesia.* Berkeley: Univ. of California Press, 1963.

White, C. M. N. Witchcraft, Divination and Magic Among the Balovale Tribes. *Africa*, 18, 1948, p.81–104.

Wilson, M. H. Witch Beliefs and Social Structure. *Amer. J. Sociol.*, 56/4, 1951, p.307–13.

See Also:

3. History and Development of Religion

Agrawala, U. S. Vedic Symbolism. *J. Ind. Hist.*, 41/2, 1963, p.517–23.

American Historical Association. *The American Historical Association Guide to Historical Literature.* N.Y.: The Macmillan Co., 1963, 962p.

Burkhardt, V. R. *Chinese Creeds and Customs.* Hong Kong: South China Morning Post, 1956, 2 vols.

Chamberlayne, J. H. The Development of Kuan Yin: Chinese Goddess of Mercy. *Numen*, 9/1, 1962, p.45–52.

Cornford, F. M. *From Religion to Philosophy: A Study in the Origins of Western Speculation.* N.Y.: Harper, 1957, 275p.

Day, C. B. *The Philosophers of China, Classical and Contemporary.* N.Y.: Philosophical Library, 1962, 426p.

Finegan, J. *The Archeology of World Religions.* Princeton: Princeton Univ. Press, 1952.

Freud, S. and Oppenheim, D. E. *Dreams in Folklore* (Trans. Under Supervision of J. Strachey). N.Y.: International Universities Press, 1958, 111p.

Gaustad, E. S. *Historical Atlas of Religion in America.* N. Y.: Harper and Row, 1962.

Harper, H. V. *Days and Customs of All Faiths.* N.Y.: Fleet Publishing Corporation, 1957, 399p.

Harris, E. and Harris, J. R. *The Oriental Cults in Roman Britain.* Leiden: E. J. Brill, 1965, 120p.

Hart, H. Religion. *Amer. J. Sociol.*, 47/6, 1942, p.888–97.

Hayes, E. C. The Evolution of Religion. *Amer. J. Sociol.*, 21/1, 1915, p.45–64.

Hultkrantz, A. Bachofen and the Mother Goddess: An Appraisal After One Hundred Years. *Ethnos*, 26, 1961, p.75–85.

Kellett, E. E. *A Short History of Religions.* London: Gollancz, 1954, 607p.

Kishimoto, H. and Howes, J. F. *Japanese Religion in the Meiji Era.* Tokyo: Obunsha, 1956.

Lancaster, J. C. *Bibliography of Historical Works Issued in the United Kingdom 1946–1956.* London: Univ. of London, Institute of Historical Research, 1957.

Levy, G. R. *The Gate of Horn.* London: Faber & Faber, 1948.

Living Religions Within the Empire. *Sociol. R.*, 16/1, 1924, p.89–116.

McCullough, W. S. (ed.) *The Seed of Wisdom: Essays in Honor of T. J. Meek.* Toronto: University Press, 1964, 200p.

Mehta, D. D. *Early Indian Religious Thought: An Introduction and Essay.* London: Luzac, 1956, 532p.

Melish, W. H. Religious Developments in the Soviet Union. *Amer. Sociol R.*, 9, 1944, p.279–86.

Murray, C. E. The Personality and Career of Satan. *J. Soc. Issues*, 18/4, 1962, p.36–54.

Niebuhr, H. R. *Radical Monotheism and Western Civilization.* N.Y.: Harper, 1960, 144p.

Nielson, F. Toynbee's "A Study of History." *Amer. J. Econ. Sociol.*, 6/4, 1947, p.451–72.

Oliver, J. H. *Demokratia: The Gods and the Free World.* Baltimore: John Hopkins Univ. Press, 1960, 192p.

Olmstead, C. E. *History of Religion in the United States.* Englewood-Cliffs, New Jersey: Prentice Hall, 1960.

Parkes, H. B. *Gods and Men: The Origins of Western Culture.* N.Y.: Alfred A. Knopf, 1959.

Parrish, F. L. A. *A History of Religion.* N.Y.: Pageant Press, 1965, 279p.

Pettazzoni, R. *The All-Knowing God: Researches Into Early Religion and Culture* (Trans. H. J. Rose). London: Methuen, 1956, 475p.

Pettazzoni, V. *Essays on the History of Religions.* Leiden: E. J. Brill, 1954.

The Religions, Conference. *Sociol. R.*, 16/4, 1924, p.283–316.

Shah, I. *Oriental Magic.* N.Y.: Rider, 1956, 206p.

Smith, D. H. Chinese Concepts of the Soul. *Numen*, 5/3, 1958, p.165–79.

Smith, D. H. Chinese Religion in the Shang Dynasty. *Numen*, 8/1, 1961, p.142–50.

Smith, T. L. Historic Waves of Religious Interest in America. *Ann. Amer. Acad. Polit. Soc. Sci.*, 332, 1960, p.9–19.

Stedman, A. R. *Living Religions: An Historical and Comparative Survey.* London: Bell, 1959, 272p.

Sweet, W. W. *Religion in the Development of American Culture, 1765–1840.* N.Y.: Scribners, 1952.

Sykes, N. *The English Religious Tradition: Sketches of Its Influence on Church, State, and Society.* London: SCM Press, 1953, 121p.

Toy, C. H. *Introduction to the History of Religion.* Cambridge: Harvard Univ. Press, 1948, 639p.

Toynbee, A. J. *A Study of History.* N.Y.: Oxford Univ. Press, 1962, 6 vols.

Verma, B. C. *Socio-Religious, Economic and Literary Condition of Bihar (From ca. 319 A.D. to 1000 A.D.).* Delhi: Munshi Ram Manohar Lal, 1962, 209p.

Walton, F. R. Religious Thought in the Age of Hadrian. *Numen,* 4/3, 1957, p.165–70.

Watt, W. M. The Place of Religion in the Islamic and Roman Empires. *Numen,* 9/2, 1962, p.110–27.

Yang, C. K. *Religion in Chinese Society.* Berkeley: Univ. of California Press, 1961.

Precursors of Modern Religion

Anthes, R. Egyptian Theology in the Third Millenium B.C. *J. Near East. Stud.,* 18/3, 1959, p.169–212.

Bell, H. I. *Cults and Creeds in Greaco-Roman Egypt.* N.Y.: Philosophical Library, 1953, 117p.

Bhattacharyya, H. *Cultural Heritage of India.* Calcutta: Ramakrishna Mission Institute of Culture, 1956.

Bonwick, J. *Egyptian Belief and Modern Thought.* Indian Hills, Colorado: Falcon Wing Press, 1956, 454p.

Brandon, S. G. F. A Problem of the Osirian Judgment of the Dead. *Numen,* 5/2, 1958, p.110–27.

Brandon, S. G. F. *Creation Legends of the Ancient Near East:* London: Hodder and Stoughton, 1963, 241p.

Branston, B. *The Lost Gods of England.* London: Thames & Hudson, 1958, 194p.

Breasted, J. H. *Development of Religion and Thought in Ancient Egypt.* N.Y.: Harper, 1959, 379p.

Budge, E. A. W. *Egyptian Magic.* Evanston, Illinois: University Books, 1958, 234p.

Budge, E. A. W. *Egyptian Ideas of the Future Life: Egyptian Religion.* N.Y.: University Books, 1959, 224p.

Budge, E. A. W. *Osiris: The Egyptian Religion of Resurrection.* N.Y.: University Books, 1961, 440p.

Campbell, J. The Historical Development of Mythology. *Daedalus,* 88/2, 1959, p.232–54.

Cerny, J. *Ancient Egyptian Religion.* London: Hutchinson House, 1952, 195p.

Clark, R. T. T. *Myth and Symbol in Ancient Egypt: With a Chart of Religious Symbols.* N.Y.: Grove Press, 1959, 292p.

Davidson, H. R. *Gods and Myths of Northern Europe.* Baltimore: Penguin Books, 1964, 251p.

de Bary, W. T., *et al.* (eds.) *Sources of Chinese Tradition.* N.Y.: Columbia Univ. Press, 1963, 2 vols.

de Coulanges, F. *The Ancient City: A Study of the Religion, Laws, and Institutions of Greece and Rome.* N.Y.: Anchor Books, 1956.

Drioton, E. *Religions of the Ancient East.* London: Burns and Oates, 1959, 166p.

Dubs, H. H. Theism and Naturalism in Ancient Chinese Philosophy. *Philos. East West,* 9/3–4, 1959–60, p.163–72.

Eastwood, C. C. *Life and Thought in the Ancient World.* Phila.: Westminster Press, 1965.

Fontenrose, J. E. *Phyton: A Study of Delphic Myth and Its Origins.* Berkeley: Univ. of California Press, 1959, 575p.

Frankfort, H. *Ancient Egyptian Religion: An Interpretation.* N.Y.: Columbia Univ. Press, 1948, 172p.

Frazer, J. G. *Adonis, Attis, Osiris.* New Hyde Park, N.Y.: University Books, 1961.

Freud, S. *Totem and Taboo* (Trans. J. Strachey). N.Y.: W. W. Norton, 1962, 172p.

Gaer, J. *How the Great Religions Began.* N.Y.: Dodd, Mead, 1956, 424p.

Goldenweiser, A. A. Origin of Totemism. *Amer. Anthropol.,* 14, 1912, p.600–7.

Guthrie, W. K. C. *The Greeks and Their Gods.* Boston: Beacon Press, 1955, 388p.

Hays, H. R. *In the Beginnings: Early Man and His Gods.* N.Y.: Putnam, 1963, 364p.

Henning, C. L. Origin of Religion. *Amer. Anthropol.,* 11, 1898, p.313–82.

Hooke, S. H. *Babylonian and Assyrian Religion.* Oxford: Blackwell, 1962, 128p.

Huang, W. S. The Origins of Chinese Culture: A Study of Totemism. In A. Leroi-Gourhan, *et al.* (eds.)—*VIe Congres International des Sciences Anthropologiques et Ethnologiques, Paris, 30 Juillet—6 Août 1960 Tome II, Ethnologie (Premier Volume).* Paris: Musée de l'Homme, 1963, p.139–43.

James, E. O. Primitive Monotheism. *Sociol. R.,* 27/3, 1935, p.328–43.

James, E. O. *Prehistoric Religion: A Study in Prehistoric Archaeology.* London: Thames & Hudson, 1957, 300p.

James, E. O. The Threshold of Religion. *Folk Lore* (London), 69, 1958, p.160–74.

James, E. O. The Religions of Antiquity. *Numen,* 7/2, 1960, p.137–47.

Jesi, F. The Thracian Herakles. *Hist. Rel.,* 3/2, 1964, p. 261–77.

Kitagawa, J. M. Prehistoric Background of Japanese Religion. *Hist. Rel.,* 2/1, 1963, p.292–328.

Knight, W. F. J. Origins of Belief. *Folk Lore* (London), 74, 1963, p.289–304.

Lockyer, J. N. *The Dawn of Astronomy: A Study of the Temple Worship and Mythology of the Ancient Egyptians.* Cambridge: M. I. T. Press, 1964, 432p.

Marconi, M. Can the Cosmogony of the Greek be Reconstructed? *Hist. Rel.,* 1/2, 1962, p.274–80.

Mavalwala, J. D. The Ancestors of the Parsi Community in Iran. *J. Ind. Hist.,* 36/2, 1958, p.101–9.

Mendelsohn, I. (ed.) *Religions of the Ancient Near East.* N.Y.: Liberal Arts Press, 1955, 284p.

Murphy, J. *The Origins and History of Religions.* Manchester: Univ. of Manchester Press, 1949.

Okladnikov, A. P. Notes on the Beliefs and Religion of the Ancient Mongols. *Acta Ethnographica,* 13/1, 1963, p.411–4.

Reumann, J. "Stewards of God": Pre-Christian Religious Application of "Oikonomos" in Greek. *J. Bibl. Lit.,* 77/4, 1958, p.399–49.

Roheim, G. *The Gates of the Dream.* N.Y.: International University Press, 1953, 554p.

Skinner, J. Ritual Matricide: A Study of the Origins of Sacrifice. *Amer. Imago,* 18/1, 1961, p.70–102.

Strouve, V. V. The Religion of the Achaemenides and Zoroastrianism. *J. World Hist.,* 6/3, 1960, p.529–45.

Swanson, G. E. *The Birth of the Gods: The Origin of Primitive Beliefs.* Ann Arbor: Univ. of Michigan Press, 1964.

Tritton, A. S. Notes on Religion in Early Arabia. *Muséon,* 72/1–2, 1959, p.191–5.

Zaehner, R. C. *The Teaching of the Magi: A Compendium of Zoroastrian Beliefs.* London: Allen & Unwin, 1956, 157p.

Zaehner, R. C. *The Dawn and Twilight of Zoroastrianism.* London: Weidenfeld and Nicolson, 1961, 371p.

See Also: 2, 6

3a. Christianity

Albright, W. F. *From Stone Age to Christianity.* Baltimore: Johns Hopkins, 1957, 432p.

Bainton, R. H. *Early Christianity.* Princeton, New Jersey: Van Nostrand, 1960, 192p.

Bainton, R. H. (ed.) *Collected Papers in Church History.* Series I. *Early and Medieval Christianity.* Princeton: Van Nostrand, 1962, 192p.
    Series II. *Studies on the Reformation.* Boston: Beacon Press, 1963, 289p.
    Series III. *Christian Unity and Religion in New England.* Boston: Beacon Press, 1964, 294p.

Bainton, R. H. *Christian Unity and Religion in New England.* Boston: Beacon Press, 1964, 294p.

Bainton, R. H. *Christendom: A Short History of Christianity and Its Impact on Western Civilization.* N.Y.: Harper, 1965.

Baker, H. C. *The Image of Man: A Study of an Idea of Human Dignity in Classical Antiquity, the Middle Ages and the Renaissance.* Cambridge: Harvard Univ. Press, 1947, 365p.

Baker, H. C. *The Wars of Truth: Studies in the Decay of Christian Humanism in the Earlier Seventeenth Century.* Cambridge: Harvard Univ. Press, 1952, 390p.

Barnett, J. H. The Easter Festival: A Study in Cultural Change. *Amer. Sociol. R.,* 14/1, 1949, p.62–70.

Barry, C. J. (ed.) *Readings in Church History*. Westminster, Maryland: Newman Press, 1960–65, 3 vols.

Bester, A. E., Jr. *Backwoods Utopias: The Sectarian and Owenite Phases of Communitarian Socialism in America: 1663–1829*. Phila.: Univ. of Pennsylvania Press, 1950.

Bettenson, H. (ed.) *Documents of the Christian Church*. London: Oxford Univ. Press, 1963, 489p.

Brandt, W. J. Church and Society in the Late Fourteenth Century: A Contemporary View. *Medievalia Humanistica*, 13, 1960, p.58–67.

Brown, L. W. *The Indian Christians of Saint Thomas: Being An Account of the Ancient Syrian Church of Malabar*. Cambridge: University Press, 1956, 315p.

Butt, A. J. The Birth of a Religion: The Origins of "Hallalujah", the Semi-Christian Religion of the Carib-Speaking Peoples of the Borderlands of British Guiana, Venezuela, and Brazil. *Timehri*, 38, 1959, p.37–48.

Carrington, P. *The Early Christian Church*. Cambridge: University Press, 1957, 2 vols.

Case, S. J. *The Origins of Christian Supernaturalism*. Chicago: Univ. of Chicago Press, 1946.

Case, S. J., *et al. A Bibliographical Guide to the History of Christianity*. N.Y.: Peter Smith, 1951, 265p.

Clark, S. D. *Church and Sect in Canada*. Toronto: Univ. of Toronto Press, 1948, 458p.

Clark, W. A. Sanctification in Negro Religion. *Soc. Forces*, 15/4, 1937, p.544–51.

Cohn, N. *The Pursuit of the Millenium: Revolutionary Messianism in Medieval and Reformation Europe and Its Bearing on Modern Totalitarian Movements*. N.Y.: Harper and Brothers, 1961, 481p.

Davies, J. G. *The Early Christian Church*. London: Weidenfeld and Nicolson, 1965, 328p.

Dawson, C. *Religion and the Rise of Western Culture*. Garden City: Doubleday, 1958.

Fernando, C. Early Christianity in Ceylon in Pre-Portuguese Times. *Ceylon Today*, 5/7, 1956, p.13–8.

Greenslade, S. L. (ed.) *The Cambridge History of the Bible: The West From the Reformation to the Present Day*. London: Cambridge Univ. Press, 1963, 590p.

Guignebert, C. *Ancient, Medieval and Modern Christianity: The Evolution of a Religion*. New Hyde Park: University Books, 1961.

Holt, S. *Terror in the Name of God: The Story of the Sons of Freedom Doukhobors*. N.Y.: Crown Publishers, 1964, 312p.

Inglis, K. S. *Churches and the Working Classes in Victorian England*. Toronto: Univ. of Toronto Press, 1963.

Judge, E. A. *The Social Patterns of Christian Groups in the First Century*. London: Tyndale Press, 1960.

LaCarriere, J. *The God-Possessed*. London: Allen and Unwin, 1964, 237p.

Latourette, K. S. *History of the Expansion of Christianity*. N.Y.: Harper & Brothers, 1937–1945, 7 vols.

Latourette, K. S. *A History of Christianity*. N.Y.: Harper and Brothers, 1953, 1516p.

Latourette, K. S. *Christianity in a Revolutionary Age: A History of Christianity in the Nineteenth and Twentieth Century*. N.Y.: Harper, 1958–1961, 5 vols.

Lawrence, C. H. (ed.) *The English Church and the Papacy in the Middle Ages*. London: Burns and Oates, 1965, 276p.

Lindsay, T. M. *History of the Reformation*. Edinburgh: T. and T. Clark, 1959, 2 vols.

Littell, F. H. *From State Church to Pluralism: A Protestant Interpretation of Religion In American History*. N.Y.: Anchor Books, 1962, 174p.

Littell, F. H. (ed.) *Reformation Studies: 16 Essays in Honor of Ronald H. Bainton*. Richmond, Virginia: Knox Press, 1962, 285p.

Mathews, S. Christian Sociology. *Amer. J. Sociol.*, 1, 1895, p.69–78, 182–94, 359–80, 457–72, 771–84; see also 2, 1896, p.108–17, 274–87, 416–32.

Matthews, W. R. The Influence of the Bible Upon the English Nation. *J. Bib. Rel.*, 7, 1939, p.23–6.

Mead, G. R. S. *Fragments of a Faith Forgotten, The Gnostics: A Contribution to the Study of the Origins of Christianity*. New Hyde Park: University Books, 1960, 633p.

Moraes, G. M. *A History of Christianity in India*. Edinburgh: W. & R. Chambers, 1965, 320p.

Roheim, G. The Garden of Eden. *Psychoanal. R.*, 27, 1940, p.1–26; see also p.177–99.

Smith, H. S., *et al. American Christianity: An Historical Interpretation With Representative Documents*. N.Y.: Scribners, 1960, 1963, 2 vols., 1963–634p.

Vassall, W. F. *The Origin of Christianity: A Brief Study of the World's Early Beliefs and Their Influence on the Early Christian Church, Including an Examination of the Lost Books of the Bible*. N.Y.: Exposition Press, 1952, 183p.

Walker, W. *A History of the Christian Church* (Rev. C. C. Richardson, *et al.*). N.Y.: Scribners, 1959.

Webber, E. *Escape to Utopia: The Communal Movement in America*. N.Y.: Hastings House, 1959.

Whalen, W. J. *Christianity and American Freemasonry*. Milwaukee: Bruce Publishing Co., 1958, 195p.

Zuck, L. H.   The Changing Meaning of the Funeral in Christian History. *Past. Psychol.*, 8, 1957, p.17–26.

See Also: 2a, 6

Cross, R. D.   5
Cullman, O.   7b3
Dawson, C.   5a2
Dolan, J. P.   5a2
Ellingsworth, P.   4a
Fromm, E.   8a2
Getlein, F.   4g1
Gibbon, E.   8a6
Grant, R. M.   5a
Hardison, O. B., Jr.   4g3
Hutchinson, J. A.   5
Hyma, A.   7b
Jackson, G.   3f4

King, N. Q.   4a1
Kingdom, R.   5a2
Legge, F.   5a2
Lortz, J.   5a2
Momigliano, A.   5a2
Neill, S. C.   7b
Nichols, J. H.   6e
Nuttall, G. F.   5d
Rosenthal, F.   5a1
Speel, C. J.   5a2
Squire, R. N.   4g1
Suzuki, D. T.   7b3
Toth, W.   5a2
Toynbee, A. J.   8a1
Trevor-Roper, H.   6
Troeltsch, E.   8a6
Westfall, R. D.   1b
Widengren, G.   3b

3a1.   Protestants

Albright, R. W.   *A History of the Protestant Episcopal Church.* N. Y.: Macmillan, 1964, 406p.

Allo, I. E.   From Sect to Denomination in English Quakerism. *Brit. J. Sociol.*, 15/3, 1964, p. 207–21.

Andersen, A. W.   *The Salt of the Earth: A History of Norwegian-Danish Methodism in America.* Nashville, Tennessee: Parthenon Press, 1962, 338p.

Armstrong, M. W.   Religious Enthusiasm and Separation in Colonial New England. *Harvard Theol. R.*, 38/2, 1945, p. 111–40.

Barclay, W. C.   *Early American Methodism, 1769–1844.* N. Y.: Board of Missions and Church Extension of the Methodist Church, 1950, 2 vol.

Bender, H.   The Pacifism of the Sixteenth Century Anabaptists. *Menn. Quart. R.*, 30/1, 1956, p. 5–19.

Billings, R. A.   The Negro and His Church: A Psychogenetic Study. *Psychoanal. R.*, 21, 1934, p. 425–41.

Black, M.   *The Scrolls and Christian Origins: Studies in the Jewish Background of the New Testament.* Edinburgh: Thomas Nelson and Sons, 1961, 206p.

Boorstin, D. J.   The Puritan Tradition. *Commentary*, 26/4, 1958, p. 288–99.

Boyd, J. L.   *A History of the Baptists in America Prior to 1945.* N. Y.: American Press, 1957, 205p.

Braithwaite, W. C.   *The Beginnings of Quakerism.* N. Y.: Cambridge Univ. Press, 1955, 607p.

Braithwaite, W. C.   *The Second Period of Quakerism.* London: Cambridge Univ. Press, 1961, 735p.

Brauer, J. C.   *Protestantism in America: A Narrative History.* Phila.: Westminster Press, 1953, 307p.

Brewer, E. D.   Sect and Church in Methodism. *Soc. Forces*, 30/3, 1952, p. 400–8.

Bridenbaugh, C.   *Mitre and Sceptre: Transatlantic Faiths, Ideas, Personalities and Politics 1689–1775.* Oxford: Oxford Univ. Press, 1962, 305p.

Brinton, H. H.   *Friends for 300 Years: The History and Beliefs of the Society of Friends Since George Fox Started the Quaker Movement.* N. Y.: Harper, 1952, 239p.

Cheney, C. R.   *From Becket to Langton: English Church Government, 1170–1213.* Manchester: Manchester Univ. Press, 1956, 212p.

Clark, W. H.   *The Oxford Group: Its History and Significance.* N. Y.: Bookman Associates, 1951, 268p.

Cohen, C.   Martin Luther and His Jewish Contemporaries. *Jew. Soc. Stud.*, 25/3, 1963, p.195–204.

Cole, C. C., Jr.   *The Social Ideas of the Northern Evangelists, 1826–1860.* N. Y.: Columbia Univ. Press, 1954.

Davies, H.   *Worship and Theology in England: From Watts and Wesley to Maurice, 1690–1850.* Princeton: Princeton Univ. Press, 1961, 355p.

Dawson, C.   *The Historic Reality of Christian Culture: A Way to the Renewal of Human Life.* N. Y.: Harper, 1960, 132p.

DeMille, G. E.   *The Episcopal Church Since 1900: A Brief History.* N. Y.: Morehouse-Gorham, 1955, 223p.

Dike, S. W.   A Study of New England Revivals. *Amer. J. Sociol.*, 15/3, 1909, p. 361–78.

Drummond, A. L.   *German Protestantism Since Luther.* London: Epworth Press, 1951, 282p.

Edwards, M. L. *John Wesley and the Eighteenth Century: A Study of His Social and Political Influence.* London: Epworth Press, 1955, 207p.

Fairweather, E. R. (ed.) *The Oxford Movement.* N. Y.: Oxford Univ. Press, 1964.

Flanders, R. B. *Nauvoo: Kingdom on the Mississippi.* Urbana: Univ. of Illinois Press, 1965.

Foulds, E. V. *The Story of Quakerism, 1652–1952.* London: Bannisdale Press, 1954, 312p.

Free, J. *Mormonism and Inspiration: A Study.* Concord, California: Pacific Publishing Co., 1962, 381p.

Fremantle, A. (ed.) *The Protestant Mystics.* N. Y.: New American Library, 1965, 317p.

Fyfe, C. H. The West African Methodists in the Nineteenth Century. *Sierra Leone Bull. Rel.*, 3/1, 1961, p.22–7.

Garvan, A. The New England Plain Style. *Comp. Stud. Society Hist.*, 3/1, 1960, p.106–22.

Gasper, L. *The Fundamentalist Movement.* The Hague: Mouton, 1963, 181p.

Gaustad, E. S. *The Great Awakening in New England.* N. Y.: Harper Brothers, 1959.

George, C. H. and George, K. *The Protestant Mind of the English Reformation.* Princeton: Princeton Univ. Press, 1961, 452p.

Grant, J. W. *Free Churchmanship in England 1870–1940: With Special Reference to Congregationalism.* London: Independent Press, 1955, 418p.

Haller, W. *The Rise of Puritanism: The Way to the New Jerusalem as Set Forth in Pulpit and Press From Thomas Cartwright to John Tilburne and John Milton.* N. Y.: Harper, 1957, 464p.

Hanley, O. T. Colonial Protestantism and the Rise of Democracy. *Amer. Eccles. R.*, 141, 1959, p.24–32.

Harkness, G. E. *Methodist Church in Thought and Action.* N. Y.: Abingdon Press, 1964.

Harrell, D. E., Jr. The Sectional Origins of the Churches of Christ. *J. South. Hist.*, 30/3, 1964, p.261–77.

Hill, M. S. The Historiography of Mormonism. *Church Hist.*, 28/4, 1959, p.418–26.

Hudson, W. S. Puritanism and the Spirit of Capitalism. *Church Hist.*, 18, 1949, p.3–16.

Hyma, A. Calvinism and Capitalism, 1555–1700. *J. Mod. Hist.*, 10, 1938, p.321–43.

Johnson, C. A. *The Frontier Camp Meeting: Religion's Harvest Time.* Dallas: Southern Methodist Press, 1955.

Klassen, P. J. *The Economics of Antibaptism 1525–60.* The Hague: Mouton and Co., 1964, 149p.

Krahn, C. *The Story of the Mennonites.* Newton, Kansas: Mennonite Publication Office, 1950, 856p.

Littell, F. H. *The Origins of Sectarian Protestantism.* N. Y.: Macmillan, 1964, 231p.

Loveland, C. O. *The Critical Years: The Reconstruction of the Anglican Church in the United States of America, 1780–1789.* Greenwich, Connecticut: Seabury Press, 1956, 311p.

Maclear, J. F. The Birth of the Free Church Tradition. *Church Hist.*, 26, 1957, p.99–131.

Marlowe, J. *The Puritan Tradition in English Life.* London: Cresset Press, 1956, 148p.

Maurer, H. H. Studies in the Sociology of Religion. *Amer. J. Sociol.*, I The Sociology of Protestantism, 30, 1924, p.257–86; II Religion and American Sectionalism: The Pennsylvania German, 30, 1925, p.408–38; III The Problems of a National Church Before 1860, 30, 1925, p.534–50; IV The Problems of Group Consensus: The Founding of the Missouri Synod, 30, 1925, p.665–82; V The Fellowship Law of a Fundamentalist Group: The Missouri Synod, 31, 1925, p.39–57; VI The Consciousness of Kind of a Fundamentalist Group, 31, 1926, p.485–506.

McGiffert, A. C. *Protestant Thought Before Kant.* N. Y.: Harper, 1961, 265p.

McNeill, J. T. *The History and Character of Calvinism.* N. Y.: Oxford Univ. Press, 1954, 370p.

Meuser, F. W. *The Formation of the American Lutheran Church: A Case Study in Lutheran Unity.* Columbus, Ohio: Wartburg Press, 1958, 327p.

Miller, P. *Orthodoxy in Massachusetts, 1630–1650.* Boston: Beacon Press, 319p.

Miller, P. and Johnson, T. H. (eds.) *The Puritans: A Sourcebook of Their Writings.* N. Y.: Harper, 1963, 2 vols.

More, P. and Cross, F. L. *Anglicanism: The Thought and Practice of the Church of England, Illustrated From the Literature of the Seventeenth Century.* London: SPCK, 1951, 811p.

Moss, C. B. *The Old Catholic Movement.* London: SPCK, 1964, 362p.

Mulder, W. *The Mormons in American History.* Salt Lake City, Utah: Univ. of Utah, 1957, 36p.

Nichols, R. H. and Nichols, J. H. *Presbyterianism in New York State: A History of the Synod and Its Predecessors.* Phila.: Westminster Press, 1963, 288p.

Peters, V. *All Things Common: The Hutterite Way of Life.* Minneapolis: Univ. of Minnesota Press, 1965, 233p.

Pierce, P. B. Origin of the "Book of Mormon." *Amer. Anthropol.*, 1, 1899, p.675–94.

Posey, W. B. *The Presbyterian Church in the Old Southwest, 1788–1838.* Richmond, Virginia: Knox Press, 1952, 192p.

Posey, W. B. *The Baptist Church in the Lower Mississippi Valley, 1776–1845.* Lexington: Univ. of Kentucky, 1957, 166p.

Powell, S. C. *Puritan Village.* Garden City: Doubleday & Co., 1965.

Quick, G. Some Aspects of the African Watchtower Movement in Northern Rhodesia. *Int. R. Missions,* 29/114, 1940, p.216–25.

Reese, T. R. Religious Factors in the Settlement of a Colony: Georgia in the Eighteenth Century. *J. Rel. Hist.,* 1/2, 1961, p.206–16.

Rightmyer, N. W. *Maryland's Established Church.* Baltimore: Church Historical Society for the Diocese of Maryland, 1956, 239p.

Schneider, H. W. The Developments in Protestantism During the 19th Century Throughout the World. *J. World Hist.,* 6/1, 1960, p. 97–121.

Sisk, G. N. Negro Churches in the Alabama Black Belt, 1875–1917. *J. Presb. Hist. Society,* 33/2, 1955, p.87–92.

Smith, C. H. *The Story of the Mennonites* (Rev. C. Krahn). Newton, Kansas: Mennonite Publication Office, 1957, 856p.

Starkey, M. L. *The Devil in Massachusetts: A Modern Inquiry Into the Salem Witch Trials.* N.Y.: Knopf, 1950, 310p.

Stephenson, G. M. *The Puritan Heritage.* N. Y.: The Macmillan Co., 1952.

Swihart, A. K. *Luther and the Luthern Church, 1483–1960.* N. Y.: Philosophical Library, 1960, 703p.

Symonds, J. *Thomas Brown and the Angels: A Study in Enthusiasm.* London: Hutchinson, 1961, 175p.

Taylor, P. A. M. *Expectations Westward: The Mormons and the Emigration of Their British Converts in the Nineteenth Century.* London: Oliver and Boyd, 1965, 294p.

Teall, J. L. Witchcraft and Calvinism in Elizabethan England: Divine Power and Human Agency. *J. Hist. Ideas,* 23/1, 1962, p.21–36.

VanBaumer, F. L. The Church of England and The Common Corps of Christendom. *J. Mod. Hist.,* 16, 1944, p.1–21.

VanBaumer, F. L. England: The Turk and The Common Corps of Christendom. *Amer. Hist. R.,* 50, 1944, p.26–48.

Werner, Ern. Popular Ideologies in Late Medieval Europe: Taborite Chiliasm and Its Antecedents. *Comp. Stud. Society Hist.,* 2, 1959–1960, p.344–63.

Whitemore, L. B. *Struggle for Freedom: History of the Phillipine Independent Church.* Greenwich, Connecticut: Seabury Press, 1961, 228p.

Williams, G. H. Studies in the Radical Reformation (1517–1618): A Bibliographical Survey of Research Since 1939. *Church Hist.,* 27/1, 1958, p.46–69; see also 27/2, p.124–60.

Wilson, W. E. *The Angel and the Serpent: The Study of New Harmony.* Bloomington: Indiana Univ. Press, 1964.

Yule, G. Bibliography: Puritanism and English Society 1558–1660. *J. Rel. Hist.,* 2/2, 1963, p.270–6.

See Also:

American Church Union   5e3
Berkhofer, R. F., Jr.   5e2
Birnbaum, N.   6c
Bodo, J. R.   5
Cohen, A.   6b
Cross, W. R.   6c
Doherty, R. W.   6c
Eister, A. W.   7d
Fox, C. E.   5e4
Froom, L. R. E.   6d
Furniss, N. F.   4a
Gabriel, R. H.   4g5
Gould, J. E.   6c
Gray, E. E.   5e2
Hair, P. E. H.   9
Heddendorf, R.   8a2
Hostetler, J. A.   9
Hughley, J.   5
Iglehart, C.   2a1
James, S. V.   4b
Jones, W. L.   4h
Landis, J. T.   5
Lord, F. T.   5a1
Mackenzie, K. N.   5d
Maclear, J. F.   7b2
Marrow, R. E.   4
McFaran, D. M.   5e1
Merton, R. K.   1b
Meyer, C. S.   6e
Miller, R. M.   5
Morgan, E. S.   7b3
Mueller, C. E.   7a3
Niebuhr, H. R.   4j3 (2)
Norwood, F. A.   8a4
Nyholm, P. C.   6e
Pope, L.   6a
Posey, W. B.   5a2

Shanahan, W. O.   5d
Smith, E. A.   7a1
Thomas, W. T.   5e3
Tillich, P.   6c

Varg, P. A.   5e3
Watson, B.   2a1
Williamson, H. R.   5e3
Wilson, R. C.   5

3a2.   *Catholics*

Barlow, F.   *The English Church 1000–1066: A Constitutional History.*   London: Longmans, Green, 1965, 324p.

Bossy, J.   The Character of Elizabethan Catholicism. *Past Present*, 21, 1962, p.39–59.

Bourke, J.   Gnosticism and Christianity: The Nag-Hammadi Discoveries. *Blackfriars*, 42/448, 1961, p.4–19.

Brandon, S. G. F.   The Historical Element in Primitive Christianity. *Numen*, 2/3, 1955, p.156–67.

Brown, W. E.   *The Catholic Church in South Africa: From Its Origins to the Present Day* (Ed. M. Derrick). N. Y.: P. J. Kenedy, 1960, 384p.

Burns, C. D.   The Religious Order in the West. *Sociol. R.*, 3/1, 1910, p.24–34.

Butsche, J.   Negro Catholics in the United States. *Cath. Hist. R.*, 3, 1917, p.33–51.

Cardoza, M.   The Holy See and the Question of the Bishop-elect of Rio, 1833–39. *Americas*, 10/1, 1953, p.3–74.

Chamberlayne, J. H.   From Sect to Church in British Methodism. *Brit. J. Sociol.*, 15/2, 1964, p.139–49.

Claudia, I. H. M.   *Dictionary of Papal Pronouncements: Leo XIII to Pius XII, 1878–1957.* N.Y.: Kenedy and Sons, 1958, 216p.

Code, J. B.   A Selected Bibliography of the Religious Orders and Congregations of Women Founded Within the Boundaries of the United States, 1727–1850. *Cath. Hist. R.*, 23, 1937, p.331–51; see also 26, 1940, p.222–45.

Coulton, G. G.   *Five Centuries of Religion.* Cambridge: University Press, 1929–50, 4 vols.

Daniel-Rops, H.   *Cathedral and Crusade: Studies of the Medieval Church, 1050–1350.* N. Y.: E. P. Dutton, 1957.

Daniel-Rops, H.   *The Church in the Dark Ages.* N. Y.: E. P. Dutton, 1959.

Danielou, J. and Marrov, H.   *The First Six Hundred Years* (Trans. V. Cronin). Vol. 1. *The Christian Centuries.* N. Y.: McGraw-Hill Book Co., 1964, 522p.

Decarreaux, J.   *Monks and Civilization.* N. Y.: Doubleday and Co., 1964, 397p.

Diamant, A.   *Austrian Catholics and the First Republic: Democracy, Capitalism and the Social Order, 1918–1934.* Princeton: Princeton Univ. Press, 1960.

Ellis, J. T. (ed.)   *Documents of American Catholic History.* Milwaukee: Bruce Publishing Co., 1956, 677p.

Ellis, J. T.   *Catholics in Colonial America.* N. Y.: Taplinger, 1964.

Furfey, P. H.   Christian Social Thought in the First and Second Centuries. *Amer. Cath. Sociol. R.*, 1/1, 1940, p.13–20.

Garrison, W. E.   *Religion and Civil Liberty in the Roman Catholic Tradition.* Chicago: Willett, Clark and Co., 1947.

Hales, E. E. Y.   *The Catholic Church in the Modern World: A Survey From the French Revolution to the Present.* Garden City, N. Y.: Hanover House, 1958, 312p.

Harnack, A.   *The Mission and Expansion of Christianity in the First Three Centuries* (Trans. J. Moffett). N. Y.: Harper, 1962, 527p.

Hughes, E. C.   The Industrial Revolution and the Catholic Movement in Germany. *Soc. Forces*, 14/2, 1935, p.286–92.

Kirkham, E. K.   *A Survey of American Church Records.* Salt Lake City, Utah: Deseret Book Co., 1959, 1960, 2 vols.

Lietzmann, H.   *History of the Early Church.* N.Y.: Meridian, 1961, 2 vols.

McAvoy, T. T.   The Catholic Church in the United States Between Two Wars. *R. Polit.*, 4/4, 1942, p.409–31.

McAvoy, T. T.   *The Americanist Heresy in Roman Catholicism: 1895–1900.* Notre Dame: Univ. of Notre Dame, 1963, 322p.

Mollat, G.   *The Popes at Avignon, 1305–1378* (Trans. J. Love). N. Y.: Thomas Nelson & Sons, 1963, 360p.

Moody, J. N., *et al.* (eds.)   *Church and Society: Catholic Social and Political Thought and Movements, 1789–1950.* N. Y.: Arts, 1953, 914p.

Murphy, Rob. J.   The Catholic Church in the United States During the Civil War Period (1852–1866). *Amer. Cath. Hist. Society Phila. Rec.*, 39, 1928, p.271–346.

Nuesse, C. J. The Social Thought Among American Catholics in the Colonial Period. *Amer. Cath. Sociol. R.*, 7, 1946, p.43–52.

O'Connor, T. F. Writings on United States Catholic History, 1946: A Selective Bibliography. *Americas*, 4, 1948, p.501–9.

Perry, M. "Preparation for Salvation" in Seventeenth Century New England. *J. Hist. Ideas*, 4/3, 1943, p.253–86.

Petry, R. C. Survey: Medieval Church History. *Church Hist.*, 26, 1957, p.169–73.

Procko, B. P. *A Brief History of the Eastern Rites.* Bridgeport, Pennsylvania: Chancellor Press, 1956, 16p.

Rogier, A., *et al.* (eds.) *The Christian Centuries: A New History of the Catholic Church.* N. Y.: McGraw-Hill, 1964–65, 5 vols.

Shannon, J. P. *Catholic Colonization on the Western Frontier.* New Haven: Yale Univ. Press, 1957, 302p.

Shaw, I. P. *Nationality and the Western Church Before the Reformation.* Naperville, Illinois: A. R. Allenson, 1959.

Shaw, P. E. *The Catholic Apostolic Church, Sometimes Called Irvingite: A Historical Study.* N. Y.: King's Crown Press, 1946, 264p.

Sheppard, L. C. *The Mass in the West.* London: Burns and Oates, 1962, 112p.

Ullman, W. *The Growth of Papal Government in the Middle Ages: A Study in the Ideological Relations of Clerical to Lay Power.* N. Y.: Barnes & Noble, 1956, 482p.

Vidler, A. R. *A Century of Social Catholicism 1820–1920.* London: SPCK, 1963, 171p.

Vig Naux, G. The Catholics in France Since the Armistice. *R. Polit.*, 5/2, 1943, p.194–215.

Vollmar, E. R. *The Catholic Church in America: An Historical Bibliography.* New Brunswick, New Jersey: Scarecrow Press, 1956, 354p.

Welsh, E. A. The Catholic Church in Present Day Russia. *Cath. Hist. R.*, 18, 1932, p.177–204.

See Also:

Beales, A. C. F.   4g4
Cantor, N. F.   4a1
Chapman, S. H.   4f1
Confraternity of Christian Doctrine   7b1
Costello, B. D.   4b
de la Costa, H.   5e4
Diamant, A.   5
Ellis, J. T.   9
Frend, W. H. C.   6b
Gasparini, E.   5a1
Hanson, R. P. C.   8a2
Hatch, E.   6c
Hesketh, C.   5a2
Kaiser, M. L.   4g4
Kenton, E.   5e2
Koren, H. J.   7a1
Kots, S. O.   6c
Loomis, L. R.   5a1
Malone, G. K.   6c
Menczer, B.   4a
Metzger, C. H.   5d
Meyer, D.   4a
Morner, M.   4a
Neundorfer, L.   8a2
Nuesse, C. J.   7b3
Periodical Literature   9
Petry, R. C.   4
Phelan, J. L.   5e4
Sharp, J. K.   4f4
Smalley, B.   4g4
Smith, E. A.   5a2
Snell, M. M.   5
Tavard, G. H.   6c
Thomas, W. I.   7b3
Trimble, W. R.   5a2
Windell, G. G.   4a
Wise, J. E.   4g4

3a3.   Orthodox

Benz, E. *The Eastern Orthodox Church: Its Thought and Life.* N. Y.: Doubleday & Co., 1963.

Fedotov, G. P. *The Russian Religious Mind: Kievan Christianity, the Tenth to the Thirteenth Centuries.* N. Y.: Harper & Row, 1960, 432p.

Hoover, C. B. Religion in Soviet Russia. *S. Atlantic Quart.*, 30, 1931, p.113–24.

Leen, W. The Origin and Present Condition of the Russian Orthodox Church. *Eccles. Rec.*, 42, 1910, p.400–16.

Palmieri, F. A. The Failure of the Russian Church. *Cath. Mind*, 114, 1921, p.199–209.

Richards, G. W. The Church and the Religion of Russia. *Amer. J. Theol.*, 22, 1918, p.541–61.

Schmemann, A. *The Historical Road of the Eastern Orthodoxy* (Trans. L. W. Keisch). N. Y.: Holt, 1963, 342p.

Simpson, J. Y. Religion in Russia Today. *Hibbert J.*, 14, 1916, p.393–408.

Soué, B. I. Religion in the Soviet Union. *Contemp. Russia*, 1, 1937, p.322–40; see also 2, 1938, p.422–55.

Spinka, M. Slavonic Studies in Church History. *Slavonic R.*, 5, 1926, p.114–27.

Tisserant, E. *Eastern Christianity in India: A History of the Syro-Malabar Church From the Earliest Time to the Present Day.* Calcutta: Orient Longmans, 1959, 266p.

Widdrington, P. E. T. What Has Happened to the Russian Church? *Christendom*, 2, 1937, p.74–83.

Zernov, N. *Eastern Christendom: A Study of the Origin and Development of the Eastern Orthodox Church.* N. Y.: G. P. Putnam's Sons, 1961, 326p.

See Also:

Bennett, E. M.   4a1
Curtis, J. S.   4a, 4a1
Lawrence, J.   4a1
Meyendorff, J.   2a3
Phillippou, A. J.   2a3
Runicman, S.   5a2
Ware, T.   4a1

3b. Judaism

Baron, S. W. The Jewish Factor in Medieval Civilization. *Proc. Amer. Acad. Jew. Res.*, 12, 1942, p.1–48.

Baron, S. W. *A Social and Religious History of the Jews.* N. Y.: Columbia Univ. Press, 1952–1960, 9 vols.

Ben-Horin, M., *et al.* (eds.) *Studies and Essays in Honor of Abraham A. Neuman.* Leiden: E. J. Brill, 1962, 650p.

Bentwich, N. The Social Transformation of Anglo-Jewry 1883–1960. *Jew. J. Sociol.*, 2/1, 1960, p.16–24.

Brenner, A. B. The Covenant With Abraham. *Psychoanal. R.*, 39, 1952, p.34–52.

Chambers, W. T. Ancient Palestine: The Evolution of an Advanced Religion. *Southw. Soc. Sci. Quart.*, 20/3, 1939, p.283–91.

Cohen, I. The Jewish Community. *Sociol. R.*, 3/3, 1910, p.216–26.

Dunn, S. P. The Roman Jewish Community: A Study in Historical Causation. *Jew. J. Sociol.*, 2/1, 1960, p.185–201.

Efros, I. L. *Ancient Jewish Philosophy: A Study in Metaphysics and Ethics.* Detroit: Wayne State Univ., 1964, 199p.

Ehrlich, E. L. *A Concise History of Israel: From the Earliest Times to the Destruction of the Temple in A.D. 70* (Trans. J. Barr). London: Darton, Longman & Todd, Ltd., 1962, 153p.

Finkelstein, L. (ed.) *The Jews: Their History, Culture and Religion.* N. Y.: Jewish Publication Society, 1949, 4 vols.

Gamoran, M. *Days and Ways: The Story of Jewish Holidays and Customs.* N. Y.: Union of American Hebrew Congregation, 1956, 205p.

Gaster, T. H. *Passover: Its History and Tradition.* London: Abelard-Schuman, 1958, 102p.

Golb, N. The Dietary Laws of the Damascus Covenant in Relation to Those of the Karaites. *J. Jew. Stud.*, 8/1–2, 1957, p.51–69.

Goldman, L. M. *The History of the Jews in New Zealand.* Wellington: A. H. & A. W. Reed, 1958, 272p.

Grayzel, S. *Through the Ages: The Story of the Jewish People.* Phila.: Jewish Publication Society, 1947.

Grayzel, S. *A History of Contemporary Jews: From 1900 to the Present.* The Jewish Publication Society of America, Inc., 1960, 192p.

Grinstein, H. B. *The Rise of the Jewish Community of New York, 1654–1860.* Phila: Jewish Publication Society, 1945, 645p.

Harstein, J. I. (ed.) *The Jews in American History: A Resource Book for Teachers of Social Studies and American History.* N. Y.: Anti-Defamation League of B'nai B'rith, 1955, 100p.

Heschel, A. J. The Eastern European Era in Jewish History. *Yivo Ann. Jew. Soc. Sci.*, 1, 1946, p.86–106.

Husik, I. *A History of Mediaeval Jewish Philosophy.* N. Y.: Meridian Books, 1958, 466p.

Kage, J. *With Faith and Thanksgiving: The Story of Two Hundred Years of Jewish Immigration and Immigrant Aid Effort in Canada.* Montreal: Eagle Publishing Co., 1962, 288p.

Katz, J. Jewry and Judaism in the Nineteenth Century. *J. World Hist.*, 4/4, 1958, p.881–900.

Lestchinsky, J. The Industrial and Social Structure of the Jewish Population of Interbellum Poland. *Yivo Ann. Jew. Soc. Sci.*, 11, 1956–57, p.243–69.

Levinger, A. *Jewish Adventures in America: The Story of 300 Years of Jewish Life in the United States.* N. Y.: Bloch Publishing Co., 1955, 243p.

Levy, A. *History of the Sunderland Jewish Community.* London: Macdonald, 1956, 326p.

Liebman, S. B. The Jews of Colonial Mexico. *Hisp. Amer. Hist. R.*, 43/1, 1963, p.95–108.

Lipman, V. D. (ed.) *Three Centuries of Anglo-Jewish History: A Volume of Essays.* Cambridge: W. Heffer and Sons, 1961, 201p.

Meek, T. J. *Hebrew Origins.* N.Y.: Harper, 1950, 246p.

Merrill, G. The Role of the Sephardic Jews in the British Caribbean Area During the Seventeenth Century. *Caribbean Stud.*, 4/3, 1964, p.32–49.

Moscati, S. Israel's Predecessors: A Re-Examination of Certain Current Theories. *J. Bib. Rel.*, 24, 1956, p.245–54.

Noth, M. *The History of Israel.* N. Y.: Harper, 1958, 479p.

Parkes, J. *End of an Exile.* London: Vallentine Mitchell, 1954, 192p.

Parkes, J. *A History of the Jewish People.* London: Weidenfeld and Nicolson, 1962, 254p.

Pessin, D. *History of the Jews in America.* N.Y.: United Synagogue Commission on Jewish Education, 1957, 317p.

Pinson, K. S. (ed.) Studies on the Epoch of the Jewish Catastrophe, 1933–1945. *Yivo Ann. Jew. Soc. Sci.*, 8, 1953, 303p. (entire issue).

Pinson, K. S. (ed.) Studies in American Jewish History and Culture. *Yivo Ann. Jew. Soc. Sci.*, 9, 1954, 398p.

Plaut, W. G. *The Jew in Minnesota: The First Seventy-Five Years.* N. Y.: American Jewish Historical Society, 1959, 347p.

Plaut, W. G. *The Rise of Reform Judaism.* N. Y.: World Union for Progressive Judaism, 1963, 288p.

Proctor, S. Jewish Life in America: Over Three Hundred Years of Freedom. *Soc. Sci.*, 32/2, 1957, p.151–4.

Reik, T. *Mystery on the Mountain: The Drama of the Sinai Revelation.* N. Y.: Harper, 1959, 210p.

Reik, T. *Pagan Rites in Judaism: From Sex Initiation, Magic, Mooncult, Tattooing, Mutilation and Other Primitive Rituals to Family Loyalty and Solidarity.* N. Y.: Farrar, Straus and Cudahy, 1964, 206p.

Robinson, J. and Friedman, P. *Guide to Jewish History Under Nazi Impact.* N. Y.: Yivo Institute for Jewish Research, 1960, 425p.

Roth, C. *The Jewish Contribution to Civilization.* London: East and West Library, 1956, 295p.

Roth, C. *The Jews in the Renaissance.* Phila.: Jewish Publication Society of America, 1959, 380p.

Sachar, H. M. *The Course of Modern Jewish History.* Cleveland: World Publishing Co., 1958.

Sack, B. G. *History of the Jews in Canada* (Trans. R. Novek). Montreal: Harvest House, 1965, 318p.

Schurer, E. *Jewish People in the Time of Jesus.* N. Y.: Schocken Books, 1961, 428p.

Segal, J. B. *The Hebrew Passover From Earliest Times to A. D. 70.* London: Oxford Univ. Press, 1963, 294p.

Simon, M. *Jewish Religious Conflicts.* London: Hutchinson Univ. Library, 1950, 176p.

Snatzky, J. Warsaw Jews in the Polish Cultural Life of the Early 19th Century. *Yivo Ann. Jew. Soc. Sci.*, 5, 1950, p.41–54.

Speiser, E. A. (ed.) *At the Dawn of Civilization* (World History of the Jewish People, Vol. 1). New Brunswick: Rutgers Univ. Press, 1964, 388p. (1st of a Series of 20 Vols., Under Editorship of B. Netanyahu).

Stern, H. S. The Ethics of the Clean and the Unclean. *Judaism*, 6/3, 1957, p.319–27.

Vetulani, A. The Jews in Medieval Poland. *Jew. J. Sociol.*, 4/2, 1962, p.274–94.

Wallis, L. Biblical Sociology. *Amer. J. Sociol.*, 14, 1908, p.145–70, 306–28, 497–533; see also: 15, 1909, p.214–43; 16, 1910, p. 392–419; 17, 1911, p.61–70, 329–50.

Waxman, M. (ed.) *Tradition and Change: The Development of Conservative Judaism.* N.Y.: Burning Bush Press, 1958, 477p.

Weber, M. *Ancient Judaism* (Trans. H. H. Gerth and D. Martindale). Glencoe: Free Press, 1952.

Widengren, G. Tradition and Literature in Early Judaism and in the Early Church. *Numen*, 10/1, 1963, p.42–83.

Willner, D. and Kohls, M. Jews in the High Atlas Mountains of Morocco: A Partial Reconstruction. *Jew. J. Sociol.*, 4/2, 1962, p.206–41.

Wiznitzer, A. *Jews in Colonial Brazil.* N. Y.: Columbia Univ. Press, 1960, 227p.

Rosenthal, F. 5a1
Scholem, G. G. 7b3
Shunami, S. 9

Vorspan, A. 5
Weiss, J. G. 2b
Werblowsky, R. J. 7b1

3c. *Hinduism*

Banerjee, P. Early History of Vaishnavism. *Indo-Asian Cult.*, 13/2, 1964, p.120–9.

Banerjee, P. Some Aspects of the Early History of Saivism. *Indo-Asian Cult.*, 14/3, 1965, p.215–31.

Bhavan, B. V. *Hinduism Through the Ages.* Bombay: Bharatiya Vidya Bhavan, 1956, 303p.

Bose, A. Evolution of Civil Society and Caste System in India. *Int. R. Soc. Hist.*, 3/1, 1958, p.97–121.

Chattopadhyaya, S. *The Evolution of Theistic Sects in Ancient India Up to the Time of Samkarācārya.* Calcutta: Progressive Publishers, 1962, 205p.

Cokhake, B. G. *Ancient India: History and Culture.* London: Asia Publishing House, 1959, 224p.

Cokhake, B. G. *Indian Thought Through the Ages: A Study of Some Dominant Concepts.* N.Y.: Asia Publishing House, 1961, 236p.

Eliot, C. *Hinduism and Buddhism: An Historical Sketch.* N.Y.: Barnes & Noble, 1962, 3 vols.

Kosambi, D. D. *Myth and Reality: Studies in the Formation of Indian Culture.* Bombay: Popular Prakashan, 187p.

Kuper, H. An Ethnographic Description of Kavady: A Hindu Ceremony in South Africa. *Afr. Stud.*, 18/3, 1959, p.118–32.

Majumdar, A. K. A Note on the Development of Radha Cult. *Ann. Bhandarker Orient. Inst.*, 36/3–4, 1955, p.231–57.

Parvi, S. S. The Philosophy of Caste With Special Reference to the Gupta Age. *Orissa Hist. Res. J.*, 9/3–4, 1961, p.83–96.

Parvi, S. S. Untouchability in the Early Indian Society. *J. Ind. Hist.*, 39/1, 1961, p.1–13.

Rocher, L. and Rocher, R. Sacredness of Power in Ancient India According to the Texts of Dharma. *Ann. Cent. Rel.*, 1, 1961, p.123–39.

Rudrappa, J. Divine Grace (Saktipata) According to Saivism. *Quart. J. Mythic Society*, 49/1, 1958, p.59–67.

Weber, M. *The Religion of India: The Sociology of Hinduism and Buddhism* (Trans. H. H. Gerth and D. Martindale). Glencoe: Free Press, 1958, 392p.

Zimmer, H. R. *Myths and Symbols in Indian Art and Civilization.* N.Y.: Pantheon Books, 1947.

See Also: 2c, 4j1, 6

Albinski, H. S. 4a
Banerjea, J. N. 4g1
Hutton, J. H. 4j1
Leuba, J. H. 7b3
Pal, R. 4a1
Sarma, R. 4j1
Thomas, P. 4j4

3d. *Mohammedanism*

Ahmad Khan, M. Bibliographical Introduction to Modern Islamic Development in India and Pakistan, 1700–1955. *J. Asiat. Society Pakistan*, 4 (Supplement), 1959, 170p.

al-Faruqi, I. R. A. *Urubah and Religion. A Study of the Fundamental Ideas of Arabism and of Islam as Its Highest Moment of Consciousness.* Amsterdam: Djambatan, 1962, 287p., vol. 1.

Arberry, A. J. *Aspects of Islamic Civilization, as Depicted in the Original Texts.* London: Allen and Unwin, 1964, 408p.

Arberry, L. *Sufism: An Account of the Mystics of Islam.* London: Allen & Unwin, 1950, 141p.

Cobb, S. *Islamic Contributions to Civilization.* Washington, D.C.: Avalon Press, 1963, 84p.

Davison, R. H. *Reform in the Ottoman Empire, 1856–1876.* Princeton: Princeton Univ. Press, 1963, 479p.

Dodge, B. *Al-Azhar: A Millennium of Muslim Learning.* Washington: Middle East Institute, 1961, 239p.

Gee, T. W. A Century of Muhammadan Influence in Bugunda, 1852–1951. *Uganda J.*, 22/2, 1958, p.139–50.

Gibb, H. A. R. *Studies on the Civilization of Islam.* Boston: Beacon Press, 1962, 369p.

Hill, A. H.   The Beginnings of Islam in the Far East. *J. Rel. Hist.*, 1/1, 1960, p.72–87.

Hitti, P. K.   *History of the Arabs from the Earliest Times to the Present.* London: Macmillan, 1960, 822p.

Hitti, P. K.   *The Near East in History.* Princeton: D. Van Nostrand, 1961, 543p.

Hollister, J. H.   *The Shi'a of India.* London: Luzac, 1953, 440p.

Hourani, A. H.   *Arabic Thought in the Liberal Age, 1798–1939.* N.Y.: Oxford Univ. Press, 1962.

Imamuddin, S. M.   *A Political History of Muslim Spain.* Dacca: Najmah & Sons, 1961, 286p.

Khadduri, M. and Liebesny, H. J. (eds.)   *Law in the Middle East.* Washington: Middle East Institute, 1955, 381p.

Krymsky, A. E.   A Sketch of the Development of Sufism Up to the End of the Third Century of the Hijra. *Islamic Quart.*, 5, 1960, p.109–25.

Lewis, B.   Some Observations on the Significance of Heresy in the History of Islam. *Stud. Islam.*, 1, 1953, p.43–63.

Mahmud, S. F.   *A Short History of Islam.* London: Oxford Univ. Press, 1963, 724p.

Misra, S. C.   *Muslim Communities in Gujarat: Preliminary Studies in Their History and Social Organization.* N.Y.: Asia Publishing House, 1964, 207p.

Nabi, M. N.   *Development of Muslim Religious Thought in India From 1200 A. D. to 1450 A. D.* Aligarh, India: The Aligarh Muslim Univ. Press, 1962, 210p.

Nizami, K. A.   Some Aspects of Khangah Life in Medieval India. *Stud. Islam.*, 8, 1957, p.51–69.

Qureshi, I. H.   *The Muslim Community of the Indo-Pakistan Sub-Continent (610–1947): A Brief Historical Analysis.* The Hague: Mouton and Co., 1962, 334p.

Rauf, M. A.   *A Brief History of Islam.* London: Oxford Univ. Press, 1964, 128p.

Rochlin, S. A.   Origin of Islam in the Eastern Cape. *Afr. Notes News*, 12/1, 1956, p.21–5.

Roff, W. R.   The Malayo-Muslim World of Singapore at the Close of the Nineteenth Century. *J. Asian Stud.*, 24/1, 1964, p.75–90.

Rosenthal, F.   *A History of Muslim Historiography.* Leiden: E. J. Brill, 1952, 558p.

Rosenthal, F.   *The Muslim Concept of Freedom Prior to the Nineteenth Century.* Leiden: E. J. Brill, 1960, 133p.

Roy, M. N.   *The Historical Role of Islam.* Calcutta: Renaissance Publishers, 1958, 91p.

Saunders, J. J.   *A History of Medieval Islam.* London: Routledge and Kegan Paul, 1965, 220p.

Sauvaget, J.   *Introduction to the History of the Muslim East: A Bibliographical Guide Based on the Second Edition as Recast by Claude Cahen.* Berkeley: Univ. of California Press, 1964, 252p.

Schimmel, A.   The Origin and Early Development of Sufism. *J. Pakistan Hist. Society*, 7/2, 1959, p.55–67.

Smith, W. C.   *Islam in Modern History.* Princeton: Princeton Univ. Press, 1957.

von Grunebaum, G. E. (ed.)   Studies in Islamic Cultural History. *Amer. Anthropol. Assoc. Mem.*, 76, 1954, 60p.

von Grunebaum, G. E.   *Medieval Islam: A Study in Cultural Orientation.* Chicago: Univ. of Chicago Press, 1961, 378p.

Watt, W. M.   Philosophy and Social Structure in Almohad Spain. *Islamic Quart.*, 8/1-2, 1964, p.46–51.

Zwemer, S. M.   Islam in Ethiopia and Eritrea. *Muslim World*, 26, 1936, p.5–15.

See Also: 2d, 6

Allen, H.   5
Anderson, J. N. D.   6a
Arberry, A. J.   7a1
Arnold, T. W.   4g1, 7a1
Benda, H. J.   5d
Berg, C.   6b
Coulson, N. J.   1c
Cragg, K.   4a
Dodge, B.   4g4
Gibb, H. A. R.   2d
Glubb, J. B.   5d
Hardy, M. L. J.   1c
Khadduri, M.   1c
Kirkpatrick, C.   5
Lange-Poole, S.   4a1
Loewenthal, R.   8a4
Muir, W.   6c
Myers, E. A.   5a
Rice, D. T.   4g1
Rosenthal, E. I.   4a
Siddiqi, M. Z.   4g3
Speel, C. J.   5a2
Stern, S. M.   5e1
Trimingham, J. S.   2d
Wolf, E. R.   6b

3e. Buddhism

Bapat, P. V. *2,500 Years of Buddhism*. Delhi: Publications Division, Ministry of Information and Broadcasting, 1956, 503p.

Barua, B. M. The Role of Buddhism in Indian Life and Thought. *Ind. Cult.*, 12/2, 1946–47, p.97–110.

Boribal Buribhand, L. *The History of Buddhism in Thailand* (Trans. L. Suriyabongs). Bangkok: Chatra Press, 1955, 32p.

Ch'en, K. *Buddhism in China: A Historical Survey*. Princeton: Princeton Univ. Press, 1964, 560p.

Ch'en, K. Chinese Communist Attitudes Towards Buddhism in Chinese History. *China Quart.*, 22, 1965, p.14–30.

Chia, C., *et al*. *Collected Essays on the History and Philosophical Thought of Chinese Buddhism*. Taipei, Taiwan: China Culture Publishing Foundation, 1957, 3 vols.

Conze, E. *Buddhism: Its Essence and Development*. N.Y.: Harper, 1959, 212p.

Conze, E., *et al*. (eds.) *Buddhist Texts Through the Ages*. Oxford: B. Cassirer, 1954, 322p.

Dasgupta, S. *An Introduction to Tantric Buddhism*. Calcutta: Univ. of Calcutta, 1950, 235p.

Davids, T. W. R. *Buddhist India*. Calcutta: S. Gupta 1957, 158p.

Dumoulin, H. *History of Zen*. N.Y.: Pantheon Books, 1963.

Dutt, S. *Early Buddhist Monachism*. N.Y.: Asia Publishing House, 1960, 172p.

Finot, L. Outline of the History of Buddhism in Indo-China. *Ind. Hist. Quart.*, 2, 1926, p.673–89.

Getty, A. *The Gods of Northern Buddhism: Their History, Iconography and Progressive Evolution Through the Northern Buddhist Countries*. Rutland, Vermont: C. E. Tuttle, Co., 1962, 220p.

Guenther, H. V. The Philosophical Background of Buddhist Tantrism. *J. Orient. Stud.*, 5, 1959–60, p.45–64.

Jayanama, D. Buddhism and Its Democratic Traditions in Thailand. *Thailand Today*, 1940, p.38–42.

Mal, B. *The Religion of Buddha and Its Relation to Upanishadic Thought*. Hoshiarpur: Vishveshvarand Publications, 1960, 310p.

Morgan, K. W. (ed.) *The Path of the Buddha: Buddhism Interpreted by Buddhists*. N.Y.: Ronald Press, 1956, 432p.

Pande, G. C. *Studies in the Origins of Buddhism*. Allahabad: Univ. of Allahabad, Dept. of Ancient History, Culture and Archaeology, 1957, 600p.

Saunders, E. D. *Buddhism in Japan: With an Outline of Its Origins in India*. Phila.: Univ. of Pennsylvania Press, 1964, 345p.

Snellgrove, D. L. *Buddhist Himalaya: Travels and Studies in Quest of the Origins and Nature of Tibetan Religion*. Oxford: Cassirer, 1957, 234p.

Tuskamoto, Z. The Early Stages in the Introduction of Buddhism Into China (Up to the Fifth Century). *J. World Hist.*, 6/3, 1960, p.546–72.

Varma, V. P. The Origins and Sociology of the Early Buddhist Philosophy of Moral Determinism. *Philos. East West*, 13/1, 1963, p.25–47.

Wales, H. G. O. An Early Buddhist Civilization in Eastern Siam. *J. Siam Society*, 45/1, 1957, p.42–60.

Warder, A. K. On the Relationship Between Early Buddhism and Other Contemporary Systems. *Bull. School Orient. Afr. Stud.*, 18/1, 1956, p.43–63.

Wright, A. F. *Buddhism in Chinese History*. N.Y.: Atheneum Publishers, 1965, 144p.

Wylie, T. Mar-Pā's Tower: Notes of Local Hegemons in Tibet. *Hist. Rel.*, 3/2, 1964, p.278–91.

Zigmund-Cerbu, A. The Sadangayoga. *Hist. Rel.*, 3/1, 1963, p.128–34.

3f. Other Religions

Beckwith, M. W. Some Religious Cults in Jamaica. *Amer. J. Psychol.*, 34, 1923, p.32–45.

Beesley, C. A. The Religion of the Maya. *El Palacio*, 50, 1943, p.8–21.

Berndt, R. M. *Djanggawul: An Aboriginal Religious Cult of the North-Eastern Arnhemland.* N.Y.: Philosophical Library, 1953, 308p.

Bourke, J. G. Notes Upon the Religion of the Apache Indians. *Folk Lore* (London), 2, 1891, p.419–54.

Brackett, A. G. The Shoshonies, or, Snake Indians: Their Religion, Superstitions and Manners. *Smithsonian Inst. Ann. Rep. 1879,* p.328–33.

Brundage, B. C. *Empire of the Inca.* Norman: Univ. of Oklahoma Press, 1963, 396p.

Burland, C. A. Maya Theology. *New World Antiq.*, 8/3, 1961, p.42–3.

Caso, A. *The Aztecs: Peoples of the Sun* (Trans. L. Dunham). Lorman, Oklahoma: Univ. of Oklahoma, 1958, 125p.

Chadwick, N. K. Notes on Polynesian Mythology. *J. Roy. Anthropol. Inst.*, 60, 1930, p.425–46.

Chafe, W. L. Linguistic Evidence for the Relative Age of Iroquois Religious Practices. *Southw. J. Anthropol.*, 20/3, 1964, p.278–85.

Chinnery, E. W. F. and Haddon, A. C. Five New Religious Cults in British New Guinea. *Hibbert J.*, 1917, p.458–60.

Coleman, B. The Religion of the Ojibwa of Northern Minnesota. *Primitive Man*, 10, 1937, p.35–57.

Cooper, J. M. *The Gros Ventres of Montana, Part II: Religion and Ritual.* Washington: Catholic Univ. Press, 1956, 491p.

Cory, H. Religious Beliefs and Practices of the Sukuma Nyamwezi Tribal Groups. *Tanganyika Notes Rec.*, 54, 1960, p.14–25.

Dandekar, R. N. *Vedic Bibliography.* Poona: Univ. of Poona, 1961, 2 vols.

David, H. S. The Earliest Stage of Tamil Religion. *Tamil Cult.*, 9/4, 1961, p.395–401.

DeAngelo, J. and Freeland, L. S. A New Religious Cult in North Central California. *Amer. Anthropol.*, 31/2, 1929, p.265–70.

DeLeon, P. D. *The Incas.* Norman: Univ. of Oklahoma, 1959, 397p.

Dorsey, J. O. A Study of Siouan Cults. *Smithsonian Inst., Bur. Ethnol. 1889–90,* 11, 1894, p.351–544.

Dorsinfang-Smets, A. The Search for Salvation Among the American Indians. *Ann. Cent. Rel.*, 2, 1962, p.113–26.

DuBois, C. G. The Religion of the Luiseno Indians of Southern California. *Univ. Calif. Public. Amer. Archaeol. Ethnol.*, 8/3, 1908.

Dubs, H. H. The Archaic Royal Tou Religion. *T'Oung Pao*, 46/3–5, 1958, p.217–59.

Fisher, R. G. An Outline of Pueblo Indian Religion. *El Palacio*, 1938, p.169–79.

Fortune, R. F. Manus Religion. *Oceania*, 2/1, 1931, p.74–108.

Gifford, E. W. Miwok Cults. *Univ. Calif. Public. Amer. Archaeol. Ethnol.*, 18/3, 1926, p.391–408.

Gifford, E. W. Southern Maidu Religious Ceremonies. *Amer. Anthropol.*, 29/3, 1927, p.214–57.

Goodwin, G. White Mountain Apache Religion. *Amer. Anthropol.*, 40, 1938, p.24–37.

Goodwin, G. A Comparison of Navaho and White Mountain Apache Ceremonial Forms and Categories. *Southw. J. Anthropol.*, 1/4, 1945, p.498–506.

Greenwood, W. The Upraised Hand, or the Spiritual Significance of the Rise of the Ringatu Faith. *J. Polynesian Society*, 51/1, 1942, p.1–81.

Hallowell, A. I. Some Empirical Aspects of Northern Saulteaux Religion. *Amer. Anthropol.*, 36/3, 1934, p.389–404.

Hallowell, A. I. Bear Ceremonialism in the Northern Hemisphere. *Amer. Anthropol.*, 28, 1926, p.1–175.

Herskovits, M. J. The Panan, An Afrobahian Religious Rite of Transition. *Mem. Inst. Fran. Afr. Noire*, 27, 1953, p.113–40.

Hungate, M. Religious Beliefs of the Nebraska Indians. *Nebraska Hist.*, 19, 1939, p.207–25.

James, E. O. *The Cult of the Mother Goddess.* N.Y.: F. A. Praeger, 1959, 300p.

Keller, A. G. The Study of Homeric Religion. *Amer. J. Sociol.*, 15/5, 1910, p.641–56.

Kindaichi, K. The Concepts Behind the Ainu Bear Festival (Trans. M. Yoshida). *Southw. J. Anthropol.*, 5/4, 1949, p.345–50.

Kramer, S. N. *The Sumerians: Their History, Culture and Character.* Chicago: Univ. of Chicago Press, 1963, 355p.

Loeb, E. M. The Eastern Kuksu Cult. *Univ. Calif. Public. Amer. Archaeol. Ethnol.*, 33/2, 1933, p.139–231.

Loeb, E.M. The Western Kuksu Cult. *Univ. Calif. Public. Amer. Archaeol. Ethnol.*, 33/1, 1932, p.1–137.

Low, D. A. *Religion and Society in Buganda, 1875–1900.* Kampala: East African Institute of Social Research, 1957.

Malan, V. D. and Jesser, C. J. *Dakota Indian Religion: A Study of Conflict in Values.* Brookings, South Dakota: South Dakota State College, Agricultural Experiment Station Bulletin, 473, 1959, 64p.

McIlwraith, T. F. The Feast of the Dead: Historical Background. *Anthropologica*, 6, 1958, p.83–7.

Megvel, L. P. *Aztec Thought and Culture* (Trans. J. G. Davis). Norman, Oklahoma: Univ. of Oklahoma Press, 1963, 241p.

Nyuak, L. Religious Rites and Customs of the Iban or Dyaks of Sarawak. *Anthropos*, 1, 1906, p.11–23, 165–84, 403–25.

Opler, M. E. and Rittle, W. E. The Death Practives and Eschautology of the Kiowa Apache. *Southw. J. Anthropol.*, 17/4, 1961, p.383–94.

Penniman, T. K. The Arunta Religion. *Sociol. R.*, 21/1, 1929, p.20–37.

Radcliffe-Brown, A. R. *The Andaman Islanders.* Glencoe: Free Press, 1948, 510p.

Radin, P. Religion of the North American Indians. *J. Amer. Folklore*, 27, 1915, p.335–73.

Radin, P. *Monotheism Among Primitive Peoples.* N.Y.: Pantheon, 1954.

Ray, V. The Kolaskin Cult. *Amer. Anthropol.*, 38, 1936, p.67–75.

Reichard, G. A. Distinctive Features of Navaho Religion. *Southw. J. Anthropol.*, 1/2, 1945, p.199–220.

Robbins, W. J. Some Aspects of the Pueblo Indian Religion. *Harvard Theol. R.*, 34, 1941, p.25–47.

Roediger, V. M. *Ceremonial Customs of the Plains Indians.* Berkeley: Univ. of California Press, 1961, 251p.

Roheim, G. Primitive High Gods. *Psychoanal. Quart.*, 3/Pt.2, 1934, p.1–133.

Sapir, E. Religious Ideas of the Takelma Indians of Southwestern Oregon. *J. Amer. Folklore*, 20, 1907, p.33–49.

Sebeok, T. A. and Ingemann, F. J. *Studies in Cheremis: The Supernatural.* N.Y.: Wenner-Gren Foundation, 1956, 357p.

Séjourné, L. *Burning Water: Thought and Religion in Ancient Mexico* (Trans. I. Nicholson). N.Y.: Vanguard Press, 1956, 192p.

Shashibhusan, D. *Obscure Religious Cults as Background of Bengali Literature.* Calcutta: Univ. Calcutta, 1946, 501p.

Silva, F. A. Terena Religion. *Acta Americana*, 1946, p.214–23.

Spence, L. The Gods of the Maya. *Hibbert J.*, 32, 1934, p.261–8.

Spence, L. *The Religion of Ancient Mexico.* London: Watts & Co., 1945, 126p.

Steward, J. H. Myths of the Owens Valley Paiute. *Univ. Calif. Public. Amer. Archaeol. Ethnol.*, 34/5, 1936, p.355–439.

Stewart, O. C. Aboriginal Indian Religions. *Southw. Lore*, 21/4, 1956, p.50–3.

Stiehl, R. The Origin of the Cult of Sarapis. *Hist. Rel.*, 3/1, 1963, p.21–33.

Stoevesandt, G. The Sect of the Second Adam. *Africa*, 1934, p.479–82.

Sullivan, R. J. The Problem of Maya Religion. *Thought*, 11, 1936, p.459–75.

Von Cles-Reden, S. *Realm of the Great Mother Goddess: The Story of the Megalith Builders* (Trans. E. Mosbacher). Englewood Cliffs, New Jersey: Prentice-Hall, 1962, 321p.

Wallace, A. F. C. The Cultural Composition of Handsome Lake Religion. *Bull. Bur. Amer. Ethnol.*, 180, 1961, p.143–51.

Waterman, T. T. The Religious Practices of the Dieueño Indians. *Univ. Calif. Public. Amer. Archaeol. Ethnol.*, 8/6, 1910, p.272–358.

Wax, M. The Pawnees in Search of Paradise Lost. *Archiv. Sociol. Rel.*, 1/4, 1957, p.113–22.

Willetts, R. F. *Cretan Cults and Festivals.* N.Y.: Barnes & Noble, 1962, 362p.

Williams, R. H. B. *Jaino Yoga: A Survey of the Mediaeval Śrâvakâcâras.* London: Oxford Univ. Press, 1963, 296p.

Wing-Sou Lou, D. Rain Worship Among the Ancient Chinese and the Nahua-Maya Indians. *Bull. Inst. Ethnol. Acad. Sinica*, 4, 1957, p.31–102.

Wittfogel, K. and Goldfrank, E. S. Some Aspects of Pueblo Mythology and Society. *J. Amer. Folkore*, 61, 1943, p.17–30.

Chai, C. and Chai, W. (eds. and trans.) *The Humanist Way in Ancient China: Essential Works of Confucianism.* N.Y.: Bantam Books, 1965, 373p.

Chang, C. N.   The Significance of Mencius. *Philos. East West*, 8/1–2, 1958, p.37–48.

Chang, C. Y.   *Creativity and Taoism.* N.Y.: Julian Press, 1963.

Eiichi, K.   The New Confucianism and Taoism in China and Japan From the Fourth to the Thirteenth Centuries A. D. *J. World Hist.*, 6/4, 1960, p.801–29.

Kaizuka, S.   Confucianism in Ancient Japan. *J. World Hist.*, 5/1, 1959, p.41–58.

Levenson, J. R.   *Confucian China and Its Modern Fate.*
Berkeley, California: Univ. of California Press, 1958–65, 3 vols.

Welch, H. H.   *The Parting of the Way: Lao Tzu and the Taoist Movement.* Boston: Beacon Press, 1957, 204p.

Yang, K. P. and Henderson, G.   An Outline History of Korean Confucianism. *J. Asian Stud.*, 18, 1958, 1959, p.259–76, 81–9.

See Also:

Chan, W. T.   1c
Levenson, J. R.   6c
Welch, H.   9a1
Wilhelm, H.   4a1
Wu-chi, L.   2h2

3f2.   *Ghost Dance*

DuBois, C. G.   The 1870 Ghost Dance. *Univ. Calif. Anthropol. Rec.*, 3/1, 1939.

Gayton, A. H.   The Ghost Dance of 1870 in South Central California. *Univ. Calif. Public. Amer. Archaeol. Ethnol*, 28, 1930, p.57–82.

Hill, W.   The Navaho Indians and the Ghost Dance of 1890. *Amer. Anthropol.*, 46, 1944, p.523.

Kroeber, A. L.   Ghost Dance in California. *J. Amer. Folklore*, 17, 1904, p.32–5.

Lesser, A.   Cultural Significance of the Ghost Dance. *Amer. Anthropol.*, 35, 1933, p.108–15.

Miller, D. H.   *Ghost Dance.* N.Y.: Duell, Sloan & Pearce, 1959, 318p.

Mooney, J.   The Ghost-Dance Religion and the Souix Outbreak of 1890. *Rep. Bur. Amer. Ethnol.*, 14/Pt. 2, 1896, p.641-1136.

3f3.   *Peyote Cults*

Brant, C. S.   Peyotism Among the Kiowa Apache and Neighboring Tribes. *Southw. J. Anthropol.*, 6/2, 1950, p.212–22.

Campbell, T. N.   Origin of the Mescal Bean Cult. *Amer. Anthropol.*, 60/1, 1958, p.156–60.

Dustin, C. B.   *Peyotism and New Mexico.* Farmington, New Mexico: 1960, 51p.

LaBarre, W.   *The Peyote Cult.* Hamden, Connecticut: Shoe String Press, 1959, 188p.

Opler, M. K.   The Influence of Aboriginal Pattern and White Contact on a Recently Introduced Ceremony, The Mescalero Peyote Cult. *J. Amer. Folklore*, 49, 1936, p.143–66.

Opler, M. K.   The Use of Peyote by the Carrizo and Lipan Apache Tribes. *Amer. Anthropol.*, 40/2, 1938, p.271–85.

Opler, M. K.   The Character and History of the Southern Ute Peyote Rite. *Amer. Anthropol.*, 42, 1940, p.463–78.

Opler, M. K.   Fact and Fancy in Ute Peyotism. *Amer. Anthropol.*, 44, 1942, p.151–9.

Shonle, R.   Peyote: The Giver of Visions. *Amer. Anthropol.*, 27, 1925, p.53–7.

Slotkin, J. S.   Peyotism 1521–1891. *Amer. Anthropol.*, 57, 1955, p.202–30.

Slotkin, J. S.   *The Peyote Religion: A Study in Indian-White Relations.* Glencoe: Free Press, 1956, 195p.

Stewart, O. C.   The Southern Ute Peyote Cult. *Amer. Anthropol.*, 43/2, 1941, p.303–8.

See Also:

Stewart, O. C.   7d
Voget, F. W.   6b

Eros, J. The Rise of Organized Free Thought in Mid-Victorian England. *Sociol. R.*, 2/1, 1954, p.98–120.

Gilmore, M. P. *The World of Humanism, 1453–1517.* N. Y.: Harper, 1952, 326p.

Jackson, G. The Origins of Spanish Anarchism. *Southw. Soc. Sci. Quart.*, 36/2, 1955, p.135–47.

McLachlan, H. J. *Socinianism in Seventeenth Century England.* N. Y.: Oxford Univ. Press, 1951, 352p.

Parke, D. B. *The Epic of Unitarianism: Original Writings From the History of Liberal Religion.* Boston: Beacon Press, 1957, 164p.

Wilbur, E. M. *A Bibliography of the Pioneers of the Socinian-Unitarian Movement in Modern Chris-*

tianity in Italy, Switzerland, Germany, Holland. Rome: Edizioni di storia e letteratura, 1950, 80p.

Wright, C. *The Beginnings of Unitarianism in America.* Boston: Starr King Press, 1955.

See Also:

Marty, M. E.   7c
Moody, J. N.   7c
Reed, H. A.   4a1
Salisbury, W. S.   6c
Sfeir, G. N.   4a1
Timasheff, N. S.   4a1
Van Baumer, F.   6
Winkler, H.   7c

3f5.   Witchcraft and Shamanism

Dixon, R. B. Some Aspects of the American Shaman. *J. Amer. Folklore*, 21, 1908, p.1–12.

Hocart, A. M. Medicine and Witchcraft in Eddystone of the Solomons. *J. Roy. Anthropol. Inst.*, 55, 1925, p.221–70.

Hoffman, W. J. Pictography and Shamanistic Rites of the Ojibwa. *Amer. Anthropol.*, 1, 1888, p.209–29.

Kelley, I. T. Southern Paiute Shamanism. *Univ Calif. Anthropol. Rec.*, 2/4, 1939, p.151–67.

Kluckhohn, C. Navaho Witchcraft. *Pap. Peabody Mus. Archaeol. Ethnol.*, 22/2, 1944.

Layard, J. W. Malekula: Flying Tricksters, Ghosts, Gods and Epileptics. *J. Roy. Anthropol. Inst.*, 60, 1930, p.501–24; see also p.525–50.

Lea, H. C. *Materials Toward a History of Witchcraft.* N. Y.: Thomas Yoseloff, 1957, 3 vols.

Lethbridge, T. C. *Witches: Investigating an Ancient Religion.* London: Routledge & Kegan Paul, 1962, 162p.

Park, W. Z. Paviotso Shamanism. *Amer. Anthropol.*, 36/1, 1934, p.98–113.

Petroff, L. Magical Beliefs and Practices in Old Bulgaria. *Midwest Folkl.*, 7/4, 1957, p.214–20.

Rose, E. *A Razor For a Goat: A Discussion of Certain Problems in the History of Witchcraft and Diabolism.* Toronto: Univ. of Toronto Press, 1962, 257p.

Summers, M. *The Geography of Witchcraft.* Evanston: University Books, 1958, 623p.

Summers, M. *The History of Witchcraft and Demonology.* N.Y.: Universal Books, 1956, 353p.

Williams, C. W. S. *Witchcraft.* N. Y.: Meridian Books, 1959, 316p.

Williams, F. E. Some Aspects of Papian Sorcery. *Sociol. R.*, 27/2, 1935, p.220–31.

See Also:

Baroja, C. F.   2h6
Davies, R. T.   7b3
Eliade, M.   7a1
Gardner, G. B.   1a
Honigmann, J. J.   8a5
Langton, E.   2h
Macalpine, I.   5b1
Makkay, J.   5a3
Masters, R. E. L.   5b1
Pfautz, H. W.   8a2
Swanton, J. R.   8a3

4. Religion as Related to Other Social Institutions and Behavior

Abrecht, P. The Social Thinking of the World Council of Churches. *Ecumen. R.*, 17/3, 1965, p.241–50.

Bailey, K. K. *Southern White Protestantism in the Twentieth Century.* N.Y.: Harper & Row, 1964.

Barnes, R. P. *Under Orders: The Churches and Public Affairs.* Garden City, N.Y.: Doubleday, 1961, 138p.

Basilius, H. A. (ed.) *Contemporary Problems in Religion.* Detroit: Wayne State Univ. Press, 1956.

Belshaw, C. S. The Significance of Modern Cults in Melanesian Development. *Australian Outlook*, 4, 1950, p.116–25.

Bensman, J. and Rosenberg, B. *Mass, Class and Bureaucracy.* Englewood Cliffs: Prentice Hall, 1963.

Bernard, J. *American Community Behavior.* N.Y.: Dryden Press, 1949.

Brandon, S. G. F. *Man and His Destiny in the Great Religions: An Historical and Comparative Study Containing the Wilde Lectures in Natural and Comparative Religion Delivered in the University of Oxford, 1954–1957.* Manchester: Manchester Univ. Press, 1962, 442p.

Eliade, M. *Rites and Symbols of Initiation: The Mysteries of Birth and Rebirth.* N.Y.: Harper & Row, 1965, 175p.

Frankenberg, R. *Village on the Border: A Social Study of Religion, Politics and Football in a North Wales Community.* London: Cohen & West, 1957, 163p.

Freedman, M. Religion and Society in South-Eastern China. *Man*, 57, 1957, p.56–7.

Fremantle, A. (ed.) *The Social Teachings of the Church.* N.Y.: New American Library, 1963, 320p.

Gurian, W. and Fitzsimons, M. A. (eds.) *The Catholic Church in World Affairs.* Notre Dame: Univ. of Notre Dame, 1954.

Halvorson, L. W. (ed.) *The Church in a Diverse Society.* Minneapolis: Augsburg Publishing House, 1964.

Harte, T. J. *Introduction to Social Encyclicals.* Washington: Catholic Univ. Press, 1953, 75p.

Herberg, W. Religion in a Secularized Society. *R. Rel. Res.*, 3/4, 1962, p.145–58; see also 4/1, p.35–45.

Horton, P. B. The Social Orientation of the Church. *Sociol. Soc. Res.*, 24/5, 1940, p.423–32.

Hughes, E. J. *The Church and the Liberal Society.* Notre Dame: Univ. of Notre Dame Press, 1961, 310p.

Hultkrantz, A. The Indians and the Wonders of Yellowstone: A Study of the Interrelations of Religion, Nature and Culture. *Ethnos*, 19/1–4, 1954, p.34–68.

James, E. O. *The Social Function of Religion.* Nashville: Cokesbury Press, 1940.

Laski, H. J. *The American Democracy.* N.Y.: Viking Press, 1948.

Lenski, G. E. Religion's Impact on Secular Institutions. *R. Rel. Res.*, 4/1, 1962, p.1–16.

Lenski, G. E. *The Religious Factor.* Garden City: Doubleday & Co., 1961.

Luckmann, T. Four Protestant Parishes in Germany: A Study in the Sociology of Religion. *Soc. Res.*, 26/4, 1959, p.423–48.

Maddox, J. G. *Technical Assistance by Religious Agencies in Latin America.* Chicago: Univ. of Chicago Press, 1956, 139p.

Marrow, R. E. *Northern Methodism and Reconstruction.* East Lansing: Michigan State Univ. Press, 1956, 269p.

McAvoy, T. T. *Roman Catholicism and the American Way of Life.* Norte Dame: Univ. of Notre Dame Press, 1960.

Millman, H. The Jewish Community Center as an Arm of the Organized Jewish Community. *J. Jew. Commun. Serv.*, 42/1, 1965, p.27–36.

Moberg, D. O. Religion and Society in the Netherlands and in America. *Soc. Compass*, 9/1–2, 1962, p.10–9.

Morrison, S. A. *Middle East Survey: The Political, Social and Religious Problems.* London: SCM Press, 1954, 198p.

O'Connor, D. A. *Catholic Social Doctrine.* Westminster, Maryland: Newman Press, 1956, 204p.

Petry, R. C. *Christian Eschatology and Social Thought: A Historical Essay on the Social Implications of Some*

Selected Aspects in Christian Eschatology to A. D. 1500. N.Y.: Abingdon Press, 1956, 415p.

Pope, L. Religion as a Social Force in America. *Soc. Action*, 1953, p.2–15.

Presler, H. H. Religion as Function of Life Situation. *Man India*, 39/4, 1959, p.285–300.

Radcliffe-Brown, A. R. *Religion and Society.* London: Royal Anthropological Institute of Great Britain and Ireland, 1945.

Rosenthal, H. M. On the Function of Religion in Culture. *R. Rel.*, 5, 1941, p.148–71; see also p.290–309.

Schiffman, J. and Bellamy, E. *Selected Writings on Religion and Society.* N.Y.: Liberal Arts Press, 1955, 139p.

Schroeder, W. W. and Obenhaus, V. *Religion in American Culture: Unity and Diversity in a Midwestern County.* N.Y.: Macmillan Co., 1964.

Schulyer, J. B. The Industry Council Idea: Is it Adaptable to the United States. *Amer. Cath. Sociol. R.*, 18/4, 1957, p.290–300.

Spann, J. R. (ed.) *The Church and Social Responsibility.* N.Y.: Abingdon-Cokesbury Press, 1953, 273p.

Spencer, M. Social Contribution of Congregational and Kindred Churches. *Sociol. R.*, 35/3–4, 1943, p.57–68.

Spitzer, A. The Culture Organization of Catholicism. *Amer. Cath. Sociol. R.*, 19/1, 1958, p.2–12.

Stoops, J. D. Religion and Social Institutions. *Amer. J. Sociol.*, 18/6, 1913, p.796–807.

Sturm, D. A Critique of American Protestant Social and Political Thought. *J. Polit.*, 26/4, 1964, p.896–913.

Tawney, R. H. Religious Thought on Social and Economic Questions in the Sixteenth and Seventeenth Centuries. *J. Polit. Econ.*, 31, 1923, p.461–93, 637–74, 804–25.

Tillich, P. Protestantism in the Present World Situation. *Amer. J. Sociol.*, 43, 1937, p.236–48.

Toynbee, A. J. Churches and Civilizations. *Yale R.*, 37/1, 1947, p.1–8.

Wearmouth, R. F. *The Social and Political Influence of Methodism in the Twentieth Century.* London: Epworth Press, 1957, 256p.

Williams, M. J. *Catholic Social Thought: Its Approach to Contemporary Problems.* N.Y.: Ronald Press, 1950, 567p.

Williams, R. M., Jr. *American Society.* N.Y.: Alfred A. Knopf, 1963.

Yinger, J. M. *Religion in the Struggle for Power.* Durham: Duke Univ. Press, 1946.

See Also: 2, 3, 5, 7

Caporale, R.   2a2
Carter, P.   2a1
Cauthen, L. K.   6b
Chakerian, C. G.   1g
Comeroy, R.   2a1
Comte, A.   8a6
Dicker, H.   2b
Freeman-Grenville, G. S. P.   7b3
Glock, C. Y.   6
Godin, A.   4h
Goldstein, S. E.   1g
Hsu, F. L. K.   1b
Johnson, F. E.   8b
Lee, R. and Marty, M.   5
Lehrer, L.   7f
Leventman, S.   2b
Lumen Vitae   8a4, 6e
Lynn, R. L.   1g
Miller, H. M.   5
Moody, J. N.   3a2
Nottingham, E. K.   8a2
Radhakrishnam, S.   1c
Ross, E. J.   7b3
Ryan, J. A.   6b
Sacher, H.   6b
Snell, M. M.   5
Sumner, W. G.   8a6
Sykes, N.   3
Tawney, R. H.   4b
Taylor, G.   6a
Tillich, P. J.   8a5
Toynbee, A. J.   3
Turner, V. W.   4d
Webber, E.   3a
Welty, E.   4d
Williams, M.   2a2
Williams, M. J.   2a2

4a. Religion and Political Behavior

Abbot, F. The Jama'at-I-Islami of Pakistan. *Mid. East J.*, 11/1, 1957, p.37–51.

Albinski, H. S. The Place of the Emperor Asoka in Ancient Indian Political Thought. *Midwest J. Polit. Sci.*, 2/1, 1958, p.62–75.

al Masdoosi, A. A. *Living Religions of the World: A Socio-Political Study.* Karachi: Aisha, Bawany Wakf, 1962.

Almond, G. A. The Political Ideas of Christian Democracy. *J. Polit.*, 10/4, 1948, p.734–63.

Antcliffe, H. Religions and Politics in Holland. *Contemp. R.*, 1037, 1952, p.282–5.

Arendt, H. Religion and Politics. *Confluence*, 2/3, 1953, p.105–26.

Barnard, F. M. Christian Thomasius: Enlightenment and Bureaucracy. *Amer. Polit. Sci. R.*, 59/2, 1965, p.430–8.

Barnes, S. M. The Politics of French Christian Labour. *J. Polit.*, 21/1, 1959, p.105–22.

Bennett, J. C. *When Christians Make Political Decisions.* N.Y.: Association Press, 1964, 123p.

Binder, L. Problems of Islamic Political Thought in the Light of Recent Developments in Pakistan. *J. Polit.*, 20/4, 1958, p.655–75.

Blanshard, P. *Communism, Democracy and Catholic Power.* Boston: Beacon Press, 1951.

Blanshard, P. *God and Man in Washington.* Boston: Beacon Press, 1960, 251p.

Bollen, J. D. The Temperance Movement and the Liberal Party in New South Wales Politics 1900–1904. *J. Rel. Hist.*, 1/2, 1961, p.160–82.

Bone, R. C. The Dynamics of Dutch Politics. *J. Polit.*, 24/1, 1962, p.23–49.

Bouscaren, A. T. The European Christian Democrats. *West. Polit. Quart.*, 2/1, 1949, p.59–73.

Brown, J. R. Theology and Public Policy. *Soc. Order*, 7/7, 1957, p.296–303.

Cady, J. F. Religion and Modernization in the Far East: Religion and Politics in Modern Burma. *Far East. Quart.*, 12/2, 1953, p.149–62.

Campion, D. R. Catholicism and Ethnocentrism. *Soc. Order*, 10/4, 1960, p.149–59.

Chejne, A. *Succession to the Rule in Islam.* Lahore: S. M. Ashraf, 1960, 151p.

Christie, A. The Political Use of Imported Religion: An Historical Example From Java. *Archiv. Sociol. Rel.*, 9/17, 1964, p.53–62.

Clark, S. D. The Religious Sect in Canadian Politics. *Amer. J. Sociol.*, 51/3, 1945, p.207–16.

Cohen, S. P. Rulers and Priests: A Study in Cultural Control. *Comp. Stud. Society Hist.*, 6/2, 1963–64, p.199–216.

Cragg, K. *Counsels in Contemporary Islam.* Edinburg: Edinburg Univ. Press, 1965, 270p.

Curtiss, J. S. Religion as a Social Problem in Soviet Russia. *Soc. Prob.*, 7/4, 1960, p.328–39.

Daalder, H. Parties and Politics in the Netherlands. *Polit. Stud.*, 3/1, 1955, p.1–16.

Davis, H. R. and Good, R. C. (eds.) *Reinhold Niebuhr on Politics: His Political Philosophy and its Application to Our Age as Expressed in His Writings.* N.Y.: Scribners, 1960, 364p.

de Albornoz, A. F. C. *The Basis of Religious Liberty.* N.Y.: Association Press, 1963, 182p.

Desai, A. R. National Integration and Religion. *Sociol. Bull.*, 12/1, 1963, p.53–65.

DeSantis, V. P. American Catholics and McCarthyism. *Cath. Hist. R.*, 51/1, 1965, p.1–30.

Dodge, G. H. *The Political Theory of the Hugenots of the Dispersion With Special Reference to the Thought and Influence of Pierre Jurieu.* N.Y.: Columbia Univ. Press, 1947, 287p.

Domenach, J. M. Religion and Politics. *Confluence*, 3/4, 1954, p.390–401.

Dunn, E. S. Catholics in the 79th Congress. *Amer. Cath. Sociol. R.*, 7/4, 1946, p.259–66.

Dunn, E. S. Catholics in the 80th Congress. *Amer. Cath. Sociol. R.*, 9/4, 1948, p.254–8.

Earl, D. M. *Emperor and Nation in Japan: Political Thinkers of the Tokugawa Period.* Seattle: Univ. of Washington Press, 1964, 270p.

Ebersole, L. Religion and Politics. *Ann. Amer. Acad. Polit. Soc. Sci.*, 332, 1960, p.101–11.

Eisenstadt, S. N. Religious Organizations and Political Process in Centralized Empires. *J. Asian Stud.*, 21/3, 1962, p.271–94.

Elazar, D. Churches as Molders of American Politics. *Amer. Behav. Sci.*, 4/9, 1961, p.15–8.

Ellingsworth, P. Christianity and Politics in Dahomey, 1843–1867. *J. Afr. Hist.*, 5/2, 1964, p.209–20.

Fall, B. B. The Political-Religious Sects of Viet-Nam. *Pac. Aff.*, 28/3, 1955, p.235–53.

Farnham, W. D. The Religious Issue in American Politics: An Historical Commentary. *Queen's Quart.*, 68/1, 1961, p.47–65.

Fernau, F. W. *Moslems on the March: People and Politics in the World of Islam* (Trans. E. W. Dickes). N.Y.: Knopf, 1954, 312p.

Fitzgerald, W. J. The Idea of Democracy in Contemporary Catholicism. *R. Rel.*, 12/2, 1948, p.148–65.

Fogarty, M. P. *Christian Democracy in Western Europe, 1820-1953.* London: Routledge and Kegan Paul, 1957.

Fry, C. L. The Religious Affiliations of American Leaders. *Sci. Monthly*, 36, 1933, p.241–9.

Fuchs, L. H. *The Political Behavior of American Jews.* Glencoe: Free Press, 1956, 220p.

Furniss, N. F. *The Mormon Conflict, 1850–1859.* New Haven: Yale Univ. Press, 1960, 311p.

Germino, D. L. Two Types of Recent Christian Political Thought. *J. Polit.*, 21/3, 1959, p.455–86.

Good, R. C. The National Interest and Political Realism: Niebuhr's "Debate" With Margenthay and Kenan. *J. Polit.*, 22/4, 1960, p.597–619.

Guiart, J. Cargo Cult and Political Evolution in Melanesia. *Mankind*, 4/6, 1951, p.227–9.

Gusfield, J. R. *Symbolic Crusade: Status, Politics and the American Temperance Movement.* Urbana: Univ. of Illinois Press, 1963.

Hales, E. E. Y. *Pio Nono: A Study in European Politics and Religion in the Nineteenth Century.* London: Eyre & Spottiswoode, 1954.

Halperin, S. *The Political World of American Zionism.* Detroit: Wayne State Univ. Press, 1961.

Hertzberg, A. The Protestant "Establishment," Catholic Dogma and the Presidency. *Commentary*, 30/4, 1960, p.277–85.

Hiscocks, R. Some Liberal Marxists and Left-Wing Catholics in Contemporary Poland. *Canad. J. Econ. Polit. Sci.*, 30/1, 1964, p.12–21.

Hodgkin, T. L. Islam, History and Politics. *J. Mod. Afr. Stud.*, 1/1, 1963, p.91–7.

Holloway, V. H. Power Politics and the Christian Conscience. *Soc. Action*, 15, 1950, p.5–35.

Hunt, G. L. (ed.) *Calvinism and The Political Order.* Phila.: Westminster Press, 1965, 224p.

Iqbal, S. M. Political Thought in Islam. *Sociol. R.*, 1/3, 1908, p.249–61.

Jay, R. R. *Religion and Politics in Rural Central Java.* Yale Southeast Asia Studies, Cultural Report, 12, 1963, 117p.

Jucker, M. The Vatican and Italian Democracy. *Polit. Quart.*, 20, 1949, p.352–63.

Kaplan, M. M. Religion and Democracy. *R. Rel.*, 12/2, 1948, p.179–92.

Karunakaran, K. P. Interrelation Between Religion and Politics in Pakistan. *India Quart.*, 14/1, 1958, p.43–62.

Kingdom, R. The First Expression of Theodore Beza's Political Ideas. *Archiv. Reform. Gesch.*, 46, 1955, p.88–100.

Krahn, C. Russia: Messianism—Marxism. *J. Bib. Rel.*, 31/3, 1963, p.210–5.

Kulkarni, C. M. *Essays in Hindu Polity.* Bombay: New Book Centre, 1963, 104p.

Kumar Gupta, S. Moslems in Indian Politics, 1947–1960. *India Quart.*, 18/4, 1962, p.355–81.

Lal, K. S. *Twilight of the Sultanate: A Political, Social and Cultural History of the Sultanate of Delhi from the Invasion of Timur to the Conquest of Babur, 1398–1526.* London: Asia Publishing House, 1963, 358p.

Landon, F. C. The Catholic Anti-Communist Role Within Australian Labor. *West. Polit. Quart.*, 9/4, 1956, p.884–99.

Laponce, J. A. The Religious Background of Canadian M. P.'s. *Polit. Stud.*, 6/3, 1958, p.253–8.

Larkin, E. Mounting the Counter-Attack: The Roman Catholic Hierarchy and the Destruction of Parnellism. *R. Polit.*, 25/2, 1963, p.157–82.

Lasswell, H. D. and Cleveland, H. (eds.) *The Ethic of Power: The Interplay of Religion, Philosophy, and Politics.* N.Y.: Harper, 1962, 509p.

Lee, R. W. General Aspects of Chinese Communist Religious Policy with Soviet Comparisons. *China Quart.*, 19, 1964, p.161–73.

Levenson, J. R. Confucian and Taipang "Heaven": The Political Implications of Clashing Religious Concepts. *Comp. Stud. Society Hist.*, 4/4, 1962, p.436–53.

Levitt, A. *Vaticanism: The Political Principles of the Roman Catholic Church.* N.Y.: Vantage Press, 1960, 160p.

Lewis, B. Communism and Islam. *Int. Aff.*, 30/1, 1954, p.1–12.

Long, N. Bandawe Mission Station and Local Politics, 1878–1886. *Human Prob. Brit. Cent. Afr.*, 32, 1962, p.1–22.

Luthera, V. P. Ancient Indian Polity-Theocratic or Secular? *Mod. R.*, 98/1, 1955, p.37–43.

Mavrinac, A. A. The Liberal Dilemma and the Christian Debt to Liberalism. *R. Polit.*, 22/3, 1960, p.375–92.

Maynard, T. *The Catholic Church and the American Idea.* N.Y.: Appleton-Century-Crofts, 1953.

McAvoy, T. T. The Formation of the Catholic 'Minority' in the United States, 1820–1860. *R. Polit.*, 10, 1948, p.13–34.

Menczer, B. (ed.) *Catholic Political Thought, 1789–1848.* Notre Dame: Univ. of Notre Dame, 1962, 205p.

Mendelson, E. M. Religion and Authority in Modern Burma. *World Today*, 16/3, 1960, p.110–18.

Meyer, D. *The Protestant Search for Political Realism: 1919–1941.* Berkeley: Univ. of California Press, 1960.

Miller, W. L. The "Religious Revival" and American Politics. *Confluence*, 4/1, 1955, p.44–56.

Miller, W. L. *The Protestant and Politics.* Phila.: Westminster Press, 1958, 92p.

Mizami, K. A. *Some Aspects of Religion and Politics in*

India During the 13th Century. Bombay: Asia Publishing House, 1965, 421p.

Morall, J. B. *Political Thought in Medieval Times.* London: Hutchinson, 1958, 152p.

Morner, M. *The Expulsion of the Jesuits from Latin America.* N.Y.: Alfred A. Knopf, 1965, 224p.

Morrison, K. F. *The Two Kingdoms: Ecclesiology in Carolingian Political Thought.* Princeton: Princeton Univ. Press, 1964, 297p.

Mosca, G. Church Sects and Parties (Trans. H. D. Kahn). *Soc. Forces,* 14/1, 1933, p.53–63.

Mulder, W. Immigration and the Mormon Question: An International Episode. *West. Polit. Quart.,* 9/2, 1956, p.416–33.

Najjar, F. M. Islam and Modern Democracy. *R. Polit.,* 20/2, 1958, p.164–80.

Niebuhr, H. R. *Christian Realism and Political Problems.* N.Y.: Scribners, 1953, 203p.

Nishimura, K. The Christian in Japanese Politics. *Japan. Christ. Quart.,* 29, 1963, p.165–74.

Nivolon, F. The Vietnam Buddhist Crisis. *Far East. Econ. R.,* 42/2, 1963, p.126–7.

Noether, E. P. Political Catholicism in France and Italy. *Yale R.,* 44/4, 1955, p.569–83.

Odegard, P. H. (ed.) *Religion and Politics.* New Brunswick, N.Y.: Oceania, 1960.

O'Neill, J. M. *Catholicism and American Freedom.* N.Y.: Harper & Row, 1952.

Ong, W. J. American Catholicism and America. *Thought,* 27/117, 1952–53, p.521–41.

Pennar, J. (ed.) *Islam and Communism.* N.Y.: Institute for the Study of the U.S.S.R., 1960, 72p.

Pfaff, R. H. Disengagement From Traditionalism in Turkey and Iran. *West. Polit. Quart.,* 16/1, 1963, p.79–98.

Pike, J. A. and Pyle, J. W. *The Church, Politics and Society: Dialogues on Current Problems.* N.Y.: Morehouse-Gorham Co., 1955, 159p.

Porterfield, A. L. The Church and Social Well-Being. *Sociol. Soc. Res.,* 31/3, 1947, p.213–9.

Powers, F. J. *Papal Pronouncements on the Political Order.* Westminster, Maryland: Newman Press, 1952, 245p.

Problems of Christian Democracy in Italy. *World Today,* 15/12, 1959, p.481–91.

Proshansky, H. M. and Evans, R. I. (eds.) American Political Extremism in the 1960's. *J. Soc. Issues,* 19/2, 1963, p.1–112.

Roberts, H. L. *Foreign Affairs Bibliography: A Selected and Annotated List of Books on International Affairs, 1952–1962.* N.Y.: R. R. Bowker, Co., 1964; see earlier editions.

Robertson, D. B. *The Religious Foundations of Leveller Democracy.* N.Y.: King's Crown Press, 1951, 175p.

Rosenthal, E. I. Some Reflections on the Separation of Religion and Politics in Modern Islam. *Islamic Stud.* (Karachi), 1964, p.249–84.

Rosenthal, E. I. *Political Thought in Medieval Islam.* Cambridge: Cambridge Univ. Press, 1958, 324p.

Roucek, J. S. American Ethnic and Religious Minorities in American Politics. *Politico,* 24/1, 1959, p.84–100.

Roy, R. L. *Communism and the Churches.* N.Y.: Harcourt, Brace & Co., 1960, 495p.

Sayeed, K. B. The Jama'at-I-Islami Movement in Pakistan. *Pac. Aff.,* 30/1, 1957, p.59–68.

Scigliano, R. Vietnam: Politics and Religion. *Asian Survey,* 4/1, 1964, p.666–73.

Seidler, G. L. Islam as a Political Doctrine. *Ann. Univ. M. Curie-Sklodowska,* 8, 1961, p.1–46.

Shenton, J. P. The Coughlin Movement and the New Deal. *Polit. Sci. Quart.,* 73/3, 1958, p.352–73.

Simpson, G. E. Political Cultism in West Kingston, Jamaica. *Soc. Econ. Stud.,* 4/2, 1955, p.133–49.

Szulc, T. Communists, Socialists and Christian Democrats. *Ann. Amer. Acad. Polit. Soc. Sci.,* 360, 1965, p.99–109.

Taylor, J. V. *Christianity and Politics in Africa.* London: Penguin Books, 1957, 127p.

Totten, G. Buddhism and Socialism in Japan and Burma. *Comp. Stud. Society Hist.,* 2/3, 1960, p.265–92.

Truman, T. C. *Catholic Action and Politics.* N.Y.: Hillary House, 1963.

Truman, T. C. Catholics and Politics in Australia. *West. Polit. Quart.,* 12/2, 1959, p.527–34.

Tull, C. J. *Father Coughlin & the New Deal.* Syracuse: Syracuse Univ. Press, 1965, 292p.

Varma, V. P. Studies in Hindu Political Thought and its Metaphysical Foundations. *J. Bihar Res. Society,* 39/1–2, 1953, p.49–85.

Vetterli, R. *Mormonism, Americanism, and Politics.* Salt Lake City: Ensign Publishing Co., 1961, 735p.

Vlavianos, B. J. and Gross, F. (eds.) *Struggle for Tomorrow: Modern Political Ideologies of the Jewish People.* N.Y.: Liberal Arts, 1954, 303p.

Weddanis, H. M. The Attitudes of the Churches to Politics. *Polit. Quart.,* 30/1, 1959, p.33–43.

Weil, E.   Religion and Politics.   *Confluence*, 4/2, 1955, p.202–14.

White, M.   Religion, Politics and the Higher Learning. *Confluence*, 3/4, 1954, p.402–12.

Wills, G.   *Politics and Catholic Freedom.*   Chicago: Henry Regnery, 1964, 302p.

Wolin, S. S.   Politics and Religion: Luther's Simplistic Imperative.   *Amer. Polit. Sci. R.*, 50, 1956, p.24–42.

Wolin, S. S.   Calvin and the Reformation: The Political Education of Protestantism.   *Amer. Polit. Sci. R.*, 51, 1957, p.428–53.

Woodhouse, A. S. P.   Puritanism and Democracy.   *Canad. J. Econ. Polit. Sci.*, 4/1, 1938, p.1–21.

Woodhouse, A. S. P. (ed.)   *Puritanism and Liberty.*   Chicago: Univ. of Chicago Press, 1951.

Woodhouse, A. S. P.   Religion and some Foundations of English Democracy.   *Philos. R.*, 61, 1952, p.503–31.

Zariski, R.   Intra-Party Conflict in a Dominant Party: The Experience of Italian Christian Democracy.   *J. Polit.*, 27/1, 1965, p.3–34.

Nationalism

Ansari, Z. I.   Contemporary Islam and Nationalism: A Case Study of Egypt.   *Welt Islams*, 7/1–4, 1961, p.3–38.

Aziz, K. K.   *British and Muslim India: A Study of British Public Opinion Vis-á-Vis the Development of Muslim Nationalism in India, 1857–1947.*   London: Heinemann, 1963, 278p.

Baron, S. W.   *Modern Nationalism and Religion.*   N.Y.: Meridian Books, 1960, 363p.

Beckingham, C. F.   Islam and Turkish Nationalism in Cyprus.   *Welt Islams*, 5/1–2, 1957, p.65–83.

Binder, L.   Pakistan and Modern Islamic-Nationalist Theory.   *Mid. East J.*, 11/4, 1957, p.382–96.

Boskoff, A., *et al.*   Empire, Nationality, and Religion.   In W. J. Cahnman and A. Boskoff (eds.)—*Sociology and History.*   N.Y.: Free Press of Glencoe, 1964, p.244–339.

Dawn, C. E.   From Ottomanism to Arabianism: The Origin of an Ideology.   *R. Polit.*, 23, 1961, p.378–400.

Gökalp, Z.   *Turkish Nationalism and Western Civilization: Selected Essays* (Trans. and Ed. N. Berkes).   London: Allen and Unwin, 1959, 336p.

Guiart, J.   Forerunners of Melanesian Nationalism.   *Oceania*, 22/2, 1951, p.81–90.

Harris, C. P.   *Nationalism and Revolution in Egypt: The Role of the Muslim Brotherhood.*   The Hague: Mouton & Co., 1964, 276p.

Heimsath, C. H.   *Indian Nationalism and Hindu Social Reform.*   Princeton: Princeton Univ. Press, 1964, 379p.

Hodgkin, T. L.   Islam and National Movements in West Africa.   *J. Afr. Hist.*, 3/2, 1962, p.323–7.

Holtom, D. C.   *Modern Japan and Shinto Nationalism.*   Chicago: Univ. of Chicago Press, 1947.

Huxley, A.   *The Devils of Louden.*   N.Y.: Harper & Row, 1965, 340p.

Keddie, N. R.   Religion and Irreligion in Early Iranian Nationalism.   *Comp. Stud. Society Hist.*, 4/3, 1962, p.265–95.

Kennedy, J. J.   *Catholicism, Nationalism and Democracy in Argentina.*   Notre Dame: Univ. of Notre Dame Press, 1958, 219p.

Lottich, K. V.   *Poland, Champion of Latin Christianity: Education and Nationalism Under the Communist Regime.*   Zurich: International Institute of Arts and Letters, 1963, 81p.

Malik, H.   *Moslem Nationalism in India and Pakistan.*   Washington: Public Affairs Press, 1963, 355p.

Marmorstein, E.   Religious Opposition to Nationalism in the Middle East.   *Int. Aff.*, 1952, p.344–59.

Muslim Nationalism in the Indian Subcontinent: Lyndmila Gordon—Polonskaya and Her Critics.   *Cent. Asian R.*, 13/2, 1965, p.131–48.

Peshkin, A.   Education, the Muslim Elite and the Creation of Pakistan.   *Comp. Educ. R.*, 6/2, 1962, p.152–9.

Salem, E.   Nationalism and Islam.   *Muslim World*, 52/4, 1962, p.277–87.

Van Der Kroef, J. M.   The Role of Islam in Indonesian Nationalism and Politics.   *West. Polit. Quart.*, 11/1, 1958, p.33–54.

Von Der Mehden, F. R.   Marxism and Early Indonesian Islamic Nationalism.   *Polit. Sci. Quart.*, 73/3, 1958, p.335–51.

Von Der Mehden, F. R.   *Religion and Nationalism in Southeast Asia: Burma, Indonesia, the Philippines.*   Madison: Univ. of Wisconsin Press, 1963, 253p.

Windell, G. G.   *The Catholics and German Unity, 1866–1871.*   Minneapolis: Univ. of Minnesota Press, 1954, 312p.

4a1. Church-State Relations

Acton, L. *Essays on Church and State* (Ed. D. Woodruff). N. Y.: Viking Press, 1953.

Ahmad, A. The Sufi and the Sultan in Pre-Mughul India. *Islam*, 38/1–2, 1962, p.142–53.

Ahmad, I. Sovereignty in Islam. *Pakistan Hor.*, 11/3, 1958, p.141–5; see also 11/4, p.244–57.

Anderson, P. B. *People, Church and State in Modern Russia*. N. Y.: Macmillan, 1944, 240p.

Arasaratnam, S. Oratorians and Predikants: The Catholic Church in Ceylon Under Dutch Rule. *Ceylon J. Hist. Soc. Stud.*, 1/2, 1958, p.216–22.

Armstrong, G. T. Church and State Relations: The Chances Wrought by Constantine. *J. Bib. Rel.*, 32/1, 1964, p.1–7.

Aubrey, E. E. Church and State in Contemporary Protestant Thought: With Special Reference to the American Scene. *J. Rel.*, 29/3, 1949, p.171–80.

Badi, J. *Religion in Israel Today: The Relationship Between State and Religion*. N. Y.: Bookman Associates, 1959.

Bains, J. S. (ed.) *Studies in Political Science*. Bombay: Asia Publishing House, 1961.

Bainton, R. H. The Struggle for Religious Liberty. *Church Hist.*, 10, 1941, p.95–124.

Baker, D. L. Israel and Religious Liberty. *J. Church State*, 7/3, 1965, p.403–24.

Barker, E. *Church, State, and Education*. Ann Arbor: Univ. of Michigan Press, 1957, 217p.

Barrett, P. *Religious Liberty and the American Presidency: A Study in Church-State Relations*. N. Y.: Herder & Herder, 1963, 166p.

Becker, H. Church and State in the Cosmos of Crete. *Int. R. Soc. Hist.*, 1/2, 1956, p.253–9.

Belshaw, H. Church and State in Ashanti. *Int. R. Missions*, 35, 1946, p. 408–15.

Benda, H. Indonesian Islam Under the Japanese Occupation, 1942–1945. *Pac. Aff.*, 28/4, p.350–62.

Bennett, E. M. The Russian Orthodox Church and the Soviet State, 1946–1956: A Decade of New Orthodoxy. *J. Church State*, 7/3, 1965, p.425–39.

Bennett, J. C. *Christians and the State*. N. Y.: Scribners, 1958, 302p.

Benz, E. *Buddhism or Communism: Which Holds the Future of Asia* (Trans. R. Winston and C. Winston). N. Y.: Doubleday and Co., 1965, 234p.

Beth, L. P. Toward a Modern American Theory of Church-State Relationships. *Polit. Sci. Quart.*, 70/4, 1955, p.573–97.

Beth, L. P. *The American Theory of Church and State*. Gainesville: Univ. of Florida Press, 1958, 183p.

Binder, L. *Religion and Politics in Pakistan*. Berkeley: Univ. of California Press, 1963.

Bociurkiw, B. R. Church and State in Soviet Union. *Int. J.*, 14/3, 1959, p.182–9.

Boles, D. E. Chinese Confusianism and Communist Power. *World Aff. Quart.*, 30/3, 1959, p.226–40.

Boller, P. F. *George Washington and Religion*. Dallas: Southern Methodist Univ. Press, 1963.

Bosworth, W. A. *Catholicism and Crisis in Modern France*. Princeton: Princeton Univ. Press, 1962.

Braham, R. L. (ed.) *The Destruction of Hungarian Jewry: A Documentary Account*. N.Y.: Pro Arte for the World Federation of Hungarian Jews, 1963, 969p., 2 vols.

Bramsted, E. The Position of the Protestant Church in Germany, 1871–1933. *J. Rel. Hist.*, 2/2, 1963, p.314–34.

Brilling, B. The Struggle of the VAAD ARBA ARAZOT for the Jewish Right of Religious Worship in Breslau in the 17th Century. *Yivo Ann. Jew. Soc. Sci.*, 1956–57, p.163–86.

Brinsmade, R. B. The Religious Crisis in Mexico: The View of a Liberal. *Southw. Polit. Soc. Sci. Quart.*, 9/1, 1928, p.57–66.

Broderick, F. L. (ed.) Liberalism and the Mexican Crisis of 1927: A Debate Between Norman Thomas and John A. Ryan. *Cath. Hist. R.*, 45/3, 1959, p.309–26.

Brotz, H. The Position of the Jews in English Society. *Jew. J. Sociol.*, 1/1, 1959, p.94–113.

Brown, B. E. Religious Schools and Politics in France. *Midwest J. Polit. Sci.*, 2/2, 1958, p.160–78.

Burns, R. E. The Irish Popery Laws: A Study of Eighteenth-Century Legislation and Behavior. *R. Polit.*, 24/4, 1962, p.485–508.

Cahill, G. A. Irish Catholicism and English Toryism. *R. Polit.*, 19/1, 1957, p.62–76.

Callis, H. G. *China, Confuscian and Communist*. N. Y.: H. Holt & Co., 1959, 562p.

Cameron, R. E. Papal Finance and the Temporal Power, 1815–1871. *Church Hist.*, 26, 1957, p.132–42.

Caponigri, A. R. (ed.) *Modern Catholic Thinkers: An Anthology*. N. Y.: Harper, 1960, 636p.

Carpentier, G. W. Church and State in Africa Today. *Civilisations*, 3/4, 1953, p.519–43.

Carrasco, P. The Civil Religious Hierarchy in Mesoamerican Communities: Pre-Spanish Background and Colonial Development. *Amer. Anthropol.*, 63/3, 1961, p.483–97.

Chubaty, N. Political Background of the Religious Persecution in the Ukraine by Moscow. *Ukranian Quart.*, 11/1, 1955, p.56–65.

Church and State in Argentina: Factors in Peron's Downfall. *World Today*, 12/2, 1956, p.58–66.

Church and State in Poland. *World Today*, 14/10, 1958, p.418–29.

Church of England, National Assembly, Social and Industrial Council. *The National Church and the Social Order: An Enquiry into the Principles That Have Governed the Attitude of the Anglican Church Toward the State and the Secular Order, Conducted by the Social and Industrial Council of the Church Assembly*. Westminster, London: Church Information Board of the Church Assembly, 1956, 166p.

Cleven, N. The Ecclesiastical Policy of Maximilion of Mexico. *Hisp. Amer. Hist. R.*, 1929, p.317–60.

Cochrane, A. C. *The Church's Confession Under Hitler*. Phila.: Westminster Press, 1962, 317p.

Cockburn, J. H. *Religious Freedom in Eastern Europe*. Richmond: John Knox Press, 1953, 140p.

Cody, J. Religion and Politics in Modern Burma. *Far East. Quart.*, 12, 1953, p.149–62.

Conrad, R. *Communist Control of Religion: A Sociological Case Study of the Protestant Church in East Germany*. Maxwell Air Force Base, Alabama: Air Research and Development Command, Human Resources Research Institute, 1954, 28p.

Constantelos, D. J. Paganism and the State in the Age of Justinian. *Cath. Hist. R.*, 50, 1964, p.372–80.

Copeland, E. L. The Japanese Government and Protestant Christianity: 1889–1900. *Contemp. Japan*, 22/10–12, 1954, p.650–71.

Coughlin, B. J. *Church and State in Social Welfare* N.Y.: Columbia Univ. Press, 1965, 383p.

Coulborn, R. Debate: The State and Religion. *Comp. Stud. Society Hist.*, 1/4, 1959, p.383–93.

Coulborn, R. The State and Religion: Iran, India and China. *Comp. Stud. Society Hist.*, 1/1, 1958, p.44–57.

The Cross and the Party. *East. Europe*, 6/12, 1957, p.3–11.

Crow, R. E. Religious Sectarianism in the Lebanese Political System. *J. Polit.*, 24/3, 1962, p.489–520.

Cuninggim, M. *Freedom's Holy Light*. N.Y.: Harper, 1955, 192p.

Curran, F. X. *Catholics in Colonial Law*. Chicago: Loyola Univ. Press, 1963, 129p.

Curran, J. A. *Militant Hinduism in Indian Politics: A Study of the R. S. S.* N.Y.: Inst. Pac. Rel., 1951, 94p.

Curtiss, J. S. *The Russian Church and the Soviet State, 1917–1950*. Boston: Little, Brown, 1953, 387p.

D'arcy, M. C. *Communism and Christianity*. N.Y.: Devin-Adair Co., 1957, 241p.

Darries, H. *Constantine and Religious Liberty* (Trans. R. H. Bainton). New Haven: Yale Univ. Press, 1960, 141p.

Dawson, J. M. *America's Way in Church, State, and Society*. N.Y.: MacMillan, 1953.

de la Costa, H. Church and State in the Philippines During the Administration of Bishop Salzar, 1581–1594. *Hisp. Amer. Hist. R.*, 30/3, 1950, p.314–35.

Dildine, H. G. Bolsheviks, Icons, and Patriarchs. *Northw. Missouri State Teachers Coll. Stud.*, 11/1, 1947, p.3–35.

Dolan, E. Postwar Poland and the Church. *Amer. Slavic E. Europ. R.* (Phila.), 14/1, 1955, p.84–92.

Dredmeier, C. *Kingship and Community in Early India.* Stanford: Stanford Univ. Press, 1962, 369p.

Dulce, B. and Richter, E. J. *Religion and the Presidency: A Recurring American Problem.* N.Y.: Macmillan, 1962, 245p.

Ebenstein, W. *Church and State in Franco Spain.* Princeton: Princeton Univ. Press, 1960, 53p.

Ebersole, L. *Church Lobbying in the Nation's Capital.* N.Y.: Macmillan & Co., 1951, 195p.

Ehler, S. Z. (ed. and trans.) *Church and State Through The Centuries: A Collection of Historic Documents with Commentaries.* Westminster, Maryland: Newman Press, 1954, 625p.

Ehler, S. Z. *Twenty Centuries of Church and State: A Survey of Their Relations in Past and Present.* Westminster, Maryland: Newman Press, 1957, 160p.

Ellis, L. E. Dwight Marrow and the Church–State Controversy in Mexico. *Hisp. Amer. Hist. R.*, 38/4, 1958, p.482–505.

Feizulin, G. The Persecution of the National–Religious Traditions of the Moslems in the U.S.S.R. *Caucasian R.*, 3, 1956, p.69–76.

Ferris, H. *The Christian Church in Communist China, to 1952.* Lackland Air Force Base, Texas: Air Force Personnel and Training Research Center, Air Research and Development Command, 1956, 76p.

Fletcher, W. C. *A Study in Survival: The Church in Russia, 1927–43.* N.Y.: Macmillan Co., 1965, 176p.

Fortescue, A. Russia and the Catholic Church. *Studies*, 4, 1915, p.184–205.

Foster, P. *Two Cities: A Study of the Church–State Conflict.* Westminster, Maryland: Newman Press, 1955, 110p.

Friedman, I. The Austro-Hungarian Government and Zionism: 1897–1918. *Jew. Soc. Stud.*, 27/3, 1965, p.147–67; 27/4, p.236–49.

Garbett, C. *Church and State in England.* London: Hoddes & Stoughton, 1950.

Gearing, F. O. *Priests and Warriors: Social Structures for Cherokee Politics in the 18th Century.* Menasha, Wisconsin: Amer. Anthropological Association, 1962, 124p.

Geyer, A. F. *Piety and Politics: American Protestantism in the World Arena.* Richmond, Virginia: John Knox Press, 1963, 173p.

Gianella, D. A. (ed.) *Religion and the Public Order, 1963.* Chicago: Univ. of Chicago, 1964, 338p.

Gilbert, A. A Catalogue of Church-State Problems. *Rel. Educ.*, 1961, p.424–30.

Goerner, E. A. *Peter and Caesar: The Catholic Church and Political Authority.* N.Y.: Herder and Herder, 1965, 282p.

Gregory, J. S. Church and State in Victoria, 1851–72. *Hist. Stud. Australia, New Zealand*, 5/20, 1953, p.361–78.

Grosschmid, G. B. The Kremlin and the Eastern Catholic Church. *Ukranian Quart.*, 9/4, 1953, p.324–34.

Gsovski, V. (ed.) *Church and State Behind the Iron Curtain: Czechoslovakia, Hungary, Poland, Romania, With an Introduction on the Soviet Union.* N.Y.: Published for the Mid-European Studies Center of the Free Europe Committee by Praeger, 1955, 311p.

Guterman, S. L., *et al.* Symposium on Church and State in Education. *Comp. Educ. R.*, 7/1, 1963, p.28–46.

Guttman, A. From Brownson to Eliot: The Conservative Theory of Church and State. *Amer. Quart.*, 17/3, 1965, p.483–500.

Hackett, C. W. Mexican Church & State Dispute. *Curr. Hist.*, 1929, p.688–91.

Hackett, C. W. Mexican Church and State End Three-Year Conflict. *Curr. Hist.*, 1929, p.918–21.

Hackett, C. W. Mexico Reopens War on Church. *Curr. Hist.*, 1932, p.205–7.

Hackett, C. W. Mexico's War on the Church. *Curr. Hist.*, 1934, p.343–6.

Hadjibeyli, D. J. The Campaign Against the Clergy in Azerbaidzhan. *Caucasian R.*, 4, 1957, p.78–85.

Haller, W. *Elizabeth I and the Puritans.* Ithaca, N.Y.: Cornell Univ. Press, 1964, 40p.

Hammett, H. D. Separation of Church and State: By One Wall or Two? *Church State*, 7/2, 1965, p.190–206.

Herberg, W. The Sectarian Conflict Over Church and State. *Commentary*, 14/5, 1952, p.450–62.

Herberg, W. Communism, Democracy, and the Churches. *Commentary*, 19/4, 1955, p.386–93.

Hertzberg, A. Church, State and Jews. *Commentary*, 35/4, 1963, p.277–88.

Hesdtander, T. Church and State in Sweden. *Amer. Scand. R.*, 50/1, 1962, p.15–24.

Hillerbrand, H. J.   An Early Anabaptist Treatise on the Christian and the State. *Menn. Quart. R.*, 32/1, 1958, p.28–48.

Hillerbrand, H. J.   The Anabaptist View of the State. *Menn. Quart. R.*, 32/2, 1958, p.83–111.

Hoben, A.   American Democracy and the Modern Church. *Amer. J. Sociol.*, 22/4, 1917, p.489–502.

Holt, A. E.   Organized Religion as a Pressure Group. *Ann. Amer. Acad. Polit. Soc. Sci.*, 179, 1935, p.42–9.

Homrighausen, E. G.   Roman Catholic Strategy and the Separation Issue. *Theol. Today*, 15, 1958, p.128–30.

Howerth, I. W.   Church and State in Mexican Education. *Soc. Frontier*, 1937, p.46–9.

Hughey, J. D.   Ebb tide of Religious Liberty in Spain. *J. Rel.*, 35/4, 1955, p.242–51.

Hughey, J. D.   *Religious Freedom in Spain: Its Ebb and Flow.* London: Carey Kingsgate Press, 1955, 211p.

Hunt, C. L.   The Life Cycles of Dictatorships as Seen in Treatment of Religious Institutions. *Soc. Forces*, 27/4, 1949, p.365–9.

Jacob, P. E.   Religious Freedom: A Good Security Risk. *Ann. Amer. Acad. Polit. Soc. Sci.*, 1955, p.41–50.

James, E. K.   Church and State in Mexico. *Ann. Amer. Acad. Polit. Soc. Sci.*, 208, 1940, p.112–20.

Jemolo, A. C.   On Religious Freedom in Italy. *Confluence*, 2/4, 1953, p.49–58.

Jemolo, A. C.   *Church and State in Italy, 1850–1950* (Trans. D. Moore). Oxford: Blackwell, 1960, 344p.

Johnson, A. W. and Yost, F. H.   *Separation of Church and State in the United States.* Minneapolis: Univ. of Minnesota Press, 1948, 279p.

Jones, C. L.   Roots of the Mexican Church Conflict. *For. Aff.*, 14/1, 1935, p.135–45.

Kantonen, T. A.   The Finnish Church and Russian Imperialism. *Church Hist.*, 20, 1951, p.3–13.

Karson, M.   The Catholic Church and the Political Development of American Trade Unionism (1900–1918). *Indust. Lab. Relat. R.*, 4, 1951, p.527–42.

Khadduri, M.   Nature of the Islamic State. *Islamic Cult.*, 21, 1947, p.327–31.

Khan, M. S.   Religion and the State in Turkey. *Pakistan Hor.*, 11/3, 1958, p.146–55; see also 11/4, p.221–37.

King, N. Q.   *The Emperor Theodosius and the Establishment of Christianity.* Phila.: Westminster Press, 1961.

Kinney, C. B.   *Church and State: The Struggle for Separation in New Hampshire, 1630–1900.* N.Y.: Teachers College, Columbia Univ. Press, 1955, 198p.

Kritzeck, J.   Islam and Arab Nationalism. *Politico*, 28/1, 1963, p.88–99.

Lange-Poole, S.   *Mediaeval India Under Mohammadan Rule.* London: Luzac & Co., 1964, 314p.

La Noue, G. R.   *Bibliography of Doctrinal Dissertations Undertaken in American and Canadian Universities, 1940–1962, on Religion and Politics.* N.Y.: Department of Religious Liberty, National Council of Churches of Christ in U.S.A., 1963, 49p.

Laurencena, E.   Argentina and Its Struggles with Church-State Relations. *Liberty*, 53/1, 1958, p.5–9.

Law Library, Library of Congress.   *The Church and State under Communism, Volume I, Part I: The U.S.S.R.* Washington: U.S. Gov't. Printing Office, 1964, 24p.; see other volumes.

Lawrence, J.   Soviet Policy Towards the Russian Churches, 1958–64. *Soviet Stud.*, 16/3, 1965, p.276–84.

Lecler, J. S. J.   *The Two Sovereignties: A Study of the Relationship Between Church and State.* N.Y.: Philosophical Library, 1952, 186p.

Lehrman, H.   Religion by Fiat in Israel: Ben Gurion Tacks Around the Church-State Issue. *Commentary*, 8, 1949, p.110–7.

Leiper, H. S.   Religion Confronts Caesarism. *Ann. Amer. Acad. Polit. Soc. Sci.*, 1935, p.176–82.

Levenson, J. R.   The Place of Confucius in Communist China. *China Quart.*, 12, 1962, p.1–18.

Lewis, H. R. J.   The Outlook for a Devil in the Colonies or a Colonial Viewpoint on Witchcraft, Homicide, and the Supernatural. *J. Afr. Adm.*, 11/1, 1959, p.15–21.

Lewy, G.   *The Catholic Church and Nazi Germany.* N.Y.: McGraw-Hill, 1964.

Lippman, W.   Church and State in Mexico: The American Mediation. *For. Aff.*, 8, 1929, p.186–207.

Lugan, A. A.   Church and State in Mexico. *Curr. Hist.*, 33/5, 1931, p.672–6.

Lunt, W. E.   *Financial Relations of the Papacy with England, 1327–1534.* Cambridge, Massachusetts: Mediaeval Acad. Amer., 1962, 840p.

Lyon, J.   Some Aspects of English Catholicism During the Eighteenth Century. *Duquesne R.*, 10/2, 1965, p.117–37.

Machin, G. I. T.   *The Catholic Question in English Politics, 1820–1830.* N.Y.: Oxford Univ. Press, 1964, 227p.

MacKinnon, V. S.   Freedom? or Toleration? The Problem of Church and State in the United States. *Public Law*, 1959, p.374–95.

Maclear, J. F.   "The True American Union" of Church and State: The Reconstruction of the Theocratic Tradition. *Church Hist.*, 28/1, 1959, p.41–62.

Malden, R. H. *The English Church and Nation*. London: S.P.C.K., 1953, 434p.

Mallick, A. R. *British Policy and the Muslims in Bengal, 1757–1856: A Study of the Development of the Muslims of Bengal with Special Reference to their Education*. Dacca: Asiatic Society of Pakistan, 1961, 360p.

Mallinson, V. and DeCoster, S. Church and State Education in Belgium. *Comp. Educ. R.*, 4/1, 1960, p.43–8.

Masland, J. W. Communism and Christianity in China. *J. Rel.*, 32/3, 1952, p.198–206.

Mayer, H. (ed.) *Catholics and Free Society: An Australian Symposium*. Melbourne: F. N. Cheshire, 1961, 223p.

McGrath, M. B. *The Compatability of Catholic Schools and Democratic Standards*. Washington: Catholic Univ. Press, 1948.

Medlin, W. K. *Moscow and East Rome: A Political Study of the Relations of Church and State in Muscovite, Russia*. Geneva: Libr. E. Droz., 1952, 252p.

Mendelson, E. M. Buddhism and the Burmese Establishment. *Archiv. Sociol. Rel.*, 9/17, 1964, p.85–96.

Meyer, P. Stalin Follows in Hitler's Footsteps. *Commentary*, 15/1, 1953, p.1–18.

Meyer, P. Soviet Anti-Semitism in High Gear. *Commentary*, 15/2, 1953, p.115–20.

Meyer, P. Has Soviet Anti-Semitism Halted? *Commentary*, 18/1, 1954, p.1–9.

Mizzi, F. P. Church-State Relations in Malta. *Amer. Eccles. R.*, 152/4, 1965, p.233–48.

Moir, J. S. *Church and State in Canada West: 3 Studies in the Relation of Denominationalism and Nationalism, 1841–1867*. Ontario: Univ. of Toronto, 1959, 223p.

Moody, J. N. (ed.) *Church and Society: Catholic Social and Political Thought and Movements, 1789–1950*. N.Y.: Arts, Inc., 1953.

Morrison, C. C. *The Separation of Church and State in America*. Chicago: Willett, Clark & Co., 1947.

Mueller, W. A. *Church and State in Luther and Calvin*. Garden City: Doubleday, 1965, 187p.

Murray, A. V. *The State and the Church in a Free Society*. Cambridge, University Press, 1958, 190p.

Nambiar, V. K. Religious Freedom and the Secular State in India. *Soc. Action*, 14/8, 1964, p.351–63.

National Committee for a Free Europe. *The Red and the cution in the Baltic Countries, 1940–1952*. Ed. Lithuanian, Latvian, and Estonian Sections. N.Y.: National Committee for a Free Europe, 1952, 26p.

National Committee for a Free Europe. *The Red and the Black: The Church in the Communist State*. N.Y.: Research and Publication Service, 1953, 75p.

Nemec, L. *Church and State in Czechoslovakia: Historically, Juridically and Theologically Documented*. N.Y.: Vantage Press, 1955, 577p.

Nichols, J. H. *Democracy and the Churches*. Phila.: Westminster Press, 1951.

Nichols, J. H., *et al.* Debate: The State and Religion. *Comp. Stud. Society Hist.*, 1/4, 1959, p.383–93.

Nichols, R. F. *Religion and American Democracy*. Baton Rouge: Louisiana State Univ. Press, 1959.

Oaks, D. P. (ed.) *The Wall Between Church and State*. Chicago: Univ. of Chicago Press, 1963.

O'Brien, G. D. State, Academy and Church. *J. Rel.*, 42/2, 1962, p.75–86.

Orthodox Observance and New Soviet Rites in Alma-ata Oblast. *Cent. Asian R.*, 13/1, 1965, p.61–8.

O'Sullivan, J. M. Religious Policy of the Soviet Union. *Studies*, 22, 1933, p.205–20.

Outerbridge, L. M. *The Lost Churches of China*. Phila.. Westminster Press, 1953, 237p.

Parker, T. M. *Christianity and the State in Light of History*. London: A.&C. Black, 1955, 177p.

Party and Church. *Soviet Stud.*, 6/4, 1955, p.396–404.

Payne, E. A. The Baptists of the Soviet Union. *Ecumen. R.*, 7/2, 1955, p.161–8.

Peterson, W. H. The American Federal System and Church-State Relations. *West. Polit. Quart.*, 16/3, 1963, p.590–608.

Pfeffer, L. *Church, State and Freedom*. Boston: Beacon Press, 1953.

Pfeffer, L. Some Current Issues in Church and State. *West. Reserve Law R.*, 1961, p.9–33.

Poliakov, L. Official Anti-Semitism in Old Russia. *Commentary*, 22/1, 1956, p.41–6.

Polier, S. Observations on Church-State Problems in America and the Interest of the American Jewish Community. *Jew. J. Sociol.*, 1/1, 1959, p.69–79.

Poppe, N. The Destruction of Buddhism in the U.S.S.R. *Bull. Inst. Study U.S.S.R.*, 3/7, 1956, p.14–20.

Pothacamury, T. Church and State in India. *Soc. Action*, 6/9, 1956, p.383–90.

Quelquejay, C. Anti-Islamic Propaganda in Kazakhstan Since 1953. *Mid. East J.*, 13/3, 1959, p.319–27.

Recent Doctoral Dissertations in Church and State. *Church State*, 7/2, 1965, p.301–5; see other issues.

Reed, H. A. Secularism and Islam in Turkish Politics. *Curr. Hist.*, 32, 1957, p.333–8.

Rosenthal, E. I. The Role of Islam in the Modern National State. *Yearbook World Aff.*, 16, 1962, p.98–121.

Roshwald, M. Ancient Hebrews and Government. *Judaism*, 4/2, 1955, p.167–74.

Rotnem, V. and Folsom, F. G., Jr. Recent Restrictions Upon Religious Liberty. *Amer. Polit. Sci. R.*, 36/6, 1942, p.1053–68.

Roucek, J. S. The Role of Religion in American Politics. *J. Hum. Relat.*, 11/3, 1963, p.350–62.

Roucek, J. S. and Lottich, K. V. Church and State Relationship in Poland. *Politico*, 25/3, 1960, p.512–24.

Rudolph, L. I. and Rudolph, S. H. The Political Role of Indian Caste: Associations. *Pac. Aff.*, 33/1, 1960, p.5–22.

Rulland, W. B. Church-State Relations in America: Status and Trends. *Soc. Forces*, 28/1, 1949, p.83–6.

Ryan, J. A. and Moorhouse, F.X.M. *The State and the Church.* N.Y.: Macmillan Co., 1922.

Samuel, E. State and Religion in Israel. *Polit. Quart.*, 26/4, 1955, p.380–8.

Sandero, T. G. *Protestant Concepts of Church and State: Historical Backgrounds and Approaches for the Future.* N.Y.: Holt, Rinehart, and Winston, 1964, 339p.

Sarkisyanz, E. Communism and Lamaist Utopianism in Central Asia. *R. Polit.*, 20/4, 1958, p.623–33.

Sayeed, K. B. Religion and Nation-Building in Pakistan. *Mid. East J.*, 17/3, 1963, p.279–91.

Scarangello, A. Church and State in Italian Education. *Comp. Educ. R.*, 5/3, 1962, p.199–207.

Schmitt, K. M. The Clergy and the Independence of New Spain. *Hisp. Amer. Hist. R.*, 34/3, 1954, p.289–312.

Schmitt, K. M. The Diaz Conciliation Policy on State and Local Levels 1876-1911. *Hisp. Amer. Hist. R.*, 40/4, 1960, p.513–32.

Scholes, W. V. Church and State at the Mexican Constitutional Convention, 1856–1857. *The Americas*, 4, 1947, p.151–74.

Schram, S. R. *Protestantism and Politics in France.* Alencon: Imprimerie Corbiere et Jugain, 1952, 272p.

Sfeir, G. N. Islam as the State Religion: A Secularist Point of View in Syria. *Muslim World*, 45, 1955, p.242–9.

Shields, C. V. *Democracy and Catholicism in America.* N.Y.: McGraw-Hill, 1958, 310p.

Shires, N. M. The Conflict Between Queen Elizabeth and Roman Catholicism. *Church Hist.*, 1947, p.221–33.

Shuck, L. E., Jr. Church and State in Argentina. *West. Polit. Quart.*, 2/4, 1949, p.527–44.

Singer, S. A. The Expulsion of the Jews from England in 1290. *Jew. Quart. R.*, 55/2, 1964, p.117–36.

Smith, H. M. *Henry VIII and the Reformation.* London: Macmillan, 1948, 480p.

Smith, W. C. *Pakistan as an Islamic State.* Lahore: Shaikh Mujammad Ashraf, 1954, 114p.

Stedman, M. S. Church, State, People: The Eternal Triangle. *West. Polit. Quart.*, 16/3, 1963, p.610–23.

Strayer, J. R. The State and Religion: An Exploratory Comparison in Different Cultures. *Comp. Stud. Society Hist.*, 1/1, 1958, p.38–43.

Swiggett, G. L. Conflict of Church and State in Mexico. *World Aff.* (Wash., D.C.), 1936, p.40–2.

Theodorson, G. A. The Religious Institutions in the Soviet Orbit. *J. Hum. Relat.*, 9/2, 1961, p.240–53.

Tillich, P. The Totalitarian State and the Claims of the Church. *Soc. Res.*, 1, 1934, p.405–33.

Timasheff, N. S. The Anti-Religious Campaign in the Soviet Union. *R. Polit.*, 17/3, 1955, p.329–44.

Timasheff, N. S. Urbanization, Operation Antireligion and the Decline of Religion in the U.S.S.R. *Amer. Slavic E. Europ. R.*, 14/2, 1955, p.224–38.

Truman, T. C. Church and State in Australia: The Teaching of the Catholic Church on Intervention in Politics. *Australian Quart.*, 30/4, 1958, p.35–43.

Tussman, J. (ed.) *The Supreme Court on Church and State.* N.Y.: Oxford Univ. Press, 1962, 305p.

Ukranian Catholic Priests Resident in Rome. *First Victims of Communism: White Book on the Religious Persecution in (The) Ukraine* (Trans. from Italian). Rome: Analecta O.S.B.M., 1953, 114p.

United States Congress, Select Committee on Communist Aggression. *Treatment of Jews by the Soviet.* Seventh Interim Report of Hearings Before the Select Committee on Communist Aggression, House of Representatives, Eighty-third Congress, Second Session, N.Y., 22 and 23 September 1954. Washington: U.S. Govt. Print. Office, 1954, 120p.

Van der Meulen, D. Muslims Problems Connected with an Independent Indonesia. *Muslim World*, 37, 1947, p.292–300.

Vidal, F. S. Religious Brotherhoods in Moroccan Politics. *Mid. East J.*, 4, 1950, p.427–46.

Walker, F. J. *Catholic Education and Politics in Upper Canada.* Toronto: Dent and Sons, 1955.

Walsh, G. G. Church and State in the U.S. *U.S. Cath. Hist. Society Rec. Stud.*, 37, 1948, p.3–12.

Ward, H. F. Organized Religion, the State, and the Economic Order. *Ann. Amer. Acad. Polit. Soc. Sci.*, 256, 1948, p.72–83.

Ware, T. *Eustratios Argenti: A Study of the Greek Church Under Turkish Rule.* Oxford: Clarendon Press, 1964, 196p.

Warren, R. L. Facism and the Church. *Amer. Sociol. R.*, 6, 1941, p.45–51.

Webb, L. C. *Church and State in Italy, 1947–1957.* Carlton: Melbourne Univ. Press, 1958, 60p.

Webster, R. A. *The Cross and the Faces: Christian Democracy and Fascism in Italy.* Stanford, California: Stanford Univ. Press, 1960, 229p.

Wells, R. H. The Financial Relations of the Church and State in Germany, 1919–1937. *Polit. Sci. Quart.*, 53/1, 1938, p.36–59.

Wheeler, G. *Racial Problems in Soviet Muslim Asia.* N.Y.: Oxford Univ. Press, 1960.

Wiarda, H. J. The Changing Political Orientation of the Church in the Dominican Republic. *Church State*, 7/2, 1965, p.238–54.

Wilhelm, H. The Reappraisal of Neo-Confucianism. *China Quart.*, 23, 1965, p.122–39.

Wilkowski, S. *The Roman Catholic Church in People's Poland.* Warsaw: Published by the Central Priests' Committee Affiliated to the Organization of Fighters for Freedom and Democracy, 1953, 129p.

Wilson, N. H. Dutch Schools and Religious Segmentation. *Comp. Educ. R.*, 3/2, 1959, p.19–24.

Winder, R. B. Islam as the State Religion: A Muslim Brotherhood View in Syria. *Muslim World*, 64, 1954, p.215–26.

Wolin, S. S. Richard Hooker and English Conservatism. *West. Polit. Quart.*, 6/1, 1953, p.28–47.

Woodard, W. P. Religion-State Relations in Japan. *Contemp. Japan*, 24/7–9, 1956, p.460–83; see also: 24/10–12, 1957, p.640–7; 25/1, p.81–116.

Woodruff, D. *Church and State.* N.Y.: Hawthorne Books, 1961, 128p.

Zela, S. *Trial of Vatican Agents in Czechoslavakia (Bishop Zela and Accomplices).* Prague: Orbis, 1951, 219p.

Zernov, N. Peter the Great and the Establishment of the Russian Church. *Church Quart. R.* (London), 125, 1938, p.265–93.

Divine Kingship

Bradbury, R. E. Divine Kingship in Benin. *Nigeria*, 62, 1959, p.186–207.

Cantor, N. F. *Church, Kingship and Lay Investiture in England 1089–1135.* Princeton: Princeton Univ. Press, 1958, 349p.

de Heusch, L. Aspects of the Sacredness of Power in Africa: Power and the Sacred. *Ann. Cent. Rel.*, 1, 1961, p.139–58.

de Heusch, L. Towards a Dialectic of the Sacredness of Power. *Ann. Cent. Rel.*, 2, 1962, p.15–48.

Drekmeir, C. *Kingship and Community in Early India.* Stanford: Stanford Univ. Press, 1962, 369p.

Fakhry, M. The Theocratic Idea of the Islamic State in Recent Controversies. *Int. Aff.*, 30/4, 1954, p.450–62.

Fox, P. W. Louis XIV and the Theories of Absolutism and Divine Right. *Canadian J. Econ. Polit. Sci.*, 26/1, 1960, p.128–42.

Frankfort, H. *Kingship and Gods: A Study of Ancient Near Eastern Religion as the Integration of Society and Nature.* Chicago: Univ. of Chicago Press, 1948.

Geanakoplos, D. J. Church and State in the Byzantine Empire: A Reconsideration of the Problem of Caesaropapism. *Church Hist.*, 34/4, 1965, p.381–403.

Ghoshal, U. N. A Comparison Between Ancient Indian and Medieval European Theories of the Divine Origin and Nature of Kingship. *Indian Hist. Quart.*, 31/3, 1955, p.263–66.

Gonda, J. Ancient Indian Kingship From the Religious Point of View. *Numen*, 3/1, 1956, p.36–71; see also: 3/2, p.122–55; 4/1, 1957, p.24–58; 4/2, p.127–64.

Hadfield, L. P. *Traits of Divine Kingship in Africa.* London: Watts, 1949, 134p.

Lloyd, P. C. Sacred Kingship and Government Among the Yoruba. *Africa*, 30/3, 1960, p.221–37.

Lutz, H. F. Kingship in Babylonia, Assyria, and Egypt. *Amer. Anthropol.*, 26, 1924, p.435–53.

Meyerowitz, E. L. R. *The Divine Kingship in Ghana and Ancient Egypt.* London: Faber and Faber, 1960, 260p.

Morris, J. S. The Divine Kingship of the Aga Khan: A Study of Theocracy in East Africa. *Southw. J. Anthropol.*, 14/4, 1958, p.454–72.

Pettersson, O. *Chiefs and Gods: Religious and Social Elements in the South Eastern Bantu Kingship.* Lund: Gleemp, 1953, 405p.

Riad, M. The Divine Kingship of the Shilluk and Its Origin. *Archiv. Volkerk.*, 14, 1959, p.141–284.

Richards, A. I. (ed.) *East African Chiefs: A Study of Political Development In Some Uganda and Tanganyka Tribes.* N.Y.: Praeger, 1960, 419p.

Spellman, J. W. *Political Theory of Ancient India: A*

Study of Kingship From Earliest Times to Circa A.D. 300. Oxford: Clarendon Press, 1964, 288p.

Wales, H. G. O. *The Mountain of God: A Study in Early Religion and Kingship.* London: Bernard Quaritch, 1953, 1174p.

Wilson, M. *Divine Kings and the "Breath of Men."* Cambridge: Cambridge Univ. Press, 1959, 27p.

International Relations

Adler, C. and Margalith, A. M. *With Firmness in the Right: American Diplomatic Action Affecting Jews, 1840–1945.* N.Y.: American Jewish Committee, 1946, 489p.

Batlleri, M. Some International Aspects of the Acitivity of the Jesuits in the New World. *Americas,* 14/4, 1958, p.432–6.

Byrd, R. O. Quakerism and Foreign Policy. *Int. Spec.,* 12/1, 1958, p.38–56.

Engel-Janosi, F. The Roman Question in the Diplomatic Negotiations of 1869–70. *R. Polit.,* 3/3, 1941, p.319–49.

Graham, R. A. and Harnett, R. C. *Diplomatic Relations with the Vatican.* N.Y.: The American Press, 1952, 48p.

Grubb, K. and Booth, A. R. The Church and International Relations. *Yearbook World Aff.,* 17, 1963, p.219–35.

Jensen, D. *Diplomacy and Dogmatism: Bernardio De Mendoza and The French Catholic League.* Cambridge: Harvard Univ. Press, 1964, 322p.

Khan, Z. Islam and International Relations. *Int. Spec.,* 10/11, 1956, p.308–22.

Kitagawa, J. M. Buddhism and Asian Politics. *Asian Surv.,* 2/5, 1962, p.1–11.

Natsir, M. *Some Observations Concerning the Role of Islam in National and International Affairs.* Ithaca: Southeast Asia Program, Dept. of Far Eastern Studies, Cornell Univ. Press, 1954, 141p.

O'Dea, T. F. American Catholics and International Life. *Soc. Order,* 10/6, 1960, p.243–65.

Parzen, H. Conservative Judaism and Zionism (1896–1922). *Jew. Soc. Stud.,* 23/4, 1961, p.235–64.

Proctor, J. H. (ed.) *Islam and International Relations.* N.Y.: F. A. Praeger, 1965, 221p.

Psomiades, H. J. Soviet Russia and the Orthodox Church in the Middle East. *Mid. East J.,* 11/4, 1957, p.371–81.

Riga, P. J. Communism and John XXIII. *Co-Existence,* 2, 1964, p.130–8.

Sarkar, B. K. Hindu Theory of International Relations. *Amer. Polit. Sci. R.,* 13, 1919, p.400–14.

Slater, R. L. *World Religions and World Community.* N.Y.: Columbia Univ. Press, 1963, 299p.

Smith, D. The U.S. and the Vatican. *Nat. Eng. R.,* 138/827, 1952, p.24–6.

Spector, I. Soviet Influence on Islamic Peoples. *Curr. Hist.,* 32, 1957, p.351–6.

Spector, I. *The Soviet Union and the Muslim World.* Seattle: Univ. of Washington Press, 1959, 328p.

Stock, L. F. (ed.) *Consular Relations Between the United States and the Papal States: Instructions and Dispatches.* Washington: American Catholic Historical Association, 1945, 467p.

Teller, J. L. *The Kremlin, the Jews, and the Middle East.* N.Y.: T. Yoseloff, 1957, 202p.

Thompson, K. W. Beyond National Interest: A Critical Evaluation of Reinhold Neibuhr's Theory of International Politics. *R. Polit.,* 17/2, 1955, p.733–746.

Tobias, R. *Communist—Christian Encounter in East Europe.* Indianapolis: School of Religion Press, 1956, 567p.

White, L. T. The Church and International Relations. *J. Appl. Sociol.,* 10, 1926, p.562–9.

Zenkovsky, S. *Pan-Turkism and Islam in Russia.* Cambridge: Harvard Univ. Press, 1960, 345p.

Legal Studies

Anderson, J. N. D. Law and Custom in Muslim Areas in Africa: Recent Developments in Nigeria. *Civilisations,* 7/1, 1957, p.17–29.

Anderson, J. N. D. Waqfs in East Africa. *J. Afr. Law,* 3/3, 1959, p.152–64.

Baierl, J. J. *The Catholic Church and the Modern State: A Study of Mutual Juridical Claims.* Rochester, N.Y.: St. Bernard's Seminary, 1955, 243p.

Calogero, G. Church and State in Italy. The Constitutional Issues. *Int. Aff.,* 35/1, 1959, p.33–42.

Chaij, F. Religious Liberty in the Argentine Constitution. *Liberty,* 53/1, 1958, p.9–12.

Curry, J. W. *Public Regulation of the Religious Use of Land.* Charlottesville, Virginia: The Michie Co., 1964, 429p.

Derrett, J. D. M. The Administration of a Hindu Law by the British. *Comp. Stud. Society Hist.,* 4/1, 1961, p.10–52.

Derrett, J. D. M. *Introduction to Modern Hindu Law.* Bombay: Oxford Univ. Press, 1963, 653p.

Derrett, J. D. M. Law and the Social Order in India Before the Muhammadan Conquests. *J. Econ. Soc. Hist. Orient.*, 7/1, 1964, p.73–120.

deZayas, F. *The Law and Philosophy of the Zakât.* Beirut: Khayats, 1960, 420p.

Duff, E. Church-State in the American Environment: An Historical and Legal Survey. *Soc. Order*, 10/9, 1960, p.385–402.

Ericson, J. E. and McCrocklin, J. H. From Religion to Commerce: The Evolution and Enforcement of Blue Laws in Texas. *Southw. Soc. Sci. Quart.*, 45/1, 1964, p.50–8.

Eusden, J. D. *Puritans, Lawyers, and Politics in Early Seventeenth Century England.* New Haven: Yale Univ. Press, 1958, 238p.

Faruki, K. A. *Islamic Jurisprudence.* Karachi: Pakistan Publishing House, 1962, 337p.

Fyzee, A. A. A. *Outlines of Muhammadan Law.* Bombay: Indian Branch, Oxford Univ. Press, 1955, 445p.

Fyzee, A. A. A. Muhammadan Law in India. *Comp. Stud. Society Hist.*, 5, 1962–3, p.401–15.

Glendhill, A. *The Republic of India: The Development of Its Laws and Constitution.* London: Stevens and Sons, 1964, 412p.

Gorton, B. E. Peyote and the Arizona Court Decision. *Amer. Anthropol.*, 63/6, 1961, p.1334–7.

Grebstein, S. N. (ed.) *Monkey Trial: The State of Tennessee vs. John Thomas Scopes.* Boston: Houghton Mifflin, 1960, 212p.

Halliburton, R., Jr. The Nation's First Anti-Darwin Law: Passage and Repeal. *Southw. Soc. Sci. Quart.*, 41/2, 1960, p.123–35.

Hough, R. L. The Jehovah's Witnesses Cases in Retrospect. *West. Polit. Quart.*, 6/1, 1953, p.18–92.

Howe, M. de W. *Cases on Church and State in the United States.* Cambridge: Harvard Univ. Press, 1952, 393p.

Katz, W. G. *Religion and American Constitutions.* Evanston, Illinois: Northwestern Univ. Press, 1964, 112p.

Kauper, P. G. Church and State: Cooperative Separatism. *Michigan Law R.*, 60/1, 1961, p.1–40.

Kauper, P. G. *Religion and the Constitution.* Baton Rouge: Louisiana State Univ. Press, 1964, 137p.

Khadduri, M. Islam and the Modern Law of Nations. *Amer. J. Int. Law*, 50/2, 1956, p.358–72.

Kim, R. C. C. The Constitutional Legacy of the Jehovah's Witnesses. *Southw. Soc. Sci. Quart.*, 45/2, 1964, p.125–34.

Krislov, S. Church, State and Kashruth: Some Hidden Dimensions of Pluralism. *Jew. Soc. Stud.*, 25/3, 1963, p.174–85.

Kurland, P. *Religion and the Law: Of Church and State and Supreme Court.* Chicago: Aldine Publishing Co., 1962.

Lardner, L. A. How Far Does the Constitution Separate Church and State? *Amer. Polit. Sci. R.*, 45/1, 1951, p.110–32.

Larkin, M. J. M. The Vatican, French Catholics, and the Associations Cultuelles. *J. Mod. Hist.*, 36, 1964, p.298–317.

Laundy, P. Parliament and the Church. *Parliamentary Aff.*, 12/3–4, 1959, p.445–60.

Marnell, W. H. *The First Amendment: The History of Religious Freedom in America.* Garden City: Doubleday, 1964, 247p.

Masland, J. W. Treatment of the Conscientious Objector Under the Selective Service Act of 1940. *Amer. Polit. Sci. R.*, 36, 1942, p.697–701.

McGrath, J. J. *Church and State in American Law: Cases and Materials.* Milwaukee: Bruce Publishing Co., 1962, 414p.

McLaughlin, R. *A History of State Legislation Affecting Private Elementary and Secondary Schools in the United States, 1870–1945.* Washington: Catholic Univ. Press, 1946, 348p.

Michael, F. The Role of Law in Traditional Nationalist and Communist China. *China Quart.*, 9, 1962, p.124–48.

Moehlman, C. H. *The Wall of Separation Between Church and State: An Historical Study of Recent Criticism of the Religious Clause of the First Amendment.* Boston: Beacon, 1951, 239p.

Murray, R. K. The Constitutional Position of the Church of Scotland. *Pub. Law*, 2, 1958, p.155–62.

Needham, J. Human Laws and the Laws of Nature in China and the West. *J. Hist. Ideas*, 12/1, 1951, p.3–23; see also 12/2, p.194–230.

Niemeyer, E. V., Jr. Anticlericalism in the Mexican Constitutional Conventions of 1916–1917. *Americas*, 11/1, 1954, p.31–49.

Pal, R. *The History of Hindu Law.* Calcutta: Univ. of Calcutta Press, 1959, 445p.

Quadri, A. A. *Islamic Jurisprudence in the Modern World: A Reflection Upon Comparative Study of the Law.* Bombay: N.M. Tripathi Private Ltd., 1963, 366p.

Rudolph, L. I. and Rudolph, S. H. Barristers and Brahmans in India: Legal Cultures and Social Change. *Comp. Stud. Society Hist.*, 8/1, 1965, p.24–9.

Schacht, J. Problems of Modern Islamic Legislation. *Studia Islamica*, 12, 1960, p.99–129.

Schacht, J. *An Introduction to Islamic Law.* Oxford: Clarendon Press, 1964, 304p.

Stewart, O. C. Peyote and the Arizona Court Decision. *Amer. Anthropol.*, 63/6, 1961, p.1334.

Vanalystyne, W. W. Constitutional Separation of Church and State: The Quest for a Neutral Position. *Amer. Polit. Sci. R.*, 57, 1963, p.865–82.

Wood, J. E., *et al.* *Church and State in Scripture, History and Constitutional Law.* Waco, Texas: Baylor Univ. Press, 1958, 148p.

Woodard, W. P. Study on Religious Juridical Persons Law. *Contemp. Japan*, 25/3, 1958, p.418–70; see also: 25/4, 1959, p.635–57; 26/1, p.96–115; 26/2, p.293–312.

Zabel, O. H. *God and Caesar in Nebraska: A Study of the Legal Relationship of Church and State, 1854–1954.* Lincoln: The Univ. of Nebraska Press, 1955, 198p.

See Also:

American Council of Education   4g
Anderson, J. N. D.   4e2
Black, E. C.   6b
Blau, J. L.   5c
Callahan, D.   4g4
Carlton, F. T.   4b
Chinna Durai, J.   8a5
Conference on Religion   4g
Coughlin, B. J.   1g
Coulson, N. J.   1c
Cruickshank, M.   4g
Cunningham, C. E.   6
Diamant, A.   7b3

Drake, W. E.   4g
Drinan, R.   5d
Duncan, H. D.   6a
El Hajji,   6a
Florin, H. W.   5e
Foik, P. J.   5a2
Gluckman, M.   6b
Hall, D.   7a1
Hamilton, H. D.   4g6
Hanley, T. L.   3a1
Haycock, B. G.   7a1
Hill, R.   5e1
Hurley, M. J.   4g
Kawai, K.   7a1
Khadduri, M.   3d
Knox, R. A.   6c
Knovitz, M. R.   1c
Kosok, P.   7a1
Kotb, S.   2d
Kucera, D. W.   4g
Latourette, K. S.   5e
Lockmiller, D. A.   4b
Maududi, A.   2d
McFarlan, D. M.   5e1
Meislin, B. J.   4b
Mervin, W.   5e3
Nader, L.   1c
O'Neill, J. M.   4g
Oullet, F.   3g
Parker, T. W.   5d
Pinson, K. S.   3b
Pratt, J. W.   4g5
Robinson, J.   3b
Sacks, B.   4g
Scanlon, D.   4g
Sibley, M. Q.   7b3
Skoczylas, E.   5a2
Smith, D. E.   6

4a2.   *Voting and Elections*

Baggaley, A. R. Religious Influence on Wisconsin Voting, 1928–1960. *Amer. Polit. Sci. R.*, 56/1, 1962, p.66–70.

Bates, W. Catholic Congressional Voting—Is It Truly Liberal? *Soc. Order*, 6/3, 1956, p.104–6.

Brenner, S. Patterns of Jewish-Catholic Democratic Voting and the 1960 Presidential Vote. *Jew Soc. Stud.*, 26/3, 1964, p.169–79.

Butcher, P. The Puritans at the Polls. *J. Hum. Relat.*, 5/2, 1957, p.49–55.

Cosman, B. Religion and Race in Louisiana Presidential Politics. *Southw. Polit. Soc. Sci. Quart.*, 43/3, 1962, p.235–41.

Dawidowicz, L. S. and Goldstein, L. J. *Politics in a Pluralist Democracy: Studies of Voting in the 1960 Election.* N.Y.: Institute of Human Relations Press, 1963, 100p.

Edelman, M. Sources of Popular Support for the Italian Christian Democratic Party in the Post-War Decade. *Midwest J. Polit. Sci.*, 2/2, 1958, p.143–59.

Farrelly, D. G. "Rum, Romanism and Rebellion" Resurrected. *West. Polit. Quart.*, 8/2, 1955, p.262–70.

Fenton, J. *The Catholic Vote.* New Orleans: Hauser Press, 1960.

Fuchs, L. H. American Jews and the Presidential Vote. *Amer. Polit. Sci. R.*, 49/2, 1955, p.385–401.

Fuchs, L. H.   The Religious Vote: When, Why and How Much. *Cath. World*, 200, 1965, p.285–93.

Gargan, E. T.   Radical Catholics of the Right. *Soc. Order*, 11/9, 1961, p.409–19.

Glantz, O.   Protestant and Catholic Voting Behavior in a Metropolitan Area. *Pub. Opin. Quart.*, 23/1, 1959, p.73–82.

Greer, S.   Catholic Voters and the Democratic Party. *Pub. Opin. Quart.*, 25/4, 1961, p.611–25.

Gupta, S. K.   Moslems in Indian Politics, 1947–1960. *India Quart.*, 18/4, 1962, p.355–81.

Hadden, J. K.   An Analysis of Some Factors Associated With Religion and Political Affiliation in a College Population. *J. Sci. Stud. Rel.*, 2/2, 1963, p.209–16. See also: J. M. Buss—Comment, 3/2, 1964, p.245–6; J. K. Hadden—Reply, 4/2, 1965, p.248–9.

Johnson, G. B., Jr.   Ascetic Protestantism and Political Preference. *Pub. Opin. Quart.*, 26/1, 1962, p.35–46.

Johnson, G. B., Jr.   Ascetic Protestantism and Political Preference in the Deep South. *Amer. J. Sociol.*, 69/4, 1964, p.359–65.

Kitzinger, U.   The French General Election, 1958: II. Personal Regional and Religious Factors: Strasbourg Nord-Sud. *Polit. Stud.*, 17/2, 1959, p.157–73.

Litt, E.   Status, Ethnicity and Patterns of Jewish Voting Behavior in Baltimore. *Jew. Soc. Stud.*, 22, 1960, p.159–64.

Marculies, H. F.   Anti-Catholicism in Wisconsin Politics, 1914–1920. *Mid-America*, 44/1, 1962, p.51–6.

Marquis, L. C.   Religious Diffusion and Political Consensus in the United States. *Parliamentary Aff.*, 17/2, 1964, p.200–6.

McKinney, M. M.   Religion and Elections. *Pub. Opin. Quart.*, 8/1, 1944, p.110–4.

Meisel, J.   Religious Affiliation and Electoral Behaviour: A Case Study. *Canad. J. Econ. Polit. Sci.*, 22/4, 1956, p.481–96.

Moore, E. A.   *A Catholic Runs for President. The Campaign of 1928*. N.Y.: Ronald Press, 1956, 220p.

O'Shea, H. E. and Engel, G.   Some Current Student Attitudes Toward Presidential Candidates of Different Categories. *J. Psychol.*, 51, 1961, p.233–46.

Postal, B.   Can A Jew be Elected President in Our Time? *Jew. Digest*, 1959, p.1–10.

Rose, A. M.   The Mormon Church and Utah Politics: An Abstract of a Statistical Study. *Amer. Sociol. R.* 7, 1942, p.853–4.

Rothman, S.   The American Catholic and the Radical Right. *Soc. Order*, 13/4, 1963, p.5–8.

Rothney, G. O.   The Denominational Basis of Representation in the Newfoundland Assembly, 1919–1962. *Canad. J. Econ. Polit. Sci.*, 28/4, 1962, p.557–70.

Rueckert, G. L. and Crane, W.   Christian Demo Union Deviancy in the German Bundestag. *J. Polit.*, 24/3, 1962, p.477–88.

Schran, P.   Muslim Legislators in India: Profile of a Minority Elite. *J. Asian Stud.*, 23/2, 1964, p.253–67.

Scoble, H. M. and Epstein, L. D.   Religion and Wisconsin Voting in 1960. *J. Polit.*, 26/2, 1964, p.381–96.

Silva, R. C.   *Rum, Religion and Votes: 1928 Reexamined*. University Park: Pennsylvania State Univ., 1962.

Smylie, J. H.   The Roman Catholic Church, the State and Al Smith. *Church Hist.*, 29/3, 1960, p.321–43.

Zeender, J. K.   The German Catholics and the Presidential Election of 1925. *J. Mod. Hist.*, 35, 1963, p.366–81.

4b.   *Religion and Economic Behavior*

Abell, A. I.   The Reception of Leo XIII's Labor Encyclical in America, 1891-1919. *R. Polit.*, 7/4, 1945, p.464–95.

Abu, A. S. M.   Economic Policy in Islam. *Islamic R.*, 45, 1957, p.7–14.

Ahmad Khan, M.   *Economics of Islam: A Comparative Study*. Lahore: Nuhammad Ashraf, 1947, 191p.

Al-Kader, A. A.   Land Property and Land Tenure in Islam. *Islamic Quart.*, 5/1–2, 1959, p.4–11.

Arrington, L. J.   *Orderville, Utah: A Pioneer Mormon Experiment in Economic Organization*. Logan: Utah State Agricultural College, 1954, 44p.

Bahadur, R. P.   The Economics of Casteism. *Ind. J. Econ.*, 36/142, 1956, p.325–36.

Bareau, A.   Indian and Ancient Chinese Buddhism: Institutions Analogous to the Jisa. *Comp. Stud. Society Hist.*, 3/4, 1961, p.443–51.

Baron, S. W.   *Social and Religious History of the Jews*. N.Y.: Columbia Univ. Press, 1952–60, 11 vols.

Baroni, G.   The Church and the War on Poverty. *Amer. Eccles. R.*, 153/3, 1965, p.184–97.

Beattie, J. H. M.   A Note on the Connexion Between Spirit Mediumship and Hunting in Bunyoro, With Special Reference to Possession by Animal Ghosts. *Man*, 63, 1963, p.188–9.

Beidelman, T. O.   *A Comparative Analysis of the Jajmani System*. Locust Valley, N.Y.: J. J. Augustin, 1959, 86p.

Bennett, J. C., *et al.* *Christian Values and Economic Life.* N.Y.: Harper, 1954, 272p.

Bernardin, J. L. Revenue Procurement in Catholic Schools. *Cath. Educ. R.*, 49/6, 1951, p.514–23.

Bonne, A. Trends in Occupational Structure and Distribution of Income Among the Jewish Population in Israel. *Jew. J. Sociol.*, 1/2, 1959, p.242–9.

Bose, A. and Jodha, N. S. The Jajmani System in a Desert Village. *Man India*, 45/2, 1965, p.105–26.

Bressler, M. and Westoff, C. F. Catholic Education, Economic Values and Achievement. *Amer. J. Sociol.*, 69/3, 1963, p.225–32.

Browne, H. J. *The Catholic Church and the Knights of Labor.* Washington: Catholic Univ. Press, 1949, 415p.

Bursk, E. C. (ed.) *Business and Religion: A New Depth Dimension in Management.* N.Y.: Harper and Brothers, 1959, 212p.

Cahill, A. E. Catholicism and Socialism: The 1905 Controversy in Australia. *J. Rel. Hist.*, 1, 1960, p.88–101.

Cahnman, W. J. Role and Significance of the Jewish Artisan Class. *Jew. J. Sociol.*, 7/2, 1965, p.207–14.

Carlton, F. T. Technological Advance, Government and Religion. *Sociol. Soc. Res.*, 41/2, 1956, p.115–20.

Chapman, S. H. Church Real Estate. *Amer. J. Econ. Sociol.*, 7/4, 1948, p.439–60.

Chaudhary, R. L. *Hindu Woman's Right to Property: Past and Present.* Calcutta: F.K.D. Mukhopadhyay, 1961, 156p.

Ch'en, K. The Economic Background of the Hui-Ch'ang Suppression of Buddhism. *Harvard J. Asiat. Stud.*, 19/1–2, 1956, p.67–105.

Chiang, A. C. Religion, Proverbs, and Economic Mentality. *Amer. J. Econ. Sociol.*, 20/3, 1961, p.253–64.

Child, J. Quaker Employers and Industrial Relations. *Sociol. R.*, 12/3, 1964, p.293–315.

Clark, S. D. The Religious Sect in Canadian Economic Development. *Canad. J. Econ. Polit. Sci.*, 12/4, 1946, p.439–53.

Connell, F. J. Catholics in Labor Unions. *Amer. Eccles. R.*, 116/6, 1947, p.422–31.

Costello, B. D. Catholics in American Commerce and Industry, 1925–1945. *Amer. Cath. Sociol. R.*, 17/3, 1956, p.219–33.

Cronin, J. F. *Catholic Social Principles: The Social Teachings of the Catholic Church Applied to American Economic Life.* Milwaukee: Bruce Publishing Co., 1950.

Curtis, R. F. Occupational Mobility and Church Participation. *Soc. Forces*, 38/4, 1960, p.315-9.

Demant, V. A. *Religion and the Decline of Capitalism.* London: Faber, 1952, 204p.

Desmonde, W. H. *Magic, Myth and Money: The Origin of Money in Religious Ritual.* N.Y.: Free Press of Glencoe, 1962, 208p.

Diamond, H. M. Property and Cult. *Amer. J. Sociol.*, 32/2, 1926, p.264–70.

Eberhard, W. Economic Activities of a Chinese Temple in California. *J. Amer. Orient. Society*, 82, 1962, p.362–71.

El-Saaty, H. The Role of Islam in the Social and Economic Development of the United Arab Republic. In *Transactions of the Fifth World Congress of Sociology, Washington, D.C., 1962.* Louvain: International Sociological Association, 1964, p.55–67, vol. III.

Fischel, W. J. The Jewish Merchant Colony in Madras (Fort St. George) During the 17th and 18th Centuries: A Contribution to the Economic and Social History of the Jews in India. *J. Econ. Soc. Hist. Orient.*, 3/1, 1960, p.78–107; 3/2, p.175–95.

Gannon, R. B. The Challenge of Finance in Catholic Schools. *Cath. School J.*, 51/9, 1951, p.287–9.

Garvin, M. H. Trends in Christian Trade Unionism. *Soc. Order*, 6/10, 1956, p.465–8.

Geertz, C. Religious Belief and Economic Behavior in a Central Javanese Town: Some Preliminary Considerations. *Econ. Develop. Cult. Change*, 4/2, 1956, p.134–58.

George, C. H. and George, K. Protestantism and Capitalism in Pre-Revolutionary England. *Church Hist.*, 27/4, 1958, p.351–71.

Gist, N. P. Occupational Differentiation in South India. *Soc. Forces*, 33/2, 1954, p.129–38.

Goitein, S. D. The Origin and Nature of the Muslim Friday Worship. *Muslim World*, 49/3, 1959, p.183–95.

Goody, J. R. *Death, Property and the Ancestors: A Study of Mortuary Customs of the Lodagaa of West Africa.* Stanford: Stanford Univ. Press, 1962, 452p.

Gould, H. A. The Hindu Jajmani System: A Case of Economic Particularism. *Southwest. J. Anthropol.*, 14/4, 1958, p.428–37.

Gould, H. A. A Jajmani System of North India: Its Structure, Magnitude and Meaning. *Ethnology*, 3/1, 1964, p.12–41.

Greeley, A. M. Influence of the "Religious Factor" on Career Plans and Occupational Values of College Graduates. *Amer. J. Sociol.*, 68/6, 1963, p.658–71.

Greeley, A. M. *Religion and Career: A Study of College Graduates.* N.Y.: Sheed & Ward, 1963.

Greenfield, J.   The Role of the Jews in the Development of the Clothing Industry in the United States. *Yivo Ann. Jew. Soc. Sci.*, 2/3, 1948, p.180–204.

Gremillion, J. B.   *The Catholic Movement of Employers and Managers: A Study of UNIPAC.* Rome: Gregorian Univ. Press, 1961.

Gulati, I. S. and Gulati, K. S.   *The Undivided Hindu Family: A Study of Its Tax Privileges.* Bombay: Asia Publishing House, 1962, 96p.

Habib, I.   Usury in Medieval India. *Comp. Stud. Society Hist.*, 6/4, 1964, p.393–419.

Habib, I.   *The Agrarian System of Mughal India, 1556–1707.* Bombay: Asia Publishing House, 1963, 453p.

Hardman, J. B. S.   Jewish Workers in the American Labor Movement. *Yivo Ann. Jew. Soc. Sci.*, 7, 1952, p.229–54.

Harrod, H.   Religious Institutions and the Culture of Poverty. *J. Rel. Thought*, 21/2, 1964–65, p.81–94.

Hasen, N. M.   The Protestant Ethic as a General Precondition for Economic Development. *Canad. J. Econ. Polit. Sci.*, 29/4, 1963, p.462–74.

Hoover, C. B.   Economic Forces in the Evolution of Civil and Canon Law. *Southw. Polit. Soc. Sci. Quart.*, 10/1, 1929, p.42–55.

Horton, W. R. G.   God, Man, and the Land in a Northern Ibo Village-Group. *Africa*, 26/1, 1956, p.17–28.

Hoult, T. F.   Economic Class Consciousness in American Protestantism. *Amer. Sociol. R.*, 15, 1950, p.97–100; see also 17, 1952, p.349–50.

Hurvitz, N.   Sources of Motivation and Achievement of American Jews. *Jew. Soc. Stud.*, 23, 1961, p.217–34.

Isaac, E.   Religious Factors in the Geography of Animal Husbandry. *Diogenes*, 44, 1963, p.59–80.

Islamic Socialism: The Pakistan Way.   *Cent. Asian R.*, 13/1, 1965, p.55–60.

James, S. V.   *A People Among Peoples: Quaker Benevolence in Eighteenth Century America.* Cambridge: Harvard Univ. Press, 1963, 405p.

Jonassen, C. T.   The Protestant Ethic and the Spirit of Capitalism in Norway. *Amer. Sociol. R.*, 12, 1947, p.676–86.

Kamm, J. O.   The Christian Concept of Business. *Amer. J. Econ. Sociol.*, 9/2, 1950, p.235–8.

Keller, E. A.   *Christianity and American Capitalism.* Chicago: Heritage, 1953, 92p.

Kennedy, W. F.   The Christian Conscience and Economic Growth: A Symposium. *Soc. Order*, 7/4, 1957, p.149–69.

Kerins, J. L.   The Catholic Sociologist and the Sociology of Industry. *Amer. Cath. Sociol. R.*, 8/1, 1947, p.12–23.

Knight, F. H. and Merriam, T. W.   *The Economic Order and Religion.* London: Routledge and Kegan Paul, 1947, 242p.

Kollmorgen, W. M.   The Agricultural Stability of the Old Order Amish and Old Order Mennonites of Lancaster County, Pa. *Amer. J. Sociol.*, 49/3, 1943, p.233–41.

Krausz, E.   Occupation and Social Advancement in Anglo-Jewry. *Jew. J. Sociol.*, 4/1, 1962, p.82–90.

Kumar, D.   Caste and Landlessness in South India. *Comp. Stud. Society Hist.*, 4/3, 1962, p.337–63.

Larkin, E.   Socialism and Catholicism in Ireland. *Church Hist.*, 33/4, 1964, p.462–83.

Lawrence, P.   Religion: Help or Hindrance to Economic Development in Paua and New Guinea. *Mankind*, 6/1, 1963, p.3–11.

Leach, W. H.   Financing the Local Church. *Ann. Amer. Acad. Polit. Soc. Sci.*, 332, 1960, p.70–9.

Lipman, V. D.   Trends in Anglo-Jewish Occupations. *Jew. J. Sociol.*, 2/1, 1960, p.202–18.

Lockmiller, D. A.   The Settlement of the Church Property Question in Cuba. *Hisp. Amer. Hist. R.*, 1937, p.488–98.

Maeda, T.   Influence of Ancestor Worship on Inheritance in Japanese Village Communities: Some Case Studies. *Jap. Sociol. R.*, 10/2, 1960, p.87–106.

Marcus, A.   Jews as Entrepreneurs in Weimar, Germany. *Yivo Ann. Jew. Soc. Sci.*, 7, 1952, p.175–203.

Mathur, K. S.   Caste and Occupation in a Malwa Village. *East. Anthropol.*, 12/1, 1958, p.47–61.

May, H. F.   *Protestant Churches and Industrial America.* N.Y.: Harper, 1949.

Mayer, A. J. and Sharp, H.   Religious Preference and Worldly Success. *Amer. Sociol. R.*, 27/2, 1962, p.218–27.

McCune, E. B.   The Role of the Temple in the Social and Economic Life of India. *Bull. Inst. Trad. Cult.*, 1, 1960, p.5–19.

McKee, A. F.   The Market Principle and Roman Catholic Thought. *Kyklos*, 17/1, 1964, p.65–83.

Meislin, B. J. and Cohen, M. L.   Background of the Biblical Law Against Usury. *Comp. Stud. Society Hist.*, 6, 1963–64, p.250–67.

Mendelsohn, E.   The Jewish Socialist Movement and the Second International, 1889–1914. *Jew. Soc. Stud.*, 3, 1964, p.131–45.

Miller, R. J. Buddhist Monastic Economy: The Jisa Mechanism. *Comp. Stud. Society Hist.*, 3/4, 1960–61, p.427–39.

Miller, R. M. American Protestantism and the Abolition of the Twelve-Hour Day in the Steel Strike, 1919–23. *Southw. Soc. Sci. Quart.*, 37/2, 1956, p.137–48.

Millican, C. N. *Church Financing by Financial Institutions in the United States, 1946-1952.* Gainesville, Florida: Univ. of Florida Press, 1954.

Mintz, J. S. *Mohammed, Marx and Marhaen: The Roots of Indonesian Socialism.* N.Y.: F. A. Praeger, 1965, 246p.

Misha, V. *Hinduism and Economic Growth.* Bombay: Oxford Univ. Press, 1962, 219p.

Mohan, R. P. (ed.) *Technology and Christian Culture.* Washington: Catholic Univ. Press, 1960, 144p.

Monroe, P. English and American Christian Socialism. *Amer. J. Sociol.*, 1/1, 1895, p.50–68.

Morgan, B. *Christians, the Church and Property: Ethics and the Economy in a Supramarket World.* Phila.: Westminster Press, 1963.

Muelder, W. G. *Religion and Economic Responsibility.* N.Y.: Scribner's, 1953.

Munby, D. L. *God and the Rich Society: A Study of Christians in a World of Abundance.* London: Oxford Univ. Press, 1961, 209p.

Nelson, B. *Religious Traditions and the Spirit of Capitalism: From the Church Fathers to Jeremy Bentham.* N.Y.: Harper & Row, 1964.

Niehoff, A. Caste and Industrial Organization in North India. *Admin. Sci. Quart.*, 3/4, 1959, p.494–508.

Niida, N. The Industrial and Commercial Guilds of Peking and Religion and Fellow Countrymanship as Elements of Their Coherence. *Folkl. Stud.*, 9, 1950, p.179–206.

Oberg, K. A Comparison of Three Systems of Primitive Economic Organization. *Amer. Anthropol.*, 45, 1943, p.572–87.

O'Farrell, P. J. The History of the New South Wales Labor Movement, 1880–1910: A Religious Interpretation. *J. Rel. Hist.*, 2/1, 1962, p.133–51.

Orenstein, D. E. Exploration of Function in the Interpretation of Jajmani. *Southw. J. Anthropol.*, 18/4, 1962, p.302–16.

Perry, E. L. Socio-Economic Factors and American Fundamentalism. *R. Rel. Res.*, 1/2, 1959, p.57–61.

Pieris, R. Economic Development and Ultramundaneity. *Archiv. Sociol. Rel.*, 8/15, 1963, p.95–100.

Pirinen, K. The Bible and the Account Book. *Turku Instit. Sociol.*, 6, 1959, p.147–53.

Pitcher, A. The Church and the American Achievement Culture. *Foundations*, 3, 1960, p.292–305.

Pocock, D. F. Notes on Jajmani Relationships. *Contrib. Ind. Sociol.*, 6, 1962, p.78–95.

Raftis, J. A. Western Monasticism and Economic Organization. *Comp. Stud. Society Hist.*, 3/4, 1960–61, p.452–70.

Rasmussen, A. T. *Christian Responsibility in Economic Life: Christian Perspectives on Social Problems.* Phila.: Westminster Press, 1965.

Reich, N. The Role of the Jews in the American Economy. *Yivo Ann. Jew. Soc. Sci.*, 5, 1950, p.197–204.

Ryan, J. A. and Johnson, F. E. (eds.) Industrial Relations and the Churches. *Ann. Amer. Acad. Polit. Soc. Sci.*, 103, 1923, p.1–143.

Samuelsson, K. *Religion and Economic Action* (Trans. E. G. French). N.Y.: Harper & Row, 1964.

Saran, A. K. Hinduism and Economic Development in India. *Archiv. Sociol. Rel.*, 8/15, 1963, p.87–94.

Sargent, L. Occupational Status in a Religious Group. *R. Rel. Res.*, 4/3, 1963, p.149–55.

Schmidt, A. Some Notes on the Influence of Religion on Economics in a Likar Subculture, West Africa. *Afr. Stud.*, 10/1, 1951, p.13–26.

Schwantes, R. S. Religion and Modernization in the Far East: Christianity Versus Science—A Conflict of Ideas in Meiji Japan. *Far East. Quart.*, 12/2, 1953, p.123–32.

Selsam, H. and Martel, H. (eds.) *Reader in Marxist Philosophy: From the Writings of Marx, Engels, and Lenin.* N.Y.: International Publishers, 1963, 384p.

Sharma, K. N. Occupational Mobility of Castes in a North Indian Village. *Southw. J. Anthropol.*, 17/2, 1961, p.146–64.

Sharma, R. S. Usury in Early Medieval India (A.D. 400–1200). *Comp. Stud. Society Hist.*, 8/1, 1965, p.56–77.

Sheikh, N. A. *Some Aspects of the Constitution and the Economics of Islam.* Woking, Surrey: The Woking Muslim Mission and Literary Trust, 1961, 246p.

Siefer, G. *The Church and Industrial Society: A Survey of the Worker-Priest Movement and Its Implications for the Christian Mission.* London: Darton, Longman and Todd, 1964, 355p.

Smith, R. W. Religious Influences in the Background of the British Labour Party. *Southw. Soc. Sci. Quart.*, 37/4, 1957, p.355–69.

Smythe, H. H. and Katz, D. The Jew in American Labor and Industry. *J. Hum. Relat.*, 3/3, 1955, p.22–9.

Spargo, J. Christian Socialism in America. *Amer. J. Sociol.*, 15/1, 1910, p.16–20.

Stein, B. The Economic Function of a Medieval South Indian Temple. *J. Asian Stud.*, 19/2, 1960, p.163–176.

Tawney, R. H. Religious Thought on Social and Economic Questions in the Sixteenth and Seventeenth Centuries. *J. Polit. Econ.*, I The Medieval Background. 31, 1923, p.461–93; II The Collision of Standards, 31, 1923, p.637–74; III The Social Ethics of Puritanism, 31, 1923, p.804–25.

Thorner, I. Ascetic Protestantism, Gambling and the One-Price System. *Amer. J. Econ. Sociol.*, 15/2, 1956, p.161–72.

Timasheff, N. S. Nationalization in Europe and the Catholic Social Doctrine. *Amer. Cath. Sociol. R.*, 8/2, 1947, p.111–30.

Trigger, B. G. The Jesuits and the Fur Trade. *Ethnohistory*, 12/1, 1965, p.30–53.

Twitchett, D. C. The Monasteries and China's Economy in Medieval Times. *Bull. School Orient. Afr. Stud.*, 12/3, 1957, p.526–49.

Watson, G. How Christian Pacifists View the Class Struggle. *J. Educ. Sociol.*, 9/3, 1935, p.130–41.

Wax, M. Ancient Judaism and the Protestant Ethic. *Amer. J. Sociol.*, 65/5, 1960, p.449–55.

Weber, M. *The Protestant Ethic and the Spirit of Capitalism* (Trans. T. Parsons). N.Y.: Scribners, 1958.

Wertheim, W. F. Religion, Bureaucracy and Economic Growth. In *Transactions of the Fifth World Congress of Sociology, Washington, D.C., 1962.* Louvain: International Sociological Association, 1964, p.73–86, vol. III.

Wichmann, A. A. Buddhism, Economic Development, and Neutralism in Burma. *Southw. Soc. Sci. Quart.*, 46/1, 1965, p.20–7.

Yamamoto, T. and Yamamoto, S. Religion and Modernization in the Far East: The Anti-Christian Movement in China, 1922–1927. *Far East. Quart.*, 12/2, 1953, p.133–48.

Zweig, F. The Jewish Trade Union Movement in Israel. *Jew. J. Sociol.*, 1/1, 1959, p.23–42.

See Also: 4a, 1f, 8a6

Allensmith, W. 7b3
Andreski, S. 5a2
Antonovsky, A. 4f1
Bailey, F. G. 4j1
Baltzell, E. D. 4j3
Bellah, R. 6e

Bester, A. E., Jr. 3a
Boisen, A. T. 6e
Boulding, K. 6b
Brooks, H. E. 5b2
Cantril, H. 4g
Considine, J. 5e
Cronin, J. F. 5
Curry, J. E. 4a1
Deshen, S. A. 6a
Dicker, H. 2b
Donnelly, J. F. 7a3
Dubalen, M. T. 7a1
Dynes, R. R. 4j3
Ebert, M. L. 6
Eister, A. W. 2d
Fanfani, A. 8a2
Frumkin, R. M. 5b1
Fry, C. L. 4a
George, C. H. 7b3
Goldstein, B. 6c
Griswold, A. W. 2a1
Gustafson, J. 7b3
Harris, M. D. 4f2
Hill, C. 8a6
Hodson, W. 3a
Hughes, E. C. 3a2
Inglis, K. S. 3a
Isaac, J. 4f
Karson, M. 4a1
Kosa, J. 4e, 8a6
Landon, F. C. 4a
Leslie, P. 7a
Lestchinsky, J. 3b
Marx, K. 8a2
Mendelsohn, E. 4b
Merrill, G. 3b
Mittler, R. 7a1
Parsons, T. 8a6
Petrie, J. 7a
Pope, L. 6a
Reese, T. R. 3a1
Reyburn, W. D. 4e
Robertson, A. 8a1
Rowe, W. L. 6e
Samuelsson, K. 8a6
Schnepp, G. J. 7d
Schütte, K. H. 5e1
Scoville, W. C. 5a2
Taylor, R. W. 6
Verma, B. C. 3
Veroff, J. 7b3
Ward, H. F. 4a1
Wearnouth, R. F. 6b
White, E. A. 7b3

4c. Religion and Child-Rearing Practices

Aptekman, D. M. Causes of the Vitality of the Ceremony of Baptism Under Modern Conditions. *Soviet Sociol.*, 4/2, 1965, p.10–6.

Barnett, L. D. The Kibbutz as a Child-Rearing System: A Review of the Literature. *J. Marr. Fam.*, 27/3, 1965, p.348–9.

Batten, S. Z. The Church as a Maker of Conscience. *Amer. J. Sociol.*, 7/5, 1902, p.611–28.

Bushnell, J. La Virgen De Gudalupe as Surrogate Mother in San Juan Atzingo. *Amer. Anthropol.*, 60/2, 1958, p.261–5.

Carstairs, G. M. Hindu Personality Formation—Unconscious Processes. *R. Int. D'Ethnopsychol. Norm. Pathol.*, 1/1, 1956, p.5–18.

Eaton, J. W. Adolescence in a Communal Society. *Ment. Hyg.*, 48/1, 1964, p.66–73.

Fichter, J. H. Religion and Socialization Among Children. *R. Rel. Res.*, 4, 1962, p.24–33.

Fishman, J. Childhood Indoctrination for Minority Group Membership. *Daedalus*, 90, 1961, p.329–49.

Gans, W. G. Enforceability of Antenuptial Agreements Providing for the Religious Education of Children. *J. Fam. Law*, 1, 1961, p.227–40.

Godin, A. and Van Roey, B. Immanent Justice and Divine Protection. *Lumen Vitae*, 14/1, 1959, p.129–48.

Greeley, A. M. *Strangers in the House: Catholic Youth in America.* N.Y.: Sheed and Ward, 1961, 179p.

Harms, E. The Development of Religious Experience in Children. *Amer. J. Sociol.*, 50/2, 1944, p.112–22.

Hess, R. D. and Torney, J. V. Religion, Age and Sex in Children's Perception of Family Authority. *Child Devel.*, 33/4, 1962, p.781–9.

Horton, P. B. The Church as a Socializing Agency. *J. Educ. Sociol.*, 15/1, 1941, p.46–54.

Josephina, S. A Study of Some Religious Terms for Six-Year Old Children. *Rel. Educ.*, 56, 1961, p.24–5.

Keith-Lucas, A. *The Church Children's Home in a Changing World.* Chapel Hill: Univ. of North Carolina Press, 1962, 92p.

Koppe, W. A. and Wright, H. D. Children's Potential Religious Concepts. *Character Potential*, 2/2, 1964, p.83–96.

Kunz, P. R. Religious Influences on Paternal Discipline and Achievement Demands. *Marr. Fam. Liv.*, 25/2, 1963, p.224–5.

Lehrer, L. The Psychology of the Jewish Child in America. *Yivo Ann. Jew. Soc. Sci.*, 1, 1946, p.195–216.

Malewska, H. E. Religious Puritanism. Rigid Ethics and Severity in Upbringing. *Polish Sociol.*, 1/2, 1961, p.71–8.

McGovern, C. *Services to Children in Institutions.* Washington: National Conference of Catholic Charities, 1948, 452p.

Merzbach, A. Home Punishment of Children in the Jewish Community of Palestine: A Survey of Two Thousand Five Hundred Jewish Children. *Hum. Relat.*, 2/4, 1949, p.305–18.

Mintz, S. W. and Wolf, E. R. An Analysis of Ritual Co-Parenthood (Compadrazgo). *Southw. J. Anthropol.*, 6/4, 1950, p.341–68.

Nash, D. and Berger, P. The Child, The Family and the 'Religious Revival' in Suburbia. *J. Sci. Stud. Rel.*, 2/1, 1962, p.85–93.

Parsons, R. T. Kono Religion and Preparation for Adult Life. *Sierra Leone Bull. Rel.*, 3/1, 1961, p.11–5.

Press, I. The Incidence of Compadrazgo Among Puerto Ricans in Chicago. *Sociol. Econ. Stud.*, 12, 1963, p.475–80.

Rakes, W. R. Equity and the Antenuptial Agreement to Raise Children in a Particular Religion. *J. Fam. Law*, 4, 1964, p.53–62.

Smith, R. Spiritual, Ethical and Moral Values for Children in Foster Care. *Child Wel.*, 40, 1961, p.20–4. See also: Butters, R.—Comments: How to Help Children Develop Spiritual, Ethical and Moral Values, p.24–6.

Syden, M. Religious Education for the Jewish Retarded Child. *Amer. J. Ment. Defic.*, 64, 1960, p.689–94.

Thomas, J. L. Religious Blackout of the Pre-School Child. *America*, 36, 1952, p.608–10.

Thomas, J. L. Religious Training in the Roman Catholic Family. *Amer. J. Sociol.*, 57/2, 1951, p.178–83.

Underwood, F. W. and Honigmann, I. A Comparison of Socialization and Personality in Two Simple Societies. *Amer. Anthropol.*, 49, 1947, p.557–77.

Wiesinger, R. The Parent-Daughter Relationship Among the Hindus. *Sociologus*, 15/2, 1965, p.143–61.

Zenter, H. Durkheim, Mental Health and Religious Socialization. *Sociol. Inq.* 34/1, 1964, p.92–107.

Carey, M. A.   4e
Elkind, D.   7b2 (2)
Koppe, W. A.   4g

Putney, S.   5g
Shirley, R. W.   4i
Synon, M.   7b3

4d.   Religion and Ethical Behavior

Ames, E. S.   Morale and Religion. *Amer. J. Sociol.*, 47/3, 1941, p.384–93.

Beach, W.   Freedom and Authority in Protestant Ethics. *J. Rel.*, 32/1, 1952, p.108–18.

Beach, W. and Niebuhr, H. R. (eds.) *Christian Ethics: Sources of the Living Tradition*. N.Y.: Ronald Press, 1955, 496p.

Bennett, J. C.   *Christian Ethics and Social Policy*. N.Y. Scribners, 1946.

Bergman, R. D.   Group Standards in a Protestant Congregation. *R. Rel. Res.*, 4/2, 1963, p.96–104.

Binkley, O. T.   *The Churches and the Social Conscience*. Indianapolis: National Foundation Press, 1949, 39p.

Birmingham, W. and Cunneen, J. E. (eds.) *Cross Currents of Psychiatry and Catholic Morality*. N.Y.: Pantheon, 1964, 396p.

Bishop, S. H.   The Church and Charity. *Amer. J. Sociol.*, 18/3, 1912, p.369–80.

Bolles, R. C.   Psychological Determinism and the Problem of Morality. *J. Sci. Stud. Rel.*, 2/2, 1963, p.182–9.

Bonhoeffer, D.   *Ethics* (Ed. E. Bethge; Trans. N. H. Smith). London: SCM Press, 1955, 342p.

Brandt, R. B.   *Hopi Ethics: A Theoretical Analysis*. Chicago: Univ. of Chicago Press, 1954, 398p.

Brown, P.   Religious Morality. *Mind*, 72/286, 1963, p.235–44.

Brown, W.   Emotions and Morals. *Sociol. R.*, 5/3, 1912, p.215–33.

Calhoun, R. L.   Moral Obligation and Religious Conviction. *Confluence*, 4/2, 1955, p.174–93.

Campbell, J.   *Honour, Family and Patronage: A Study of Institutions and Moral Values in a Greek Mountain Community*. Oxford: Clarendon Press, 1964, 393p.

Carlson, E. M.   *The Church and the Public Conscience*. Phila.: Muhlenberg Press, 1956, 104p.

Cary-Elwes, C.   *Law, Liberty and Love: A Study in Christian Obedience*. London: Holder & Sons, 1950, 256p.

Cleveland, H. and Lasswell, H. D. (eds.) *Ethics and Bigness: Scientific, Academic, Religious, Political, and Military*. N.Y.: Harper, 1962, 542p.

Dahlke, H. O.   Values and Group Behavior in Two Camps

for Conscientious Objectors. *Amer. J. Sociol.*, 51/1, 1945, p.22–33.

Dasgupta, S. *Development of Moral Philosophy in India*. N.Y.: Frederick Ungar, 1965, 246p.

Dawson, C.   Civilization and Morals. *Sociol. R.*, 17/3, 1925, p.174–81.

Donaldson, D. M.   *Studies in Muslim Ethics*. London: S.P.C.K., 1953.

Dumond, D. L.   Democracy and Christian Ethics. *J. Negro Hist.*, 46/1, 1961, p.1–11.

Ellis, A.   Does Morality Require Religious Sanction? *Controversy*, 1, 1959, p.24–8.

Fisher, G. W.   Toward a Christian Social Ethic and Action. *Rel. Life*, 27, 1958, p.199–207.

Friedman, M.   Social Responsibility in Judaism. *J. Rel. Health*, 2/1, 1962, p.42–60.

Friedman, M.   The Transmoral Morality. *J. Sci. Stud. Rel.*, 3/2, 1964, p.174–80. See also: N. Piedescalzi–Comments, 4/2, 1965, p.237–42; M. Friedman–Reply, p.242–6.

Gauchhwal, B. S.   The Sphere and Significance of Ethics, Morality and Religion in Hindu Tradition. *Philos. East West*, 13/4, 1964, p.339–659.

Gokhale, B. G.   The Buddhist Social Ideals. *Ind. Hist. Quart.*, 32/2-3, 1956, p.141–7.

Gross, L.   *God and Freud: Religion Looks Anew at Love and Sin*. N.Y.: David McKay, 1959, 215p.

Hall, R. K.   *Shūshin: The Ethics of a Defeated Nation*. N.Y.: Teachers College, Columbia Univ. Press, 1949, 244p.

Harper, E. B.   Hoylu: A Belief Relating Justice and the Supernatural. *Amer. Anthropol.*, 59/5, 1957, p.801–16.

Henry, C. F. H.   *Aspects of Christian Social Ethics*. Grand Rapids: W. R. Eerdmans, 1964.

Hiltner, S.   Clinical and Theological Notes on Responsibility. *J. Rel. Health*, 2/1, 1962, p.7–20.

Jaffe, N. F.   The Dynamics of Benefice Among East European Jews. *Soc. Forces*, 27/3, 1949, p.238–47.

Johnson, G. B., Jr.   Do Holiness Sects Socialize in Dominant Values? *Soc. Forces*, 39/4, 1961, p.309–16.

Karnik, H. R.   Morals in the Brahmanas (Based on Legends Found in Them). *J. Univ. Bombay*, 28/2, 1959, p.85–127.

Kaufmann, W. *Religion from Tolstoy to Camus: Basic Writings on Religious Truth and Morals*. N.Y.: Harper, 1951.

Kenney, J. F. The Principle of Subsidiarity. *Amer. Cath. Sociol. R.*, 16/1, 1955, p.31–7.

King, W. L. *In the Hope of Nibbana: Essay on the Theravada Buddhist Ethics*. London: Luzac, 1964, 298p.

Korth, F. N. Moral Philosophy in Church Law. *Hosp. Progr.*, 40, 1959, p.87.

Lacy, C. *Conscience of India: Moral Traditions in the Modern World*. N.Y.: Holt, Rinehart & Winston, 1965, 299p.

London, P., *et al.* Religion, Guilt and Ethical Standards. *J. Soc. Psychol.*, 63, 1964, p.145–59.

MacBeath, A. *The Relationship of Primitive Morality and Religion*. Glascow: Jackson, Son & Co., 1949.

Maclagan, W. G. *The Theological Frontier of Ethics*. London: George Allen and Unwin, 1961, 202p.

Madden, W. A. Victorian Morality: Ethics not Mysterious. *R. Polit.*, 23/4, 1961, p.458–71.

Mattuck, I. I. *Jewish Ethics*. London: Hutchinson's, 1953.

McCullough, J. R. Indian Theism and the Importance of Moral Acts. *R. Rel.*, 21/1–2, 1956, p.5–16.

McLaughlin, W. G. Pietism and the American Character. *Amer. Quart.*, 17/2, 1965, p.163–86.

Messenger, J. C., Jr. The Christian Concept of Forgiveness and Anang Morality. *Pract. Anthropol.*, 6/3, 1959, p.97–102.

Middleton, R. and Putney, S. Religion, Normative Standards and Behavior. *Sociometry*, 25/2, 1962, p.141–52.

Midgley, L. C. Paul Tillich's New Science of Values. *West. Polit. Quart.*, 15/2, 1962, p.235–53.

Morris, J. F. Symposium: The Development of Moral Values in Children: II The Development of Adolescent Value Judgements. *Brit. J. Educ. Psychol.*, 28, 1958, p.1–14.

Mueller, F. H. The Principle of Subsidiarity in the Christian Tradition. *Amer. Cath. Sociol. R.*, 4/3, 1943, p.144–57.

Niebuhr, H. R. *The Responsible Self*. N.Y.: Harper and Row, 1963, 183p.

Parsons, E. C. Links Between Religion and Morality in Early Culture. *Amer. Anthropol.*, 17, 1915, p.41–57.

Payne, E. K. Nurturing Ethical Growth in College. *J. Hum. Relat.*, 2/2, 1954, p.44–59.

Phillips, D. Z. Moral and Religious Conceptions of Duty: An Analysis. *Mind*, 73/291, 1964, p.406–12.

Pike, E. R. *Ethics of the Great Religions, With Some Account of Their Origins, Scriptures and Practices*. London: Watts, 1948, 247p.

Pitcher, A. Darwinism and Christian Ethics. *J. Rel.*, 40/4, 1960, p.256–66.

Poffenberger, T. and Olmsted, D. Human Behavior in Times of "Morality" and "Piety". *Merr.–Palm. Quart.*, 5/1, 1958, p.23–45.

Powers, R. H. The Earthly City of Jean-Jacques Rousseau. *Southw. Soc. Sci. Quart.*, 40/2, 1959, p.125–38.

Putney, S. and Middleton, R. Ethical Relativism and Anomia. *Amer. J. Sociol.*, 67/4, 1962, p.430–8.

Rahbar, D. *God of Justice: A Study in the Ethical Doctrine of the Qur'an*. N.Y.: Humanities Press, 1961.

Ramsey, P. *Basic Christian Ethics*. N.Y.: Scribners, 1950, 404p.

Ramsey, P. (ed.) *Faith and Ethics: The Theology of H. Richard Niebuhr*. N.Y.: Harper, 1957, 314p.

Retting, S. and Pasamanick, B. Changes in Moral Value Over Three Decades, 1929–1958. *Soc. Problems*, 6, 1959, p.320–8.

Retting, S. and Pasamanick, B. Invariance in Factor Structure of Moral Value Judgements From American and Korean College Students. *Sociometry*, 25/1, 1962, p.73–84.

Satterwhite, J. H. The Bible in Theology and Ethics. *J. Bib. Rel.*, 19, 1951, p.63–6, 80.

Schenk, W. *The Concern for Social Justice in the Puritan Revolution*. N.Y.: Longmans, Green & Co., 1948.

Searle, R. W. The Church's Responsibility for Good Citizenship. *Amer. J. Econ. Sociol.*, 9/1, 1947, p.117–24.

Sellers, J. E. *The South and Christian Ethics*. N.Y.: Association Press, 1962, 190p.

Shaw, D. and Campbell, E. Internalizations of a Moral Norm and External Support. *Sociol. Quart.*, 3, 1962, p.57–71.

Sorokin, P. A. *The Ways and Power of Love: Types, Factors, and Techniques of Moral Transformation*. Boston: Beacon Press, 1954.

Thompson, K. W. *Christian Ethics and the Dilemmas of Foreign Policy*. Durham: Duke Univ. Press, 1959.

Tibawi, A. L. The Idea of Guidance in Islam From an Educational Point of View. *Islamic Quart.*, 3/2, 1956, p.139–56.

Titus, H. H. Christian Ethics and Contemporary Social Issues. *J. Bib. Rel.*, 15, 1947, p.215–9.

Turner, V. W. Ritual Symbolism, Morality and Social Structure Among the Ndembu. *Hum. Prob. Brit. Centr. Afr.*, 30, 1961, p.1–10.

Upadhye, A. N. The Ethics of the Jainas. *Indo-Asian Cult.*, 5/2, 1956, p.183–91.

Wallis, L. Social Conscience and the Bible. *Amer. J. Econ. Sociol.*, 3/4, 1944, p.613–29.

Welty, E. *Handbook of Christian Social Ethics*. N.Y.: Herder & Co., 1960, 4 vols.

Winter, G. Society and Morality: The French Tradition. *R. Rel. Res.*, 5/1, 1963, p.11–21.

See Also: 1c, 2g, 3f, 4, 5c, 7

Albert, E. M. 9
Ballard, E. G. 7c
Bennett, J. C. 5b2
Bidwell, C. E. 4g
Boehm, L. 5a3
Bokser, B. Z. 7a2
Campbell, E. Q. 7a3 (2)
Chung, A. 7a1
Dore, R. P. 4f1
Dougherty, D. 7b3

Ferm, V. 9
Folsom, J. K. 8a2
Forde, D. 2h
Friedrichs, R. W. 4j2
Furfey, P. H. 7a2
Griffin, C. S. 6a
Harmond, N. B. 7a2
Harms, E. 7b
Hastings, J. 9
Hodges, D. C. 4j3
Holbrook, C. A. 4g6
Holloway, C. 4a
James, W. 8a2
Jonasson, C. 4b
Lasswell, H. D. 4a
MacKinnon, F. B. 1c
Martinos, A. 9
Meyer, A. E. 1e
Naess, A. 8a2
Papanek, H. 1e
Parker, A. 6d
Robertson, D. B. 4a
Sanders, I. T. 4e
Thomas, G. F. 1c
Williams, R. M. 5a2

4e. *Religion and Marriage and the Family*

Anderson, N. The Mormon Family. *Amer. Sociol. R.*, 2, 1937, p.601–8.

Baber, R. E. Religion and the Family. *Ann. Amer. Acad. Polit. Soc. Sci.*, 256, 1948, p.92–100.

Baker, L. G., Jr. Changing Religious Norms and Family Values. *J. Marr. Fam.*, 27/1, 1965, p.6–12.

Bardis, P. D. Familism Among Jews in Suburbia. *Soc. Sci.*, 36/3, 1961, p.190–6.

Bardis, P. D. Main Features of the Ancient Hebrew Family. *Soc. Sci.*, 38/3, 1963, p.168–83.

Barta, R. and O'Reilly, C. T. Some Dating Patterns and Attitudes Toward Marriage of 174 Catholic College Students. *Amer. Cath. Sociol. R.*, 13/3, 1952, p.240–8.

Bell, R. R. and Plumberg, L. Courtship, Intimacy and Religious Background. *Marr. Fam. Liv.*, 21/4, 1959, p.356–60.

Berger, P. L. and Nash, D. The Child, the Family, and the "Religious Revival" in Suburbia. *J. Sci. Stud. Rel.*, 2/1, 1962, p.85–93.

Brav, S. R. (ed.) *Marriage and the Jewish Traditions: Toward a Modern Philosophy of Family Living*. N.Y.: Philosophical Library, 1951, 218p.

Brown, B. F. The Relation of Theology and Philosophy to the Forms of Marriage. *J. Fam. Law*, 1/1, 1961, p.126–37.

Burchinal, L. G., *et al.* Comparison of State and Diocese-Reported Marriage Data for Iowa 1953–57. *Amer. Cath. Sociol. R.*, 23/1, 1962, p.21–9.

Burchinal, L. G. Marital Satisfaction and Religious Behavior. *Amer. Sociol. R.*, 22, 1957, p.306–10.

Carey, M. A. *A Bibliography for Christian Formation in the Family*. Glen Rock, New Jersey: Paulist Press, 1964, 175p.

Chamberlayne, J. H. Kinship Relationships Among the Early Hebrews. *Numen*, 10/2, 1963, p.153–64.

Chatterjee, H. Conception of Hindu Marriage. *Calcutta R.*, 141/2, 1956, p.147–52.

Chites, T., *et al.* An Experiment in Marriage Counseling by Three New Jersey Churches. *Past. Psychol.*, 12, 1961, p.29–34.

Christensen, H. T. Mormon Fertility: A Survey of Student Opinion. *Amer. J. Sociol.*, 53/4, 1948, p.270–5.

Christensen, H. T. and Cannon, K. L. Temple Versus Nontemple Marriages in Utah: Some Demographic Considerations. *Soc. Sci.*, 39/1, 1964, p.26–33.

Christina, M. Study of the Catholic Family Through Three Generations. *Amer. Cath. Sociol. R.*, 3/3, 1942, p.144–53.

Clemens, A. M. *Marriage and the Family: An Integrated Approach for Catholics.* Englewood Cliffs, New Jersey: Prentice-Hall, 1957, 356p.

Dohen, D. Religious Practice and Marital Patterns in Puerto Rico. *Amer. Cath. Sociol. R.*, 20/3, 1959, p.203–18.

Dyer, D. T. and Luckey, E. B. Religious Affiliation and Selected Personality Scores as They Relate to Marital Happiness of a Minnesota College Sample. *Marr. Fam. Liv.*, 23/1, 1961, p.40–7.

El Daghestani, K. The Evolution of the Moslem Family in the Middle Eastern Countries. *Int. Soc. Sci. Bull.*, 5/4, 1953, p.681–91.

Fairchild, R. W. and Wynn, J. C. *Families in the Church: A Protestant Survey.* N.Y.: Association Press, 1961.

Falkenberg, J. *Kin and Totem: Group Relations of Australian Aborigines in the Port Keats District.* N.Y.: Humanities Press, 1962, 272p.

Fodor, R. The Impact of the Nazi Occupation of Poland on the Jewish Mother-Child Relation. *Yivo Ann. Jew. Soc. Sci.*, 11, 1956-57, p.270–85.

Franzblau, A. N. A New Look at the Psychodynamics of Jewish Family Living. *J. Jew. Comm. Serv.*, 35, 1958, p.57–71.

Gough, E. K. Brahman Kinship in a Tamil Village. *Amer. Anthropol.*, 58/5, 1956, p.826–53.

Harries, L. Mission Research and the African Marriage Survey. *Int. R. Missions*, 39, 1950, p.94–9.

Harrison, C. Religion and Family Among the Haidas (Queen Charlotte Islands). *Anthropol. Inst. Great Brit. J.*, 21, 1892, p.14–27.

Hatch, D. L. and Hatch, M. G. An Unhappy Family: Some Observations on the Relationship Between the Calvinistic Ethic and Interpersonal Relations over Four Generations. *Marr. Fam. Liv.*, 24/3, 1962, p.213–23.

Hulett, J. E., Jr. Social Role and Personal Security in Mormon Polygamy. *Amer. J. Sociol.*, 45/4, 1940, p.542–53.

Joffe, N. F. *The American Jewish Family: A Study.* N.Y.: National Council of Jewish Women, 1954, 41p.

Jones, A. H. Sex, Educational and Religious Influences on Moral Judgements Relative to the Family. *Amer. Sociol. R.*, 8, 1943, p.405–11.

Kapadia, K. M. Changing Patterns of Hindu Marriage and Family. *Sociol. Bull.* (Bombay), 4/2, 1955, p.161–92.

Kapadia, K. M. *Marriage and Family in India.* London: Oxford Univ. Press, 1958, 318p.

Katz, J. Family, Kinship and Marriage Among Ashkenazim in the Sixteenth to Eighteenth Centuries. *Jew. J. Sociol.*, 1/1, 1959, p.4–22.

Kauffman, J. H. Interpersonal Relations in Traditional and Emergent Families Among Midwest Mennonites. *Marr. Fam. Liv.*, 23, 1961, p.247–52.

Kimwra, Y. Religious Affiliation of War Brides in Hawaii and Their Marital Adjustment. *Soc. Process*, 26, 1963, p.88–95.

Kosa, J., *et al.* Marriage, Career and Religiousness Among Catholic College Girls. *Marr. Fam. Liv.*, 24/4, 1962, p.376–80.

Kuper, H. An Interpretation of Hindu Marriages in Durban. *Afr. Stud.*, 16/4, 1957, p.221–35.

Kurian, G. *The Indian Family in Transition: A Case Study of Kerala Syrian Christians.* Hague: Mouton Co., 1961, 142p.

Landis, J. T. Religiousness, Family Relationships, and Family Values in Protestant, Catholic and Jewish Families. *Marr. Fam. Liv.*, 22/4, 1960, p.341–7.

Layard, J. On Psychic Consciousness. *Eranos Jahrbuch*, 28, 1959, p.277–344.

Levine, R. A. Witchcraft and Co-Wife Proximity in Southwestern Kenya. *Ethnology*, 1/1, 1962, p.39–45.

Lowy, S. The Extent of Jewish Polygamy in Talmudic Times. *J. Jew. Stud.*, 9/3-4, 1958, p.115–38.

Mace, D. R. *Hebrew Marriage: A Sociological Study.* N.Y.: Philosophical Library, 1953, 271p.

Madan, T. Is the Brahmanic Gotra a Grouping of Kin? *Southw. J. Anthropol.*, 18/1, 1962, p.59–75.

Madan, T. The Hindu Joint Family. *Man*, 62, 1962, p.88–9.

Malinowski, B. *The Family Among the Australian Aborigines: A Sociological Study.* N.Y.: Schocken Books, 1963, 322p.

Mandelbaum, D. G. The Family in India. *Southw. J. Anthropol.*, 4/2, 1948, p.123–39.

Mitchell, W. E. Descent Groups Among New York City Jews. *Jew. J. Sociol.*, 3/1, 1961, p.121–8.

Moray, V. E. The Patterns of Caste and Family in Wai Taluka. *J. Univ. Bombay*, 28/1, 1959, p.74–5.

Mudd, E. and Krich, A. (eds.) *Man and Wife.* N.Y.: Norton and Co., 1957.

Nahas, K. The Family in the Arab World. *Marr. Fam. Liv.*, 16/4, 1954, p.293–300.

Nelson, L. Education and the Changing Size of Mormon Families. *Rural Sociol.*, 17, 1952, p.335–42.

O'Leary, M. The Catholic Marriage Advisory Council. *Clergy R.*, 16, 1961, p.463–9.

Parson, R. T. Kono Religion and Marriage and Procreation. *Sierra Leone Bull. Rel.*, 2/1, 1960, p.11–7.

Phillips, A. (ed.) *Survey of African Marriage and Family Life.* N.Y.: Oxford Univ. Press, 1953, 462p.

Prasad, T. Fate of a Barren Woman in Hindu Society. *Ind. Folklore*, 2/1, 1959, p.15–9.

Reggs, M. D. Protestant Family Life Education: Current Theory and Practice. *Marr. Fam. Liv.*, 19/3, 1957, p.253–5.

Reis, R. H. and Hoene, R. A Study of Catholic Consanguineous Marriages. *Amer. Eccles. R.*, 142, 1960, p.145–63.

Reuss, C. Research Findings on the Effects of Modern Day Religion on Family Living. *Marr. Fam. Liv.*, 16/3, 1954, p.221–5.

Reyburn, W. D. Polygamy, Economy and Christianity in the Eastern Cameroons. *Pract. Anthropol.*, 6/1, 1959, p.1–19.

Rosenfeld, H. An Analysis of Marriage and Marriage Statistics for a Moslem and Christian Arab Village. *Int. Archiv. Ethnogr.*, 48/1, 1957, p.32–62.

Samenfink, J. A. A Study of Some Aspects of Marital Behavior as Related to Religious Control. *Marr. Fam. Liv.*, 20/2, 1958, p.163–9.

Sanders, I. T. *The Community: An Introduction to a Social System.* N.Y.: Ronald Press, 1958.

Sarma, J. Formal and Informal Relations in the Hindu Joint Household of Bengal. *Man India*, 31, 1951, p.57–71.

Schlesinger, B. The Changing Patterns in the Hindu Joint Family System of India. *Marr. Fam. Liv.*, 23, 1961, p.170–5.

Schnepp, G. J. and Roberts, L. Residential Propinquity and Mate Selection on a Parish Basis. *Amer. J. Sociol.*, 58/1, 1952, p.45–50.

Schreiber, W. I. Amish Wedding Days. *J. Amer. Folklore*, 73/287, 1960, p.12–7.

Schull, W., *et al.* Kuroshima: The Impact of Religion on an Island's Genetic Heritage. *Hum. Biol.*, 34/4, 1962, p.271–98.

Selfors, S., *et al.* Values in Mate Selection: Education Versus Religion. *Marr. Fam. Liv.*, 24/2, 1962, p.399–401.

Smith, E. L. *Bundling Among the Amish.* Akron: Applied Arts, 1961, 34p.

Smith, R. T. and Jayawardena, C. Hindu Marriage Customs in British Guiana. *Soc. Econ. Stud.*, 7/2, 1958, p.178–94.

Spooner, B. Kinship and Marriage in Eastern Persia. *Sociologus*, 15/1, 1965, p.22–31.

Symposium: The Family and Religion. *Rel. Educ.*, 52/2, 1957, p.83–132.

Tao, P. L. K. The Family System in China. *Sociol. R.*, 6/1, 1913, p.47–54.

Theophane, M. Family Customs in the Old Testament. *Amer. Cath. Sociol. R.*, 16/3, 1955, p.198–201.

Thomas, J. L. *The Catholic Viewpoint on Marriage and the Family.* N.Y.: Hanover House, 1958, 191p.

Thomas, J. L. Christian Humanism and Marriage. *Soc. Order*, 6/3, 1956, p.110–6.

Thomas, J. L. The Factor of Religion in the Selection of Marriage Mates. *Amer. Sociol. R.*, 16/4, 1951, p.487–91.

Thomas, J. L. Family Values in a Pluralistic Society. *Amer. Cath. Sociol. R.*, 23/1, 1962, p.30–40.

Thomas, J. L. Some Characteristics of CANA Conference Personnel in Chicago. *Amer. Cath. Sociol. R.*, 17/4, 1956, p.338–49.

Thomas, J. L. *The American Catholic Family.* Englewood Cliffs: Prentice-Hall, 1956.

Van Der Kroef, J. M. Woman and the Changing Marriage Patterns of Indonesia. *Amer. Cath. Sociol. R.*, 18/2, 1957, p.113–27.

Vimala, V. C. Symbolism in Marriage Ritual of the South Indian Brahmans. *J. Psychol. Res.*, 1/2, 1957, p.69–78.

Wallin, P. and Clark, A. L. Religiosity, Sexual Gratification and Marital Satisfaction in the Middle Years of Marriage. *Soc. Forces*, 42/3, 1964, p.303–9.

West, R. A. The Mormon Village Family. *Sociol. Soc. Res.*, 23/4, 1939, p.353–9.

Westermarck, E. Marriage Customs in Morocco. *Sociol. R.*, 5/3, 1912, p.187–201.

Wood, L. F. Church Programs in Marriage Education. *Ann. Amer. Acad. Polit. Soc. Sci.*, 272, 1950, p.171–9.

Wu, C. C. The Chinese Family: Organization, Names, and Kinship Terms. *Amer. Anthropol.*, 29, 1927, p.316–25.

Young, K. Sex Roles in Polygynous Mormon Families. In T. M. Newcomb, *et al.* (eds.)—*Readings in Social Psychology.* N.Y.: Henry Holt, 1947, p.373–83.

Young, P. V. The Reorganization of the Jewish Family Life in America. *Soc. Forces*, 7/2, 1928, p.238–44.

See Also: 4c, 4i, 7

Bachi, R.   5b2
Bell, R. R.   5a3
Brenner, A. B.   4i
Buck, C. F.   9
Burchinal, L. G.   4j3 (2)
Busia, K. A.   7b3
Cahnman, W. J.   4j
Campbell, J. K.   4d
Cressman, C. P.   7a1
De Jong, G.   7b2
Denton, W.   7a
Douglas, W.   7a
Faron, L. C.   7b3
Freedman, R.   5b2 (2)
Goode, W. J.   6c
Goodwin, H. M.   7a1
Jaffe, A. J.   5b2
Karve, D. D.   7a
Khatri, A. A.   6c

Kirk, D.   5b2
Koehler, J. G.   7a4
Lehrman, N. S.   8a6
Marie, L.   5b2
Marshall, D. G.   5b2
Mayer, A. J.   5b2
Mulvaney, B.   5b2
Nuesse, C. J.   4f2
Rankin, R. P.   7a1
Ross, A.   4f1
Runeberg, A.   8a5
Sawyerr, H.   8a2
Scanzoni, J.   7a
Stycos, J. M.   7a1
Thomas, J. L.   4f1
Tinque, A. M.   7a1
Wessel, H.   5b
Yaukey, D.   5a3
Young, K.   2a1

4e1.   Divorce

Ayres, J.   Divorce and the Archbishop. *Twent. Cent.*, 157/939, 1955, p.416–22.

Bonnel, J. S.   Counseling with Divorced Persons. *Past. Psychol.*, 9/86, 1958, p.11–5.

Bukowski, A. F.   The Stability of the Marriages of Catholic College Students. *Amer. Cath. Sociol. R.*, 12/1, 1951, p.11–6.

Change of Religion as Grounds for Divorce: Case Note. *J. Fam. Law*, 2, 1962, p.61–6.

Freeman, H. E. and Showel, M.   Familism and Attitude Toward Divorce. *Sociol. Soc. Res.*, 36, 1952, p.312–8.

Kunz, P. R.   Mormon and Non-Mormon Divorce Patterns. *J. Marr. Fam.*, 26/2, 1964, p.211–3.

Monahan, T. R. and Kephart, W. M.   Divorce and Desertion by Religious and Mixed Religious Groups. *Amer. J. Sociol.*, 59/5, 1954, p.454–65.

Rooney, E.   Polish Americans and Family Disorganization. *Amer. Cath. Sociol. R.*, 18/1, 1957, p.47–51.

Sandell, W. L.   Marriage, Divorce and the Church. *Hibbert J.*, 56, 1958, p.235–8.

Sokol, R. P.   Considerations in Advising Episcopal Clients on Divorce: A Study of the Marriage Canons of the Episcopal Church. *J. Fam. Law*, 2, 1962, p.226–40.

Winnett, A. R.   *Divorce and Remarriage in Anglicanism.* N.Y.: St. Martin's Press, 1958, 284p.

4e2.   Marriage Law

Anderson, J. N. D.   Muslim Marriages and the Courts in East Africa. *J. Afr. Law*, 1/1, 1957, p.14–22.

Derrett, J. D. M.   The History of the Juridical Framework of the Joint Hindu Family. *Contrib. Indian Sociol.*, 6, 1962, p.17–47.

Derrett, J. D. M.   Illegitimates: A Test for Modern Hindu Family Law. *J. Amer. Orient. Society*, 81/3, 1961, p.251–61.

Diwan, P.   The Hindu Marriage Act, 1955. *Int. Comp. Law Quart.*, 6/2, 1957, p.263–72.

Farran, D. D'O.   *Matrimonial Law of the Sudan: Being a Study of the Divergent Religious and Civil Laws in an African Society.* London: Butterworths, 1963, 325p.

Faruki, K. A.   Islamic Family Law in Pakistan in the Context of Modern Reformist Movements in the World of Islam. *Islamic R.*, 1965, May, p.5–8; June, p.8–12.

Feroze, M. R.   The Reform of Family Laws in the Muslim World. *Islamic Res.*, 1, 1962, p.109–33.

Finestein, I.   An Aspect of the Jews and English Marriage Law During the Emancipation. *Jew. J. Sociol.*, 7/1, 1965, p.3–21.

Hamid, I. A.   Dissolution of Marriage in Islamic Law. *Islamic Quart.*, 3/3–4, 1957, p.165–76.

Lobingier, C. S.   Primitive Malay Marriage Law. *Amer. Anthropol.*, 12, 1910, p.250–6.

Naamani, I. T.   Marriage and Divorce in Jewish Law. *J. Fam. Law*, 2, 1962, p.177–200.

Sen, S.   The Hindu Marriage Act, 1955. *Mod. R.*, 98/2, 1955, p.120–4.

See Also:

Gulati, I. S.   4b

4e3.   Mixed Marriage

Barron, M. L.   The Incidence of Jewish Intermarriage in Europe and America. *Amer. Sociol. R.*, 11/1, 1946, p.11–2.

Besanceney, P. H.   Interfaith Marriages of Catholics in the Detroit Area. *Sociol. Anal.*, 26/1, 1965, p.38–44.

Besanceney, P. H.   Unbroken Protestant, Catholic Marriages Among Whites in the Detroit Area. *Amer. Cath. Sociol. R.*, 23/1, 1962, p.3–20.

Beuma, D. H.   Religiously Mixed Marriages: Denominational Consequences in the Christian Reformed Church. *Marr. Fam. Liv.*, 25/4, 1963, p.428–32.

Bossard, J. H. S. and Boll, E. S.   *One Marriage, Two Faiths: Guidance on Interfaith Marriage.* N.Y.: Ronald Press, 1957.

Bossard, J. H. S. and Letts, H.   Mixed Marriages Involving Lutherans: A Research Report. *Marr. Fam. Liv.*, 18/4, 1956, p.308–11.

Burchinal, L. G.   Membership Groups and Attitudes Toward Cross-Religious Dating and Marriage. *Marr. Fam. Liv.*, 22, 1960, p.248–53.

Burchinal, L. G. and Chancellor, L. E.   Ages of Marriage, Occupation of Grooms and Interreligious Marriage Rates. *Soc. Forces*, 40/4, 1962, p.348–54.

Burchinal, L. G. and Chancellor, L. E.   *Factors Related to Interreligious Marriages in Iowa, 1953–1957.* Ames: Agricultural and Home Economics Experiment Station, Iowa State Univ. of Science and Technology, 1962.

Burchinal, L. G. and Chancellor, L. E.   Proportions of Catholics, Urbanism, and Mixed-Catholic Marriage Among Iowa Counties. *Soc. Problems*, 9/4, 1962, p.359–65.

Burchinal, L. G. and Chancellor, L. E.   Survival Rates Among Religiously Homogamous and Interreligious Marriages. *Soc. Forces*, 41/4, 1963, p.353–62.

Cahnman, W. J. (ed.)   *Intermarriage and Jewish Life: A Symposium.* N.Y.: The Herzl Press and the Jewish Reconstructionist Press, 1963, 212p.

Chancellor, L. E. and Monahan, T.   Religious Preference and Inter-Religious Mixtures in Marriage and Divorces in Iowa. *Amer. J. Sociol.*, 61/3, 1955, p.233–9.

Cizon, F. A.   Interethnic and Interreligious Marriage Patterns in Parish X. *Amer. Cath. Sociol. R.*, 15/3, 1954, p.244–55.

Engelman, U. Z.   Intermarriage Among Jews in Switzerland, 1888-1920. *Amer. J. Sociol.*, 34, 1928, p.516–23.

Frumkin, R. M.   Jewish-Gentile and Interfaith Dating on a College Campus. *Ethos*, 5/4, 1960, p.5–7.

Glick, P. C.   Intermarriage and Fertility Patterns Among Persons in Major Religious Groups. *Eugenics Quart.*, 7/1, 1960, p.31–8.

Gordon, A. I.   *Intermarriage: Interfaith, Interracial, Interethnic.* Boston: Beacon, 1964.

Heer, D. M.   The Trend of Interfaith Marriages in Canada, 1922-1957. *Amer. Sociol. R.*, 27/2, 1962, p.245–50.

Heiss, J. S.   Interfaith Marriage and Marital Outcome. *Marr. Fam. Liv.*, 23/3, 1961, p.228–33.

Heiss, J. S.   Premarital Characteristics of the Religiously Intermarried in an Urban Area. *Amer. Sociol. R.*, 25, 1960, p.47–55.

Kannan, C. T.   Intercaste Marriage in Bombay. *Sociol. Bull.*, 10/2, 1961, p.53–68.

Kenkel, W. F., *et al.*   Religious Socialization, Present Devoutness and Willingness to Enter a Mixed Religious Marriage. *Sociol. Anal.*, 26/1, 1965, p.30–7.

Kennedy, R. J.   Single or Triple Melting Pot: Intermarriage in New Haven, 1870–1950. *Amer. J. Sociol.*, 58/1, 1953, p.56–9.

Kirshenbaum, D.   *Mixed Marriage and the Jewish Future.* N.Y.: Bloch Publishing Co., 1958, 144p.

Landis, J. T.   Marriages of Mixed and Non-Mixed Religious Faiths. *Amer. Sociol. R.*, 14, 1949, p.401–7.

Leiffer, M. H.   Mixed Marriages and Church Loyalties. *Christ. Cent.*, 66, 1949, p.78–80.

Leiffer, M. H.   Mixed Marriages and the Children. *Christ. Cent.*, 66, 1949, p.106–8.

Levinson, M. and Daniel, J. Jews Who Intermarry. *Yivo Ann. Jew. Soc. Sci.*, 12, 1958/1959, p.103–130.

Locke, H. J., *et al.* Interfaith Marriages. *Soc. Problems*, 4/4, 1957, p.329–33.

Mayer, J. E. *Jewish-Gentile Courtships: An Exploratory Study of a Social Process.* Glencoe, Illinois: The Free Press, 1961, 237p.

Newell, W. H. Inter-Caste Marriage in Kugti Village, Uper Budl Nadl, Brahmaur Tahsil, Chamba District, Miachel Pradesh, India. *Man*, 63, 1963, p.55–7.

Prince, A. J. A Study of 194 Cross-Religion Marriages. *Fam. Life Coord. R.*, 11/1, 1962, p.3–7.

Reiss, P. J. The Trend in Interfaith Marriages. *J. Sci. Stud. Rel.*, 5/1, 1965, p.64–7.

Resnik, R. B. Some Sociological Aspects of Intermarriage of Jew and Non-Jew. *Soc. Forces*, 12/1, 1933, p.94-102.

Slotkin, J. S. Adjustment in Jewish-Gentile Intermarriages. *Soc. Forces*, 21/2, 1942, p.226–30.

Sweeting, G. *Mixed Marriages.* Grand Rapids, Michigan: Zondervan Publishing House, 1957, 28p.

Thomas, J. L. Out-Group Marriage Patterns of Some Selected Ethnic Groups. *Amer. Cath. Sociol. R.*, 15/1, 1954, p.6–18.

See Also:

Brown, J. 4j3
Marcson, S. 7d
Vernon, G. M. 8a4

4f. Religion and Community

Bachi, R. The Demographic Development of Italian Jewry from the Seventeenth Century. *Jew. J. Sociol.*, 4/2, 1962, p.172–91.

Baer, G. *Population and Society in the Arab East* (Trans. H. Szoki). N.Y.: F. A. Praeger, 1964.

Berger, P. L. The Problem of Christian Community in Modern Society. *Luth. World*, 7, 1960, p.14–22.

Blackwell, G. W., *et al. Church and Community in the South.* Richmond, Virginia: John Knox, 1949, 411p.

Blochinger, A. *The Modern Parish Community* (Trans. G. Stevens). N.Y.: P. J. Kenedy and Sons, 1965, 263p.

Bogue, D. J. *The Population of the United States.* Glencoe: Free Press, 1959.

Bronsztejn, S. The Jewish Population of Poland in 1931. *Jew. J. Sociol.*, 6/1, 1964, p.3–29.

Bronsztejn, S. A Questionnaire Inquiry into the Jewish Population of Wrocaw. *Jew. J. Sociol.*, 7/2, 1965, p.246–75.

Burchard, W. W. A Comparison of Urban and Rural Churches. *Rural Sociol.*, 28/3, 1963, p.271–8.

Burchinal, L. G. Farm-Nonfarm Differences in Religious Beliefs and Practices. *Rural Sociol.*, 26/4, 1961, p.414–8.

Chapman, S. H. Spatial Fixity in New Haven Churches. *Sociol. Soc. Res.*, 29/3, 1945, p.213–7.

Committee for the Demography of Jews in the Netherlands. Dutch Jewry: A Demographic Analysis, Part I. *Jew. J. Sociol.*, 3/2, 1961; see also Part II, 4/1, 1962, p.47–71.

Datta, J. M. Geographical Distribution of the Brahmans in India. *Mod. R.*, 103/4, 1958, p.318–20.

Datta, J. M. Influence of Religious Beliefs on the Geographical Distribution of Brahmans in Bengal. *Man India*, 42/2, 1962, p.89–103.

deKok, J. A. Numerical Relations Between Catholics and Protestants in the Netherlands, 1580-1880. *Soc. Compass*, 11/3-4, 1964, p.37–40.

Dynes, R. R. The Relation of Community Characteristics to Religious Organization and Behavior. In M. B. Sussman (ed.)—*Community Structure and Analysis.* N.Y.: Thomas Y. Crowell Co., 1959, p.253–68.

Engelmann, U. Z. Jewish Statistics in the U.S. Census of Religious Bodies (1850-1936). *Jew. Soc. Stud.*, 9/2, 1947, p.127–74.

Erskine, H. G. The Polls: Church Attendance. *Public Opin. Quart.*, 28/4, 1964, p.671–9; see also The Polls: Personal Religion, 29/1, 1965, p.145–57; The Polls: Organized Religion, 29/2, p.326–37.

Fry, C. L. Organized Religion. *Amer. J. Sociol.*, 35/6, 1930, p.1042–51.

Gabriel, K. R. Nuptiality and Fertility of Origin Groups in Israel. *Jew. J. Sociol.*, 2/1, 1960, p.74–97.

Gibb, H. A. R. The Community in Islamic History. *Proc. Amer. Philos. Society*, 107/2, 1963, p.173–6.

Gibbons, W. J., *et al.* (Compilers, eds.) *Basic Ecclesiastical Statistics for Latin America, 1960.* Mary Knoll: Maryknoll Publications, 1960, 86p.

Glanz, R. The Immigration of German Jews up to 1880. *Yivo Ann. Jew. Soc. Sci.*, 2/3, 1948, p.81–99.

Glanz, R. Source Materials on the History of Jewish Immigration to the United States, 1800-1880. *Yivo Ann. Jew. Soc. Sci.*, 6, 1951, p.73–156.

Halevi, H. S. The Demography of Jewish Communities in Eastern Europe. *Jew. J. Sociol.*, 2, 1960, p.103–9.

Harris, F. The Christian Associations and the Community. *Soc. Forces*, 4/4, 1926, p.776–80.

Holloway, M. *Heavens on Earth: Utopian Communities in America, 1680-1880.* London: Turnstile Press, 1951, 240p.

Holt, A. E. The Ecological Approach to the Church. *Amer. J. Sociol.*, 33/1, 1927, p.72–9.

Houtart, F. A Sociological Study of the Evolution of the American Catholics. *Soc. Compass*, 2/5-6, 1955, p.189–216.

International Catholic Migration Commission. Migration Facts and Figures: Catholic Migration Movements to Latin America. *Migration News*, 9/3, 1960, p.20–1.

Isaac, J. Cultural and Economic Problems of Jewish Migration in the Post-War World. *Jew. J. Sociol.*, 1/2, 1959, p.234–41.

Jitodai, T. T. Migrant Status and Church Attendance. *Soc. Forces*, 43/2, 1964, p.241–8.

Kaufman, H. F. *Religious Organization in Kentucky.* Lexington, Kentucky: Agricultural Experiment Station Bulletin, 524, 1948.

Kelly, G. A. and Coogan, T. What is Our Real Catholic Population. *Amer. Eccles. R.*, 110, 1944, p.368–77.

Kincheloe, S. C. Church and Community: *J. Rel. Thought*, 3/1, 1946, p.63–76; see also 3/2, p.163–84; 4/1, p.73–85.

Kissman, J. The Immigration of Rumanian Jews up to 1914. *Yivo Ann. Jew. Soc. Sci.*, 2/3, 1948, p.160–179.

Krausz, E. *Leeds Jewry: Its History and Social Structure.* Cambridge: Heffer, 1964, 150p.

Lazerwitz, B. A Comparison of Major United States Religious Groups. *J. Amer. Stat. Assoc.*, 56, 1961, p.568–79.

Lazerwitz, B. Jews In and Out of New York City. *Jew. J. Sociol.*, 3/2, 1961, p.254–60.

Martin, R. D. The Church and Changing Ecological Dominance. *Sociol. Soc. Res.*, 25/3, 1941, p.46–57.

Meisel, T. The Jews of Mexico. *Yivo Ann. Jew. Soc. Sci.*, 2/3, 1948, p.295–312.

Myers, G. Patterns of Church Distribution and Movement. *Soc. Forces*, 40/4, 1962, p.354–63.

Nuesse, C. J. and Harte, T. (eds.) *The Sociology of the Parish: An Introductory Symposium.* Milwaukee: Bruce Publishing Co., 1951, 354p.

O'Dea, T. F. Geographical Position and Mormon Behavior. *Rural Sociol.*, 19/4, 1954, p.358–64.

Pearl, R. Some Notes on the Census of Religious Bodies, 1926. *J. Soc. Psychol.*, 2, 1931, p.417–32.

Petersen, W. Religious Statistics in the United States. *J. Sci. Stud. Rel.*, 1/2, 1962, p.155–64.

Prais, S. J. Statistical Publication on the Jewish Population of Great Britain: A Bibliography. *Jew. J. Sociol.*, 1/1, 1959, p.136–8.

Rosenberg, L. The Demography of the Jewish Community in Canada. *Jew. J. Sociol.*, 1/2, 1959, p.217–33.

Rosenwaike, I. The Jewish Population of Argentina. *Jew. Soc. Stud.*, 22/4, 1960, p.195–214.

Roucek, J. S. On Religion and Immigration. *Sociologica Religiosa*, 7, 1963, p.52–64.

Schever, J. F. Church Parish Population Profiles. *Amer. Cath. Sociol. R.*, 12, 1956, p.131–42.

Sherrard, T. D. and Murray, R. C. The Church and Neighborhood Community Organization. *Soc. Work*, 10/3, 1965, p.3–14.

Slusser, G. H. *The Local Church in Transition: Theology, Education, and Ministry.* Phila.: Westminster Press, 1964.

Some Data About Religious Communities. *Soviet Stud.*, 7/4, 1956, p.471–2.

Sorokin, P. A. Rural-Urban Differences in Religious Culture, Beliefs and Behavior. *Publ. Amer. Sociol. Society*, 23, 1929, p.224–5.

Taylor, L. and Jones, A. R., Jr. *Rural Life and Urbanized Society.* N.Y.: Oxford Univ. Press, 1964.

Thoen, C. M. and Godfrey, J. Some Remarks on the Inquiry into the Activities of Catholic Organizations in the Field of International Migration. *Soc. Compass*, 3/5-6, 1955, p.400–8.

Zelinsky, W. An Approach to the Religious Geography of the United States: Patterns of Church Membership in 1952. *Ann. Assoc. Amer. Geog.*, 51, 1961, p.139–93.

Cohen, P. S.   2b
Coughenour, C. M.   8a2
Cowhig, J. D.   7b1
Dall, E. E.   2a1
Datta, J. M.   6c
Fenton, R. A.   5a1
Freedman, M.   2b
Goldstein, I.   2b
Greeley, A. M.   2a2
Hammond, P. E.   6e
Illich, I. D.   7a1
Institute of Jewish Affairs   2b
Kage, J.   3b
Klausner, S. Z.   7b3
Landis, B. Y.   6c
Lazerwitz, B.   7b1
Leent, J. A. A.   8a2
Madge, C.   4j1

Mann, W. E.   2
Marie, L.   5b2
Marriott, M.   4j1
Massarik, F.   2b
Miller, A. W.   6c
Muetler, E. W.   5a2
Rebirth of Muslim Communal   6c
Reuss, C.   8a4
Rodehaver, M.   7b
Schuyler, J. B.   8a1
Shannon, J. P.   3a2
Shapiro, J.   7b
Strizower, S.   2b
Swanstrom, E. E.   7b3
Tillyand, F.   2a1
Tonnies, F.   8a6
Ward, C. K.   2a2
Weintraub, D.   7d

4f1.   Urban Areas

Abell, A. I.   The Catholic Factor in Urban Welfare: The Early Period, 1850–1880.   *R. Polit.*, 14/3, 1952, p.289–324.

Antonovsky, A.   Aspects of New Haven Jewry: A Sociological Study.   *Yivo Ann. Jew. Soc. Sci.*, 10, 1956, p.128–64.

Bienenstok, T.   Social Life and Authority in East European Jewish Shtetel Community.   *Southw. J. Anthropol.*, 6/3, 1950, p.238–54.

Bigman, S. K.   *The Jewish Population of Greater Washington in 1956: Report on an Interview Survey of Size, Social Characteristics, Residential Mobility, Community Participation, and Observance of Some Traditional Jewish Practices.*   Washington: Jewish Community Council of Greater Washington, 1957, 173p.

Boskoff, A.   *The Sociology of Urban Regions.*   N.Y.: Appleton-Century-Crofts, 1962.

Chapman, S. H.   The Development of the Catholic Church in New Haven, Connecticut.   *Amer. Cath. Sociol. R.*, 5/3, 1944, 161–8.

Clark, D.   Catholics and Urban Affairs.   *Soc. Order*, 10/2, 1960, p.53–7.

Clark, D.   *Cities in Crisis: The Christian Response.*   N.Y: Sheed and Ward, 1960, 177p.

Clark, D.   Modern Christians and the Wealth of Cities.   *Soc. Order*, 11/1, 1961, p.12–22.

Cowgill, D. O.   The Ecology of Religious Preference in Wichita.   *Sociol. Quart.*, 1/1, 1960, p.25–38.

Cox, H.   *The Secular City: Secularization and Urbaniza-tion in Theological Perspective.*   N.Y.: Macmillan, 1965, 276p.

Cross, R. D.   The Changing Image of the City Among American Catholics.   *Cath. Hist. R.*, 48, 1962, p.33–52.

Curtis, J. H., *et al.*   Urban Parishes as Social Areas.   *Amer. Cath. Sociol. R.*, 18/4, 1957, p.319–25.

Deardorff, N. R.   The Religio-Cultural Background of New York City's Population.   *Milbank Memor. Fund. Quart.*, 33/2, 1955, p.152–60.

Dore, R. P.   *City Life in Japan.*   Berkeley: Univ. of California Press, 1958.

Dumont, F.   An Investigation of Religions Practiced in an Urban Milieu.   *Rech. Sociol.*, 1/4, 1960, p.500–2.

Engelman, G. S.   A New Church for a New City.   *City Church*, 1953, p.2–5.

Etzioni, A.   The Ghetto: A Re-evaluation.   *Soc. Forces*, 37/3, 1959, p.255–62.

Fichter, J. H.   Urban Mobility and Religious Observance.   *Amer. Cath. Sociol. R.*, 11/3, 1950, p.130–9.

Fichter, J. H.   Conceptualizations of the Urban Parish.   *Soc. Forces*, 31/1, 1952, p.43–6.

Fichter, J. H.   *Social Relations in the Urban Parish.*   Chicago: Univ. of Chicago Press, 1954.

Fischel, W. J.   The City in Islam.   *Mid. East. Aff.*, 7/6–7, 1956, p.227–32.

Golomb, E.   Model Theoretical Considerations on the Organization of Urban Pastoral Work.   *Soc. Compass*, 10/4–5, 1963, p.357–75.

Greeley, A. M. The Urban Parish Under a Microscope. *Soc. Order*, 9/7, 1959, p.335–9.

Gringauz, S. The Ghetto as an Experiment of Jewish Social Organization. *Jew. Soc. Stud.*, 17/1, 1943, p.3–20.

Hirsch, R. G. *Judaism and Cities in Crisis.* N.Y.: Union of American Hebrew Congregations, 1961, 103p.

Hollingshead, A. B. *Elmtown's Youth.* N.Y.: John Wiley & Sons, 1961.

Jones, E. The Distribution and Segregation of Roman Catholics in Belfast. *Sociol. R.*, 4/2, 1956, p.167–89.

Kincheloe, S. C. The Sociological Study of Religion in the City: The Perspective of Social Interaction. *R. Rel. Res.*, 6/2, 1965, p.77–81.

Kincheloe, S. C. The Theoretical Perspectives for the Sociological Study of Religion in the City: Ecological and Anthropological Perspectives, In Special Reference to the Growth and Distribution of Religious Institutions and People in Metropolitan Areas. *R. Rel. Res.*, 6/2, 1965, p.63–76.

Kloetzli, W. *The City Church: Death or Renewal.* Phila.: Muhlenberg Press, 1961, 224p.

Laidlow, W. The Church and the City Community. *Amer. J. Sociol.*, 16/6, 1911, p.794–804.

Lee, R. (ed.) *Cities and Churches: Readings on the Urban Church.* Phila.: Westminster Press, 1962, 366p.

Lenski, G. E. Religion and the Modern Metropolis. *R. Rel. Res.*, 1/1, 1959, p.24–9.

Lestchinsky, J. The Jews in the Cities of the Republic of Poland. *Yivo Ann. Jew. Soc. Sci.*, 1, 1946, p.156–77.

Levy, C. S. Social Action, Social Work and Jewish Social Philosophy in Jewish Community Center Practice. *J. Jew. Commun. Serv.*, 40/1, 1963, p.124–34.

Lipman, V. D. Social Topography of a London Congregation 1863–1963. *Jew. J. Sociol.*, 61, 1964, p.69–74.

Miller, K. *Man and God in the City.* N.Y.: Friendship Press, 1954.

Oelsner, P. The Jewish Ghetto of the Past. *Yivo Ann. Jew. Soc. Sci.*, 1, 1946, p.24–43.

Parrinder, E. G. *Religion in an African City.* N.Y.: Oxford Univ. Press, 1953, 211p.

Parsons, A. The Pentacostal Immigrants: A Study of an Ethnic Central City Church. *J. Sci. Stud. Rel.*, 4/2, 1965, p.183–197.

Pin, E. Can the Urban Parish Be a Community? *Soc. Compass*, 8/6, 1961, p.503–34.

Reisman, L. The New Orleans Jewish Community. *Jew. J. Sociol.*, 4/1, 1962, p.100–23.

Rischin, M. *The Promised City: New York's Jews 1870–1914.* Cambridge: Harvard Univ. Press, 1962, 342p.

Rosenberg, S. E. *The Jewish Community in Rochester.* N.Y.: Columbia University Press, 1954, 325p.

Rosenwaike, I. The Utilization of Census Tract Data in the Study of the American Jewish Population. *Jew. Soc. Stud.*, 25/1, 1963, p.42–56.

Ross, A. *The Hindu Family and Its Urban Setting.* Toronto: Univ. of Toronto Press, 1961.

Rubin, I. Chassidic Community Behavior. *Anthropol. Quart.*, 37/3, 1964, p.138–48.

Sanua, V. D. Patterns of Identification With the Jewish Community in the U.S.A. *Jew. J. Sociol.*, 6/2, 1964 p.190–212.

Schmelz, O. The Jewish Population of Jerusalem. *Jew. J. Sociol.*, 6/2, 1964, p.243–63.

Schmidt, N. J. An Orthodox Jewish Community in the United States: A Minority Within a Minority. *Jew. J. Sociol.*, 7/2, 1965, p.176–206.

Schroeder, W. W. Conceptualization of Urbanization. *R. Rel. Res.*, 5/2, 1964, p.74–9.

Schulyer, J. B. Potential Elements of Organization and Disorganization in the Parish: As Seen in Northern Parish. *Amer. Cath. Sociol. R.*, 18/2, 1957, p.98–117.

Seger, I. *Responsibility for the Community: A New Norm Confronts Tradition in Lutheran City Churches.* Totowa, New Jersey: The Bedminster Press, 1963, 366p.

Shippey, F. A. *Protestantism in Indianapolis.* Indianapolis: The Church Federation of Indianapolis, 1946.

Singer, M. The Great Tradition in a Metropolitan Center: Madras. *J. Amer. Folklore*, 71/281, 1958, p.347–88.

Sirjamaki, J. *The Sociology of Cities.* N.Y.: Random House, 1964.

Smythe, C. *Church and Parish: Studies in Church Problems Illustrated From the Parochial History of St. Margaret's, Westminster.* London: SPCK, 1955, 262p.

Sullenger, T. E. The Church in an Urban Society. *Sociol. Soc. Res.*, 41/5, 1957, p.361–6.

Tcherikower, E. Jewish Immigrants to the United States, 1881–1900. *Yivo Ann. Jew. Soc. Sci.*, 6, 1951, p.157–76.

Thomas, J. L. The Urban Impact on Catholic Families. *Amer. Cath. Sociol. R.*, 10, 1949, p.258–67.

Topley, M. The Emergence and Social Functions of Chinese Religious Associations in Singapore. *Comp. Stud. Society Hist.*, 3/3, 1961, p.289–314.

Wells, C. D.   Urban Experience and Religious Loyalty. *Sociol. Soc. Res.*, 16/2, 1931, p.157–63.

Wickham, E. R.   *Church and People in an Industrial City.* London: Lutterworth Press, 1957.

Wirth, L.   The Ghetto. *Amer. J. Sociol.*, 33/1, 1927, p.57–71.

Younger, G. D.   *The Church and Urban Power Structure: Christian Perspectives on Social Problems.* Phila: Westminster Press, 1963, 88p.

Younger, G. D.   "Success" and "Failure" in Inner-City Churches. *Christ. Crisis*, 1960, p.171–5.

See Also:

Allah, I.   4j1
Besanceney, P. H.   4e3 (2)
Beynon, E. D.   2h5
Coates, C. H.   7a1
Cowhig, J. D.   5a3
deLaney, M. M.   3b
Dunn, S. P.   3b
Evans, D.   1g
Fichter, S.   2a2
Ginsberg, M.   2b
Glantz, O.   4a2
Gordon, W. H.   2b
Grimes, A.   5c
Grinstein, H. B.   3b

Heiss, J. S.   4e3
Hepple, L. M.   4f2
Hill, C. S.   4j2
Horowitz, I. L.   2b
Kennedy, R. J.   4e3
Kollmorgen, W. M.   4b
Krausze, E.   2b
Lee, E. G.   4h
Lee, R.   5c
Lowi, T.   2b
Mann, H. H.   4j1
Michonneau, G.   6c
Mitchell, W. E.   4e
O'Brien, R. W.   4j3
Parringer, G.   2
Porter, J.   5a3
Roff, W. R.   3d
Rudavsky, D.   4g4
Sanderson, R. W.   6e
Schellenberg, J.   7b2
Seidman, H.   5b
Smith, P. M.   5a1
Snatzky, J.   3b
Srole, L.   5b1
Stanley, M.   6e
Sullenger, T. E.   6e
Takenaka, M.   5e
Timaseff, N. S.   4a1
Ward, C. K.   7a

4f2.   Rural Areas

Alexander, F. D.   Religion in a Rural Community of the South. *Amer. Sociol R.*, 6, 1941, p.241–51.

Anderson, W. A.   Social Participation and Religious Affiliation in Rural Areas. *Rural Sociol.*, 9/3, 1944, p.242–50.

Berreman, G. D.   Himalayan Rope-Sliding and Village Hinduism: An Analysis. *Southw. J. Anthropol.*, 17/4, 1961, p.326–42.

Bertrand, A. L. (ed.)   *Rural Sociology: An Analysis of Contemporary Rural Life.* N.Y.: McGraw-Hill Book Co., 1958.

Briggs, L. C. and Guede, N. L.   No More For Ever: A Saharan Jewish Town. *Pap. Peabody Mus. Archaeol. Ethnol.*, 55/1, 1964, 108p.

Brunner, E. deS.   The Rural Church at its Best. *Soc. Forces*, 2/1, 1923, p.80–1.

Buie, T. S.   The Land and the Rural Church. *Rural Sociol.*, 9/3, 1944, p.251–6.

Bultena, L.   Rural Churches and Community Integration. *Rural Sociol.*, 9/3, 1944, p.257–64.

Coughenour, C. M. and Hepple, L. M.   *The Church in Rural Missouri: Religious Groups in Rural Missouri.* Columbia, Missouri: Agricultural Experiment Station Research Bulletin, 663B, 1957.

DeJong, G. F. and Ford, T. R.   Religious Fundamentalism and Denominational Preference in the Southern Appalachian Region. *J. Sci. Stud. Rel.*, 5/1, 1965, p.24–33.

Doll, E. E.   Social and Economic Organization in Two Pennsylvania German Religious Communities. *Amer. J. Sociol.*, 57/2, 1951, p.168–77.

Dollard, J.   *Caste and Class in a Southern Town.* N.Y.: Doubleday & Co., 1949.

Eliot, T. D.   The Rural Church as a Social Unit. *Soc. Forces*, 2/1, 1923, p.82–3.

Embree, J. F.   *A Japanese Village: Suye Mura.* London: Kegan Paul, 1946, 268p.

Felton, R. A.   *These are My Brethren: A Study of 570 Negro Churches and 1542 Negro Homes in the Rural South.* Madison, N.Y.: Dept. of the Rural Church, Drew Theol. Sem., 1950, 102p.

Fishman, A. (ed.) *The Religious Kibbutz Movement.* N.Y.: Jewish Agency for Palestine, 1957, 195p.

Garnett, W. E. *The Virginia Rural Church and Related Influences, 1900–1950.* Blackburg: Virginia Agricultural Experimental Station Bulletin, 479, 1957.

Gillin, J. L. The Church and the Rural Community. *Amer. J. Sociol.,* 16/6, 1911, p.696–702.

Hamilton, C. H. and Garnett, W. E. *The Role of the Church in Rural Community Life in Virginia.* Virginia Agricultural Experiment Station Bulletin, 267, 1929.

Harris, M. D. and Ackerman, J. *Town and Country Churches and Family Farming.* N.Y. National Council of Churches of Christ in the U.S.A., 1960, 102p.

Hepple, L. M. *The Church in Rural Missouri: Rural-Urban Churches Compared.* Columbia, Missouri: Agricultural Experiment Station Research Bulletin, 633E, 1959.

Hobbs, S. H., Jr. Conference Viewpoints on Religion in Country Life. *Soc. Forces,* 3/2, 1925, p.304–7.

Hunter, E. A. *The Small Town and the Country Church.* Nashville: Abingdon Press, 1947.

Johannes, M. E. *A Study of the Russian German Settlements in Ellis County, Kansas.* Washington: Catholic Univ. Press, 1946, 164p.

Jordon, R. H. The Social Functions of Churches in Oakville. *Sociol. Soc. Res.,* 40/2, 1955, p.107–11.

Kammer, E. J. *A Socio-Economic Survey of the Marsh Dwellers of Four Southeastern Louisiana Parishes.* Washington: Catholic Univ. Press, 1941, 180p.

Kaufman, H. F. *Rural Churches in Kentucky, 1947.* Kentucky Agricultural Experiment Station Bulletin 530, 1949.

La Farge, O. *Santa Eulalia: The Religion of a Cuchumatan Indian Town.* Chicago: Univ. of Chicago Press, 1947.

Losey, J. E. *The Rural Church Situation in Indiana.* Lafayette, Indiana: Purdue Univ. Agricultural Experiment Station, 153, 1957.

Mather, W. G. *The Rural Churches of Allegany County.* Cornell Agricultural Experiment Station Bulletin, 587, 1934.

Mueller, E. W. and Ekola, G. (eds.) *The Silent Struggle for Mid-America: The Church in Town and Country Today.* Minneapolis: Augsburg Publishing House, 1963, 167p.

Nelson, L. *The Mormon Village: A Pattern and Technique of Land Settlement.* Salt Lake City: Univ. of Utah Press, 1952, 296p.

Nuesse, C. J. Membership Trends in a Rural Catholic Parish. *Rural Sociol.,* 22/2, 1957, p.123–30.

Nuesse, C. J. Recent Catholic Fertility in Rural Wisconsin. *Rural Sociol.,* 28/4, 1963, p. 379–93.

Opler, M. E. The Place of Religion in a North Indian Village. *Southw. J. Anthropol.,* 15/3, 1959, p.219–26.

Prag, A. Some Demographic Aspects of Kibbutz Life in Israel. *Jew. J. Sociol.,* 4/1, 1962, p. 39–46.

Salisbury, W. S. *The Organization and Practice of Religion in a Small City.* Oswego, N.Y.: Ontario Press, 1950, 40p.

Samson, A'D. *Church Groups in Four Agricultural Settings in Montana.* Bozeman, Montana: Montana Agricultural Experiment Station Bulletin 538, 1958, 43p.

Scheifele, T. C. and Mather, W. G. *Closed Rural Pennsylvania Churches.* Pennsylvania Agricultural Experiment Station Bulletin 512, 1949.

Schwab, H. *Jewish Rural Communities in Germany.* London: Cooper, 1957, 93p.

Skrabanek, R. L. The Rural Church: Characteristics and Problems. In A. Bertrand (ed.)—*Rural Sociology: An Analysis of Contemporary Rural Life.* N.Y.: McGraw-Hill Book Co., 1958, p.237–52.

Vidich, A. J. and Bensman, J. *Small Town in Mass Society: Class, Power and Religion in a Rural Community.* Garden City: Doubleday, 1960.

Wagley, C. The Social and Religious Life of a Guatemalan Village. *Amer. Anthropol. Assoc. Memoir,* 71, 1949, 150p.

Wolters, G. The Human Crop of a Rural Catholic Parish. *Rural Sociol.,* 21/3–4, 1956, p.297–8.

Kaplan, B. 4h
Klietsch, 6e
Majumdar, D. N. 4j1
Mijakana, T. S. 6b
Nash, D. 4c
Neusse, C. J. 4j3
Orestein, H. 4j1
Powell, S. C. 3a1
Rich, M. 5a1

Rose, P. I. 5a
Rosenfeld, H. 4e
Rosenthal, C. S. 4j3
Samson, A'd. 7a
Tubiville, G. 5a2
West, R. A. 4e
Wilson, W. E. 3a1
Winsberg, D. 2b
Wolf, E. R. 8a5

4f3. Suburban Areas

Dodson, D. W. Religion in Suburbia. *J. Educ. Sociol.*, 32/8, 1959, p.365–73.

Ferkiss, V. C. Suburbia: A Religious Problem? *Soc. Order*, 10/2, 1960, p.84–8.

Gans, H. J. Progress in a Suburban Jewish Community: Forest Park Revisited. *Commentary*, 23, 1957, p.113–22.

Gersh, H. The New Suburbanites of the 50's. *Commentary*, 17/3, 1954, p.209–21.

Gordon, A. I. *Jews in Suburbia.* Boston: Beacon Press, 1959.

Greeley, A. M. *The Church and the Suburbs.* N.Y.: Sheed & Ward, 1959.

Greeley, A. M. Suburban Parish. *Commonwealth*, 1959, p.537–9.

Leinberger, H. The Church in the "New Suburb." *Rel. Educ.*, 50/1, 1955, p.11–4.

Marty, M. E. The Suburban Church: A Second Look. *City Church*, 1962, p.5–8,13.

Miller, K. Our Growing Suburbs and Their Churches. *Rel. Life*, 1955, p.516–22.

Nash, D. J. and Berger, P. L. Church Commitment in an American Suburb. *Archiv. Sociol. Rel.*, 13, 1962, p.105–20.

Simon, E. Suburbia: Its Affect on the American Jewish Teen-Ager. *J. Educ. Sociol.*, 36/3, 1962, p.124–33.

Winter, G. The Church in Suburban Captivity. *Christ. Cent.*, 1955, p.1112–4, 1134.

Winter, G. *The Suburban Captivity of the Churches.* Garden City: Doubleday & Co., 1961.

See Also:

Bardis, P. O. 4e
Berger, P. L. 4e
Eaton, J. W. 7a1 (2)
Farwell, P. T. 1g
Senn, M. 4j2
Zimmer, B. G. 7b1

4f4. Rural/Urban Transition

Adler, S. and Connolly, T. E. *From Ararat to Suburbia: The History of the Jewish Community of Buffalo.* Phila.: Jewish Publication Society of America, 1960, 498p.

Blizzard, S. W. Churching the Rural-Urban Fringe. *City Church*, 1953, p.11–2.

Douglass, T. B. Ecological Changes and the Church. *Ann. Amer. Acad. Polit. Soc. Sci.*, 332, 1960, p.80–8.

Fiawoo, D. K. Urbanization and Religion in Eastern Ghana. *Sociol. R.*, 7/1, 1959, p.83–97.

Fishman, J. A. Moving to the Suburbs: Its Possible Impact on the Role of the Jewish Minority in American Community Life. *Phylon*, 24/2, 1963, p.146–53.

Greene, S. E. Reurbanization Faces the Church. *Christ. Cent.*, 1958, p.551–2.

Schaffer, A. The Rural Church in a Metropolitan Area. *Rural Sociol.*, 24/3, 1959, p.236–45.

Sharp, J. K. *History of the Diocese of Brooklyn, 1853–1953: The Catholic Church on Long Island.* N.Y.: Fordham Univ. Press, 1954, 392p/365p., 2 vols.

Wells, C. D. Adapting the Church to the City. *Sociol. Soc. Res.*, 15/4, 1931, p.317–22.

See Also:

Clark, C. A. 6c
Dynes, R. R. 7b1
Thomas, W. I. 7b3

Alilunas, L. J.   The Image of Public Schools in Roman-Catholic American History Textbooks. *Hist. Educ. Quart.*, 3/3, 1963, p.159–65.

Atkinson, N.   The School Structure in the Republic of Ireland. *Comp. Educ. R.*, 9, 1964, p.276–80.

Barnes, S. B.   The Entry of Science and History in the College Curriculum, 1865–1914. *Hist. Educ. Quart.*, 4/1, 1964, p.44–58.

Barth, P. J.   *Franciscan Education and the Social Order in Spanish North America: 1520–1821.*   Chicago: Univ. of Chicago Press, 1945.

Bartlett, L. E.   *Bright Galaxy: Ten Years of Unitarian Fellowships.*   Boston: Beacon Press, 1960, 255p.

Bidwell, C. E. and Kazamias, A. M.   Religion, Politics and Popular Education: An Historical Comparison of England and America. *Comp. Educ. R.*, 6/2, 1962, p.97–110.

Bidwell, C. E. and Vieland, R. S.   College Education and Moral Orientations: An Organizational Approach. *Admin. Sci. Quart.*, 8, 1963, p.166–91.

Boehm, L.   The Development of Conscience: A Comparison of Students in Catholic Parochial Schools and in Public Schools. *Child Devel.*, 33/3, 1962, p.591–602.

Brickman, W. W.   Public Aid to Religious Schools. *Rel. Educ.*, 55, 1960, p.279–88.

Brothers, J. B.   *Church and School: A Study of the Impact of Education on Religion.*   Liverpool: Liverpool Univ. Press, 1964, 187p.

Brown, L. B.   Religious Belief in Two Student Societies. *Australian J. Psychol.*, 14, 1962, p.202–9.

Cantril, H.   Educational and Economic Composition of Religious Groups. *Amer. J. Sociol.*, 48/5, 1943, p.574–9.

Chamberlin, J. G.   *Parents and Religion: A Preface to Christian Education.*   Phila.: Westminster Press, 1963.

Christiansen, J. R., *et al.*   Church Participation and College Desires of Rural Youth in Utah. *Rural Sociol.*, 28/2, 1963, p.176–85.

Clegg, A. A., Jr.   Church Groups and Federal Aid to Education, 1933–1939. *Hist. Educ. Quart.*, 4, 1964, p.137–54.

Conference on Religion and Public Education. *Religion and Public Education: Proceedings of a Conference.*   Washington: American Council on Education, 1945, 76p.

Contemporary American Morality and Religious and Character Education. *Rel. Educ.*, 58/2, 1963, p.82–246.

Cruickshank, M.   *Church and State in English Education, 1870 to the Present Day.*   N.Y.: St. Martin's Press, 1963, 200p.

Dawson, C.   Education and the Crisis of Christian Culture. *Lumen Vitae*, 1/2, 1946, p.204–15.

deKadt, E. J.   Locating Minority Group Members: Two British Surveys of Jewish University Students. *Jew. J. Sociol.*, 6/1, 1964, p.30–51.

deLissovoy, V.   A Sociological Approach to Religious Literacy. *J. Educ. Sociol.*, 27/9, 1954, p.419–24.

Deutscher, I. and Montague, A.   Professional Education and Conflicting Value Systems: The Role of Religious Schools in the Educational Aspirations of Nursing Students. *Soc. Forces*, 32, 1956, p.126–31.

Drake, W. E.   God-State Idea in Modern Education. *Hist. Educ. Quart.*, 3/2, 1963, p.81–98. See also: T. Smith-Response, p.99–101.

Drouin, E. G.   *The School Question: A Bibliography on Church-State Relations in American Education, 1940–1960.*   Washington: Catholic Univ. Press, 1963, 261p.

Eby, F.   *The Development of Modern Education.*   Englewood Cliffs, New Jersey: Prentice Hall, 1952, 719p.

Ecumenicism and Religious Education. *Lumen Vitae*, 19/3, 1964, p.411–532; see also 19/4, p.609–730.

Fisher, J. E.   Patterns of Interaction Between Religious and Educational Institutions. *Silliman J.*, 2/4, 1955, p.312–25.

Garnett, A. C.   The Impact of Modern Scholarship on Christianity. *J. Bib. Rel.*, 21, 1953, p.154–62.

Garrity, F. D.   A Study of Some Secondary Modern School Pupils Attitudes Towards Religious Education. *Rel. Educ.*, 56, 1961, p.141–3.

Greeley, A. M. and Rossi, P. H.   Correlates of Parochial School Attendance. *School R.*, 72/1, 1964, p.52–73.

Grensichen, H. W.   Theological Education in Africa. *Int. R. Missions*, 52/206, 1963, p.155–62.

Hilliard, F. H.   The Influence of Religious Education Upon the Development of Children's Moral Ideas. *Brit. J. Educ. Psychol.*, 29, 1959, p.50–9.

Hochwalt, G.   Catholic Education Today. *Ave Maria*, 85/17, 1957, p.12–5.

Holman, C. T.   Psychological Techniques in Campus Religious Work. *Rel. Educ.*, 35, 1940, p.101–8.

Horton, P. B. Student Interest in the Church. *Rel. Educ.*, 35, 1940, p.215–9.

Hunt, R. L. Religion and Education. *Ann. Amer. Acad. Polit. Soc. Sci.*, 332, 1960, p.89–100.

Hurley, M. J. *Church-State Relationships in Education in California.* Washington: Catholic Univ. Press, 1949, 183p.

Hutchinson, B. Robert Grosseteste: The Role of Education in the Reform of Thirteenth Century Society. *Hist. Educ. Quart.*, 5/1, 1965, p.26–39.

Kohlbrenner, B. J. Religion and Higher Education: An Historical Perspective. *Hist. Educ. Quart.*, 1/2, 1961, p.45–56.

Koppe, W. A. A Developmental Theory of Character Education. *R. Rel. Res.*, 6/1, 1964, p.23–8.

Kucera, D. W. *Church-State Relationships in Education in Illinois.* Washington: Catholic Univ. Press, 1955, 252p.

Lang, K. and Lang, G. E. Resistance to School Desegregation: A Case Study of Backlash Among Jews. *Sociol. Inq.*, 35/1, 1965, p.94—106.

Lennon, R. T. A Comparison of the Educational Achievement of Public and Parochial Elementary School Pupils. *Cath. Educ. R.*, 46/10, 1948, p.647–52.

Linguistic Philosophy and Christian Education: A Symposium. *Rel. Educ.*, 60/1, 1965, p.3–48.

Little, L. C. *Researches in Personality, Character and Religious Education.* Pittsburgh: Univ. of Pittsburgh Press, 1962, 215p.

Little, L. C. (ed.) *Wider Horizons in Christian Adult Education.* Pittsburgh: Univ. of Pittsburgh Press, 1962, 338p.

Little, L. C. *A Bibliography of Doctoral Dissertations on Adults and Adult Education.* Pittsburgh: Univ. of Pittsburgh Press, 1963, 163p.

Maitland, D. J. Puritan Attitudes Toward Learning. *Christ. Schol.*, 40, 1957, p.101–8.

McCoy, R. F. *American School Administration: Public and Catholic.* N.Y.: McGraw-Hill Book Co., 1961, 489p.

McKinney, R. I. *Religion in Higher Education Among Negroes.* New Haven: Yale Univ. Press, 1945, 165p.

McPheeters, A. A. Interest of the Methodist Church in the Education of Negroes. *Phylon*, 10/4, 1949, p.343–9.

Nakosteen, M. *History of Islamic Origins of Western Education.* Boulder, Colorado: Univ. of Colorado Press, 1964, 361p.

Newman, H. L. A Study in Bible Credit for College Entrance (Committee Report). *J. Bib. Rel.*, 2, 1934, p.71–80.

O'Neill, J. M. *Religion and Education Under the Constitution.* N.Y.: Harper & Row, 1949.

Parsons, T. Religious Perspectives in College Teaching: Sociology and Social Psychology. In H. N. Fairchild (ed.)—*Religious Perspectives in College Teaching.* N.Y.: Ronald Press, 1952, p.286–337.

Perez, L. S. The Problems of Jewish University Youth in the Argentine. *In Dispersion*, 2, 1963, p.89–98.

Powell, T. *The School Bus Law: A Case Study in Education, Religion, and Politics.* Middletown, Connecticut: Wesleyan Univ. Press, 1960, 334p.

Race Relations and Religious Education. *Rel. Educ.*, 59/1, 1964, p.2–120.

Reines, C. W. Public Support of Rabbis, Scholars and Students in the Jewish Past. *Yivo Ann. Jew. Soc. Sci.*, 7, 1952, p.84–109.

Robinson, S. B. Problems of Education in Israel. *Comp. Educ. R.*, 7/2, 1963, p.125–41.

Rossi, P. and Rossi, A. Background and Consequences of Parochial School Education. *Harvard Educ. R.*, 27/3, 1957, p.168–99.

Rossi, P. and Rossi, A. Background and Consequences Education in America. *Daedalus*, 90, 1961, p.300–28.

Sacks, B. *The Religious Issue in the State Schools of England and Wales, 1902–1914.* Albuquerque: Univ. of New Mexico Press, 1961, 292p.

Scanlon, D. Church, State and Education in Sub-Sahara Africa: An Overview. *Int. R. Educ.*, 9/4, 1963–64, p.438–47.

Scherer, R. P., *et al.* Annotations of Doctoral Dissertations Relevant to Religious Education, 1962. *Rel. Educ.*, 58/6, 1963, p.491–528, 537 (see other issues).

Scott, R. B. Turkish Village Attitudes Toward Religious Education. *Muslim World*, 55/3, 1965, p.222–9.

Sheehy, M. S. The Confessional as a Procedure in Student Counseling. *Rel. Educ.*, 25, 1930, p.709–15.

Sjogren, J. Religious Education in Sweden. *Rel. Educ.*, 58/3, 1963, p.298–301, 328.

Smith, M. B. A Comparison of the Growth of School Enrollments in Public And Non-Public Schools of the United States, 1927 to 1947–48. *J. Educ. Sociol.*, 25/8, 1952, p.495–511.

Stone, C. L. *Church Participation and Social Adjustment of High School and College Youth.* Washington Agricultural Experiment Stations, Institute of Agricultural Sciences, State College of Washington Bulletin, 550, 1954.

Symposium: Research in Religious Development. *Rel. Educ.*, 59/3, 1964, p.234–57.

Taylor, M. J. (ed.) *Religious Education: A Comprehensive Survey.* N.Y.: Abingdon Press, 1960, 446p.

Thomas, J. H. Religious Language as Symbolism. *Rel. Stud.*, 1/1, 1965, p.89–93.

Thompson, S. *Motif Index of Folk-Literature: A Classification of Narrative Elements in Folktales, Ballads, Myths, Fables, Mediaeval Romances, Exempla, Fabliaux, Jest-Books and Local Legends.* Bloomington: Indiana Univ. Press, 1955–1958, 6 vols.

Tibawi, A. L. *British Interests in Palestine, 1800–1901: A Study of Religious and Educational Enterprises.* N.Y.: Oxford Univ. Press, 1961, 280p.

Vincent, P. Glascow Jewish School Children. *Jew. J. Sociol.*, 6/2, 1964, p.220–31.

Wilks, I. The Growth of Islamic Learning in Ghana. *J. Hist. Society Nigeria*, 2/4, 1963, p.409–17.

Young, G. W., *et al.* The Religion of the Post-War College Student. *J. Psychol.*, 25, 1948, p.3–33.

Zoborowski, M. The Place of Book Learning in Traditional Jewish Culture. *Harvard Educ. R.*, 19, 1949, p.87–107.

See Also: 1h, 4a, 5a, 5e

Barker, E.   4a1
Blizzard, S. W.   7a1
Brickman, W. W.   5a

Bruder, E. E.   7a4
Cassirer, E.   1c
Fichter, J. H.   7b3
Furley, O.   4j2
Greeley, A. M.   7b1
Guterman, S. L.   4a1
Havens, J.   8a4
Holmer, P. L.   1b
Howerth, I. W.   4a1
Jones, A. H.   4e
Kane, J. J.   5a2
Kimpel, B. F.   1c
Kosa, J.   4e
Lottich, K. V.   4a
Mallinson, V.   4a1
Morris, J. F.   4d
Muntz, E. E., Jr.   7a3
Naegele, K. D.   7a4
Nelson, L.   4e
Pelissner, J.   8a4
Péshkin, A.   4a
Redekop, C.   6a
Reggs, M. D.   4e
Religion and the Intellectuals   8
Scarangello, A.   4a1
Schroeder, W. W.   1f
Selfors, S.   4e
Spoerl, D. T.   7b3
Stark, R.   1b
Synon, M.   7b3
Wilson, N. H.   4a1

4g1.   Art and Music

Arnold, T. W. *Painting in Islam: A Study of the Place of Pictorial Art in Muslim Culture.* N.Y.: Dover Publications, 1965, 159p.

Banerjea, J. N. *The Development of Hindu Iconography.* Calcutta: Univ. of Calcutta, 1956.

Bhattacharya, B. *The Indian Buddhist Iconography.* Calcutta: K. L. Mukhepadhyaya, 1958, 478p.

Brodbeck, A. J. Religion and Art as Socializing Agencies: A Note on the Revision of Marxist and Freudian Theories. *Psychol. Rep.*, 3/2, 1957, p.161–65.

Bush, W. T. Religion and Art. *J. Philos.*, 27, 1930, p.5–14.

Coomaraswamy, A. K. *Christian and Oriental Philosophy of Art.* N.Y.: Dover Publications, 1956.

Davidson, J. L. *The Lotus Sutra in Chinese Art: A Study in Buddhist Art to the Year 1000.* New Haven: Yale Univ. Press, 1954, 105p.

Eversole, F. (ed.) *Christian Faith and the Contemporary Arts.* N.Y.: Abingdon Press, 1962, 255p.

Fellerer, K. G. *History of Catholic Church Music* (Trans. F. A. Brunner). N.Y.: Taplinger Publishing Co., 1960, 235p.

Getlein, F. and Getlein, D. *Christianity in Art.* Milwaukee: Bruce Publishing Co., 1959, 196p.

Gordon, A. K. *The Iconography of Tibetan Lamaism.* Tokyo: C. E. Tuttle, 1959, 131p.

Groslier, B. P. and Arthaud, J. *The Arts and Civilization of Angkor* (Trans. E. Smith). N.Y.: Praeger, 1957, 230p.

Grottanelli, V. L. Asonu Worship Among the Nzema: A Study in Akan Art and Religion. *Africa*, 31/1, 1961, p.46–60.

Hasumi, T. *Zen in Japanese Art.* N.Y.: Philosophical Library, 1962, 113p.

Hooper, W. L. *Church Music in Transition.* Nashville, Tennessee: Broadman Press, 1963.

Horton, R.   The Kalabari Ekine Society: A Borderland of Religion and Art. *Africa*, 33/2, 1963, p.94–114.

James, E. O.   *From Cave to Cathedral: Temples and Shrines of Prehistoric Classical and Early Christian Time*. N.Y.: Frederick A. Praeger, 1965, 404p.

Kluckhohn, C. and Wyman, L. C.   An Introduction to Navaho Chant Practice, With an Account of the Behaviors Observed in 4 Chants. *Amer. Anthropol. Assoc. Mem.*, 53, 1946, p.1–204.

Kuruppu, J.   The Influence of Buddhism on the Arts of Ceylon. *Maha Bodhi*, 65/10, 1957, p.388–93.

Male, E.   *The Gothic Image: Religious Art in France of the Thirteenth Century* (Trans. D. Nussey). N.Y.: Harper and Brothers, 1958, 415p.

Maus, C. P.   *The Church and the Fine Arts*. N.Y.: Harper, 1960, 902p.

McLaughlin, W. B.   Symbolism and Mysticism in the Spirituals. *Phylon*, 1963, p.69–77.

Merriam, A. P. and D'Azevedo, W. L.   Washo Peyote Songs. *Amer. Anthropol.*, 59/4, 1957, p.615–41.

Rattray, R. S., *et al.   Religion and Art in Ashanti*. London: Oxford Univ. Press, 1954, 414p.

Reifenberg, A.   *Ancient Hebrew Arts*. N.Y.: Schocken, 1950.

Rice, D. T.   *Islamic Art*. London: Thames and Hudson, 1965, 286p.

Routley, E.   *Twentieth Century Church Music*. N.Y.: Oxford Univ. Press, 1964, 244p.

Rowland, B.   Religious Art East and West. *Hist. Rel.*, 2/1, 1962, p.11–32.

Roy, N. R.   Contribution of Buddhism to Art. *Maha Bodhi*, 65/15, 1957, p.161–70.

Schmitz, C. A.   *Wantoat: Art and Religion of the Northeast New Guinea Papuans* (Trans. G. E. Van Baaren-Pape). The Hague: Mouton, 1963, 159p.

Seckel, D.   *The Art of Buddhism* (Trans. A. E. Keep). N.Y.: Crown Publishers, 1965.

Segy, L.   African Sculpture and Animism. *J. Hum. Relat.*, 2/1, 1953, p.76–87.

Squire, R. N.   *Church Music, Musical and Hymnological Developments in Western Christianity*. St. Louis: Bethany Press, 1962, 317p.

Strauss, H.   Jewish Art as a Minority Problem. *Jew. J. Sociol.*, 2/1, 1960, p.147–71.

van der Leeuw, G.   *Sacred and Profane Beauty: The Holy in Art* (Trans. D. E. Green). N.Y.: Holt, Rinehart & Winston, 1963, 357p.

Vogt, V. O.   *Art and Religion*. Boston: Beacon Press, 1960, 269p.

Weiss, P.   *Religion and Art*. Milwaukee: Marquette Univ. Press, 1963, 97p.

Wellesz, E.   *History of Byzantine Music and Hymnography*. N.Y.: Oxford Univ. Press, 1961.

Weman, H.   *African Music and the Church in Africa*. Uppsala, Sweden: Lundequist, 1960, 296p.

Werner, E.   *The Sacred Bridge: The Interdependence of Liturgy and Music in Synagogue and Church During the First Millenium*. N.Y.: Columbia Univ. Press, 1959, 618p.

Wyman, L. C. and Kluckhohn, C.   Navaho Classification of Their Song Ceremonials. *Amer. Anthropol. Assoc. Mem.*, 50, 1938, 38p.

Zimmer, H. R.   *The Art of Indian Asia* (Ed. J. Campbell). N.Y.: Pantheon, 1955, 2 vols.

See Also:

Bucher, F.   7f
Leaño, I.   7b3
Mountford, C. P.   2h
Zimmer, H.   3c

4g2.   *Communication*

Boyd, M.   *Crisis in Communication: A Christian Examination of the Mass Media*. Garden City: N.Y.: Doubleday, 1957, 128p.

Case, L. D.   Origins of Methodist Publishing in America. *Pap. Biblio. Society Amer.*, 59/1, 1965, p.12–27.

Dimock, E. C., Jr.   The Goddess of Snakes in Medieval Bengali Literature. *Hist. Rel.*, 1/2, 1962, p.307–21.

Fogel, H. H.   Colonial Theocracy and a Secular Press. *Journalism Quart.*, 37/4, 1960, p.525–32.

Fraenkel, J.   *The Jewish Press of the World*. London:

Cultural Department of the World Jewish Congress, 1954, 49p.

Fraenkel, J.   The Jewish Press of the Diaspora. *In Dispersion*, 2, 1963, p.147-56.

Gillmor, D. M.   Freedom in Press Systems and the Religious Variable. *Journalism Quart.*, 39/1, 1961–62, p.15–26.

Goddijn, W.   Propaganda and the Continuity of Religious Groups. *Soc. Compass*, 7/5–6, 1960, p.449–60.

Gurian, W.   The Catholic Publicist. *R. Polit.*, 17/1, 1955, p.5–18.

Lee, A. M. The Press and Public Relations of Religious Bodies. *Ann. Amer. Acad. Polit. Soc. Sci.*, 256, 1948, p.120–31.

Majumdar, D. N. *Caste and Communication in an Indian Village.* Bombay: Asia Publishing House, 1958, 358p.

Marty, M. E. *The Improper Opinion: Mass Media and the Christian Faith.* Phila.: Westminster Press, 1961, 144p.

Marty, M. E., *et al. The Religious Press in America.* N.Y.: Holt, Rinehart and Winston, 1963.

McCormack, W. The Forms of Communication in Virataiva Religion. *J. Amer. Folklore*, 71/281, 1958, p.325–35.

McCornack, R. B. Attitudes Towards Religious Matters in Mexican School History Textbooks. *Americas*, 15/3, 1959, p.235–47.

Millard, W. J. Reader Characteristics and Content Preferences for a Denominational Magazine. *Journalism Quart.*, 41/3, 1964, p.433–6.

Moreau, J. L. *Language and Religious Language: A Study in the Dynamics of Translation.* Phila.: Westminster Press, 1961, 207p.

Parker, E. C., *et al. The Radio-Television Audience and Religion.* N.Y.: Harper & Brothers, 1955.

Reyburn, W. D. Christianity and Ritual Communication. *Pract. Anthropol.*, 10/4, 1963, p.145–59.

Severson, A. L. Nationality and Religious Preferences as Reflected in Newspaper Advertisements. *Amer. J. Sociol.*, 44/4, 1939, p.540–5.

Shaw, T. and Shaw, G. *Through Ebony Eyes: Evangelism Through Journalism in West Africa.* London: United Society for Christian Literature, Lutterword Press, 1956, 96p.

Stroupe, H. S. *The Religious Press in the South Atlantic States, 1802–1865: An Annotated Bibliography With Historical Introduction and Notes.* Durham, North Carolina: Duke Univ. Press, 1956, 172p.

Stuhlmuller, C. The Bible and the World of Books. *Crosscurrents*, 15/3, 1965, p.305–23.

Turner, H. W. *Profile Through Preaching: A Study of the Sermon Texts Used in a West African Independent Church.* London: Edinburg House Press for World Council of Churches, 1965, 88p.

Vleck, J. V., Jr. and Wolf, C. U. Reader-Appeal of Religious Articles. *Amer. Sociol. R.*, 7, 1942, p.828–32.

Wolseley, R. E. The Church Press: Bulwark of Denominational Sovereignty. *Christendom*, 11, 1946, p.490–500.

Wonderly, W. L. and Nida, E. A. Cultural Differences and the Communication of Christian Values. *Pract. Anthropol.*, 10/6, 1963, p.241–8.

Wright, L. B. The Significance of Religious Writings in the English Renaissance. *J. Hist. Ideas*, 1/1, 1940, p.59–68.

See Also:

Clark, W. K. 7a1
Eulau, H. 7d
Gonda, J. 8a2
Hutchinson, J. 7f
Kaplan, S. 5a3
Klamke, E. D. 1c
Krug, M. M. 1d
Saab, H. 5a
Schneider, L. 8a1 (2)
Wakefield, D. 8a1
Welmers, W. E. 5a3

4g3. Literature

Baker, C. The Place of the Bible in American Fiction. *Theol. Today*, 17, 1960, p.53–76.

Braden, C. S. The Bible in Contemporary Drama. *J. Bib. Rel.*, 19, 1951, p.177–82.

Charles, L. H. Drama in Shaman Exorcism. *J. Amer. Folklore*, 66/260, 1953, p.95–122.

Frye, R. M. *Perspective on Man: Literature and the Christian Tradition.* Phila.: Westminster Press, 1961, 207p.

Guenther, H. V. The Concept of Mind in Buddhist Tantrism. *J. Orient. Stud.*, 3/2, 1956, p.261–77.

Haller, W. *The Elect Nation: The Meaning and Relevance of Foxe's Book of Martyrs.* N.Y.: Harper and Row, 1964, 259p.

Hardison, O. B., Jr. *Christian Rite and Christian Drama in the Middle Ages.* Baltimore, Maryland: Johns Hopkins Univ. Press, 1965.

Hsiang-Kuang, C. Buddhist Studies in China and Its Impact on Chinese Literature and Thought. *Chinese Cult.*, 4/4, 1963, p.43–59.

Merkelbach, R. Origin and Religious Meaning of Greek Tragedy and Comedy: According to the *Erigone* of Eratosthenes. *Hist. Rel.*, 3/2, 1964, p.175–190.

Panichas, G. A. (ed.) Literature and Religion. *Comp. Lit. Stud.*, 2/4, 1965, p.289–385.

Pollins, H. Sociological Aspects of Anglo-Jewish Literature. *Jew. J. Sociol.*, 2/1, 1960, p.25–41.

Puknat, S. B. *Religious Forms and Faith in the Volksbuch.* Berkeley: Univ. of California Press, 1952, 428p.

Roth, L. Religion and Literature. *Hibbert J.*, 60, 1961, p.24–34.

Scott, N. A., Jr. *Modern Literature and the Religious Frontier.* N.Y.: Harper, 1958, 138p.

Siddiqi, M. *Hadīth Literature: Its Origin, Development, Special Features and Criticism.* Calcutta: Calcutta Univ. Press, 1961, 211p.

Steinberg, A. H. Jewish Characters in Fugitive American Novels of the Nineteenth Century. *Yivo Ann. Jew. Soc. Sci.*, 11, 1956–57, p.105–21.

Sutton, J. Christian Literature Work in Malaya and Singapore. *Int. R. Missions*, 48/190, 1959, p.216–21.

Upadhye, A. N. The Literature and Philosophy of the Jainas. *Indo-Asian Cult.*, 4/4, 1956, p.440–9.

Weales, G. *Religion in Modern English Drama.* Phila.: Univ. of Pennsylvania Press, 1961, 317p.

Wheeler, B. M. Research Abstract: Religious Themes in Contemporary Literature 1959–1962. *J. Bib. Rel.*, 32/1, 1964, p.50–6; see also 32/2, p.133–8.

White, C. S. J. Sufism in Medieval Hini Literature. *Hist. Rel.*, 5/1, 1965, p.114–32.

See Also:

Alilunas, L. J.   1d
Dasgupta, S.   3e
Freud, S.   8a6
May, R.   7f
Olson, B. E.   7b3
Shashibhusan, D.   3f
Verma, B. C.   3
Voigt, G. P.   7a
Widengren, G.   3b

4g4.   Parochial Schools

Barrett, D. N. and Blair, M. J. Undergraduate Sociology Programs in Catholic Colleges in the United States, 1942–1964. *Sociol. Anal.*, 26/1, 1965, p.45–50.

Beales, A. C. F. Catholic Education in England. *Lumen Vitae*, 1/3, 1946, p.456–66.

Beales, A. C. F. *Education Under Penalty: English Catholic Education From the Reformation to the Fall of James II.* London: Univ. of London, 1960, 306p.

Browne, H. J. The American Parish School in the Last Half Century. *Bull. Nat. Cath. Educ. Assoc.*, 50/1, 1952, p.323–34.

Callahan, D. (ed.) *Federal Aid and Catholic Schools.* Baltimore: Helican, 1964, 160p.

Chapman, S. H. Church Schools: Some Factors in the Relation Among Private, Public, and Parochial Schools. *J. Educ. Sociol.*, 18/5, 1945, p.340–50.

Church History in Religious Education. *Lumen Vitae*, 14/2, 1959, p.225–344.

Clippinger, J. A Survey of Church-Related Colleges. *J. Bib. Rel.*, 13, 1945, p.196–200.

Cottle, W. C. and Watson, E. P. Counseling and Guidance Services in Catholic Schools. *Cath. Counselor*, 2, 1958, p.43–5.

Curtin, J. R. *Attitudes of Parents Toward Catholic Education.* Washington: Catholic Univ. Press, 1954.

Defarrari, R. J. Sociology in the Program of the Catholic General College. *Amer. Cath. Sociol. R.*, 13/2, 1952, p.89–102.

Denty, V. D. Religious Education at American Catholic Colleges. *Lumen Vitae*, 14/3, 1959, p.549–53.

Dodge, B. *Muslim Education in Medieval Times.* Washington: Middle East Institute, 1962, 105p.

Donovan, J. D. Family Socialization and Faculty Publication: A Study of the Academic Man in the Catholic College. *Amer. Cath. Sociol. R.*, 24/2, 1963, p.115–26.

Draz, S. M. A. Al Azhar. *Int. Soc. Sci. Bull.*, 5/4, 1953, p.698–701.

Duskin, A. M. and Redelheim, U. A. *Jewish Education in the United States.* N.Y.: American Association for Jewish Education, 1959.

Ebisawa, A. The Jesuits and Their Cultural Activities in the Far East. *J. World Hist.*, 5/2, 1959, p.244–74.

Ellis, J. T. *The Formative Years of the Catholic University of America.* Washington: American Catholic Historical Association, 1946, 415p.

Espy, R. H. W. *The Religion of College Teachers: The Beliefs, Practices, and Religious Preparations of Faculty Members in Church-Related College.* N.Y.: Association Press, 1951, 216p.

Fernan, J. J. The College Religion Course: The Freshman Year. *Lumen Vitae*, 4/2, 1949, p.332–7.

Fichter, J. H. *The Parochial School: A Sociological Study.* Notre Dame: Univ. of Notre Dame, 1958.

Fishman, J. A. Degree of Bilingualism in a Yiddish School

and Leisure Time Activities. *J. Soc. Psychol.*, 36/2, 1952, p.155–65.

Fleshler, A. D. The Sociological and Educational Significance of Jewish Schools in New York. *J. Educ. Sociol.*, 2/5, 1929, p.278–89.

Frain, T. J. A Survey of the Lay Catechists Teaching Public School Pupils. *Cath. Educ. R.*, 53/4, 1955, p.238–54.

Goodman, M. A Research Note on Jewish Education on Merseyside, 1962. *Jew. J. Sociol.*, 7/1, 1965, p.30–45.

Greeley, A. M. Anti-Intellectualism in Catholic Colleges. *Amer. Cath. Sociol. R.*, 23/4, 1962, p.350–68. See also: R. A. Lamanna—Note on Catholic Anti-Intellectualism, 24/1, 1963, p. 57–8; A. M. Greeley—Rejoinder, 24/2, p.167.

Hoffner, J. Replacement of Professors in Theological Colleges and Faculties. *Soc. Compass*, 8/4, 1961, p.291–303.

Hornsby, G. Church and Education in the Lake Nyasa Region of Tanganyika. *Comp. Educ. R.*, 6/1, 1962, p.63–8.

Janowsky, O. I. Adult Jewish Education—Analysis of a Survey. *Jew. Educ.*, 36/1, 1965, p.17–23.

Joseph, H. Jewish Education in Great Britain. *In Dispersion*, 1, 1962, p.43–53.

Kaiser, M. L. *The Development of the Concept and Function of the Catholic Elementary School in the American Parish.* Washington: Catholic Univ. Press, 1955.

Kaminetsky, J. The Hebrew Day School Movement. *School Society*, 82/2069, 1955, p.105–7.

Kraft, C. F. Religion in the Church-Related College. *J. Bib. Rel.*, 14, 1946, p.69–75.

Kramer, W. A. *Lutheran Schools of the Lutheran Church-Missouri Synod.* St. Louis: The Lutheran Church-Missouri Synod, 1961.

La Farge, J. Race Relations in the Curriculum of the Catholic College. *Amer. Cath. Sociol. R.*, 2/2, 1944, p.97–103.

La Farge, J. Religious Education of American Negro. *Lumen Vitae*, 2/1, 1947, p.4–20.

Levinson, B. M. The Intelligence of Applicants for Admission to Jewish Day Schools. *Jew. Soc. Stud.*, 19, 1957, p.129–40.

Levitats, I. The Organization and Management of Jewish Schools in America. *Yivo Ann. Jew. Soc. Sci.*, 11, 1956–57, p.82–104.

Levy, C. S. The Special Purpose of the Jewish School of

Social Work. *Jew. Soc. Work Forum*, 1/1, 1963, p.7–16.

Lienhardt, P. The Mosque College of Lamu and Its Social Background. *Tanganyika Notes Rec.*, 5, 1959, p.228–42.

Mang, W. The Extent of Democratization in Catholic Educational Institutions. *Amer. Cath. Sociol. R.*, 2/1, 1941, p.57–64.

Marie, N. Statistics of Religious Educators. *Cath. Educ.*, 27/5, 1957, p.291–2, 344.

Matthews, Z. K. Christian Education in a Changing Africa. *Int. R. Missions*, 52/205, 1963, p.38–46.

McAvoy, T. T. The Philosophers and American Catholic Education. *Cath. Educ. R.*, 47, 1949, p.579–85.

McGreal, M. N. *The Role of the Teaching Sisterhood in American Education.* Washington: Catholic Univ. Press, 1951.

McManus, W. E. Financing Catholic Education. *Cath. School J.*, 51/4, 1951, p.137–40.

Murray, J. C. The Religious School in a Pluralist Society. *Cath. Mind*, 54/1125, 1956, p.502–11.

Nardi, N. Jewish Education in the United States: Changes and Prospects. *In Dispersion*, 1, 1962, p.22–42.

National Catholic Welfare Conference. *The Official Guide to Catholic Educational Institutions in the United States: With a Special Section on Religious Communities.* Washington, D.C.: National Catholic Welfare Conference, 1959.

Niebuhr, H. R., *et al.* *The Advancement of Theological Education.* N.Y.: Harper, 1957.

O'Brien, R. E. The Cost of Parochial Education in Chicago. *J. Educ. Sociol.*, 2/6, 1929, p.479–86. See also: Administrative Management of Teachers in the Elementary Schools of the Roman Catholic Church in Chicago, 2/8, p.479–86; Relations Between the Public and Catholic Schools of Chicago, 3/2, p.121–9.

Odsthuizen, G. C. Theological Education in South Africa. *Int. R. Missions*, 52/207, 1963, p.279–88.

Power, T. *Home and School Relationships in the Catholic Elementary Schools of a Number of Selected Dioceses.* Washington: Catholic Univ. Press, 1950.

Present Trends in Children's Religious Education. *Lumen Vitae*, 12/4, 1957, p.671–716.

Rothman, S. The Politics of Catholic Parochial Schools: An Historical and Comparative Analysis. *J. Polit.*, 25/1, 1963, p.49–71.

Ruberu, T. R. Educational Work of the Christian Missionary Societies in Ceylon During the Early Years of British Rule. *Ceylon J. Hist. Soc. Stud.*, 3/2, 1960, p.157–65; see also: 4/1, 1961, p.50–8; 4/2, p.157–68; 6/1, 1963, p.71–83.

Rudavsky, D.   Trends in Jewish School Organization and Enrollment in New York City, 1917–1950. *Yivo Ann. Jew. Soc. Sci.*, 10, 1956, p.45–81.

Ryan, C. J.   The Lay Teacher in the Catholic School. *Homil. Pastoral R.*, 48/8, 1948, p.575–81.

Sloyan, G. S.   Undergraduate Studies in Sacred Doctrine at one U.S. University. *Lumen Vitae*, 15/4, 1960, p.712–22.

Smalley, B.   *The Study of the Bible in the Middle Ages.* Notre Dame: Univ. of Notre Dame Press, 1964.

Steinberg, B.   Jewish Schooling in Great Britain. *Jew. J. Sociol.*, 6/1, 1964, p.52–68.

Wagner, H., *et al.*   Religious Background and Higher Education. *Amer. Sociol. R.*, 24, 1959, p.852–6.

Watkin, E. I.   *The Catholic Campus.* N.Y.: Macmillan, 1963, 204p.

Wise, J. E.   Jesuit School Beginnings. *Hist. Educ. Quart.*, 1/1, 1961, p.28–31.

Wyckoff, D. C.   The Protestant Day School. *School Society*, 82/2069, 1955, p.98–101.

Yarri, A.   "Ner Tamid" Societies in Poland and Lithuania. *Jew. Soc. Stud.*, 21/2, 1959, p.118–31.

See Also:

Allen, Y., Jr.   7a
Bainton, R. H.   7a4
Boehm, L.   5a3

Bruder, E. E.   7a4
Cash, W. L.   7a4
Cragg, D. B.   7b3
Daneman, E. A.   1e
Dodge, B.   3d
Doerr, H.   7a4
Elliot, H. S.   5b1
Ferguson, P.   5e4
Gans, W. G.   4c
Hake, A.   5e1
Hassenger, R.   4h
Hiltner, S.   7a1
Houtart, F.   5e
Huppeler, V. K.   1f
Jamison, W. G.   7a4
Kerins, J. L.   7a4
Kimber, J. A. M.   7b3
Kosa, J.   7b3
Lauerman, L. L.   1g
Lee, J. M.   7a4
Martin, J. A., Jr.   7a4
McClure, R. B.   5b
McLaughlin, R.   4a1
McManus, W. E.   5a2
Mihanovich, C. S.   7b3
Mulvaney, B. G.   1f
Newman, E. V.   5e4
Presbyterian Church   5e3
Rossi, P. H.   7b2
Sandron, C.   7b2
Southard, S.   7a4
Walker, F. J.   4a1
Walsh, M. E.   5c

4g5.   *Secular Schools*

American Council of Education.   *The Function of Public Schools in Dealing With Religion.* Washington: American Council of Education, 1953, see other reports.

The Anti-Religious Campaign in Higher Education. *Soviet Stud.*, 6/3, 1955, p.312–5.

Azneer, J. L.   Religious Holiday Observance in Public Schools. *Rel. Educ.*, 55, 1960, p.293–6.

Beach, W.   Graduate Study in Religion at Duke University. *J. Bib. Rel.*, 31/1, 1963, p.36–9.

Boles, D. E.   *The Bible, Religion, and the Public Schools.* Ames: Iowa State Univ. Press, 1965, 408p.

Brooks, B. A.   The Place of the Study of Religion in the Liberal Arts Curriculum in the Light of Recent Theories of the Higher Learning. *J. Bib. Rel.*, 6, 1938, p.187–94.

Brothers, J. B.   Religion in the British Universities: The Findings of Some Recent Surveys. *Archiv. Sociol. Rel.*, 18, 1964, p.71–82.

Cantelon, J. E.   *A Protestant Approach to the Campus Ministry.* Phila.: Westminster Press, 1964, 127p.

Chamberlin, J. G.   *Churches and the Campus.* Phila.: Westminster Press, 1963, 189p.

Cohen, J.   Religion and the Public Schools. *J. Jew. Commun. Serv.*, 33/1, 1956, p.36–40.

Compton, R. J.   Christianity and Liberal Education. *J. Bib. Rel.*, 23, 1955, p.251–5.

Eadie, D. G.   Religion on the Campus. *Foundations*, 4, 1961, p.358–62.

Gabriel, R. H.   *Religion and Learning at Yale: The Church of Christ in College and University, 1757–1957.* New Haven: Yale Univ. Press, 1958.

Gernant, L.   Religion at a State-Owned Institution: The Western Michigan College Story. *Rel. Educ.*, 52/5, 1957, p.375–583.

Green, V. H. H.   *Religion at Oxford and Cambridge: A*

History, 1160–1960. London: S C M Press, 1964, 392p.

Greenberg, M.   The Jewish Student at Yale: His Attitude Toward Judaism. *Yivo Ann. Jew. Soc. Sci.,* 1, 1946, p.217–40.

Grissom, R. L., *et al.*   Some Experiments in Teaching with the Clergy in the University of Nebraska College of Medicine. *J. Med. Educ.,* 34, 1959, p.1000–2.

Hammond, P. E.   The Campus Ministry and Academic Values: An Interpretation of Some Findings in a Questionnaire Survey. *J. High. Educ.,* 36/5, 1965, p.274–8.

Herberg, W.   The Religious Stirring on the Campus. *Commentary,* 13/2, 1952, p.242–8.

Hofmann, J.   Toward an Understanding of the Jewish College Student. *Rel. Educ.,* 60/6, 1965, p.443–50.

Jacobs, J. A.   The Present Dilemma of Religious Education. *J. Educ. Sociol.,* 4/4, 1930, p.225–32.

Jones, W. M.   Religion in School and Society. *Sociol. R.,* 38/1, 1946, p.22–3.

Jospe, A.   *Judaism on the Campus.* Washington: B'nai Brith Hillel Foundations, 1963, 126p.

Karpas, M. R.   The Schools and Religion: A Study to Identify the Advocates of Religious Instruction in the Public Schools. *J. Hum. Relat.,* 13/1, 1965, p.13–20.

Kirkpatrick, C.   Students Projects and the Sociology of Religion. *Soc. Forces,* 12/1, 1933, p.57–64.

Lanning, J. T.   The Church and the Enlightenment in the Universities. *Americas,* 15/4, 1959, p.333–49.

Meland, B. E.   The Study of Religion in a Liberal Arts College. *J. Bib. Rel.,* 5, 1937, p.62–9.

Michaelson, R.   *The Study of Religion in American Universities.* New Haven, Connecticut: The Society for Religion in Higher Education, 1965, 164p.

Mitchell, F. W.   Religious Instruction and Observances in the Public Schools of New Zealand. *Comp. Educ. R.,* 7, 1963, p.297–300.

Pratt, J. W.   Religious Conflict in the Development of the New York Public School System. *Hist. Educ. Quart.,* 5/2, 1965, p.110–20.

Rudavsky, D.   Hebraic Studies in Colleges and Universities. *Rel. Educ.,* 59/4, 1964, p.330–7.

Shedd, C. P.   Religion in the Colleges. *J. Bib. Rel.,* 8, 1940, p.179–87.

Snavely, G. E.   *The Church and the Four-Year College: An Appraisal of Their Relation.* N.Y.: Harper, 1955, 216p.

Strachan, M. and Beardslee, A. M. (eds.)   *The Christian Faith and Youth Today: Proceedings of the Conference on Religion in Education Held at Atlantic City, October 1956.* Greenwich, Connecticut: Seabury Press, 1957, 88p.

Stroup, H.   Coordinating Councils of Religious Organizations in Public Colleges and Universities. *R. Rel. Res.,* 4/3, 1963, p.171–8.

Symposium: Religion on the Campus. *Rel. Educ.,* 60/4, 1965, p.258–89.

Symposium: Religion in the Public Schools. *Rel. Educ.,* 59/6, 1964, p.442–78, 504.

Tangri, S. S.   Intellectuals and Society in Nineteenth Century India. *Comp. Stud. Society Hist.,* 3/4, 1961, p.368–94.

Thalheimer, F.   Continuity and Change in Religiosity: A Study of Academicians. *Pac. Sociol. R.,* 8/2, 1965, p.101–8.

Thayer, V. T.   *Religion in Public Education.* N.Y.: Viking, 1947.

Thayer, V. T.   *The Attack Upon the American Secular School.* Boston: The Beacon Press, 1951.

Wagner, H. R. and Brown, R. J.   Catholic Students in Non-Catholic Colleges, *Sociol. Anal.,* 26/2, 1965, p.82–95.

Williams, G. H.   Religion in the Public Schools of Our Democracy. *Rel. Educ.,* 51, 1956, p.374–7.

Withey, R. A., Jr.   Role of Religion in Higher Education. *School Society,* 26/1975, 1952, p.257–61.

See Also:

Segal, B. E. 5a2, 5a3
Shuttleworth, F. K. 7b
Smith, S. A. 7a1

Strommen, M. 7b
Vinacke, W. E. 7b3
Wonderly, W. K. 5e

4g6. *Teaching of Religion*

Adams, D. E. The Teaching of Religion in the Liberal Arts College. *J. Bib. Rel.*, 2, 1934, p.56–60.

Adar, Z. The Teaching of the Bible in Israel and the Problem of Religious Education. In A. M. Duskin and C. Frankenstein (eds.)—*Studies in Education.* Jerusalem: The Hebrew University, 1963, p.77–104, vol. 13.

Bausani, A. Can Monotheism be Taught? *Numen*, 10/3, 1963, p.167–201.

Branigan, J. J. *The Teaching of Religion in Catholic Schools.* London: Macmillan, 1954, 332p.

Brown, N. C. (ed.) *The Study of Religion in the Public Schools: An Appraisal.* Washington, D. C.: American Council on Education, 1958.

Butler, J. D. *Religious Education.* N.Y.: Harper & Row, 1962, 231p.

Chamberlin, J. G. *Freedom and Faith: New Approaches to Christian Education.* Phila.: Westminster Press, 1965.

Committee on Religion and Education of the American Council of Education—*The Function of the Public Schools in Dealing With Religion.* Washington, D. C.: American Council on Education, 1953.

Cross, E. A. Bible-Study in State Colleges and High Schools. *Amer. J. Sociol.*, 20/5, 1915; p.700–5.

Cutler, E. Two Experiments in Teaching Religion to Pre-College Students. *J. Bib. Rel.*, 15, 1947, p.100–4.

Elwood, D. J. The Lost Dimension in the University Curriculum. *Silliman J.*, 10/1, 1963, p.5–22.

Fairchild, E. M. Ethical Instruction in School and Church. *Amer. J. Sociol.*, 4/4, 1899, p.433–47.

Finch, S. M. and Kroon, E. H. Some Educational Factors in the Religious Education of Children. *Rel. Educ.*, 54, 1959, p.36–43.

Hamilton, H. D. God in the Classroom: The New York Regents' Prayer Case. *Soc. Sci.*, 38/2, 1963, p.92–8.

Holbrook, C. A. Changing Emphases in Courses in Christian Ethics. *J. Bib. Rel.*, 23, 1955, p.95–102.

Johnson, P. E. College Courses in Religion. *J. Bib. Rel.*, 10, 1942, p.147–50, 183–4.

Kobayashi, V. N. The Quest for Experience: Zen, Dewey, and Education. *Comp. Educ. R.*, 5/3, 1962, p.217–22.

Lampe, M. W. Teaching Religion in a State University. *J. Bib. Rel.*, 17, 1949, p.17–8.

Lee, D. D. *Religious Perspectives of College Teaching in Anthropology.* New Haven: E. W. Hazen Foundation, 1951, 22p.

Lottich, K. V. Religious Values in Intercultural Education: An Experimental College Colloquium on World Civilization. *J. Hum. Relat.*, 11/5, 1963, p.616–25.

Lovell, F. B. Religious Syncretism and Undergraduate Biblical Courses. *J. Bib. Rel.*, 9, 1941, p.23–7.

Newman, H. L. A Study of Instruction in Bible in Secondary Schools. *J. Bib. Rel.*, 2, 1934, p.80–3.

Newman, H. L. The Needs and Opportunities for the Teaching of Bible and Religion in Preparatory Schools (Committee Report). *J. Bib. Rel.*, 4, 1936, p.25–8.

Noss, J. B. Changing Perspectives in Courses in World Religions. *J. Bib. Rel.*, 23, 1955, p.89–94.

Oullet, F. Elementary School Teaching: Responsibility of Church or State? *Rech. Sociog.*, 2/2, 1961, p.171–87.

Quimby, C. W. Teaching Materials in Church Schools as Related to College. *J. Bib. Rel.*, 4, 1936, p.28–31.

Raghavan, V. Methods of Popular Religious Instruction in South India. *J. Amer. Folklore*, 71/281, 1958, p.336–46.

Rosmarin, T. W. The Aims and Methods of Jewish Adult Education. *J. Bib. Rel.*, 5, 1937, p.69–74.

Simonitsch, R. G. *Religious Instruction in Catholic Colleges for Men.* Washington: Catholic Univ. Press, 1952, 327p.

Sloyan, G. S. *The Recognition of Certain Christian Concepts in the Social Studies in Catholic Elementary Education.* Washington: Catholic Univ. Press, 1948.

Therese, M. Presenting Basic Christian Principles in High School Sociology. *Amer. Cath. Sociol. R.*, 12/2, 1951, p.84–93.

Training Religious Educators. *Lumen Vitae*, 14/3, 1959, p.395–528.

Tuttle, H. S. Aims of Courses in Religion. *J. Soc. Psychol.*, 31/2, 1950, p.305–9.

See Also:
Assunta, M. 2a

102

4h.   *Religion and Personality*

Academy of Religion and Mental Health. *Religion in the Developing Personality.* N.Y.: New York Univ. Press, 1960.

Aitken, B. Temperament in Native American Religion. *J. Roy. Anthropol. Inst.,* 60, 1930, p.363–87.

Allinsmith, W. Conscience and Conflict: The Moral Force in Personality. *Child Devel.,* 28, 1957, p.469–76.

Allport, G. W. *The Individual and His Religion.* N.Y.: Macmillan, 1950.

Allport, G. W. *Religion in the Developing Personality.* N.Y.: New York Univ. Press, 1960.

Armstrong, R. G., *et al.* Religious Attitudes and Emotional Adjustment. *J. Psychol. Stud.,* 13, 1962, p.35–47.

Beck, R. N. *The Meaning of Americanism: An Essay on the Religious and Philosophical Basis of the American Mind.* N.Y.: Philosophical Library, 1956, 180p.

Bettelheim, B. *Symbolic Wounds: Puberty Rites and the Envious Male.* Glencoe: Free Press, 1954, 286p.

Bieri, J. and Lobeck, R. Self Concept Differences in Relation to Identifications, Religion and Social Class. *J. Abnorm. Soc. Psychol.,* 62, 1961, p.94–8.

Boisen, A. T. The Genesis and Significance of Mystical Identification in Cases of Mental Disorder. *Psychiatry,* 15, 1952, p.287–96.

Boisen, A. T. Inspiration in the Light of Psychopathology. *Past. Psychol.,* 11, 1960, p.10–8.

Bowers, M. K. Friend or Traitor? Hypnosis in the Service of Religion. *Int. J. Clin. Exp. Hypnosis,* 7, 1959, p.205–15.

Boyer, L. B. Christian "Neurosis." *J. Amer. Psychoanal. Assoc.,* 3/3, 1955, p.467–88.

Brown, D. G. and Lowe, W. L. Religious Beliefs and Personality Characteristics of College Students. *J. Soc. Psychol.,* 33/1, 1951, p.103–29.

Brown, L. B. Religious Belief and Reports of Childhood Experiences. *Psychol. Rep.,* 10/1, 1962, p.269–70.

Brown, W. *Personality and Religion.* London: Univ. of London Press, 1946.

Caffrey, A. M. *Youth in a Catholic Parish.* Washington: Catholic Univ. Press, 1941, 310p.

Callahan, D. *The Mind of the Catholic Layman.* N.Y.: Scribners, 1963, 208p.

Carstairs, G. M., *et al.* Rorschach Responses of Hindus and Bhils. *J. Soc. Psychol.,* 51/2, 1960, p.217–27.

Clark, W. H. A Study of Some of the Factors Leading to Achievement and Creativity, With Special Reference to Religious Scepticism and Belief. *J. Soc. Psychol.,* 41/1, 1955, p.57–70.

Dreger, R. M. Expressed Attitudes and Needs of Religious Persons Compared With Those Determined by Projective Techniques. *J. Genet. Psychol.,* 1958, p.217–24.

Dreger, R. M. Some Personality Correlates of Religious Attitudes as Determined by Projective Techniques. *Psychol. Monographs,* 66/3, 1952, 18p.

Elkind, D. Age Changes in the Meaning of Religious Identity. *R. Rel. Res.,* 6/1, 1964, p.36–40.

Erikson, E. H. *Young Man Luther: A Study in Psychoanalysis and History.* N.Y.: Norton, 1962, 288p.

Evoy, J. J. and Christophe, V. F. *Personality Development in Religious Life.* N.Y.: Sheed & Ward, 1963, 247p.

Farr, C. B. and Howe, R. L. The Influence of Religious Ideas on the Etiology, Symptomology and Prognosis of the Psychoses: With Special Reference to Social Factors. *Amer. J. Psychiat.,* 11, 1932, p.845–64.

Fichter, J. H. Religious Values and the Social Personality. *Amer. Cath. Sociol. R.,* 17/2, 1956, p.109–11.

Fichter, J. H. Social Background of Religious and Laity. *Soc. Order,* 8/4, 1958, p.168–78.

Firth, R. W. Religious Belief and Personal Adjustment. *J. Roy. Anthropol.,* 78/1–2, 1948, p.25–43.

Fishman, J. A. Patterns of American Self-Identification Among Children of a Minority Group. *Yivo Ann. Jew. Soc. Sci.,* 10, 1956, p.212–66.

Fleege, H. The American Adolescent and Religion. *Lumen Vitae,* 2/3, 1947, p.397–420.

Francesco, E. A Pervasive Value: Conventional Religiosity. *J. Soc. Psychol.,* 57, 1962, p.467–70.

Fukuyama, Y. Wonder Letters: An Experimental Study of the Religious Sensitivities of Children. *Rel. Educ.*, 58/4, 1963, p.377–83.

Glenn, V. M. Religious Self-Identification. *Pac. Sociol. R.*, 5/1, 1962, p.40–3.

Godin, A. Faith and the Psychological Development of Children and Adolescents. *Lumen Vitae*, 13, 1958, p.297–311.

Godin, A. (ed.) *Child and Adult Before God: Thought and Research.* Brussels: Lumen Vitae Press, 1961.

Grafton, T. H. God in the Personality Paradigm. *R. Rel. Res.*, 5/1, 1963, p.21–30.

Guertin, W. and Schmidt, A. W. Constellations of Religious Attitudes of Paranoid Schizophrenics. *Psychol. Rep.*, 1/4, 1955, p.319–22.

Halpern, L. Some Data on the Psychic Morbidity of Jews and Arabs in Palestine. *Amer. J. Psychiat.*, 94, 1938, p.1215–22.

Hamilton, T. Social Optimism and Pessimism in American Protestantism. *Pub. Opin. Quart.*, 6/2, 1942, p.280–3.

Hanawalt, N. G. Feelings of Security and of Self-Esteem in Relation to Religious Belief. *J. Soc. Psychol.*, 59/2, 1963, p.347–54.

Hassenger, R. Religious Values and Personality Traits in Catholic College Women. *Insight*, 3/1, 1964, p.37–48.

Heiermann, F. Sainthood. *Amer. J. Sociol.*, 25/1, 1919, p.24–40.

Held, O. C. A Comparative Study of the Performance of Jewish and Gentile College Students on the American Council Psychological Examination. *J. Soc. Psychol.*, 13/2, 1941, p.407–11.

Hoult, T. F. and Reckham, C. W. Religion as a Cultural Factor in One Aspect of the Personality of Selected College Students. *J. Educ. Sociol.*, 31/2, 1957, p.75–81.

Johnson, B. H. Personality Traits of Workers in the Field of Religion. *Rel. Educ.*, 38, 1943, p.325–9.

Jones, M. B. Religious Values and Authoritarian Tendency. *J. Soc. Psychol.*, 48, 1958, p.83–9.

Jones, W. L. Some Psychological Conditions of the Development of Methodism Up to 1850. *Brit. J. Psychol.*, 42, 1951, p.345–54.

Kaplan, A. Maturity in Religion. *Bull. Phila. Assoc. Psychoanal.*, 13, 1963, p.101–19.

Kaplan, B. and Plaut, T. F. A. *Personality in a Communal Society: An Analysis of the Mental Health of the Hutterites.* Lawrence, Kansas: Univ. of Kansas Publications, 1956, 116p.

Leary, T., *et al.* (eds.) *The Psychedelic Experience: A Manual Based on the Tibetan Book of the Dead.* N.Y.: University Books, 1964, 159p.

Lee, E. G. *Mass Man and Religion.* London: Hutchinson, 1946, 160p.

Lehrer, L. The Jewish Elements in the Psychology of the Jewish Child in America. *Yivo Ann. Jew. Soc. Sci.*, 1, 1946, p.195–216.

Lengermann, J. J. and D'Antonio, W. V. Religion, Dogmatism and Community Leadership: An Extension of the Theories of the Open and Closed Mind. *Sociol. Anal.*, 25/3, 1964, p.141–58.

Lesser, G. S. Religion and the Defensive Responses in Children's Fantasy. *J. Proj. Tech.*, 23, 1959, p.64–8.

Levinson, B. M. The Socio-Economic Status, Intelligence and Personality Traits of Jewish Homeless Men. *Yivo Ann. Jew. Soc. Sci.*, 11, 1956–57, p.122–41.

Levinson, B. M. Traditional Jewish Cultural Values and Performance on the Wechsler Tests. *J. Educ. Psychol.*, 50, 1959, p.177–81.

Loewenstein, R. *Christians and Jews: A Psychoanalytic Study.* N.Y.: International Universities Press, 1951, 224p.

Long, B. H. Catholic-Protestant Differences in Acceptance of Others. *Sociol. Soc. Res.*, 49/2, 1965, p.166–72.

Lowe, W. L. Psychodynamics in Religious Delusions and Hallucinations. *Amer. J. Psychoth.*, 7, 1953, p.454–62.

Martin, C. and Nichols, R. C. Personality and Religious Belief. *J. Soc. Psychol.*, 56, 1962, p.3–8.

McKenna, H. V. Religious Attitudes and Personality Traits. *J. Soc. Psychol.*, 54, 1961, p.379–88.

Mischel, W. and Mischel, F. Psychological Aspects of Spirit Possession. *Amer. Anthropol.*, 60, 1958, p.249–60.

Moberg, D. O. The Christian Religion and Personal Adjustment in Old Age. *Amer. Sociol. R.*, 18, 1953, p.87–90.

Moloney, J. C. Mother, God, and Superego. *J. Amer. Psychoanal. Assoc.*, 2/1, 1954, p.120–51.

Moore, S. A Catholic Neurosis? *Clergy R.*, 46, 1961, p.641–7.

Mukerjee, R. Roots of Religion. *Soc. Forces*, 8/1, 1929, p.10–6.

Muller, W. Mazdak and the Alphabet: Mysticism of the East. *Hist. Rel.*, 3/1, 1963, p.72–82.

Nash, C. B. Correlation Between ESP and Religious Value. *J. Parapsychol.*, 22, 1958, p.204–9.

Nicholson, R. A. *The Idea of Personality in Sufism.* Lahore: Shaikh Muhammed Ashrof, 1964, 106p.

Oates, W. E. *Religious Dimensions of Personality.* N.Y.: Association Press, 1957, 320p.

Oates, W. E. The Religious Understanding of Personality. *Past. Psychol.*, 8/79, 1957, p.46–50.

Oguchi, I. Authoritarianism in Japanese Religion. *Rel. East West*, 1, 1955, p.10–5.

O'Reilly, C. T. Religious Practice and Personal Adjustments of Older People. *Sociol. Soc. Res.*, 42/2, 1957, p.119–21.

Ostow, M. and Scharfstein, B. A. *The Need to Believe.* N.Y.: International Universities Press, 1954.

Pan, J. S. Personal Adjustments of Old People: A Study of Old People in Protestant Church Homes for the Aged. *Sociol. Soc. Res.*, 35, 1950, p.3–11.

Parsons, A. Expressive Symbolism in Witchcraft and Delusion: A Comparative Study. *R. Int. D'Ethnopsychol. Norm. Pathol.*, 1/2, 1956, p.99–119.

Plodnick, D. The Effect of Culture Change Upon the Personalities of Second-Generation Reservation Indians. *Yivo Ann. Jew. Soc. Sci.*, 2/3, 1948, p.252–61.

Rath, R. and Sircar, N. C. The Cognitive Background of Six Hindu Caste Groups Regarding the Low Caste Untouchables. *J. Soc. Psychol.*, 51/2, 1960, p.295–306.

Reik, T. *Dogma and Compulsion.* N.Y.: International Universities Press, 1951.

Sadler, A. W. Glossolalia and Possession: An Appeal to the Episcopal Study Commission. *J. Sci. Stud. Rel.*, 4/1, 1964, p.84–90.

Sanua, V. D. Minority Status Among Jews and the Psychological Adjustment. *Jew. J. Sociol.*, 4/2, 1962, p.242–53.

Schermerhorn, R. A. (ed.) *Psychiatric Index for Interdisciplinary Research: A Guide to the Literature.* Washington, D. C.: U.S. Department of Health, Education and Welfare, 1964, p.873–78.

Schroeder, T. A "Living God" Incarnate. *Psychoanal. R.*, 19, 1932, p.36–46.

Shanker Asthana, H. Some Aspects of Personality Structuring in Indian (Hindu) Social Organization. *J. Soc. Psychol.*, 44/2, 1956, p.155–63.

Shinn, R. L. (ed.) *The Search for Identity: Essays on the American Character.* N.Y.: Harper and Row, 1964, 204p.

Slater, E. Neurosis and Religious Affiliation. *J. Ment. Sci.*, 93, 1947, p.392–8.

Smith, E. L. Personality Differences Between Amish and Non-Amish Children. *Rural Sociol.*, 23/4, 1958, p.371–6.

Solomon, D. (ed.) *LSD: The Consciousness-Expanding Drug.* N.Y.: G. P. Putnam's Sons, 1964, 273p.

Sorokin, P. A. (ed.) *Forms and Techniques of Altruistic and Spiritual Growth: A Symposium.* Boston: Beacon Press, 1954.

Spilka, B. Some Personality Correlates of Interiorized and Institutionalized Religious Belief. *Psychol. News.*, 47, 1958, p.397–405.

Stimson, J. Some Religious-Ethnic Differences in Interaction Rates. *Psychol. Rep.*, 7, 1960, p.345–56.

Sward, K. Temperament and Religious Experience. *J. Soc. Psychol.*, 2, 1931, p.374–96.

Taylor, W. S. Basic Personality in Orthodox Hindu Culture Patterns. *J. Abnorm. Soc. Psychol.*, 43, 1948, p.3–12.

Thouless, R. H. *Authority and Freedom: Some Psychological Problems of Religious Belief.* London: Hodder & Staughton, 1954.

Tkacik, A. Conscience: Conscious and Unconscious. *J. Rel. Health*, 4/1, 1964, p.75–85.

Vergote, A. Psychological Conditions of Adult Faith. *Lumen Vitae*, 15/4, 1960, p.623–34.

von Kaam, A. *Religion and Personality.* Englewood Cliffs, New Jersey: Prentice-Hall, 1964, 170p.

Welford, A. T. Is Religious Behavior Dependent Upon Affect or Frustration? *J. Abnorm. Soc. Psychol.*, 42, 1947, p.310–9.

Wells, C. D. Religious Personality Types. *Sociol. Soc. Res.*, 16/3, 1932, p.232–41.

White, E. *Christian Life and the Unconscious.* N.Y.: Harper & Brothers, 1955.

Wolff, M. S. Notes on the Vodoun Religion in Haiti With Reference to Its Social and Psychodynamics. *R. Int. D'Ethnopsychol.*, 1/2, 1956, p.209–40.

Cockrum, L. V. 7a4
Durkheim, E. 5a3
Dyer, D. T. 4e
Eaton, J. W. 5b1
Eliade, M. 8a5
Ellis, F. H. 7e
Fine, R. 8a6
Freud, S. 8a6
Frumkin, R. M. 5b1
Gilliand, A. R. 7b2
Guntrip, H. 1e
Harms, E. 7b
Hawley, F. 2a1
Hiltner, S. 8a4
Hofmann, H. 5b1
Houston, J. 7b3
Hsi, Flk, 7b
James, W. 7b3
Jekels, L. 8a2
Johnson, E. H. 7a4
Johnson, P. E. 8a2
Jung, C. G. 6
Kaufman, M. R. 5b1
Kaufman, W. C. 5a2
Kligerman, C. 7a
Kuhlen, R. 7b2
Leavy, S. A. 7d
Lennard, H. L. 7b3
Lewit, D. W. 5a
Little, L. C. 4g (2)

Lowe, W. L. 7b3
Maves, P. B. 5b1
McCann, R. 5b1
Meissner, W. W. 9
Mukerjee, R. 1a
Murphy, R. J. 5b2
Oates, W. E. 5b1 (2), 7a4
O'Doherty, E. F. 5b1
Oetting, E. R. 1e
Pfister, O. R. 5b1
Photiadis, J. D. 7b1
Religious Psychology, Thought 8a3
Ribeiro, R. 7a1
Roberts, H. W. 7a
Róheim, G. 5b1
Rokeach, M. 6d, 7b3
Roy, R. L. 7b3
Rusk, G. Y. 7b2
Sato, K. 1e
Smith, R. O. 7a4
Spoerl, D. T. 5a2
Stromnen, M. 7b
Vernon, G. N. 7b2
Wallace, A. F. C. 8a2
Webb, S. C. 7b
White, G. E. 7a4
Wright, J. C. 5b1
Yarnall, H. 2a1
Young, K. 4e
Zenner, W. P. 7b3

4i. Religion and Sexual Behavior

Bailey, D. S. *Homosexuality and the Western Christian Tradition.* London: Longmans, Green, 1955, 181p.

Bainton, R. H. Christianity and Sex, an Historical Survey. *Past. Psychol.,* 3/26, 1952, p.10–26, 82; see also 4/21, 1953, p.12–29.

Bigham, T. J. Pastoral and Ethical Notes on Problems of Masturbation. *Past. Psychol.,* 11, 1960, p.19–23.

Bodde, D. Sexual Sympathetic Magic in Han China. *Hist. Rel.,* 3/2, 1964, p.292–9.

Bowman, C. C. Cultural Ideology and Heterosexual Reality: A Preface to Sociological Research. *Amer. Sociol. R.,* 49, 1949, p.624–33.

Brav, S. R. *Since Eve: A Sex Ethic Inspired by Hebrew Scripture.* N.Y.: Pageant Press, 1959, 204p.

Brenner, A. B. Onan, the Levirate Marriage and the Genealogy of the Messiah. *J. Amer. Psychoanal. Assoc.,* 10/4, 1962, p.701–21.

Buckley, M. J. *Morality and the Homosexual: A Catholic Approach to a Moral Problem.* Westminster, Maryland: Newman Press, 1960, 214p.

Carney, R. E. and McKeachier, W. J. Religion, Sex, Social Class Probability of Success, and Student Personality. *J. Sci. Stud. Rel.,* 3/1, 1963, p.32–42.

Cole, W. G. *Sex in Christianity and Psychoanalysis.* N.Y.: Oxford, 1955.

Dedman, J. The Relationship Between Religious Attitude and Attitude Toward Pre-Marital Sex Relations. *Marr. Fam. Liv.,* 21, 1959, p.171–6.

Edwards, A. *The Jewel in the Lotus: A Historical Survey of the Sexual Culture of the East.* London: Thames & Hudson, 1961, 293p.

Ellis, A. and Abarbanel, A. (eds.) *The Encyclopedia of Sexual Behavior.* N.Y.: Hawthorne Books, 1961, 2 vols.

Epstein, L. *Sex Laws and Customs in Judaism.* N.Y.: Bloch, 1948.

Feucht, O. E., *et al.* *Sex and the Church: A Sociological, Historical and Theological Investigation of Sex Attitudes.* St. Louis: Concordia Publishing House, 1961, 277p.

Goldberg, B. Z. *The Sacred Fire: The Story of Sex in Religion.* N.Y.: University Books, 1959, 288p.

Gordon, P. *Sex and Religion.* N.Y.: Social Sciences Publishers, 1949, 320p.

Hart, H. and Annella, M. Comparative Sex Mores Among Protestant and Catholic Sociology Students. *Amer. Cath. Sociol. R.,* 24/1, 1963, p.54–6.

Lindenfeld, F. A Note of Social Mobility, Religiosity, and Students' Attitudes Toward Pre-Marital Sexual Relations. *Amer. Sociol. R.,* 25, 1960, p.81–4.

Madigan, F. C. and Vance, R. B. Differential Sex Morality: A Research Design. *Soc. Forces,* 35/3, 1957, p.193–9.

Marukawa, H. Sexual Observances as a Religious Rite in Japan. *Tenri J. Rel.,* 2, 1959, p.5–17.

Patai, R. *Sex and Family in the Bible and the Middle East.* N.Y.: Doubleday, 1959, 282p.

Rommetveit, R. *Social Norms and Roles: Explorations in the Psychology, and Enduring Social Pressures With Empirical Contributions From Inquiries into Religious Attitudes and Sex Roles of Adolescents From Some Districts in Western Norway.* Minneapolis: Univ. of Minnesota Press, 1955, 167p.

Schneider, D. M. Political Organization, Supernatural Sanctions and the Punishment for Incest on Yap. *Amer. Anthropol.,* 59/5, 1957, p.791–800.

Schroeder, T. Witchcraft and the Erotic Life. *J. Nervous Ment. Disease,* 72, 1930, p.640–51.

Shirley, R. W. and Rommey, A. K. Love Magic and Socialization Anxiety: A Cross-Cultural Study. *Amer. Anthropol.,* 64/5, 1962, p.1028–31.

Tanner, R. E. S. The Relationships Between the Sexes in a Coastal Islamic Society: Pangani District, Tanganyika. *Afr. Stud.,* 21/2, 1962, p.70–82.

Taylor, G. R. *Sex in History.* London: Thames & Hudson, 1959, 338p.

Van der Kroef, J. M. Transvestitism and the Religious Hermaphrodite in Indonesia. *J. East Asiatic Stud.,* 3, 1959, p.257–65.

Van Gulik, R. H. *Sexual Life in Ancient China: A Preliminary Survey of Chinese Sex and Society From ca. 1500 B.C. till 1644 A.D.* Leiden: E. J. Brill, 1961, 392p.

Wallin, P. Religiosity, Sexual Gratification, and Marital Satisfaction. *Amer. Sociol. R.,* 22, 1957, p.300–5.

Wayman, A. Female Energy and Symbolism in the Buddhist Tantras. *Hist. Rel.,* 2/1, 1962, p.73–111.

Wood, R. W. *Christ and the Homosexual: Some Observations.* N.Y.: Vantage Press, 1960, 221p.

See Also: 1e, 4e, 4h, 4j4, 7g

Bell, R. R.   4e
Bier, W. C.   7a1
Chruch of England   5g
Cole, W. G.   1e
Derrett, J. D. M.   4e2
Jones, A. H.   4e
Kabiraj, S.   7f
Kavolis, V.   7b3
Layard, J.   4e
Malinowski, B.   8a6
Marshall, D. G.   5b2
Masters, R. E. L.   5b1
Mudd, E.   4e
Schroeder, T.   4h
Strizower, S.   2b
Wallim, P.   4e

4j.   *Religion and Social Differentiation*

Cahnman, W. J. Religion and Nationality. *Amer. J. Sociol.,* 49/6, 1944, p.524–7.

Fichter, J. H. Social Status of American Religious Personnel. *Christus Rex,* 11/1, 1957, p.427–38.

Fichter, J. H. Urban Mobility and Religious Observance. *Amer. Cath. Sociol. R.,* 9/3, 1950, p.130–9.

Greenberg, J. H. Islam and Clan Organization of the Housa. *Southw. J. Anthropol.,* 3/3, 1947, p.193–211.

Jung, L. Judaism in the New World Order: Human Equality and Social Reconstruction. *Amer. J. Econ. Sociol.,* 4/3, 1945, p.385–9.

Kallner, G. Differences in Mobility Among Jewish Groups in Israel. *Jew. J. Sociol.,* 3/2, 1961, p.264–74.

Kosa, J. and Nash, J. Social Ascent of Catholics. *Soc. Order,* 8, 1958, p.98–103.

Lane, R., Jr. Research Note on Catholics as a Status Group. *Sociol. Anal.,* 26/2, 1965, p.110–12.

McAvoy, T. T. The American Catholic Minority in the Later Nineteenth Century. *R. Polit.,* 15/3, 1953, p.275–302.

Mehok, W. J. Mobility Within the Society of Jesus. *Soc. Compass,* 10/2, 1963, p.211–7.

Mihanovich, C. S. The Mobility of Eminent Catholic Laymen. *Amer. Cath. Sociol. R.,* 1/2, 1940, p.92–9.

Mol, J. J. Churches and Immigrants: Sociological Study of the Mutual Effect of Religion and Immigrants Adjustment. *Res. Group Europ. Mig. Prob.*, 9 (Supplement 5), 1961.

Piekostewski, J. *The Religious Problem of Refugees in the U. S. A.* London: Veritas, 1960, 128p.

See Also: 2c, 3c, 5a, 5c

Ajayi, J. F.   5e1
Brewer, E. D.   7b3
Cain, L. D., Jr.   8a1
Carney, R. E.   4i
Clark, A. H.   7b3
Curtis, J. H.   4f1
Dumond, D. L.   4d
Fishman, J. A.   4c, 4d
Gordon, M. M.   7d

Grimes, A. P.   5c
Kane, J. J.   1f
Lee, J. O.   2
Lee, R.   5c
Mathew, D.   2a2
Obenhaus, V.   7b1
Perry, H. F.   7c
Photidias, J. D.   7b3
Rosenblum, A. L.   7b3
Schuyler, J. B.   7b1
Spiro, M. E.   7d
Stimson, J.   4h
Tavuchis, N.   7a1
Wearnouth, R. F.   6b
Yinger, J. M.   6
Zenner, W. P.   7b3

4j1.   Caste

Aberle, E. K. G.   Criteria of Caste Ranking in South India. *Man India*, 39/2, 1959, p.115–26.

Allah, I.   Caste, Patti and Faction in the Life of a Punjab Village. *Sociologus*, 8/2, 1958, p.170–86.

Ansari, G.   *Muslim Caste in Uttar Pradesh.* Lucknow: Ethnographic and Folk Culture Society, 1960, 83p.

Bailey, F. G.   *Caste and the Economic Frontier: A Village in Highland Orissa.* N.Y.: The Humanities Press, 1958, 292p.

Bailey, F. G.   Closed Social Stratification in India. *Archiv. Europ. Sociol.*, 4/1, 1963, p.107–24.

Barua, P. L.   The Doctrine of Caste in Early Buddhism. *J. Asiatic Society Pakistan*, 4, 1959, p.134–56.

Bhat, J. N.   Untouchability in India. *Civilisations*, 4/4, 1954, p.565–70.

Bhowmick, P. K. and Bhattacharya, B.   Caste, Occupation and Status. *Man India*, 37/1, 1957, p.81–3.

Bose, N. K.   Some Aspects of Caste in Bengal. *J. Amer. Folklore*, 71/281, 1958, p.397–412.

Bose, N. K.   Some Observations on Nomadic Castes in India. *Man India*, 36/1, 1956, p.1–6.

Bougle, C.   The Essence and the Reality of the Caste System. *Contrib. Ind. Sociol.*, 2, 1958, p.7–30.

Bulsara, J. F.   'Gnyati-Band-han' or Caste Barriers: What are They? *Ind. J. Adult Educ.*, 19/3, 1958, p.5–12.

Chandrashekharaiyah, K.   Mobility Patterns Within the Caste. *Sociol. Bull.*, 11, 1961, p.62–7.

Chattopadhyaya, B.   Caste in the Vedas. *Calcutta R.*, 145/3, 1957, p.237–42.

Damle, Y. B.   Reference Group Theory With Regard to Mobility in Caste. *Soc. Action*, 13/4, 1963, p.190–9.

Damle, Y. B.   Caste in Maharashtra. *J. Univ. Poona*, 9, 1958, p.87–98.

D'Souza, V. S.   Caste and Endogamy: A Reappraisal of the Concept of Caste. *J. Anthropol. Society Bombay*, 11/1, 1959, p.11–42.

Dube, S. C.   Ranking Castes in Telengana Villages. *East. Anthropol.*, 8/3–4, 1955, p.182–90.

Dumont, L.   "Tribe and Caste" in India. *Contrib. Ind. Sociol.*, 6, 1962, p.120–2.

Dumont, L. and Pocock, D. (eds.)   Caste. *Contrib. Ind. Sociol.*, 2, 1958, 63p.

Freed, S. A.   An Objective Method for Determining the Collective Caste Hierarchy of an Indian Village. *Amer. Anthropol.*, 65/4, 1963, p.879–91.

Ghurye, G. S.   *Caste and Class in India.* Bombay: Popular Book Depot, 1957, 316p.

Gould, H. A.   Castes, Outcastes, and the Sociology of Stratification. *Int. J. Comp. Sociol.*, 1/2, 1960, p.220–38.

Gould, H. A.   The Adaptive Functions of Caste in Contemporary Indian Society. *Asian Surv.*, 3/9, 1963, p.427–38.

Guha, U.   Caste Among Rural Bengali Muslims. *Man India*, 45/2, 1965, p.167–9.

Gupta, B. K. D.   Caste-Mobility Among the Mahato of South Manbhum. *Man India*, 42/3, 1962, p.228–36.

Gupta, R.   Caste Ranking and Inter-Caste Relations Among the Muslims of a Village in North-Western U. P. *East. Anthropol.*, 10/1, 1956, p.30–42.

Harper, E. B.   Ritual Pollution as an Integrator of Caste and Religion. *J. Asian Stud.*, 23, 1964, p.151–97.

Hutton, J. H. *Caste in India: Its Nature, Function and Origins.* Bombay: Oxford Univ. Press, 1951.

Kapadia, K. M. Caste in Transition. *Sociol. Bull.,* 11, 1961, p.73–90.

Kausalyayana, B. A. How to Get Rid of Untouchability. *Maha Bodhi,* 63/5, 1955, p.173–9.

Madge, C. Caste and Community in India and Thailand —A Contrast. *Ind. J. Adult Educ.,* 19/3, 1958, p.13–5.

Mahar, P. M. A Multiple Scaling Technique for Caste Ranking. *Man India,* 39/2, 1959, p.127–47.

Majumdar, D. N., *et al.* Inter-Caste Relations in Gohanakallan, A Village Near Lucknow. *East. Anthropol.,* 8/3–4, 1955, p.191–214.

Mandelbaum, D. G. Role Variation in Caste Relations. In T. N. Madan and G. Sarana (eds.) *Indian Anthropology: Essays in Honor of D. N. Majumdar.* Bombay: Asia Publishing House, 1962, p.310–24.

Mann, H. H. The Untouchable Classes of an Indian City. *Sociol. R.,* 5/1, 1912, p.42–55.

Marriot, M. Interactional and Attributional Theories of Caste Ranking. *Man India,* 39, 1959, p.92–107.

Marriot, M. *Caste Ranking and Community Structure in Five Regions of India and Pakistan.* Poona: Deccan College Postgraduate and Research Institute, 1960, 75p.

Mayer, A. C. Some Hierarchical Aspects of Caste. *Southw. J. Anthropol.,* 12/2, 1956, p.117–44.

Mayer, A. C. The Dominant Caste in a Region of Central India. *Southw. J. Anthropol.,* 14/4, 1958, p.407–27.

Mayer, A. C. *Caste and Kinship in Central India.* Berkeley: Univ. of Calif. Press, 1960, 295p.

Naik, T. B. Religion and the Anavils of Surat. *J. Amer. Folklore,* 71/281, 1958, p.389–96.

Nanavatty, M. C. Casteism and Social Education: Role of the Social Education Worker. *Ind. J. Adult Educ.,* 19/3, 1958, p.47–61.

Nanavatty, M. C. Seminar on Casteism and Removal of Untouchability: A Review. *Ind. J. Adult Educ.,* 16/4, 1955, p.41–56.

Nimbark, A. Status Conflicts Within a Hindu Caste. *Soc. Forces,* 43/1, 1964, p.50–7.

Orenstein, H. *Gaon: Conflict and Cohesion in an Indian Village.* Princeton: Princeton Univ. Press, 1965, 341p.

Pocock, D. F. "Difference" in East Africa: A Study of Caste and Religion in Indian Society. *Southw. J. Anthropol.,* 13/4, 1957, p.289–300.

Pocock, D. F. Inclusion and Exclusion: A Process in the Caste System of Guijerat. *Southw. J. Anthropol.,* 13/1, 1957, p.19–31.

Rambiritch, B. and Van Den Berghe, L. Caste in a Natal Hindu Community. *Afr. Stud.,* 20/4, 1961, p.217–25.

Rath, R. and Sircar, N. C. Intercaste Relationship as Reflected in the Study of Attitudes and Opinions of Six Hindu Caste Groups. *J. Soc. Psychol.,* 51, 1960, p.3–25.

Rudolph, L. I. The Modernity of Tradition: The Democratic Incarnation of Caste in India. *Amer. Polit. Sci. R.,* 59/4, 1965, p.975–89.

Ryan, B. *Caste in Modern Ceylon: The Sinhalese System in Transition.* New Brunswick, New Jersey: Rutgers Univ. Press, 1953, 371p.

Sarma, J. The Secular Status of Castes. *East. Anthropol.,* 12/2, 1958, 1959, p.87–106.

Sarma, R. *Sudras in Ancient India: A Survey of the Position of the Lower Orders Down to Circa A. D. 500.* Patna: Motilal Banarsidass, 1958, 318p.

Silverberg, J. Caste-Ascribed "Status" Versus Caste-Irrelevant Roles. *Man India,* 39/2, 1959, p.148–62.

Srinivas, M. N. Caste in Modern India. *J. Asian Stud.,* 16/4, 1957, p.529–48.

Srinivas, M. N. *Caste in Modern India, and Other Essays.* London: Asia Publishing House, 1962, 171p.

Srinivas, M. N. The Dominant Caste in Rampura. *Amer. Anthropol.,* 61/1, 1959, p.1–16.

Srinivas, M. N., *et al.* Caste: A Trend Report and Bibliography. *Curr. Sociol.,* 8/1, 1959, p.133–84.

Stroup, H. The Caste System in Hinduism. *J. Hum. Relat.,* 5/4, 1957, p.64–79.

Thakkar, K. K. The Problem of Casteism and Untouchability. *Ind. J. Soc. Work,* 17/1, 1956, p.44–9.

Venkataraman, S. R. Seminar on Casteism and Removal of Untouchability-Report. *Ind. J. Soc. Work,* 16/4, 1956, p.305–9.

Vidyarthi, L. P. The Extensions of an Indian Priestly Caste. *Man India,* 39/1, 1959, p.28–35.

von Fürer-Haimendorf, C. Status Differences in a High Hindu Caste of Nepal. *East. Anthropol.,* 12/4, 1959, p.223–33.

von Fürer-Haimendorf, C. Caste in the Multi-Ethnic Society of Nepal. *Contrib. Ind. Sociol.,* 4, 1960, p.12–32.

Wood, E. Caste Ranking. *Man India,* 42/3, 1962, p.247–9.

Yalman, N. On the Purity of Women in the Castes of Ceylon and Malabar. *J. Roy. Anthropol. Inst.,* 93/1, 1963, p.25–58.

Zinkin, T. *Caste Today.* London: Oxford Univ. Press, 1962, 69p.

4j2.   Race and Slavery

Abrams, C.   Only the Very Best Christian Clientele. *Commentary*, 19/1, 1955, p.10–7.

Achille, L. T.   The Catholic Approach to Interracialism in France. *Amer. Cath. Sociol. R.*, 3/1, 1942, p.22–7.

Alexander, S. T.   *Quaker Testimony Against Slavery and Racial Discrimination: An Anthology.* London: Friends Home Service Committee for Race Relation Committee, 1958, 63p.

Ali, M.   Slavery Amongst the Ancients, Christianity and Islam. *Islamic R.*, 45/10, 1957, p.7–10.

Augustine, D.   The Catholic College Men and the Negro. *Amer. Cath. Sociol. R.*, 8/3, 1947, p.204–8.

Bennett, J. H.   *Bondsmen and Bishops: Slavery and Apprenticeship on the Codrington Plantations of Barbados, 1710–1838.* Berkeley: Univ. of California Press, 1958, 176p.

Bernard, R.   Some Anthropological Implications of the Racial Admission Policy of the U. S. Sisterhoods. *Amer. Cath. Sociol. R.*, 19, 1958, p.124–33.

Brenman, M.   Minority-Group Membership and Religious, Psychosexual, and Social Patterns in a Group of Middle-Class Negro Girls. *J. Soc. Psychol.*, 12/1, 1940, p.179–96.

Congar, Y. M. J.   *The Catholic Church and the Race Question.* Paris: UNESCO, 1953.

Culver, D. W.   *Negro Segregation in the Methodist Church.* New Haven: Yale Univ. Press, 1953.

Daniel, V. E.   Ritual and Stratification in Chicago Negro Churches. *Amer. Sociol. R.*, 7/3, p.352–61.

Fichter, J. H.   American Religion and the Negro. *Daedalus*, 94/4, 1965, p.1085–106.

Fichter, J. H.   The Catholic South and Race. *Rel. Educ.*, 59/1, 1964, p.30–3.

Friedrichs, R. W.   Christians and Residential Exclusion: An Empirical Study of a Northern Dilemma. *J. Soc. Issues*, 15/4, 1959, p.14–23.

Furley, O.   Moravian Missionaries and Slaves in the West Indies. *Caribbean Stud.*, 5/2, 1965, p.3–16.

Gell, C. W. M.   Colour and the South African Church. *Afr. South*, 1/2, 1957, p.64–76.

Hill, C. S.   *West Indian Migrants and the London Churches.* London: Oxford Univ. Press, 1963, 102p.

Malalasekera, G. P. and Jayatilleko, K. N.   *Buddhism and the Race Question.* Paris: UNESCO, 1958, 73p.

Mason, P.   *Christianity and Race.* London: Lutterworth, 1956, 174p.

Miller, R. M.   The Attitudes of American Protestantism Toward the Negro, 1919–1939. *J. Negro Hist.*, 41/3, 1956, p.215–40.

Miller, R. R.   *Slavery and Catholicism.* Durham, North Carolina: North State Publishers, 1957, 259p.

O'Neill, J. E. (ed.)   *A Catholic Case Against Segregation.* N.Y.: Macmillan, 1961, 155p.

Pope, L.   The Negro and Religion in America. *R. Rel. Res.*, 5/3, 1964, p.142–52.

Senn, M.   Race, Religion and Suburbia. *J. Intergr. Relat.*, 3/2, 1962, p.159–70.

Tilson, C. E.   *Segregation and the Bible.* N.Y.: Abingdon Press, 1958, 176p.

Triandis, H. C. and Triandis, L. M.   Race, Social Class, Religion and Nationality as Determinants of Social Distance. *J. Abnorm. Soc. Psychol.*, 61, 1960, p.110–8.

Washington, J. R., Jr.   *Black Relgion: The Negro and Christianity in the United States.* Boston: Beacon Press, 1964, 308p.

Weatherford, W. D.   *The American Churches and the Negro.* Boston: Christopher, 1957.

Young, E. F.   Race and Religion. *Sociol. Soc. Res.*, 13/5, 1929, p.459–64.

See Also:

Bernard, R.   7b3
Breathett, G.   5e2
Brink, W.   6b
Burns, W. H.   8a1
Butsche, J.   3a2
Clark, H.   5c
Conference on Christian. . .   5c
Cosman, B.   4a2
Felton, R. A.   4f2, 7a
Fisk University   7d
Foley, A. S.   7e (2)
Harte, T. J.   7b3

Hill, S. S.   5c
La Farge, J. K.   4g4, 5c (3)
Lang, K.   4g
McKinney, R. I.   4g
McPeeters, A. A.   4g
Osborne, W.   5c
Pipes, W. H.   7a
Posey, W. B.   5c
Rice, M. H.   7b3
Root, R.   5c
Sisk, G. N.   3a1
Tiryakian, E. A.   5c
Tumin, M. M.   5a2
Worthy, W.   2d

4j3.   Social Status

Baltzell, E. D.   *Philadelphia Gentlemen: The Making of a National Upper Class.* Glencoe: The Free Press, 1958, 440p.

Baltzell, E. D.   *The Protestant Establishment: Aristocracy and Caste in America.* N.Y.: Random House, 1964.

Bronk, D. W.   The Religion of Jesus and the Disinherited. In T. H. Johnson (ed.)— *In Defense of Democracy.* N.Y.: Putnam, 1949.

Brown, J.   Social Class, Intermarriage and Church Membership in a Kentucky Community. *Amer. J. Sociol.*, 57/3, 1951, p.232–42.

Burchinal, L. G.   Some Social Status Criteria and Church Membership and Church Attendance. *J. Soc. Psychol.*, 49, 1959, p.53–64.

Burchinal, L. G. and Chancellor, L. E.   Social Status, Religious Affiliation and Ages at Marriage. *Marr. Fam. Liv.*, 25/2, 1963, p.219–20.

Burchinal, L. G. and Kenkel, W. F.   Religious Identification and Occupational Status of Iowa Grooms, 1953–1957. *Amer. Sociol. R.*, 27/4, 1962, p.526–32.

Cochran, J. W.   The Church and the Working Man. *Ann. Amer. Acad. Polit. Soc. Sci.*, 30/3, 1907, p.13–27.

Cohn, W.   Jehovah's Witnesses as a Proletarian Movement. *Amer. Scholar*, 24, 1955, p.281–98.

Coleman, J. S.   Social Cleavage and Religious Conflict. *J. Soc. Issues.* 12/3, 1956, p.44–56.

Danzig, D.   The New Status of Religious Groups. *J. Intergr. Relat.*, 2/1, 1960–61, p.18–26.

Davies, J. K.   The Mormon Church: Its Middle-Class Propensities. *R. Rel. Res.*, 4/2, 1963, p.84–95.

Demerath, N. J., III.   *Social Class in American Protestantism.* Chicago: Rand McNally, 1965.

Demerath, N. J., III.   Social Stratification and Church Involvement: The Church-Sect Distinction Applied to Individual Participation. *R. Rel. Res.*, 2/4, 1961, p.146–54.

Dillingham, H. C.   Protestant Religion and Social Status. *Amer. J. Sociol.*, 70/4, 1965, p.416–22.

Dynes, R. R.   Church-Sect Typology and Socio-Economic Status. *Amer. Sociol. R.*, 20, 1955, p.555–60.

Ford, T. R.   Status, Residence and Fundamental Religious Beliefs in the Southern Appalachians. *Soc. Forces*, 39/1, 1960, p.41–9.

Freedman, M.   Jews, Chinese and Some Others. *Brit. J. Sociol.*, 10, 1959, p.61–70.

Friedman, N. L.   German Lineage and Reform Affiliation: American Jewish Prestige Criteria in Transition. *Phylon*, 26/2, 1965, p.140–7.

Goldschmidt, W. R.   Class Denominationalism in Rural California Churches. *Amer. J. Sociol.*, 49/4, 1944, p.348–55.

Groner, F.   The Social Standing of Catholics in the Federal Republic of Germany. *Soc. Compass*, 9/5–6, 1962, p.539–53.

Hodges, D. C.   The Class Significance of Ethical Traditions. *Amer. J. Econ. Sociol.*, 20/3, 1963, p.241–52.

Kosa, J.   Patterns of Social Mobility Among American Catholics. *Soc. Compass*, 9/4, 1962, p.361–71.

Moberg, D. O.   Does Social Class Shape the Church? *R. Rel. Res.*, 1/3, 1960, p.110–5.

Niebuhr, H. R.   *The Social Sources of Denominationalism.* New Brunswick, New Jersey: Shoestring Press, 1954.

Niebuhr, H. R.   *The Kingdom of God in America.* New Brunswick, New Jersey: Shoestring Press, 1956.

Nuesse, C. J.   The Relation of Financial Assessment to Status in a Rural Parish. *Amer. Cath. Sociol. R.*, 9/1 1948, p.26–38.

O'Brien, R. W.   Some Socio-Economic Comparisons of Six Seattle Jewish Congregations. *J. Hum. Relat.*, 2/3, 1954, p.39–47.

Pope, L.   Religion and the Class Structure. *Ann. Amer. Acad. Polit. Soc. Sci.*, 256, 1948, p.84–91.

Poppers, H. L.   The Declassé in the Babylonian Jewish Community. *Jew. Soc. Stud.*, 20/3, 1958, p.153–79.

Rahim, A.   The Rise of Hindu Aristocracy Under the Bengal Nawabs. *J. Asiat. Society Pakistan*. 6, 1961, p.176–224.

Rosenthal, C. S.   Social Stratification of the Jewish Community in a Small Parish Town. *Amer. J. Sociol.*, 59/1, 1953, p.1–10.

Schommer, C. O., *et al.*   Socio-Economic Background and Religious Knowledge of Catholic College Students. *Amer. Cath. Sociol. R.*, 21/3, 1960, p.229–37.

Small, A. W.   The Church and Class Conflicts. *Amer. J. Sociol.*, 60/6, 1955, p.54–74; see also 24/5, 1919, p.481–501.

Stark, R.   Class, Radicalism and Religious Involvement in Great Britain. *Amer. Sociol. R.*, 29/5, 1964, p.698–706.

Vernon, G. M.   Religious Groups and Social Class—Some Inconsistencies. *Pap. Michigan Acad. Sci. Arts Letters*, 45, 1960, p.295–301.

Yeld, E. R.   Islam and Social Stratification in Nigeria. *Brit. J. Sociol.*, 11/2, 1960, p.112–28.

Ziegler, G. H.   Social Farness Between Hindus and Moslems. *Sociol. Soc. Res.*, 33, 1949, p.188–95.

See Also:

Allen, J.   7a
Bieri, J.   4h, 5a3
De Jong, G.   7b2
Dollard, J.   4f2
Goldscheider, C.   5b2
Hoult, T. F.   4b
Kleiner, R. J.   5b1 (2)
Levinson, B. M.   4h
Litt, E.   4a2
Messing, S. D.   5b1
Muntz, E. E.   7a3
Sargent, L.   4b
Vidich, A. J.   4f2

4j4.   Women

Awad, B. A.   The Status of Women in Islam. *Islamic Quart.*, 8/1–2, 1964, p.17–24.

Coomaraswamy, A. K.   Sati: A Vindication of the Hindu Woman. *Sociol. R.*, 6/2, 1913, p.117–35.   See also: H. M. Swanwick—Note, p.136–8.

Cormack, M. L.   *The Hindu Woman*.   London: Asia Publishing House, 1962, 200p.

Horner, I. B.   Women in East Buddhism. *Middle Way*, 32/1, 1957, p.13–8; see also p.67–72.

Lichtenstadter, I.   The Muslim Woman in Transition, Based on Observations in Egypt and Pakistan. *Sociologus*, 7/1, 1957, p.23–38.

Lustéguy, P.   *The Role of Women in Tonkinese Religion and Property* (Trans. C. A. Messner).   New Haven: Human Relations Area Files, 1954, 149p.

Peiris, W.   Women in Buddhism. *Ceylon Today*, 9/10, 1960, p.6–9.

Sahgal, M. M.   Condition of Women in India. *Civilisations*, 1/4, 1951, p.13–20.

Schmideler, E.   Woman in the Catholic Tradition. *Soc. Forces*, 20/4, 1942, p.478–82.

Scott, G.   The Position of Women in Burma. *Sociol. R.*, 6/2, 1913, p.139–46.

Thomas, P.   *Indian Women Through the Ages*.   N.Y.: Asia Publishing House, 1964, 392p.

See Also:

Chaudhary, R. L.   4b
Hansen, H. H.   2d, 7b
Van der Kroef, J.   4e

5. Religion and Social Issues

Allen, H. Islam and Modern Social-Economic Problems. *J. Rel.*, 14, 1934, p.44–52.

Bodo, J. R. *The Protestant Clergy and Public Issues, 1812–1848.* Princeton: Princeton Univ. Press, 1954, 291p.

Bowers, S. The Church and Social Welfare. *Soc. Order,* 10/1, 1960, p.25–9.

Cronin, J. F. *Social Principles and Economic Life.* Milwaukee: Bruce Publishing Co., 1959.

Cross, R. D. (ed.) *Walter Rauschenbusch: Christianity and the Social Crisis.* N.Y.: Harper & Row, 1964.

Davis, J. *Religion in Action.* N.Y.: Philosophical Library, 1956, 319p.

Diamant, A. *Austrian Catholics and the Social Question, 1918–1933.* Gainesville: Univ. of Florida Press, 1959, 81p.

Duff, E. *The Social Thought of the World Council of Churches.* N.Y.: Association Press, 1954.

Furfey, P. H. The Churches and Social Problems. *Ann. Amer. Acad. Polit. Soc. Sci.,* 256, 1948, p.101–9.

Glasner, S. *A Self Survey of a Congregation's Social Attitudes.* N.Y.: Union of American Hebrew Congregations, 1959.

Glock, C. Y. and Ringer, B. B. Church Policy and Attitudes of Ministers and Parishioners on Social Issues. *Amer. Sociol. R.,* 21/2, 1956, p.148–56.

Houtart, F. H. Social Problems of the Church in Europe. *Amer. Cath. Sociol. R.,* 15/3, 1954, p.230–43.

Hughley, J. N. *Trends in Protestant Social Idealism.* N.Y.: King's Crown Press, 1948.

Hutchinson, J. A. (ed.) *Christian Faith and Social Action.* N.Y.: Scribners, 1953.

Judson, E. The Church and Its Social Impact. *Ann. Amer. Acad. Polit. Soc. Sci.,* 30/3, 1907, p.1–12.

Kincheloe, S. C. Major Reactions of City Churches. *Rel. Educ.,* 23, 1928, p.868–74.

Kirkpatrick, C. Religion and Humanitarianism: A Study of Institutional Implications. *Psychol. Monographs,* 63/9, 1949.

Landis, J. T. Social Action in American Protestant Churches. *Amer. J. Sociol.,* 52/6, 1947, p.517-22.

Lee, R. and Marty, M. E. (eds.) *Religion and Social Conflict.* N.Y.: Oxford Univ. Press, 1964.

Miller, H. M. *Compassion and Community: An Appraisal of the Church's Changing Role in Social Welfare.* N.Y.: Association Press, 1961, 288p.

Miller, R. M. *American Protestantism and Social Issues, 1919–1939.* Chapel Hill: Univ. of North Carolina Press, 1958, 385p.

Newton, C. A. Father Coughlin and His National Union for Social Justice. *Southw. Soc. Sci. Quart.,* 41/3, 1960, p.341–9.

Nordskog, J. E. Organized Religion and Social Reform. *Sociol. Soc. Res.,* 22/2, 1937, p.128–37.

Shack, W. A. Religious Ideas and Social Action in Gurage Bond-Friendship. *Africa,* 33/3, 1963, p.198–208.

Snell, M. M. The Catholic Social-Reform Movement. *Amer. J. Sociol.,* 5/1, 1899, p.16–50.

Spann, J. R. (ed.) *The Christian Faith and Secularism.* Nashville: Abingdon-Cokesbury, 1952.

Symanowski, H. The Christian Witness in an Industrial Society (Trans. G. H. Kehm). Phila.: Westminster Press, 1964, 160p.

Vorspan, A. and Lipman, E. J. *Justice and Judaism: The Work of Social Action.* N.Y.: Union of American Hebrew Congregations, 1956, 271p.

White, L. T. The Church and Social Problems. *J. Appl. Sociol.,* 10, 1926, p.447–60.

White, L. T. The Church and Industrial Problems. *J. Appl. Sociol.,* 11, 1926, p.72–6.

Wilson, R. C. *Authority, Leadership and Concern: A Study in Motive and Administration in Quaker Relief.* London: G. Allen & Unwin, 1949, 80p.

See Also: 1g, 1h, 9

Acton, L.   4al
Basiluis, H. A.   4
Chakerian, C. G.   1g

113

5a. Relations Between Religious Groups

Anathil, G. M. Are Hindu Renascent Movements a Help or an Obstacle for the Spreading of Christianity in India. *Neue Z. Miss.-Wiss.*, 17/3, 1961, p.224–32.

Anstels, R. T. Christianity and Bantu Philosophy: Observations on the Thought and Work of Placide Temels. *Int. R. Missions*, 52/207, 1963, p.316–22.

Baeck, L. *Judaism and Christianity* (Trans. W. Kaufmann). Phila.: Jewish Publication Society of America, 1958, 292p.

Bagchi, P. C. *India and China: A Thousand Years of Cultural Relations*. Bombay: Hind Kitabs, Ltd., 1950, 234p.

Barlow, R. B. *Citizenship and Conscience: A Study in the Theory and Practice of Religious Toleration in England During the Eighteenth Century*. Phila.: Univ. of Pennsylvania Press, 1962, 348p.

Bennett, J. C. Cultural Pluralism: The Religious Dimension. *Soc. Order*, 11/2, 1961, p.54–64.

Berline, P. Russian Religious Philosophers and the Jews. *Jew. Soc. Stud.*, 9/4, 1947, p.271–318.

Bhattacharya, T. P. Brahma Cult and Buddhism. *J. Bihar. Res. Society*, 42/1, 1956, p.91–115.

Bhattacharya, T. P. Brahma Cult and Jainism. *J. Bihar. Res. Society*, 42/1, 1956, p.82–90.

Bishop, L. K. Catholic-Protestant Relations in the United States. *J. Hum. Relat.*, 1960, p.29–47.

Braden, C. S. Hindu Interpretations of the Bible and Jesus. *J. Bib. Rel.*, 12, 1944, p.42–7.

Braden, C. S. Christian-Jewish Relations Today. *J. Bib. Rel.*, 13, 1945, p.94–105.

Brickman, W. W. The Meeting of East and West in Educational History. *Comp. Educ. R.*, 5/2, 1961, p.82–9.

Brinton, H. H. *Quakerism and Other Religions*. Wallingford, Pennsylvania: Pendle Hill, 1957, 40p.

Brown, R. M. and Scott, D. (eds.) *The Challenge to Reunion*. N.Y.: McGraw-Hill Book Co., 1963.

Brown, W. N. Religion and Language as Forces Affecting Unity in Asia. *Ann. Amer. Acad. Polit. Soc. Sci.*, 318, 1958, p.8–17.

Buber, M. *Two Types of Faith: A Study of the Interpenetration of Judaism and Christianity* (Trans. N. P. Goldhawk). N.Y.: The Macmillan Co., 1961, 177p.

Callaway, T. N. Christianity and the Religions of Japan. *R. Exp.*, 58, 1961, p.50–66.

Callaway, T. N. Christian's Attitude Toward Other Religions in Japan. *Japan. Christ. Quart.*, 29, 1963, p.220–6.

Carman, J. B. The Present Encounter Between Christianity and Hinduism in India. *R. Exp.*, 58, 1961, p.67–90.

Copeland, E. L. *Christianity and World Religions*. Nashville: Convention Press, 1963.

Cragg, K. The Christian Church and Islam Today. *Muslim World*, 42/1–4, 1952, p.11–22, 112–23, 207–17, 277–87.

Davidson, R. H. Turkish Attitudes Concerning Christian-Muslim Equality in the Nineteenth Century. *Amer. Hist. R.*, 49/4, 1954, p.844–64.

Davies, P. E. Early Christian Attitudes Toward Judaism and the Jews. *J. Bib. Rel.*, 13, 1945, p.72–82.

Dean, J. P., *et al.* Jews and Their Neighbors: Majority-Minority Interaction in America. *Jew. Soc. Stud.*, 17/3, 1955, p.77–114.

Devanandan, P. D. The Christian Attitude and Approach to Non-Christian Religions. *Int. R. Missions*, 41, 1952, p.177–84.

Dewick, E. C. *The Christian Attitude to Other Religions* (Hulsean Lectures). Cambridge: University Press, 1953.

Dykstra, J. W. Problems of a Religiously Pluralistic Society. *Sociol. Soc. Res.*, 45/4, 1961, p.401–6.

El-Hajji, A. A. Christian States in Northern Spain During the Umayyad Period (138–366 A.H./A.D. 755–976). The Borders of Those States, Their Kings, Internal Relations: Influence on Their Relations and Motives for Their Diplomatic Relations With the Muslims. *Islamic Quart.*, 9/1–2, 1965, p.46–55.

Fox, G. G. Early Jewish Attitudes Toward Jesus, Christians, and Christianity. *J. Bib. Rel.*, 13, 1945, p.83–93.

Frye, R. N. (ed.) *Islam and the West: Proceedings of the*

Harvard Summer School Conference on the Middle East, July 25–27, 1955. The Hague: Mouton & Co., 1956.

Goitein, S. D. *Jews and Arabs: Their Contacts Through the Ages.* N.Y.: Schocken, 1955.

Goitein, S. D. Muhammad's Inspiration by Judaism. *J. Jew. Stud.,* 9/3–4, 1958, p.149–62.

Golden, H. L. Jew and Gentile in the New South. *Commentary,* 20/5, 1955, p.403–12.

Golden, H. L. *Jewish Roots in the Carolinas: A Pattern of American Philo-Semitism.* Greensboro, North Carolina: Deal Printing Co., 1955, 72p.

Gowing, P. G. Resurgent Islam and the Maro Problem in the Philippines. *South E. Asia J. Theol.,* 4/1, 1962, p.57–65.

Grant, R. M. *Gnosticism and Early Christianity.* N.Y.: Columbia Univ. Press, 1950, 227p.

Griffiths, B. Hinduism and Christianity in India. *Blackfriars,* 41/485, 1960, p.364–72.

Hair, P. E. H. Freetown Christianity and Africa. *Sierra Leone Bull. Rel.,* 6/2, 1964, p.13–21.

Hedenquist, G. (ed.) *The Church and the Jewish People.* London: Edinborough Press, 1954, 211p.

Hertzberg, A., *et al. The Outbursts That Await Us: Three Essays on Religion and Culture in America.* N.Y.: Macmillan, 1963, 181p.

Hsiang-Kuang, C. Victory of the Confucian School in China. *United Asia,* 7/3, 1955, p.150–1.

Hunt, C. L. Moslem and Christian in the Philippines. *Pac. Aff.,* 28/4, 1955, p.331–49.

Jonas, H. *The Gnostic Religion: The Message of the Alien God and the Beginnings of Christianity.* Boston: Beacon Press, 1958, 302p.

Katz, J. *Exclusiveness and Tolerance: Studies in Jewish-Gentile Relations in Medieval and Modern Times.* Oxford: Oxford Univ. Press, 1961.

Koper, H. The Swazi Reaction to Missions. *Afr. Stud.,* 5/3, 1946, p.177–88.

Lamb, G. (trans.) *Tolerance and the Catholic: A Symposium.* N.Y.: Sheed & Ward, 1955.

Landon, K. P. *Southeast Asia: Crossroad of Religion.* Chicago: Univ. of Chicago Press, 1949, 215p.

Lewit, D. W. Minority Group Belonging, Social Preference, and the Marginal Personality. *J. Abnorm. Soc. Psychol.,* 58, 1959, p.357–62.

Lioneh, E. Judaism and the Religions of the Far East. *Judaism,* 6, 1957, p.224–35.

Loehlin, C. H. Sikhs and Christians in the Punjab. *Int. R. Missions,* 51/204, 1962, p.451–60.

Magoulias, H. J. A Study in Roman Catholic and Greek Orthodox Church Relations on the Island of Cyprus Between the Years A.D. 1196 and 1360. *Greek Orth. Theol. R.,* 10, 1964, p.75–106.

Maillart, E. Nepal, Meeting Place of Religions. *Geogr. Mag.,* 19/6, 1956, p.273–88.

Marinoff, I. Christian Minorities in Israel. *Contemp. R.,* 1081, 1956, p.2–24.

McDonald, E. *The Catholic Church and Secret Societies in the United States.* N.Y.: U. S. Catholic Historical Society, 1946, 220p.

Muelder, W. G. Institutional Factors Affecting Unity and Disunity. *Ecumen. R.,* 8/2, 1956, p.113–26.

Myers, E. A. *Arabic Thought and the Western World in the Golden Age of Islam.* N.Y.: Frederick Ungar Publishing Co., 1964, 156p.

Noss, G. S. Some Japanese Interpretations of the Bible. *J. Bib. Rel.,* 22, 1954, p.87–92.

Paranivatana, S. Religious Intercourse Between Ceylon and Siam in the 13th–15th Centuries. *J. Roy. Asiat. Society Ceylon Br.,* 32, 1932, p.190–213.

Parkes, J. *The Foundations of Judaism and Christianity.* Chicago: Quadrangle Books, 1960, 344p.

Perkins, W. A. Christian Youth in the Middle East. *Ecumen. R.,* 7/4, 1955, p.347–52.

Qureshi, I. H. Relations Between the Hindus and the Muslims in the Subcontinent of India and Pakistan. *Civilisations,* 5/1, 1955, p.43–51.

Raisin, J. S. *Gentile Reactions to Jewish Ideals (With Special Reference to Proselytes).* N.Y.: Philosophical Library, 1953, 876p.

Reichelt, G. M. Chinese Religion and Christianity. *R. Exp.,* 58, 1961, p.25–34.

Rivkin, E. Unitive and Divisive Factors in Judaism. *Civilisations,* 7/4, 1957, p.529–43.

Rose, P. I. Small-Town Jews and Their Neighbors in the United States. *Jew. J. Sociol.,* 3/2, 1961, p.174–91.

Ross, F. H. A Re-Examination of Christian Attitudes Toward Other Faiths. *J. Bib. Rel.,* 21, 1953, p.79–83.

Saab, H. Communication Between Christianity and Islam. *Mid. East J.,* 18/1, 1964, p.41–62.

Schermerhorn, R. A. Where Christians are a Minority. *Antioch R.,* 21/4, 1961–62, p.497–509.

Skinner, E. P. Christianity and Islam Among the Mossi. *Amer. Anthropol.,* 60/6, 1958, p.1102–19.

Smylie, J. H. Phases in Protestant–Roman Catholic Relations in the United States. *Rel. Life,* 34/2, 1965, p.258–69.

Sorokin, P. A. *Altruistic Love, A Study of American*

"Good Neighbors" and Christian Saints. Boston: Beacon Press, 1950, 253p.

Strizower, S. Jews as an Indian Caste. *Jew. J. Sociol.*, 1/1, 1959, p.43–57.

Survey of Church Union Negotiations, 1961–1963. *Ecum. R.*, 1964, 16/4, p.406–43; see also earlier issues.

Synan, E. A. *The Popes and the Jews in the Middle Ages.* N.Y.: Macmillan, 1965, 256p.

Tavard, G. H. *The Catholic Approach to Protestantism.* N.Y.: Harper & Brothers, 1955, 160p.

Thomas, J. L. Catholicism in a Pluralistic Society. *Soc. Order*, 11/9, 1961, p.385–95.

Tillich, P. *Christianity and the Encounter of the World Religions.* N.Y.: Columbia Univ. Press, 1963, 97p.

Unwoki, T. The Influence of Non-Christian Religions on Japanese Life and Thought. *Japan. Christ. Quart.*, 30/2, 1964, p.134–9; 30/3, p.197–206.

Upadhyaya, G. *Buddhism and Hinduism.* Banaras: Banaras Hindu Univ., 1956, 58p.

von Garbe, R. *India and Christendom: The Historical Connections Between Their Religions* (Trans. L. G. Robinson). LaSalle, Illinois: Open Court Publishing Co., 1959, 298p.

Watt, W. M. The Meeting of Religions: A Sociological View. *Aryan Path.*, 27/11, 1956, p.486–90.

Wieder, N. *The Judean Scrolls and Karaism.* London: East and West Library, 1962, 296p.

See Also: 4, 5e, 6

Archer, J. C.   2h
Gordon, A. I.   4e3
Hermanns, M.   2c
Kritzeck, J.   8a4, 8a5
Lange-Poole, S.   4a1
Matthijssen, A. J. M.   7b2
Ottenberg, S.   7a1
Roucek, J. S.   4f
Sandmel, S.   7b3
Scharper, P.   2a2
Williamson, S. G.   6b

5a1. Ecumenical Movements

Barnes, R. P. The Ecumenical Movement. *Ann Amer. Acad. Polit. Soc. Sci.*, 332, 1960, p.135–45.

Beazley, G. G., Jr. (ed.) Consultation on Church Union: Its History and Progress. *Mid-Stream*, 2/4, 1963, 159p.

Bedwell, H. K. *Black Gold: The Story of the International Holiness Mission in South Africa, Which United With the Church of the Nazarene, Nov. 29, 1952, at Acornhoek, Transvaal.* Kansas City: Beacon Hill Press, 1953, 128p.

Bell, G. K. A. (ed.) *Documents on Christian Unity: A Selection from the First and Second Series, 1920–1930.* London: Oxford Univ. Press, 1955, 271p.

Berger, P. L. A Marked Model for the Analysis of Ecumenicity. *Soc. Res.*, 30/1, 1963, p.77–94.

Bilheimer, R. S. *The Quest for Christian Unity.* N.Y.: Association Press, 1952, 181p.

Bolles, D. C. National Council of Churches in the U. S. A. I. Purpose and Program. *J. Hum. Relat.*, 4/3, 1956, p.47–58. See also: A. Kramer and J. O. Lee—II Achievements in Racial and Cultural Areas, p.59–68.

Braden, C. S. The Christian Encounter With World Religions. *J. Church State*, 7/3, 1965, p.388–402.

Bryson, L., *et al.* (eds.) *Approaches to National Unity: Fifth Symposium.* N.Y.: Conference on Science, Philosophy and Religion in Their Relation to the Demo-cratic Way of Life. Dist. by Harper and Brothers, 1945, 1037p.

Carpenter, J. H. Churches Work Together in Federation. *J. Educ. Sociol.*, 23/5, 1950, p.291–301.

Clinchy, E. R. *The Growth of Good Will: A Sketch of Protestant-Catholic-Jewish Relations.* N.Y.: National Conference of Christians and Jews, 1953.

Coleman, F. P. Ecumenicism in the Anglican Communion. *Lumen Vitae*, 20/2, 1965, p.325–38.

Crow, P. A., Jr. *The Ecumenical Movement in Bibliographical Outline.* N.Y.: National Council of Churches of Christ in the U. S. A., 1965, 80p.

Cullman, O., *et al.* Comments on the Decree of Ecumenism Enacted in the Second Vatican Council and Promulgated on November 21st, 1964. *Ecumen. R.*, 17/2, 1965, p.93–112.

de Laney, M. M. Social Interaction of Three Denominations in the Inner City. *R. Rel. Res.*, 1/2, 1959, p.50–6.

Diamond, M. L. Catholicism in America: The Emerging Dialogue. *Judaism*, 1960, p.307–18.

Dolan, J. P. Medieval Christian Tolerance and the Muslim World. *Muslim World*, 51, 1961, p.280–7.

Ehrenstrom, N. and Muelder, W. G. *Institutionalism and Church Unity.* N.Y.: Association Press, 1963.

Estep, W. R. *Church Union and Southern Baptists.* Fort Worth: Baptist Book Store, 1955, 165p.

Felton, R. A. *Cooperative Churches.* N.Y.: Home Missions Council, 1947.

Froendt, A. H. *An Ecumenical Bibliography.* N.Y.: World Council of Churches, 1959, 32p.

Georgiadis, H. The Ecumenical Role of the Catholic Eastern Churches. *Dublin R.,* 505, 1965, p.234–44.

Goddall, N. *The Ecumenical Movement, What It Is and What It Does.* London: Oxford Univ. Press, 1964, 257p.

Gowing, P. G. The Idea of a Church Catholic: Reformed and Evangelical. *Silliman J.,* 10/1, 1963, p.23–37.

Hargreaves, J. R. The Rural Community and Church Federation. *Amer. J. Sociol.,* 20/2, 1914, p.249–60.

Hartt, J. N. Theological Aspects of Emerging International, Interracial and Interreligious Relationships. *Civilisations,* 7/4, 1957, p.544–50.

Heideman, E. Reformed Ecumenicity 1888–93. *Reformed R.,* 18/1, 1964, p.16–25.

Heiler, F. Can Christian and Non-Christian Co-operate? *Hibbert J.,* 52, 1954, p.107–18.

Hyslop, R. D. Conditions for New Ventures in Theological Meeting. *Civilisations,* 7/4, 1957, p.551–6.

Jenkins, D. T. The Ecumenical Movement and Its Non-Theological Factors. *Ecumen. R.,* 3/4, 1951, p.339–46.

Jenkins, D. T. *Europe and America: Their Contributions to the World Church.* Phila.: Westminster Press, 1951, 72p.

Johnson, F. E. The Jewish Question as an Ecumenical Problem. *Ecumen. R.,* 7, 1955, p.225–31.

Jung, M., *et al. Relations Among Religions Today: A Handbook of Policies and Principle.* Leiden: E. J. Brill, 1963, 178p.

Knight, G. A. F. *Jews and Christians: Preparation for Dialogue.* Phila: Westminster Press, 1965.

Laidlow, W. Plea and Plan for a Co-operative Church Parish System in Cities. *Amer. J. Sociol.,* 3/6, 1898, p.795–808.

Lee, R. *The Social Sources of Church Unity.* Nashville: Abingdon Press, 1960.

Leeming, B. *The Churches and the Church: A Study of Ecumenism Developed From the Lauriston Lectures for 1957.* London: Darton Longman and Todd, 1960, 340p.

Loomis, L. R. *The Council of Constance: The Unification of the Church* (Ed. and Annotated J. H. Mundy and K. M. Woody). N.Y.: Columbia Univ. Press, 1961, 562p.

Loos, A. W. (ed.) *Religious Faith and World Culture.* N.Y.: Prentice-Hall, 1951, 294p.

Lord, F. T. *Baptist World Fellowship: A Short History of the Baptist World Alliance.* London: Carey Kingsgate Press, 1955, 185p.

Mackie, R. C. The Responsibility of the Churches in the World Council. *Ecumen. R.,* 8/1, 1955, p.8–17.

Mackie, R. C. and West, C. C. (eds.) *The Sufficiency of God: Essays on the Ecumenical Hope in Honor of W. A. Visser't Hooft.* Phila.: Westminster Press, 1963, 240p.

Marshall, R. P. and Taylor, M. J. *Liturgy and Christian Unity.* Englewood Cliffs, New Jersey: Prentice Hall, 1965, 186p.

Marty, M. E. The Future of the Denominations in an Ecumenical Era. *Cath. World,* 200, 1964, p.34–41.

Mathews, S. The Christian Church and Social Unity. *Amer. J. Sociol.,* 5/4, 1900, p.456–69.

McCaughey, J. D. Church Union in Australia. *Ecumen. R.,* 17/1, 1965, p.38–53.

McNeill, J. T. *Unitive Protestantism.* Virginia: John Knox Press, 1964, 352p.

Meliton, M. The Re-Encounter Between the Eastern Church and the Western Church. *Ecumen. R.,* 17/4, 1965, p.301–20.

Miegge, M. Is Ecumenism a Cultural Rather Than a Theological Phenomenon? *Communio Viatorum,* 7/1, 1964, p.16–24.

Miller, J. Q. *Christian Unity: Its Relevance to the Community.* Strasburg, Virginia: Shenandoah Publishing House, 1957, 122p.

Mode, P. G. Aims and Methods of Contemporary Church-Union Movements in America. *J. Theol.,* 24/2, 1920, p.224–51.

Nakosteen, M. *History of the Islamic Origins of Western Civilization, A.D. 800–1350.* Boulder: Univ of Colorado Press, 1964, 361p.

Neill, S. C. *Christian Faith and Other Faiths: The Christian Dialogue With Other Religions. The Moorhouse Lectures, Melbourne, 1960.* London: Oxford Univ. Press, 1962, 241p.

O'Neill, C. (ed.) *Ecumenism and Vatican II.* Milwaukee: Bruce Publishing Co., 1964.

Paul, R. S. British Churches and the Ecumenical Future. *Ecumen. R.,* 8/2, 1956, p.178–87.

Pfeffer, L., *et al.* Interreligious Relationship. *J. Intergr. Relat.,* 1/2, 1960, p.81–103.

117

Plattner, F. A. *Christian India*. London: Thames K. Hudson, 1957, 147p.

Proudfoot, L. Towards Muslim Solidarity in Freetown. *Africa*, 31/2, 1961, p.147–57.

Rayner, K. The American Episcopal Church and the Anglican Communion, 1865–1900. *J. Rel. Hist.*, 3/2, 1964, p.158–74.

Rich, M. *The Rural Church Movement*. Columbia, Missouri: Juniper Knoll Press, 1957.

Rosenthal, F. The Rise of Christian Hebraism in the Sixteenth Century. *Hist. Judaica*, 7/2, 1945, p.167–91.

St. John, H. *Essays in Christian Unity, 1928–1954*. Westminster, Maryland: Newman Press, 1955, 144p.

Sanderson, R. W. *Church Cooperation in the U. S.: The Nation-Wide Backgrounds and Ecumenical Significance of State and Local Council of Churches in Their Historical Perspectives*. N.Y.: Association of Council Secretaries, 1961, 272p.

Schaller, L. E. Connectionalism: The New Polity? *Christ. Cent.*, 81/27, 1964, p.858–61.

Sjölander, R. *Presbyterian Reunion in Scotland, 1907–1921* (Trans. E. J. Sharpe). Edinburg: T. & T. Clark, 1964, 416p.

Smith, P. M. Protestant Comity in Metropolitan Pittsburgh. *Amer. Sociol. R.*, 8, 1943, p.425–32.

Sundkler, B. G. M. *The Church of South India: The Movement Towards Union*. London: Lutterworth Press, 1954, 457p.

Swilder, L. J. (ed.) *Scripture and Ecumenism*. Pittsburgh: Duquesne Univ. Press, 1964, 197p.

Tillich, P. and Tavard, G. H. An Ecumenical Dialogue. *Dublin R.*, 504, 1965, p.162–81.

Villain, M. *Unity: A History and Some Reflections* (Trans. J. R. Foster). Baltimore: Helicon Press, 1963.

Vischer, L. (ed.) *A Documentary History of the "Faith and Order Movement," 1927–1963*. St. Louis: Bethany Press, 1963, 246p.

Visser't Hooft, W. A. Various Meanings of Unity and the Unity Which the World Council of Churches Seeks to Promote. *Ecumen. R.*, 8/1, 1955, p.18—29.

Visser't Hooft, W. A. (ed.) *The New Delhi Report: The Third Assembly of the World Council of Churches*. N.Y.: Association Press, 1962, 448p.

Wedel, T., *et al.* The One Church and Our Many Churches: Toward What Sort of Union? *Rel. Life*, 24/2, 1955, p.163–94.

Wesley, C. H. The Significance of Oneness: Principle or Expediency. *J. Hum. Relat.*, 2/1, 1953, p.57–69.

Wilson, E. Notes on Gentile Pro-Semitism. *Commentary*, 22, 1956, p.329–35.

World Council of Churches. *Six Ecumenical Surveys: Preparatory Material for the Second Assembly of the World Council of Churches, 1954*. N.Y.: Harper & Bros., 1954.

Zeitlin, S. The Ecumenical Council: Vatican II and the Jews. *Jew. Quart. R.*, 56/2, 1965, p.93–111.

Syncretism

Aung, H. *Folk Elements in Burmese Buddhism*. London: Oxford Univ. Press, 1962, 140p.

Barnett, J. H. *The American Christmas: A Study in National Culture*. N.Y.: Macmillan Co., 1954, 173p.

Beekman, J. Cultural Extensions in the Chol Church. *Pract. Anthropol.*, 7/2, 1960, p.54–61.

Brohm, J. Buddhism and Animism in a Burmese Village. *J. Asian Stud.*, 22/2, 1963, p.155–67.

Courtois, V. *Mary in Islam*. Calcutta: Oriental Institute, Islamic Section, 1954, 79p.

Dougall, J. W. C. African Separatist Churches. *Int. R. Missions*, 45, 1956, p.257–66.

Fernandez, J. W. The Idea and Symbol of the Savior in a Gabon Syncretistic Cult: Basic Factors in the Mythology of Messianism. *Int. R. Missions*, 53/211, 1964, p.281–9.

Gasparini, E. Studies in Old Slavic Religion, "Ubrus". *Hist. Rel.*, 2/1, 1962, p.112–39.

Grant, F. C. (ed.) *The Hellenistic Religions: The Age of Syncretism*. N.Y.: Liberal Arts Press, 1953, 196p.

Greenberg, J. H. *The Influence of Islam on a Sudanese Religion*. Seattle: Univ. of Washington Press, 1957, 83p.

Grottanelli, V. L. Pre-Existence and Survival in Nzema Beliefs. *Man*, 61, 1961, p.1–5.

Henderson, A. C. *Brothers of the Light: The Penitentes of the Southwest*. Chicago: Rio Grande Press, 1962, 126p.

Ilogu, E. The Problem of Indigenization in Nigeria. *Int. R. Missions*, 49/194, 1960, p.167–82.

Jusuf, H. *Glimpses of Medieval Indian Culture*. Bombay: Asia Publishing House, 1959, 165p.

Kleivan, I. *Mitârtut: Vestiges of the Eskimo Sea-Woman Cult in West Greenland*. København: C. A. Reitzel, 1960, 30p.; also appeared as *Medd. Grønland*, 161/5, 1960, p.1–30.

Kurath, G. P. Afro-Wesleyan Liturgical Structures. *Midwest Folkl.*, 13/1, 1963, p.29–32.

Leach, E. R. Pulleyar and the Lord Buddha: An Aspect

of Religious Syncretism in Ceylon. *Psychoanal. Psychoanal. R.*, 49/2, 1962, p.81–102.

Levi, C. *Christ Stopped at Eboli.* N.Y.: Farrar, Straus, & Co., 1947, 268p.

Mandic, O. Pagan Elements in the Rural Type of Revealed Religion. In *Transactions of the Fifth World Congress of Sociology, Washington, D. C., 1962, Vol. III.* Louvain, International Sociological Association, 1964, p.69–72.

Messenger, J. C., Jr. Reinterpretations of Christian and Indigenous Belief in a Nigerian Nativist Church. *Amer. Anthropol.*, 62, 1960, p.268–78.

Moss, L. W. and Cappannari, S. C. The Black Madonna: An Example of Culture Borrowing. *Sci. Monthly*, 76, 1953, p.319–24.

Oakes, M. *The Two Crosses of Todos Santos: Survivals of Mayan Religious Ritual.* N.Y.: Pantheon Books, 1951, 274p.

Parrinder, E. G. Islam and West African Indigenous Religion. *Numen*, 6/2, 1959, p.130–41.

Samarin, W. J. Gbeya Prescientific Attitudes and Christianity. *Pract. Anthropol.*, 6/4, 1959, p.179–82.

Sawyerr, H. Traditional Sacrificial Rituals and Christian Worship. *Sierra Leone Bull. Rel.*, 2/1, 1960, p.18–26.

Singh, P. N. Sources of Hindu Influence on Oraons Living in Purnea District. *J. Soc. Res.*, 7/1–2, 1964, p.70–86.

Smirnova, I. S. Some Religious Survivals Among the Black Sea Adygei. *Soviet Anthropol. Archeol.*, 3/1, 1964, p.3–8.

Turner, H. W. Searching and Syncretism: A West African Documentation. *Int. R. Missions*, 49/194, 1961, p.189–94.

Turner, H. W. Pagan Features in West African Independent Churches. *Pract. Anthropol.*, 12/3, 1965, p.145–51.

Walters, M. The Penitents: A Folk Observance. *Soc. Forces*, 6/2, 1927, p.253–6.

Webster, J. B. *The African Churches Among the Yoruba 1888–1922.* N.Y.: Oxford Univ. Press, 1964, 236p.

Zimmerman, C. The Cult of the Holy Cross: An Analysis of Cosmology and Catholicism in Quintana Roo. *Hist. Rel.*, 3/1, 1963, p.50–71.

See Also:

5a2.   *Conflict Between Religious Groups*

Ashby, P. H. *Conflict of Religions.* N.Y.: Scribners, 1955.

Bathgate, J. and Chandran, J. R. Indian Communism and the Christian Church. *Int. R. Missions*, 39, 1951, p.79–85.

Berkhoeffer, R. F., Jr. Protestants, Pagans, and Sequences Among the North American Indians, 1760–1860. *Ethnohistory*, 10/3, 1963, p.201–32.

Bettelheim, B. and Janowitz, M. *Dynamics of Prejudice.* N.Y.: Harper, 1950, 279p.

Bird, B. A Consideration of the Etiology of Prejudice. *J. Amer. Psychoanal. Assoc.*, 5/3, 1957, p.490–513.

Boisguerin, R. The Religious Persecution in China. *Asian R.*, 52/190, 1956, p.150–3.

Clasper, P. D. The Buddhist-Christian Encounter in Burma. *R. Exp.*, 58, 1961, p.35–49.

Clinchy, E. R. The Efforts of Organized Religion. *Ann. Amer. Acad. Polit. Soc. Sci.*, 244, 1946, p.128–36.

Daniel, N. *Islam and the West: The Making of an Image.* Edinburgh: Edinburgh Univ. Press, 1960, 443p.

Drummond, R. H. Japan's New Religions and the Christian Community. *Christ. Cent.*, 81/50, 1964, p.1521–3.

Earthy, E. D. The Impact of Mohammedanism on Paganism in the Liberian Hinterland. *Numen*, 2/3, 1955, p.206–16.

Fairbank, J. K.   Patterns Behind the Tientsin Massacre. *Harvard J. Asiat. Stud.*, 20/3-4, 1957, p.480–511.

Fisher, W. S.   Black Magic Feuds. *African Stud.*, 8/1, 1949, p.20–72.

Gordon, K. H.   Religious Prejudice in an Eight-Year Old Boy. *Psychoanal. Quart.*, 34/1, 1965, p.102–7.

Gray, C. H.   The Correlation of Social Cleavages and the Intensity of Intergroup Conflict. *Australian New Zealand J. Sociol.*, 1/2, 1965, p.70–84.

Gunson, N.   An Account of the Mamaia or Visionary Heresy of Tahiti, 1826–1841. *J. Polynes. Society*, 71/2, 1962, p.209–43.

Hager, D. J., *et al.* (eds.)   Religious Conflicts in the United States. *J. Soc. Issues*, 12/3, 1956, p.1–66.

Harkness, G. E.   *Conflicts in Religious Thought.* N.Y.: H. Holt & Co., 1929, 362p.

Hughes, K.   Christianity and Islam in West Africa. *Christ. Cent.*, 81/9, 1964, p.264–7; see also, 81/10, p.298–302.

Joseph, J.   *The Nestorians and Their Muslim Neighbors.* Princeton: Princeton Univ. Press, 1961.

LaViolette, F. E.   *The Struggle for Survival: Indian Cultures and the Protestant Ethic in British Columbia.* Toronto: Univ. of Toronto Press, 1961, 201p.

Legge, F.   *Forerunners and Rivals of Christianity.* New Hyde Park, N.Y.: University Books, 1964, 462p.

Marrow, A.   *Changing Patterns of Prejudice: A New Look at Today's Racial Religious and Cultural Tensions.* Phila.: Chilton, 1962, 271p.

Mather, R.   The Conflict of Buddhism With Native Chinese Ideologies. *R. Rel.*, 20, 1955, p.25–37.

Myers, G.   *The History of Bigotry in the United States.* N.Y.: G. P. Putnam's Sons, 1960.

Pfeffer, L.   Issues that Divide. *J. Soc. Issues*, 12/3, 1956, p.21–39.

Pfeffer, L.   *Creeds in Competition.* N.Y.: Harper Brothers, 1958.

Pike, R. and Cowan, F.   Mushroom Ritual Versus Christianity. *Pract. Anthropol.*, 6/4, 1959, p.145–50.

Pi-Sunyer, O.   Religion and Witchcraft: Spanish Attitudes and Pueblo Reactions. *Anthropologica*, 2/1, 1960, p.66–75.

Pos, A.   Buddhist Propaganda in the Western World and the Christian Answer. *Free Univ. Quart.*, 8, 1961, p.26–42.

Pratt, S. A. J.   Spiritual Conflicts in a Changing African Society. *Ecumen. R.*, 8/2, 1956, p.154–62.

Proudfoot, L.   Mosque-Building and Tribal Separatism in Freetown East. *Africa*, 29/4, 1959, p.405–16.

Raab, E. (ed.)   *Religious Conflict in America: Studies in the Problems Beyond Bigotry.* Garden City: Doubleday, 1964.

Raikar, Y. A.   A Study in the Islamic Invasions of India. *J. Maharaja Sayajiro*, 8/1, 1959, p.11–20.

Reyburn, W. D.   The Spiritual, the Material, and the Western Reaction in Africa. *Pract. Anthropol.*, 6/2, 1959, p.78–83.

Runciman, S.   *A History of the Crusades:* Cambridge: Cambridge Univ. Press, 1951–62, 378p., 2 vols.

Samarrai, A. I.   The Muslims in the South Seas and the Beginning of the Portuguese Challenge. *Islamic R.*, 45/12, 1957, p.27–9.

Serruys, H.   Early Mongols and the Catholic Church. *Neue Z. Miss.-Wiss.*, 19/3, 1963, p.161–9.

Speel, C. J.   The Disappearance of Christianity From North Africa in the Wake of the Rise of Islam. *Church Hist.*, 1960, p.379–95.

Spencer, R. F.   The Problem of Buddhism in the U. S. *Maha Bodhi*, 59, 1951, p.356–66.

Spilka, B. and Reynolds, J. F.   Religion and Prejudice: A Factor-Analytic Study. *R. Rel. Res.*, 6/3, 1965, p.163–8.

Sweetman, J. W.   Muslim's View of Christianity. *Moslem World*, 34, 1944, p.278–84.

Trimingham, J. S.   *The Christian Church and Islam in West Africa.* London: SCM Press, 1955, 55p.

Tumin, M. M.   *Supplement to Segregation and Desegregation.* N.Y.: Anti-Defamation League of B'nai B'rith, 1960, 32p.

Tumin, M. M. (ed.)   *Segregation and Desegregation: A Digest of Recent Research.* N.Y.: Anti-Defamation League of B'nai B'rith, 1957, 112p.

Visser't Hooft, W. A.   *The Ecumenical Movement and the Racial Problem.* Paris: UNESCO, 1954.

Von der Kroef, J.   Culture Contact and Culture Conflict in Western New Guinea. *Anthropol. Quart.*, 32/3, 1959, p.134–60.

Williams, R. M., Jr.   Religion, Value-Orientations and Intergroup Conflict. *J. Soc. Issues*, 12/3, 1956, p.12–20.

Zubek, J. P.   The Doukhobors: A Genetic Study on Attitudes. *J. Soc. Psychol.*, 36/2, 1952, p.223–39.

Anti-Semitism

Ackerman, N. W. and Jahoda, M.   *Anti-Semitism and Emotional Disorder.* N.Y.: Harper, 1950, 135p.

Ackerman, N. W. and Jahoda, M.   Toward a Dynamic Interpretation of Anti-Semitic Attitudes. *Amer. J. Orthopsychiat.*, 18/1, 1948, p.163–73.

Adorno, T. W., *et al.* *The Authoritarian Personality*. N.Y.: Harper, 1950, 990p.

Andreski, S. An Economic Interpretation of Anti-Semitism in Eastern Europe. *Jew. J. Sociol.*, 5/2, 1963, p.201–13.

Bergman, S. Some Methodological Errors in the Study of Anti-Semitism. *Jew. Soc. Stud.*, 5/1, 1943, p.43–60.

Berkowitz, L. Anti-Semitism and the Displacement of Aggression. *J. Abnorm. Soc. Psychol.*, 59/2, 1959, p.182–7.

Bernstein, P. F. *Jew Hate as a Sociological Problem* (Trans. D. Saraph). N.Y.: Philosophical Library, 1951, 300p.

Bieber, H. Anti-Semitism in the First Years of the German Republic. *Yivo Ann. Jew. Soc. Sci.*, 4, 1949, p.123–45.

Brown, J. Christian Teaching and Anti-Semitism. *Commentary*, 24/6, 1957, p.494–501.

Byrnes, R. F. *Antisemitism in Modern France: The Prologue to the Dreyfus Affair*. New Brunswick, New Jersey: Rutgers Univ. Press, 1950.

Engel, G., *et al.* An Investigation of Anti-Semitic Feelings in Two Groups of College Students: Jewish and Non-Jewish. *J. Soc. Psychol.*, 48/1, 1958, p.75–82.

Epstein, B. R. Anti-Semitism in the United States—1957 Report. *J. Hum. Relat.*, 6/1, 1957, p.52–8.

Flannery, E. H. *The Anguish of the Jews: 2000 Years of Anti-Semitism*. N.Y.: Macmillan, 1965, 332p.

Galtung, J. *Anti-Semitism in the Making: A Study of American High School Students*. Oslo: Inst. Soc. Res., 1960, 118p.

Gergel, N. The Pogroms in the Ukraine in 1918–21. *Yivo Ann. Jew. Soc. Sci.*, 1951, p.237–52, vol. 6.

Ginsberg, M. Anti-Semitism. *Sociol. R.*, 35/1-2, 1943, p.1–11.

Glenn, J. Circumcision and Anti-Semitism. *Psychoanal. Quart.*, 29, 1960, p.395–9.

Gough, H. G. Studies of Social Intolerance: I. Some Psychological and Sociological Correlates of Anti-Semitism; II. A Personality Scale for Anti-Semitism; III. Relationship of the Pr Scale to Other Variables. *J. Soc. Psychol.*, 33/2, 1951, p.237–46, 247–55, 257–62.

Haim, S. C. Arabic Anti-Semitic Literature: Some Preliminary Notes. *Jew. Soc. Stud.*, 17/4, 1955, p.307–14.

Halperin, S. Zionist and Christian America: The Political Use of Reference Groups. *Southw. Soc. Sci. Quart.*, 40, 1959, p.225–37.

Halperin, S. Zionist Counterpropaganda: The Case of the American Council for Judaism. *Southw. Soc. Sci. Quart.*, 41, 1961, p.450–63.

Hays, M. V. *Europe and the Jews: The Pressure of Christendom on the People of Israel for 1900 Years*. Boston: Beacon Press, 1960, 352p.

Ichheiser, G. The Jews and Anti-Semitism. *Sociometry*, 9/1, 1946, p.92–108.

Isaac, J. *The Teaching of Contempt: Christian Roots of Anti-Semitism*. N.Y.: Holt, Rinehart & Winston, 1964.

Jocz, J. Jewish-Christian Controversy Concerning Israel. *Int. R. Missions*, 37, 1948, p.382–92.

Kagan, H. E. *Changing the Attitude of Christians Toward Jews*. N.Y.: Columbia Univ. Press, 1952, 155p.

Kahler, E. Forms and Features of Anti-Judaism. *Soc. Res.*, 6/4, 1939, p.455–88.

Kane, J. J. Anti-Semitism Among Catholic College Students. *Amer. Cath. Sociol. R.*, 8/3, 1947, p.209–18.

Kaufman, W. C. Status, Authoritarianism, and Anti-Semitism. *Amer. J. Sociol.*, 62/4, 1957, p.379–82.

Kren, G. Race and Ideology. *Phylon*, 23/2, 1962, p.167–77.

Leschnitzer, A. *The Magic Background of Modern Anti-Semitism: An Analysis of the German-Jewish Relationship*. N.Y.: International University Press, 1956, 236p.

Lever, H. The Defacement of a Ghetto Exhibition. *Jew. J. Sociol.*, 6/2, 1964, p.213–9.

Levinson, P. J. and Sanford, R. N. A Scale for the Measurement of Anti-Semitism. *J. Abnorm. Soc. Psychol.*, 47, 1952, p.749–58.

Lipman, E. J. and Varspan, A. *A Tale of Ten Cities*. N.Y.: Union of Hebrew Congregations, 1962, 344p.

Lovsky, F. Christian-Jewish Relations: Some French Points of View. *Int. R. Missions*, 44, 1955, p.274–91.

Massing, P. W. *Rehearsal for Destruction: A Study of Political Anti-Semitism in Imperial Germany*. N.Y.: Harper, 1949.

Mayer, C. Anti-Judaism Reconsidered. *Soc. Res.*, 1940, p.169–83.

Parkes, J. *An Enemy of the People: Anti-Semitism*. N.Y.: Penguin, 1945, 153p.

Parkes, J. *The Emergence of the Jewish Problem, 1878–1939*. Oxford: Oxford Univ. Press, 1946.

Parkes, J. *Anti-Semitism*. Chicago: Quadrangle Books, 1964.

Parkes, J. *The Conflict of the Church and the Synagogue: A Study in the Origins of Anti-Semitism*. Cleveland: World Publishing Co., 1961, 430p.

Perry, T. W. *Public Opinion, Propaganda, and Politics in Eighteenth-Century England: A Study of the Jew*

Bill of 1753. Cambridge: Harvard Univ. Press, 1962, 215p.

Pinson, K. S. (ed.) *Essays on Anti-Semitism.* N.Y.: Conference on Jewish Relations, 1946, 269p.

Polakov, L. European Anti-Semitism East and West. *Commentary*, 23/6, 1957, p.553–60.

Robb, J. H. *Working-Class Anti-Semite: A Psychological Study in a London Borough.* London: Travistock Publications, 1954, 239p.

Second, P. F. and Saumer, E. Identifying Jewish Names: Does Prejudice Increase Accuracy? *J. Abnorm. Soc. Psychol.*, 61, 1960, p.144–5.

Segal, B. E. Fraternities, Social Distance and Anti-Semitism Among Jewish and Non-Jewish Undergraduates. *Sociol. Educ.*, 38/3, 1965, p.251–64.

Seydewitz, R. and Seydewitz, M. *Anti-Semitism in West Germany.* Berlin: Committee for German Unity, 1956, 80p.

Silberner, E. *Western European Socialism and the Jewish Problem, 1800–1918: A Selective Bibliography.* Jerusalem: Hebrew Univ., 1955, 62p.

Silberner, E. The Anti-Semitic Tradition in Modern Socialism. In R. Bachi (ed.)—*Scripta Hierosolymitana. Vol. 3: Studies in Economic and Social Sciences.* Jerusalem: Hebrew Univ., 1956, p.378–96.

Simmel, E. (ed.) *Anti-Semitism: A Social Disease.* N.Y.: International Universities Press, 1946, 140p.

Skoczylas, E. *The Realities of Soviet Anti-Semitism.* Phila.: Univ. of Pennsylvania, 1965, 72p.

Sobel, B. Z. Legitimation and Anti-Semitism as Factors in the Functioning of a Hebrew-Christian Mission. *Jew. Soc. Stud.*, 23/3, 1961, p.170–6.

Spoerl, D. T. The Jewish Stereotype, The Jewish Personality, and Jewish Prejudice. *Yivo Ann. Jew. Soc. Sci.*, 7, 1952, p.268–76.

Steinberg, M. *A Partisan Guide to the Jewish Problem.* N.Y.: Bobbs-Merrill, 1945.

Tumin, M. M. *An Inventory and Appraisal of Research on American Anti-Semitism.* N.Y.: Freedom Books, 1961, 185p.

United Nations, Sub-Commission on Prevention of Discrimination and Protection of Minorities. *Manifestations of Anti-Semitism and Other Forms of Racial Prejudice and Religious Intolerance of a Similar Nature.* N.Y.: United Nations, 1960, 45p.

Wrong, D. H. The Psychology of Prejudice and the Future of Anti-Semitism in America. *Eur. J. Sociol.*, 6/2, 1965, p.311–28.

Yaffe, R. A. Anti-Semitism in the United States. *In Dispersion*, 2, 1963, p.15–34.

Barbour, H. *The Quakers in Puritan England.* New Haven: Yale Univ. Press, 1964, 272p.

Beach, W., *et al.* Issues Between Catholics and Protestants at Mid-Century. *Rel. Life*, 23/2, 1954.

Bien, D. D. Religious Persecution in the French Enlightenment. *Church Hist.*, 30, 1961, p.325–33.

Billington, R. A. Anti-Catholic Propaganda and the Home Missionary Movement, 1800–1860. *Miss. Valley Hist. R.*, 22/3, 1935, p.361–84.

Billington, R. A. Tentative Bibliography of Anti-Catholic Propaganda in the U.S., 1800–1860. *Cath. Hist. R.*, 12, 1933, p.492–513.

Burns, R. E. The Belfast Letters, The Irish Volunteers, 1778–79, and the Catholics. *R. Polit.*, 21/4, 1959, p.678–91.

Colacci, M. *The Doctrinal Conflict Between Roman Catholic and Protestant Christianity.* Minneapolis: Denison, 1962, 269p.

Cross, J. L. The American Protective Association: A Sociological Analysis of the Periodic Literature of the Period, 1890–1900. *Amer. Cath. Sociol. R.*, 10, 1949, p.172–87.

Davies, H. *Christian Deviations: The Challenge of the New Spiritual Movements.* Phila.: Westminster Press, 1965, 144p.

Dawson, C. *The Dividing of Christendom.* N.Y.: Sheed and Ward, 1965, 304p.

Dodd, C. H., *et al. More Than Doctrine Divides the Churches.* N.Y.: World Council of Churches, 1952.

Dolan, J. P. *History of the Reformation: A Conciliatory Assessment of Opposite Views.* N.Y.: Desclee Co., 1965, 417p.

Dornbusch, S. M. and Irle, R. D. The Failure of Presbyterian Union. *Amer. J. Sociol.*, 64/4, 1959, p.352–5.

Ellul, J. On the Cultural and Social Factors Influencing Church Division. *Ecumen. R.*, 1952, p.269–75.

Flynn, F. T. The Problem of Religious Tensions. *Amer. Cath. Sociol. R.*, 8/1, 1947, p.24–30.

Foik, P. J. Anti-Catholic Parties in American Politics, 1776–1860. *Amer. Cath. Hist. Society Phila. Rec.*, 36, 1925, p.41–69.

Friedman, R. Conception of the Anabaptists. *Church Hist.*, 1940, p.341–65.

Furniss, N. F. *The Fundamentalist Controversy, 1918–1931.* New Haven: Yale Univ. Press, 1954.

Furniss, N. F. The Fundamentalist Controversy in the Twenties. In H. A. Quint, *et al.* (eds.)—*Main Prob-*

lems in American History. Homewood, Illinois: Dorsey Press, 1964, vol. II.

Glock, C. Y. Issues that Divide: A Postscript. *J. Soc. Issues*, 12/3, 1956, p.40–3.

Greenslade, S. L. *Schism in the Early Church*. N.Y.: Harper & Brothers, 1953.

Gutton, J. *Great Heresies and Church Councils*. N.Y.: Harper and Row, 1965, 191p.

Harbison, H. Will Versus Reason: The Dilemma of the Reformation in Historical Perspective. *J. Bib. Rel.*, 9, 1941, p.203–16.

Hayward, V. E. W. (ed.) *African Independent Church Movements*. London: Edinburgh House Press, 1963, 94p.

Herberg, W. Protestant-Catholic Tensions in Pluralistic America. *Yale Div. News*, 1960, p.3–11.

Hesketh, C. *The Dark Hours: Catholic Life in Seventeenth-Century Scotland*. Glascow: Catholic Truth Society of Scotland, 1954, 21p.

Horton, D. *Christian Deviations: The Challenge of the Sects*. London: SCM Press, 1961.

Hromadka, J. Social and Cultural Factors in Our Divisions. *Ecumen. R.*, 1952, p.52–8.

Kane, J. J. Protestant-Catholic Tensions. *Amer. Sociol. R.*, 16, 1951, p.663–72. See also: C. L. Hunt—Comment, p.845; and C. D. Alston, 17, 1952, p.236–7.

Kane, J. J. *Catholic-Protestant Conflicts in America*. Chicago: Regnery, 1955.

Kennedy, G. The Problem of Church Union. *Rel. Life*, 31, 1962, p.563–71.

Kingdom, R. *Geneva and the Coming of the Wars of Religion in France*. Geneve: Librairie E. Droz, 1956, 163p.

Kinzer, D. L. *An Episode in Anti-Catholicism: The American Protective Association*. Seattle: Univ. of Washington Press, 1964, 342p.

Lamb, U. Religious Conflicts in the Conquest of Mexico. *J. Hist. Ideas*, 17/4, 1956, p.526–52.

Loram, C. T. The Separatist Church Movement. *Int. R. Missions*, 15/59, 1926, p.476–82.

Lortz, J. *The Reformation* (Trans. J. C. Dwyer). Westminster, Maryland: Newman Press, 1964, 261p.

McAvoy, T. T. The Catholic Minority After the Americanist Controversy 1899–1917; A Survey. *R. Politics*, 21/1, 1959, p.53–82.

McManus, W. E. The Catholic School and the Community. *Cath. Action*, 33/11, 1951, p.6–8, 18.

Momigliano, A. (ed.) *The Conflict Between Paganism and Christianity in the Fourth Century*. Oxford: Clarendon Press, 1963, 222p.

Mootsi, L. and Mkele, N. A Separatist Church: I B and LA Lika-Krestu. *Afr. Stud.*, 5/1, 1946, p.106–25.

Mueller, E. W. and Giles, C. *The Silent Struggle for Mid-America: The Church in Town and Country Today*. Minneapolis: Augsburg Publishing House, 1963.

New, J. F. *Anglican and Puritan: The Basis of Their Opposition, 1558–1640*. Stanford: Stanford Univ. Press, 1964.

Parry, H. J. Protestants, Catholics and Prejudice. *Int. J. Opin. Att. Res.*, 3, 1949, p.205–13.

Pickering, W. S. F. *Anglican-Methodist Relations: Some Institutional Factors*. London: Darton, Longman & Todd, 1961.

Popkin, R. H. Skepticism and the Counter Reformation in France. *Archiv. Reform. Gesch.*, 51, 1960, p.56–86.

Posey, W. B. *Religious Strife on the Southern Frontier*. Baton Rouge: Louisiana State Univ. Press, 1965.

Ray, J. M. Anti-Catholicism and Know-Nothingism in Rhode Island. *Amer. Eccles. R.*, 148, 1963, p.27–36.

Runciman, S. *The Eastern Schism: A Study of the Papacy and the Eastern Churches During the Eleventh and Twelfth Centuries*. Oxford: Clarendon Press, 1955, 189p.

Runciman, S. The Schism Between the Eastern and Western Churches. *Anglic. Theol. R.*, 44, 1962, p.337–50.

Scoville, W. C. *The Persecutions of Huguenots and French Economic Development, 1680–1720*. Berkeley: Univ. of California Press, 1960, 497p.

Shapiro, L. Religious Tensions in the United States: A Social Problem. *Amer. Cath. Sociol. R.*, 8/1, 1947, p.31–7.

Smith, E. A. The Role of the Presbyterian Schism of 1837–1838. *Church Hist.*, 29, 1960, p.44–63.

Sugrue, T. A. *A Catholic Speaks His Mind on America's Religious Conflict*. N.Y.: Harper, 1951.

Toth, W. Trinitarianism Versus Antitrinitarianism in the Hungarian Reformation. *Church Hist.*, 13/4, 1944, p.255–68.

Trimble, W. R. *The Catholic Laity in Elizabethan England, 1558–1603*. Cambridge, Massachusetts: Harvard Univ. Press, 1964, 290p.

Tubeville, G. Religious Schism in the Methodist Church: A Sociological Analysis of the Pine Grove Case. *Rural Sociol.*, 14, 1949, p.29–39.

Vokes, F. E. The Opposition to Montanism From

Church and State in the Christian Empire. *Studia Patristica*, 4, 1961, p.518–26.

Wagoner, W. D., *et al.* The Protestant Ecumenical Dilemma. *Christ. Cent.*, 81/11, 1964, p.329–32.

Weima, J. Authoritarianism, Religious Conservatism, and Sociocentric Attitudes in Roman Catholic Groups. *Hum. Relat.*, 18/3, 1965, p.231–9.

Welbourn, F. B. *East African Rebels: A Study of Some Independent Churches.* London: SCM Press, 1961, 258p.

Workman, H. B. *Persecution in the Early Church.* N.Y.: Abingdon Press, 1960, 155p.

Zahn, G. C. The Content of Protestant Tensions: Fears of Catholic Aims and Methods. *Amer. Cath. Sociol. R.*, 18/3, 1957, p.205–12.

See Also:

Achutegui, P. S.   6c
Armstrong, W.   3a1
Bainton, R. H.   3a
Baltzell, E. D.   4j3
Benz, E.   4a1
Bone, R. C.   4a
Bridenbaugh, C.   3a1
Celnik, M.   9
Cohen, P. A.   5e3
Coleman, J. S.   4j3
Cooley, J. K.   6
Deutsch, M.   5g
Elkin, A. P.   7f
Feagin, J. R.   7b3
Firth, R.   7f
Furniss, N. F.   4a

Goode, W. J.   1a
Griffith, G.   6b
Hertzberg, A.   4a
Holt, S.   3a
Hughes, E. C.   6b
Lal, K. S.   4a
Leakey, L. S. B.   6c
Levenson, J. R.   4a
Lindsay, T. M.   3a
Marcules, H. F.   4a2
Maxwell, M.   6c
Morton-Williams, P.   8a3
Norton, G. R.   6e
Olson, B. E.   7b3
Orestein, H.   4j1
Perez, L. S.   4g
Pernoud, R.   5e
Poliakov, L.   4a1
Pulzer, P. G. J.   4a
Radcliffe-Brown, A. R.   7f
Reitlinger, G.   5c
Reyburn, W. D.   4e
Shepperson, G.   6c
Shires, H.   5a2
Siegel, M.   7b3
Singer, S. A.   4a1
Smith, W. C.   2d
Stroup, H. H.   7b3
Trachtenberg, J.   7b3
Trevor-Roper, H.   6
Weima, J.   7b3
Welbourn, F. B.   2a1
Whitemore, L. B.   3a1
Wilson, N. H.   4a1
Yamamoto, T.   4b
Zuck, L. H.   6c

5a3. *Differential Behavior of Members of Religious Groups*

Batemen, M. M. and Jensen, J. S. The Effect of Religious Background on Modes of Handling Anger. *J. Soc. Psychol.*, 47, 1958, p.133–141.

Bell, R. R. and Buerkle, J. V. Mothers and Mothers-In-Law as Role Models in Relation to Religious Background. *Marr. Fam. Liv.*, 25/4, 1963, p.485–6.

Bieri, J., *et al.* Psychosocial Factors in Differential Social Mobility. *J. Soc. Psychol.*, 58/1, 1962, p.183–200.

Blum, B. S. and Mann, J. H. The Effect of Religious Membership on Religious Prejudice. *J. Soc. Psychol.*, 52, 1960, p.97–101.

Boehm, L. The Development of Conscience: A Comparison of Upper-Middle Class Academically Gifted Children Attending Catholic and Jewish Parochial Schools. *J. Soc. Psychol.*, 59, 1963, p.101–10.

Bonney, M. E. A Study of Friendship Choices in Colleges in Relation to Church Affiliation, In-Church Preferences, Family Size, and Length of Enrollment in College. *J. Soc. Psychol.*, 29/2, 1949, p.153–66.

Clark, E. T. Nontheological Factors in Religious Diversity. *Ecumen. R.*, 3/4, 1951, p.347–56.

Cowhig, J. D. and Schnore, L. F. Religious Affiliation and Church Attendance in Metropolitan Centers. *Amer. Cath. Sociol. R.*, 23/2, 1962, p.113–27.

Cragg, G. R. Disunities Created by Differing Patterns of Church Life. *Ecumen. R.*, 1952, p.276–81.

Crowther, B. Note on Religious Group Differences in Interaction Profiles: A Replication Study. *Psychol. Rep.*, 10/2, 1962, p.459–64.

Dean, D. G. and Reeves, J. A. Anomie: A Comparison of a Catholic and a Protestant Sample. *Sociometry*, 25/2, 1962, p.209–12.

Douglass, H. P. Cultural Differences and Recent Religious Divisions. *Christendom*, 1945, p.89–105.

Durkheim, E. *Suicide* (Trans. J. A. Spaulding and G. Simpson). Glencoe: Free Press, 1951.

Dykstra, J. W. Parochial Divisions in American Life. *Christ. Cent.*, 1958, p.465–7.

Garrison, W. E. Social and Cultural Factors in Our Divisions. *Ecumen R.*, 1952, p.43–51.

Giles, H. H. Community Conflicts Related to Religious Difference. *J. Intergr. Relat.*, 2/2, 1962, p.145–8.

Harris, A. and Watson, G. Are Jewish or Gentile Children More Clannish? *J. Soc. Psychol.*, 24/1, 1946, p.71–6.

Jouard, S. M. Religious Denomination and Self-Disclosure. *Psychol. Rep.*, 8/3, 1961, 446p.

Kaplan, S. The Anglicization of the East European Jewish Immigrant as Seen by The London *Jewish Chronicle*, 1870–1897. *Yivo Ann. Jew. Soc. Sci.*, 10, 1956, p.267–79.

Kruijt, J. P. The Influence of Denominationalism on Social Life and Organizational Patterns. *Archiv. Sociol. Rel.*, 8, 1959, p.105–11.

Linsky, A. S. Religious Differences in Lay Attitudes and Knowledge on Alcholism and Its Treatment. *J. Sci. Stud. Rel.*, 5/1, 1965, p.41–50.

Murray, J. C. The Problems of a Catholic Approach to the Non-Catholic Mind in Great Britain. *Lumen Vitae*, 1/1, 1946, p.135–53.

Nimkoff, M. F. and Wood, A. L. Effect of Majority Patterns on the Religious Behavior of a Minority Group. *Sociol. Soc. Res.*, 30/4, 1946, p.282–9.

Porter, J. Differentiating Features of Orthodox, Conservative, and Reform Jewish Groups in Metropolitan Philadelphia. *Jew. Soc. Stud.*, 25/3, 1963, p.186–94.

Pratt, K. C. Differential Selection of Intelligence According to Denominational Preference of College Freshmen. *J. Soc. Psychol.*, 8, 1937, p.301–10.

Sanua, V. D. The Socio-Cultural Aspects of Schizophrenia: A Comparison of Protestant and Jewish Schizophrenics. *Int. J. Soc. Psychiat.*, 9/1, 1963, p.27–36.

Sappenfield, B. R. The Responses of Catholic, Protestant, and Jewish Students to the Monaco Checklist. *J. Soc. Psychol.*, 20/2, 1944, p.295–9.

Segal, B. E. Contact, Compliance and Distance Among Jewish and Non-Jewish Students. *Soc. Problems*, 13/1, 1965, p.66–74.

Shuey, A. M. Differences in Performance of Jewish and Non-Jewish Students on the American Council Psychological Examination. *J. Soc. Psychol.*, 15/2, 1942, p.245–54.

Skolnick, J. H. Religious Affiliation and Drinking Behavior. *Quart. J. Stud. Alcohol*, 19, 1958, p.452–70.

Woolston, H. B. Religious Consistency. *Amer. Sociol. R.*, 2, 1937, p.380–8.

Yaukey, D. *Fertility Differences in a Modernizing Country.* Princeton: Princeton Univ. Press, 1961, 204p.

See Also:

Baltzell, E. D. 4j3
Beattie, J. H. M. 4b
Beidelman, T. O. 4b
Demerath, N. J., III 4j3 (2)
Eaton, J. W. 5b1
Fetter, G. C. 7b3
Freedman, R. 5b2 (2)
Glick, P. C. 4e3
Goldenweiser, A. A. 3
Gould, H. A. 4b
Hart, H. 4i
Held, O. C. 4h
Higgins, E. 5b2
Jaffe, A. F. 5b2
Kenkel, W. F. 4e3
Knopfelmacher, F. 7b3
Landis, J. T. 4e3
Loewenstein, R. 4h
Mulvaney, B. 5b2
Obenhaus, V. 7b3
Prothro, E. 7b3
Robbins, R. 6c
Smith, E. L. 4h
Stark, R. 7b3
Stark, W. 4j3
Stimson, J. 4h
Ziegler, G. H. 4j3

5b. Religion and Health

Bainton, R. H. The Churches and Alcohol. *Quart. J. Stud. Alcohol*, 6, 1945, p.45–58.

Bawden, C. R. The Supernatural Element in Sickness and Death According to Mongol Tradition. *Asia Major*, 8/2, 1961, p.215–57.

Binkley, O. T. Attitudes of the Churches. In R. G. McCarthy (ed.)—*Drinking and Intoxication.* Glencoe, Illinois: Free Press, 1959, p.325–30.

Blanten, S. Analytical Study of a Cure at Lourdes. *Psychoanal. Quart.*, 9, 1940, p.348–62.

Boisen, A. T. Religious Experience and Psychological Conflict. *Amer. Psychol.*, 13, 1958, p.568–70.

Browne, S. G. *Medicine and Faith in a Primitive Community.* London: Tindale Press, 1959, 11p.

Bruder, E. E. The Myth of the Healing Team. *J. Rel. Health*, 2/1, 1962, p.61–73.

Burch, T. K. Patterns of Induced Abortion and Their Socio-Moral Implications in Postwar Japan. *Soc. Compass*, 3/4, 1956, p.178–88.

Burstein, S. R. Demonology and Medicine in the Sixteenth and Seventeenth Centuries. *Folk Lore* (London), 67/1, 1956, p.16–33.

Carter, P. H. The Use of the Bible by Protestant Healing Groups. *J. Theol.*, 5, 1963, p.43–53.

Chellappa, D. Christian Medical Work and the Indian Church. *J. Christ. Med. Assoc. India*, 34, 1959, p.221–6.

Clinebell, H. J., Jr. Philosophical-Religious Factors in the Etiology and Treatment of Alcoholism. *Quart. J. Stud. Alcohol*, 24, 1963, p.473–88.

Dicks, R. L. The Religious Function of the Nurse. *Amer. J. Nursing*, 39, 1939, p.1109–12.

Doniger, S. (ed.) *Healing: Human and Divine. Man's Search for Health and Wholeness Through Science, Faith and Prayer.* N. Y.: Association Press, 1957, 254p.

Dunbar, H. F. Medicine, Religion, and the Infirmities of Mankind. *Ment. Hyg.*, 18/1, 1934, p.16–25.

Eaton, J. W. and Mayer, A. J. *Man's Capacity to Reproduce: The Demography of a Unique Population.* Glencoe: Free Press, 1954, 59p.

Elgood, C. The Medicine of the Prophet. *Med. Hist.*, 6/2, 1962, p.146–53.

Farris, C. D. Prohibition as a Political Issue. *J. Polit.*, 23/3, 1961, p.507–25.

Fecher, C. J. Health and Longevity of Today's Sisters. *Soc. Compass*, 8/4, 1961, p.347–54.

Friess, H. L. (ed.) Religion and Health. *R. Rel.*, 1946, vol. 10.

Ghalioungui, P. *Magic and Medical Science in Ancient Egypt.* London: Hodder and Stoughton, 1963, 189p.

Gladstone, I. *Ministry and Medicine in Human Relations.* N.Y.: International Universities Press, 1955, 173p.

Gordon, B. L. Biblical and Talmudic Medicine. *Hebrew Med. J.*, 1, 1960, p.223–31.

Gramberg, K. P. Leprosy and the Bible. *Trop. Geog. Med.*, 11, 1959, p.127–39.

Gusfield, J. R. Social Structure and Moral Reform: A Study of the Women's Christian Temperance Union. *Amer. J. Sociol.*, 61/3, 1955, p.221–32.

Havens, J. A Working Paper: Memo on the Religious Implications of the Consciousness-Changing Drugs. *J. Sci. Stud. Rel.*, 3/2, 1964, p.216–66. See also: C. M. Owens—Comments, 4/2, 1965, p.246–8.

Henry, F. E. and Kemp, C. F. Religion in the Life of the Mentally Retarded. *J. Rel. Health*, 4/1, 1964, p.59–65.

Hoffman, L. Problem Patient: The Christian Scientist. *Med. Econ.*, 33, 1956, p.265–83.

Hultkrantz, A. The Masters of the Animals Along the Wind River Shoshoni. *Ethnos*, 26/4, 1961, p.198–218.

Jayne, W. A. *The Healing Gods of Ancient Civilizations.* New Hyde Park, N.Y.: University Books, 1962, 569p.

Jordon, G. R., Jr. L. S. D. and Mystic Experience. *J. Bib. Rel.*, 31, 1963, p.114–23.

Kahn, M. Some Observations on the Role of Religion in Illness. *Soc. Work*, 3/3, 1958, p.83–9.

Kanin, E. J. Value Conflicts in Catholic Device-Contraceptive Usage. *Soc. Forces*, 35/3, 1956, p.238–43.

Khare, R. S. Ritual Purity and Pollution in Relation to Domestic Sanitation. *East. Anthropol.*, 15/2, 1962, p.125–39.

Kiev, A. Brief Note: Primitive Hotistic Medicine. *Int. J. Soc. Psychiat.*, 8/1, 1961–62, p.58–61.

Kocher, P. H. The Idea of God in Elizabethan Medicine. *J. Hist. Ideas*, 11/1, 1950, p.3–29.

Kreyer, V. (ed.) The Church and the Physically Handicapped. *Past. Psychol.*, 16/155, 1965, p.5–44.

Landis, B. Y. A Survey of Local Church Activities and Pastoral Relating to Problems of Alcoholism. *Quart. J. Stud. Alcohol*, 8, 1948, p.636–56.

Levey, M. Fourteenth Century Muslim Medicine and the Hisba. *Med. Hist.*, 7/2, 1963, p.176–81.

Levin, S. Obstetrics in the Bible. *J. Obstet. Gynaec. Brit. Emp.*, 67, 1960, p.490–8.

Lieban, R. W. The Dangerous Ingkantos: Illness and Social Control in a Philippine Community. *Amer. Anthropol.*, 64/2, 1962, p.306–11.

Loewen, J. A. Shamanism, Illness, and Power in Toba Church Life. *Pract. Anthropol.*, 12/6, 1965, p.250–80.

Lorimer, F., *et al.* An Inquiry Concerning Some Ethical

Principles Relating to Human Reproduction. *Soc. Compass*, 4/5–6, 1957, p.201–12.

Maclure, H. L. Religion and Disease in Sierra Leone. *Sierra Leone Bull. Rel.*, 4/1, 1962, p.29–34.

Mayer, A. J. and Marx, S. Social Change, Religion, and Birth Rates. *Amer. J. Sociol.*, 62, 1957, p.401–7.

McClure, R. B. Paramedical Training and the Christian Church in India. *J. Christ. Med. Assoc. India*, 35, 1960, p.205–8.

Mischel, F. Faith Healing and Medical Practice in the Southern Caribbean. *Southw. J. Anthropol.*, 15/4, 1959, p.407–17.

Mowrer, O. H. Symposium on Relationship Between Religion and Mental Health. *Amer. Psychol.*, 13, 1958, p.565–79.

Offner, C. B. and Van Straelen, H. *Modern Japanese Religions With Special Emphasis Upon Their Doctrine of Healing*. N.Y.: Twayne Publishers, 1963, 296p.

Ojiamob, H. H. The Psychology of Witchcraft. *East. Afr. J.*, 2/4, 1965, p.23–5.

Palmer, C. The Role of Religion in Rehabilitation. *Rehab. Lit.*, 23/12, 1962, p.362–70.

Paterson, D. E. Co-operation in the Ministry of Healing in India. *J. Christ. Med. Assoc. India*, 35, 1960, p.83–92.

Paulsen, A. E. Religious Healing. *J. Amer. Med. Assoc.*, 86/29, 1926, p.1519–24, 1617–23, 1692–7.

Paulsen, A. E. Religious Healing. *Ment. Hyg.*, 10/3, 1926, p.541–95.

Podmore, F. *From Mesmer to Christian Science: A Short History of Mental Healing*. New Hyde Park, N.Y.: University Books, 1963, 306p.

Ratan, R. A Study in Magic and Medicine. *Vanyajti*, 3/2, 1955, p.67–72.

Romano, O. I. V. Charismatic Medicine, Folk-Healing and Folk Sainthood. *Amer. Anthropol.*, 67/5, Part I, 1965, p.1151–73.

Rosenberg, M. The Dissonant Religious Context and Emotional Disturbance. *Amer. J. Sociol.*, 68/1, 1962, p.1–10.

Rosenbloom, J. R. Notes on Jewish Drug Addicts. *Psychol. Rep.*, 5/4, 1959, p.769–72.

Roth, J. A. Ritual and Magic in the Control of Contagion. *Amer. Sociol R.*, 22, 1957, p.310–4.

Salsman, L. Spiritual and Faith Healing. *J. Past. Care*, 11, 1957, p.146–55.

Schneck, J. M. The Hypnotic Trance, Magico-Religious Medicine, and Primitive Initiation Rites. *Psychoanal. R.*, 41, 1954, p.182–90.

Scott, W. R. Potentials for Ministry in Medical Work. *J. Christ. Med. Assoc. India*, 34, 1959, p.352–7.

Seidman, H., *et al.* Death Rates in New York City by Socio-Economic Class and Religious Groups and by Country of Birth, 1949–1951. *Jew. J. Sociol.*, 4/2, 1962, p.254–73.

Smith, H. Do Drugs Have Religious Import? *J. Philos.*, 61/18, 1964, p.517–30.

Snyder, F. Studies of Drinking in Jewish Culture. *Quart. J. Stud. Alcohol*, 16, 1955, p.101–77, 263–89, 504–32, 700–42.

Stern, B. An Indian Shaker Initiation and Healing Service. *Soc. Forces*, 7/3, 1929, p.432–4.

Stringham, J. A. Christian Medical Counseling. *J. Christ. Med. Assoc. India*, 39, 1964, p.22–30.

Sutherland, R. L. Therapeutic Goals and Ideals of Health. *J. Rel. Health*, 3/2, 1964, p.119–35.

Swanton, J. R. Religious Beliefs and Medical Practices of the Creek Indians. *Amer. Ethnol. Bur. Ann. Report*, 42, 1924–5, p.473–672.

Thorner, I. Ascetic Protestantism and Alcoholism. *Psychiatry*, 16, 1953, p.167–76.

Walters, O. S. The Religious Background of Fifty Alcoholics. *Quart. J. Stud. Alcohol*, 18, 1957, p.405–16.

Walters, O. S. Metaphysics, Religion, and Psychotherapy. *J. Counseling Psychol.*, 5/4, 1958, p.243–52.

Wardwell, W. I. Christian Science Healing. *J. Sci. Stud. Rel.*, 4/2, 1965, p.175–81.

Welmers, W. E. Secret Medicines, Magic and Rites of the Kpelle Tribe in Liberia. *Southw. J. Anthropol.*, 5/3, 1949, p.208–43.

Wendland, L. V. Some Religious Feelings of the Post-Poliomyelitic. *J. Soc. Psychol.*, 38/1, 1953, p.99–108.

Wessel, H. *Natural Childbirth and the Christian Family*. N.Y.: Harper & Row, 1963, 287p.

Wilder, E. W. The Christian Medical Worker. *J. Christ. Med. Assoc. India*, 34, 1959, p.227–9.

Wilder, E. W. The Pattern of Christian Medical Work in Changing India. *Int. R. Missions*, 48/190, 1959, p.190–7.

Zimmer, H. R. *Hindu Medicine* (Ed. L. Edelstein). Baltimore: Johns Hopkins Univ. Press, 1948, 203p.

See Also: 1e, 2h, 3f, 4h, 5g, 7b3

Allaman, R. 7a1
Anbunathan, C. 5e3
Backman, E. L. 7b1

Berkowitz, L.   5a2
Bronner, A.   1e
Dittman, A. T.   2h3
Duetscher, I.   4g
Ewers, J. C.   2h
Ferm, V.   7a1
Gelfand, M.   7a1
Goldstein, B.   6c
Green, J. J.   6b
Hocart, A. M.   3f5

Houston, J.   7b3
Houtart, F.   5e
Knight, J. A.   1e
Landis, B. Y.   7a3
Linsky, A. S.   5a3
McDill, T. H.   9
Peel, R.   2a
Solomon, D.   4h
Ware, J. T.   7a1
Zenter, H.   4c

5b1.   *Mental Illness*

Academy of Religion and Mental Health. *Religion, Culture and Mental Health.* N.Y.: New York Univ. Press, 1961.

Academy of Religion and Mental Health. *Research in Religion and Health: Proceedings of the Fifth Academy Symposium of the Academy of Religion and Mental Health.* N.Y.: Fordham Univ. Press, 1963, 165p.; see other issues.

Alpert, D. B.   Religion and State Hospital. *Ment. Hyg.,* 27/4, 1963, p.574–80.

Anderson, G. C.   The Partnership of Theologians and Psychiatrists. *J. Rel. Health,* 3/1, 1963, p.56–69.

Armstrong, R. G.   Mental Illness Among American Jews. *Jew. Soc. Stud.,* 27/2, 1965, p.103–11.

Bagchi, B. K.   Mental Hygiene and the Hindu Doctrine of Relaxation. *Ment. Hyg.,* 20/3, 1936, p.424–40.

Barnes, C. R.   Is There a Technique for the Cure of Souls? *Rel. Educ.,* 24, 1929, p.619–23.

Blackman, E. A.   Mental Hygiene Clinic in the Church. *Rel. Educ.,* 24, 1929, p.636–9.

Blain, D.   Organized Religion and Mental Health. *J. Rel. Health,* 4/2, 1965, p.164–73.

Boisen, A. T.   *The Exploration of the Inner World: A Study of Mental Disorder and Religious Experience.* N.Y.: Harper, 1962, 322p.

Bowman, K. M.   Religious Problems in Clinical Cases. *Rel. Educ.,* 24, 1929, p.631–5.

Clinebell, H. J., Jr.   The Future of the Speciality of Pastoral Counseling. *Past. Psychol.,* 16/158, 1965, p.18–24, 26.

Davis, T. K.   The Bible and Neurology in New Amsterdam. *J. Nerv. Ment. Dis.,* 86, 1937, p.147–51.

Devereaux, G.   The Origin of Shamanistic Powers as Reflected in a Neurosis: A Brief Clinical Communication. *R. Inter. D'Ethnopsychol. Norm. Pathol.,* 1/1, 1956, p.19–30.

Devereaux, G.   Shamans as Neurotics. *Amer. Anthropol.,* 63/5, pt. 1, 1961, p.1088–90. See also: M. K. Opler— On Devereaux's Discussion of Ute Shamanism. *Amer. Anthropol.,* p.1091–3.

Dimock, H. S.   Mental Hygiene Attainments Interpreted for Religious Education. *Rel. Educ.,* 25, 1930, p.674–7.

Dunbar, H. F.   Mental Hygiene and Religious Teaching. *Ment. Hyg.,* 19/3, 1935, p.353–72.

Eaton, J. W. and Weil, R. J.   *Cultural and Mental Disorders: A Comparative Study of the Hutterites and Other Populations.* Glencoe: Free Press, 1955.

Elliot, H. S.   Mental Hygiene and Religious Education. *Rel. Educ.,* 24, 1929, p.616–8.

Feifel, H.   Symposium on Relationships Between Religion and Mental Health. *Amer. Psychol.,* 13, 1958, 565ff.

Fein, L. G.   Religious Observance and Mental Health: A Note. *J. Past. Care,* 12, 1958, p.99–101.

Fodor, N.   People Who Are Christ. *Psychoanal. Psychoanal. R.,* 45, 1958, p.100–19.

Ford, J. C.   *Religious Superiors, Subjects and Psychiatrists.* Westminster, Maryland: The Newman Press, 1963.

Freed, S. A. and Freed, R. S.   Spirit Possession as Illness in a North Indian Village. *Ethnology,* 3/2, 1964, p.152–71.

Frumkin, R. M. and Frumkin, M. S.   Religion, Occupation and Major Mental Disorders: A Research Note. *Hum. Relat.,* 6/1, 1958, p.98–101.

Gluckman, R. M.   The Chaplin as a Member of the Diagnostic Clinical Team. *Ment. Hyg.,* 37, 1953, p.278–82.

Godin, A.   Mental Health in Christian Life. *J. Rel. Health,* 1/1, 1961, p.41–54.

Gotten, N. and Patten, C. A.   The Delusions of Spiritualism: Psychiatric Reactions. *Amer. J. Psychiat.,* 13, 1934, p.1331–47.

Haydon, A. E. Spiritual (Religious) Values and Mental Hygiene. *Ment. Hyg.*, 14/4, 1930, p.779–90.

Hiltner, S. The Contributions of Religion to Mental Health. *Ment. Hyg.*, 24/3, 1940, p.366–77.

Hofmann, H. *Religion and Mental Health.* N.Y.: Harper, 1961.

Jahoda, G. Traditional Healers and Other Institutions Concerned with Mental Illness in Ghana. *Int. J. Soc. Psychiat.*, 7/4, 1961, p.245–68.

Johnson, P. E. New Religions and Mental Health. *J. Rel. Health*, 3/4, 1964, p.327–34.

Kaufman, M. R. Religious Delusions in Schizophrenia. *Int. J. Psychoanal.*, 20/3–4, 1939, p.363–76.

Kelley, M. W. Depression in the Psychoses of Members of Religious Communities of Women. *Amer. J. Psychol.*, 118, 1961, p.423–5.

Kelley, M. W. The Incidence of Hospitalized Mental Illness Among Religious Sisters in the U. S. *Amer. J. Psychiat.*, 115, 1958, p.72–5.

Kiev, A. (ed.) *Magic, Faith and Healing: Studies in Primitive Psychiatry Today.* N.Y.: Free Press of Glencoe, 1964.

Kirkpatrick, M. E. Mental Hygiene and Religion. *Ment. Hyg.*, 24/3, 1940, p.378–89.

Klein, D. C. The Minister and Mental Health: An Evaluation. *J. Past. Care*, 13, 1959, p.230–6.

Kleiner, R. J., *et al.* Mental Disorder and Status Based on Religious Affiliation. *Hum. Relat.*, 12/3, 1959, p.273–6.

Kleiner, R. J., *et al.* Mental Disorder and Status Based on Protestant Subgroup Membership. *J. Soc. Psychol.*, 58/2, 1962, p.345–8.

Krige, J. D The Magical Thought Patterns of the Bonter in Relation to Health Services. *Afr. Stud.*, 3, 1944, p.1–13.

La Barre, W. Religion, Rorschachs and Tranquilizers. *Amer. J. Orthopsychiat.*, 29, 1959, p.688–98.

Larson, R. F. Attitudes and Opinions of Clergymen About Mental Health and the Causes of Mental Illness. *Ment. Hyg.*, 49/1, 1965, p.52–9.

Lawson, D. W. Religious Programs for the Mentally Retarded Residing in Institutions. *Amer. J. Ment. Defic.*, 66, 1961, p.459–63.

Macalpine, I. and Hunter, R. A. *Schizophrenia, 1677: A Psychiatric Study of an Illustrated Autobiographical Record of Demoniacal Possession.* London: W. Dawson, 1956.

Malzberg, B. The Prevalence of Mental Disease Among Jews. *Ment. Hyg.*, 14/4, 1930, p.926–46.

Malzberg, B. Mental Disease Among Jews: A Second Study With a Note on the Relative Prevalence of Mental Defect and Epilepsy. *Ment. Hyg.*, 15/4, 1931, p.766–74.

Malzberg, B. Mental Disease Among Jews in New York State, 1920–1952. *Yivo Ann. Jew. Soc. Sci.*, 10, 1956, p.279–99.

Masters, R. E. L. *Eros and Evil: The Sexual Psychopathology of Witchcraft.* N.Y.: Julian Press, 1962, 322p.

Maves, P. B. (ed.) *The Church and Mental Health.* N.Y.: Scribner's, 1953.

McCann, R. *The Churches and Mental Health.* N.Y.: Basic Books, 1962.

McComb, S. Spiritual Healing in Europe. *Ment. Hyg.*, 12, 1928, p.706–21.

Messing, S. D. Group Therapy and Social Status in the Zar Cult of Ethiopia. *Amer. Anthropol.*, 60, 1958, p.1120–6.

Misiak, H. Psychosomatic Medicine and Religion. *Cath. World*, 1953, p.342–5.

Moloney, J. C. The Psychosomatic Aspects of Myths. *Amer. Imago*, 18/1, 1961, p.57–64.

Moore, T. V. Insanity in Priests and Religious. *Amer. Eccles. R.*, 95, 1936, p.485–96.

Noveck, S. (ed.) *Judaism and Psychiatry: Two Approaches to the Personal Problems and Needs of Modern Man.* N.Y.: The National Academy for Adult Jewish Studies of the United Synagogue of America, 1956, 198p.

Oates, W. E. *Religious Factors in Mental Illness.* London: Allen & Unwin, 1957.

Oates, W. E. The Role of Religion in the Psychoses. *J. Past. Care*, 3, 1949, p.21–30.

O'Doherty, E. F. *Religion and Personality Problems.* Staten Island, N.Y.: Alba House, 1964, 240p.

O'Doherty, E. F. and McGrath, S. C. (eds.) *The Priest and Mental Health.* Staten Island, N.Y.: St. Paul Publications, 1963, 251p.

Opler, M. K. (ed.) *Culture and Mental Health: Cross Cultural Studies.* N.Y.: MacMillan, 1960, 533p.

Patry, F. L. Mental Hygiene in Religion. *Rel. Educ.*, 33, 1938, p.209–11.

Pfister, O. R. *Christianity and Fear: A Study in History and in the Psychology and Hygiene of Religion* (Trans. W. H. Johnston). N.Y.: Macmillan & Co., 1948, 589p.

Reynolds, B. C. The Church and Individual Security. *Amer. J. Orthopsychiat.*, 3, 1933, p.44–54.

Roberts, B. H. and Myers, J. K. Religion, National

Origin, Immigration and Mental Illness. *Amer. J. Psychiat.*, 110, 1954, p.759–64.

Roger, L. and Hollingshead, A. The Puerto Rican Spiritualist as a Psychiatrist. *Amer. J. Sociol.*, 67, 1961, p.17–21.

Roheim, G. *Magic and Schizophrenia* (Eds. W. Muensterberger and S. H. Posinsky). N.Y.: International Universities Press, 1955, 230p.

Scully, A. W. The Work of a Chaplain in a State Hospital for Mental Disorder. *J. Nerv. Ment. Dis.*, 101, 1945, p.264–7.

Silver, D. J. The Retarded Child and Religious Education: A Case Study. *Rel. Educ.*, 52/5, 1957, p.361–4.

Sisney, V. V. and Shewmaker, K. L. Group Psychotherapy in a Church Setting. *Past. Psychol.*, 15/146, 1964, p.36–40.

Smet, W. Religious Experience in Client-Centered Therapy. In M. B. Arnold and J. A. Gasson(eds.)— *The Human Person.* N.Y.: Ronald Press, 1954, p.539–47.

Srole, L. and Langer, T. Religious Origins. In L. Srole, et al.—*Mental Health in the Metropolis: Midtown Manhattan Study.* N.Y.: McGraw-Hill, 1962.

Stubblefield, H. W. The Ministry and Mental Retardation. *J. Rel. Health*, 3/2, 1964, p.136–47.

Stubblefield, H. W. *The Church's Ministry to the Mentally Retarded.* Nashville: Broadman Press, 1965.

Suttie, I. D. Religion: Racial Character and Mental and Social Health. *Brit. J. Med.Psychol.*, 12, 1932, p.289–314.

Van Dusen, W. LSD and the Enlightenment of Zen. *Psychologia*, 4, 1961, p.11–6.

Vaughan, R. P. Mental Illness Among Religious. *R. for Rel.*, 18, 1959, p.25–6.

Vaughan, R. P. Religious Belief, Values, and Psychotherapy. *J. Rel. Health*, 2/3, 1963, p.198–209.

Wallace, A. F. C. Dreams and the Wishes of the Soul: A Type of Psychoanalytic Theory Among the Seventeenth Century Iroquois. *Amer. Anthropol.*, 60/2, 1958, p.234–49.

Weatherhead, L. D. *Psychology, Religion, and Healing.* Nashville, Tennessee: Abingdon-Cokesbury Press, 1957.

Whittaker, M. L. Adolescent Religion in Relation to Mental Hygiene. *Rel. Educ.*, 27, 1932, p.811–7.

Wright, E. D. Personal Counseling in the Chicago Central Y.M.C.A. *Rel. Educ.*, 25, 1930, p.729–34.

Wright, J. C. Personal Adjustment and its Relationship to Religious Attitudes and Certainty. *Rel. Educ.*, 54, 1959, p.521–3.

See Also:

Adler, M. D.   7a1
Allport, G. W.   1f, 7a1
Boisen, A. T.   1e, 4h (2)
Bowers, M. K.   7a4
Bowman, H. L.   1g
Bruder, E. E.   7a1 (3)
Christensen, C. W.   7a4
Draper, E.   1e
Ekstein, R.   1e
Freed, E. X.   7b3
Kagan, M.   7a1
Kaplan, B.   4h
Khatri, A. A.   6c
Kiev, A.   7b2
Klink, T. W.   7a1
Knight, J. A.   1e
LaBarre, W.   7b2
Landis, C.   7b3
Lorand, S.   1e
Ranck, J. G.   7b3
Sanua, V. D.   5a3
Schaer, H.   8a6
Schermerhorn, R. A.   4h
Wise, C. A.   7a1

5b2.   *Population Growth and Control*

Abrams, R. H. The Bishops of the Protestant Episcopal Church and Birth Control. *J. Soc. Psychol.*, 7/2, 1936, p.229–36.

Ahearn, N. Regulation of Offspring and the Roman Catholic Church. *Eugenics Quart.*, 6/1, 1959, p.23–5.

Bachi, R. and Matras, J. Family Size Preferences of Jewish Maternity Cases in Israel. *Milbank Memor. Fund Quart.*, 42/2, pt. 1, 1964, p.38–56.

Baker, O. E. Some Implications of Population Trends to the Christian Church. *Amer. Cath. Sociol. R.*, 3/2, 1942, p.80–92.

Bennett, J. C. Protestant Ethics and Population Control. *Daedalus*, 88/3, 1959, p.454–9.

Betancour, J. and de Souse, L. G. Current Population Changes in Latin America and the Implications for Religious Institutions and Behavior. *Amer. Cath. Sociol. R.*, 20/1, 1959, p.25–42.

Birmingham, W. (ed.) *The Roman Catholic Church and Contraception*. N.Y.: New American Library, 1964.

Blacker, C. P. Population, Religion and Birth Control. *Eugenics R.*, 51/4, 1960, p.217–20.

Brooks, H. E. and Franklin, J. H. An Empirical Study of the Relationships of Catholic Practice and Occupational Mobility to Fertility. *Milbank Memor. Fund Quart.*, 36/3, 1958, p.222–81.

Cambell, F. Birth Control and the Christian Churches. *Pop. Stud.*, 14/2, 1960, p.131–47.

Casey, T. J. Catholics and Family Planning. *Amer. Cath. Sociol. R.*, 21/2, 1960, p.125–35.

Day, L. H. Fertility Differentials Among Catholics in Australia. *Milbank Memor. Fund Quart.*, 42/2, pt. 1, 1964, p.57–83.

de Vries, E. Population Growth and Christian Responsibility. *Ecumen. R.*, 13/1, 1960, p.36–41.

Eaton, J. W. and Mayer, A. J. The Social Biology of Very High Fertility Among the Hutterites: The Demography of a Unique Population. *Hum. Biol.*, 25, 1953, p.206–64.

Fagley, R. M. Doctrines and Attitudes of Major Religions in Regard to Fertility. *Ecumen. R.*, 17/4, 1965, p.332–44.

Fagley, R. M. *The Population Explosion and Christian Responsibility*. N.Y.: Oxford Univ. Press, 1960.

Fonseca, A. The Church and the Control of Population. *Soc. Action*, 8/5–6, 1958, p.218–25.

Ford, J. C. and Kelly, G. Will the Church's Teachings on Birth Control Change? *Cath. World*, 1963, p.87–93.

Fox, J. R. Therapeutic Rituals and Social Structure in Cohiti Pueblo. *Hum. Relat.*, 13/4, 1960, p.291–304.

Freedman, R. and Whelpton, P. K. Fertility Planning and Fertility Rates by Religious Interests and Denominations. *Milbank Memor. Fund Quart.*, 29, 1950, p.294–343.

Freedman, R., *et al.* Socio-Economic Factors in Religious Differentials in Fertility. *Amer. Sociol. R.*, 26/4, 1961, p.608–14.

Goldscheider, C. Ideological Factors in Jewish Fertility Differentials. *Jew. J. Sociol.*, 7/1, 1965, p.92–104.

Goldscheider, C. Socio-Economic Status and Jewish Fertility. *Jew. J. Sociol.*, 7/2, 1965, p.221–37.

Higgins, E. Differential Fertility Outlook and Patterns Among Major Religious Groups in Johannesburg. *Soc. Compass*, 11/1, 1964, p.23–62.

Jackson, J. M. The World Population Problem: The Catholic Viewpoint. *Christus Rex*, 15/1, 1961, p.40–9.

Jaffe, A. J. Religious Differentials in the Net Reproduction Rate. *J. Amer. Stat. Assoc.*, 34, 1939, p.335–42.

Kelly, G. A. *Birth Control and Catholics*. N.Y.: Doubleday, 1963.

Kelly, G. A. *Overpopulation: A Catholic View*. N.Y.: The Paulist Press, 1960, 95p.

Kirk, D. Recent Trends of Catholic Fertility: Current Research in Human Fertility. *Milbank Memor. Fund Quart.*, 1955, p.93–105.

Kiser, C. V. and Whelpton, P. K. Social Psychological Factors Affecting Fertility: Summary of Chief Findings and Implications for Future Studies. *Milbank Memor. Fund Quart.*, 36, 1958, p.282–329.

Marie, L. Is the Catholic Birth Rate Declining? *Amer. Cath. Sociol. R.*, 5/3, 1944, p.177–84.

Marshall, D. G. The Decline of Family Fertility and its Relationship to Nationality and Religious Background. *Rural Sociol.*, 15, 1950, p.42–9.

Mulvaney, B. G. Notes of Sociological Interest: How Catholics and Non-Catholics Differ in Fertility. *Amer. Cath. Sociol. R.*, 7/2, 1946, p.124–7.

Murphy, R. J. Psychodynamic Factors Affecting Fertility in the United States. In R. F. Winch (ed.)—*Selected Studies in Marriage and the Family*. N.Y.: Henry Holt, 1959.

Rieterman, C. Birth Control and Catholics. *J. Sci. Stud. Rel.*, 4/2, 1965, p.213–33.

Rosenthal, E. Jewish Fertilities in the U.S. *Eugenics Quart.*, 8/4, 1961, p.198–217.

Ryan, B. Institutional Factors in Sinhalese Fertility. *Milbank Memor. Fund. Quart.*, 30/4, 1952, p.359–81.

Shuster, G. N. (ed.) *The Problem of Population: Practical Catholic Applications*. Notre Dame: Univ. of Notre Dame Press, 1964, 185p.

Stouffer, S. A. Trends in the Fertility of Catholics and Non-Catholics. *Amer. J. Sociol.*, 41/2, 1935, p.43–66.

Stycos, J. M. and Back, K. Contraception and Catholicism in Jamaica. *Eugenics Quart.*, 5/4, 1958, p.216–20.

Sulloway, A. W. *Birth Control and Catholic Doctrine*. Boston: Beacon Press, 1959.

Thomas, J. L. The Catholic Position on Population Control. *Daedalus*, 88/3, 1959, p.444–53.

Van Heck, F. Roman-Catholicism and Fertility in the

Netherlands: Demographic Aspects of Priority Status. *Pop. Stud.*, 10, 1956, p.125–38.

Whelpton, P. K. and Kiser, C. V. Social and Psychological Factors Affecting Fertility. *Eugenics R.*, 51, 1959, p.35–42.

Wichmann, A. A. Burma: Agriculture, Population and Buddhism. *Amer. J. Econ. Sociol.*, 24, 1965, p.71–84.

Zimmerman, A. *Overpopulation: A Study of Papal Teachings on the Problem With Special Reference to Japan.* Washington: Catholic Univ. Press, 1957, 328p.

Zimmerman, A. The Alleged Danger of Imminent World Overpopulation. *Amer. Cath. Sociol. R.*, 18/1, 1957, p.10–32.

See Also:

Glick, P. C.   4e3
Nuesse, C. J.   4f2
Rokeach, M.   7b2
Wells, W. R.   7b
Yaukey, D.   5a3

5c.   *Religion and Civil Rights/Human Rights*

Aaron, B. The Garvey Movement: Shadow and Substance. *Phylon*, 4/4, 1947, p.337–42.

Allport, G. W. Religion and Prejudice. *Crane R.*, 2, 1959, p.8–9.

Barber, H. W. Religious Liberty V. The Police Power. *Amer. Polit. Sci. R.*, 41/2, 1947, p.226–47.

Blanshard, P. *American Freedom and Catholic Power.* Boston: Beacon Press, 1949.

Blau, J. L. (ed.) *Cornerstones of Religious Freedom in America.* Boston: Beacon Press, 1949.

Briefs, G. The Disputes Between Catholicism and Liberalism in the Early Decades of Capitalism. *Soc. Res.*, 4/1, 1937, p.52–73.

Cantwell, D. M. Race Relations: As Seen by a Catholic. *Amer. Cath. Sociol. R.*, 7/4, 1946, p.242–58.

Catchings, L. M. Interracial Activities in Southern Churches. *Phylon*, 13/1, 1952, p.54–6.

Clark, H. *The Church and Residential Segregation.* New Haven: College & University Press, 1964.

Conference on Christian Citizenship in a Multi-Racial Society. *The Christian Citizen in a Multi-Racial Society: A Report of the Rosetten-Ville Conference, July, 1949.* Strand, C. P.: Christian Council of South Africa, 1949, 107p.

Coogan, J. Improving Racial Attitudes Among Catholics. *Amer. Cath. Sociol. R.*, 7/2, 1946, p.118–123.

Cranston, M. Pope John XXIII on Peace and The Rights of Man. *Polit. Quart.*, 34, 1963, p.380–90.

Drinan, R. *Religion, the Courts and Public Policy.* N.Y.: McGraw-Hill, 1963, 261p.

Fogarty, M. P., and Hughes, N. S. Catholicism and Democracy. *Commentary*, 26/2, 1958, p.119–26.

Goldberg, B. Z. *The Jewish Problem in the Soviet Union.* N.Y.: Crown Publishers, 1961.

Grimes, A. P. *Equality in America: Religion, Race and Urban Majority.* N.Y.: Oxford Univ. Press, 1964.

Harte, T. J. *Catholic Organizations Promoting Negro-White Race Relations in the United States.* Washington: Catholic Univ. Press, 1947, 173p.

Haselden, K. *The Racial Problem in Christian Perspective.* N.Y.: Harper & Brothers, 1959, 222p.

Hassum, H. C. Social Rights of Muslim Women. *Asian R.*, 52/198, 1956, p.158–60.

Haynes, G. E. The Church and Negro Progress. *Ann. Amer. Acad. Polit. Soc. Sci.*, 130, 1928, p.264–71.

Hero, A. O., Jr. Southern Jews, Race Relations, and Foreign Policy. *Jew. Soc. Stud.*, 27/4, 1965, p.213–35.

Hill, S. S. Southern Protestantism and Racial Integration. *Rel. Life*, 33/3, 1964, p.421–9.

Houser, G. M. Racism Sits in the Pews. *Fellowship*, 13, 1947, p.26–7.

Hughes, H. S. How Democratic is Christian Democracy? *Commentary*, 5/5, 1958, p.379–84.

Hurley, P. S. Role of the Churches in Integration. *J. Intergr. Relat.*, 1/3, 1960, p.41–6.

Jernegen, M. W. Slavery and Conversion in the American Colonies. *Amer. Hist. R.*, 21/3, 1916, p.504–27.

Kelsey, G. D. Protestantism and Democratic Intergroup Living. *Phylon*, 8/1, 1947, p.77–82.

Kelsey, G. D. *Racism and the Christian Understanding of Man.* N.Y.: Scribner's, 1965, 195p.

Kluckhohn, C., *et al.* *Religion and Our Racial Tensions.* Cambridge: Harvard Univ., 1945.

Kramer, A. Racial Integration in Three Protestant Denominations. *J. Educ. Sociol.*, 28/1, 1954, p.59–68, 96.

LaFarge, J. *The Catholic Viewpoint on Race Relations.* Garden City, N.Y.: Hanover House, 1960, 192p.

LaFarge, J. *The Catholic Viewpoint on Race Relations.* Garden City, N.Y.: Hanover House, 1960, 192p.

LaFarge, J. American Catholicism and the Negro, 1962. *Soc. Order,* 12/4, 1962, p.153–61.

Lee, R. The Church in a Case of Neighborhood Exclusion. *Phylon,* 13/4, 1952, p.338–40.

Lincoln, C. E. The Church and Race Relations. *Phylon,* 17, 1956, p.343–8.

Loecher, F. S. The Protestant Church and the Negro: Recent Pronouncements. *Soc. Forces,* 26/2, 1947, p.197–201.

Loecher, F. S. *The Protestant Churches and the Negro: A Pattern of Segregation.* N.Y.: Association Press, 1948.

Manhattan, A. *Catholic Imperialism and World Freedom.* London: Watts, 1952, 510p.

Maston, T. B. *Segregation and Desegregation: A Christian Approach.* N.Y.: Macmillan, 1959.

Miller, P., *et al. Religion and Freedom of Thought.* N.Y.: Doubleday, 1954.

Mol, J. J. Integration Versus Segregation in the New Zealand Churches. *Brit. J. Sociol.,* 16/2, 1965, p.140–9.

Northwood, L. K. Ecological and Attitudinal Factors in Church Desegregation. *Soc. Prob.,* 6/2, 1958, p.150–63.

Osborne, W. The Church and the Negro: A Crisis in Leadership. *Crosscurrents,* 15/2, 1965, p.129–50.

Papers and Proceedings of a Conference on Negro-Jewish Relations in the United States. *Jew. Soc. Stud.,* 27/1, 1965, p.3–66.

Paton, D. M. (ed.) *Church and Race in South Africa.* London: SCM Press, 1958, 128p.

Pope, L. *The Kingdom Beyond Caste.* N.Y.: Friendship Press, 1957, 170p.

Posey, W. B. The Baptists and Slavery in the Lower Mississippi Valley. *J. Negro Hist.,* 41/2, 1956, p.117–30.

Prestwood, C. M. Dilemmas of Deep South Clergy. *Christ. Today,* 1961, p.308–9.

Reimers, D. M. *White Protestantism and the Negro.* N.Y.: Oxford University Press, 1965, 236p.

Reinders, R. C. The Churches and the Negro in New Orleans, 1850–1860. *Phylon,* 22/3, 1961, p.241–8.

Root, R. *Progress Against Prejudice: The Church Confronts the Race Problem.* N.Y.: Friendship Press, 1957, 165p.

Rossi, P. New Directions for Race Relations Research. *R. Rel. Res.,* 5/3, 1964, p.125–32.

Scarlett, W. (ed.) *The Christian Demand for Social Justice.* N.Y.: New American Library, 1949.

Tiryakian, E. A. Race, Equality and Religion. *Theol. Today,* 17/4, 1961, p.455–65.

Walsh, M. E. Courses on Race Relations in Catholic Colleges. *Amer. Cath. Sociol. R.,* 2/1, 1941, p.23–33.

Waltz, A. K. and Wilson, R. L. Minister's Attitudes Toward Integration. *Phylon,* 19/2, 1958, p.195–9.

Williams, R. M., Jr., *et al. Strangers Next Door: Ethnic Relations in American Communities.* Englewood Cliffs: Prentice-Hall, 1964.

See Also: 1c, 4d, 4j, 5a2

Abrams, C.   4j2
Adjei, A.   5e1
Augustine, D.   4j2
Bernard, R.   4j2
Breathett, G.   5e2
Bruder, E. E.   7a1
Campbell, E. Q.   7a3 (2)
Clark, H.   7a3
Congar, Y. M. J.   4j2
Culver, D. W.   4j2
Edwards, L. P.   7b3
Eighmy, J. L.   7b3
Feagin, J. R.   7b3
Ford, J. C.   5b2
Frankino, S. P.   5g
Friedrichs, R. W.   4j2
Garrison, W. E.   3a2
Harte, T. J.   7b3
Haynes, L.   2a1
Hill, C. S.   4j2
Hunt, C. L.   4a1
Johnson, J.   7a4
Johnston, R. F.   2a1
Lang, K.   4g
Leavy, G.   (3a1)
Linguistic Philosophy and Christian . . .   4g
Malalasekera, G. P.   4j2
Marrow, R. E.   4
Mason, P.   4j2
Miller, R. R.   4j2
Muelder, W. G.   7a4
Murphy, R. J.   3a2
Nelson, W. S.   7a3
Northwood, L. K.   7b3
O'Neill, J. E.   4j2
Perry, T. N.   5a2
Pope, L.   4j3
Rice, M. H.   7b3

5d.   Religion and Peace and War

Abrams, R. H.   The Churches and the Clergy in World War II. *Ann. Amer. Acad. Polit. Soc. Sci.*, 256, 1948, p.110–9.

Bainton, R. H.   *Christian Attitudes to War and Peace: An Historical Survey and Critical Re-Evaluation.* N.Y.: Abingdon Press, 1960, 299p.

Bainton, R. H.   The Churches Shift on War. *Rel. Life*, 12, 1943, p.1–13.

Barish, L. (ed.)   *Rabbis in Uniform: The Story of the American Jewish Military Chaplain.* N.Y.: J. David, 1962, 347p.

Baron, S. W.   Impact of Wars on Religion. *Polit. Sci. Quart.*, 67/4, 1952, p.534–72.

Ben-Ami, A.   Insitutional Lag and Neofunctions: The Case of the Latin Kingdom of Jerusalem. *Comp. Stud. Society Hist.*, 7/4, 1965, p.409–28.

Benda, H.   *The Cresent and the Rising Sun: Indonesian Islam Under the Japanese Occupation 1942–1945.* The Hague: W. Van Hoeve, 1958, 320p.

Boardman, E. P.   Christian Influences upon the Ideology of the Taiping Rebellion. *Far East. Quart.*, 10/2, 1951, p.115–24.

Braden, C. S.   *War, Communism and World Religions.* N.Y.: Harper & Brothers, 1953.

Dewart, L.   *Christianity and Revolution: The Lesson of Cuba.* N.Y.: Herder and Herder, 1963, 316p.

Droba, D. D.   Churches and War Attitudes. *Sociol. Soc. Res.*, 15/6, 1932, p.547–52.

Ellis, F. H.   Patterns of Aggression and the War Cult in Southwestern Pueblos. *Southw. J. Anthropol.*, 7/2, 1951, p.177–201.

Ellsworth, C. S.   American Churches and the Mexican War. *Amer. Hist. R.*, 45/2, 1940, p.301–26.

Esco Foundation.   *Palestine: A Study of Jewish, Arab and British Policies.* New Haven: Yale Univ. Press, 1947.

Fisher, M. M.   The Negro Church and the World War. *J. Rel.*, 5/5, 1925, p.483–99.

Glubb, J. B.   *The Great Arab Conquests:* London: Hodder and Stoughton, 1963, 384p.

Gregory, J. S.   British Missionary Reaction to the Taiping Revolution in China. *J. Rel. Hist.*, 2, 1963, p.204–18.

Hershberger, G. F.   *The Mennonite Church in the Sec-* ond World War. Scottdale, Pennsylvania: Mennonite Publishing House, 1951.

Hicks, G.   The Parsons and the War. *Amer. Mercury*, 1927, p.129–42.

Johnson, F. E.   The Impact of the War on Religion in America. *Amer. J. Sociol.*, 48/3, 1942, p.353–60.

Kahn, R. A.   The Law of Nations and the Conduct of War in the Early Times of the Standing Army. *J. Polit.*, 6/1, 1944, p.77–105.

Kaufmann, I.   *American Jews in World War II.* N.Y.: Dial, 1947.

Kerwin, J. G.   The Church and the Garrison State. *R. Polit.*, 1/2, 1939, p.179–90.

Khadduri, M.   *War and Peace in the Law of Islam.* Baltimore: Johns Hopkins Press, 1955.

Kinsolving, A. L.   War and Our Religious Condition. *Virginia Quart. R.*, 21, 1945, p.355–67.

Korn, B. W.   *American Jewry and the Civil War.* Cleveland: World Publishing Co., 1961, 329p.

Lewy, G.   The Uses of Insurrection: The Church and Franco's War. *Continuum*, 3/3, 1965, p.267–90.

Linton, R.   Totemism and the A. E. F. *Amer. Anthropol.*, 26, 1924, p.296–300.

Mackenzie, K. M.   *The Robe and the Sword: The Methodist Church and the Rise of Imperialism.* Washington, D. C.: Public Affairs Press, 1961.

McAvoy, T. T.   American Catholics and the Second World War. *R. Polit.*, 6, 1944, p.131–50.

McKenna, J. C.   Ethics and War: A Catholic View. *Amer. Polit. Sci. R.*, 54, 1960, p.647–58.

McNeill, J. T.   Asceticism Versus Militarism in the Middle Ages. *Church Hist.*, 5, 1936, p.3–28.

Metzger, C. H.   *Catholics and the American Revolution: A Study in Religious Climate.* Chicago: Loyola Univ. Press, 1962, 306p.

Moellering, R. L.   *Modern War and the American Churches: A Factual Study of the Christian Conscience on Trial From 1939 to the Cold War Crisis of Today.* N.Y.: American Press, 1956, 141p.

National Peace Congress of Catholic Clergy.   *The Catholic Priest in the Fight for Peace: Addresses and Resolutions From the National Peace Congress of Catholic*

Clergy, Held in Prague. Prague: Czech Catholic Charita, 1951, 61p.

Nuttall, G. F. *Christian Pacifism in History.* Oxford: Oxford Univ. Press, 1958.

Palmieri, F. A. The Church and the Russian Revolution. *Cath. World,* 105, 1917, p.661–70; see also 107, 1918, p.323–36, p.764–76.

Parker, T. W. *The Knights Templars in England.* Tucson, Arizona: Univ. of Arizona Press, 1963, 195p.

Pernoud, R. *The Crusades.* London: Secker and Warburg, 1962, 295p.

Poland, B. C. *French Protestantism and the French Revolution: A Study in Church and State, Thought and Religion, 1685–1815.* Princeton: Princeton Univ. Press, 1957, 315p.

Polish Legation, U. S. *German Revisionism: Its Threat to Peace-Statements of Polish Catholics.* Washington: Polish Embassy, 1952, 20p.

Reynolds, R. The Russian Church and the Revolution. *Contemp. R.,* 113, 1918, p.397–405.

Salmon, J. H. M. *The French Religious Wars in English Political Thought.* Oxford: Clarendon Press, 1959, 203p.

Sanchez, J. M. *Reform and Reaction: The Politico-Religious Background of the Spanish Civil War.* Chapel Hill: Univ. of North Carolina Press, 1964, 231p.

Shanahan, W. O. *German Protestants Face the Social Question.* Notre Dame: Univ. of Notre Dame Press, 1954, 2 vols.

Sibley, M. Q. The Political Theories of Modern Religious Pacifism. *Amer. Polit. Sci. R.,* 37/3, 1943, p.439–54.

Siedenburg, F. War and the Catholic Church. *Amer. J. Sociol.,* 31/3, 1925, p.336–77.

Stratman, F. M. *War and Christianity Today.* Westminster, Maryland: Newman Press, 1956.

Sturzo, L. Modern Wars and Catholic Thought. *R. Polit.,* 3/2, 1941, p.155–87.

Sulxma, A. Russian Orthodox Church as a Tool of Soviet "Peace Policy." *Ukranian Quart.,* 14/1, 1958, p.49–57.

Sweeney, E. B. Nationalism and Internationalism Through the Churches: The Catholic Church and the Promotion of Peace Attitudes. *J. Educ. Sociol.,* 10/6, 1937, p.338–42. See also: L. Minsky—Jewish Efforts for International Good Will, p.342–7; R. P. Barnes—The Protestant Churches and International Attitudes, p.348–52.

Swomley, J. M., Jr. *The Military Establishment.* Boston: Beacon Press, 1964, 266p.

Szajkowski, Z. Demands for Complete Emancipation of German Jewry During World War I. *Jew. Quart. R.,* 55/4, 1965, p.350–63.

Von Elbe, J. The Evolution of the Concept of the Just War in International Law. *Amer. J. Int. Law,* 33/4, 1939, p.665–88.

Wieman, H. N. Teaching Religion in War Time. *J. Bib. Rel.,* 11, 1943, p.75–80.

Zahn, G. C. *German Catholics and Hitler's Wars.* London: Sheed & Ward, 1963.

See Also: *4a, 5c, 6, 7b*

5e. Religion and Missions

Anderson, G. H. *Bibliography of the Theology of Missions in the Twentieth Century.* N.Y.: Missionary Research Library, 1960.

Anderson, G. H. (ed.) *The Theology of the Christian Mission.* N.Y.: McGraw-Hill, 1961, 341p.

Beals, R. L. On the Study of Missionary Policies. *Amer. Anthropol.,* 61/2, 1959, p.298–301.

Beckmann, J. Roman Catholic Missions 1963–64. *Int. R. Missions,* 54/213, 1965, p.76–80.

Bibliography on World Missions and Evangelism. *Int. R. Missions,* 54/216, 1965, p.526–42. (Note: Each Volume Contains Such a Bibliography.)

Brown, D. G. Missions and Cultural Diffusion. *Amer. J. Sociol.,* 50/3, 1944, p.214–9.

Capen, E. Modern Principles of Foreign Missions. *Ann. Amer. Acad. Polit. Soc. Sci.*, 30/3, 1907, p.33–44.

Church Missionary Society. *Bibliography of Books and Pamphlets on Christian Missions.* London: Church Missionary Society, 1959, 50p.

Clasper, P. D. The Denominational Missionary and the Organization Man. *Foundations*, 2, 1959, p.57–71.

Considine, J. J. *The Missionary's Role in Socio-Economic Betterment.* Westminster, Maryland: The Newman Press, 1960, 320p.

Devanandan, P. D. Hindu Missions to the West. *Int. R. Missions*, 48/192, 1959, p.398–408.

Duignan, P. Early Jesuit Missionaries: A Suggestion for Further Study. *Amer. Anthropol.*, 60, 1958, p.725–32.

Ethnologie Religieuse: Afrique-Oceanie. Roma: Apud Aedes Pontificiae Universitatis Gregorianae, 1964, 258p. (Coll.: Studia Missionalia XIV); See other issues.

Fathauer, G. H., *et al.* A Symposium on Modern Missions. *J. Hum. Relat.*, 12/2, 1964, p.189–219.

Florin, H. W. Government Aid and Mission Operations. *J. Church State*, 7/3, 1965, p.350–73.

Harr, W. C. (ed.) *Frontiers of the Christian World Mission Since 1938: Essays in Honor of Kenneth Scott Latourette.* N.Y.: Harper, 1962, 310p.

Horner, N. A. *Cross and Crucifix in Mission: A Comparison of Protestant-Roman Catholic Mission Strategy.* Nashville: Abingdon, 1965, 223p.

Houtart, F. and Dhooghe, J. The Study of the Educational, Health and Social Activities of Christian Religious Bodies in the Developing Countries. *Soc. Compass*, 11/6, 1964, p.49–52.

Kittler, G. D. *The White Fathers.* London: Allen, 1957, 319p.

Korb, G. M. The Scientific Scrutiny of Mission Methods. *Amer. Eccles. R.*, 144/2, 1961, p.114–21.

Kraemer, H. The Role and Responsibility of the Christian Mission. *Civilisations*, 7/4, 1957, p.557–70.

Lamott, W. C. *Revolutuion in Missions: From Foreign Missions to the World Mission of the Church.* N.Y.: Macmillan, 1954, 228p.

Latourette, K. S. Colonialism and Missions: Progressive Separation. *J. Church State*, 7/3, 1965, p.330–49.

Latourette, K. S. The Present Status of Foreign Missions. *Ann. Amer. Acad. Polit. Soc. Sci.*, 256, 1948, p.63–71.

Luznetak, L. J. Toward an Applied Missionary Anthropology. *Anthropol. Quart.*, 34/4, 1961, p.165–76.

Mission and Service. *Int. R. Missions*, 54/216, 1965, p.417–94.

Neill, S. *Christian Missions.* London: Hodder and Stoughton, 1965, 622p.

Newbigin, L. A Survey of the Year 1963–4. *Int. R. Missions*, 54/213, 1965, p.3–75; see other issues.

North American Foreign Mission Agencies. N.Y.: Missionary Research Library, 1964, 80p.

Orchard, R. K. *Missions in a Time of Testing.* Phila.: Westminster Press, 1965.

Orchard, R. K. (ed.) *Witness in Six Continents.* Edinburgh: Edinburgh House Press, 1964, 200p.

Ortega Y Medina, J. A. An Analysis of the Missionary Methods of the Puritans. *Americas*, 14/2, 1957, p.125–34.

Orthodoxy and Mission. *Int. R. Missions*, 54/215, 1965, p.273–359.

Parks, R. E. Missions and the Modern World. *Amer. J. Sociol.*, 50/3, 1944, p.177–83.

Reischaver, A. R. Non-Christian Religions and Christian Leadership. *Int. R. Missions*, 43, 1954, p.179–85.

Richardson, W. J. (ed.) *The Modern Mission Apostolate: A Symposium.* Maryknoll, N.Y.: Maryknoll Publications, 1965, 308p.

Scott, W. H. Some Contrasts in Missionary Patterns. *Int. R. Missions*, 54/215, 1965, p.315–24.

Sullivan, R. E. The Papacy and Missionary Activity in the Early Middle Ages. *Medieval Stud.*, 17, 1955, p.66–106.

Takenaka, M. Urban and Industrial Evangelism in the United States: A Critical Reflection. *Int. R. Missions*, 52/207, 1963, p.303–15.

Vallier, I. Church, Society and Labor Resources: An Interdenominational Comparison. *Amer. J. Sociol.*, 68/1, 1962, p.21–33.

Van Hardenberg, P. Petro-Apostolate Among Non-Catholics, Exercised by "The Ladies of Bethany" Holland. *Lumen Vitae*, 1/4, 1946, p.612–34.

Wonderly, W. L. and Nida, E. A. Linguistics and Christian Missions. *Anthropol. Ling.*, 5/1, 1963, p.104–44.

See Also: 2, 3, 4g, 5a, 7a, 7c

5e1.   Africa

Adjei, A. Imperialism and Spiritual Freedom: An African View. *Amer. J. Sociol.*, 50/3, 1944, p.189–98.

Ajayi, J. F. A. *Christian Missions in Nigeria, 1841–1891: The Making of a New Elite.* Evanston, Illinois: Northwestern Univ. Press, 1965.

Aquina, M. A Note on Missionary Influence of Shona Marriage. *Human Prob. Brit. Centr. Afr.*, 33, 1963, p.68–79.

Bane, M. J. *Catholic Pioneers in West Africa.* London: Burns, Oates and Washbourne, 1956, 220p.

Barnett, A. Christian Home and Family Life in Kenya Today. *Int. R. Missions*, 49, 1960, p.420–6.

Bernander, G. A. *The Rising Tide: Christianity Challenged in East Africa* (Trans. H. D. Friberg). Rock Island, Illinois: Augustana Press, 1957, 70p.

Birkeli, F. The Church in Madagascar. *Int. R. Missions*, 46/182, 1957, p.155–63.

Cutler, A. The Ninth Century Spanish Martyrs' Movement and the Origins of Western Christian Missions to the Muslims. *Muslim World*, 55/4, 1965, p.321–39.

Desai, A. R. (ed.) *Christianity in Africa as Seen by Africans.* Denver: Alan Swallow, 1962.

Forde, D., *et al. Missionary Statesmanship in Africa: A Present Day Demand Upon the Christian Movement.* Hartford: Hartford Seminary Foundation, 1953, 99p.

Gale, H. P. *Uganda and the Mill Hill Fathers.* London: Macmillan, 1959, 334p.

Green, S. Blantyre Missions. *Nyasaland J.*, 10/2, 1957, p.6–17.

Green-Wilkinson, F. O. Christianity in Central Africa. *Afr. Aff.*, 62/247, 1963, p.114–24.

Groves, C. P. *The Planting of Christianity in Africa.* London: Lutterworth Press, 1958, 390p.

Hake, A. An Urban Mission Course in Nairobi. *Int. R. Missions*, 52/206, 1963, p.173–81.

Hill, R. Government and Christian Missions in the Anglo-Egyptian Sudan, 1899–1914. *Mid. East Stud.*, 1/2, 1965, p.113–34.

Hooker, J. R. Witnesses and Watchtower in the Rhodesias and Nyasaland. *J. Afr. Hist.*, 6/1, 1965, p.91–106.

Ilogu, E. Christianity and Ibo Traditional Religion. *Int. R. Missions*, 54/215, 1965, p.335–42.

Johnson, T. S. *The Story of a Mission: The Sierra Leone Church: First Daughter of the C. M. S.* London: SPCK, 1953, 148p.

Kuper, H. The Swazi Reaction to Missions. *Afr. Stud.*, 5/3, 1946, p.177–89.

McFarlan, D. M. *Calabar, the Church of Scotland Mission, 1846–1946.* London: T. Nelson, 1946, 183p.

Northcott, C. *Christianity in Africa.* Phila.: Westminster Press, 1963.

Parsons, R. T. Missionary-African Relations. *Civilisations*, 3/4, 1953, p.505–18.

Pretorius, J. L. The Story of the Dutch Reformed Church Mission in Nyasaland. *Nyasaland. J.*, 10/1, 1957, p.11–22.

Sawyerr, H. Christian Evangelistic Strategy in West Africa. *Int. R. Missions*, 54/215, 1965, p.343–52.

Schütte, K. H. The Catholic Church and Agriculture in Africa. *Neue Z. Miss.—Wiss.*, 14/1, 1958, p.1–14.

Slade, R. M. *English-Speaking Missions in the Congo Independent State (1878–1908)*. Bruselles: Academie Royale Des Sciences Coloniales, 1959, 432p.

Stern, S. M. The Early Islamic Missionaries in North West Persia and in Khurāsān and Transoxaniá. *Bull. School Oriental Afr. Stud.*, 23/1, 1960, p.56–90.

Stuart, M. *Land of Promise: The Story of the Church in Uganda*. London: Highway, 1957, 112p.

Tannous, A. I. Missionary Education in Lebanon: A Study in Acculturation. *Soc. Forces*, 21/3, 1943, p.338–43.

Taylor, J. V. *The Growth of the Church in Buganda: An Attempt at Understanding*. London: SCM Press, 1958, 288p.

Taylor, J. V. The Uganda Church Today. *Int. R. Missions*, 46/182, 1957, p.136–44.

Taylor, J. V. *Processes of Growth in an African Church*. London: SCM Press, 1958, 30p.

5e2. The Americas

Barber, J. B. *Climbing Jacob's Ladder: Story of the Work of the Presbyterian Church, U. S. A. Among the Negroes*. N.Y.: Board of National Missions Presbyterian Church in U. S. A., 1952, 103p.

Berkhoeffer, R. F., Jr. *Salvation and the Savage: An Analysis of Protestant Missions and American Indian Response, 1787–1862*. Lexington: Univ. of Kentucky Press, 1965, 186p.

Breathett, G. Catholic Missionary Activity and the Negro Slave in Haiti. *Phylon*, 22/3, 1962, p.78–85.

Christelow, A. Father Joseph Neumann, Jesuit Missionary to the Tarahumares. *Hisp. Amer. Hist. R.*, 1939, p.423–42.

Forrest, E. R. *Missions and Pueblos of the Old Southwest*. Chicago: Rio Grande Press, 1962, 386p.

Goncalves, A. De C. Evangelism in Brazil Today. *Int. R. Missions*, 48/191, 1959, p.302–8.

Gray, E. E. and Gray, L. R. *Wilderness Christians: The Moravian Mission to the Delaware Indians*. Ithaca, N.Y.: Cornell Univ. Press, 1956, 354p.

Hendricks, F. K. The First Apostolic Mission to Chile. *Hisp. Amer. Hist. R.*, 1942, p.644–69.

Hickerson, H. William T. Boutwell of the American Board and the Pillager Chippewa. *Ethnohistory*, 12/1, 1965, p.1–29.

Jesset, T. E. Christian Missions to the Indians of Oregon. *Church Hist.*, 28/2, 1959, p.147–56.

Kenton, E. (ed.) *Black Gown and Redskins: Adventure and Travels of the Early Jesuit Missionaries in North America, 1610–1791*. London: Longmans, Green, 1956, 527p.

Kevane, R. A. Papal Volunteers for Latin America. *Amer. Eccles. R.*, 152/5, 1965, p.298–306.

King, L. T. Spanish Mission to Virginia: A Settlement That Failed. *Americas*, 8/11, 1956, p.19–22.

Loewen, J. A. The Church Among the Choco Indians of Panama. *Pract. Anthropol.*, 10/3, 1963, p.97–108.

Loth, J. H. *Catholicism on the March: The California Missions*. N.Y.: Vantage Press, 1961, 93p.

Loughran, E. The First Episcopal Sees in Spanish America. *Hisp. Amer. Hist. R.*, 1930, p.167–87.

Mattison, R. H. Indian Missions and Missionaries on the Upper Missouri to 1900. *Nebraska Hist.*, 38/1, 1957, p.127–54.

Nida, E. A. The Relationship of Social Structure to the Problem of Evangelism in Latin America. *Pract. Anthropol.*, 5/3, 1958, p.101–23.

Obermüller, R. *Evangelism in Latin America*. London: Lutterworth, 1957, 32p.

Pearce, R. H. The "Ruines of Mankind": The Indian and the Puritan Mind. *J. Hist. Ideas*, 13/2, 1952, p.200–17.

Robinson, D. F. The Indian Church in a Sponsor Oriented Society. *Pract. Anthropol.*, 9/2, 1962, p.90–3.

Schusky, E. L. Mission and Government Policy in Dakota Indian Communities. *Pract. Anthropol.*, 10/3, 1963, p.109–14.

Scopes, W. (ed.) *The Christian Ministry in Latin America and the Caribbean*. N.Y.: Commission on World Mission and Evangelism, World Council of Churches, 1962, 267p.

Wallis, E. E. *The Dayuma Story: Life Under Auca Spears*. N.Y.: Harper, 1960, 288p.

Williamson, H. A. The Moravian Mission and Its Impact on the Labrador Eskimo. *Arctic Anthropol.*, 2/2, 1964, p.32–6.

Wonderly, W. L. Social Anthropology, Christian Missions, and the Indians of Latin America. *Pract. Anthropol.*, 6/2, 1959, p.55–64.

American Church Union. *Christianity in India: An Historical Summary Having Particular Reference to the Anglican Communion and to the Church of South India.* N.Y.: American Church Publications Committee, 1954, 47p.

Anbunathan, C. Should a Regional Church Body Control the Medical Mission. *J. Christ. Med. Assoc. India,* 35, 1960, p.4–6.

Arasaratnam, S. Reverend Philippus Baldaeus: His Pastoral Work in Ceylon 1656–1665. *Ceylon J. Hist. Soc. Stud.,* 3/1, 1960, p.27–37.

Barton, W. Untouchability and Foreign Missions in India. *Contemp. R.,* 1072, 1955, p.244–8.

Bathgate, J. Christian Participation in Rural Development in India. *Int. R. Missions,* 52, 1963, p.289–99.

Berndt, C. H. Anthropology and Mission Activity. *S. Pacific,* 10/2, 1958, p.38–43.

Bruce, M. The Church of England and South India. *Ecumen. R.,* 8/1, 1955, p.42–54.

Cary-Elwes, C. *China and the Cross: A Survey of Missionary History.* N.Y.: P. J. Kenedy, 1957, 323p.

Cattell, E. L. The Christian Impact on India. *Int. R. Missions,* 51/202, 1962, p.153-62.

Cohen, P. A. The Anti-Christian Tradition in China. *J. Asian Stud.,* 20/2, 1961, p.169–80.

deSilva, K. M. *Social Policy and Missionary Organizations in Ceylon, 1840–1855.* London: Longmans, 1965, 328p.

Doi, M. The Implications of the Ecumenical Council for Catholic-Protestant Relations in Mission Work in Japan. *Japan. Christ. Quart.,* 30/2, 1964, p.100-5.

Hollis, A. M. *Paternalism and the Church: A Study of South Indian Church History.* London: Oxford Univ. Press, 1962, 114p.

Johnson, S. E. Early Christianity in Asia Minor. *J. Bibl. Lit.,* 77/1, 1958, p.1–17.

Kuhn, I. S. *Ascent to the Tribes: Pioneering in North Thailand.* London: China Inland Mission, 1956, 253p.

Lacy, C. The Missionary Exodus from China. *Pac. Aff.,* 28/4, 1955, p.301–14.

Meersman, A. The Franciscans in India. *Neue Z. Miss.-Wiss.,* 13/3, 1957, p.208–16.

Mervin, W. C. and Jones, F. P. (eds.) *Documents on the Three-Self Movement: Source Materials for the Study of the Protestant Church in Communist China.* N.Y.: National Council of Churches of Christ in the U. S. A., 1963.

Presbyterian Church in the U. S. A., Board of Foreign Missions. *Education in West Pakistan: A Study of the Schools and Educational Needs Related to Lahore Church Council Conference, Lahore, Pakistan, 1955.* N.Y.: Ecumenical Mission, Board of Foreign Missions, Presbyterian Church in the U. S. A., 1956, 172p.

Scott, R. W. Christian Missionary Decline in India. *Pac. Aff.,* 30/4, 1957, p.366–76.

Short, F. Asian Impressions. *Int. R. Missions,* 46/181, 1957, p.37–51.

Spae, J. Japan's Religions and Morality in Missionary Perspective. *Japan. Christ. Quart.,* 29, 1963, p.227–33.

Spae, J. *Christian Corridors to Japan.* Tokyo: Oriens Institute for Religious Research, 1965, 266p.

Thomas, P. *Colonists and Foreign Missionaries of Ancient India.* Ernakulam, Kerala: Joseph Thamasons, 1963, 96p.

Thomas, W. T. *Protestant Beginnings in Japan: The First Three Decades, 1859–1889.* Tokyo: Charles E. Tuttle, 258p.

Varg, P. A. *Missionaries, Chinese, and Diplomats: The American Protestant, Missionary Movement in China, 1890–1952.* Princeton: Princeton Univ. Press, 1958, 335p.

Welmers, W. E. African Languages and Christian Missions. *Civilisations,* 3/4, 1953, p.545–61.

Williamson, H. R. *British Baptists in China, 1845–1952.* London: Casey Kingsgate, 1958, 382p.

Yoder, F. R. Rural Missions in Japan. *Sociol. Soc. Res.,* 21/3, 1937, p.213–6.

5e4.   Pacific Islands

Aston, C. W. W. *Challenge in Polynesia.* Sydney: Australian Board of Missions, 1957, 32p.

de la Costa, H. *Jesuits in the Philippines, 1581–1768.* Cambridge: Harvard Univ. Press, 1961, 633p.

Ferguson, P. The Contribution of the Missions to Education in Papua and New Guinea. *Australian Terr.,* 3/1, 1963, p.4–9.

Fox, C. E. *Lord of the Southern Isles: Being the Story of the Anglican Mission in Melanesia, 1849–1949.* London: Mowbray, 1958, 272p.

Harrisson, B. Near to Ngadju (Rhinish Missionaries in South Borneo, 1836–1913). *Sarawak Mus. J.*, 9/13–14, 1959, p.121–31.

Koskinen, A. A. *Missionary Influence as a Political Factor in the Pacific Islands.* Helsinki: Suomalainen Tiedaekatemian Toimituksia Annales Academiae Scientiarum Fennicae, 1953, 163p.

Meller, N. Missionaries to Hawaii: Shapers of the Island's Government. *West. Polit. Quart.*, 11/4, 1958, p.788–99.

Nelson, H. N. The Missionaries and the Aborigines in the Port Phillip District. *Hist. Stud. Australia New Zealand*, 12/45, 1965, p.57–67.

Newman, E. V. Missions and Education in the Pacific. *Int. R. Missions*, 50/197, 1961, p.158–64.

Pelzer, K. J. Western Impact on East Sumatra and North Tapanuli: The Roles of the Planter and the Missionary. *J. Southe. Asian Hist.*, 2/2, 1961, p.66–71.

Phelan, J. L. *The Hispanization of the Philippines.* Madison: Univ. of Wisconsin, 1959.

Preiss, G. The Church in Tahiti. *Int. R. Missions*, 46/184, 1957, p.401–9.

Probowinoto, B. The Christian Churches in Mid-Java. *Int. Missions*, 45/178, 1956, p.174–9.

Van Der Kroef, J. M. Conflicts of Religious Policy in Indonesia. *Far East. Survey*, 22, 1953, p.121–5.

5f. Religion and Age

Beekman, A. J. Youth and Religion in a Changing World. *Soc. Compass*, 8/5, 1961, p.447–68.

Botz, P. Spiritual Aspects of Care for the Aged. *Hosp. Progr.*, 41, 1960, p.62–5.

Covalt, N. K. The Meaning of Religion to Older People. *Geriatrics*, 15, 1960, p.658–64.

Culver, E. T. *New Church Programs With the Aging.* N.Y.: Association Press, 1961, 152p.

Goldman, R. J. *Religious Thinking From Childhood to Adolescence.* London: Routledge and K. Paul, 1964, 274p.

Gray, R. M. and Moberg, D. O. *The Church and the Older Person.* Grand Rapids: William B. Eerdmans Publishing Co., 1962.

Harth, C. J. Religion and Its Relation to the Aging. *Maryland Med. J.*, 9, 1960, p.126–7.

Hiltner, S. and Menninger, K. (eds.) *Constructive Aspects of Anxiety.* N.Y.: Abingdon Press, 1963, 173p.

MacIver, R. M. (ed.) *Dilemmas of Youth in America Today.* N.Y.: Harper, 1961, 141p.

Maves, P. B. Aging, Religion, and the Church. In C. Tibitts (ed.)—*Handbook of Social Gerontology.* Chicago: Univ. of Chicago Press, 1960.

Maves, P. B. and Cedarleaf, J. L. *Older People and the Church.* N.Y.: Abingdon, 1949, 272p.

Moberg, D. O. Religious Activities and Personal Adjustment in Old Age. *J. Soc. Psychol.*, 43/2, 1956, p.261–8.

Orbach, H. L. Aging and Religion. *Geriatrics*, 16, 1961, p.530–40.

Pan, J. S. A Comparison of Factors in the Personal Adjustment of Old People in Protestant Church Homes for the Aged and Old People Living Outside Institutions. *J. Soc. Psychol.*, 35/2, 1952, p.195–203.

Rosen, B. C. *Adolescence and Religion: The Jewish Teenager in American Society.* Cambridge, Massachusetts: Schenkman Publishing Co., 1965, 218p.

Schnepp, G. J. and Kurz, J. T. Length of Life of Male Religious. *Amer. Cath. Sociol. R.*, 14/3, 1953, p.156–61.

Scudder, D. L. (ed.) *Organized Religion and the Older Person.* Gainesville: Univ. of Florida Press, 1958.

Van Dyke, P. and Pierce-Jones, J. The Psychology of Religion of Middle and Late Adolescence: A Review of Empirical Research. *Rel. Educ.*, 58/6, 1963, p.529–37.

Waterman, L. Religion and Religious Observance in Old Age. In C. Tibbitts (ed.)—*Living Through the Older Years.* Ann Arbor: Univ. of Michigan Press, 1949, p.99–112.

Wershow, H. J. The Older Jews of Albany Park: Aspects of the Aged and Its Interaction With a Gerontological Research Project. *Gerontologist*, 4/4, 1964, p.198–202.

5g. Religion and Social Deviance

Barrett, D. N. Penal Values in Canonical and Sociological Theory. *Amer. Cath. Sociol. R.*, 21/2, 1960, p.98–116.

Cedarleaf, J. L. The Chaplain's Role With Delinquent Boys in an Institution. *Fed. Probation*, 18, 1954, p.40–5.

Celestine, Sr. Juvenile Delinquency and the Catholic Home: A Study of Juvenile Court Records in Duluth During the Years 1934–1939 Inclusively. *Amer. Cath. Sociol. R.*, 1/4, 1940, p.198–216.

Church of England Moral Welfare Council. *Sexual Offenders and Social Punishment.* Westminster: Church Information Board, 1956, 120p.

Deutsch, M. The 1960 Swastika-Smearing: Analysis of the Apprehended Youth. *Merr.-Palm. Quart.*, 8/2, 1962, p.99–120.

Dominic, M. Religion and the Juvenile Delinquent. *Amer. Cath. Sociol. R.*, 15/3, 1954, p.256–64.

Falk, G. J. Religion, Personal Integration and Criminality. *J. Educ. Sociol.*, 35/4, 1961, p.159–61.

Frankino, S. P. The Manacles and the Messenger: A Short Study in Religious Freedom in the Prison Community. *Cath. Univ. Law R.*, 14/1, 1965, p.30–66.

Goldberg, N. Jews in the Police Records of Los Angeles, 1933–1947. *Yivo Ann. Jew. Soc. Sci.*, 5, 1950, p.261–91, vol. 5.

Hager, D. J. Religion, Delinquency and Society. *Soc. Work*, 2/3, 1957, p.16–21.

Hersch, L. Delinquency Among Jews: A Comparative Study of Criminality Among the Jewish and Non-Jewish Population of the Polish Republic. *J. Crim. Law Crimin.*, 27, 1936, p.515–38.

Hersch, L. Complementary Data on Jewish Delinquency in Poland: General Considerations Suggested by Its Study. *J. Crim. Law Crimin.*, 27, 1937, p.857–73.

Hersch, L. Jewish and Non-Jewish Criminality in Poland, 1932–1937. *Yivo Ann. Jew. Soc. Sci.*, 1, 1946, p.178–194.

Holcomb, E. P. *The Role of Religion in the Prevention of Juvenile Delinquency.* Dallas: Southern Methodist Univ., 1956, 174p.

Hoyles, A. J. *Religion in Prison.* N.Y.: Philosophical Library, 1955, 146p.

Kvaraceus, W. C. Delinquent Behavior and Church Attendance. *Sociol. Soc. Res.*, 28, 1944, p.284–9.

Liguori, M. The Central Verein, A Non-Institutional Social Control. *Amer. Cath. Sociol. R.*, 2/3, 1941, p.153–8.

McCallum, D. K. Consensus and Control: The Kunapipi Ritual and Attendant Taboo. *East. Anthropol.*, 18/2, 1965, p.80–8.

Middlemore, M. The Treatment of Bewitchment in a Puritan Community. *Int. J. Psychoanal.*, 15, 1934, p.41–58.

Minen, J. R. Church Membership and Commitments of Prisoners. *Hum. Biol.*, 3, 1931, p.429–36.

Nagel, W. H. Criminality and Religion. *Soc. Compass*, 8/1, 1961, p.3–34.

Oberholzer, E., Jr. *Delinquent Saints: Disciplinary Action in the Early Congregational Churches of Massachusetts.* N.Y.: Columbia Univ. Press, 1956, 379p.

Protestant Episcopal Church in the U. S. A., Joint Commission on Alcoholism. *Alcohol, Alcoholism, and Social Drinking: An Official Publication.* Greenwich, Connecticut: Seabury Press, 1958, 28p.

Putney, S. and Middleton, R. Rebellion, Conformity and Parental Religious Ideologies. *Sociometry*, 24, 1961, p.125–35.

Rhodes, H. T. F. *The Satanic Mass: A Sociological and Criminological Study.* N.Y.: Citadel Press, 1955, 232p.

Smith, P. M. Organized Religion and Criminal Behavior. *Sociol. Soc. Res.*, 33/5, 1949, p.362–7.

Smith, P. M. Role of the Church in Delinquency Prevention. *Sociol. Soc. Res.*, 35/3, 1951, p.183–90.

Snyder, C. R. *Alcohol and the Jews: A Cultural Study of Drinking and Sobriety.* Glencoe: Free Press, 1958, 226p.

Tiebout, H. M. and Coburn, M. Character Building and Stealing. *Rel. Educ.*, 24, 1929, p.935–40.

Travers, J. F. and Davis, R. G. Study of Religious Motivation and Delinquency. *J. Educ. Sociol.*, 34/5, 1961, p.205–20.

Trawick, A. M. The City Church and the Problem of Crime. *Amer. J. Sociol.*, 20/2, 1914, p.220–48.

Wattenberg, W. W. Church Attendance and Juvenile Misconduct. *Sociol Soc. Res.*, 34/3, 1950, p.195–202.

Webb, R. and Webb, M. *The Churches and Juvenile Delinquency.* N.Y.: Association Press, 1957, 64p.

Wenger, S. B. What Prison Inmates Think of God. *Rel. Educ.*, 40, 1945, p.39–43.

Whalen, E. A. Religion and Suicide. *R. Rel. Res.*, 5/2, 1964, p.91–110.

6. Religion and Social Change

Alagoma, D. Cargoes on the Move. *West Afr. R.*, 33/409, 1962, p.10–5.

All-Africa Church Conference, Ibadan, Nigeria, 1958. *The Church in Changing Africa: Report*. N.Y.: International Missionary Council, 1958, 106p.

Barnes, S. H. Quebec Catholicism and Social Change. *R. Polit.*, 23/1, 1961, p.52–76.

Bellah, R. N. (ed.) *Religion and Progress in Modern Asia*. N.Y.: Free Press, 1965, 272p.

Berger, M. Social and Political Change in the Moslem-Arab World. *World Polit.*, 10/4, 1958, p.629–38.

Bourdeaux, M. *Opium of the People: The Christian Religion in the USSR*. London: Faber, 1965, 244p.

Braden, C. S. Why are the Cults Growing? *Christ. Cent.*, 1944, p.45–7, 78–80, 108–10, 137–40.

Cline, W. Notes on Cultural Innovations in Dynastic Egypt. *Southw. J. Anthropol.*, 4/1, 1948, p.1–30.

Cooley, J. K. *Baal, Christ and Mohammed: Religion and Revolution in North America*. N.Y.: Holt, Reinhart and Winston, 1965, 253p.

Cunningham, C. E. Order and Change in An Atoni Diarchy. *Southw. J. Anthropol.*, 21/4, 1965, p.359–82.

Ebert, M. L. and Schnepp, G. J. *Industrialism and the Popes*. N.Y.: Kenedy, 1953, 245p.

Edmonson, M. S. Nativism, Syncretism and Anthropological Science. *Mid. Amer. Res. Inst. Publ.*, 1960, p.183–202.

Eliade, M. Crisis and Renewal in History of Religions. *Hist. Rel.*, 5/1, 1965, p.1–17.

Fernandez, J. W. African Religious Movements: Types and Dynamics. *J. Mod. Afr. Stud.*, 3/4, 1965, p.418–46.

Fernando, C. The Role of the Christian Church in the New Asia. *New Lanka* (Columbo), 7/3–4, 1956, p.68–82.

Forster, A. and Epstein, B. R. *Danger on the Right*. N.Y.: Random House, 1964, 294p.

Friend, J. A. N. *Demonology, Sympathetic Magic and Witchcraft: A Study of Superstition as it Persists in Man and Affects Him in a Scientific Age*. London: C. Griffin, 1961, 173p.

Gibb, H. A. R. Unitive and Divisive Factors in Islam. *Civilisations*, 7/4, 1957, p.507–14.

Glazer, N. and Moynihan, D. P. *Beyond the Melting Pot: The Negroes, Puerto Ricans, Jews, Italians and Irish of New York City*. Cambridge, Massachusetts: MIT Press, 1963, 360p.

Glock, C. Y. and Stark, R. *Religion and Society in Tension*. Chicago: Rand, McNally and Co., 1965, 336p.

Goody, J. Anomie in Ashanti? *Africa*, 27/4, 1957, p.356–63.

Greenslade, S. L. *The Church and the Social Order; A Historical Sketch*. London: SCM Press, 1948, 128p.

Hammer, R. *Japan's Religious Ferment*. London: S. C. M. Press, 1961.

Hammond, P. E. Religion and the 'Informing' of Culture. *J. Sci. Stud. Rel.*, 3, 1963, p.97–106.

Hodgson, M. G. S. Modernity and the Islamic Heritage. *Islamic Res.*, 2, 1962, p.89–129.

Hogbin, H. I. *Transformation Scene: The Changing Culture of a New Guinea Village*. London: Routledge & Paul, 1951, 326p.

Hostetler, J. A. Persistence and Change Patterns in Amish Society. *Ethnology*, 3/2, 1964, p.185–98.

Houtart, F. *The Challenge to Change: The Church Confronts the Future*. N.Y.: Sheed and Ward, 1964, 212p.

Howes, R. G. *The Church and the Change: An Initial Study of the Role of the Roman Catholic Church in the Changing American Community*. Boston: St. Paul Editions, 1961, 180p.

James, M. Christianity in the Emergent Africa. *Présence Afr.* (Dakar), 9/9–10, 1956, p.238–44.

Jung, C. G. *Civilization in Transition: The Collected Works of C. G. Jung* (Trans. R. F. C. Hull; Eds. H. Read, *et al.*). N.Y.: Pantheon Books, 1964, 618p.

Keesing, F. M. *Cultural Change: An Analysis and Bibliography of Anthropological Sources*. Stanford: Stanford Univ. Press, 1953, 242p.

Kerekes, T. (ed.) *The Arab Middle East and Muslim Africa.* N.Y.: Praeger, 1961, 126p.

Khurana, B. K. Bhagti Movements. *Bull. Trib. Res. Inst.,* 2/4, 1959, p.68–76.

Kitagawa, J. M. (ed.) *Modern Trends in World Religions.* LaSalle, Illinois: Open Court Publishing Co., 1959, 286p.

Klee, J. B. Religion as Facing Forward in Time. *Exist. Inq.,* 1/2, 1960, p.19–32.

Kraft, C. M. Mission in a World of Rapid Social Change. *Pract. Anthropol.,* 10/6, 1963, p.271–9.

Kumlien, W. F. *Basic Trends of Social Change in South Dakota: Religious Organization.* Agricultural Experiment Station, South Dakota State College, Bulletin 348, 1941.

Latif, S. A. Islam and Social Change. *Int. Soc. Sci. Bull.,* 5/4, 1953, p.691–7.

Lerner, D. *The Passing of Traditional Society: Modernizing the Middle East.* Glencoe: Free Press, 1958, 466p.

Le Von Baumer, F. *Religion and the Rise of Skepticism.* N.Y.: Harcourt Brace, 1960, 308p.

Lichtenstadter, I. *Islam and the Modern Age.* N.Y.: Bookman Associates—Twayne Publishers, 1958, 228p.

Licorish, D. N. *Tomorrow's Church in Today's World: A Study of the Twentieth-Century Challenge to Religion.* N.Y.: Exposition Press, 1956, 172p.

MacLean, D. A. The Christian Basis for a New World Order. *Amer. J. Econ. Sociol.,* 1/3, 1942, p.239–64; see also 1/4, p.415–30; 2/1, p.81–96; 2/2, 1943, p.211–29.

Mahar, P. M. Changing Caste Ideology in a North Indian Village. *J. Soc. Issues,* 14/4, 1958, p.51–65.

Manikan, R. B. *Christianity and the Asian Revolution.* Madras: Christian Literature Society, 1955, 293p.

McKinnon, D. Religious Trends. *Sociol. R.,* 39/1, 1947, p.94–5.

Miller, R. C. (ed.) *The Church and Organized Movements.* N.Y.: Harper, 1946.

Miller, R. J. Monasteries and Culture Change in Inner Mongolia. *Asiat. Forsch.,* 2, 1959, p.152.

Neal, M. A. *Values and Interests in Social Change.* Englewood Cliffs: Prentice-Hall, 1965.

Panikkar, K. M. *Hindu Society at Crossroads.* Bombay: Asia Publishing House, 1955, 102p.

Randall, J. H., Jr. The Churches and the Liberal Tradition. *Ann. Amer. Acad. Polit. Soc. Sci.,* 256, 1948, p.148–64.

Rauschenbusch, W. The Stake of the Church in the Social Movement. *Amer. J. Sociol.,* 3/1, 1897, p.18–30.

Schilling, B. N. The English Case Against Voltaire: 1789–1800. *J. Hist. Ideas,* 4/2, 1943, p.193–216.

Schuyler, J. P. Potential Elements of Organization and Disorganization in the Parish—As Seen in Northern Parish. *Amer. Cath. Sociol. R.,* 18/2, 1957, p.98–112.

Sexton, P. C. *Spanish Harlem: Anatomy of Poverty.* N.Y.: Harper & Row, 1965.

Smith, D. E. *India as a Secular State.* Princeton: Princeton Univ. Press, 1963, 518p.

Sorokin, P. A. *Social and Cultural Dynamics: A Study of Change in Major Systems of Art, Truth, Ethics, Law and Social Relationships.* London: Owen, 1959, 718p.

Stirling, P. Religious Change in Republican Turkey. *Mid. East J.,* 12/4, 1958, p.395–408.

Szcesniak, B. The Russian Revolution and Religion. Notre Dame: Univ. of Notre Dame Press, 1959, 289p.

Tamney, J. The Prediction of Religious Change. *Sociol. Anal.,* 26/2, 1965, p.72–81.

Taylor, R. W. and Thomas, M. M. *Mud Walls and Steel Mills: God and Man at Work In India.* N.Y.: Friendship Press, 1963, 128p.

Tiryakian, E. A. (ed.) *Sociological Theory, Values, and Sociocultural Change: Essays in Honor of Pitirim A. Sorokin.* N.Y.: Free Press of Glencoe, 1963, 302p.

Trevor-Roper, H. Religion: The Reformation and Social Change. *Hist. Stud.,* 4, 1965, p.18–45.

Troeltsch, E. *Protestantism and Progress.* Boston: Beacon Press, 1958.

Van Der Kroef, J. M. Culture Contact and Culture Change in Western New Guinea. *Anthropol. Quart.,* 32/3, 1959, p.134–60.

Visser't Hooft, W. A. *No Other Name: The Choice Between Syncretism and Christian Universalism.* London: SCM Press, 1963.

Yinger, J. M. Religion and Social Change: Functions and Dysfunctions of Sects and Cults Among the Disprivileged. *R. Rel. Res.,* 4/2, 1963.

See Also: 2, 3, 5, 7d

6a. *Religion and the Maintenance of Social Order*

Ahler, J. G. and Tamney, J. B. Some Functions of Religious Ritual in a Catastrophe. *Sociol. Anal.*, 25/4, 1964, p.212–30.

Anderson, J. N. D. *Islamic Law in the Modern World.* N.Y.: New York Univ. Press, 1959, 100p.

Anderson, J. N. D. Law as a Social Force in Islamic Culture and History. *Bull. School Orient. Afr. Stud.*, 20, 1957, p.13–40.

Augsburger, A. D. Control Patterns and the Behavior of Mennonite Youth. *Menn. Quart. R.*, 39/3, 1965, p.192–203.

Bennisen, A. Traditional Islam in the Customs of the Turkic Peoples of Central Asia. *Mid. East J.*, 12/2, 1958, p.227–33.

Bigler, R. M. The Rise of Political Protestantism in Nineteenth Century Germany: The Awakening of Political Consciousness and the Beginnings of Political Activity in the Protestant Clergy of Pre-March Prussia. *Church Hist.*, 34/4, 1965, p.423–44.

Bohn, F. The Ku Klux Klan Interpreted. *Amer. J. Sociol.*, 30/4, 1925, p.385–407.

Bolle, K. W. *The Persistence of Religion: An Essay on Tantrism and Sri Aurobindo's Philosophy.* Leiden: E. J. Brill, 1965, 134p.

Boyer, W. W., Jr. Religion and the Police Power in Wisconsin. *Marquette Law R.*, 37/1, 1953, p.2–34.

Brandon, S. G. F. The Ritual Perpetuation of the Past. *Numen*, 6/2, 1959, p.112–29.

Brown, L. B. and Pallant, D. J. Religious Belief and Social Pressure. *Psychol. Rep.*, 10, 1962, p.813–4.

Chroust, A. H. The Function of Law and Justice in the Ancient World and the Middle Ages. *J. Hist. Ideas*, 7/3, 1946, p.298–320.

Collins, J. M. The Indian Shaker Church: A Study of Continuity and Change in Religion. *Southw. J. Anthropol.*, 6, 1950, p.399–411.

Concepcion, M. Ritual Mourning: Culturally Specified Crowd Behaviour. *Anthropol. Quart.*, 35/1, 1962, p.1–9.

Coulson, N. J. Doctrine and Practice in Islamic Law. *Bull. School Orient. Afr. Stud.*, 18/2, 1956, p.211–26.

Coulson, N. J. Muslim Custom and Case-Law. *Welt Islams*, 6/1–2, 1959, p.13–24.

Deshen, S. A. A Case of Breakdown of Modernization in an Israeli Immigrant Community. *Jew J. Sociol.*, 7/1, 1965, p.63–91.

Duncan, H. D. *Communication and Social Order.* N.Y.: Bedminster Press, 1962.

Edelmann, A. T. *Latin America Government & Politics: The Dynamics of a Revolutionary Society.* Homewood, Illinois: Dorsey Press, 1965.

Ellwood, C. A. Man's Social Destiny. *Sociol. R.*, 22/1, 1930, p.43–51.

Embree, J. F. Some Social Functions of Religion in Rural Japan. *Amer. J. Sociol.*, 47/2, 1941, p.184–9.

Esbergenov, K. On the Struggle Against Survivals of Obsolete Customs and Rites. *Soviet Anthropol. and Archeol.*, 3/1, 1964, p.9–20.

Evans-Pritchard, E. E. The Nuer Conception of Spirit in its Relation to the Social Order. *Amer. Anthropol.*, 55, 1953, p.201–14.

Faron, L. C. Symbolic Values and the Integration of Society Among the Mapuche of Chile. *Amer. Anthropol.*, 64/6, 1962, p.1151–64.

Fichter, J. H. The Parish and Social Integration. *Soc. Compass*, 7/1, 1960, p.39–47.

Friess, H. L. Dogmatic Religion in a Democratic Society. *Amer. J. Econ. Sociol.*, 4/2, 1945, p.193–201.

Fyzee, A. A. A. Islamic Law and Theology in India. *Mid. East J.*, 8/2, 1954, p.163–83.

Glock, C. Y. Religion and the Integration of Society. *R. Rel. Res.*, 2/2, 1960, p.49–61.

Good, A. Religion. In J. S. Roucek, (ed.)—*Social Control.* Princeton: D. Van Nostrand, 1956, p.101–16.

Griffin, C. S. Religious Benevolences as Social Control. *Miss. Valley Hist. R.*, 44/3, 1957, p.423–44.

Hunt, C. L. Religious Ideologies as a Means of Social Control. *Sociol. Soc. Res.*, 33, 1949, p.180–7.

Ishwaran, K. Customary Law in Village India. *Int. J. Comp. Sociol.* (Dharwar), 5/2, 1964, p.228–43.

Jaspan, M. A. In Quest of New Law: The Perplexity of

Legal Syncretism in Indonesia. *Comp. Stud. Society Hist.*, 7/3, 1965, p.252–66.

Khadduri, M. The Juridical Theory of the Islamic State. *Muslim World*, 1951, p.181–5.

Lauquier, H. C. Cultural Change Among Three Generations of Greeks. *Amer. Cath. Sociol. R.*, 22/3, 1961, p.223–32.

Leis, P. E. "Collective Sentiments" as Represented in Ijaw Divination. *J. Folklore Inst.* (Hague), 1/3, 1964, p.167–79.

Lieban, R. W. Shamanism and Social Control in a Philippine City. *J. Folklore Inst.*, 2/1, 1965, p.43–54.

Mehden, F. V. Burma's Religious Campaign Against Communism. *Pac. Aff.*, 33/3, 1960, p.290–9.

Mills, L. O. The Relationship of Discipline to Pastoral Care in Frontier Churches, 1800–1850: A Preliminary Study. *Past. Psychol.*, 16/159, 1965, p.22–32, 34.

Ostow, M. The Nature of Religious Control. *Amer. Psychol.*, 13/10, 1958, p.571–4.

Ostow, M. The Nature of Religious Controls. *Past. Psychol.*, 12/114, 1961, p.19–23.

Oxnam, G. B. The Church and the Social Order. *J. Appl. Sociol.*, 7, 1923, p.109–14.

Photiadis, J. D. The American Business Creed and Denominational Identification. *Soc. Forces*, 44/1, 1965, p.92–100.

Pope, L. *Millhands and Preachers: A Study of New Gastonia*. New Haven: Yale Univ. Press, 1965, 369p.

Priolkar, A. K. *The Goa Inquisition: Being a Quatercentenary Commemoration Study of the Inquisition in India, With Accounts Given by Dr. Dellon and Dr. Buchanan*. Bombay: A. K. Priolkar, 1961, 189p.

Queen, S. A., *et al. The American Social System: Social Control, Personal Choice, and Public Decision*. Boston: Houghton Mifflin Co., 1956.

Quinlan, P. T. Solidarity Among the Amish. *Amer. J. Econ. Sociol.*, 6/4, 1947, p.561–3.

Rao, P. S. V. *Tradition in Religion. Bull. Inst. Trad. Cult.*, 1957, p.19–28.

Redekop, C. and Hostetler, J. A. Education and Boundary Maintenance in Three Ethnic Groups. *R. Rel. Res.*, 5/2, 1964, p.80–91.

Ross, E. A. Social Control: Religion. *Amer. J. Sociol.*, 2/3, 1896, p.433–45.

Siddiqi, M. The Role of Islamic Tradition in Pakistan. *Confluences*, 2/4, 1953, p.117–28.

Sirvaitis, C. P. *Religious Folkways in Lithuania and their Conservation Among the Lithuanian Immigrants in the United States*. Washington: Catholic Univ. Press, 1952, 49p.

Smith, W. *Confuscianism in Modern Japan: A Study of Conservatism in Japanese Intellectual History*. Tokyo: Hokuseido Press, 1959, 285p.

Squisher, E. Chinese Intellectuals Under Western Impact, 1838–1900. *Comp. Stud. Society Hist.*, 1/1, 1958, p.26–37.

Stockwood, M. A Church Living in the Past. *Nat. Eng. R.*, 149/898, 1957, p.259–63.

Taylor, G. The Social Function of the Church. *Amer. J. Sociol.*, 5/3, 1899, p.305–21.

Watt, W. M. *Islam and the Integration of Society*. London: Routledge, Kegan Paul, 1961.

Wermlund, S. Religious Speech Community and Reinforcement of Belief. *Acta Sociol.*, 3/2–3, 1958, p.132–46.

Whiting, J. W. M. Sorcery, Sin and the Super-ego: A Cross-Cultural Study of Some Mechanisms of Social Control. In M. R. Jones (ed.)—*Nebraska Symposium on Motivation*. Lincoln: Univ. of Nebraska Press, 1959.

Zakuta, L. Membership in a Becalmed Protestant Movement. *Canad. J. Econ. Polit. Sci.*, 24, 1958, p.190–202.

Zborowsky, M. The Children of the Covenant. *Soc. Forces*, 29/4, 1951, p.351–64.

Zimmerman, F. K. Religion and Conservative Social Force. *J. Abnorm. Soc. Psychol.*, 28, 1934, p.473—4.

Bascom, W.   African Culture and the Missionary. *Civilisations*, 3/4, 1953, p.451–504.

Bentwich, N.   *Religious Foundations of Internationalism.* N.Y.: Bloch Publishing Co., 1960, 303p.

Berg, C.   The Islamisation of Java. *Studia Islamica*, 4, 1955, p.11–42.

Bernard, G. and Caprasse, P.   Religious Movements in the Congo: A Research Hypothesis. *Cah. Econ. Soc.*, 3/1, 1965, p.49–60.

Bilheimer, R. S.   International Church Assistance and Rapid Social Change. *Ecumen. R.*, 9/4, 1957, p.402–9.

Black, E. C.   The Tumultuous Petitioners: The Protestant Association in Scotland 1778–1780. *R. Polit.*, 25/2, 1963, p.183–211.

Boulding, K.   Religious Foundations of Economic Progress. *Harvard Bus. R.*, 30, 1952, p.33–40.

Brink, W. and Harris, L.   *The Negro Revolution in America.* N.Y.: Simon & Shuster, 1963.

Cauthen, K.   *The Impact of American Religious Liberalism.* N.Y.: Harper & Row, 1962, 290p.

Chang, C.   Buddhism as a Stimulus to Neo-Confucianism. *Oriens Extremus*, 2, 1955, p.157–66.

Clark, R. M., *et al.*   Social Effects of Change in Religious Outlook Among Indians Villagers. *Sociol. R.*, 33/1–2, 1941, p.37–55.

Cohen, A.   The Fifth Monarchy Mind: Mary Cary and the Origins of Totalitarianism. *Soc. Res.*, 31/2, 1964, p.195–213.

Coleman, J. S.   Current Political Movements in Africa. *Ann. Amer. Acad. Polit. Soc. Sci.*, 298, 1955, p.95–108.

Crane, W. H.   Alienation in the New African Society. *Soc. Compass*, 12/6, 1965, p.367–78.

Cronin, J. F.   *Christianity and Social Progress: Mater et Magistra Clarifies.*   Baltimore: Helicon Press, 1965.

Descola, J.   *Conquistadors.*   London: Allen & Unwin, 1957, 404p.

Dorey, F. D.   Religion. In E. F. Frazier (ed.)—*The Integration of the Negro into American Society.* Papers Contributed to the 14th Annual Conference of the Division of the Social Sciences, 1951, Washington, D. C.

Essien-Udom, E. U.   *Black Nationalism: A Search for Identity in America.*   Chicago: Univ. of Chicago Press, 1962, 367p.

Foa, U. G.   Social Change Among Yemenite Jews Settled in Jerusalem. *Sociometry*, 11/1–2, 1948, p.75–99.

Frend, W. H. C.   *The Donatist Church: A Movement of Protest in Roman North Africa.*   N.Y.: Oxford Univ. Press, 1952, 360p.

Geisfield, J. R.   Social Structure and Moral Reform: A Study of the Woman's Christian Temperance Union. *Amer. J. Sociol.*, 61, 1955, p.221–32.

Gluckman, M.   *Rituals of Rebellion in South-East Africa.* Manchester: Manchester Univ. Press, 1954, 36p.

Godwin, G. and Kaut, O.   A Native Religious Movement Among the White Mountain and Cibecue Apache. *Southw. J. Anthropol.*, 10/4, 1954, p.385–404.

Green, J. J.   The Organization of the Catholic Total Abstinence Union of America, 1866–1884. *Amer. Cath. Hist. Society*, Phila. Records, 61, 1950, p.71–97.

Griffiths, G.   The Revolutionary Character of the Revolt of the Netherlands. *Comp. Stud. Society Hist.*, 2, 1960, p.453–69.

Groves, C. P.   The Impact of Christianity Upon African Life. *Corona*, 13/1, 1961, p.12–6.

Hermanns, M.   The Impact of Buddhism on Persia, the Near East and Europe. *J. Anthropol. Society Bombay*, 10/2, 1958, p.1–16.

Hobsbawn, E. J.   *Primitive Rebels: Studies in Archaic Forms of Social Movement in the Nineteenth and Twentieth Centuries.*   N.Y.: Frederick Praeger, 1963.

Holt, J. B.   Holiness Religion: Cultural Shock and Social Reorganization. *Amer. Sociol. R.*, 5, 1940, p.740–7.

Howard, P.   *The World Rebuilt: The True Story of Frank Buchman and The Achievements of Moral Re-Armament.*   N.Y.: Duell, Sloan, & Pearce, 1951.

Hughes, E. C.   *French Canada in Transition.*   London: K. Paul, French Trubner & Co., 1946.

Hutchinson, B.   Some Social Consequences of Missionary Activity Among South Africa Bantu. *Pract. Anthropol.*, 6/2, 1959, p.67–76.

Jeffreys, M. D. W.   Some Rules of Directed Culture Change Under Roman Catholicism. *Amer. Anthropol.*, 58/4, 1956, p.721–31.

Jelavich, C. and Jelavich, B.   The Call to Action: Religion, Nationalism, Socialism. *J. Centr. Europ. Aff.*, 23/1, 1963, p.3–11.

Jones, A. H.   Were Ancient Heresies National or Social Movements in Disguise? *J. Theol. Stud.*, 10, 1959, p.280–98.

King, W. L.   Millennialism as a Social Ferment. *Rel. Life*, 1951–2, p.33–44.

Klingberg, F. J.   *Codrington Chronicle: An Experiment*

in Anglican Altruism on a Barbados Plantation, 1710-1834. Berkeley: Univ. of California Press, 1949, 157p.

Krader, L. A Nativistic Movement in Western Siberia. *Amer. Anthropol.*, 58/2, 1956, p.282–92.

Lasswell, H. D. Religion and Modernization in the Far East: Commentary. *Far East. Quart.*, 12/2, 1953, p.163–172.

Latourette, K. S. The Contribution of the Religion of the Colonial Period to the Ideals and Life of the United States. *Americas*, 14, 1958, p.340–55.

Laue, J. H. A Contemporary Revitalization Movement in American Race Relations: The "Black Muslims." *Soc. Forces*, 42, 1964, p.315–23.

Lawrence, P. Lutheran Influences on Madang Societies. *Oceania*, 27/2, 1956, p.73–89.

Levy, H. S. Yellow Turban Religion and Rebellion at the End of Han. *J. Amer. Orient. Society*, 76/4, 1956, p.214–27.

Lewis, W. H. Islam, A Rising Tide in Tropical Africa. *R. Polit.*, 19/4, 1957, p.446–61.

Linton, R. Nativistic Movements. *Amer. Anthropol.*, 45, 1943, p.230–40.

Madhavtirtha, S. The Re-Construction of Society. *J. Hum. Relat.*, 2/2, 1954, p.7–15.

Mair, L. P. Independent Religious Movements in Three Continents. *Comp. Stud. Society Hist.*, 1/2, 1959, p.113–35.

Malalasekera, G. P. Buddhism on the March. *Ceylon Today*, 12/4, 1963, p.9–13.

Mathews, S. The Service of the Church to Social Advance. *Soc. Forces*, 2/4, 1924, p.546–8.

Mathews, S. The Significance of the Church to the Social Movement. *Amer. J. Sociol.*, 4/5, 1899, p.603-10.

McCombe, J. H. Value Judgements of Peruvian Indians Altered by Evangelical Christian Experience. *Pract. Anthropol.*, 7/6, 1960, p.276–8.

Michaud, P. The Yellow Turbans. *Monum. Serica*, 17, 1958, p.47–127.

Millet, J. H. The Catholic Action Rural Movement. *Amer. Eccles. R.*, 117/5, 1947, p.348–60.

Miyakawa, T. S. *Protestants and Pioneers*. Chicago: Univ. of Chicago Press, 1964.

Morris, W. D. *The Religious Origins of Social Revolt*. London: G. Allen & Unwin, 1949, 240p.

Nikki, K. Religion and Irreligion in Early Iranian Nationalism. *Comp. Stud. Society Hist.*, 4/3, 1962, p.265-95.

Noble, D. W. The Religion of Progress in America, 1890–1914. *Soc. Res.*, 22/4, 1955, p.417–40.

Ross, E. The Impact of Christianity in Africa. *Ann. Amer. Acad. Polit. Soc. Sci.*, 298, 1955, p.161–9.

Runes, D. D. *The Hebrew Impact on Western Civilization*. N.Y.: Philosophical Library, 1951, 922p.

Ryan, J. A. The Bishop's Program of Social Reconstruction. *Amer. Cath. Sociol. R.*, 5/1, 1944, p.25–33.

Sacher, H. Zionism and Its Programme. *Sociol. R.*, 5/1, 1912, p.35–41.

Smith, W. C. Missionary Activities and the Acculturation of Backward Peoples. *J. Appl. Sociol.*, 7/4, 1923, p.175–86.

Spicer, E. H. Social Structure and the Acculturation Process: Social Structure and Cultural Process in Yaqui Religious Acculturation. *Amer. Anthropol.*, 60/3, 1958, p.433–41.

Stuntz, H. Christian Missions and Social Cohesion. *Amer. J. Sociol.*, 50/3, 1944, p.184–8.

Trimingham, J. S. and Fyfe, C. H. The Early Expansion of Islam in Sierra Leone. *Sierra Leone Bull. Rel.*, 2/2, 1960, p.33–9.

Turner, H. W. The Church of the Lord: The Expansion of a Nigerian Independent Church in Sierra Leone and Ghana. *J. Afr. Hist.*, 3/1, 1962, p.91–110.

Van Velsen, J. The Missionary Factor Among the Lakeside Tonga of Nyasaland. *Human Prob. Brit. Centr. Afr.*, 26, 1959, p.1–32.

Voget, F. W. The American Indian in Transition: Reformation and Status Innovations. *Amer. J. Sociol.*, 62, 1957, p.369–77.

Walzer, M. Puritanism as a Revolutionary Ideology. *Hist. Theory*, 3/1, 1964, p.59–90.

Wearnouth, R. F. *Methodism and the Working-Class Movement of England*. London: Epworth Press, 1947, 290p.

Wertheim, W. F. Religious Reform Movements in South and Southeast Asia. *Archiv. Sociol. Rel.*, 12, 1961, p.53–62.

Williams, E. Protestantism as a Factor of Cultural Change in Brazil. *Econ. Develop. Cult. Change*, 3/4, 1955, p.321–33.

Williamson, S. G. and Dickson, K. A. (eds.) *Akan Religion and the Christian Faith: A Comparative Study of the Impact of Two Religions*. London: Oxford Univ. Press, 1965, 186p.

Wilson, M. H. *Communal Rituals of the Nyakyusa*. London: N.Y.: Oxford Univ. Press, 1959, 228p.

Wolf, E. R. The Social Organization of Mecca and the

Origins of Islam. *Southw. J. Anthropol.*, 7, 1951, p.329–56.

Wrigley, C. C.   The Christian Revolution in Buganda. *Comp. Stud. Society Hist.*, 2/1, 1959, p.33–48.

Zürcher, E.   *The Buddhist Conquest of India.*   Leiden: E. J. Brill, 1959, 2 vols.

See Also: 2, 3, 5, 7

6c.   *Changes in Religion Itself*

Abbot, M. M.   *A City Parish Grows and Changes.* Washington: Catholic Univ. Press, 1953, 94p.

Ahlstrom, S. F.   Theology and the Present Day Revival. *Ann. Amer. Acad. Polit. Soc. Sci.*, 332, 1960, p.20–36.

A'La Maududi, S. A.   *A Short History of the Revivalist Movements in Islam* (Trans. al-Ashcari). Lahore: Islamic Publications Ltd., 1963, 156p.

Altholz, J. L.   *The Liberal Catholic Movement in England: The Rambler and Its Contributors, 1848–1864.* London: Burns & Oates, 1962, 251p.

Badeau, J. S.   Islam and the Modern Middle East. *For. Aff.*, 38, 1959, p.61–74.

Barclay, H. B.   Process in the Arab Sudan. *Human Org.*, 24/1, 1965, p.43–8.

Berkes, N.   *The Development of Secularism in Turkey.* Montreal: McGill Univ. Press, 1964, 538p.

Bernhardt, W. H.   The Present and Future of Religious Liberalism. *J. Bib. Rel.*, 11, 1943, p.195–201.

Birnbaum, N.   The Zwinglian Reformation in Zurich. *Archiv. Sociol. Rel.*, 6, 1959, p.15–30.

Boaz, F.   Northern Elements in the Mythology of the Navaho. *Amer. Anthropol.*, 8, 1897, p.371–7.

Bodrogi, T.   Colonization and Religious Movements in Melanesia. *Acta Ethnog. Acad. Scient. Hung.*, 2, 1951, p.259–90.

Braden, C. S.   Religion in Post-War Japan. *J. Bib. Rel.*, 21, 1953, p.147–53.

Braden, C. S.   *Spirits in Rebellion: The Rise and Development of New Thought.* Dallas: Southern Methodist Univ. Press, 1963, 571p.

Briggs, L. P.   The Syncretism of Religions in Southeast Asia, Especially in the Kmer Empire. *J. Amer. Orient. Society*, 71/4, 1951, p.230–49.

Brown, L. C.   The Islamic Reformist Movement in North Africa. *J. Mod. Afr. Stud.*, 2/1, 1964, p.55–63.

Brzezenski, Z. K.   Deviation Control: A Study in the Dynamics of Doctrinal Conflict. *Amer. Polit. Sci. R.*, 56/1, 1962, p.15–22.

Camps, A.   Crisis of Islam in West Pakistan. *Soc. Compass*, 9/3, 1963, p.221–37.

Cato, A. C.   Disintegration, Syncretization and Change in Fijian Religion. *Mankind*, 5/3, 1956, p.101–6.

Clark, C. A.   *Rural Churches in Transition.* Nashville: Broadman Press, 1959.

Cohn, B. S.   Changing Traditions of a Low Caste. *J. Amer. Folklore*, 71/281, 1958, p.413–21.

Comhaire, J. L.   Religious Trends in African and Afro-American Urban Societies. *Anthropol. Quart.*, 261, 1953, p.201–7.

Constas, H.   The U.S.S.R.—From Charismatic Sect to Bureaucratic Society. *Admin. Sci. Quart.*, 6/3, 1961, p.282–98.

Cragg, K.   The Intellectual Impact of Communism Upon Contemporary Islam. *Mid. East J.*, 8/2, 1954, p.127–38.

Cressy, E. Recent Developments in the Religions of China. *J. Bib. Rel.*, 15, 1947, p.75–80.

Cross, R. D. Changing Image of Catholicism in America. *Yale R.*, 48, 1959, p.562–75.

Cross, W. R. *The Burned-Over District: The Social and Intellectual History of Enthusiastic Religion in Western New York, 1800–1850.* Ithaca: Cornell Univ. Press, 1950, 383p.

Curran, C. A. Some Psychological Aspects of Vatican Council II. *J. Sci. Stud. Rel.*, 2/2, 1963, p.190–4.

Datta, J. M. Proportion of the Brahmans in India's Population is Decreasing. *Mod. R.*, 103/3, 1958, p.230–2.

Davidson, W. The Plight of Rural Protestantism. *Rel. Life*, 15/3, 1946, p.337–90.

Davies, H. The Continental Liturgical Movement in the Roman Catholic Church. *Canadian J. Theol.*, 10/3, 1964, p.148–65.

Davis, M. *The Emergence of Conservative Judaism.* Phila.: Jewish Publication Society of America, 1963, 528p.

Dawson, C. Prevision in Religion. *Sociol. R.*, 26/1, 1934, p.41–54.

de Achutegui, P. and Miguel, B. A. *Religious Revolution in the Philippines: The Life and Church of Gregorio Aglipay.* Manila: Ateneo de Manila, 1961, 555p.

Devanandan, P. D. The Renascence of Hinduism in India. *Ecumen. R.*, 11/1, 1958, p.52–65.

Doherty, R. W. Religion and Society: The Hicksite Separation of 1827. *Amer. Quart.*, 17/1, 1965, p.63–80.

Draak, M. Migration Over the Sea. *Numen*, 9/2, 1962, p.81–98.

Duker, A. G. On Religious Trends in American Jewish Life. *Yivo Ann. Jew. Soc. Sci.*, 4, 1949, p.51–63.

Eaton, S. G. Culture Change and Reintegration Found in the Cults of West Kingston, Jamaica. *Proc. Amer. Philos. Society*, 99/2, 1955, p.89–92.

Eggan, R. and Pacyaya, A. The Sapilada Religion: Reformation and Accommodation Among the Igorots of Northern Luzon. *Southw. J. Anthropol.*, 18/2, 1962, p.95–113.

Eister, A. W. The Oxford Movement: A Typological Analysis. *Sociol. Soc. Res.*, 34, 1950, p.116–24.

Famminella, F. X. The Impact of Italian Migration on American Catholicism. *Amer. Cath. Sociol. R.*, 22/3, 1961, p.233–41.

Firey, W. Informal Organization and the Theory of Schism. *Amer. Sociol. R.*, 13/1, 1948, p.15–24.

Firth, R. W. and Pillius, J. S. *A Study in Ritual Modification.* London: Royal Anthropological Institute, 1964, 31p.

Fosselman, D. H. *Transition in the Development of a Downtown Parish.* Washington: Catholic Univ. Press, 23p.

Francis, E. K. The Russian Mennonites: From Religious to Ethnic Group. *Amer. J. Sociol.*, 54/2, 1948, p.101–7.

Fuchs, P. Development and Changes in the Institution of the Priest Headman in Southern Wadai, Sudan. *Sociologus*, 11/2, 1961, p.174–86.

Fuse, T. M. Religions, Society and Accommodation: Some Remarks on Neo-Orthodoxy in American Protestantism. *Soc. Compass*, 12/6, 1965, p.345–58.

Glazer, N. The Jewish Revival in America. *Commentary*, 1955, p.483–9; see also 1956, p.17–24.

Goldin, J. Of Change and Adaptation in Judaism. *Hist. Rel.*, 4/2, 1965, p.269–94.

Goldstein, B. and Eichhorn, R. L. The Changing Protestant Ethic; Rural Patterns in Health, Work and Leisure. *Amer. Sociol. R.*, 26/4, 1961, p.557–65.

Goode, W. J. *World Revolution and Family Patterns.* N.Y.: Free Press, 1963.

Gould, J. E. *The Chautauqua Movement: An Episode in the Continuing American Revolution.* N.Y.: State University of New York, 1961, 108p.

Gowing, P. G. Scripture and Tradition: Trends in Protestant Theology Today. *Silliman J.*, 10/4, 1963, p.399–414. See also: H. E. Chandlee—An Anglican Response, p.415–20.

Guenther, H. V. Indian Buddhist Thought in Tibetan Perspective: Infinite Transcendence Versus Finiteness. *Hist. Rel.*, 3/1, 1963, p.83–105.

Hales, E. E. Y. *Pope John and His Revolution.* London: Eyre and Spottiswoode, 1965, 238p.

Halpern, B. Sectarianism and the Jewish Community. *J. Jew. Commun. Serv.*, 42/1, 1965, p.6–17.

Handy, R. T. The American Religious Depression, 1925–35. *Church Hist.*, 29, 1960, p.3–16.

Hanson, P. M. *Jesus Christ Among the Ancient Americans.* Independence, Missouri: Herald Press, 1959, 204p.

Hatch, E. *The Influence of Greek Ideas on Christianity.* N.Y.: Harper, 1957.

Herberg, W. America's New Religiousness. *Commentary*, 20/3, 1955, p.240–7.

Herberg, W. The Postwar Revival of the Synagogue. *Commentary*, 9/4, 1950, p.315–25.

Herberg, W.   Religious Trends in American Jewry. *Judaism*, 3/3, 1954, p.229–40.

Herberg, W.   There is a Religious Revival! *R. Rel. Res.*, 1/2, 1959, p.45–50.

Hooker, W. W.   The Significance of Numa's Religious Reforms. *Numen*, 10/2, 1963, p.87–132.

Hostetler, J. A.   Old World Extinction and New World Survival of the Amish: A Study of Group Maintenance and Dissolution. *Rural Sociol.*, 20/3–4, 1955, p.212–9.

Hudson, W. S. (ed.)   *Baptist Concepts of the Church: A Survey of the Historical and Theological Issues Which Have Produced Changes in Church Order.* Chicago: Judson Press, 1959, 239p.

Hutchison, W. R.   *The Transcendentalist Ministers: Church Reform in the New England Renaissance.* New Haven: Yale Univ. Press, 1959, 240p.

Iglehart, C. W.   Current Religious Trends in Japan. *J. Bib. Rel.*, 15, 1947, p.81–5.

Isaacs, H. R.   *India's Ex-Untouchables.* N.Y.: John Day Co., 1965, 188p.

Jeffery, A.   Present Day Movements in Islam. *Moslem World*, 33/3, 1943, p.165–86.

Johns, A. H.   The Role of Sufism in the Spread of Islam to Malaya and Indonesia. *J. Pakistan Hist. Society*, 9/3, 1961, p.143–61.

Kaplan, M. M.   The Effect of Intercultural Contacts upon Judaism. *J. Rel.*, 14, 1934, p.53–61.

Kato, G.   Some New Aspects of the Religious Belief in Mt. Fuji. *Bull. Japan Society*, 2/22, 1957, p.2–10.

Khatri, A. A.   Social Change in the Caste Hindu Family and its Possible Impact on Personality and Mental Health. *Sociol. Bull.*, 11, 1961, p.146–65.

Kincheloe, S. C.   The Behavior Sequence of a Dying Church. *Rel. Educ.*, 24, 1929, p.329–45.

Kitagawa, J. M.   The Buddhist Transformation in Japan. *Hist. Rel.*, 4/2, 1965, p.319–36.

Knox, R. A.   Religion and Civilization: The Rise of the Omni-Competent State. *Sociol. R.*, 39/1, 1947, p.13–22.

Kot, S.   Opposition to the Pope by the Polish Bishops, 1557–1560: Three Unique Polish Reformation Pamphlets. *Oxford Slav. Pap.*, 4, 1953, p.38–70.

Kraemer, H.   *From Mission Field to Independent Church: Report on a Decisive Decade in the Growth of Indigenous Churches in Indonesia.* London: S C M Press, 1958, 186p.

Kurungala, L.   Experiments in Ceylon. *Ecumen. R.*, 8/1, 1955, p.36–41.

Lambert, R. D.   Current Trends in Religion: A Summary. *Ann. Amer. Acad. Polit. Soc. Sci.*, 332, 1960, p.146–55.

Landis, B. Y.   Trends in Church Membership in the United States. *Ann. Amer. Acad. Polit. Soc. Sci.*, 332, 1960, p.1–8.

Lawson, J. C.   *Modern Greek Folklore and Ancient Greek Religion.* New Hyde Park, N.Y.: University Books, 1964, 620p.

Leakey, L. S. B.   *Mau Mau and Kikuyu.* London: Methuen and Co., 1952, 115p.

Leuba, J. H.   *The Reformation of the Churches.* Boston: The Beacon Press, 1950, 219p.

Levenson, J. R.   The Breakdown of Confucianism: Liang Ch'i-ch'ao Before Exile-1873–1898. *J. Hist. Ideas*, 11/4, 1950, p.448–85.

Levenson, J. R.   *Confucian China and Its Modern Fate: The Problem of Intellectual Continuity.* Berkeley: Univ. of California Press, 1958, 223p.

Lewis, B.   Islamic Revival in Turkey. *Int. Aff.*, 1952, p.38–48.

Lloyd, A. H.   The Passing of the Supernatural. *J. Philos.*, 7, 1910, p.533–53.

MacKeen, A. M. W.   The Sufi-Quam Movement. *Muslim World*, 53, 1963, p.212–5.

Mahar, P. M.   Changing Religious Practices of an Untouchable Caste. *Econ. Develop. Cult. Change*, 8/3, 1960, p.279–87.

Malefijt, A. de W.   Animism and Islam Among the Japanese in Surinam. *Anthropol. Quart.*, 37/3, 1964, p.149–55.

Malone, G. K.   Catechitical Crisis: What is "Common Catholic Teaching." *Amer. Eccles. R.*, 152/2, 1965, p.100–14.

Marcus, J. T.   The Mystique: Movement and Order. *Amer. J. Econ. Sociol.*, 19/3, 1960, p.231–9.

Marty, M. E.   *The New Shape of American Religion.* N.Y.: Harper, 1959, 180p.

Maxwell, M.   The Division in the Ranks of the Protestants in Eighteenth Century France. *Church Hist.*, 27/2, 1958, p.107–23.

McClellan, C.   Shamanistic Syncretism in Southern Yukon. *Trans. New York Acad. Sci.*, 19/2, 1956, p.130–7.

McLoughlin, W. G.   *Modern Revivalism: Charles Grandison Finney to Billy Graham.* New York: Ronald Press, 1959.

McMinn, J. B.   Fusion of the Gods: A Religio-Astrological Study of the Interpenetration of the East and West in Asia Minor. *J. Near East. Stud.*, 15/4, 1956, p.201–13.

McNeill, J. T. *Modern Christian Movements*. Phila.: Westminster, 1954.

Meade, S. E. *The Lively Experiment: The Shaping of Christianity in America*. N.Y.: Harper & Row, 1963.

Messenger, J. C., Jr. Religious Acculturation Among the Anang Ibibio. In W. R. Bascom and M. J. Herskovits—*Continuity and Change in African Cultures*. Chicago: Univ. of Chicago Press, 1959, p.279–329.

Metraux, A. Paganism and Christianity Among the Bolivian Indians. *Inter-Amer. Quart.*, 1940, p.53–60.

Michonneau, G. *Revolution in a City Parish*. Westminster, Maryland: Newman Press, 1950.

Miller, A. W. The Changing Anglo-Jewish Community. *Commentary*, 30/5, 1960, p.398–403.

Mischel, F. African 'Powers' in Trinidad: The Shango Cult. *Anthropol. Quart.*, 30/2, 1957, p.45–9.

Mohler, M. Conversion of the Churches From Wet to Dry. *Curr. Hist.*, 25, 1926, p.6–13.

Moos, F. Some Aspects of Park Chang No Kyo—A Korean Revitalization Movement. *Anthropol. Quart.*, 37/3, 1964, p.110–21.

Morris, R. E. Problems Concerning the Institutionalization of Religion. *Amer. Cath. Sociol. R.*, 17/2, 1956, p.98–108.

Muelder, W. G. From Sect to Church. *Christendom*, 1945, p.450–62.

Muir, W. *The Caliphate: Its Rise, Decline and Fall*. Beirut: Khayats Publishers and Booksellers, 1963, 628p.

Murphy, R. Organizational Change and the Individual: A Case Study of the Religious Community. *Sociol. Anal.*, 25/2, 1964, p.91–8.

Natarajan, S. *A Century of Social Reform in India*. Bombay: Asia Publishing House, 1962, 223p.

Nielson, F. The Return to Mysticism. *Amer. J. Econ. Sociol.*, 2/4, 1943, p.503–16.

Nketia, J. H. The Contribution of African Culture to Christian Worship. *Int. R. Missions*, 47/187, 1958, p.265–78.

O'Brien, J. F. The Socialization of the American Church in the Last Quarter of the Nineteenth Century. *Soc. Forces*, 2/5, 1924, p.700–5; see also 3/2, 1925, p.297–304.

O'Dea, T. F. Catholic Sectarianism: A Sociological Analysis of the So-Called Boston Heresy Case. *R. Rel. Res.*, 3/2, 1961, p.49–63.

O'Dea, T. F. Five Dilemmas in the Institutionalization of Religion. *J. Sci. Stud. Rel.*, 1/1, 1961, p.30–9. See also: J. M. Yinger—Comment, p.40–1.

O'Dea, T. F. Mormonism and the Avoidance of Sectarian Stagnation: A Study of Church, Sect, and Incipient Nationality. *Amer. J. Sociol.*, 60/3, 1954, p.285–93.

Oosthuiyen, G. C. Confessional Developments in the Churches in Asia and Africa. *South E. Asia J. Theol.*, 5/5, 1964, p.22–33.

Osekre, B. A. *Genealogy of Morals Among the Ghana Peoples: Religion in Transition: Ancient Ghana, Gold Coast, Ghana*. Cape Coast, Ghana: Mfantsiman Press, 1958, 11p.

Parenti, M. The Black Muslims: From Revolution to Institution. *Soc. Res.*, 31/2, 1964, p.175–94.

Parsons, E. C. Spanish Elements in the Kachina Cult of the Pueblos. *Proc. Twenty-Third Int. Cong. Amer.*, 1928, p.582–603.

Pfautz, H. W. Christian Science: A Case Study of the Social Psychological Aspect of Secularization. *Soc. Forces*, 34, 1956, p.246–51.

Pipes, R. Moslems of Soviet Central Asia: Trends and Prospects. *Mid. East J.*, 9/2, 1955, p.147–162; see also 9/3, p.295–308.

Pitt, M. Recent Developments in Religion in India. *J. Bib. Rel.*, 15, 1947, p.69–74.

Rapoport, R. N. Changing Navaho Religious Values. *Pap. Peabody Mus. Amer. Archeol. Ethnol.*, 41/2, 1954, 152p.

The Rebirth of a Muslim Communal Organization in Andhra. *Cent. Asian R.*, 13/3, 1965, p.232–8.

Redfield, R. *The Primitive World and Its Transformations*. Ithaca: Cornell Univ. Press, 1953.

Reed, H. A. Revival of Islam in Secular Turkey. *Mid. East J.*, 8/3, 1954, p.267–82.

Reed, H. A. Revival of Religious Feeling in the U.S.S.R. *World Today*, 10/10, 1954, p.439–47.

Riley, C. L. and Hogood, J. A Recent Nativistic Movement Among the Southern Tepehuan Indians. *Southw. J. Anthropol.*, 15/4, 1959, p.355–60.

Robbins, R. American Jews and American Catholics: Two Types of Social Change. *Sociol. Anal.*, 26/1, 1965, p.1–17. See also: T. F. O'Dea—Comment, p.18–20.

Ryan, B., *et al.* Secularization Process in a Ceylon Village. *East. Anthropol.*, 11/3, 1958, p.155–61.

Salem, E. Arab Reformers and the Reinterpretation of Islam. *Muslim World*, 55/4, 1965, p.311–20.

Salisbury, W. S. Religion and Secularization. *Soc. Forces*, 36/3, 1958, p.197–245.

Sanders, A. J. Iglesia NI Cristo: Factors Contributing to

Its Growth and Its Future. *South E. Asia J. Theol.*, 4/1, 1962, p.43–56.

Sanderson, R. W. Measuring the Progress of White Protestant Churches. *Amer. J. Sociol.*, 38/3, 1932, p.432–6.

Schlegel, S. A. The UPI Expiritistas: A Case Study in Cultural Adjustment. *J. Sci. Stud. Rel.*, 4/2, 1965, p.198–212.

Schmitt, K. M. The Clergy and the Enlightenment in Latin America: An Analysis. *Americas*, 15/4, 1959, p.381–91.

Scotch, N. Magic, Sorcery and Football Among the Urban Zulus: A Case of Reinterpretation Under Acculturation. *J. Conf. Resol.*, 5/1, 1961, p.70–4.

Scott, W. H. The Philippine Independent Church in History. *Silliman J.*, 10/3, 1963, p.298–310.

Seifert, F. The Religious Frontier: New Approaches to Old Problems. *Soc. Process*, 26, 1963, p.70–3.

Seznex, J. *The Survival of the Pagan Gods: The Mythological Tradition and its Place in Renaissance Humanism and Art*. N.Y. Pantheon Books, 1953, 376p.

Sharabi, H. The Transformation of Ideology in the Arab World. *Mid. East J.*, 19/4, 1965, p.471–86.

Shepperson, G. The Politics of African Church Separatist Movements in British Central Africa, 1892–1916. *Africa*, 24/3, 1954, p.233–46.

Smith, M. W. Synthesis and Other Processes in Sikhism. *Amer. Anthropol.*, 50/1, 1948, p.457–62.

Smith, T. L. *Revivalism and Social Reform: Protestantism on the Eve of the Civil War*. N.Y.: Harper, 1965, 253p.

Smith, W. C. Sociology and the Social Gospel. *Sociol. Soc. Res.*, 32, 1947, p.609–15.

Smith, W. C. Islam in the Modern World. *Curr. Hist.*, 32, 1957, p.321–5.

Spitzer, A. and Spitzer, M. L. Religious Reorganization Among the Montana Blackfeet. *R. Rel. Res.*, 2/1, 1960, p.19–35.

Steinberg, S. Reformed Judaism: The Origin and Evolution of a "Church Movement." *J. Sci. Stud. Rel.*, 5/1, 1965, p.117–29.

Suttles, W. The Plateau Prophet Dance Among the Coast Salish. *Southw. J. Anthropol.*, 13/4, 1957, p.352–96.

Tavard, G. H. The Catholic Reform in the Sixteenth Century. *Church Hist.*, 26, 1957, p.275–88.

Thompson, D. E. Maya Paganism in Christianity. *Mid. Amer. Res. Inst. Publ.*, 19, 1960, p.1–36.

Tillich, P. *The Protestant Era*. Chicago: Univ. of Chicago Press, 1948, 323p.

Toch, H. H., *et al.* "Secularization in College:" An Exploratory Study. *Rel. Educ.*, 59/6, 1964, p.490–501, 504.

Toynbee, A. J. The Future of Religion. *Twent. Cent.*, 170/1010, 1961, p.114–39.

Turner, H. W. The Church of the Lord: The Expansion of a Nigerian Independent Church in Sierra Leone and Ghana. *J. Afr. Hist.*, 3/1, 1962, p.91–110.

Van Stone, J. W. Some Aspects of Religious Change Among Native Inhabitants in West Alaska and the Northwest Territories. *Arctic Anthropol.*, 2/2, 1964, p.21–4.

Von Fürer-Haimendorf, C. Pre-Buddhist Elements in Sherpa Belief and Ritual. *Man*, 55, 1955, p.49–52.

Wallace, A. F. C. New Religious Beliefs Among the Delaware Indians, 1600–1900. *Southw. J. Anthropol.*, 12/1, 1956, p.1–21.

Wallace, A. F. C. Revitalization Movements. *Amer. Anthropol.*, 53/2, 1956, p.264–81.

Watkin, E. I. *The Church in Council*. London: Darton, Longman and Todd, 1960, 227p.

Wayman, A. Buddhist Dependent Origination and the Sāṁkhya Gunas. *Ethnos*, 27, 1962, p.14–22.

Weisberger, B. A. *They Gathered at the River: The Story of the Great Revivalists and their Impact Upon Religion in America*. Boston: Little, Brown, 1958.

White, R. C. The Ever-Changing Church. *Southw. Polit. Soc. Sci. Quart.*, 6/3, 1925, p.256–75.

Whitley, O. R. The Sect-To-Denomination Process in An American Religious Movement: The Disciples of Christ. *Southw. Soc. Sci. Quart.*, 1955, p.275–81.

Williams, C. R. The Welsh Religious Revival. *Brit. J. Sociol.*, 3, 1952, p.242–59.

Wilson, W. H. The Church and the Country Life Movement. *Soc. Forces*, 2/1, 1923, p.23–8.

Wonderly, W. L. Pagan and Christian Concepts in a Mexican Indian Culture. *Pract. Anthropol.*, 5/5-6, 1958, p.197–202.

Wyon, O. *Living Springs: New Religious Movements in Western Europe*. Phila.: Westminster Press, 1963, 120p.

Yetiv, I. Marseilles Jewry at the Crossroads. *In Dispersion*, 2, 1963, p.99–112.

Yinger, J. M. Religion and Social Change: Problems of Integration and Pluralism Among the Privileged. *R. Rel. Res.*, 4/3, 1963, p.129–48.

Zald, M. and Denton, P. From Evangelism to General

Service: The Transformation of the YMCA. *Admin. Sci. Quart.*, 8/2, 1963, p.214–34.

Zuck, L. H. Anabaptism: Abortive Counter Revolt Within the Reformation. *Church Hist.*, 26, 1957, p.211–26.

See Also: 2, 3, 5d, 5e, 7d

6d.   *Messiahs and Prophets of Religion*

Aberle, D. F.   The Prophet Dance and Reactions to White Contact. *Southw. J. Anthropol.*, 15/1, 1959, p.74–83. See also: L. Spier, *et al.*—Comment, p.84–8.

Afnan, R.   *The Great Religious Prophets: Moses, Zoraster, Jesus.* N.Y.: Philosophical Library, 1960, 459p.

Akiwowo, A.   The Place of Mojolo Agebebi in the African Nationalist Movements: 1890–1917. *Phylon*, 26/2, 1965, p.122–39.

Andersson, E.   *Lundquist: Messianic Popular Movements in the Lower Congo.* Up Sala: Studia Ethnographica Upsaliensia, 1958, 287p.

Anesaki, M.   *Nichiren: The Buddhist Prophet.* Cambridge: Harvard Univ. Press, 1949, 160p.

Arlow, J. A.   The Consecration of the Prophet. *Psychoanal. Quart.*, 20, 1951, p.374–97.

Bailey, P.   *Wovoka, The Indian Messiah.* Los Angeles: Westernlore Press, 1957.

Barber, B.   Acculturation and Messianic Movements. *Amer. Sociol. R.*, 6/5, 1941, p.663–9.

Barclay, H. B.   Muslim "Prophets" in the Modern Sudan. *Muslim World*, 54/4, 1964, p.250–5.

Berger, P. L.   Charisma and Religious Innovation: The Social Location of Isrealite Prophecy. *Amer. Sociol. R.*, 28/6, 1963, p.940–50.

Bernardi, B.   *The Mugwe, a Failing Prophet: A Study of a Religious and Public Dignitary of the Meru of Kenya.* London, N.Y.: Oxford Univ. Press, 1959, 211p.

Braden, C. S. *Jesus Compared: A Study of Jesus and Other Great Founders of Religions.* Englewood Cliffs, New Jersey: Prentice-Hall, 1957, 230p.

Cantril, H. and Sherif, M. The Kingdom of Father Divine. *J. Abnorm. Soc. Psychol.*, 33, 1938, p.147–67.

Cook, S. The Prophets: A Revivalistic Folk Religious Movement in Puerto Rico. *Caribbean Stud.*, 4/4, 1965, p.20–35.

Deardorff, M. H. The Religion of Handsome Lake: Its Origin and Development. In "Symposium on Local Diversity in Iroquois Culture," ed. W. N. Fenton— *Bull. Bur. Amer. Ethnol.*, 149, 1951, p.79–197.

Dobson, W. A. C. H. *Mencius.* Toronto: Univ. of Toronto Press, 1963, 215p.

Duchesne-Guillemin, J. Heraclitus and Iran. *Hist. Rel.*, 3/1, 1963, p.34–49.

Eberhardt, J. Messianism in South Africa. *Archiv. Sociol. Rel.*, 1, 1957, p.31–56.

Emmet, D. Prophets and Their Societies. *J. Roy. Anthropol. Inst.*, 86, 1956, p.13–24.

Faucett, L. W. *Six Great Teachers of Morality: Gotama Budda and Jesus, Moses and Mohammed, Confucius and Socrates: A Classified Arrangement in Twenty Parts for the Study and Comparison of Their Teachings* (Eds. I. Maki and K. Watanable). Tokyo: Shinozaki Shorin, 1958, 551p.

Fletcher, A. C. The Indian Messiah. *J. Amer. Folklore*, 4, 1891, p.57–60.

Foucher, A. *The Life of Buddha: According to the Ancient Texts and Movements of Gidia* (Trans. S. B. Boas). Middletown, Connecticut: Wesleyan Univ. Press, 1963, 272p.

Fox, R. C., *et al.* The Second Independence: A Case Study of the Kwilu Rebellion in the Congo. *Comp. Stud. Society Hist.*, 8/1, 1965, p.78–109.

Froom, L. R. E. *The Prophetic Faith of Our Fathers.* Washington: Review Herald, 1946–54, 4 vols.

Guiart, J. John Frum Movement in Tanna. *Oceania*, 22/3, 1952, p.165–77.

Halsey, J. J. The Genesis of a Modern Prophet. *Amer. J. Sociol.*, 9/3, 1906, p.310–28.

Heizer, R. F. A California Messianic Movement of 1801 Among the Chumash. *Amer. Anthropol.*, 43/1, 1914, p.128–9.

Herold, A. F. *The Life of Buddha, According to the Legends of Ancient India* (Trans. P. C. Blum). Tokyo: C. E. Tuttle, 1954, 286p.

Heymann, F. G. *John Zizka and the Hussite Revolution.* Princeton: Princeton Univ. Press, 1955, 521p.

Hodgson, M. G. S. Al-Darasi and Hamza in the Origin of the Druze Religion. *J. Amer. Orient. Society*, 82/1, 1962, p.5–20.

Hoebel, E. A. The Comanche Sun Dance and Messianic Outbreak of 1873. *Amer. Anthropol.*, 43/2, 1941, p.301–3.

Hoult, T. F. Messiah for Millionaires. *Christ. Reg.*, 129, 1950, p.15–6.

Kamma, F. C. Messianic Movements in Western New Guinea. *Int. R. Missions*, 41/162, 1952, p.148–60.

Kincheloe, S. C. The Prophet as a Leader. *Sociol. Soc. Res.*, 12/5, 1928, p.461–8.

Köbben, A. J. F. Prophetic Movements as an Expression of Social Protest. *Int. Archiv. Ethnogr.*, 49/1, 1960, p.117–64.

Lanternari, V. Messianism: Its Historical Origin and Morphology. *Hist. Rel.*, 2/1, 1962, p.52–72.

Lanternari, V. *The Religions of the Oppressed: A Study of Modern Messianic Cults.* N.Y.: Alfred Knopf, 1963.

Manheim, E. Recent Types of Charismatic Leadership. In J. S. Roucek (ed.)—*Social Control.* Princeton: D. Van Nostrand, 1956, p.545–57.

Martin, M. L. *The Biblical Concept of Messianism and Messianism in South Africa.* Morija, Basutoland: M. Sesuto Book Depot, 1964, 207p.

Martindale, D. *Social Life and Cultural Change.* Princeton: Van Nostrand, 1962.

Metraux, A. A Quechua Messiah in Eastern Peru. *Amer. Anthropol.*, 44/1, 1942, p.721–5.

Mitchell, R. C. African Prophet Movements. *Christ. Cent.*, 81/47, 1964, p.1427–9.

Myers, E. D. The Psychology of Prophecy. *J. Bib. Rel.*, 5, 1937, p.55–62.

Olson, R. A New Messianic Cult in Japan. *Kroeber Anthropol. Society Pap.*, 8/9, 1953, p.78–81.

Parker, A. The Code of Handsome Lake, The Seneca Prophet. *New York State Mus. Bull.*, 163, 1913.

Postal, S. K. Hoax Nativism at Caughnawaga: A Control Case for the Theory of Revitalization. *Ethnology*, 4/3, 1965, p.266–81.

Rahman, F. *Prophecy in Islam.* N.Y.: Macmillan, 1958, 118p.

Reid, I. DeA. Negro Movements and Messiahs, 1900–1949. *Phylon*, 10/4, 1949, p.362–8.

Rokeach, M. *The Three Christs of Ypsilanti: A Narrative Study of Three Lost Men.* N.Y.: A. A. Knopf, 1964, 336p.

Rotberg, R. The Lenshina Movement of Northern Rhodesia. *Human Prob. Brit. Centr. Afr.*, 29, 1961, p.63–78.

Rowley, H. H. *Prophecy and Religion in Ancient China and Israel.* London: Athlone, 1956, 154p.

Schwartz, T. *The Paliau Movement in the Admiralty Islands, 1946–1954.* N.Y.: American Museum of Natural History, 1962, 421p.

Smith, M. G. *Black Puritan.* Kingston: Department of Extra-Mural Studies, Univ. of West Indies, Kingston, Jamaica, 1963, 139p.

Smith, M. G., *et al. The Ras Tafari Movement in Kingston, Jamaica.* Mona, Jamaica: Univ. College of the West Indies, 1960, 54p.

Stark, W. Psychology of Social Messianism. *Soc. Res.*, 25, 1958, p.145–57.

Sundkler, B. G. M. Bantu Messiah and White Christ. *Pract. Anthropol.*, 7/4, 1960, p.170-6.

Sundkler, B. G. M. *Bantu Prophets in South Africa.* N.Y.: Oxford Univ. Press, 1961.

Turner, H. W. African Prophet Movements. *Hibbert J.*, 61, 1963, p.112–6.

Van Der Kroef, J. M. Racial Messiahs. In E. T. Thompson and E. C. Hughes—*Race, Individual and Collective Behavior.* Glencoe: Free Press, 1958, p.357–64.

Van Nuys, K. Evaluating the Pathological in Prophetic Experience (Particularly in Ezekiel). *J. Bib. Rel.*, 21, 1953, p.244–51.

Wallace, A. F. C. Handsome Lake and the Great Revival in the West. *Amer. Quart.*, 1952, p.149–65.

Watt, W. M. *Muhammad at Mecca.* Oxford: Clarendon Press, 1953.

Watt, W. M. *Muhammad at Medina.* Oxford: Clarendon Press, 1956.

White, E. Bungan: A New Kayan Belief. *Sarawak Mus. J.*, 7/8, 1956, p.472–75.

Whitley, C. F. The Date and Teaching of Zarathustra. *Numen*, 4/3, 1957, p.215–27.

Wilder, A. N. Jesus and the Charismatic Type. *J. Bib. Rel.*, 9, 1941, p.51–4.

Willner, A. R. and Willner, D. The Rise and Role of Charismatic Leaders. *Ann. Amer. Acad. Polit. Soc. Sci.*, 358, 1965, p.77–88.

Wilson, W. D. *Messiahs: Their Role in Civilization.* Washington: American Council in Public Affairs, 1943, 217p.

See Also: 3, 5a, 7a

Barnett, H. G.   2a1
Brenner, A. B.   4i
Dawson, C.   6c
Elgood, C.   5b
Festinger, L.   2h
Goitein, S. D.   5a
Justus, M. V. D. K.   7b2
Meng, H.   7a4
Reik, T.   3b
Romano, O. I., V   5b
Salisbury, W. S.   7b
Wach, J.   7a1

6e.   *Effects of Social Change on the Church*

Abell, A. I. *Urban Impact on American Protestantism, 1865–1900.* Hamden, Connecticut: Archon, 1962, 275p.

Abrecht, P. *The Churches and Rapid Social Change.* Garden City: Doubleday & Co., 1961.

Beaven, A. W. The Meaning for Religions of the Trend Toward Nationalism. *Ann. Amer. Acad. Polit. Soc. Sci.*, 174, 1934, p.65–75.

Bellah, R. N. Religious Aspects of Modernization in Turkey and Japan. *Amer. J. Sociol.*, 64/1, 1958, p.1–5.

Best, E. E. Christian Faith and Cultural Crisis: The Japanese Case. *J. Rel.*, 41, 1961, p.28–37.

Boisen, A. T. Factors Which Have to do With the Decline of the Country Church. *Amer. J. Sociol.*, 22, 1916, p.177–92.

Boisen, A. T. Economic Distress and Religious Experi-ence: A Study of the Holy Rollers. *Psychiatry*, 2/2, 1939, p.185–94.

Boisen, A. T. *Religion in Crisis and Custom: A Sociological and Psychological Study.* N.Y.: Harper, 1955, 271p.

Breines, A. R. An Elite as Response to Crisis in Religious Organization. *Amer. Cath. Sociol. R.*, 20/1, 1959, p.43–52.

Bromley, O. G. *The Church and Contemporary Change.* N.Y.: Macmillan, 1950, 132p.

Cuber, J. F. Church Doctrines in a Changing World. *Rel. Educ.*, 33, 1938, p.112–7.

D'Antonio, W. V. and Pike, F. (eds.) *Religion, Revolution and Reform: New Forces for Change in Latin America.* N.Y.: Frederick A. Praeger, 1964.

Davis, J. The Minister and the Economic Order. *J. Educ. Sociol.*, 10/5, 1937, p.269–79.

Faris, N. A. and Husayn, M. T.—*The Cresent in Crisis: An Interpretative Study of the Modern Arab World.* Lawrence: Univ. of Kansas, 1955, 191p.

Gaustad, E. S. The Theological Effects of the Great Awakening in New England. *Miss. Valley Hist. R.*, 40/4, 1954, p.681–706.

Gillispie, C. C. *Genesis and Geology: The Impact of Scientific Discoveries Upon Religious Beliefs in the Decades Before Darwin.* N.Y.: Harper & Row, 1959, 306p.

Goldschmidt, D. Israel and the Modern World. *Soc. Compass*, 9/3, 1962, p.215–20.

Graybeal, D. M. Churches in a Changing Culture. *R. Rel. Res.*, 2/3, 1961, p.121–6.

Hammond, P. E. The Migrating Sect: An Illustration from Early Norwegian Immigration. *Soc. Forces*, 41/3, 1963, p.275–83.

Harrison, S. S. Caste and the Andhra Communists. *Amer. Polit. Sci. R.*, 50/2, 1956, p.378–404.

Holt, A. E. Religion. *Amer. J. Sociol.*, 34/1, 1928, p.172–6; see also 34/6, 1929, p.1116–28.

Houtart, F. and Tonna, B. The Implications of Change for the Church in Malta. *Soc. Compass*, 7/5–6, 1960, p.461–74.

Klietsch, R. G. Social Change: Ethnicity and the Religious System in a Rural Community. *Cath. Sociol. R.*, 24/3, 1963, p.222–30.

Latourette, K. S., *et al.* Do We Live in a Post-Christian Age? *Rel. Life*, 33/2, 1964, p.170–285.

Locher, G. W. Myth in a Changing World. *Bijdrag. Taal-Land Volkenk.*, 112/2, 1956, p.169–92.

Mead, M. *New Lives for Old: Cultural Transformation, Manus 1928–1953.* N.Y.: Marrow, 1956, 548p.

Melady, T. P. The Impact of Africa on Recent Developments in the Roman Catholic Church. *Race*, 7/2, 1965, p.147–56.

Meyer, C. S. Lutheran Immigrant Churches Face the Problems of the Frontier. *Church Hist.*, 1960, p.440–62.

Modern Environment and Religion. *Lumen Vitae*, 6/1–2, 1951, p.7–362.

Nichols, J. H. *History of Christianity, 1650–1950: Secularization of the West.* N.Y.: Ronald Press, 1956, 493p.

Norton, G. R. The Emergence of New Religious Organizations in South Africa: A Discussion of Causes. *J. Roy African Society*, 40, 1941, p.48–67.

Nyholm, P. C. *The Americanization of the Danish Lutheran Churches in America.* Minneapolis: Augsburg Publishing House, 1963, 480p.

Peel, R. *Christian Science: Its Encounter with American Culture.* Garden City: Doubleday, 1965, 224p.

Rowe, W. L. Changing Rural Class Structure and the Jajmani System. *Hum. Org.*, 22/1, 1963, p.41–4.

Sanderson, R. W. *The Church Serves the Changing City.* N.Y.: Harper Brothers, 1955.

Schneider, H. W. The Influence of Darwin and Spencer on American Philosophical Theology. *J. Hist. Ideas*, 6/1, 1945, p.3–18.

Sommerfeld, R. *The Church of the Twenty-First Century: Prospects and Proposals.* St. Louis: Concordia, 1965.

Stanley, M. Church Adaptation to Urban Social Change: A Typology of Protestant City Congregations. *J. Sci. Stud. Rel.*, 2/1, 1962, p.64–73.

Sullenger, T. E. and Lindevall, G. The Urban Church in a Changing Social Scene. *Sociol. Soc. Res.*, 30/3, 1946, p.197–200.

Talmon, Y. Pursuit of the Millennium: The Relation Between Religions and Social Change. *Eur. J. Sociol.*, 3/1, 1962, p.125–48.

Thomas, J. L. The New Immigration and Cultural Pluralism. *Amer. Cath. Sociol. R.*, 15/4, 1954, p.310–22.

Welch, H. H. Buddhism Under the Communists. *China Quart.*, 6, 1961, p.1–14.

White, E. A. *Science and Religion in American Thought: The Impact of Naturalism.* Stanford Univ. Press, 1952, 117p.

Young, F. W. Adaptation and Pattern Integration of a California Sect. *R. Rel. Res.*, 1/4, 1960, p.137–50.

See Also: 2, 3, 5, 9b

Bernander, G. A.   5e1
Brothers, J.   4g, 7a1
Fletcher, W. C.   4a1
Graebner, O. E.   7a
Howes, R. G.   6
Lee, J. M.   7a4
Levenson, J. R.   4a1
Masland, J. W.   4a1
O'Dea, T.   2a2
Palmieri, F. A.   5d
Pratt, S. A. J.   5a2
Timasheff, N. S.   4a1
Tuveson, E. L.   7b3
Von Grunebaum, G.   7f
Weisinger, H.   7b3

7.   The Impact of Religious Belief on Behavior

Argyle, M.   *Religious Behavior*. London: Routledge and Kegan Paul, 1958.

Bram, J.   Spirits, Mediums, and Believers in Contemporary Puerto Rico.   *Trans. New York Acad. Sci.*, 20/4, 1958, p.340–7.

Dodds, E. R.   *Pagan and Christian in An Age of Anxiety: Some Aspects of Religious Experience from Marcus Aurelius to Constantine*. Cambridge: The University Press, 1965, 144p.

Saunders, E. D.   Symbolic Gestures in Buddhism. *Artibus Asiae*, 21/1, 1958, p.47–63.

Troeltsch, E.   *Christian Thought: Its History and Application* (Ed. B. F. von Hogel). N.Y.: Meridian Books, 1957, 191p.

Wach, J.   *Types of Religious Experience*. Chicago: Univ. of Chicago Press, 1951.

Wood, H. G.   *Belief and Unbelief Since 1850*. London: Cambridge Univ. Press, 1955, 143p.

Znaniecki, F.   *Social Relations and Social Roles*. San Francisco: Chandler Publishing Co., 1965.

See Also: 1a, 4, 5

Birmingham, W.   5b2
Cock, S. W.   8a4
Dynes, R. R.   4f
Kluckhohn, C.   3f5
Moore, E. A.   4a2
Moore, T. V.   5b1
Robinson, M. S.   9
Sadler, A. W.   4h
Siegman, E. W.   8a2
Woodhouse, A. S. P.   4a

7a.   *The Religious Leader and His Roles*

Allen, P. J.   The Growth of Strata in Early Organizational Development. *Amer. J. Sociol.*, 68/1, 1962, p.34–46.

Allen, Y., Jr.   *A Seminary Survey*. N.Y. Harper and Brothers, 1960, 640p.

Bamberger, B. J.   The American Rabbi: His Changing Role. *Judaism*, 3, 1954, p.488–97.

Barbeau, M.   Medicine-Men on the North Pacific Coast. *Nat. Mus. Canada Bull.*, 15/42, 1958, p.95.

Bhowmick, P. K.   Social and Religious Officials of the Lodha Caste. *Man India*, 35/2, 1956, p.119–26.

Blizzard, S. W.   The Minister's Dilemma. *Christ. Cent.*, 1956, p.508–9.

Blizzard, S. W.   Role Conflicts of the Urban Minister. *City Church*, 1956, p.13–5.

Blizzard, S. W.   The Parish Minister's Self-Image of His Master Role. *Past. Psychol.*, 9, 1958, p.25–32.

Blizzard, S. W.   The Parish Minister's Self-Image and Variability in Community Culture. *Past. Psychol.*, 10, 1959, p.27–36.

Bloomhill, G.   *Witchcraft in Africa*. London: Bailey & Swinten, 1962, 172p.

Bodenstein, W. and Raum, O. F.   A Present Day Zulu Philosopher. *Africa*, 30/2, 1960, p.166–81.

Bowers, M. K.   *Conflicts of the Clergy. A Psychodynamic Study with Case Histories*.   N.Y.: Thomas Nelson and Sons, 1963, 252p.

Bunnik, R. J.   The Ecclesiastical Minister and Marriage: An Attempt at Clarification. *Soc. Compass*, 12/1–2, 1965, p.53–100.

Campbell, E. T.   The Changing Nature of the Ministry. *Reformed R.*, 17/2, 1963, p.16–26.

Camps, A.   Searching After the Straight Path: The Role of the Religious Leader, The Pir, in the Islam of West Pakistan. *Soc. Compass*, 11/6, 1964, p.23–8.

Chapman, S. H.   The Contemporary Pastorate. *Amer. Sociol. R.*, 9, 1944, p.595–602.

Christensen, J. B.   The Adaptive Function of Fanti Priesthood. In W. R. Bascom and M. J. Herskovits—*Continuity and Change in African Cultures*. Chicago: Univ. of Chicago Press, 1959, p.257–78.

Denton, W.   Role Attitudes of the Minister's Wife. *Past. Psychol.*, 12/119, 1961, p.17–23.

Douglas, W. *Ministers' Wives*. N.Y.: Harper & Row, 1965, 288p.

Duncan, H. G. Reactions of Ex-Ministers Toward the Ministry. *J. Rel.*, 12, 1932, p.101–15.

Felton, R. A. *Go Down Moses: A Study of Twenty-One Successful Negro Rural Pastors*. Madison, New Jersey: Drew Theol. Seminary, 1952.

Fichter, J. H. Priests as Interviewers. *Soc Order*, 9/6, 1959, p.275–9.

Fichter, J. H. A Comparative View of the Parish Priest. *Archiv. Sociol. Rel.*, 8/16, 1963, p.44–8.

Fichter, J. H. *Priest and People*. N.Y.: Sheed & Ward, 1965.

Foley, A. S. *God's Men of Color: The Colored Catholic Priests of the United States, 1854–1954*. N.Y.: Farrar, Straus, 1955, 322p.

Foley, A. S. The Status and Role of the Negro Priest in the American Catholic Clergy. *Amer. Cath. Sociol. R,*, 16/2, 1955, p.83–93.

Gelbep, S. M. *The Failure of the American Rabbi: A Program for the Revitalization of the Rabbinate in America*. N.Y.: Twayne Publishers, 1961.

Graebner, O. E. Pastor and People at Kennedy's Casket. *R. Rel. Res.*, 6/2, 1965, p.107–17.

Gustafson, J. M. The Clergy in the U. S. *Daedalus*, 92, 1963, p.727–44.

Hadden, J. K. A Study of the Protestant Ministry of America. *J. Sci. Stud. Rel.*, 5/1, 1965, p.10–23.

Hiltner, S. (ed.) The Minister and Money. *Past. Psychol.*, 16/152, 1965, p.5–48.

Honeywell, R. J. *Chaplains in the United States Army*. Washington: Office of Chief of Chaplains, Dept. of Army, 1958.

Hori, I. On the Concept of Hijiri (Holy Man). *Numen*, 5/2, 1958, p.128–60.

Horn, W. M. The Image of the Ministry. *Luther. Quart.*, 13, 1961, p.192–210.

Howegawa, C. The Hongwanji Buddhist Minister in Hawii: A Study of an Occupation. *Soc. Process*, 26, 1963, p.73–9.

Isherwood, S. Effects of a Clergy Examiner on Responses to a Religious Attitude Questionnaire. *Bull. Maritime Psychol. Assoc.*, 11/1, 1962, p.7–10.

James, E. O. *The Nature and Function of Priesthood: A Comparative and Anthropological Study*. N.Y.: Barnes and Noble, 1961, 336p.

Karve, D. D. (ed.) *The New Brahmans: Five Maharashtrian Families*. Berkeley: Univ. of California Press, 1963, 303p.

Kligerman, C. A Psychoanalytic Study of the Confessions of St. Augustine. *J. Amer. Psychoanal. Assoc.*, 5/3, 1957, p.469–84.

Klink, T. W. The Ministry and Medicine: A New Examination. *Past. Psychol.*, 10, 1959, p.39–45.

Knight, R. P. Practical and Theoretical Considerations in the Analysis of a Minister. *Psychoanal. R.*, 24, 1937, p.350–64.

Knowles, D. D. *The Religious Orders in England*. N.Y.: Cambridge Univ. Press, 1948–1959, 3 vols.

Landis, B. Y. (ed.) *The Clergyman's Fact Book 1964–1965*. N.Y.: M. Evans and Co., 1963, 311p., see other issues.

Lavaud, B. *The Meaning of the Religious Life* (Trans. G. Le Bras). Westminster, Maryland: Newman Press, 1955, 81p.

LeClerq, J. *The Religious Vocation*. N.Y.: Kennedy, 1955.

Leslie, P. *The Deployment and Payment of the Clergy*. London: Church Information Office, 1964, 311p.

Loeb, E. M. Shaman and Seer. *Amer. Anthropol.*, 31/1, 1929, p.80–4.

Loeb, E. M. The Shaman of Niue. *Amer. Anthropol.*, 26/3, 1924, p.393–402.

Magner, J. A. *The Catholic Priest in the Modern World*. Milwaukee: Bruce Publishing Co., 1957, 291p.

Mayne, P. *The Saints of Sind*. Garden City, N.Y.: Doubleday, 1956, 254p.

McLoughlin, W. G., Jr. *Billy Sunday Was His Real Name*. Chicago: Univ. of Chicago Press, 1955, 324p.

Miller, N. Changing Patterns of Leadership in the Jewish Community. *Jew. Soc. Stud.*, 17/3, 1955, p.179–82. See also: A. G. Duker—Historical and Sociological Factors in Jewish Communal Leadership: Comment on Norman Miller, p.183–92; H. L. Lurie—Motivations and Social Change: Comment on Norman Miller, p.193–4.

Moore, E. H. and Mammer, C. Ministers in Retirement. *Sociol. Soc. Res.*, 32, 1948, p.920–7.

Mugrauer, B. Variations in Pastoral Role in France. *Amer. Cath. Sociol. R.*, 9/1, 1950, p.15–24.

Naylor, R. E. *The Baptist Deacon*. Nashville: Broadman Press, 1955, 138p.

Niebuhr, H. R. and Williams, D. D. (eds.) *The Ministry in Historical Perspective*. N.Y.: Harper & Row, 1956.

Oates, W. E. *The Christian Pastor*. Phila.: Westminster Press, 1964, 258p.

O'Malley, F. The Thinker in the Church: The Spirit of Newman. *R. Polit.*, 21/1, 1959, p.5–23.

Paton, D. M. (ed.) *New Forms of Ministry.* N.Y.: Friendship Press, 1965, 102p.

Petrie, J. (Trans.) *The Worker-Priests: A Collective Documentation.* N.Y.: Macmillan, 1956, 204p.

Pipes, W. H. *Say Amen Brother: Old Time Negro Preaching. A Study on American Frustration.* N.Y.: William-Frederick Press, 1951, 210p.

Poage, G. and Lievin, G. (Trans. and Eds.) *Today's Vocation Crisis: A Summary of the Studies and Discussions on Vocations to the States of Perfection, Dec. 10–16, 1961.* Cork: The Mercier Press, 1962, 435p.

Poeisz, J. The Pastoral Significance of Catholic Associations. *Soc. Compass,* 6/6, 1959, p.213–25.

Proyser, P. W. (ed.) St. Augustine's Confessions: Perspectives and Inquiries. *J. Sci. Stud. Rel.,* 5/1, 1965, p.130–52; to be continued.

Rodehaver, M. Ministers on the Move: A Study of Mobility in Church Leadership. *Rur. Sociol.,* 13, 1948, p.400–10.

Rodehaver, M. and Smith, L. M. Migration and Occupational Structure: The Clergy. *Soc. Forces,* 29/4, 1951, p.416–21.

Samson, A'D. *Church Pastors in Four Agricultural Settings in Montana.* Bozeman, Montana: Montana Agricultural Experiment Station Bulletin, 539, 1958, 26p.

Scanzoni, J. Resolution of Occupational-Conjugal Role Conflict in Clergy Marriages. *J. Marr. Fam. Liv.,* 27/3, 1965, p.396–402.

Scholefield, H. B. Psychoanalysis and the Parish Ministry. *J. Rel. Health,* 2/2, 1963, p.112–28.

Schreuder, O. The Parish Priest as a Subject of Criticism. *Soc. Compass,* 7/2, 1960, p.111–26.

Smith, M. W. Shamanism in the Shaker Religion of Northwest America. *Man,* 54, 1954, p.119–22.

Sprague, T. W. Some Notable Features in the Authority Structure of a Sect. *Soc. Forces,* 21/3, 1943, p.344–50.

Suzuki, D. T. *Training of the Zen Buddhist Monk.* N.Y.: University Books, 1959.

Tanner, R. E. S. The Magician in Northern Sukumaland, Tanganyika. *Southw. J. Anthropol.,* 13/4, 1957, p.355–51.

Tanner, R. E. S. The Sorcerer in Northern Sukumaland, Tanganyika. *Southw. J. Anthropol.,* 12/4, 1956, p.437–43.

Vacca, V. Social and Political Aspects of Egyptian and Yamani Sufism. *J. Pakistan Hist. Society,* 8, 1960, p.233–59.

Van Noord, G. Promoting Mental Health in the Pastor. *Rel. R.,* 13, 1961, p.9–17.

Van Zeller, H. *The Benedictine Nun.* Baltimore, Maryland: Helicon, 1965, 271p.

Voigt, G. P. The Protestant Minister in American Fiction. *Luth. Quart.,* 11, 1959, p.3–13.

Von den Ende, W. M. I. The Personal and Functional Elements in Pastoral Care. *Soc. Compass,* 8/1, 1961, p.35–48.

Ward, C. K. *Priests and People: A Study in the Sociology of Religion.* Liverpool, England: University Press, 1961, 182p.

Wesister, D. *Patterns of Part-Time Ministry in Some Churches in South America.* London: World Dominion Press, 1964, 48p.

Winstedt, R. O. *The Malay Magician Being Shaman, Saiva, and Sufi.* London: Routledge and Paul, 1951, 160p.

Wulff, I. The So-Called Priests of the Ngadju Dyaks. *Folklore,* 2, 1960, p.121–32.

See Also: 1g, 4a, 4g, 5b, 5e

Abrams, R. H.   5b2
Busjan, C.   7b3
Clinebell, H. J., Jr.   5b
Considine, J.   5e
Davies, H.   6e
Fagley, R. M.   5b2
Fecher, C. J.   5b
Ford, J. C.   5b1
Freud, S.   8a6
Gearing, F. O.   4a1
Gluckman, R. M.   5b1
Hutchison, W. R.   6c
Kelley, I. T.   3f5
Kelley, M. W.   5b1 (2)
Little, L. C.   9
Lloyd, P. C.   4a1
McLoughlin, W. G.   6c
Mehok, W. J.   4j
Menges, R. J.   9
Metaux, A.   6d
Morris, J. S.   4a1
Neal, M. A.   6
Niebuhr, H. R.   4g4
O'Brien, K. R.   2a2
Richardson, W. J.   5e
Scott, R. W.   5e3
Scott, W. H.   6c
Swanton, J. R.   8a3
Symonds, J.   3a1
Vaughn, R. P.   5b1
Vidyarthi, L. P.   4j1
Weisberger, B. A.   6c

Adler, M. D.   An Analysis of Role Conflicts of the Clergy in Mental Health Work. *J. Past. Care*, 19/2, 1965, p.65–75.

Alexander, F.   Buddhistic Training as an Artificial Catatonia. *Psychoanal. R.*, 18, 1931, p.129–45.

Allaman, R.   The Clinically Trained Chaplain in the Child-Care Institution. *Child Welfare*, 39/1, 1960, p.6–9.

Allport, G. W.   Mental Health: A Generic Attitude. *J. Rel. Health*, 4/1, 1964, p.7–21.

Arberry, A. J.   *Sufism: An Account of the Mystics of Islam.* London: Allen & Unwin, 1950, 141p.

Arnold, T. W.   *The Preaching of Islam: A History of the Propagation of the Muslim Faith.*   Lahore: Shukh Muhammad Ashaf, 1965, 508p.

Bennett, G. W.   The Social Environment and Its Influence on Counseling Procedure in the Rural Church. *Past. Psychol.*, 10, 1959, p.31–6.

Bier, W. C. (ed.)   *Personality and Sexual Problems in Pastoral Psychology.*   N.Y.: Fordham Univ. Press, 1964.

Binkley, O. T. (ed.)   Pastoral Psychology and the Rural Ministry. *Past. Psychol.*, 10/96, 1959.

Blizzard, S. W.   The Roles of the Rural Parish Minister, the Protestant Seminaries, and the Sciences of Human Behavior. *Rel. Educ.*, 50/6, 1955, p.383–92.

Blizzard, S. W.   The Protestant Parish Minister's Integrating Roles. *Rel. Educ.*, 53, 1958, p.374–80.

Bolino, A. C.   Brigham Young an Entrepreneur. *Amer. J. Econ. Sociol.*, 18/2, 1959, p.181–92.

Bourke, J. G.   The Medicine-Men of the Apache. *Rep. Bur. Amer. Ethnol.* (Washington, D. C.), 9, 1887–1888, p.443–603.

Boverman, M.   Collaboration of Psychiatrist and Clergyman: A Case Report.   The Psychiatrist's Viewpoint. *Fam. Proc.*, 3/2, 1964, p.251–62. See also J. R. Adams, p.262–72.

Braude, L.   The Rabbi: Some Notes on Identity Clash. *Jew. Soc. Stud.*, 22/1, 1960, p.43–52.

Brothers, J. B.   Social Change and the Role of the Priest. *Soc. Compass*, 10/6, 1963, p.477–89.

Bruder, E. E.   A Clinically Trained Ministry in the Mental Hospital.   *Quart. R. Psychiat. Neurol.*, 2, 1947, p.543–52.

Bruder, E. E.   Training the Mental Hospital Chaplain. *J. Past. Care*, 11, 1957, p.136–45.

Bruder, E. E. (ed.)   The Expanding Role of the Pastor

in Mental Health Work. *Past. Psychol.*, 16/154, 1965, p.5–37.

Burke, F. L. and McCreanor, F. J.   *Training Missionaries for Community Development: A Report on Experiences in Ghana.*   Princeton, New Jersey: Jill de Grazia, 1960, 86p.

Carlough, W. L.   Pastoral Responsibility in Counseling. *Reformed R.*, 17/1, 1963, p.20–5.

Chadwick, N. K.   Shamanism Among the Tartars of Central Asia. *J. Roy. Anthropol. Inst.*, 66, 1936, p.75–112.

Chapman, S. H.   The Minister: Professional Man of the Church. *Soc. Forces*, 23/2, 1944, p.202–6.

Chung, A. C.   The Moral Philosophy of Mencius. *Chinese Cult.*, 4/2, 1962, p.42–70.

Clark, W. K. (ed.)   *The Digest of Research in Religious Speaking.*   1/1, 1963, see other issues.

Coates, C. H. and Kistler, R. C.   Role Dilemmas of Protestant Clergymen in a Metropolitan Community. *R. Rel. Res.*, 6/3, 1965, p.147–52.

Cobb, L. R., *et al.*   Barriers in Pastoral Counseling Research. *Ment. Hyg.*, 49/3, 1965, p.337–40.

The Connecticut Conference on Pastoral Counseling.   Washington, D. C.: U. S. Public Health Service, 1960.

Cotter, J. B. D.   The Monastic Idea in Protestantism Today. *Church Quart. R.*, 1963, p.218–28.

Courtois, V.   On Mullas and Mullaism. *Notes Islam*, 1952, p.102–5.

Cressman, C. P.   Ministers and Marriage Instruction. *Soc. Forces*, 20/3, 1942, p.378–81.

Cumming, E. and Harrington, C.   Clergyman as Counselor. *Amer. J. Sociol.*, 69/3, 1963, p.234–43.

Curran, C. A.   Counseling, Psychotherapy, and the Unified Person. *J. Rel. Health*, 2/2, 1963, p.95–111.

Demal, W.   *Pastoral Psychology in Practice.*   Cork, Ireland: Mercier Publishing Co., 1955, 297p.

Doniger, S. (ed.)   *The Minister's Consultation Clinic: Pastoral Psychology in Action.*   Great Neck, N.Y.: Channel Press, 1955, 316p.

Dorjahn, V. R.   Some Aspects of Temne Divination. *Sierra Leone Bull. Rel.*, 4/1, 1962, p.1–8.

Dubalen, M. T.   *The Worker Priests.*   N.Y.: Student League for Industrial Democracy, 1955, 60p.

Dutt, S.   *Buddhist Monks and Monasteries of India: Their History and Their Contribution to Indian Culture.*   London: Allen & Unwin, 1962, 397p.

Eaton, J. W., *et al.*   *Pastoral Counseling in a Metropolitan*

Suburb. Pittsburgh: Southeastern Community Guidance Association, 1961.

Eaton, J. W., *et al.* Pastoral Counseling in a Metropolitan Suburb. *J. Past. Care*, 17, 1963, p.93–105.

Edgar, G. W. The Chaplain and Mental Hygiene. *Amer. J. Sociol.*, 52/5, 1947, p.420–3.

Eliade, M. *Shamanism: Archaic Techniques of Ecstacy* (Trans. W. R. Trask). Princeton: Princeton Univ. Press, 1964.

Evans, T.Q. The Brethren Pastor: Differential Concepts of An Emerging Role. *J. Sci. Stud. Rel.*, 3/1, 1963, p.43–51.

Farag. F. R. *Sociological and Moral Studies in the Field of Coptic Monasticism.* Leiden: E. J. Brill, 1964, 148p.

Feldman, A. J. *The American Reform Rabbi: A Profile of a Profession.* N.Y.: Bloch Publishing Co., 1965, 242p.

Ferguson, E. Jewish and Christian Ordination: Some Observations. *Harvard Theol. J.*, 56, 1963, p.13–9.

Ferm, V. *A Dictionary of Pastoral Psychology.* N.Y.: Philosophical Library, 1954, 336p.

Fichter, J. H. *Religion as an Occupation: A Study in the Sociology of Professions.* Notre Dame: Univ. of Notre Dame Press, 1961, 295p.

Fichter, J. H. The Religious Professional. *R. Rel. Res.*, 1, 1960, p.89–101, 150–70.

Fortune, R. F. *Sorcerers of Dobu.* London: Routledge & Kegan Paul, 1963, 318p.

Freeman, R. S. J. and Freeman, H. A. *Counseling: A Bibliography (With Annotations).* N.Y.: The Scarecrow Press, 1964, p.71–283.

Geertz, C. The Javanese Kijaji: The Changing Role of a Cultural Broker. *Comp. Stud. Society Hist.*, 2/2, 1960, p.228–50. See also: L. Binder—Comment, p.250–7.

Gelfand, M. *Witch Doctor: Traditional Medicine Man of Rhodesia.* London: Harvill Press, 1964, 191p.

George, K. and George, C. H. Roman Catholic Sainthood and Social Status: A Statistical and Empirical Study. *J. Rel.*, 35/1, 1955, p.85–98.

Giles, E. (ed.) *Documents Illustrating Papal Authority.* Naperville, Illinois: A. R. Allenson, 1952.

Goddijn, H. P. M. The Monastic Community Life in Our Times. *Soc. Compass*, 12/1–2, 1965, p.101–13.

Godin, A. *The Pastor as Counselor* (Trans. B. Philips). N.Y.: Holt, Rinehart, and Winston, 1965, 182p.

Goldstein, S. I. The Roles of an American Rabbi. *Sociol. Soc. Res.*, 38, 1953, p.32–7.

Goodwin, H. M. Marriage Counseling and the Minister. *J. Rel. Health*, 3/2, 1964, p.176–83.

Gross, G. A. and Fritze, H. P. The Function of a Chaplain in Psychotherapy. *Bull. Menninger Clin.*, 16/4, 1952, p.136–41.

Gustafson, J. M. An Analysis of the Problem of the Role of the Minister. *J. Rel.*, 34/3, 1954, p.187–91.

Haeberlin, H. Sbetetda'q: A Shamanistic Performance of the Coast Salish. *Amer. Anthropol.*, 20, 1918, p.249–57.

Hagopian, E. C. The Status and Role of the Marabout in Pre-Protectorate Morroco. *Ethnology*, 3/1, 1964, p.42–52.

Hagstrom, W. O. The Protestant Clergy as a Profession: Status and Prospects. *Berk. Pub. Soc. Inst.*, 3/1, 1957, p.1–12.

Hall, D. The Position of the Chiefs in Northern Rhodesia: Spiritual and Material Leadership in Tribal Life. *Afr. World*, 1959, p.11–2.

Hammond, P. E. and Mitchell, R. E. Segmentation of Radicalism: The Case of the Protestant Campus Minister. *Amer. J. Sociol.*, 71/2, 1965, p.133–43.

Hammond-Tooke, W. D. The Initiation of a Baca Isangoma Diviner. *Afr. Stud.*, 14/1, 1955, p.16–22.

Harper, E. B. Shamanism in South India. *Southw. J. Anthropol.*, 13/3, 1957, p.267–87.

Haycock, B. G. The Kingship of Cush in the Sudan. *Comp. Stud. Society Hist.*, 7/4, 1965, p.461–80.

Henderson, R. W. *The Teaching Office in the Reformed Tradition: A History of the Doctoral Ministry.* Phila.: Westminster Press, 1962, 277p.

Henze, A. *The Pope and the World* (Trans. M. Michael). N.Y.: Viking Press, 1965, 133p.

Hiltner, S. *Clinical Pastoral Training.* N.Y.: Federal Council of Churches of Christ in America, 1945, 176p.

Hiltner, S. and Colston, L. G. *The Context of Pastoral Counseling.* N.Y.: Abingdon Press, 1961, 272p.

Hopkins, L. C. The Shaman or Chinese Wu: His Inspired Dancing and Versatile Character. *J. Roy. Asiatic Society*, 1945, p.3–16, pts. I–II.

Hori, I. Self Mummified Buddhas in Japan. *Hist. Rel.*, 1/2, 1962, p.222–42.

Horton, R. Kalabari Diviners and Oracles. *Odù*, 1/1, 1964, p.3–16.

Illich, I. D. The Pastoral Care of Puerto Rican Migrants in New York. *Soc. Compass*, 5/5–6, 1958, p.256–60.

Jackson, G. F. The Pastoral Counselor: His Identity and Work. *J. Rel. Health*, 3, 1964, p.250–80.

Jammes, J. M. The Social Role of the Priest. *Amer. Cath. Sociol. R.*, 16/2, 1955, p.94–103.

Kagan, M. and Kliger, P. I. An Exploratory Study of Mental Health Workshops for Clergymen. *Proc. W. Va. Acad. Sci.*, 32, 1960, p.201–24.

Kawai, K. The Divinity of the Japanese Emperor. *Polit. Sci.* (Wellington), 10/2, 1958, p.3–14.

King, A. A. *Liturgies of the Religious Orders*. N.Y.: Longmans Green, 1955, 431p.

Klausner, S. Role Adaptation of Pastors and Psychiatrists. *J. Sci. Stud. Rel.*, 4/1, 1964, p.14–39.

Klink, T. W. How the Minister Can Recognize Serious Mental Illness. *Past. Psychol.*, 10, 1959, p.43–8.

Koren, H. J. *The Spiritans: A History of the Congregation of the Holy Ghost*. Pittsburgh: Duquesne Univ. Press, 1958, 641p.

Kosok, P. Astronomy, the Priesthood and the State: New Aspects of Ancient Nazca. *Z. Ethnol.*, 84/1, 1959, p.5–18.

Lamotte, E. *The Spirit of Ancient Buddhism* (Trans. R. Toulmin). Venezia-Roma: Istituto Per La Collaborazione Culturale, 1961, 80p.

Lawton, G. The Psychology of Spiritualist Mediums. *Psychoanal. R.*, 19, 1932, p.418–45.

Leiffer, M. H. *The Role of the District Superintendent in the Methodist Church*. Evanston, Illinois: Bureau of Social & Religious Research, 1960.

Leroi, J. *Monks and Monasteries of the Near East* (Trans. P. Collin). London: George Harrapp and Co., 1963, 208p.

Madigan, F. C. Role Satisfactions and Length of Life in a Close Population. *Amer. J. Sociol.*, 67/6, 1962, p.640–9.

Mehok, W. J. What Do Jesuits Do? *Soc. Compass*, 8/6, 1961, p.567–74.

Mental Health Aspects of Pastoral Counseling. U. S. Public Health Service, Washington, D. C., 1958.

Miller, B. D. The Web of Tibetan Monasticism. *J. Asian Stud.*, 20/2, 1961, p.197–203.

Needham, R. The Left Hand of Mugwe: An Analytical Note on the Structure of Meru Symbolism. *Africa* (London), 30/1, 1960, p.20–33.

Nelson, J. O. Vocation, Theism, and Testing. *Past. Psychol.*, 9/89, 1958, p.33–40.

Nigg, W. *Warriers of God: The Great Religious Orders and Their Founders* (Ed. and Trans. M. Ilford). N.Y.: A. Knopf, 1959, 353p.

Nottingham, J. C. Sorcery Among the Akamba in Kenya. *J. Afr. Adm.*, 11/1, 1959, p.2–14.

Oates, W. E. *Premarital Pastoral Care and Counseling*. Nashville: Broadman Press, 1958, 71p.

Oates, W. E. *Protestant Pastoral Counseling*. Phila.: Westminster Press, 1962, 256p.

Opler, M. E. The Creative Role of Shamanism in Mescalero Apache Mythology. *J. Amer. Folklore*, 59/233, 1946, p.268–81.

Opler, M. E. Notes on Chiricahua Apache Culture: Supernatural Power and the Shaman. *Primitive Man*, 20/1–2, 1947, p.1–14.

Ottenberg, S. Ibo Oracles and Intergroup Relations. *Southw. J. Anthropol.*, 14/3, 1958, p.295–317.

Parsons, R. T. The Missionary and the Cultures of Man. *Int. R. Missions*, 45/178, 1956, p.161–8.

Potter, C. F. *The Great Religious Leaders: A Revision and Updating of "The Story of Religion" in the Light of Recent Discovery and Research Including the Qumran Scrolls*. N.Y.: Simon & Schuster, 1958, 493p.

Radin, P. *The Trickster*. N.Y.: Philosophical Library, 1956, 211p.

Rankin, R. P. The Ministerial Calling and the Minister's Wife. *Past. Psychol.*, 11, 1960, p.16–8, 20–2.

Ribeiro, R. Projective Mechanisms and the Structuralization of Perceptions in Afro-Brazilian Divination. *R. Int. D'Ethnopsychol. Norm. Pathol.*, 1/2, 1956, p.161–81.

Roberts, H. W. The Rural Negro Minister: His Work and Salary. *Rural Sociol.*, 12, 1947, p.285–95.

Roberts, R. G. Mind Over Matter—Magical Performances in the Gilbert Islands. *J. Polynes. Society*, 63/1, 1954, p.17–25.

Robinson, M. E. The Function of the Priest. *Sociol. R.*, 9/1, 1916, p.27–39.

Rohner, K. *Bishops: Their Status and Function*. Baltimore: Helicon Press, 1965, 80p.

Sauneron, S. *The Priests of Ancient Egypt*. N.Y.: Grove Press, 1960, 191p.

Scherer, R. P. New Light on Ministerial Compensation. *Past. Psychol.*, 16/155, 1965, p.45–51.

Schnitzer, J. Rabbis and Counseling: Report on a Project. *Jew. Soc. Stud.*, 20, 1958, p.131–52.

Schumacher, H. C. Mental Hygiene and the Pastoral Ministry. *Cath. Charit. R.*, 22, 1938, p.274–6.

Severn, W. *Magic and Magicians*. N.Y.: D. McKay, 1958, 178p.

Shah, I. *The Secret Lore of Magic: Books of the Sorcerers*. London: F. Muller, 1957, 314p.

Smith, E. A. *The Presbyterian Ministry in American*

Culture: A Study in Changing Concepts 1700–1900. Phila.: Westminster Press, 1962, 269p.

Smith, M. S.   Parish Clergymen's Role Images as Pastoral Counselors. *J. Past. Care*, 14, 1960, p.21–8.

Smith, S. A.   *The American College Chaplaincy.* N.Y.: Association Press, 1954.

Smith, Wilf. C.   Occupational Attitudes and the Minister. *Past. Psychol.*, 14/133, 1963, p.29–34.

Smith, W. J.   Psychoanalysis and Pastoral Counseling. *Amer. Eccles. R.*, 153/2, 1965, p.82–95.

Stycos, J. M.   The Potential Role of Turkish Village Opinion Leaders in a Program of Family Planning. *Pub. Opin. Quart.*, 29/1, 1965, p.120–30.

Sutherland, R. L.   The Pastor and the Mental Health Team. *J. Rel. Health*, 4/1, 1964, p.22–9.

Tavuchis, N.   *Pastors and Immigrants: The Role of a Religious Elite in the Absorption of Norwegian Immigrants.* The Hague: Mouton, 1963.

Thomas, S. F.   Evangelism in the Hospital. *J. Christ. Med. Assoc. India*, 35, 1960, p.352–7.

Thomson, D. F., *et al.*   Medicineman and Sorcerer in Arnhem Land. *Man*, 61, 1961, p.97–102.

Tinque, A. M.   The Minister's Role in Marriage Preparation and Premarital Counseling. *Marr. Fam. Liv.*, 20/1, 1958, p.11–7.

Tonna, B.   The Allocation of Time Among Clerical Activities: A Study of a Brussels Parish. *Soc. Compass*, 10/1, 1963, p.93–106.

Turner, V. W.   *Ndembu Divination: Its Symbolism and Techniques.* Manchester: Manchester Univ. Press, 1961, 85p.

Von Fürer-Haimendorf, C.   The Role of the Monastery in Sherpa Society. *Ethnologica*, 2, 1960, p.12–28.

Voss, L. E.   Using a Religious Counselor in an Institution. *J. Past. Care*, 12, 1958, p.94–8.

Wach, J.   Master and Disciple: Two Religio-Sociological Studies. *J. Rel.*, 42/1, 1962, p.1–21.

Wade, A. L. and Berremen, J. V.   Are Ministers Qualified for Marriage Counseling? *Sociol. Soc. Res.*, 35/2, 1950, p.106–12.

Wagoner, W. D.   *Bachelor of Divinity: Uncertain Servants in Seminary and Ministry.* N.Y.: Association Press, 1964.

Waley, A.   *The Nine Songs: A Study of Shamanism in Ancient China.* London: Allen & Unwin, 1955, 64p.

Wallace, W. J. and Taylor, E. S.   Hupa Sorcery. *Southw. J. Anthropol.*, 6/2, 1950, p.188–96.

Ware, J. T.   An Aspect of Pastoral Theology. *Ment. Hyg.*, 21/1, 1937, p.30–45.

Waterman, M. L.   Pastoral Decision: To Counsel or Refer. *J. Past. Care*, 14, 1960, p.34–8.

Weiner, H.   Billy Graham: Respectable Evangelism. *Commentary*, 24/3, 1957, p.257–62.

Welch, H. H.   The Chang T'ien Shik and Taoism in China. *J. Orient. Stud.*, 4, 1957–58, p.188–212.

West, C. C.   *Communism and the Theologians.* N.Y.: Macmillan, 1963, 399p.

Williams, M. O., Jr.   The Psychological-Psychiatric Appraisal of Candidates for Missionary Service. *Past. Psychol.*, 9/84, 1958, p.41–4.

Williams, T. J. and Campbell, A. W.   *The Park Village Sisterhood.* London: S P C K, 1965, 174p.

Wise, C. A.   The Clergy and Community Education for Mental Hygiene. *Ment. Hyg.*, 25/1, 1941, p.30–42.

Wise, C. A.   *Pastoral Counseling.* N.Y.: Harper, 1951, 231p.

Wise, C. A. (ed.)   The Ministry as a Vocation. *Past. Psychol.*, 9/89, 1958, p.7–54.

Wolcott, L.   Missionary Training: The Commercial Non-Academic Orientation. *Int. R. Miss.*, 49, 1960, p.410–4.

Wynn, J. and Hunt, J.   Experiment of a Family Casework Agency as a Training Source for Pastoral Counseling. *Marr. Fam. Liv.*, 4/4, 1962, p.381–3.

Younghusband, F.   Lamaism in Tibet. *Sociol. R.*, 4/2, 1911, p.98–109.

See Also:

Holman, C. T.   4g
Hoyles, A. J.   5g
Kenton, E.   5e2
Kincheloe, S.   6d
Kittler, G. D.   5e
Klein, D. C.   5b1
Leach, W.   4b
Lehrman, N. S.   1e
McCabe, A. R.   1g
McDonnell, K.   1e
McGreal, M. N.   4g4
National Peace Congress   5d
O'Doherty, E. F.   5b1
Posinsky, S. H.   2h4
Roftis, J.   4b

Roger, L.   5b1
Salem, E.   6c
Schroeder, W. W.   7b2
Scully, A. W.   5b1
Sheehy, M. S.   4g
Stubblefield, H. W.   5b1 (2)
Sullivan R. E.   5e
Swihart, A. K.   3a1
Textor, R. B.   8a1
Turner, H. W.   4g3
Van Hardenberg, P.   5e
Wheeler, W. F.   1e
Wilder, A. N.   6d
Wilson, M.   4a1

7a2.   As a Believer

Bokser, B. Z.   Codes of the American Rabbinate. *Ann. Amer. Acad. Polit. Soc. Sci.*, 297, 1955, p.59–63.

Furfey, P. H.   The Code of the Catholic Clergy. *Ann. Amer. Acad. Polit. Soc. Sci.*, 297, 1955, p.64–69.

Harmon, N. B.   Ethics of the Protestant Clergy. *Ann. Amer. Acad. Polit. Soc. Sci.*, 297, 1955, p.70–75.

Holland, J. B. and Loomis, C. P.   Goals of Rural Ministers. *Sociometry*, 11/3, 1948, p.217–29.

Kling, F. R.   Value Structures and the Minister's Purpose. *Past. Psychol.*, 12/112, 1961, p.13–23.

Lobsang, R. T.   *The Third Eye: The Autobiography of a Tibetan Lama.*   London: Secker and Warburg, 1956, 256p.

O'Donovan, T. R. and Deegan, A. X.   A Comparative Study of the Orientations of a Selected Group of Church Executives. *Sociol. Soc. Res.*, 48/3, 1964, p.330–39.

Smith, L. M.   The Clergy: Authority Structure, Ideology, and Migration. *Amer. Sociol. R.*, 18, 1953, p.242–48.

Southard, S.   Faithful Commitment to the Ministry. *Past. Psychol.*, 14/139, 1963, p.31–36.

Strunk, O., Jr.   Men, Motives and the Ministry. *Rel. Educ.*, 54, 1959, p.429–34.

Strunk, O., Jr.   Theological Students: A Study in Perceived Motive. *Personnel Guid. J.*, 36, 1958, 320–22.

Torbet, R. G.   The Discipline of Ministers. *Foundations*, 4, 1961, 321–31.

Vollmer, H. M.   Member Commitment and Competence in Religious Orders. *Berkeley Pub. Soc. Instit.*, 3/1, 1957, p.13–26.

Zeitlin, J.   *Disciples of the Wise: The Opinions of American Rabbis.*   N.Y.: Teachers College, Columbia University, 1945, 233p.

See Also:

Beach, W.   5a2
Blum, B. S.   5a3
Johnson, G. B., Jr.   4a2
Raab, E.   5a2
Schneider, H. W.   6e
Smith, M.   8b
Upadhye, A. N.   4g2
Williams, R. M., Jr.   5a2

7a3.   Beliefs Related to Religion

Burchard, W. W.   Role Conflicts of Military Chaplains. *Amer. Sociol. R.*, 19, 1954, p.528–35.

Campbell, E. Q. and Pettigrew, T. P.   *Christians in Racial Crisis: A Study of the Little Rock Ministry.* Washington, D. C.: Public Affairs Press, 1959.

Campbell, E. Q. and Pettigrew, T. P.   Racial and Moral Crisis: The Role of the Little Rock Ministers. *Amer. J. Sociol.*, 64/5, 1959, p.509–16.

Clark, H.   Churchmen and Residential Segregation. *R. Rel. Res.*, 5/3, 1964, p.157–64.

Conroy, T. M.   The Ku Klux Klan and the American Clergy. *Amer. Eccles. R.*, 70, 1924, p.47–58.

Davis, J.   The Social Action Pattern of the Protestant Religious Leader. *Amer. Sociol. R.*, 1, 1936, p.105–14.

Donnelly, J. F.   The Junior Clergy Look at Organized Labor. *Amer. Eccles. R.*, 115/1, 1946, p.1–10.

Ferguson, L. W. Socio–Psychological Correlates of the Primary Attitude Scales. I. Religionism; II. Humanitarianism. *J. Soc. Psychol.*, 19, 1944, p.81–98.

Fulton, R. L. The Clergyman and the Funeral Director: A Study in Role Conflict. *Soc. Forces*, 39/4, 1961, p.317–23.

Hamelin, L. Numerical Secular Evolution of the Catholic Clergy in Quebec. *Rech. Sociog.*, 212, 1961, p.189–241.

Hattori, V. Confucius' Conviction of His Heavenly Mission. *Harvard J. Asiat. Stud.*, 1, 1936, p.96–108.

Landis, B. Y. A Survey of Official Church Statements on Alcoholic Beverages. *Quart. J. Stud. Alcohol*, 6, 1946, p.515–39.

Larson, R. F. Psychiatric Orientations of a Selected Sample of New England Clergy. *Ment. Hyg.*, 49/3, 1965, p.341–6.

Mueller, G. E. Calvin's Institutes of the Christian Religion as an Illustration of Christian Thinking. *J. Hist. Ideas*, 4/3, 1943, p.287–300.

Muntz, E. E., Jr. Opinions of Divinity and Law Students on Social Class. *J. Educ. Sociol.*, 34/5, 1961, p.221–9.

Nelson, W. S. (ed.) The Christian Abby in Race Relations. N.Y.: Harper, 1948, 256p.

Oehrtman, M. L. Chaplaincy Service for the Mentally Retarded. *Amer. J. Ment. Defic.*, 60, 1955, p.253–7.

Pugh, T. J. A Comparative Study of the Values of a Group of Ministers and Two Groups of Laymen. *J. Soc. Psychol.*, 33/2, 1951, p.225–35.

Rafton, H. P. *The Roman Catholic Church and Democracy: The Teachings of Pope Leo XIII.* Boston: Beacon Press, 1951.

Rankin, H. W. Political Values of the American Missionary. *Amer. J. Sociol.*, 13/2, 1907, p.145–82.

Webb, N. J. and Kobler, F. J. Clinical-Empirical Techniques for Assessing the Attitudes of Religious Toward Psychiatry. *J. Soc. Psychol.*, 55, 1961, p.245–51.

Wolch, C. How Ontario Clergy Look at Alcoholism: Denominational or Individual Differences Revealed by Study of Experience and Views. *Alcoholism Res.*, 4/4, 1957, p.1–7.

See Also:

7a4.   Social Psychological Background

Allen, P. J. Childhood Backgrounds of Success in a Profession. *Amer. Sociol. R.*, 20/2, 1955, p.186–90.

Bainton, R. H. *Yale and the Ministry: A History of Education for the Christian Ministry at Yale From the Founding in 1701.* N.Y.: Harper & Brothers, 1957, 297p.

Beaven, A. W. Should Theological Seminaries Prepare Their Students to Deal With Parish Family Problems? *J. Educ. Sociol.*, 8/8, 1939, p.489–504.

Bonacker, R. D. Clinical Pastoral Training for the Pastoral Ministry: Problems and Methods. *J. Past. Care*, 14, 1960, p.1–12.

Booth, G. Unconscious Motivation in the Choice of the Ministry as a Profession. *Past. Psychol.*, 9/89, 1958, p.18–24.

Bowers, M. K., *et al.* Therapeutic Implications of Analytic Group Psychotherapy of Religious Personnel. *Int. J. Group Psychother.*, 8, 1958, p.243–56.

Bruder, E. E. Some Theoretical Considerations in Clinical Pastoral Education. *J. Past. Care*, 8, 1954, p.135–46.

Bruder, E. E. and Barb, M. L. A Survey of Ten Years of Clinical Pastoral Training at Saint Elizabeth's Hospital. *J. Past. Care*, 10, 1956, p.86–94.

Cash, W. L. The Relationship of Personality Traits and Scholastic Aptitude to Academic Achievement in Theological Studies. *J. Psychol. Stud.*, 13, 1962, p.105–10.

Christensen, C. W. The Occurrence of Mental Illness in the Ministry: Personality Disorders. *J. Past. Care*, 17, 1963, p.125–35.

Cockrum, L. V. Personality Traits and Interests of Theological Students. *Rel. Educ.*, 47, 1952, p.28–32.

Comfort, R. O. Survey of Activities and Training of Selected Rural Ministers in the United States. *Rural Sociol.*, 12/4, 1947, p.374–87.

Culver, D. W. and Bridston, K. R. *Pre-Seminary Education: Report of the Lilly Endowment Study.* Minneapolis: Augsburg Publishing House, 1965.

Cunninggim, M. Changing Emphases in the Seminary Curriculum. *J. Bib. Rel.*, 23, 1955, p.110–8.

Cuthbert, M. Anthropology in Mission Training. *Pract. Anthropol.*, 12/2, 1965, p.119–22.

David-Neel, A. *Initiations and Initiates in Tibet.* N.Y.: University Books, 1959, 222p.

Davies, H. Ministers of To-Morrow, Their Duties and Training. *Hibbert J.*, 48/3, 1950, p.226–30.

Devereaux, G. Dream Learning and Individual Ritual Differences in Mohave Shamanism. *Amer. Anthropol.*, 59, 1957, p.1036–45.

Dittes, J. E. Research on Clergymen: Factors Influencing Decisions for Religious Service and Effectiveness in the Vocation. *Rel. Educ.*, 57/4, 1962, p.141–65.

Doerr, H. Sociology in the Major Seminary. *Amer. Cath. Sociol. R.*, 13/1, 1952, p.31–8.

Donovan, J. D. The American Catholic Hierarchy: A Social Profile. *Amer. Cath. Sociol. R.*, 19/2, 1958, p.98–112.

Felton, R. A. *New Ministers.* Madison, New Jersey: Drew Theological Seminary, 1949.

Gynther, M. D. and Kempson, J. O. Personal and Interpersonal Changes in Clinical Pastoral Training. *J. Past. Care*, 12, 1958, p.210–9.

Gynther, M. D. and Kempson, J. O. Seminarians and Clinical Pastoral Training: A Follow-up Study. *J. Soc. Psychol.*, 56, 1962, p.9–14.

Hall, J. O. A Note on the Relationship Between Attitudes Toward the Scientific Method and the Background of Seminarians. *Soc. Forces*, 39, 1960, p.49–52.

Hammer, H. M. A Ministerial Training Program in Community Mental Health. *Ment. Hyg.*, 49/4, 1965, p.520–4.

Harrower, M. Mental Health Potential and Success in the Ministry. *J. Rel. Health*, 4/1, 1964, p.30–58.

Harrower, M. Psychological Tests in the Unitarian Universalist Ministry. *J. Rel. Health*, 2/2, 1963, p.129–42.

Herr, V. V., *et al. Screening Candidates for the Priesthood and the Religious Life.* Chicago: Loyola Univ. Press, 1962, 230p.

Jamison, W. G. Predicting Academic Achievement of Seminary Students. *R. Rel. Res.*, 6/2, 1965, p.90–6.

Johnson, E. H. Personality and Religious Work: Results of the Berneuter Personality Inventory Given to Societies of Religion. *Amer. J. Orthopsychiat.*, 12, 1942, p.317–23.

Johnson, E. J. An Approach to Intergroup Relations in the Theological Seminary Program. *J. Intergr. Relat.*, 1/3, 1960, p.37–40.

Kerins, J. L. Sociology in the Major Seminary: The Program at Mt. St. Alphonsus Seminary. *Amer. Cath. Sociol. R.*, 13/1, 1952, p.25–31.

Kobler, F. J. Screening Applicants for Religious Life. *J. Rel. Health*, 3/2, 1964, p.161–70.

Koehler, J. G. The Minister as a Family Man. *Past. Psychol.*, 11, 1960, p.11–5.

Larson, R. F. Social and Cultural Characteristics of a Selected Sample of New England Clergymen. *R. Rel. Res.*, 6/3, 1965, p.131–7.

Lee, J. M. and Putz, L. J. (eds.) *Seminary Education in a Time of Change.* Notre Dame, Indiana: Fides Publishers, Inc., 1965, 590p.

Lincoln, C. E. Extremist Attitudes in the Black Muslim Government. *J. Soc. Issues*, 19/2, 1963, p.75–84.

Madeleva, M. The Preparation of Teachers of Religion. *Bull. Cath. Educ. Assoc.*, 46/1, 1949, p.202–4.

Maehr, M. L. and Stake, R. E. The Value Patterns of Men Who Voluntarily Quit Seminary Training. *Personnel Guid. J.*, 40, 1962, p.537–40.

Martin, J. A., Jr. The Graduate Study of Religion in a Seminary Environment. *J. Bib. Rel.*, 31/4, 1963, p.320–8.

Meng, H. Was Buddha Schizophrenic? *Psyche* (Stuttgart), 16/6, 1962, p.374–7.

Moscheles, J. Social Geography and Its Desirability in Schools of Divinity. *Sociol. R.*, 22/4, 1930, p.309–14.

Moss, B. S. *Clergy Training Today.* London: SPCK, 1964, 87p.

Muelder, W. G. Recruitment of Negroes for Theological Studies. *R. Rel. Res.*, 5/3, 1964, p.152–6.

Murray, J. C. Personality Study of Priests and Seminarians. *Homil. Pastoral R.*, 49, 1958, p.443–7.

Naegele, K. D. Clergymen, Teachers and Psychiatrists: A Study in Roles and Socialization. *Canad. J. Econ. Polit. Sci.*, 22/1, 1956, p.46–62.

Oates, W. E. (ed.) *The Minister's Own Mental Health.* Great Neck, N.Y.: Channel Press, 1955.

O'Donovan, T. R. and Deegan, A. X. Some Career Determinants of Church Executives. *Sociol. Soc. Res.*, 48/1, 1963, p.58–68.

Palmieri, F. A. The Ecclesiastical Training of the Russian Clergy. *Amer. Cath. Quart. R.*, 43, 1918, p.529–42.

Roberts, H. W. The Rural Negro Minister: His Personal and Social Characteristics. *Soc. Forces*, 27/3, 1949, p.291–300.

Sinha, S. Training of a Bhumij Medicine-Man. *Man India*, 38/2, 1958, p.111–28.

Smith, R. O. Personality and Cultural Factors Affecting

the Religion of One Hundred and Forty Divinity Students. *Rel. Educ.*, 43, 1948, p.106–11.

Southard, S.   The Spiritual Development of Successful Students. *J. Rel. Health*, 4/2, 1965, p.154–63.

Stanley, G.   Personality and Attitude Characteristics of Fundamentalist Theological Students. *Australian J. Psychol.*, 15/2, 1963, p.121–3.

Webb, S. C. and Goodling, R. A.   Test Validity in a Methodist Theology School. *Educ. Psychol. Meas.*, 18, 1958, p.859–66.

Webb, S. C., *et al.*   The Prediction of Field Work Ratings in a Theological School. *Rel. Educ.*, 53, 1958, p.534–8.

Webber, G. W.   Recruiting for the Protestant Ministry. *Christ. Cent.*, 70/17, 1953, p.504–6.

Whitlock, G. E.   Role and Self Concepts in the Choice of the Ministry as a Vocation. *J. Past. Care*, 17, 1963, p.208–12.

Wilson, C. R. and Brown, J. E.   Psychologists, Religious Superiors, and Candidates. *Amer. Eccles. R.*, 153/3, 1965, p.155–76.

Zax, M., *et al.*   A Comparative Study of Novice Nuns and College Females Using the Response Set Approach. *J. Abnorm. Soc. Psychol.*, 66/4, 1963, p.369-75.

See Also:

7b.   *The Parishioner*

Bender, I. E.   Changes in Religious Interest: A Retest After Fifteen Years. *J. Abnorm. Soc. Psychol.*, 57/1, 1958, p.41–6.

Benney, M. W., *et al.*   Christmas in an Apartment Hotel. *Amer. J. Sociol.*, 65/3, 1959, p.233–40.

Devolder, P. N.   Inquiry Into the Religious Life of Catholic Intellectuals. *J. Soc. Psychol.*, 28/1, 1948, p.39–56.

Godin, A.   Belonging to a Church: What Does it Mean Psychologically? *J. Sci. Stud. Rel.*, 3/2, 1964, p.204–15.

Greenberg, M.   Social Characteristics of the Jewish Students at the University of Maryland. *Jew. Soc. Stud.*, 23/1, 1961, p.21–37.

Grumelli, A.   Religious Behavior of Migrants. *Int. Migration Digest*, 2/2, 1965, p.158–64.

Hansen, H. H.   *Daughters of Allah: Among Muslim Women in Kurdistan.* London: Allen & Unwin, 1960, 192p.

Hsu, F. L. K.   *Under the Ancestor's Shadow: Chinese Culture and Personality.*   N.Y.: Columbia Univ. Press, 1948.

Hyma, A.   *The Brethren of the Common Life.*   Grand Rapids: Wm. B. Erdmans Publishing Co., 1950, 222p.

Koppers, W.   *Primitive Man and His World Picture* (Trans. E. Raybould). London: Sheed & Ward, 1952, 264p.

Krueger, E. T.   Negro Religious Expression. *Amer. J. Sociol.*, 38, 1932, p.22–31.

Landis, B. Y.   The Church and Religious Activity. *Amer. J. Sociol.*, 40/6, 1935, p.780–7.

Levinson, B. M.   The Problems of Jewish Religious Youth. *Genet. Psychol. Monogr.*, 60, 1959, p.309–48.

London, I. D. and Poltoratzky, N. P.   Contemporary Religious Sentiments in the Soviet Union. *Psychol. Rep.*, 3/1, 1957, p.113–30.

Neill, S. C. and Weber, H. R.   *The Layman in Christian History: A Project of the Department of the Laity of the World Council of Churches.* Phila.: Westminster Press, 1963, 408p.

Nowlan, E. H.   The Picture of the "Catholic" Which Emerges From Attitude Tests. *Lumen Vitae*, 12, 1957, p.275–85.

Radin, P.   The Religious Experiences of An American Indian. *Eranos Jahrbuch*, Bd. 18, 1950, p.249–90.

Salisbury, W. S.   Faith, Ritualism, Charismatic Leadership and Religious Behavior. *Soc. Forces*, 34/3, 1956, p.241–5.

Shapiro, J.   The Jewish Community and the Synagogue in Perspective. *J. Jew. Commun. Serv.*, 33/1, 1956, p.25–35.

Shuttleworth, F. K.   The Influence of Early Religious Home Training on Sophomore Men. *Rel. Educ.*, 2, 1927, p.57–60.

Strommen, M. *Profiles of Church Youth: Report of a Four-Year Study of 3,000 High School Lutherans.* St. Louis: Concordia Publishing House, 1963.

Stunkard, A. Some Interpersonal Aspects of an Oriental Religion. *Psychiatry,* 14, 1951, p.419–31.

Sturges, H. A. Methods of Comparing Orthodoxy and Piety. *Amer. Sociol R.,* 2, 1937, p.372–9.

Telford, C. W. A Study of Religious Attitudes. *J. Soc. Psychol.,* 31/2, 1950, p.217–30.

Thornman, D. J. *The Emerging Layman: The Role of the Catholic Layman in America.* Garden City: Doubleday, 1962, 234p.

Webb, S. C. An Exploratory Investigation of Some Needs Met Through Religious Behavior. *J. Sci. Stud. Rel.,* 5/1, 1965, p.51–8.

Wells, W. R. Religious Belief and the Population Question. *Amer. J. Psychol.,* 31, 1920, p.204–7.

Wilson, C. L. A Social Picture of a Congregation. *Amer. Sociol. R.,* 10, 1945, p.418–22.

Zegwaard, G. A. Headhunting Practices of the Asmat of Netherlands New Guinea. *Amer. Anthropol.,* 61/6, 1959, p.1020–41.

See Also: 4, 5b, 5f, 5g

Burchinal, L. G. 4f
Casey, T. J. 5b2
Fairchild, R. W. 4e
Fichter, J. H. 4h, 7a
Godin, A. (ed.) 4h
Hatch, D. L. 4e
Heiermann, F. 4h
Hulett, J. E., Jr. 4e
Jaffe, N. 4d
Kammer, E. J. 4f2
Kaplan, S. 5a3
Kevane, R. A. 5e2
MacIver, R. M. 5f
Murphy, R. J. 5b2
Nimkoff, M. 5a3
O'Dea, T. 4f
Sorokin, P. A. 4f
Sulloway, A. N. 5b2
Thomas, J. L. 4e
Trimble, W. R. 5a2
Ward, C. 7a (2)
Wenger, S. B. 5g
Woolston, H. B. 5a3

7b1. As a Church-Goer

Alland, A., Jr. "Possession" in a Revivalist Negro Church. *J. Sci. Stud. Rel.,* 1/2, 1962, p.204–13.

Anders, S. F. Religious Behavior of Church Families. *Marr. Fam. Liv.,* 17/1, 1955, p.54–7.

Anderson, G. C. Medieval Medicine for Sin. *J. Rel. Health,* 2/2, 1963, p.156–65.

Arlow, J. A. A Psychoanalytic Study of a Religious Initiation Rite: Bar Mitzvah. In *The Psychoanalytic Study of the Child.* N.Y.: International Universities Press, 6, 1951, p.353–74.

Backman, E. L. *Religious Dances in the Christian Church and in Popular Medicine.* London: Allen & Unwin, 1952.

Baron, R. R. V. The Measurement of Religious Observance Amongst Jews. *Jew. J. Sociol.,* 6/1, 1964, p.81–90.

Branford, V. The Purpose of Liturgy. *Sociol. R.,* 20/1, 1928, p.1–17.

Bultena, L. Church Membership and Church Attendance in Madison (Wisconsin). *Amer. Sociol. R.,* 14/3, 1949, p.384–9.

Confraternity of Christian Doctrine. *The Confraternity Comes of Age: A Historical Symposium.* Paterson, N.Y.: Confraternity Press, 1956, 310p.

Cowhig, J. D. Marginal Church Participants. *Sociol. Soc. Res.,* 25/1, 1940, p.57–62.

Dimock, E. C., Jr. Doctrine and Practice Among the Vaisnavas of Bengal. *Hist. Rel.,* 3/1, 1963, p.106–27.

Dynes, R. R. Rurality, Migration, and Sectarianism. *Rural Sociol.,* 21, 1956, p.25–8.

Eder, M. D. The Jewish Phylacteries and Other Jewish Ritual Observances. *Int. J. Psychoanal.,* 14, 1933, p.341–75.

Fichter, J. H. The Marginal Catholic: An Institutional Approach. *Soc. Forces,* 32/2, 1953, p.167–73.

Frerking, K. Religious Participation of Lutheran Students. *R. Rel. Res.,* 6/3, 1965, p.153–62.

Fukuyama, Y. The Major Dimensions of Church Membership. *R. Rel. Res.,* 2/4, 1961, p.154–61.

Greeley, A. M. The Religious Behavior of Graduate Students. *J. Sci. Stud. Rel.,* 5/1, 1965, p.34–40.

Greinacher, N. The Development of Applications to Leave the Church and the Transfer from one Church to Another, and Its Causes. *Soc. Compass,* 8/1, 1961, p.61–72.

Harne, E. P. and Stender, W. H. Student Attitudes Toward Religious Practices. *J. Soc. Psychol.,* 22/2, 1945, p.215–7.

Hogan, W. F. The Layman in Institutions of Religious. *R. for Rel.*, 23, 1964, p.27–32.

Horowitz, M. M. The Worship of South Indian Dieties in Martinque. *Ethnology*, 2/3, 1963, p.339–46.

Hostetler, J. A. and Mather, W. G. *Participation in the Rural Church.* University Park: Pennsylvania State Univ. Agricultural Extension Service Paper, no. 1762, Oct., 1952.

Kelly, G. A. *Catholics and the Practice of the Faith: A Census Study of the Diocese of St. Augustine.* Washington: Catholic Univ. Press, 1946, 224p.

Kingsbury, F. A. Why Do People Go to Church? *Rel. Educ.*, 32, 1937, p.50–4.

Kosa, J. and Schommer, C. O. Religious Participation, Religious Knowledge and Scholastic Aptitude: An Empirical Study. *J. Sci. Stud. Rel.*, 1/1, 1961, p.88–97.

Kreieger, E. T. Negro Religious Expression. *Amer. J. Sociol.*, 38/1, 1932, p.22–31.

Lazerwitz, B. Membership in Voluntary Associations and Frequency of Church Attendance. *J. Sci. Stud. Rel.*, 2/1, 1962, p.74–84.

Lazerwitz, B. Some Factors Associated With Variations in Church Attendance. *Soc. Forces*, 39, 1961, p.301–9.

Lipset, S. M. Religion in America: What Religious Revival? *R. Rel. Res.*, 1/1, 1959, p.17–24.

Means, R. L. Intellectuals Within the Church. *Rel. Educ.*, 55, 1960, p.341–4.

Obenhaus, V., *et al.* Church Participation Related to Social Class and Type of Center. *Rural Sociol.*, 23/3, 1958, p.298–308.

Parrinder, E. G. *Worship in the World's Religions.* London: Faber & Faber, 1961, 239p.

Photiadis, J. D. and Johnson, A. L. Orthodoxy, Church Participation and Authoritarianism. *Amer. J. Sociol.*, 69/3, 1963, p.244–8.

Pickering, W. S. F. "Religious Movements" of Church Members in Two Working Class Towns in England. *Archiv. Sociol. Rel.*, 6/11, 1961, p.129–40.

Poit, C. H. A Study Concerning Religious Belief and Denominational Affiliation. *Rel. Educ.*, 57, 1962, p.214–6.

Reik, T. *Ritual: Four Psychoanalytic Studies* (Trans. D. Bryan). N.Y.: Grove, 1962, 367p.

Rubinstein, J. Jewish Day of Atonement Census Studies. *R. Rel. Res.*, 5/1, 1963, p.30–9.

Schulyer, J. B. Religious Observance Differentials by Age and Sex in Northern Parish. *Amer. Cath. Sociol. R.*, 20/2, 1959, p.124–31.

Schulyer, J. B. The Role of the Laity in the Catholic Church. *Amer. Cath. Sociol. R.*, 20/4, 1959, p.290–307.

Somanader, S. V. O. Penances in Hindu Temples. *Ceylon Today*, 7/7, 1958, p.9–14.

Tampy, K. P. P. Religion and Worship of Kadar. *Ind. Folklore*, 2/1, 1959, p.48–50.

Verger, P. Trance States in Orisha Worship. *Odù*, 9, 1964, p.13–20.

Wakefield, G. S. *Puritan Devotion: Its Place in the Development of Christian Piety.* London: Epworth Press, 1957, 170p.

Werblowsky, R. J. Z. Zwi-Mystical and Magical Contemplation: The Kabbalists in Sixteenth Century Safed. *Hist. Rel.*, 1/1, 1961, p.9–36.

Werbner, R. P. Atonement Ritual and Guardian Spirit Possession Among Kalanga. *Africa*, 34/3, 1964, p.206–23.

Zimmer, B. G. and Hawley, A. H. Suburbanization and Church Participation. *Soc. Forces*, 37/4, 1959, p.348–54.

Zubrzycki, J. Social Participation and Primary Group Affiliation: A Case Study of a Dutch Group in Australia. *Sociologus*, 15/1, 1965, p.32–44.

See Also:

Allport, G. W., *et al.* The Religion of the Post-War College Student. *J. Psychol.*, 25, 1948, p.3–33.

Amara, I. B. Possession: Its Nature and Some Modes. *Sierra Leone Bull. Rel.*, 6/2, 1964, p.1–12.

Aubrey, E. E. The Authority of Religious Experience. *J. Rel.*, 12, 1933, p.433–49.

Bardis, P. D. Religiosity Among Jewish Students in a Metropolitan Community. *Sociol. Soc. Res.*, 49/1, 1964, p.90–5.

Braden, C. S. Why People Are Religious: A Study in Religious Motivation. *J. Bib. Rel.*, 15, 1947, p.38–45.

Breen, W. E., Jr. A Factor Analytic Study of Religious Attitudes. *J. Abnorm. Soc. Psychol.*, 54/2, 1957, p.176–9.

Brown, L. B. A Study of Religious Belief. *Brit. J. Psychol.*, 53, 1962, p.259–72.

Brown, L. B. Classifications of Religious Orientation. *J. Sci. Stud. Rel.*, 4/1, 1964, p.91–9.

Chaplin, D. P. *Children and Religion.* N.Y.: Scribners, 1961, 238p.

Cline, V. B. and Richards, J. M., Jr. A Factor Analytic Study of Religious Belief and Behavior. *J. Person. Soc. Psychol.*, 1/6, 1965, p.569–78.

Covington, G. E. *What They Believe: A Survey of Religious Faith Among Groups of College Students.* N.Y.: Philosophical Library, 1956, 109p.

DeJong, G. Religious Fundamentalism, Socio-Economic Status and Fertility Attitudes in the Southern Appalachians. *Demography*, 2, 1965, p.540–8.

Dudycha, G. J. The Religious Beliefs of College Freshman in 1930 and 1949. *Rel. Educ.*, 45, 1950, p.165–9.

Elkind, D. The Child's Conception of his Religious Denomination: I—The Jewish Child. *J. Gen. Psychol.*, 99, 1961, p.209–25.

Elkind, D. The Child's Conception of his Religious Denomination: II—The Catholic Child. *J. Gen. Psychol.*, 101, 1962, p.185–93.

Elkind, D. The Child's Conception of his Religious Denomination: III—The Protestant Child. *J. Gen. Psychol.*, 103, 1963, p.291–304.

Elkind, D. and Elkind, S. Varieties of Religious Experience in Young Adolescents. *J. Sci. Stud. Rel.*, 2/1, 1962, p.102–12.

Ellspermann, C. Knowledge of Catholic Social Teaching Among Forty-Five Catholic Industrial Workers. *Amer. Cath. Sociol. R.*, 17/1, 1956, p.10–23.

Evans-Pritchard, E. E. The Meaning of Sacrifice Among the Nuer. *J. Roy. Anthropol. Inst.*, 84/1–2, 1954, p.21–33.

Ferguson, L. W. The Sociological Validity of Primary Social Attitude Scale No. 1: Religionism. *J. Soc. Psychol.*, 23/2, 1946, p.197–204.

Ferm, V. (ed.) *The Protestant Credo.* N.Y.: Philosophical Library, 1953, 241p.

Fife, A. and Fife, A. *Saints of Sage and Saddle: Folklore Among the Mormons.* Bloomington: Indiana Univ. Press, 1956, 367p.

Ford, T. R. Religious Thought and Beliefs in the Southern Appalachians as Revealed in an Attitude Survey. *R. Rel. Res.*, 3/1, 1961, p.2–21.

From Religious Experience to a Religious Attitude. *Lumen Vitae*, 19/2, 1964, p.191–348.

Furfey, P. H. Personalistic Social Action in the Rerum Novarum and Quadragesimo Anno. *Amer. Cath. Sociol. R.*, 2/3, 1941, p.204–16.

Gilliland, A. R. Changes in Religious Beliefs of College Students. *J. Soc. Psychol.*, 37, part I, 1953, p.113–6.

Glock, C. Y. On the Study of Religious Commitment. *Rel. Educ.*, 42, 1962, p.98–110.

Gruber, A. Differences in Religious Evaluation of Adolescent Boys and Girls. *Lumen Vitae*, 12, 1957, p.301–12.

Gustavson, C. G. German Lutheranism: A Psychological Study. *J. Hist. Ideas*, 11/2, 1950, p.140–58.

Harris, G. Possession "Hysteria" in a Kenya Tribe. *Amer. Anthropol.*, 59, 1957, p.1046–66.

Hassenger, R. Varieties of Religious Orientation. *Sociol. Anal.*, 25/4, 1964, p.189–99.

Havens, J. A Study of Religious Conflict in College Students. *J. Soc. Psychol.*, 64/1, 1964, p.77–87.

Highet, J. Scottish Religious Adherence. *Brit. J. Sociol.*, 4/2, 1953, p.147–59.

Jackson, A. K. Religious Beliefs and Expressions of the Southern Highlander. *R. Rel. Res.*, 3/1, 1961, p.21–39.

Jacobsen, T. Toward the Image of Tammuz. *Hist. Rel.*, 1/2, 1962, p.189–213.

Keedy, T. C., Jr. Anomie and Religious Orthodoxy. *Sociol. Soc. Res.*, 43/1, 1958, p.34–7.

Kelsey, M. T. *Tongue Speaking: An Experiment in Spiritual Experience.* N.Y.: Doubleday and Co., 1964, 252p.

Kiev, A. Psychotherapeutic Aspects of Pentacostal Sects

Among West Indian Immigrants to England. *Brit. J. Sociol.*, 15/2, 1964, p.129–38.

Kitay, P. M. *Radicalism and Conservatism Toward Conventional Religion.* N.Y.: Teachers College, Columbia Univ. Press, 1947.

Klausner, J. *The Messianic Idea in Israel: From Its Beginning to the Completion of the Mishnah* (Trans. W. F. Stinespring). London: Allen & Unwin, 1956, 543p.

Kondo, A. Intuition in Zen Buddhism. *Amer. J. Psychoanal.*, 12, 1952, p.10–4.

Kuhlen, R. G. and Arnold, M. Age Difference in Religious Beliefs and Problems During Adolescence. *J. Genet. Psychol.*, 65, 1944, p.291–300.

LaBarre, W. Primitive Psychotherapy in Native American Cultures: Peyotism and Confession. *J. Abnorm. Soc. Psychol.*, 42, 1947, p.294–309.

Lang, K. and Lang, G. E. Decisions for Christ: Billy Graham in New York City. In M. Stein, *et al.—Identity and Anxiety: Survival of the Person in Mass Society.* N.Y.: Free Press, 1960, p.415–27.

Laski, M. *Ecstacy: A Study of Some Secular and Religious Experiences.* Bloomington: Indiana Univ. Press, 1961.

Lawrence, P. J. Children's Thinking About Religion: A Study of Concrete Operational Thinking. *Rel. Educ.*, 60/2, 1965, p.111–6.

Lewis, E. *Children and Their Religion.* N.Y.: Sheed & Ward, 1962, 316p.

Little, K. The Organization of Voluntary Associations in West Africa. *Civilisations*, 9/3, 1959, p.283–97.

Lowe, W. L. Religious Beliefs and Religious Delusions. *Amer. J. Psychoth.*, 9, 1955, p.54–61.

Maclear, J. F. Popular Anti-Clericalism in Puritan Revolt. *J. Hist. Ideas*, 17, 1956, p.443–70.

Matthijssen, A. J. M. Catholic Intellectual Emancipation in the Western Countries of Mixed Religion. *Soc. Compass*, 6/3, 1959, p.91–113.

Mavlana, M. A. The Concept of God in Islam. *Islamic R.*, 51/1–3, 1963, p.5–10.

Mavlana, M. A. The Concept of God in Islam: The Attributes of God. *Islamic R.*, 51/4–6, 1963, p.20–4.

May, L. C. A Survey of Glossolalia and Related Phenomena in Non-Christian Religions. *Amer. Anthropol.*, 58, 1956, p.75–92.

McLean, M. D. Diagnosing Patterns of Religious Belief. *Rel. Educ.*, 43, 1948, p.343–9.

Metraux, A. The Concept of Soul in Haitian Vodu. *Southw. J. Anthropol.*, 2/1, 1946, p.84–92.

Middleton, W. C. Denunciation and Religious Certainty. *J. Soc. Psychol.*, 5/2, 1934, p.254–7.

Muhiuddin, A. H. M. Prohibition of Swine Flesh in Islam. *Islamic R.*, 49/10, 1961, p.25–6.

Murphy, L. B. Backgrounds of Adolescent Religion. *Child Stud.*, 13, 1936, p.140–4.

Myers, M. S. The Role of Certain Religious Values for High School Youth. *Stud. High. Education*, No. 79, Purdue Univ., 1951.

Noble, D. S. Demoniacal Possession Among the Giryama. *Man*, 61, 1961, p.50–2.

O'Brien, E. *Varieties of Mystic Experience.* N.Y.: Holt, Rinehart & Winston, 1964.

O'Keefe, C. B. Conservative Opinion on the Spread of Deism in France, 1730–1750. *J. Mod. Hist.*, 33, 1961, p.398–406.

Parsons, E. C. The Religious Dedication of Women. *Amer. J. Sociol.*, 11/5, 1906, p.610–22.

Parsons, H. L. Religious Beliefs of Students at Six Colleges and Universities. *Rel. Educ.*, 58/6, 1963, p.538–44.

Payne, R. Knowledge of the Bible Among Protestant and Jewish University Students: An Exploratory Study. *Rel. Educ.*, 58/2, 1963, p.289–93.

Photiadis, J. D. Overt Conformity to Church Teaching as a Function of Religious Belief and Group Participation. *Amer. J. Sociol.*, 70/4, 1965, p.423–8.

Pilkington, G. W., *et al.* Changes in Religious Attitude and Practices Among Students During University Degree Courses. *Brit. J. Educ. Psychol.*, 35/2, 1965, p.150–7.

Pixley, E. and Beekman, E. The Faith of Youth as Shown by a Survey of Public Schools in Los Angeles. *Rel. Educ.*, 44, 1949, p.336–42.

Politella, J. *Mysticism and the Mystical Consciousness Illustrated from the Religions.* Kent, Ohio: Kent State Univ., 1964, 89p.

Poppleton, P. K. and Pilkington, G. W. The Measurement of Religious Attitudes in a University Population. *Brit. J. Clin. Psychol.*, 2, 1963, p.20–36.

Price, H. H. Belief "In" and Belief "That." *Rel. Stud.*, 1/1, 1965, p.5–27.

Rose, R. *Living Magic: The Realities Underlying the Psychical Practices and Beliefs of Australian Aborigines.* N.Y.: Rand McNally, 1956, 240p.

Ross, M. G. *Religious Beliefs of Youth: A Study of the Content, Origin and Life, Relevance of the Beliefs of Young People.* N.Y.: Association Press, 1950, 251p.

Rossi, P. and Greeley, A. H. The Impact of the Roman Catholic Denominational School. *School R.*, 72, 1964, p.34–51.

Rudowusky, D. Religion and Religiosity in American Jewish Life. *J. Educ. Sociol.*, 33/7, 1960, p.314–20.

Rusk, G. Y. The Spiritual Nature of Man: A Study in Catholic Psychology. *J. Soc. Psychol.*, 27/2, 1948, p.151–8.

Sandron, C. End-Primary School Cathechetical Knowledge: An Objective Examination. *Lumen Vitae*, 12, 1957, p.290–300.

Schellenberg, J., *et al.* Religiosity and Social Attitudes in an Urban Congregation. *R. Rel. Res.*, 6/3, 1965, p.142–6.

Schreuder, O. Religious Attitudes, Group Consciousness, Liturgy and Education. *Soc. Compass*, 10/1, 1963, p.29–52.

Schroeder, W. W. Lay Expectations of the Ministerial Role: An Exploration of Protestant-Catholic Differentials. *J. Sci. Stud. Rel.*, 2/2, 1963, p.217–27.

Schulyer, J. B. Religious Behavior in Northern Parish: A Study of Motivating Values. *Amer. Cath. Sociol. R.*, 19/2, 1958, p.134–44.

Sen, A. C. The Car Festival of India. *Indo-Asian Cult.*, 14/2, 1965, p.84–95.

Smith, E. W. (ed.) *African Ideas of God: A Symposium.* London: Edinburgh House Press, 1950, 308p.

Spilka, B., *et al.* The Concept of God: A Factor Analytic Approach. *R. Rel. Res.*, 6/1, 1964, p.28–36.

Stewart, K. M. Spirit Possession in Native America. *Southw. J. Anthropol.*, 2/3, 1946, p.323–39.

Sundkler, B. G. M. The Concept of Christianity in the African Independent Churches. *Afr. Stud.*, 2/4, 1961, p.203–13.

Thouless, R. H. The Tendency to Certainty in Religious Belief. *Brit. J. Psychol.*, 26, 1935, p.16–31.

Van Der Kroef, J. M. Javanese Messianic Expectations: Their Origin and Cultural Context. *Comp. Stud. Society Hist.*, 1/4, 1959, p.299–324.

Veronica, H. A Religious Maturity Scale. *Cath. Educ.*, 29, 1959, p.487–9.

Vernon, G. M. An Introduction to the Scalability of Church Orthodoxy. *Sociol. Soc. Res.*, 39/5, 1955, p.324–9.

Vernon, G. M. Religious Self-Identification. *Pac. Sociol. R.*, 5/1, 1962, p.40–3.

Vidyarthi, L. P. *The Sacred Complex in Hindu Gaya.* N.Y.: Asia Publishing House, 1961, 232p.

Wach, J. Spiritual Teachings in Islam: A Study. *J. Rel.*, 28/4, 1948, p.263–80.

Walkout, D. The Culturally Conditioned Christian. *Rel. Life*, 39, 1961, p.279–84.

Williams, J. P. *What Americans Believe and How They Worship.* N.Y.: Harper, 1962.

Willoughby, R. R. The Emotional Maturity ot Some Religious Attitudes. *J. Soc. Psychol.*, 1/4, 1930, p.532–6.

Wolff, K. H. Surrender and Religion. *J. Sci. Stud. Rel.*, 2/1, 1962, p.36–50. See also: H. Hoffmann—Comment, p. 50–2.

See Also:

Al-Karmi, H.—Prayer in Islam. *Islamic Quart.*, 9/1–2, 1965, p.37–45.

Asrani, V. A. A Modern Approach to Mystical Experience. *Main Curr. Mod. Thought*, 20/1, 1963, p.15–20.

Baker, L. G., Jr. Changing Religious Norms and Family Values. *J. Marr. Fam.*, 27/1, 1965, p.6–12.

Baldwin, N. A. People of Bible Lands and Their Attitude Toward Mental Disease. *Ment. Hyg.*, 12/2, 1928, p.378–84.

Battenhouse, R. A. The Doctrine of Man in Calvin and in Renaissance Platonism. *J. Hist. Ideas*, 9/4, 1948, p.447–71.

Beattie, J. H. M. Divination in Bunyoro, Uganda. *Sociologus*, 14/1, 1964, p.44–61.

Benedict, R. The Vision in Plains Culture. *Amer. Anthropol.*, 24, 1922, p.1–23.

Bennett, C. A. Religion and the Idea of the Holy. *J. Philos.*, 23, 1926, p.460–9.

Blake, J. A. The Compatibility of Reason and Faith. *J. Rel. Health*, 4/1, 1964, p.86–105.

Bogoras, W. Ideas of Space and Time in the Conception of Primitive Religion. *Amer. Anthropol.*, 27, 1925, p.205–66.

Borowitz, E. B. Crisis Theology and the Jewish Community. *Commentary*, 32/1, 1961, p.36–42.

Brandon, S. G. F. *History, Time and Deity: A Historical and Comparative Study of the Conception of Time in Religious Thought and Practice.* N.Y.: Barnes and Noble, 1965, 240p.

Breer, P. E. and Locke, E. A. *Task Experience as a Source of Attitudes.* Homewood, Illinois: Dorsey Press, 1965.

Butterfield, H. Reflections on Religion and Modern Individualism. *J. Hist. Ideas*, 22/1, 1961, p.33–46.

Carlyle, M. L. A Survey of Glossalia and Related Phenomena in Non-Christian Religions. *Amer. Anthropol.*, 58/1, 1956, p.75–96.

Chakravarti, C. Beef in Hindu Folklore of Bengal. *Folklore*, 6/1, 1965, p.18–22. See also P. K. Maity, 6/4, p.174–7.

Chung, A. C. The Mysticism of Buddhists. *Chinese Cult.*, 5/1, 1963, p.99–121.

Cullmann, O. *Christ and Time: The Primitive Christian Conception of Time and History.* Phila.: Westminster Press, 1964.

Dantzker, S. Some Jewish Folk Habits and Superstitions. *New York Folkl. Quart.*, 14, 1958, p.148–9.

Densmore, F. Notes on the Indian's Belief in the Friendliness of Nature. *Southw. J. Anthropol.*, 4/1, 1948, p.94–7.

Douglas, W. Religion. In N. L. Farberow (ed.)—*Taboo Topics.* N.Y.: Atherton Press, 1963, p.80–95.

Dumont, L. World Renunciation in Indian Religions. *Contrib. Ind. Sociol.*, 4, 1960, p.33–62.

Dynes, R. R. The Consequences of Sectarianism for Social Participation. *Soc. Forces*, 35, 1957, p.331–4.

Eliade, M. Mythologies of Memory and Forgetting. *Hist. Rel.*, 2/1, 1963, p.329–44.

Freed, E. X. Ethnic Identification of Hospitalized Jewish Psychiatric Patients: An Exploratory Study. *Int. J. Soc. Psychiat.*, 11/2, 1965, p.110–5.

Freeman-Grenville, G. S. P. *The Muslim and Christian Calendar.* London: Oxford Univ. Press, 1963, 87p.

Garrison, K. C. The Relationship of Certain Variables to Church-Sect Typology Among College Students. *J. Soc. Psychol.*, 56, 1962, p.29–32.

Gayton, A. H. The Orpheus Myth in North America. *Amer. Folklore*, 48/189, 1935, p.263–93.

Happold, F. C. *Mysticism: A Study and Anthology.* London: Penguin Books, 1963, 364p.

Hooke, S. H. Omens—Ancient and Modern. *Folklore*, 66/3, 1955, p.330–9.

Houston, J. Psycho-Chemistry and the Religious Consciousness. *Int. Philosoph. Quart.*, 5/3, 1965, p.397–413.

Htin, A. *Folk Elements in Burmese Buddhism.* London: Oxford Univ. Press, 1962, 140p.

Hubert, H. and Mauss, M. *Sacrifice: Its Nature and Function* (Trans. W. D. Halls). Chicago: Univ. of Chicago Press, 1964, 165p.

James, W. A Suggestion About Mysticism. *J. Philos.*, 7, 1910, p.85–92.

James, W. *The Varieties of Religious Experience: A Study in Human Nature.* N.Y.: American Library, 1958, 406p.

Jetté, J. On the Superstitions of the Len'a Indians (Middle Part of the Yukon Valley, Alaska). *Anthropos*, 6, 1911, p.95–108, 241–59, 602–15, 699–723.

Johnson, E. E. (ed.) *Patterns of Faith.* N.Y.: Harper & Brothers, 1957.

Joya, M. Some Aspects of Local Superstition. *Contemp. Japan*, 27/3, 1962, p.492–511.

Kimber, J. A. M. Interests and Personality of Bible Institute Students. *J. Soc. Psychol.*, 26, 1947, p.225–33.

Klausner, S. Why They Choose Israel. *Archiv. Sociol. Rel.*, 5/9, 1960, p.129–44.

Lamprecht, S. P. A Type of Religious Mysticism. *J. Philos.*, 24, 1927, p.701–15.

Landis, C. and Wunderlich, E. P. Religious Attitudes of Psychopathic Patients. *J. Abnorm. Soc. Psychol.*, 30, 1936, p.508–12.

Langer, J. *Nine Gates to the Chassidic Mysteries* (Trans. S. Lolly). N.Y.: David McKay, 1961, 226p.

Leuba, J. H. The Yoga System of Mental Concentration and Religious Mysticism. *J. Philos.*, 16, 1919, p.197–207.

Liebenthal, W. The Concept of God in Chinese Religion. *J. Asiat. Society Letters*, 22/2, 1956, p.137–46.

Lowe, W. L. Group Beliefs and Socio-Cultural Factors in Religious Delusions. *J. Soc. Psychol.*, 40/2, 1954, p.267–74.

Lubin, A. T. A Boy's View of Jesus. *Psychoanal. Stud. Child*, 14, 1959, p.155–8.

Makemson, M. W. Astronomy in Primitive Religion. *J. Bib. Rel.*, 22, 1954, p.163–71.

Moody, J. N. and Lawler, J. G. (eds.) *The Challenge of Mater et Magistra*. N.Y.: Herder & Herder, 1963, 280p.

Morgan, E. S. *Visible Saints: The History of a Puritan Idea*. N.Y.: New York Univ. Press, 1963.

Murphy, R. F. On Zen Marxism: Filiation and Alliance. *Man*, 63, 1963, p.17–9.

Nazmul Karim, A. K. Some Aspects of Popular Beliefs Among Muslims of Bengal. *East. Anthropol.*, 9/1, 1955, p.29–41.

Noble, D. S. The Concept of Jok. *Afr. Stud.*, 20/2, 1961, p.123–30.

Norbeck, E. Yakudoshi, a Japanese Complex of Supernaturalistic Beliefs. *Southw. J. Anthropol.*, 11/2, 1955, p.105–20.

Orenstein, H. Caste and the Concept of "Maratha" in Maharashtra. *East. Anthropol.*, 16/1, 1963, p.1–9.

Orenstein, H. The Structure of Hindu Caste Values: A Preliminary Study of Hierarchy and Ritual Defilement. *Ethnology*, 4/1, 1965, p.1–15.

Patai, R., *et al.* (eds.) *Studies in Biblical and Jewish Folklore*. Bloomington: Indiana Univ. Press, 1960, 374p.

Patterson, R. L. *Irrationalism and Rationalism in Religion*. Durham: Duke Univ. Press, 1954.

Prodipto, R. The Sacred Cow in India. *Rural Sociol.*, 20/1, 1955, p.8–15.

Putney, S. and Middleton, R. Dimensions and Correlates of Religious Ideologies. *Soc. Forces*, 39/4, 1961, p.285–90.

Ranck, J. G. Religious Conservatism-Liberalism and Mental Health. *Past. Psychol.*, 12, 1961, p.34–40.

Rath, R. and Sircar, N. C. The Mental Pictures of Six Hindu Groups About Each Other as Reflected in Verbal Stereotypes. *J. Soc. Psychol.*, 51/2, 1960, p.277–93.

Ryan, L. V. Some Czech-American Forms of Divination and Supplication. *J. Amer. Folklore*, 69/273, 1956, p.281–5.

Sandmel, S. *We Jews and Jesus*. N.Y.: Oxford Univ. Press, 1965, 163p.

Sanford, C. L. *The Quest For Paradise: Europe and the American Moral Imagination*. Urbana: Univ. of Illinois Press, 1961.

Schnepp, G. J. Social Progress,1931–46: An Estimate of a Papal Document. *Amer. Cath. Sociol R.*, 7/1, 1946, p.3–14.

Scholem, G. G. *Jewish Gnosticism, Merkabah, Mysticism and Talmudic Tradition*. N.Y.: Jewish Theological Seminary of America, 1960, 126p.

Sierksma, F. Sacred Cairns in Pastoral Cultures. *Hist. Rel.*, 2/1, 1963, p.227–41.

Slater, R. L. *Paradox and Nirvana: A Study of Religious Ultimates with Special Reference to Burmese Buddhism*. Chicago: Univ. of Chicago Press, 1951, 145p.

Speck, F. G. Penobscot Tales and Religious Beliefs. *J. Amer. Folklore*, 48, 1936, p.1–107.

Strunk, O., Jr. Perceived Relationships Between Parental and Deity Concepts. *Psychol. News.*, 10, 1959, p.222–6.

Stuart, G. C. Faith and Fact. *J. Hum. Relat.*, 2/1, 1953, p.7–23.

Suzuki, D. T. *Mysticism: Christian and Buddhism*. N.Y.: Harper, 1957, 214p.

Swanstrom, E. E. The Christian Attitude Towards Migration. *Soc. Compass*, 3/5–6, 1956, p.10–4.

Taylor, D. Carib Folk-Beliefs and Customs From Dominica, B. W. I. *Southw. J. Anthropol.*, 1/4, 1945, p.507–30.

Thomas, W. I. and Znaniecki, F. *The Polish Peasant in Europe and America*. N.Y.: Dover Publications, 1958, 4 vols.

Trinkaus, C. The Problem of Free Will in the Renaissance and the Reformation. *J. Hist. Ideas*, 10/1, 1949, p.51–62.

Tumin, M. M. and Feldman, A. S. The Miracle at

Sabana Grande. *Pub. Opin. Quart.*, 19/2, 1955, p.125–39.

Tuttle, H. S. Religion as Motivation. *J. Soc. Psychol.*, 15/2, 1942, p.255–64.

Vallette, M. F. American Mythology as Related to Asiatic and Hebrew Tradition. *Amer. Cath. Quart. R.*, 40, 1950, p.584–601.

Vilakazi, A. Changing Concepts of the Self and the Supernatural in Africa. *Ann. New York Acad. Sci.*, 96, 1962, p.670–5.

Wales, H. G. O. The Cosmological Aspect of Indonesian Religion. *J. Roy. Asiat. Society*, 3/4, 1959, p.100–39.

Watt, W. M. The Concept of the Charismatic Community in Islam. *Numen*, 7/1, 1960, p.77–90.

White, C. M. N. *Elements in Luvale Beliefs and Rituals.* Manchester: Manchester Univ. Press, 1962, 70p.

Wilder, A. N. Paul Through Jewish Eyes. *J. Bib. Rel.*, 12, 1944, p.181–7.

Zaehner, R. C. *Mysticism, Sacred and Profane.* N.Y.: Oxford Univ. Press, 1961, 234p.

Zulliger, H. Prophetic Dreams. *Int. J. Psychoanal.*, 15, 1934, p.191–208.

Attitudes Toward Church

Ackiss, T. D. Changing Patterns of Religious Thought Among Negroes. *Soc. Forces*, 23/2, 1944, p.212–5.

Adinarayan, S. P. and Rajamanickam, M. A Study of Student Attitude Toward Religion, the Spiritual and the Supernatural. *J. Soc. Psychol.*, 57/1, 1962, p.105–11.

Akesson, S. K. The Akán Concept of the Soul. *Afr. Aff.*, 64/257, 1965, p.280–91.

Allen, E. E. and Hites, R. W. Factors in Religious Attitudes of Older Adolescents. *J. Soc. Psychol.*, 55, 1961, p.265–73.

Aronfreid, J. The Nature, Variety, and Social Patterning of Moral Responses to Transgression. *J. Abnorm. Soc. Psychol.*, 63/2, 1961, p.223–40.

Barker, G. C. Some Aspects of Penitential Processions in Spain and the American Southwest. *J. Amer. Folklore*, 70/276, 1957, p.137–42.

Bharati, A. Pilgrimage in the Indian Tradition. *Hist. Rel.*, 3/1, 1963, p.135–67.

Bose, R. S. Religious Concepts of Children. *Rel. Educ.*, 24, 1929, p.831–7.

Brandon, S. G. F. (ed.) *The Savior God: Comparative Studies in the Concept of Salvation.* N.Y.: Barnes and Noble, 1963, 242p.

Brauer, J. C. Images of Religion in America. *Church Hist.*, 30, 1961, p.3–18.

Brewer, E. D. Attitudes Toward Inclusive Practices in the Methodist Church in the Southeast. *R. Rel. Res.*, 6/2, 1965, p.82–9.

Burtt, H. E. The Influence of Majority and Expert Opinion on Religious Attitudes. *J. Soc. Psychol.*, 14/2, 1941, p.269–78.

Busian, C. Priests and the Rising Generation of Priests in the Opinion of Brazilians. *Soc. Compass*, 8/4, 1961, p.317–26.

Clark, A. H. Old World Origins and Religious Adherence in Nova Scotia. *Geogr. R.*, 20/3, 1960, p.451–8.

Cragg, D. B. Religious Attitudes of Denominational College Students. *J. Soc. Psychol.*, 15/2, 1942, p.245–54.

Doherty, J. F. The Image of the Priest: A Study in Stereotyping. *Phillipine Sociol. R.*, 12/1-2, 1964, p.70–6.

Eddy, E. M. Student Perspectives on the Southern Church. *Phylon*, 25/4, 1964, p.369–81.

Fox, J. T. The Attitude of Male College Students Toward Their Church. *Amer. Cath. Sociol. R.*, 24/2, 1963, p.127–31.

George, C. H. English Calvinist Opinion on Usury, 1600–1640. *J. Hist. Ideas*, 18/4, 1957, p.455–74.

Gilliland, A. R. The Attitude of College Students Toward God and the Church. *J. Soc. Psychol.*, 11, 1940, p.11–8.

Glick, P. C. and Young, K. Justifications for Religious Attitudes and Habits. *J. Soc. Psychol.*, 17, 1943, p.45–68.

Glock, C. Y. and Ross, P. Parishioner's Views of How Ministers Spend Their Time. *R. Rel. Res.*, 2/4, 1961, p.170–5.

Godin, A. (ed.) *From Religious Experience to Religious Attitude.* Brussels: Lumen Vitae, 1964.

Harrison, W. R. A Study of Church Attitudes in the East Baton Rouge Area. *Rel. Educ.*, 1, 1952, p.39–51.

Kalir, J. The Jewish Service in the Eyes of Christian and Baptized Jews in the 17th and 18th Centuries. *Jew. Quart. R.*, 56/1, 1965, p.51–80.

Karsten, J. Cultural Adaptation of Religious Symbols in the Missions. *Lumen Vitae*, 20/3, 1965, p.499–507.

Lennard, H. L. Jewish Youth Appraising Jews and Jewishness. *Yivo Ann. Jew. Soc. Sci.*, 2/3, 1948, p.262–81.

Litt, E. Ethnic Status and Political Perspectives. *Midwest J. Polit. Sci.*, 5/3, 1961, p.276–83.

Liu, W. T. The Marginal Catholics in the South: A Revision of Concepts. *Amer. J. Sociol.*, 65/4, 1960, p.383–90.

Middleton, W. C. and Fay, P. J. Attitudes of Delinquent and Non-Delinquent Girls Toward Sunday Observance, the Bible and War. *J. Educ. Psychol.*, 32, 1941, p.555–8.

Moreton, F. E. Attitudes to Religion Among Adolescents and Adults. *Brit. J. Educ. Psychol.*, 14, 1944, p.69–79.

Opler, M. E. The Concept of Supernatural Power Among the Chiricahua and Mescalero Apaches. *Amer. Anthropol.*, 37, 1935, p.65–70.

Photiadis, J. D. and Biggar, J. Religiosity, Education, and Ethnic Distance. *Amer. J. Sociol.*, 67/6, 1962, p.666–72.

Puckett, N. N. Religious Folk-Beliefs of Whites and Negroes. *J. Negro Hist.*, 16/1, 1931, p.9–35.

Sherman, C. B. Emerging Patterns and Attitudes in American Jewish Life. *Jew. J. Sociol.*, 5/1, 1963, p.47–54.

Simpson, R. L. *The Interpretation of Prayer in the Early Church.* Phila.: Westminster Press, 1965.

Simpson, R. M. Attitude Toward the Ten Commandments. *J. Soc. Psychol.*, 4, 1953, p.223–30.

Stark, R. Through a Stained Glass Darkley: Reciprocal Protestant-Catholic Images in America. *Sociol. Anal.*, 25/3, 1964, p.159–66.

Steinbaum, I. A Study of the Jewishness of Twenty New York Families. *Yivo Ann. Jew. Soc. Sci.*, 5, 1950, p.232–55.

Stroup, H. The Attitude of the Jehovah's Witnesses Toward the Roman Catholic Church. *Rel. Making*, 2/2, 1942, p.148–63.

Strunk, O., Jr. Relation Between Self Reports and Adolescent Religiosity. *Psychol. Rep.*, 4, 1958, p.683–6.

Taves, M. J. *Factors Influencing Personal Religion of Adults.* Washington Agricultural Experiment Station Bulletin 544, State College of Washington, Pullman, Washington, 1953.

VanBaumer, F. L. The Conception of Christendom in Renaissance England. *J. Hist. Ideas*, 6/2, 1945, p.131–56.

Vinacke, W. E., *et al.* Religious Attitudes of Students at the University of Hawaii. *J. Psychol.*, 28, 1949, p.161–79.

Zenner, W. P. Ambivalence and Self-Image Among Oriental Jews in Israel. *Jew. J. Sociol.*, 5/2, 1963, p.214–23.

Death and Ancestor Worship

Argyle, A. W. The Historical Christian Attitude to Cremation. *Hibbert J.*, 1958, p.67–71.

Becker, H. and Bruner, D. K. Attitude Toward Death and the Dead and Some Possible Causes of Ghost Fear. *Ment. Hyg.*, 15/4, 1931, p.828–37.

Bouquet, A. C. Beliefs and Practices of the Jalaris in the Matter of the Life Beyond the Grave. *Numen*, 7/2–3, 1960, p.201–14.

Busia, K. A. Ancestor Worship. *Pract. Anthropol.*, 6/1, 1959, p.23–6.

Devereaux, G. Mohave Soul Concepts. *Amer. Anthropol.*, 39, 1937, p.417–22.

Du Toit, B. M. Some Aspects of the Soul-Concept Among the Bantu-Speaking Nguni-Tribes of South Africa. *Anthropol. Quart.*, 33/3, 1960, p.134–42.

Eliade, M. *Cosmos and History: The Myth of the Eternal Return.* N.Y.: Harper, 1959, 176p.

Erkes, E. The God of Death in Ancient China. *T'Oung Pao*, 35, 1940, p.185–210.

Faron, L. C. On Ancestor Propitiation Among the Mapuche of Central Chile. *Amer. Anthropol.*, 63/4, 1961, p.824–30.

Fulton, R. L. Death and the Self. *J. Rel. Health*, 3/4, 1964, p.359–68.

Green, L. C. and Beckwith, M. W. Hawaiian Customs and Beliefs Relating to Sickness and Death. *Amer. Anthropol.*, 28, 1926, p.176–208.

Hultkrantz, A. *Conceptions of the Soul Among North American Indians: A Study in Religious Ethnology.* Stockholm: Ethnographical Museum of Sweden, 1953, 544p.

Immortality and Resurrection and Ecumenical Themes. *The London Quart. and Holborn R.*, April 1965.

Kelly, W. H. Cocopa Attitudes and Practices With Respect to Death and Mourning. *Southw. J. Anthropol.*, 5/2, 1949, p.151–64.

Key, A. F. The Concept of Death in Early Israelite Religion. *J. Bib. Rel.*, 32/3, 1964, p.239–47.

König, S. Beliefs Regarding the Soul and the Future World Among Galician Ukranians. *Folk Lore* (London), 49, 1938, p.157–61.

Leaño, I. The Ibaloy Sing for the Dead. *Philippine Sociol. R.*, 13/3, 1965, p.154–82.

Loyens, W. J. The Koyukon Feast for the Dead. *Arctic Anthropol.*, 2/2, 1964, p.133–48.

Mandelbaum, D. G. Social Uses of Funeral Rites. *East. Anthropol.*, 12/1, 1958, p.5–24.

Martin, D. and Wrightman, L. S., Jr. Religion and Fears

About Death: A Critical Review of Research. *Rel. Educ.*, 59/2, 1964, p.174–76.

Martin, D. and Wrightman, L. S., Jr. The Relationship Between Religious Behavior and Concern About Death. *J. Soc. Psychol.*, 65, 1965, p.317–23.

Matz, M. Judaism and Bereavement. *J. Rel. Health*, 3/4, 1964, p.345–52.

Morton-Williams, P. Yoruba Responses to the Fear of Death. *Africa*, 30/1, 1960, p.34–40.

Wilson, G. R. The Religion of the American Slave: His Attitude Toward Life and Death. *J. Negro Hist.*, 8/1, 1923, p.41–71.

Yü, Y. S. Life and Immortality in the Mind of Han China. *Harvard J. Asiat. Stud.*, 25, 1964, 1965, p.80–122.

Zandee, J. *Death as an Enemy According to Ancient Egyptian Conceptions.* Leiden: E. J. Brill, 1960, 344p.

Social and Political Attitudes

Allinsmith, W. and Allinsmith, B. Religious Affiliation and Politico-Economic Attitude: A Study of Eight Major United States Groups. *Pub. Opin. Quart.*, 12, 1948, p.377–89.

Anisfeld, M., *et al.* The Structure and Dynamics of the Ethnic Attitudes of Jewish Adolescents. *J. Abnorm. Soc. Psychol.*, 66/1, 1963, p.31–6.

Bainton, R. H. *Christian Attitudes Toward War and Peace: A Historical Survey and Critical Re-Evaluation.* N.Y.: Abingdon Press, 1960, 299p.

Bannan, R. S. The Other Side of the Coin: Jewish Student Attitudes Toward Catholics and Protestants. *Sociol. Anal.*, 26/1, 1965, p.21–9.

Bernard, R. U. S. Protestants and Race. *Soc. Order*, 6/6, 1956, p.256–63.

Brannen, N. Sòka Gakkai's Theory of Value. *Contemp. Rel. Japan*, 5/2, 1964, p.143–54.

Brown, R. L. Attitudes Among Local Baptist Church Leaders in Washington State. *Sociol. Soc. Res.*, 47/3, 1963, p.322–31.

Cahnman, W. J. Attitudes of Minority Youth: A Methodological Introduction. *Amer. Sociol. R.*, 14/4, 1949, p.543–9.

Cossette, J. P. *Catholic Social Work and Catholic Action: A Comparative Study on the Basis of the Lay Apostolate.* Washington: Catholic Univ. Press, 1952, 529p.

Diamant, A. Austrian Catholics and the First Republic, 1918–1934: A Study in Anti-Democratic Thought. *West. Polit. Quart.*, 10/3, 1957, p.603–33.

Dougherty, D. Normative Values: Differences Between Public and Parochial School Adolescents. *Sociol. Anal.*, 26/2, 1965, p.96–109.

Dougherty, F. J. and Nuesse, C. J. Differentials in Catholic Opinion on the Admission of Displaced Persons. *Amer. Cath. Sociol. R.*, 12/4, 1951, p.207–16.

Drucker, P. E. Organized Religion and the American Creed. *R. Polit.*, 18/3, 1956, p.296–304.

Edwards, L. P. Religious Sectarianism and Race Prejudice. *Amer. J. Sociol.*, 41/2, 1935, p.167–79.

Eighmy, J. L. Recent Changes in the Racial Attitudes of Southern Baptists. *Foundations*, 5, 1962, p.354–60.

Elinson, H. Implications of Pentacostal Religion for Intellectualism, Politics and Race Relations. *Amer. J. Sociol.*, 70/4, 1965, p.403–15.

Feagin, J. R. Prejudice and Religious Types: A Focused Study of Southern Fundamentalists. *J. Sci. Stud. Rel.*, 4/1, 1964, p.3–13.

Feagin, J. R. Prejudice, Orthodoxy and the Social Situation. *Soc. Forces*, 44/1, 1965, p.46–56.

Fetter, G. C. A Comparative Study of Attitudes of Christian and of Moslem Lebanese Villagers. *J. Sci. Stud. Rel.*, 4/1, 1964, p.48–59.

Fichter, J. H. and Facey, P. W. Social Attitudes of Catholic High School Students. *Amer. Cath. Sociol. R.*, 14/2, 1953, p.94–106.

Ford, C. E. and Schinert, G. The Relation of Ethnocentric Attitudes to Intensity of Religious Practice. *J. Educ. Sociol.*, 32, 1958, p.157–62.

Gellner, E. Sanctity, Puritanism, Secularization and Nationalism in North Africa: A Case Study. *Archiv. Sociol. Rel.*, 15, 1963, p.71–86.

Godstein, B. and Eihhom, R. L. The Changing Protestant Ethic: Rural Patterns in Wealth, Work and Leisure. *Amer. Sociol. R.*, 26, 1961, p.557–65.

Groves, E. R. An Unsocial Element in Religion. *Amer. J. Sociol.*, 22/5, 1917, p.657–62.

Gustafson, J. M. Christian Attitudes Toward a Technological Society. *Theol. Today*, 16, 1959, p.173–87.

Harte, T. J. Scalogram Analysis of Catholic Attitudes Toward the Negro. *Amer. Cath. Sociol. R.*, 12/2, 1951, p.66–74.

Hirschberg, H. H. *Hebrew Humanism.* Los Angeles: California Writers, 1964, 230p.

Ilsager, H. Factors Influencing the Formation and Change of Political and Religious Attitudes. *J. Soc. Psychol.*, 29, 1949, p.253–65.

Kavolis, V. Church Involvement and Marital Status as Restraints on Non-Conforming Sexual Behavior. *J. Hum. Relat.*, 11/1, 1962, p.133–9.

Knopfelmacher, F. and Armstrong, D. B. Authoritarianism, Ethnocentrism and Religious Denomination. *Amer. Cath. Sociol. R.*, 24/2, 1963, p.99–114.

Kosa, J. and Schommer, C. O. Sex Differences in the Religious Attitudes of Catholic College Students. *Psychol. Rep.*, 10/1, 1962, p.285–6.

Lenski, G. E. Social Correlates of Religious Interest. *Amer. Sociol. R.*, 18, 1953, p.533–44.

Litt, E. Jewish Ethno-Religious Involvement and Political Liberalism. *Soc. Forces*, 39/4, 1961, p.328–32.

Luckmann, T. On Religion in Modern Society: Individual Consciousness World View and Institution. *J. Sci. Stud. Rel.*, 2/2, 1963, p.147–62.

Maitre, J. Extreme Right-Wing Catholicism and Anti-Subversive Crusade. *R. Franc. Sociol.*, 2/2, 1961, p.106–117.

Mihanovich, C. S. and Janson, E. W. Social Attitudes of Catholic High School Seniors. *Amer. Cath. Sociol. R.*, 7/3, 1946, p.170–3.

Nuesse, C. J. *The Social Thought of American Catholics, 1634–1829*. Washington: Catholic Univ. Press, 1945, 315p.

Nuesse, C. J. Social Thought Among American Catholics in the Colonial Period. *Amer. Cath. Sociol. R.*, 7/1, 1946, p.43–52.

Obenhaus, V. and Schroeder, W. W. Church Affiliation and Attitudes Toward Selected Public Questions in a Typical Midwest County. *Rural Sociol.*, 28/1, 1963, p.35–47.

Olson, B. E. *Faith and Prejudice*. New Haven: Yale Univ. Press, 1962.

Osterhaven, M. E. The Calvinistic Attitude Toward the World. *Reformed R.*, 18/4, 1965, p.30–6.

Podhoretz, N., *et al.* Jewishness and the Younger Intellectuals: A Symposium. *Commentary*, 31/4, 1961, p.306–59.

Prothro, E. T. and Jensen, J. A. Interrelations of Religious and Ethnic Attitudes in Selected Southern Populations. *J. Soc. Psychol.*, 32/1, 1950, p.45–9.

Quinney, R. V. Political Conservatism, Alienation, Fatalism: Contingency of Social Status and Religious Fundamentalism. *Sociometry*, 27/3, 1964, p.372–81.

Reines, C. W. Collectivism and Individualism in Judaism. *Judaism*, 6, 1957, p.240–7.

Rhodes, A. L. Authoritarianism and Fundamentalism of Rural and Urban High School Students. *J. Educ. Sociol.*, 34/3, 1960, p.97–105.

Rice, M. H. *American Catholic Opinion in the Slavery Controversy*. N.Y.: Philosophical Library, 1950, 160p.

Rim, Y. and Kurweil, Z. E. A Note on Attitudes to Risk-Taking of Observant and Non-Observant Jews. *Jew. J. Sociol.*, 7/2, 1965, p.238–45.

Ringer, B. B. and Glock, C. Y. The Political Role of the Church as Defined by its Parishioners. *Pub. Opin. Quart.*, 12, 1948, p.377–89.

Rokeach, M. *The Open and Closed Mind: Investigations Into the Nature of Belief Systems and Personality Systems*. N.Y.: Basic Books, 1960.

Rokeach, M. Political and Religious Dogmatism: An Alternate to the Authoritarian Personality. *Psychol. Monographs*, 70/18, 1956, p.1–43.

Rokeach, M. Paradoxes of Religious Belief: The Golden Rule Versus the Rule of Exclusion. *Trans-Action*, 2/2, 1965, p.9–12.

Rosenblum, A. L. Ethnic Prejudice as Related to Social Class and Religiosity. *Sociol. Soc. Res.*, 43/4, 1959, p.272–5.

Ross, E. J. Judaic Social Thought. *Amer. Cath. Sociol. R.*, 7/1, 1946, p.33–42.

Roy, R. L. *Apostles of Discord: A Study of Organized Bigotry and Disruption on the Fringes of Protestantism*. Boston: Beacon Press, 1957.

Salisbury, W. S. Religiosity, Regional Sub-Culture, and Social Behavior. *J. Sci. Stud. Rel.*, 2/1, 1962, p.94–101.

Sanai, M. Empirical Study of Political, Religious and Social Attitudes. *Brit. J. Psychol.*, 5, 1952, p.81–92.

Shinert, G. and Ford, C. E. The Relation of Ethnocentric Attitudes to Intensity of Religious Practice. *J. Educ. Psychol.*, 32, 1958, p.157–62.

Sibley, M. Q. and Jacob, P. E. *Conscription of Conscience: The American State and The Conscientious Objector, 1940–1947*. Ithaca: Cornell Univ. Press, 1952, 580p.

Siegel, M. "Horns, Tails and Easter Sport": A Study of a Stereotype. *Soc. Forces*, 20/3, 1942, p.382–6.

Soloviev, A. *Holy Russia: The History of a Religious-Social Idea*. N.Y.: Humanities Press, 1959.

Spoerl, D. T. Some Aspects of Prejudice as Affected by Religion and Education. *J. Soc. Psychol.*, 33, 1951, p.69–76.

Synon, M. Problems of Pupils in Acquiring Christian Social Attitudes. *Bull. Nat. Cath. Educ. Assoc.*, 49/1, 1952, p.415-8.

Tuveson, E. L. *Millennium and Utopia: A Study in the Background of the Idea of Progress*. Berkeley: Univ. of California Press, 1949.

Vaughan, J. H., Jr. The Religion and World View of the Marghi. *Ethnology*, 3/4, 1964, p.389–97.

Veroff, J., *et al.* Achievement, Motivation and Religious Background. *Amer. Sociol. R.*, 27/2, 1962, p.205–17.

Warburton, F. W. Beliefs Concerning Human Nature Among Students in a University Department of Education. *Brit. J. Educ. Psychol.*, 26/3, 1956, p.156–62.

Weima, J. Authoritarian Personality, Anti-Catholicism, and the Experience of Religious Values. *Soc. Compass*, 11/2, 1964, p.13–25.

Weisinger, H. English Attitudes Toward the Relationship Between the Renaissance and the Reformation. *Church Hist.*, 14/3, 1945, p.167–87.

Weissberg, N. C. and Proshansky, H. M. The Jewish Anti-Semite's Perceptions of Fellow Jews. *J. Soc. Psychol.*, 60/1, 1963, p.139–51.

Whitam, F. L. Subdivision of Religiosity and Race Prejudice. *R. Rel. Res.*, 3/4, 1962, p.166–74.

White, E. A. Fundamentalism Versus Modernism, 1920–1930. *Pac. Spect.*, 5/1, 1951, p.112–20.

Williamson, R. de V. Conservatism and Liberalism in American Protestantism. *Ann. Amer. Acad. Polit. Soc. Sci.*, 344, 1962, p.76–84.

Wilson, F. G. Liberals, Conservatives and Catholics. *Ann. Amer. Acad. Polit. Soc. Sci.*, 344, 1962, p.85–94.

Wilson, W. C. Extrinsic Religious Values and Prejudices. *J. Abnorm. Soc. Psychol.*, 60/2, 1960, p.286–8.

Younger, G. D. Protestant Piety and the Right Wing. *Soc. Action*, 17, 1951, p.5–35.

Zahn, G. C. Catholic Conscientious Objectors: A Portrait. *Continuum*, 3/3, 1965, p.329–37.

Witches, Sorcerers, and Spirits

Ames, D. Belief in "Witches" Among the Rural Wolof of the Gambia. *Africa*, 29/3, 1959, p.263–73.

Beidelman, T. O. Kaguru Omens: An East African People's Concepts of the Unusual, Unnatural and Supernormal. *Anthropol. Quart.*, 36/2, 1963, p.43–59.

Benedict, R. *The Concept of the Guardian Spirit in North America.* Menasha: Mem. Amer. Anthropol. Assoc., 29, 1923.

Bennett, W. *The Pendle Witches.* Burnley: Public Library, 1957, 32p.

Blunsdon, N. *A Popular Dictionary of Spiritualism.* N.Y.: Citadel, 1963, 256p.

Burland, C. A. Modern Swabian Folk-Beliefs About Witches. *Folk Lore* (London), 68/4, 1957, p.495–7.

Carneiro, R. L. The Amahuaca and the Spirit World. *Ethnology*, 3/1, 1964, p.6–11.

Coleman, S. J. *Sorcery and the Supernatural.* Douglas: Folklore Academy, 1958, 16p.

Daraul, A. *Witches and Sorcerers.* London: F. Muller, 1962, 160p.

Davies, R. T. *Four Centuries of Witch Beliefs With Special Reference to the Great Rebellion.* London: Methuen & Co., 1947.

Epstein, S. A Sociological Analysis of Witch Beliefs in a Mysore Village. *East Anthropol.*, 12/4, 1959, p.234–51.

Forde, D. Spirits, Witches and Sorcerers in the Supernatural Economy of the Yako. *J. Roy. Anthropol. Inst.*, 88/2, 1958, p.165–78.

Jahoda, G. Magic Witchcraft and Literacy: Beliefs and Attitudes Among West Africans. *Lumen Vitae*, 15, 1960, p.315–24.

Messenger, J. A Critical Reexamination of the Concept of Spirits: With Special Reference to Traditional Folklore and Contemporary Irish Folk Culture. *Amer. Anthropol.*, 64/2, 1962, p.367–73.

Michelet, J. *Satanism and Witchcraft: A Study in Mediaeval Superstition.* London: Arco, 1958, 332p.

Middleton, J. The Concept of "Bewitching" in Lugbara. *Africa*, 25/3, 1955, p.252–60.

Parrinder, E. G. African Ideas of Witchcraft. *Folk Lore* (London), 67/3, 1956, p.142–50.

Prince, R. The Yoruba Image of the Witch. *J. Ment. Sci.*, 107, 1961, p.795–805.

Saler, B. Nagual, Witch, and Sorcerer in a Quiché Village. *Ethnology*, 3/3, 1964, p.305–28.

Whitten, N. E. Contemporary Patterns of Malign Occultism Among Negroes in North Carolina. *J. Amer. Folklore*, 75, 1962, p.311–25.

Winslow, C. E. A. The Power of Ghosts. *Ment. Hyg.*, 20/1, 1936, p.1–10.

See Also:

Achille, L. T.   4j2
Alexander, S. T.   4j2
Arlow, J. A.   6d
Bainton, R. H.   5d
Beck, R. N.   4h
Blacker, C. P.   5b2
Blum, B. S.   5a3
Brenman, M.   4j2
Brill, A. A.   7d
Bryson, L.   8a2
Byrns, R. E.   4a1
Campion, D. R.   4a
Chiang, A. C.   4b
Clark, W. H.   4h
Coe, M. D.   7f
Cohn, N.   3a
Dawn, C. E.   4a

7c. The Non-Believer

Ballard, E. G.   A Use for Atheism in Ethics. *J. Rel. Health,* 2/2, 1963, p.1515–55.

Collier, K. G.   Obstacles to Religious Belief. *Hibbert J.,* 50, 1958, p.140–7.

Howes, P.   Why Some of the Best People Aren't Christian. *Sarawak Mus. J.,* 9/15–16, 1960, p.488–95.

Jacovini, J.   A Social-Psychological Study of Religious Nonbelievers. *Soc. Compass,* 12/3, 1965, p.177–86.

Klimovich, L.   What an Atheist Should Know About the Qur'an. *Islamic R.,* 47, 1959, p.39–42.

Luijpen, W. A.   *Phenomenology and Atheism* (Duquesne Studies, Philosophical Series, Vol. 17.). Pittsburgh: Duquesne Univ. Press, 1964, 344p.

Marty, M. E.   *Infidel: Freethought and American Religion.* N.Y.: Meridian, 1961.

Moody, J. N.   The Dechristianization of the French Working Class. *R. Polit.,* 20/1, 1958, p.46–69.

Perry, H. F.   The Workingman's Alienation from the Church. *Amer. J. Sociol.,* 4/5, 1899, p.621–9.

Rumke, H. C.   *The Psychology of Unbelief: Character and Temperament in Relation to Unbelief.* N.Y.: Sheed & Ward, 1962.

Schillebeeckx, E.   Theological Reflections on Religio-Sociological Interpretations of Modern 'Irreligion.' *Soc. Compass,* 10/3, 1963, p.257–84.

Winkeler, H.   Towards a Typology of Religious Personality Structures Amongst Non-Churchgoing, Lapsed Catholic Workers. *Soc. Compass,* 12/3, 1965, p.187–200.

See Also: 2g, 3f4

Gurian, W.   8a2
MacCreery, R.   2b
Moreton, F. E.   7b2

7d.   Conversion and Assimilation

Barkin, T. and Lee, R. H.   The Phoenix Jewish Community Center: An Institution in Adaptation. *J. Hum. Relat.,* 11/5, 1963, p.665–78.

Bharati, A.   The Indians in East Africa: A Survey of Problems of Transition and Adaptation. *Sociologus,* 14/2, 1964, p.169–77.

Boisen, A. T.   Conversion and Mental Health. *Int. J. Rel. Educ.,* 15, 1939, p.14–5.

Brill, A. A.   The Adjustment of the Jew to the American Environment. *Ment. Hyg.,* 2/2, 1918, p.219–31.

Brock, T. C.   Implications of Conversion and Magnitude of Cognitive Dissonance. *J. Sci. Stud. Rel.,* 1/2, 1962, p.198–203.

Cassin, H.   *San Nicandro: The Story of A Religious Phenomenon.* London: Cohen & West, 1959.

Cesarman, F. C.   Religious Conversion of Sex Offenders During Psychotherapy: Two Cases. *J. Past. Care,* 11, 1957, p.25–35.

Cowan, M. M.   A Christian Movement in Mexico. *Pract. Anthropol.,* 9/5, 1962, p.193–204.

Dababhay, Y.   Circuituos Assimilation Among Rural Hindustanis in California. *Soc. Forces,* 33/2, 1954, p.138–41.

Dawn, C. E.   Arab Islam in the Modern Age. *Mid. East J.,* 19/4, 1965, p.435–46.

Doherty, J. F. (ed.)   The Eighth Annual Baguio Religious

Acculturation Conference. *Philippine Sociol. R.,* 13/2, 1965, p.67–121.

Eaton, J. W.   Controlled Acculturation: A Survival Technique of the Hutterites. *Amer. Sociol. R.,* 17, 1952, p.331–40.

Eister, A. W.   *Drawing Room Conversion: A Sociological Account of the Oxford Group Movement.* Durham: Duke Univ. Press, 1950.

Eulau, H.   Proselytizing in the Catholic Press. *Pub. Opin. Quart.,* 11/2, 1947, p.189–97.

Fathi, A.   Mechanisms for Maintaining Jewish Identity. *Pac. Sociol. R.,* 5/1, 1962, p.44–7.

Femminella, F. X.   The Impact of Italian Migration on American Catholicism. *Amer. Cath. Sociol. R.,* 22/3, 1961, p.233–41.

Fergeson, E. H. (ed.)   Special Issue on Religious Conversion. *Past. Psychol.,* 16/156, 1965, p.5–51.

Fernández, J. W.   Christian Acculturation and Fang Witchcraft. *Cah. Et. Afr.,* 2, 1961, p.244–70.

Freed, S. A.   Suggested Type Societies in Acculturation Studies. *Amer. Anthropol.,* 59/1, 1957, p.55–68.

God Struck Me Dead: Religious Conversion Experiences and Autobiographies of Negro Ex-Slaves. Nashville, Tennessee: Social Science Institute, Fisk Univ., 1945, 218p.

Goddijn, W.   Catholic Minorities and Social Integration. *Soc. Compass,* 7/2, 1960, p.161–76.

Gordon, M. M. *Assimilation in American Life: The Role of Race, Religion and National Origins.* N.Y.: Oxford Univ. Press, 1964.

Harms, E. Ethical and Psychological Implications of Religious Conversion. *R. Rel. Res.,* 3/3, 1962, p.122–31.

Inniger, M. W. Mass Movements and Individual Conversion in Pakistan. *Pract. Anthropol.,* 10/3, 1963, p.122–6.

James, E. O. *The Ancient Gods: The History and Diffusion of Religion in the Ancient Near East and the Eastern Mediterranean.* N.Y.: G. P. Putnam's Sons, 1960, 359p.

Johnson, P. E. Conversion. *Past. Psychol.,* 10, 1959, p.51–6.

Jones, D. D. The Jew Leaves the Pale. *Sociol. Soc. Res.,* 19/1, 1934, p.26–37.

Kan, W. E. Why Has Christianity in Japan Made Such Slow Progress? *Church Quart. R.,* 157, 1956, p.157–65.

Kent, R. K. Soviet Muslims, The Arab World and the Myth of Synthesis. *J. Int. Aff.,* 13/2, 1959, p.141–8.

Kietzman, D. W. Conversion and Culture Change. *Pract. Anthropol.,* 5/5–6, 1958, p.203–10.

Landa, J. F. Conversion and the Patterning of Christian Experience in Malitbog, Central Panay, Philippines. *Philippine Sociol. R.,* 13/2, 1965, p.96–121.

Leavy, S. A. A Religious Conversion in a Four Year Old Child. *Bull. Phila. Assoc. Psychoanal.,* 7/3, 1957, p.85–90.

MacDonald, D. J. Psychological Factors in Conversion. *Amer. Eccles. R.,* 88, 1933, p.337–51.

Marcson, S. A Theory of Intermarriage and Assimilation. *Soc. Forces,* 29/1, 1950, p.75–8.

Mason, L. The Characterization of American Culture in Studies of Acculturation. *Amer. Anthropol.,* 57/6, pt. 1, 1955, p.1264–79.

Maves, P. B. Conversion: A Behavioral Category. *R. Rel. Res.,* 5/1, 1963, p.41–8.

Menes, A. The Conversion Movement in Prussia During the First Half of the 19th Century. *Yivo Ann. Jew. Soc. Sci.,* 6, 1951, p.187–205.

Motvani, H. L. Hinduization: A Study of Assimilation. *Sociol. Soc. Res.,* 15/4, 1930, p.810–23.

Navlakha, S. K. Spread of Puritanistic Cults in the Bhil Society. *Bull. Tribal Res. Inst.,* 2/4, 1959, p.14–32.

Novak, M. *A New Generation: American and Catholic.* N.Y.: Herder, 1964, 250p.

O'Flannery, E. Social and Cultural Assimilation. *Amer. Cath. Sociol. R.,* 22/3, 1961, p.195–206.

Owen, B. *The Battle for the Soul: Aspects of Religious Conversion.* Phila.: Westminster Press, 1960.

Palmer, E. N. The Religious Acculturation of the Negro. *Phylon,* 5/3, 1944, p.260–5.

Philpott, H. M. Conversion Techniques Used by the New Sects in the South. *Rel. Educ.,* 38, 1943, p.174–9.

Presler, H. H. Institutional Shifts in Religious Affiliation. *East. Anthropol.,* 13/1, 1959, p.17–26.

Rosenthal, E. Acculturation Without Assimilation: The Jewish Community of Chicago, Illinois. *Amer. J. Sociol.,* 66, 1960, p.275–88.

Saler, B. Religious Conversion and Self-Aggrandizment: A Guatemalan Case. *Pract. Anthropol.,* 12/3, 1965, p.107–14.

Salzman, L. The Psychology of Religious and Ideological Conversion. *Psychiatry,* 16, 1953, p.177–87.

Sangree, W. H. The Structure and Symbol Underlying "Conversion" in Bantu Tiriki. *Pract. Anthropol.,* 6/3, 1959, p.132–4.

Schnepp, G. J. Nationality and Leakage. *Amer. Cath. Sociol. R.,* 3/3, 1942, p.154–63.

Schnepp, G. J. Economic Status and Leakage. *Amer. Cath. Sociol. R.,* 4/2, 1943, p.76–92.

Siegel, B. J. (ed.) *Acculturation: Critical Abstracts, North America.* Stanford, California: Stanford Univ. Press, 1955, 231p.

Siegel, M. Religion in Western Guatemala: A Product of Acculturation. *Amer. Anthropol.,* 43, 1941, p.62–76.

Solomon, V. *A Handbook on Conversions to the Religions of the World.* N.Y.: Stravon Educational Press, 1965, 416p.

Spiro, M. E. The Acculturation of American Ethnic Groups. *Amer. Anthropol.,* 57/6, 1955, p.1240–52.

Stanley, G. Personality and Attitude Correlates of Religious Conversion. *J. Sci. Stud. Rel.,* 4/1, 1964, p.60–3.

Stewart, O. C. Washo-Northern Paiute Peyotism: A Study in Acculturation. *Univ. Calif. Public Amer. Archaeol. Ethnol.,* 40/3, 1944, p.133–6.

Voget, F. W. The American Indian in Transition: Reformation and Accommodation. *Amer. Anthropol.,* 58/2, 1956, p.249–63.

Weintraub, D. and Lissak, M. The Absorption of North African Immigrants in Agricultural Settlements in Israel. *Jew. J. Sociol.,* 3/1, 1961, p.29–54.

Willems, E. Acculturative Aspects of the Feast of the Holy Ghost in Brazil. *Amer. Anthropol.,* 51, 1949, p.400–8.

Zetterberg, H. L. Religious Conversion as a Change of Social Roles. *Sociol. Soc. Res.*, 36/3, 1952, p.159–66.

See Also: 5a, 5e, 6

Barber, B. 6d
Boisen, A. T. 5b1
Cassin, H. 5a1
Greenberg, J. H. 5a

Hedenquist, G. 5a
Jernegen, M. W. 5c
Pearce, R. H. 5e2
Spector, S. I. 2b
Spicer, E. H. 6b
Steward, J. H. 8a4
Tannous, A. I. 5e1
Taylor, P. A. M. 3a1

7e. *Mythology*

Clark, C. and Williams, T. B. *Pomo Indian Myths and Some of Their Sacred Meanings.* N.Y.: Vantage Press, 1954, 127p.

Gaskill, G. A. *Dictionary of All Scriptures and Myths.* N.Y.: Julian Press, 1960.

Guirand, F. *Egyptian Mythology.* London: Hamlyn, 1963, 153p.

Guirand, F. *Greek Mythology.* London: Hamlyn, 1965.

Hackin, J., *et al.* *Asiatic Mythology: A Detailed Description and Explanation of the Mythologies of all the Great Nations of Asia* (Trans. F. M. Atkinson). N.Y.: Thomas Y. Crowell, 1963, 459p.

Henderson, J. L. and Oakes, M. *The Wisdom of the Serpent: The Myths of Death, Rebirth and Resurrection.* N.Y.: G. Braziller, 1963, 262p.

Hooke, S. H. *Middle East Mythology.* Baltimore: Penguin Books, 1963, 198p.

Kaster, J. *Putnam's Concise Mythological Dictionary.* N.Y.: Putnam, 1963, 180p.

Kramer, S. N. *Mythologies of the Ancient World.* N.Y.: Doubleday, 1961, 480p.

Kroeber, A. L. *Seven Mohave Myths.* Berkeley: Univ. of California Press, 1948, 70p.

Long, C. H. *Alpha: The Myths of Creation.* N.Y.: G. Braziller, 1963, 264p.

Loomis, R. S. *The Grail, from Celtic Myth to Christian Symbol.* N.Y.: Columbia Univ. Press, 1963, 287p.

Petre, E. O. G. T. *Myth and Religion of the North.* London: George Weidenfeld & Nicolson, Ltd., 1964, 340p.

Sebeok, T. A. (ed.) *Myth: A Symposium.* Phila.: American Folklore Society, 1955, 110p.

Thomas, G. F. Myth and Symbol in Religion. *J. Bib. Rel.*, 7, 1939, p.163–71.

Velikovsky, I. *Oedipus and Ahknaton: Myth and History.* Garden City: Doubleday & Co., 1960.

Watts, A. W. *The Myths of Polarity.* N.Y.: G. Braziller, 1963.

Werner, E. T. C. *A Dictionary of Chinese Mythology.* N.Y.: Julian Press, 1961, 627p.

Zimmerman, J. E. *Dictionary of Classical Mythology.* N.Y.: Harper & Row, 1964, 300p.

See Also: 1a, 2, 3, 7a3, 7b3, 7f

Barton, R. F. 2h
Best, E. 2h
Boaz, F. 6c
Campbell, J. 3, 8a5
Cassirer, E. 1c
Clark, R. T. T. 3
Davidson, H. R. 3
Diehl, K. S. 9
Fontenrose, J. E. 3
Funk and Wagnall's 9
Gotesky, R. 1a
Guiraun, F. 9
Hyman, S. E. 8a2
Hymes, D. H. 1a
Jung, C. G. 8a2
King, W. 2e
Kluckhohn, C. 8a3 (2)
Locher, G. W. 6e
Lucier, C. 2h
Malinowski, B. 8a6
Moloney, J. C. 5b1
Monro, D. H. 8a2
Murray, H. A. 8a2
Opler, M. E. 7a1
Radin, P. 7a1
Rank, O. 1
Roheim, G. 8a3
Ross, A. 2h
Seznex, J. 6c
Slote, B. 8a2
Steward, J. H. 3f
Thompson, S. 4g
Trevett, L. D. 8a2
Tyler, H. A. 2h
Wittfogel, K. 3f
Zimmer, H. 3c

Bhatnagar, I. M. L. Tree Symbol Worship in Punjab. *Folklore*, 6/3, 1965, p.105–8.

Bucher, F. Cistercian Architectural Purism. *Comp. Stud. Society Hist.*, 3/1, 1960, p.89–105.

Cammann, S. The Magic Square of Three in Old Chinese Philosophy and Religion. *Hist. Rel.*, 1/1, 1961, p.37–80.

Coe, M. The Funerary Temple Among the Classic Maya. *Southw. J. Anthropol.*, 12, 1956, p.387–94.

Cope, G. *Symbolism in the Bible and the Church.* N.Y.: Philosophical Library, 1959, 287p.

Dillingstone, F. W. *Christianity and Symbolism.* Phila.: Westminster Press, 1955, 320p.

Eliade, M. *Images and Symbols: Studies in Religious Symbolism* (Trans. P. Mairet). N.Y.: Sheed & Ward, 1961.

Elkin, A. P. Studies in Australian Totemism: The Nature of Australian Totemism. *Oceania*, 4, 1933–34, p.113–31.

Firth, R. W. Totemism in Polynesia. *Oceania*, 1, 1930–31, p.291–321.

Fischer, J. L. Totemism on Truk and Ponape. *Amer. Anthropol.*, 59/2, 1957, p.250–65.

Fletscher, A. C. A Study From the Omaha Tribe: The Impact of the Totem. *Smithsonian Inst. Ann. Rep.*, 1897, p.877–86.

Geertz, C. Ethos, World-View and the Analysis of Sacred Symbols. *Antioch R.*, 17/4, 1957, p.421–37.

Gelfand, M. The Totem of the Tutelary Spirit (Mhondoro) and That of the Clan of the Sokonon District. *Afr. Stud.*, 20/4, 1961, p.214–6.

Ghosal, S. Tree in Folk Life. *Folklore*, 6/5, 1965, p.179–90.

Goldenweiser, A. A. Form and Content in Totemism. *Amer. Anthropol.*, 20, 1918, p.280–95.

Goodenough, E. R. *Jewish Symbols in the Greco Roman Period.* N.Y.: Pantheon Books, 1953–64, 12 vols.

Harvey, B. III. Masks at a Maskless Pueblo: The Laguna Colony Kachina Organization at Isleta. *Ethnology*, 2/4, 1963, p.478–89.

Hodgson, M. G. S. Islam and Image. *Hist. Rel.*, 3/2, 1964, p.220–60.

Hostetler, J. A. The Amish Use of Symbols and Their Function in Bounding the Community. *J. Roy. Anthropol. Inst.*, 94, 1964, p.11–22.

Hutchinson, J. A. *Language and Faith: Studies in Sign, Symbol, and Meaning.* Phila.: Westminster Press, 1963, 316p.

Johnson, F. E. (ed.) *Religious Symbolism.* N.Y.: Harper & Brothers, 1955.

Kabiraj, S. Fertility Cult and Trees. *Folklore*, 6/4, 1965, p.162–9.

Kaikini, V. M. Symbolism in Religion. *J. Anthropol. Society Bombay*, 11/2, 1961, p.20–36.

Lehrer, L. The Dynamic Role of Jewish Symbols in the Psychology of the Jewish Child in America. *Yivo Ann. Jew. Soc. Sci.*, 6, 1951, p.37–72.

Luyster, R. Symbolic Elements in the Cult of Athena. *Hist. Rel.*, 5/1, 1965, p.133–63.

Machle, E. J. Symbols in Religion. *J. Bib. Rel.*, 21, 1953, p.163–9.

May, R. (ed.) *Symbolism in Religion and Literature.* N.Y.: George Braziller, 1960, 253p.

McAllister, J. G. The Four Quartz Rocks Medicine Bundle of the Kiowa-Apache. *Ethnology*, 4/2, 1965, p.210–24.

Nair, P. T. Tree Symbol Worship Among the Nairs. *Folklore*, 6/3, 1965, p.114–24.

Newcomb, F. J., *et al.* *A Study of Navajo Symbolism.* Cambridge: Pap. Peabody Mus. Archaeol. Ethnol., 32/3, 1956, 100p.

Paranivatana, S. *The God of Adam's Peak.* Ascona, Switzerland: Artibus Asiae Publishers, 1958, 78p.

Radcliffe-Brown, A. R. Notes on Totemism in Eastern Australia. *J. Roy. Anthropol. Inst.*, 59, 1929, p.399–415.

Rank, G. The Symbolic Bow in the Birth Rites of North Eurasian Peoples. *Hist. Rel.*, 1/2, 1962, p.281–90.

Riley, O. L. *Masks and Magic.* London: Thames & Hudson, 1955, 122p.

Ross, R. G. and Van Den Haag, E. *Symbols and Civilization: Science, Morals, Religion, Art.* N.Y.: Harcourt Brace and World, 1963, 243p.

Sen Gupta, S., *et al.* Tree Symbol Worship in India. *Folklore*, 6/6, 1965, p.219–75 (entire Issue).

Troyer, J. *The Cross as Symbol and Ornament.* Phila.: Westminster Press, 1961, 126p.

Von Grunebaum, G. E. Byzantine Iconoclasm and the Influence of the Islamic Environment. *Hist. Rel.*, 2/1, 1962, p.1–10.

Westcott, J. and Morton-Williams, P. The Symbolism and Ritual Context of the Yoruba Laba Shango. *J. Roy. Anthropol. Inst.*, 92/1, 1962, p.23–37.

Wolf, E. R. The Virgin of Guadalupe: A Mexican National Symbol. *J. Amer. Folklore*, 71/279, 1958, p.34–9.

Worsley, P. M.   Totemism in a Changing Society. *Amer. Anthropol.*, 57/4, 1955, p.851–61.

See Also: 1a, 2, 3, 4g, 7b

Agrawala, U. S.   3
Arlow, J.   8a2
Bhatnagar, I. M. L.   7b3
Borton, H.   9
Bricson, L.   8a2
Buck, C. F.   9
Chaplin, D. P.   7b2
Clark, R. T. T.   3
Christensen, C. W.   7a4
Desmonde, W. H.   4b
Eliade, M.   4
Fernandez, J. W.   5a1
Garvan, A.   3a1
Ghosal, S.   7b3
Guertin, W.   4h
Heschel, A. J.   8a5

Karsten, J.   7b3
Kuhlen, R. G.   7b2
Levi-Strauss, C.   8a3
Lewis, E.   7b2
Loomis, R. S.   7e
Martin, D.   7b3
McLaughlin, W. B.   4g1
Moberg, D. O.   4h
Modre, E. H.   7a
Morgenstern, J.   8a2
Murray, H. A.   8a2
O'Reilly, C. T.   4h
Pan, J. S.   4h
Propipto, R.   7b3
Schuyler, J. B.   7b1
Simmons, L. W.   8a4
Thomas, J. H.   4g
Tillich, P.   8a2
Turner, V. W.   4d
Van Gennep, A.   8a3
Vimala, V. C.   4e
Wayman, A.   4i
Whittaker, M. L.   5b1

8.   Religion, Textbooks, Analytic Articles, and Readers

Religion and the Intellectuals: A Symposium. *Partisan R.,*
17/2–5, 1950, p.103–42, 216–56, 313–39, 456–83.

8a.   Textbooks and Analytic Articles

Boulard, F.   *An Introduction to Religious Sociology.* London: Darton Longman & Todd, 1960.

Chave, E. J.   *A Functional Approach to Religious Education.* Chicago: Univ. of Chicago Press, 1947.

Havens, J.   The Participant's versus the Observer's Frame

of Reference in the Psychological Study of Religion.
J. Sci. Stud. Rel., 1/1, 1961, p.79–87.

Hoult, T. F.   *The Sociology of Religion.*   N.Y.: Holt,
Rinehart, & Winston, 1958.

Wach, J.   *Sociology of Religion.*   Chicago: Univ. of Chicago Press, 1962, 418p.

8a1.   *Emphasis Analysis of Contemporary Religion*

Agogino, G. A.   Hypnotism: Its Role in the History of the
Supernatural. *Genus,* 20/1–4, 1964, p.78–81.

Ahlstrom, S. F.   The Levels of Religious Revival. *Confluence,* 4/1, 1955, p.32–43.

Alonso, J. M.   A Social and Psychological Typology of
Religious Identification in Spanish Catholicism. *Soc.
Compass,* 12/4–5, 1965, p.217–43.

Becker, H.   Processes of Secularisation: I. An Ideal-Typi-
cal Analysis With Special Reference to Personality
Change as Affected by Population Movement. *Sociol.
R.,* 24/2, 1932, p.138–54; see also Part II, 24/3, p.266–
86.

Beiler, I. R.   A Religious Attitude Inventory. *J. Bib. Rel.,*
12, 1944, p.188–92.

Benson, P. H.   *Religion in Contemporary Culture: A
Study of Religion Through Social Science.* N.Y.:
Harper & Bros., 1960.

Berger, P. L.   *The Precarious Vision.*   Garden City:
Doubleday & Co., 1961.

Berkes, N.   Religious and Secular Institutions in Comparative Perspective. *Archiv. Sociol. Rel.,* 8/16, 1963,
p.65–72.

Bigman, S. E.   Evaluating the Effectiveness of Religious
Programs. *R. Rel. Res.,* 2/3, 1961, p.97–121.

Borhek, J. T.   Role Orientations and Organizational Stability. *Human Org.,* 24/4, 1965, p.332–8.

Bradley, D. G.   Religious Differences and the Study of
Religions. *J. Bib. Rel.,* 25, 1957, p.32–7.

Brothers, J. B.   Perception in Socio-Religious Research.
Sociol. Religiosa, 7/9–10, 1963, p.65–70.

Burns, W. H.   Black Muslims in America: A Reinterpretation. *Race,* 5/1, 1963, p.26–37.

Cain, L. D., Jr.   Japanese-American Protestants. *R. Rel.
Res.,* 3/3, 1962, p.113–21.

Catton, W. R., Jr.   What Kind of People Does a Religious
Cult Attract? *Amer. Sociol. R.,* 22, p.561–6.

Chiari, J.   *Religion and Modern Society.*   London: Herbert Jenkins Ltd., 1964, 215p.

Coe, G. E.   The Recent Census of Religious Bodies. *Amer.
J. Sociol.,* 15/6, 1910, p.806–16.

Cogley, J. (ed.)   *Religion in America: Original Essays on
Religion in a Free Society.* N.Y.: Meridian Books,
1958, 288p.

Cox, H.   Sociology of Religion in a Post-Religious Era.
Christ. Scholar, 48/1, 1965, p.9–26.

Crawford, A. A.   'Q-Sort' as a Method of Determining
Areas of Concern in Adult Religious Education. *Rel.
Educ.,* 158/4, 1963, p.366–71.

Danziger, K.   Ideology and Utopia in South Africa: A
Methodological Contribution to the Sociology of
Knowledge. *Brit. J. Sociol.,* 41/1, 1963, p.59–76.

Davis, K. *Human Society.* N.Y.: Macmillan Co., 1948.

Donovan, J. D. The Sociologist Looks at the Parish. *Amer. Cath. Sociol. R.,* 9/2, 1950, p.66–73.

Eister, A. W. Empirical Research on Religion and Society: A Brief Survey of some Fruitful Lines of Inquiry. *R. Rel. Res.,* 6/3, 1965, p.125–30.

Eister, A. W. Some Aspects of Institutional Behavior with Reference to Churches. *Amer. Sociol. R.,* 17, 1952, p.64–9.

Elkind, D. Piaget's Semi-Clinical Interview and the Study of Spontaneous Religion. *J. Sci. Stud. Rel.,* 4/1, 1964, p.40–7.

Fischer, J. L. The Socio-Psychological Analysis of Folktales. *Curr. Sociol.,* 4/3, 1963, p.235–95.

Flam, L. The Sacred and Secularization in Contemporary Thought. *A. Cent. Rel.,* 1, 1961, p.179–86.

Fletcher, R. Religion in Modern Society. *Plain View,* 11/4, 1957, p.166–87.

Gerth, H. H. and Mills, C. W. *Character and Social Structure.* London: Routledge & Kegan Paul, 1961.

Godin, A. Importance and Difficulty of Scientific Research in Religious Education: The Problem of "Criterion." *Rel. Educ.,* 57/4, 1962, p.166–74.

Goldman, R. J. The Application of Piaget's Scheme of Operational Thinking to Religious Story Data by Means of the Guttman Scalogram. *Brit. J. Educ. Psychol.,* 35/2, 1965, p.158–70.

Goodenough, E. R. *The Psychology of Religious Experience.* N.Y.: Basic Books, 1965, 192p.

Grensted, L. W. *Psychology of Religion.* N.Y.: Oxford Univ. Press, 1952.

Guide for Interviewing the Minister and Selected Key Members of the Congregation of the Urban Church Effectiveness Study. *Soc. Compass,* 9/4, 1962, p.387–402.

Hammond, P. E. Contemporary Protestant Ideology: A Typology of Church Images. *R. Rel. Res.,* 2/4, 1961, p.161–9.

Hartt, J. N. The Philosopher, the Prophet and the Church: Some Reflections on Their Roles as Critics of Culture. *J. Rel.,* 35/3, 1955, p.147–59.

Holik, J. S. An Index of Religious Group Action. *Rural Sociol.,* 22/3, 1957, p.268–70.

Hopkins, P. *The Social Psychology of Religious Experience.* N.Y.: Paine-Whitman Publishers, 1962, 135p.

Inglis, J. Cargo Cults: The Problem of Explanation. *Oceania,* 27/4, 1957, p.249–63.

Jellema, D. Toward Investigating the 'Post-Modern Mind': A Working Paper. *J. Sci. Stud. Rel.,* 3/1, 1963, p.81–5.

Kedourie, E. Islam and the Orientalists: Some Recent Discussions. *Brit. J. Sociol.,* 7/3, 1956, p.217–25.

Klapp, O. E. *Ritual and Cult: A Sociological Interpretation.* Washington: Public Affairs Press, 1956, 40p.

Klausner, S. Methods of Data Collection in Studies of Religion. *J. Sci. Stud. Rel.,* 3/2, 1964, p.193–203.

Kraeling, C. H. Method in the Study of Religious Syncretism. *J. Bib. Rel.,* 9, 1941, p.28–34, 66.

Landis, B. Y. *Religion in the U. S.* N.Y.: Barnes and Noble, 1965.

Larson, R. F. Measuring "Infinite" Values. *Amer. Cath. Sociol. R.,* 20/3, 1959, p.194–202.

Lawson, E. D. and Stagner, R. The Ferguson Religionism Scale: A Study in Validation. *J. Soc. Psychol.,* 39/2, 1954, p.245–56.

Leach, E. R. (ed.) *Aspects of Caste in South India, Ceylon, and North West Pakistan.* N.Y.: Cambridge Univ. Press, 1960.

Levinson, B. M. Yeshiva College Subcultural Scale: An Experimental Attempt at Devising a Scale of the Internalization of Jewish Traditional Values. *J. Genet. Psychol.,* 101/2, 1962, p.375–99.

Lipset, S. M. The Study of Jewish Committees in a Comparative Context. *Jew. J. Sociol.,* 5/2, 1963, p.157–66.

Lyman, S. M. Chinese Secret Societies in the Occident: Notes and Suggestions for Research in the Sociology of Secrecy. *Canad. R. Sociol. Anthropol.,* 1/2, 1964, p.79–102.

Madigan, F. C., *et al.* Tamontaka: A Sociological Experiment. *Amer. Cath. Sociol. R.,* 19/4, 1958, p.322–36.

Mair, L. P. Witchcraft as a Problem in the Study of Religion. *Cah. Et. Afr.,* 4/3, 1964, p.337–48.

Moberg, D. O. *The Church as a Social Institution: The Sociology of American Religion.* Englewood Cliffs: Prentice Hall, 1962.

Murphy, G. A Note on Method in the Psychology of Religion. *J. Philos.,* 25, 1928, p.337–45.

Niebuhr, H. R. *Pious and Secular America.* N.Y.: Scribners, 1958.

O'Connell, J. The Withdrawal of the High God in West African Religion: An Essay in Interpretation. *Man,* 62, 1962, p.67–9. See also: Horton, R.—The High God: A Comment on Father O'Connell's paper, p.137–40.

Pande, T. The Concept of Folklore: Its Befitting Indian Symbols. *Folklore,* 6/1, 1965, p.7–17.

Paulson, I. Scientific Method in Monographs on Religion. *Amer. Anthropol.*, 63/4, 1961, p.832–3.

Potter, K. H. A Fresh Classification of India's Philosophical Systems. *J. Asian Stud.*, 21/1, 1961, p.25–32.

Prasad, I. A Brief Note on the Methodological Aspect of Studies in Caste Stereotypes. *Man India*, 41/3, 1961, 204–14.

Rebelsky, F. G. An Inquiry into the Meanings of Confession. *Merr.-Palm. Quart.*, 9, 1963, p.287–94.

Redekop, C. The Sect From a New Perspective. *Menn. Quart. R.*, 39/3, 1965, p.204–17.

Riesman, D. Some Informal Notes on American Churches and Sects. *Confluence*, 4/2, 1955, p.127–59.

Robertson, A. *Socialism and Religion: An Essay.* London: Lawrence & Wishart, 1960, 61p.

Schneider, L. and Dornbusch, S. M. Inspirational Religious Literature: From Latent to Manifest Functions of Religion. *Amer. J. Sociol.*, 62/5, 1957, p.476–81.

Schneider, L. and Dornbusch, S. M. *Popular Religion.* Chicago: Univ. of Chicago Press, 1958.

Schulyer, J. B. The Parish Studied as a Social System. *Amer. Cath. Sociol. R.*, 17/4, 1956, p.320–37.

Smith, J. E. The Structure of Religion. *Rel. Stud.*, 1/1, 1965, p.63–73.

Spiro, M. and D'Andrade, R. G. A Cross-Cultural Study of Some Super-Natural Beliefs. *Amer. Anthropol.*, 60/3, 1958, p.456–66.

Strunk, O., Jr. Note on Self-Reports and Religiosity. *Psychol. Rep.*, 4, 1958, p.29.

Sullivan, T. The Application of Shevky-Bell Indices to Parish Analysis. *Amer. Cath. Sociol. R.*, 22/2, 1961, p.168–71.

Textor, R. B. A Statistical Method for the Study of Shamanism: A Case Study From Field Work in Thailand. *Human Org.*, 21/1, 1962, p.56–60.

Thouless, R. H. Scientific Method in the Study of Psychology of Religion. *Char. Person.*, 7, 1938, p.103–8.

Toynbee, A. J. *Christianity Among the Religions of the World.* N.Y.: Scribners, 1958.

Vernon, G. M. Measuring Religion: Two Methods Compared. *R. Rel. Res.*, 3/4, 1962, p.159–65.

Vernon, G. M. *Sociology of Religion.* N.Y.: McGraw-Hill, 1962.

Vernon, G. M. and Stewart, R. L. Is American Religiosity Real? *Humanist*, 19, 1959, p.14–6.

Von Hoffman, N. and Cassidy, S. W. Interviewing Negro Pentecostals. *Amer. J. Sociol.*, 62/2, 1956, p.195–7.

Wach, J. *Church, Denomination and Sect.* Evanston, Illinois: Seabury Western Theological Seminary, 1946, 32p.

Wakefield, D. Slick-Paper Christianity. In M. R. Stein, *et al.* (eds.)—*Identity and Anxiety.* N.Y.: Free Press of Glencoe, 1960, p.410–5.

Welford, A. T. An Attempt at an Experimental Approach to the Psychology of Religion. *Brit. J. Psychol.*, 36, 1946, p.55–73.

Whitley, O. R. *Religious Behavior: Where Sociology and Religion Meet.* Englewood-Cliffs: Prentice-Hall, 1964.

Winter, G. Methodological Reflections on "The Religious Factor." *J. Sci. Stud. Rel.*, 2/1, 1962, p.52–63.

Witherington, H. C. *Psychology of Religion: A Christian Interpretation.* Grand Rapids: W. B. Eerdmans Publishing Company, 1955, 344p.

Yalman, N. On Some Binary Concepts in Sinhalese Religious Thought. *Trans. New York Acad. Sci.*, 24/4, 1962, p.408–20.

See Also:

188

8a2.   *Emphasis Theoretical Analysis of Religion*

Adams, J. L.   Religion and Ideologies.   *Confluence*, 4/1, 1955, p.72–84.

Agus, J. B.   Toynbee and Judaism.   *Judaism*, 4, 1955, p.319–32.

Arlow, J. A.   Ego Psychology and the Study of Mythology.   *J. Amer. Psychoanal. Assoc.*, 9/3, 1961, p.371–93.

Aubrey, E. E.   The Place of Definition in Religious Experience.   *J. Philos.*, 27, 1930, p.561–72.

Ball, J. (ed.)   A Theory for American Folklore: A Symposium.   *J. Amer. Folklore*, 72/285, 1959, p.197–242.

Bardis, P. D.   A Religious Scale.   *Soc. Sci.*, 36/2, 1961, p.120–3.

Bascom, W.   The Myth-Ritual Theory.   *J. Amer. Folklore*, 70/276, 1957, p.103–14.

Becker, H. and Majers, R. C.   Sacred and Secular Aspects of Human Society.   *Sociometry*, 5, 1942, p.207–29, 335–70.

Bellah, R. N.   Place of Religion in Human Action.   *R. Rel.*, 22, 1958, p.137–54.

Berger, P. L.   The Sociological Study of Sectarianism.   *Soc. Res.*, 21/4, 1954, p.467–85.

Berger, P. L. and Luckman, T.   Sociology of Religion and Sociology of Knowledge.   *Sociol. Soc. Res.*, 47/4, 1963, p.417–27.

Berthold, F., Jr.   The Meaning of Religious Experience.   *J. Rel.*, 32/4, 1952, p.263–71.

Binkley, L. J.   What Characterizes Religious Language.   *J. Sci. Stud. Rel.*, 2/1, 1962, p.18–22.   See also: J. H. Hick—Comment, p.22–4; Reply, 2/2, 1963, p.228–30.

Bleeker, C. J.   *The Sacred Bridge: Researches into the Nature and Structure of Religion.*   Leiden: E. J. Brill, 1963, 272p.

Borkenau, F.   Toynbee's Judgment of the Jews.   *Commentary*, 19, 1955, p.421–7.

Brunner, E. de S.   Harlan P. Douglass: Pioneer Researcher in the Sociology of Religion.   *J. Sci. Stud. Rel.*, 1, 1959, p.3–16, 63–7.

Bryan, G. M.   The "Kingdom of God" Concept in Sorokin and Toynbee.   *Soc. Forces*, 26, 1947, p.288–92.

Bryson, L., *et al.* (eds.)   *Symbols and Values: An Initial Study* (Thirteenth Symposium of the Conference on Science, Philosophy and Religion).   N.Y.: Harper & Bros., 1954, 827p.

Busia, K. A.   Has the Distinction Between Primitive and Higher Religions Any Sociological Significance?   *Archiv. Sociol. Rel.*, 8/16, 1963, p.22–5.

Buss, M. J.   The Meaning of "Cult" and the Interpretation of the Old Testament.   *J. Bib. Rel.*, 32/4, 1964, p.317–25.

Carrier, H.   *The Sociology of Religious Belonging.*   N.Y.: Herder & Herder, 1965, 335p.

Chaffee, G. E.   The Isolated Religious Sect as an Object for Social Research.   *Amer. J. Sociol.*, 35/4, 1930, p.618–30.

Cheney, C. O.   The Significance of Spiritualism.   *Ment. Hyg.*, 5/3, 1921, p.529–34.

Coe, G. A.   What Constitutes a Scientific Interpretation of Religion.   *J. Rel.*, 6, 1926, p.225–35.

Cohn, W.   Is Religion Universal? Problems of Definition.   *J. Sci. Stud. Rel.*, 2/1, 1962, p.25–33.   See also: S. Z. Klausner—Comment, p.33–5.

Coughenour, C. M.   An Application of Scale Analysis to the Study of Groups.   *Rural Sociol.*, 20/3–4, 1955, p.197–211.

Coulborn, R.   Toynbee's Reconsiderations: A Commentary.   *J. World Hist.*, 8/1, 1964, p.1–53.

Cuber, J. F., *et al.*   *Problems of American Society.*   N.Y.: Holt, Rinehart & Winston, 1964.

Dawson, C.   The Life of Civilizations.   *Sociol. R.*, 14/1, 1922, p.51–68.

Demaree, R. G.   Religion and Research. *Soc. Forces*, 4/2, 1925, p.365–70.

Demos, R.   The Meaningfullness of Religious Language. *Philosoph. Phenom. Res.*, 18, 1957–58, p.96–106.

Desroche, H.   Areas and Methods of a Sociology of Religion: The Work of G. LeBras (Trans. E. L. Sheppard). *J. Rel.*, 1955, p.34–47.

Downs, R. E.   On the Analysis of Ritual. *Southw. J. Anthropol.*, 17/1, 1961, p.75–80.

Dundes, A.   Earth-Diver: Creation of the Mythopoeic Male. *Amer. Anthropol.*, 64/5, 1962, p.1032–51.

Dunlap, K.   *Religion: Its Functions in Human Life.* N.Y.: McGraw-Hill Book Co., 1946.

Dunstan, J. L.   The Interdependence of Men and the Role of Religion. *Civilisations*, 7/4, 1957, p.489–99.

Dynes, R. R.   Toward the Sociology of Religion. *Sociol. Soc. Res.*, 38, 1954, p.227–32.

Eister, A. W.   Religious Institutions in Complex Societies: Difficulties in the Theoretic Specification of Functions. *Amer. Sociol. R.*, 28, 1957, p.387–91.

Ellwood, C. A.   The Social Function of Religion. *Amer. J. Sociol.*, 19/3, 1913, p.289–307.

Everett, J. R.   *Religion in Human Experience: An Introduction.* N.Y.: H. Holt, 1950, 556p.

Fairchild, E. M.   The Function of the Church. *Amer. J. Sociol.*, 2/2, 1896, p.220–33.

Falardeau, J. C.   The Parish as An Institutional Type. *Canad. J. Econ. Polit. Sci.*, 15/3, 1949, p.365–71.

Fanfani, A.   *Catholicism, Protestantism and Capitalism.* N.Y.: Sheed & Ward, 1955.

Faris, E.   What Constitutes a Scientific Interpretation of Religion. *J. Rel.*, 6, 1926, p.236–42.

Faris, E.   The Sect and the Sectarian. *Amer. J. Sociol.*, 60/6, 1955, p.75–89.

Faris, E.   Some Phases of Religion That are Susceptible to Study. *Amer. J. Sociol.*, 60/6, 1955, p.90.

Ferriols, R.   Religion and Culture. *Soc. Order.*, 10/4, 1960, p.160–4.

Fiero, M.   Religion as a Social Institution. In J. Biesanz and M. Biesanz—*Modern Society*. N.Y.: Prentice-Hall, Inc., 1954.

Firth, R. W.   Problem and Assumption in an Anthropological Study of Religion. *J. Roy. Anthropol. Inst.*, 89/2, 1959, p.129–48.

Fischoff, E.   The Protestant Ethic and the Spirit of Capitalism: The History of a Controversy. *Soc. Res.*, 11/1, 1944, p.53–77.

Fitzgibbon, G. F.   The Cyclical Theory of Christopher Dawson. *Amer. Cath. Sociol. R.*, 2/1, 1941, p.34–40.

Foa, U. G.   An Equal Interval Scale for the Measurement of Sabbath Observance. *J. Soc. Psychol.*, 27, 1948, p.273–6.

Fogarty, M. P.   The Rooting of Ideologies. *Soc. Compass*, 9/1–2, 1962, p.109–24.

Folsom, J. K.   Kinsey's Challenge to Ethnics and Religion. *Soc. Problems*, 1/4, 1954, p.164–8.

Fortes, M.   *Oedipus and Job in West African Religion.* Cambridge: Cambridge Univ. Press, 1959, 81p.

Francis, E. K.   Toward a Typology of Religious Orders. *Amer. J. Sociol.*, 55/5, 1950, p.437–49.

Fromm, E.   *Escape From Freedom.* N.Y.: Avon Books, 1965, 333p.

Fukuyama, Y.   Functional Analysis of Religious Beliefs. *Rel. Educ.*, 56, 1961, p.446–51.

Gargan, E. T. (ed.)   *The Intent of Toynbee's History: A Cooperative Appraisal.* Chicago: Loyola Univ. Press, 1961.

George, G.   The Sociology of Ritual. *Amer. Cath. Sociol. R.*, 17/2, 1956, p.109–16.

Goddijn, H. P. M.   The Sociology of Religious Orders and Congregations. *Soc. Compass*, 7/5–6, 1960, p.431–47.

Gonda, J.   Some Notes on the Study of Ancient-Indian Religious Terminology. *Hist. Rel.*, 2/2, 1962, p.243–73.

Greeley, A. M.   A Note on the Origins of Religious Differences. *J. Sci. Stud. Rel.*, 3/1, 1963, p.21–31.

Gurian, W.   Totalitarian Religions. *R. Polit.*, 14/1, 1952, p.3–14.

Hadot, J. J.   Religious Systems and Social Structure. *Ann. Sociol.*, 1960, p.391–414.

Hanson, R. P. C.   *Tradition in the Early Church.* Phila: Westminster Press, 1963, 288p.

Haydon, A. E.   What Constitutes a Scientific Interpretation of Religion? *J. Rel.*, 6, 1926, p.243–9.

Heddendorf, R.   The Sect and Religious Autonomy. *Sociol. Quart.*, 6/1, 1965, p.45–58.

Herberg, W.   Arnold Toynbee, Historian or Religious Prophet? *Queen's Quart.*, 64, 1957, p.421–33.

Herberg, W.   *Protestant-Catholic-Jew.* Garden City: Doubleday & Co., 1955.

Herrlin, O.   On Liturgy and Society. *Acta Sociol.*, 3/2–3, 1958, p.91–7.

Hertz, R.   *Death and the Right Hand* (Trans. R. Needham and C. Needham). Glencoe: Free Press, 1960, 174p.

Higham, J. Another Look at Nativism. *Cath. Hist. R.*, 44/2, 1958, p.147–58.

Hoffer, E. *The True Believer.* N.Y.: Harper, 1951.

Hostie, R. *Religion and the Psychology of Jung.* N.Y.: Sheed and Ward, 1957, 264p.

Hoult, T. F. A Functional Theory of Religion. *Sociol. Soc. Res.*, 41/4, 1957, p.277–80.

Hudson, R. L. The Social Context of Religion. *Sociol. Soc. Res.*, 30/1, 1946, p.43–7.

Hughes, E. C. The Early and Contemporary Study of Religion. *Amer. J. Sociol.*, 60/6, 1955, p. i–iv.

Hyman, S. E. The Ritual View of Myth and the Mythic. *J. Amer. Folklore*, 68/270, 1955, p.462–72.

James, E. O. The Nature and Function of Myth. *Folk Lore* (London), 68/4, 1957, p.474–82.

James, W. *Essays on Faith and Morals.* N.Y.: Longmans, Green & Co., 1949.

Jekels, L. *Selected Papers.* N.Y.: International Universities Press, 1952.

Johnson, P. E. *Psychology of Religion.* Nashville: Abingdon, 1959, 304p.

Jung, C. G. and Kerenyi, C. *Essays on a Science of Mythology: The Myth of the Divine Child and the Mysteries of Eleusis.* N.Y.: Pantheon Books, 1949, 289p.

Kling, F. R. A Study of Testing as Related to the Ministry. *Rel. Educ.*, 53/3, 1958, p.243–8.

Kluckhohn, C. Myths and Rituals: A General Theory. *Harvard Theol. R.*, 35, 1942, p.45–79.

Kluckhohn, F., *et al. Variations in Value Orientations.* Evanston, Illinois: Row, Peterson, 1961, 50p.

Kolenda, P. M. Toward a Model of the Hindu Jajmani System. *Human Org.*, 22/1, 1963, p.11–31.

Kroeber, A. L. *The Nature of Culture.* Chicago: Univ. of Chicago Press, 1952, 438p.

Kroeber, A. L. and Kluckhohn, C. *Culture: A Critical Review of Concepts and Definitions.* Cambridge: Pap. Peabody Mus. Archeol. Ethnol., 47/1, 1952, 228p.

Lake, E. F. C. Folklife and Traditions. *Folk Lore* (London), 69, 1958, p.47–51, 195–202, 265–9.

Leach, E. R. Levi-Strauss in the Garden of Eden: An Examination of Some Recent Developments in the Analysis of Myth. *Trans. New York Acad. Sci.*, 2/23, 1961, p.386–96.

Lee, R. The Sociology of Religion: Some Problems and Prospects. *Rel. Life*, 30, 1961, p.268–78.

Leferre, P. Erikson's Young Man Luther: A Contribution to the Scientific Study of Religion. *J. Sci. Stud. Rel.*, 2/2, 1963, p.248–52.

Lewis, L. S. Knowledge, Danger, Certainty and the Theory of Magic. *Amer. J. Sociol.*, 69/1, 1963, p.7–12.

Little, D. Religion and Social Analysis in the Thought of Ernst Troeltsch. *J. Sci. Stud. Rel.*, 1/1, 1959, p.17–24.

Lowie, R. H. Religion in Human Life. *Amer. Anthropol.*, 65/3, 1963, p.532–42.

Marwick, M. G. The Study of Ritual. *Afr. Stud.*, 16/3, 1957, p.181–7.

Marx, K. and Engels, F. *On Religion.* N.Y.: Schocken Books, 1964, 382p.

Matthes, J. Preconceptions and Institutionalisation: The Crucial Problem Facing Contemporary Research Work in Germany in the Field of the Sociology of Religion. *Soc. Compass*, 10/4–5, 1963, p.377–86.

Matthews, S. Theology From the Point of View of Social Psychology. *J. Rel.*, 3, 1923, p.337–51.

May, H. G. A Sociological Approach to Hebrew Religion. *J. Bib. Rel.*, 2, 1944, p.98–106.

Mayer, C. The Problem of a Sociology of Religion. *Soc. Res.*, 1936, p.337–47.

Monro, D. H. The Concept of Myth. *Sociol. R.*, 42/6, 1950, p.115–32.

Morgenstern, J. *The Fire Upon the Altar.* Chicago: Quadrangle Books, 1963, 132p.

Mow, J. B. The Natural Sources of Religion. *J. Bib. Rel.*, 23, 1955, p.25–31.

Mukerjee, R. The Way of the Transcendentalist. *Sociol. R.*, 21/3, 1929, p.197–206.

Mukerjee, R. Religious Experience: What It Is and How It Works. *Sociol. R.*, 22/2, 1930, p.97–107.

Munk, A. W. The Basis of Authority in Religion. *J. Bib. Rel.*, 20, 1952, p.255–9.

Murray, H. A. (ed.) *Myth and Mythmaking.* N.Y.: George Braziller, 1960, 381p.

Naess, A. A Systematization of Gandian Ethics of Conflict Resolution. *J. Conf. Resol.*, 2/2, 1958, p.140–55.

Nagendra, S. P. The Nature and Significance of Ritual. *East. Anthropol.*, 15/1, 1962, p.2–20.

Neundorfer, L. Office and Service: The Function of the Church in Modern Society. *Soc. Compass*, 7/4, 1960, p.283–98.

Newell, W. H. The Sociology of Ritual in Early China. *Sociol. Bull.*, 6/1, 1957, p.1–13.

Nichols, J. H.   Religion in Toynbee's History.   *J. Rel.*, 27, 1948, p.99–119.

Nottingham, E. K.   *Religion and Society.*   N.Y.: Random House, 1954.

O'Dea, T. F.   The Sociology of Religion.   *Amer. Cath. Sociol. R.*, 15/2, 1954, p.73–103.

O'Dea, T. F.   *The Sociology of Religion.*   Englewood Cliffs, New Jersey: Prentice-Hall, 1965.

Otto, M. C.   Changes in the Theory of Religion.   *Ment. Hyg.*, 14/2, 1930, p.258–71.

Page, C. H.   Bureaucracy and the Liberal Church.   *R. Rel.*, 16, 1952, p.137–50.

Parsons, T.   *Structure and Process in Modern Societies.*   Glencoe: Free Press, 1964.

Parsons, T.   *Essays in Sociological Theory.*   Glencoe: Free Press, 1949, p.194–211.

Partin, H.   Recent Trends in the Study of Religions: Some Current Problems in Methodology.   *Encounter*, 22, 1961, p.310–6.

Pemberton, P. L.   Frontiers in Studying the Religious Aspects of Human Relations.   *J. Hum. Relat.*, 3/1, 1954, p.24–43.

Pemberton, P. L.   An Examination of Some Criticism of Talcott Parsons Sociology of Religion.   *J. Rel.*, 36/4, 1956, p.241–56.

Pfautz, H. W.   The Sociology of Secularization: Religious Groups.   *Amer. J. Sociol.*, 61/2, 1955, p.121–8.

Pilling, A. R.   Statistics, Sorcery, and Justice.   *Amer. Anthropol.*, 64/5, 1962, p.1057–9.

Presler, H. H.   Variant Definitions as a Source of Oral Myth.   *Man India*, 38/3, 1958, p.186–98.

Pruyser, P. W.   Erikson's Young Man Luther: A New Chapter in the Psychology of Religion.   *J. Sci. Stud. Rel.*, 2/2, 1963, p.238–42.

Quarberg, D.   Historical Reason, Faith and the Study of Religion.   *J. Sci. Stud. Rel.*, 1/1, 1961, p.122–4.

Randall, J. H., Jr.   Romantic Reinterpretations of Religion.   *Stud. Romanticism*, 2/4, 1963, p.189–212.

Reik, T.   *Myth and Guilt.*   N.Y.: George Braziller, 1957, 432p.

Reik, T.   *The Temptation.*   N.Y.: George Braziller, 1961, 256p.

Reyburn, W. D.   Conflicts and Contradictions in African Christianity.   *Pract. Anthropol.*, 4/5, 1957, p.161–9.

Robinson, G. K.   Nationality Origin and Religious Background.   *Amer. J. Sociol.*, 44/5, 1939, p.708–20.

Robinson, M. P.   The "Lumen Vitae" Religious Projective Pictures, Presented as a Group Test.   *Lumen Vitae*, 15, 1960, p.243–57.

Rotenstreich, N.   The Revival of the Fossil Remnant—Or Toynbee and Jewish Nationalism.   *Jew. Soc. Stud.*, 24/3, 1962, p.131–43.

Roucek, J. S.   Sociology of Secret Societies.   *Amer. J. Econ. Sociol.*, 19/2, 1960, p.161–8.

Sawyerr, H.   Ancestor Worship: A Discussion of Some of the Problems Inherent in the Phrase.   *Sierra Leone Bull. Rel.*, 6/2, 1964, p.25–33.

Schmidt, P. F.   Is There Religious Knowledge?   *J. Philos.*, 55/13, 1958, p.529–38.

Schneider, L.   Problems in the Sociology of Religion.   In R.E.L. Faris (ed.)—*Handbook of Modern Sociology.*   Chicago: Rand McNally, 1964, p.770–807.

Siegman, A. W.   An Empirical Investigation of the Psychoanalytic Theory of Religious Behavior.   *J. Sci. Stud. Rel.*, 1/1, 1961, p.74–8.

Simmel, G.   *Sociology of Religion* (Trans. C. Rosenthal).   N.Y.: Philosophical Library, 1959, 76p.

Slote, B. (ed.)   *Myth and Symbol: Critical Approaches and Applications.*   Lincoln: Univ. of Nebraska Press, 1963, 196p.

Smalley, W. A.   Cultural Implications of an Indigenous Church.   *Pract. Anthropol.*, 5/2, 1958, p.51–65.

Smith, D. H.   The Significance of Confucius for Religion.   *Hist. Rel.*, 2/1, 1963, p.242–55.

Smith, M. (trans.)   *Readings From the Mystics of Islam.*   London: Luzac and Co., 1950, 144p.

Smith, M. W.   Towards a Classification of Cult Movements.   *Man*, 59, 1959, p.8–12. See also: A. F. C. Wallace, p.24–5; F. W. Voget, p.26–8; and M. W. Smith, p.28.

Smith, W. C.   The Group and the Church.   *Sociol. Soc. Res.*, 41/5, 1957, p.349–53.

Spillius, J.   Review of Radcliffe-Brown's Theory of Religion.   *Bull. Tribal Res. Inst.*, 11/2, 1958, p.32–48.

Stahmer, H.   *Religion and Contemporary Society.*   N.Y.: Macmillan Co., 1963.

Stanley, M.   Plumber or Religious Researcher?   *R. Rel. Res.*, 2/2, 1960, p.69–79.

Stark, R.   A Taxonomy of Religious Experience.   *J. Sci. Stud. Rel.*, 5/1, 1965, p.97–116.

Stark, W.   *Social Theory and Christian Thought.*   London: Routledge and Kegan Paul, 1959.

Stein, J. W.   Heaven: A Topic for Research.   *R. Rel. Res.*, 5/3, 1964, p.170–4.

Sterba, R.   On Christmas.   *Psychoanal. Quart.*, 13/1, 1944, p.79.

Strunk, O., Jr. (ed.)   *Readings in the Psychology of Religion.*   N.Y.: Abingdon Press, 1959.

Strunk, O., Jr. (ed.) *Religion: A Psychological Interpretation*. N.Y.: Abingdon Press, 1962.

Thorner, I. Prophetic and Mystic Experience: Comparison and Consequences. *J. Sci. Stud. Rel.*, 5/1, 1965, p.82–96.

Thurlings, J. M. G. Functionalism, Social Change and the Sociology of Religion. *Soc. Compass*, 8/5, 1961, p.407–23.

Tillich, P. The Religious Symbol. *Daedalus*, 87, 1958, p.3–21.

Trevett, L. D. Origins of the Creation Myth: A Hypothesis. *Amer. Psychoanal. Assoc.*, 5/3, 1957, p.461–8.

Tufari, P. Sixty Years of Psychology of Religion: Notes and Comments on a Recent Survey. *Soc. Compass*, 7/4, 1960, p.341–59.

Underhill, E. *Worship*. N.Y.: Harper & Brothers, 1957, 350p.

Underhill, E. *The Essentials of Mysticism and Other Essays*. N.Y.: E. P. Dutton, 1960, 245p.

Van de Weyer, A. The Sociology of Religion: An Essay in Interpretation. *Soc. Compass*, 8/5, 1961, p.381–6.

Voget, F. W. The Folk Society: An Anthropological Application. *Soc. Forces*, 33/2, 1954, p.105–11.

Vogt, E. Z. American Subcultural Continua as Exemplified by the Mormons and Texans. *Amer. Anthropol.*, 57/6, 1955, p.1163–72.

Von Hoffman, N. The Church: Subject of Social Research. *Soc. Order*, 6/7, 1956, p.319–27.

von Leent, J. A. A. The Sociology of Parish and Congregation. *Soc. Compass*, 8/6, 1961, p.535–58.

Von Nieuwenhuyze, C. A. O. The Prophetic Function in Islam: An Analytic Approach. *Etudes, Correspond. d'Orient*, 1/2, 1962, p.119–38; see also 3, 1963, p.99–119.

Wach, J. Sociology of Religion. In G. Gurvitch and W. Moore—*Twentieth Century Sociology*. N.Y.: Philosophical Library, 1945, p.406–37.

Wach, J. General Revelation and the Religions of the World. *J. Bib. Rel.*, 22, 1954, p.83–93.

Walker, L. Toynbee and Religion: A Catholic View. *Thomist*, 18, 1955, p.292–9.

Walker, R. E. and Firetto, A. The Clergyman as a Variable in Psychological Testing. *J. Sci. Stud. Rel.*, 4/2, 1965, p.234–6.

Wallace, A. F. C. Mazeway Resynthesis: A Biocultural Theory of Religious Inspiration. *Trans. New York Acad. Sci.*, 2/18, 1956, p.626–38.

Wallace, A. F. C., *et al.* Towards a Classification of Cult Movements: Some Further Considerations. *Man*, 59, 1959, p.25–8.

Wallis, L. Sociological Significance of the Bible. *Amer. J. Sociol.*, 12/4, 1907, p.532–52.

Weil, G. Arnold Toynbee's Conception of the Future of Islam. *Mid. East. Aff.*, 2, 1951, p.3–17.

Wendon, J. Christianity, History and Mr. Toynbee. *J. Rel.*, 36, 1956, p.139–49.

White, L. A. An Anthropological Approach to the Emotional Factors of Religion. *J. Philos.*, 2/3, 1926, p.546–54.

Williams, J. P. The Nature of Religion. *J. Sci. Stud. Rel.*, 2/1, 1962, p.3–14. See also: H. L. Friess—Comment, p.15–7.

Williams, M. J. Catholic Sociological Theory: A Review and Prospectus. *Amer. Cath. Sociol. R.*, 4/3, 1943, p.137–43.

Wilson, D. R. An Analysis of Sect Development. *Amer. Sociol. R.*, 24, 1959, p.3–15.

Woolcott, P., Jr. Erikson's Luther: A Psychiatrist's View. *J. Sci. Stud. Rel.*, 2/2, 1963, p.243–8.

Yinger, J. M. The Influence of Anthropology on Sociological Theories of Religion. *Amer. Anthropol.*, 60/3, 1958, p.487–95.

Yinger, J. M. *Religion, Society and the Individual*. N.Y.: Macmillan Co., 1957.

Yinger, J. M. *Sociology Looks at Religion*. N.Y.: Macmillan Co., 1964.

Young, B. and Hughes, J. E. Organizational Theory and the Canonical Parish. *Sociol. Anal.*, 26/2, 1965, p.57–71.

Zeligs, D. F. A Psychoanalytic Note on the Function of the Bible. *Amer. Imago*, 14, 1957, p.57–85.

Zuurdeeg, W. F. *An Analytic Philosophy of Religion*. N.Y.: Abingdon Press, 1958, 320p.

See Also:

8a3.   Primitive Religion

Barber, B.   A Socio-Cultural Interpretation of the Peyote Cult. *Amer. Anthropol.*, 43/4, 1941, p.673–5.

Brenner, A. B.   The Great Mother Goddess. *Psychoanal. R.*, 37, 1950, p.320–40.

Coriat, I. H.   Totemism in Prehistoric Man. *Psychoanal. R.*, 21, 1934, p.40–8.

Dawson, C.   Religion and Primitive Culture. *Sociol. R.*, 17/2, 1925, p.105–19.

Evans-Pritchard, E. E., *et al.   The Institutions of Primitive Society.* Glencoe: Free Press, 1954.

Firth, R. W.   The Theory of Cargo Cult: A Note on Tikopia. *Man,* 55, 1955, p.130–2.

Firth, R. W.   *The Fate of the Soul: An Interpretation of Some Primitive Concepts.* Cambridge: Cambridge Univ. Press, 1955, 46p.

Gausdal, J.   *The Santal Khuts: Contribution to Animistic Research.* London: Routledge & Kegan Paul, 1961, 217p.

Goldenweiser, A. A.   Spirit, Mana, and the Religious Thrill. *J. Philos.*, 12, 1915, p.632–40.

Goode, W. J.   Contemporary Thinking About Primitive Religion. *Sociologus,* 5/2, 1955, p.122–32.

Goode, W. J.   *Religion Among the Primitives.* N.Y.: Collier-Macmillan, 1964.

Gunckel, L. W.   Analysis of the Dieties of Mayan Inscriptions. *Amer. Anthropol.*, 8, 1897, p.397–412.

Hogg, G.   *Cannibalism and Human Sacrifice.* London: Hale, 1958, 206p.

Howells, W.   *The Heathens.* Garden City: Doubleday & Co., 1948.

Inglis, J.   Cargo Cults: The Problem of Explanation. *Oceania,* 27/4, 1957, p.249–63.

James, E. O.   Primitive Religion: Past and Present. *Folk Lore* (London), 72, 1961, p.496–509.

Jarvie, I. C.   Theories of Cargo Cults: A Critical Analysis. *Oceania,* 34/1, 1963, p.1–31; see also 34/2, p.108–36.

Klingender, F. D.   Palaeolithic Religion and the Principle of Social Evolution. *Brit. J. Sociol.*, 5/2, 1954, p.138–53.

Kluckhohn, C.   Myths and Rituals: A General Theory. *Harvard Theol. R.*, 35/1, 1942, p.45–79.

Kluckhohn, C.   Theories of Myth and the Folklorist. *Daedalus,* 88/2, 1959, p.280–90.

Kroeber, A. L.   *Anthropology.* N.Y.: Harcourt, Brace, 1948.

Lang, A.   Method in the Study of Totemism. *Amer. Anthropol.*, 14, 1912, p.368–404.

Levi-Strauss, C. *Totemism* (Trans. R. Needham). Boston: Beacon Press, 1963, 116p.

Lowie, R. H. *Primitive Religion.* N.Y.: Liveright Publishing Co., 1948, 382p.

Makkay, J. An Important Proof to the Prehistory of Shamanism. *Alba Regia,* 2, 1961–62, p.5–10.

Maringer, J. *The Gods of Prehistoric Man.* London: Weidenfeld & Nicolson, 1960, 219p.

Moore, O. K. Divination: A New Perspective. *Amer. Anthropol.,* 59/1, 1957, p.69–74.

Morton-Williams, P. The Atinga Cult Among the South-Western Yoruba: A Sociological Analysis of a Witch-Finding Movement. *Bull. Inst. Francais Afrique Noire,* 18/3–4, 1956, p.315–34.

Nash, M. Witchcraft as Social Process in a Tzeltal Community. *Amer. Indig.,* 20/2, 1960, p.121–6.

Norbeck, E. *Religion in Primitive Society.* N.Y.: Harper & Brothers, 1961, 318p.

Park, G. K. Divination and Its Social Contexts. *J. Roy. Anthropol. Inst.,* 93/2, 1963, p.195–209.

Radcliffe-Brown, A. R. *Structure and Function in Primitive Society.* Glencoe: Free Press, 1952.

Radin, P. *Primitive Religion.* N.Y.: Dover Publishers, 1957.

Roheim, G. *The Eternal Ones of the Dream: A Psychoanalytic Interpretation of Australian Myth and Ritual.* N.Y.: International Universities Press, 1945, 270p.

Stanner, W. E. H. On Aboriginal Religion: I. Lineaments of Sacrifice. *Oceania,* 30/2, 1959, p.108–27. See also: II. Sacramentalism, Rite and Myth, 30/1, 1960, p.246–78; III. Symbolism in the Higher Rites, 31/2, p.100–20; IV. Design Plan of a Riteless Myth, 31/4, 1961, p.233–58; V. Design Plan of a Mythless Rite, 32/2, p.79–108; VI. Cosmos and Society Made Correlative, 33/4, 1963, p.239–73.

Stefaniszyn, B. African Reincarnation Re-Examined. *African Stud.,* 13/3–4, 1954, p.130–46.

Steiner, F. and Bohannan, L. (eds.) *Taboo.* London: Philosophical Library, 1956, 154p.

Sumner, W. G. *Folkways: A Study of the Sociological Importance of Usages, Manners, Customs, Mores, and Morals.* N.Y.: Dover Publications, 1959, 692p.

Swanton, J. R. Shamanism and Witchcraft. *Nat. Mus. Canada Bull.,* 152/42, 1958, p.64–7.

Turner, V. W. Some Current Trends in the Study of Ritual in Africa. *Anthropol. Quart.,* 38/3, 1965, p.155–66.

Tylor, E. B. *Primitive Culture.* N.Y.: Harper & Row, 1958, 539p.

Van Eyken, A. G. M. Witchcraft and the Supernatural. *Uganda J.,* 22/2, 1958, p.151–7.

Van Gennep, A. *The Rites of Passage* (Trans. M. B. Veyedom and G. L. Chaffee). Chicago: Univ. of Chicago Press, 1960, 198p.

See Also:

Durkheim, E.   8a6
Goldenweiser, A. A.   7e
Jahoda, G.   7b3
James, E. O.   7d
Jensin, A. E.   8a5
Leslie, C.   8b
Lessa, W. A.   2h
Needham, R.   7a1
Pettersson, O.   2h
Radin, P.   3f
Spillius, J.   8a2
Swanson, G. E.   3

8a4.   *Description Or Review of Programs*

Almerich, P. The Present Position of Religious Sociology in Spain. *Soc. Compass,* 12/4–5, 1965, p.312–20.

Anzai, S. Sociology of Religion in Post-War Europe. *Jap. Sociol. R.,* 11/1, 1960, p.109–20.

Banning, W. The Sociological Institute of the Dutch Reformed Church. In *Transactions of the Second World Congress of Sociology.* London: International Sociological Association, 1954, p.47–52, vol. 1.

Birnbaum, N. Nuffield College Conference on the Sociology of Religion. *Archiv. Sociol. Rel.,* 11, 1961, p.147–9.

Blow, R. M. The Sociology of Religion in Latin America. *Amer. Cath. Sociol. R.,* 15/2, 1954, p.161–75.

Brothers, J. B. Recent Development in the Sociology of Religion in England and Wales. *Soc. Compass,* 11/3-4, 1964, p.13–9.

Bureau For Native Affairs, Netherlands, New Guinea. Anthropological Research in Netherlands, New Guinea Since 1950. *Oceania,* 29/2, 1958, p.132–63.

Cook, S. W. (ed.) *Research Plans Formulated at the Research Planning Workshop on Religious and Character Education.* N.Y.: Religious Education Association, 1961.

Cook, S. W. Review of Recent Research Bearing on Religious and Character Formation. *Rel. Educ.*, 57, 1962.

Defarrari, R. J. (ed.) *The Social Sciences in Catholic College Programs*. Washington: Catholic Univ. Press, 1954, 180p.

Delacroix, S. Parish Inquiries in France. *Amer. Cath. Sociol. R.*, 13/3, 1952, p.169–73.

Delcuve, G. Mission and Catechesis: A Report on the International Week (Eichstädt, July 1960). *Lumen Vitae*, 15/4, 1960, p.723–40.

Devanandan, P. D. A Centre For the Study of Hinduism. *Int. R. Missions*, 46, 1957, p.260–7.

Dorson, R. M. Current Folklore Theories. *Curr. Anthropol.*, 4/1, 1963, p.93–112.

Dorson, R. M. (ed.) *Folklore Research Around the World: A North American Point of View*. Bloomington: Indiana Univ. Press, 1961, 197p.

Drakeford, J. W. *Psychology in Search of a Soul: A Survey Study in the Psychology of Religion*. Nashville: Broadman Press, 1964.

Dumont, L. and Pocock, D. (eds.) Religion. *Contrib. Ind. Sociol.*, 3, 1959, p.7–87.

Early, J. D. The Sociology of Religion in the United States. *Sociol. Rel.*, 5/7, 1962, p.85–100.

Eliade, M. Recent Works on Shamanism: A Review Article. *Hist. Rel.*, 1, 1961, p.152–186.

Fishman, J. A. American Jewry As a Field of Social Science Research. *Yivo Ann. Jew. Soc. Sci.*, 12, 1958–59, p.70–101.

Friedel, F. J. Catholic Sociological Research. *Amer. Cath. Sociol. R.*, 3/3, 1942, p.129–36. See also: Liguori, *et al.*—Comments, p.137–43.

Friess, H. L. Growth in Study of Religion at Columbia University. *R. Rel.*, 19/1-2, 1954, p.13–39.

Gartner, L. P. The History of North American Jewish Communities: A Field for the Jewish Historian. *Jew. J. Sociol.*, 7/1, 1965, p.22–9.

Gauss, G. *The Teaching of Religion in American Higher Education*. N.Y.: Ronald Press, 1951, 158p.

Glock, C. Y. The Sociology of Religion. In R. K. Merton, *et al.* (eds.)—*Sociology Today*. N.Y.: Basic Books, 1959, p.153–77.

Goddijn, W. The Development of Positive Sociological Research in Relation to Religion, and the International Institute for Social-Ecclesiastical Research. *Soc. Compass*, 3/5-6, 1956, p.348–54.

Goddijn, W. The Sociology of Religion and Socio-Religious Research in the Netherlands. *Soc. Compass*, 7/4, 1960, p.360–9.

Golb, N. The Second World Congress of Jewish Studies. *Judaism*, 7/1, 1958, p.30–6.

Greeley, A. M. Areas of Research on Religion and Social Organization. *Amer. Cath. Sociol. R.*, 23/2, 1962, p.99–112.

Gregory, W. E. The Psychology of Religion: Some Suggested Areas of Research of Significance to Psychology. *J. Abnorm. Soc. Psychol.*, 1952, p.256–8.

Gustafson, J. M. Sociology of Religion in Sweden. *R. Rel. Res.*, 1/3, 1960, p.101–9.

Gustafsson, B. The State of Sociology of Protestantism in Scandinavia. *Soc. Compass*, 12/6, 1965, p.359–66.

Havens, J. The Changing Climate of Research on the College Student and His Religion. *J. Sci. Stud. Rel.*, 3/1, 1963, p.52–69.

Herberg, W. (ed.) *Four Existential Theologians*. Garden City: Doubleday & Co., 1958.

Herr, V. V. The Loyola National Institute of Mental Health Seminary Project. A Project. A Progress Report. *Amer. Cath. Sociol. R.*, 21/4, 1960, p.331–6.

Highet, J. A Review of Scottish Socio-Religious Literature. *Soc. Compass*, 11/3-4, 1964, p.21–4.

Hiltner, S. and Rogers, W. R. Research on Religion and Personality Dynamics. *Rel. Educ.*, 57/4 (Res. Suppl.), 1962, p.128–40.

Hopkins, P. A Critical Survey of the Psychologies of Religion. *Char. Person.*, 6, 1937, p.16–35.

Hormann, B. L. Towards a Sociology of Religion in Hawaii. *Soc. Process*, 25, 1961-2, p.58–66.

Hostetler, J. A. The Hutterite Society Study. *Menn. Quart. R.*, 37, 1963, p.239–42.

Hostetler, J. A. and McKusick, V. Genetic Studies of the Amish: A Summary and Bibliography. *Menn. Quart. R.*, 39/3, 1965, p.223–6.

Houtart, F. Developments in Religious Sociology. *Soc. Order*, 7, 1957, p.220–4.

Howes, J. F. New Writings on Japan's Religions: A Review Article. *Pac. Aff.*, 37/2, 1964, p.166–78.

Hultkrantz, A. Swedish Research on the Religion and Folklore of the Lapps. *J. Roy. Anthropol. Inst.*, 85/1-2, 1955, p.81–99.

International Survey: The Liturgical Movement in Various Countries. *Lumen Vitae*, 10/2-3, 1955, p.417–35.

Jackson, M. An Account of Religious Sociology in France. *Sociol. R.*, 7/2, 1959, p.19–21.

Jewish Social Studies. Papers and Proceedings of the Tercentary Conference on American Jewish Sociology. *Jew. Soc. Stud.*, 17/13, 1955, p.1–116.

Johnson, P. E. Psychology of Religion in America. *Archiv. Religions Psychol.*, 7, 1962, p.42–53.

Kauffman, J. H. Report on Mennonite Sociological Research. *Menn. Quart. R.*, 37, 1963, p.126–31.

Kooster, R. The Second European Seminar on the Sociology of Protestantism. *Soc. Compass*, 8/1, 1961, p.81–6.

Kraemer, P. Research Activities of the Sociological Institute of the Netherlands Reformed Church. *Archiv. Sociol. Rel.*, 8, 1959, p.113–9.

Kritzeck, J. Moslem—Christian Understanding in Medieval Times: A Review Article. *Comp. Stud. Society Hist.*, 4/3, 1962, p.387–401.

Kroeber, A. L. (ed.) *Anthropology Today: An Encyclopedia Inventory.* Chicago: Univ. of Chicago Press, 1953, 966p.

La Barre, W. Twenty Years of Peyote Studies. *Curr. Anthropol.*, 1/1, 1960, p.45–60.

Lambert, R. D. Untouchability as a Social Problem: Theory and Research. *Sociol. Bull.* (Bombay), 7/1, 1958, p.55–61.

Landau, J. M. Prolegomena to a Study of Secret Societies in Modern Egypt. *Mid. East Stud.*, 1/2, 1965, p.135–86.

Lenski, G. E. The Sociology of Religion in the United States: A Review of Theoretically Oriented Research. *Soc. Compass*, 9/4, 1962, p.307–37.

Loewenthal, R. Russian Contributions to the History of Islam in China. *Cent. Asiat. J.*, 7/4, 1962, p.312–5.

Long, C. H. The West African High God: History and Religious Experience. *Hist. Rel.*, 3/2, 1964, p.328–42.

Lurie, M. L. and Weinreich, M. (eds.) Jewish Social Research. *Yivo Ann. Jew. Soc. Sci.*, 1949, 4, p.147–312.

Metraux, A. Status of Folklore Research in South America. *Southw. J. Anthropol.*, 4/2, 1948, p.148–54.

Minihan, J. The Pan-Orthodox Meeting at Rhodes. *Blackfriars*, 42/498, 1961, p.507–16.

Moberg, D. O. Sociology of Religion in the Netherlands. *R. Rel. Res.*, 2/1, 1960, p.1–7.

Moore, D. H. The British Institute of Christian Education. *J. Bib. Rel.*, 7, 1939, p.27–9.

Mosse, G. L. Puritanism Reconsidered. *Archiv. Reform.*, 55/1, 1964, p.37–48.

National Council of Churches, U. S. A: Bureau of Research and Survey. *Soc. Compass*, 10/6, 1963, p.550–2.

Niles, D. T. The All Africa Conference of Churches. *Int. R. Missions*, 57/208, 1963, p.409–13.

Norwood, F. A. Methodist Historical Studies, 1930–1959. *Church Hist.*, 28/4, 1959, p.391–417; 29/1, 1960, p.74–88.

Page, F. H. The Psychology of Religion After Fifty Years. *Canad. J. Psychol.*, 5, 1951, p.60–7.

Patai, R. (ed.) *Current Jewish Social Research.* N.Y.: Theodor Herzl Foundation, 1958, 102p.

Paulson, I. Swedish Contributions to the Study of Primitive Soul Conceptions. *Ethnos*, 19/1–4, 1954, p.157–67.

Paulson, I. The Animal Guardian: A Critical and Synthetic Review. *Hist. Rel.*, 3/2, 1964, p.202–19.

Pelissner, J. The International Centre "Lumen Vitae." *Lumen Vitae*, 15/2, 1960, p.217–30.

Petry, R. C. European Church History (1946–7): (Research Abstracts). *J. Bib. Rel.*, 16, 1948, p.108–11.

Pickering, W. S. F. Protestant and Episcopalian Church Survey Centres in the United States. *Soc. Compass*, 9/4, 1962, p.351–9.

Presler, H. H. Sociology of Religion in India. *R. Rel. Res.*, 3/3, 1962, p.97–113.

Pruyser, P. W. Some Trends in the Psychology of Religion. *J. Rel.*, 40, 1960, p.113–29.

Religious Psychology, Thought and Research. *Lumen Vitae*, 12/2, 1957, p.203–390.

Reuss, C. An Appraisal of the 1936 Religious Census. *Amer. Sociol. R.*, 8, 1943, p.342–5.

Rodinson, M. Sociology of Islam. *Ann. Sociol.*, 1960, p.362–74.

Rosenmayr, L. The Sociology of Religious Phenomena in Germany and Austria Since Max Weber. *Amer. Cath. Sociol. R.*, 15/2, 1954, p.141–60.

Ross, E. J. The Sociology of Religion in France Today. *Amer. Cath. Sociol. R.*, 9/1, 1950, p.3–14.

Ross, E. J. Modern Studies in the Sociology of Religion in France and Belgium. *Amer. Cath. Sociol. R.*, 15/2, 1954, p.115–40.

Rubenstein, R. L. A Note on the Research Lag in Psychoanalytic Studies in Religion. *Jew. Soc. Stud.*, 25/2, 1963, p.133–44.

Schaub, E. L. The Present Status of the Psychology of Religion. *J. Rel.*, 2, 1922, p.362–79.

Schaub, E. L. The Psychology of Religion in America During the Past Quarter-Century. *J. Rel.*, 6, 1926, p.113–34.

Schuon, F. Studies in Shintô. *France-Asie*, 17/164, 1960, p.1435–50.

Sears, W. H. The Study of Social and Religious Systems in North American Archaeology. *Curr. Anthropol.*, 2/3, 1961, p.223–46.

Shukman, A. Muslim Republics of the U.S.S.R. *Roy. Cent. Asian J.*, 47, 1960, p.11–21.

Simmons, L. W. A Prospectus for Field-Research in the Position and Treatment of the Aged in Primitive and Other Societies. *Amer. Anthropol.*, 47, 1945, p.433–8.

The Sixth World Muslim Conference Held in Mogadiscio, Dec. 26, 1964—Jan. 2, 1965. *Mid. East J.*, 19/4, 1965, p.557–62.

Sklare, M. The Development and Utilization of Sociological Research: The Case of the American Jewish Community. *Jew. J. Sociol.*, 5/2, 1963, p.167–86.

Smith, D. E. Millenarian Scholarship in America. *Amer. Quart.*, 17/3, 1965, p.535–49.

Smith, R. Contributions of Recent Research in Sociology to Religious Education. *Rel. Educ.*, 44, 1949, p.217–24.

Sociology and Religion: Proceedings of the Hazen International Conference on the Sociology of Religion. Wetteren, Belgium: Cultra Press, 1965, 62p.

Sociology Club, University of Hawaii. *Social Process in Hawaii.* Vol. 16, "Sociology of Religion in Hawaii." Honolulu: Sociology Club, Univ. of Hawaii, 1952.

Sociology of Religion in Scandinavia. *Soc. Compass*, 10/6, 1963, p.555–7.

Southard, S. Resources and Research in Church Administration. *Past. Psychol.*, 8, 1957, p.137–46.

Spencer, A. E. C. W. The Newman Demographic Survey, 1953–1964: Reflection on the Birth, Life and Death of a Catholic Institute of Socio-Religious Research. *Soc. Compass*, 11/3–4, 1964, p.31–7.

Steeman, T. M. VIII International Conference of Religious Sociology, Barcelona, July 2–4, 1965: Religion in the Transition From a Pre-Technical to an Industrial and Urban Society. *Soc. Compass*, 12/4–5, 1965, p.323–5.

Steward, J. H. Acculturation Studies in Latin America: Some Needs and Problems. *Amer. Anthropol.*, 45/2, 1943, p.189–206.

Strunk, O., Jr. The Present Status of the Psychology of Religion. *J. Bib. Rel.*, 25, 1957, p.287–92.

Strunk, O., Jr. The Psychology of Religion: An Historical and Contemporary Survey. *Psychol. News.*, N.Y. Univ., 9, 1958, p.181–99.

Studies in Religious Sociology. *Lumen Vitae*, 11/2, 1956, p.315–38.

Turner, V. W. A Revival in the Study of African Ritual. *Rhodes-Livingstone J.*, 17, 1955, p.51–6.

Twenty-Third Annual Meeting of the Society for the Scientific Study of Religion. *Soc. Compass*, 10/6, 1963, p.542–9.

Upadhyaya, K. D. A General Survey of Indian Folklore *Midwest Folklore*, 10/4, 1960–1961, p.181–96.

Vernon, G. M. Bias in Professional Publications Concerning Interfaith Marriages. *Rel. Educ.*, 55/4, 1960, p.261–4.

Wallach, L. The Beginning of the Science of Judaism in the Nineteenth Century. *Hist. Judaica*, 8/1, 1946, p.33–60.

Ward, C. K. Sociological Research in the Sphere of Religion in Great Britain. *Sociol. Religiosa*, 3/4, 1959, p.79–94.

Ward, C. K. Socio-Religious Research in Ireland. *Soc. Compass*, 11/3–4, 1964, p.25–9.

Warnom, H. (ed.) Highlights and Recommendations for Research. *Rel. Educ.*, 55, 1960, p.51–67.

Werblowsky, R. J. Z. The 9th International Congress for the History of Religions, Tokyo, 1958. *Numen*, 5/3, 1958, p.233–7.

Wertheim, W. F. and Stuers, C. V. The Development of Non-Western Sociology of Religion in the Netherlands Since 1945. *Soc. Compass*, 12/6, 1965, p.379–86.

Whitman, L. B. Religious Research in Europe. *R. Rel. Res.*, 6/1, 1964, p.2–6.

Williams, J. P. The Present Status of Research in Religion. *J. Bib. Rel.*, 15, 1947, p.3–9.

World Council of Churches. *The Evanston Report.* London: SCM Press, 1955, 360p.

Wrijhof, P. H. Some Remarks Concerning the Parish as a Social Problem and as a Topic for Social Research in the Netherlands After 1945. *Archiv. Sociol. Rel.*, 8, 1959, p.121–3.

Yinger, J. M. Areas for Research in the Sociology of Religion. *Sociol. Soc. Res.*, 42/6, 1958, p.466–72.

Yinger, J. M. Present Status of the Sociology of Religion. *J. Rel.*, 31, 1951, p.194–210.

Zeegers, G. H. L. Sociology of Religion in the Netherlands. *Amer. Cath. Sociol. R.*, 15/2, 1954, p.176–87.

See Also:

8a5.   Comparative Religion

al Faruqi, I. R. A.   A Comparison of the Islamic and Christian Approaches to Hebrew Scripture. *J. Bib. Rel.*, 31/4, 1963, p.283–93.

Altizer, T. J.   *Oriental Mysticism and Biblical Eschatology.* Phila.: Westminster Press, 1965, 170p.

Archer, J. C.   *The Sikhs in Relation to Hindus, Moslems, Christians and Ahmadiyyas: A Study in Comparative Religion.* Princeton: Princeton Univ. Press, 1946, 353p.

Baumstark, A.   *Comparative Liturgy* (Rev. B. Botte; Trans. F. L. Cross). London: A. R. Mowbray, 1958, 249p.

Bloom, A.   A Basis for the Comparison of Religion: Christianity and Buddhism. *J. Bib. Rel.*, 24, 1956, p.269–74.

Bouquet, A. C.   *Sacred Books of the World: A Companion Sourcebook to Comparative Religion.* Melbourne: Penguin Books, 1954, 343p.

Bouquet, A. C.   *Comparative Religion.* Baltimore: Penguin Books, 1962.

Brewster, P. G.   Hantu and Loa: Some Similarities Between Malay Popular Religion and Haitian Vodun. *Archiv. Antropol. Etnol.*, 87, 1957, p.95–108.

Bridges, J. H.   A Comparison of Chinese and Western Civilization. *Sociol. R.*, 19/2, 1927, p.89–105.

Buck, H. M., Jr.   From History to Myth: A Comparative Study. *J. Bib. Rel.*, 29/3, 1961, p.219–26.

Burtt, E. A.   *Man Seeks the Divine: A Study in the History and Comparison of Religions.* N.Y.: Harper, 1964, 498p.

Campbell, J.   *The Masks of God.* N.Y.: Viking Press, 3, 1959–64, 3 vols.

Chinna Durai, J.   Hindu Law and Western Ideas. *Asian R.*, 54/197, 1958, p.39–44.

Conze, E.   Buddhist Philosophy and Its European Parallels. *Philos. East West*, 13/1, 1963, p.9–23. See also A. Wayman—Comment and Discussion, 13/4, p.361–4.

Eliade, M.   *Birth and Rebirth: The Religious Meanings of Initiation in Human Culture* (Trans. W. R. Trask). N.Y.: Harper and Brothers, 1958, 175p.

Eliade, M.   *Patterns in Comparative Religion* (Trans. R. Sheed). N.Y.: Sheed & Ward, 1958.

Fingesten, P.   *East is East: Hinduism, Buddhism, Christianity; A Comparison.* Phila.: Muhlenberg Press, 1956, 181p.

Frazer, J. G.   *The Golden Bough: Study in Comparative Religion.* N.Y.: St. Martin's Press, 1955, 13 vols.

Gardner, E. C.   Altruism in Classical Hinduism and Christianity. *J. Bib. Rel.*, 22, 1954, p.172–7.

Gladstone, R. and Gupta, G. C.   A Cross-Cultural Study of the Behavioral Aspects of the Concept of Religion. *J. Soc. Psychol.*, 60/2, 1963, p.203–11.

Herberg, W.   Judaism and Christianity: Their Unity and Difference, The Double Covenant in the Divine Economy of Salvation. *J. Bib. Rel.*, 21, 1953, p.67–78.

Heschel, A. J.   *Man's Quest for God: Studies in Prayer and Symbolism.* N.Y.: Scribners, 1954.

Hoke, H.   *Witches, Witches, Witches.* N.Y.: F. Watts, 1958, 230p.

Hole, C.   *A Mirror of Witchcraft.* London: Chatto & Windus, 1957, 260p.

Honigmann, J. J.   Parallels in the Development of Shamanism Among the Northern and Southern Athapaskans. *Amer. Anthropol.*, 51, 1949, p.512–4.

Hsu, F. L. K.   *Americans and Chinese: Two Ways of Life.* N.Y.: Henry Schuman, 1953, 457p.

Hsu, F. L. K.   *Clan, Caste and Club.* Princeton: D. Van Nostrand, 1963, 335p.

Hultkrantz, A.   Religious Tradition, Comparative Religion and Folklore. *Ethnos*, 21/1–2, 1956, p.11–29.

Hultkrantz, A.   *The North American Indian Orpheus Tradition: A Contribution to Comparative Religion.* Stockholm: Statens Etnografiska Museum, 1957, 340p.

Hume, R. E.   *The World's Living Religions with Special Reference to Their Sacred Scriptures and in Comparison with Christianity: An Historical Sketch.* Edinburgh: Clark, 1959, 335p.

James, E. O.   *Comparative Study of Religion of the Eastern World.* N.Y.: Cambridge Univ. Press, 1959.

James, E. O. The History, Science and Comparative Study of Religion. *Numen*, 1/2, 1954, p.91–105.

James, E. O. *The Worship of the Sky God: A Comparative Study in Semitic and Indo-European Religion.* N.Y.: Oxford Univ. Press, 1963.

Jensin, A. E. *Myth and Cult Among Primitive Peoples* (Trans. M. T. Childin and W. Weissleder). Chicago: Univ. of Chicago Press, 1963, 349p.

Julius, C. Cargo Cults in Papua and New Guinea. *Australian Terr.*, 2/4, 1962, p.14–20.

Keeler, C. E. *Secrets of the Cuna Earthmother: A Comparative Study of Ancient Religion Illustrated.* N.Y.: Exposition Press, 1960, 352p.

King, W. L. *Buddhism and Christianity, Some Bridges of Understanding.* Phila.: Westminster, 1962, 240p.

Kritzeck, J. *Sons of Abraham: Jews, Christians and Moslems.* Baltimore: Helicon Press, 1965, 126p.

Kroeber, A. L. The Religion of the Indians of California. *Univ. Calif. Public. Amer. Archaeol. Ethnol.*, 4/6, 1907, p.320–74.

Loeb, E. M. The Religious Organizations of North Central California and Tierra del Fuego. *Amer. Anthropol.*, 33, 1931, p.517–56.

Marcus, J. T. Time and the Sense of History: West and East. *Comp. Stud. Society Hist.*, 3/2, 1961, p.123–39.

Marett, R. R. A Sociological View of Comparative Religion. *Sociol. R.*, 1/1, 1908, p.48–60.

Marsh, G. H. A Comparative Survey of Eskimo-Aleut Religion. *Anthropol. Pap. Univ. Alaska*, 3/1, 1954, p.21–36.

Moberg, D. O. Potential Uses of Church-Sect Typology in Comparative Religious Research. *Int. J. Comp. Sociol.*, 2/1, 1961, p.47–58.

Nadel, S. F. Witchcraft in Four African Societies: An Essay in Comparison. *Amer. Anthropol.*, 54, 1952, p.18–29.

Nadel, S. F. Two Nuba Religions: An Essay in Comparison. *Amer. Anthropol.*, 57/4, 1958, p.661–79.

Niesel, W. *The Gospel and the Churches: A Comparison of Catholicism, Orthodoxy, and Protestantism* (Trans. D. Lewis). Phila.: Westminster Press, 1962, 377p.

Nola, A. M. *The Prayers of Man, From Primitive Peoples to Present Times.* N.Y.: I. Obolensky, 1961, 544p.

Osborn, A. *Buddhism and Christianity in the Light of Hinduism.* London: Rider and Co., 1959, 164p.

Parrinder, E. G. *Comparative Religion.* London: Allen & Unwin, 1962, 131p.

Parrinder, E. G. *Upanishads, Gītā and Bible: A Comparative Study of Hindu and Christian Scriptures.* London: Faber and Faber, 1962, 136p.

Parrinder, E. G. *West African Psychology: A Comparative Study of Psychological and Religious Thought.* London: Lutterworth Press, 1951, 299p.

Patai, R. Religion in Middle Eastern, Far Eastern and Western Culture. *Southw. J. Anthropol.*, 10, 1954, p.233–54.

Regamey, C. The Meaning and Significance of Spirituality in Europe and in India. *Philos. East West*, 10/3–4, 1960–61, p.105–34.

Rose, B. W. African and European Magic: A First Comparative Study of Beliefs and Practices. *Afr. Stud.*, 23/1, 1964, p.1–9.

Ross, F. H. *The Meaning of Life in Hinduism and Buddhism.* Boston: Beacon Press, 1953.

Runeberg, A. *Witches, Demons and Fertility Magic: Analysis of Their Significance and Mutual Relations in West-European Folk Religion.* Helsinki: Societas Scientiarum Fennica, 1947, 273p.

Thrupp, S. L. (ed.) *Millennial Dreams in Action: Essays in Comparative Study.* The Hague: Mouton & Co., 1962.

Tillich, P. The Social Functions of the Churches in Europe and America. *Soc. Res.*, 3, 1936, p.90–104.

Von Glasenapp, H. Buddhism and Comparative Religion. *Sino-Ind. Stud.*, 5/3–4, 1957, p.47–52.

Wach, J. Radhakrishnan and the Comparative Study of Religion. In P. A. Schilpp (ed.)—*The Philosophy of Sarvepalli Radhakrishnan.* N.Y.: Tudor Publishing Co., 1952, p.443–58.

Wach, J. *The Comparative Study of Religions.* N.Y.: Oxford Univ. Press, 1961.

Williams, J. P. A Model Parliament of Religions: A Note on Method in Comparative Religion. *J. Bib. Rel.*, 10, 1942, p.224.

Wilson, B. R. Millennialism in Comparative Perspective. *Comp. Stud. Society Hist.*, 6/1, 1963, p.93–114.

Wolf, E. R. Closed Corporate Peasant Communities in Mesoamerica and Central Java. *Southw. J. Anthropol.*, 13/1, 1957, p.1–18.

Zaehner, R. C. *At Sunday Times: An Essay in the Comparison of Religions.* London: Faber & Faber, 1958, 230p.

Zaehner, R. C. Christianity and the World Religions. *Blackfriars*, 41/482–3, 1960, p.256–71.

See Also:

8a6.   Classics and the Commentators

Becker, H.   The Development and Interaction of the Ecclesia, the Sect, the Denomination, and the Cult as Illustrative of the Dilemma of the Church.   In L. von Wiese—*Systematic Sociology* (Adapt. H. Becker). Gary, Indiana: N. Paul Press, 1950.

Becker, H.   Sacred and Secular Societies Considered With Reference to Folk, State, and Similar Classifications. *Soc. Forces*, 28/4, 1950, p.361–76.

Becker, H.   Current Sacred-Secular Theory and Its Development. In H. Becker and A. Boskoff (eds.)—*Modern Sociological Theory*. N.Y.: Dryden Press, 1957, p.133–85.

Becker, H. and Bruner, D. K.   Some Aspects of Taboo and Totemism. *J. Soc. Psychol.*, 3/3, 1932, p.337–53.

Bidney, D.   The Ethnology of Religion and the Problem of Human Evolution. *Amer. Anthropol.*, 56/1, 1954, p.1–18.

Comte, A., *et al.*   Religion and Social Structure. In T. Parsons, *et al.* (eds.)—*Theories of Society*. N.Y.: Free Press of Glencoe, 1961.

Durkheim, E.   *The Elementary Forms of Religious Life* (Trans. J. W. Swain). N.Y.: Collier Books, 1961.

Ehnmark, E.   Religion and Magic: Frazer, Söderblom, and Häagerström. *Ethnos*, 21/1–2, 1956, p.1–10.

Flam, L.   Salvation in Thought From Hegel to Sartre. *Ancient Rel.*, 2, 1962, p.219–28.

Gibbon, E.   *The Triumph of Christendom in the Roman Empire* (Ed. J. B. Bury). N.Y.: Harper, 1958.

Haddon, A. C.   Dr. Frazer on Totemism and Exogamy. *Sociol. R.*, 4/1, 1911, p.37–43.

Halbwachs, M.   *Sources of Religious Sentiment*. N.Y.: Free Press of Glencoe, 1962.

Hawthorn, H. B.   A Test of Simmel on the Secret Society: The Doukhobors of British Columbia. *Amer. J. Sociol.*, 62, 1956, p.1–7.

Hill, C.   *Society and Puritanism in Pre-Revolutionary England*. N.Y.: Schocken Books, 1964, 520p.

Hiltner, S.   Darwin and Religious Development. *J. Rel.*, 40/4, 1960, p.282–95.

Homans, G. C.   Anxiety and Ritual: The Theories of Malinowski and Radcliffe-Brown. *Amer. Anthropol.*, 43, 1941, p.164–72.

Leach, E. R.   The Golden Bough or Gilded Twig. *Daedalus*, 90, 1961, p.371–87.

Leuba, J. H.   Professor William James' Interpretation of Religious Experience. *Int. J. Ethics*, 15, 1904, p.323–39.

Lobowicz, N.   Karl Marx's Attitude Toward Religion. *R. Polit.*, 26/3, 1964, p.319–52.

Malinowski, B.   *Magic, Science and Religion and Other Essays*. Boston: Beacon Press, 1948.

Malinowski, B.   *Sex, Culture, and Myth*. N.Y.: Harcourt, Brace & World, 1962, 346p.

Martland, T. R., Jr.   *The Metaphysics of William James and John Dewey: Process and Structure in Philosophy and Religion*. N.Y.: Philosophical Library, 1963, 210p.

Marx, K.   *A World Without Jews* (Trans. D. D. Runes). N.Y.: Philosophical Library, 1959, 51p.

Pareto, V.   *Mind and Society: A Treatise on General Sociology*. N.Y.: Dover Publishers, 1963, 4 vols.

Parsons, T.   *The Structure of Social Action*. Glencoe: Free Press, 1949.

Perry, R. B.   *The Thought and Character of William James*. N.Y.: Harper, 1948, 400p.

Pfuetze, P. E. *Self, Society, Existence: Human Nature and Dialogue in the Thought of George Herbert Mead and Martin Buber*. N.Y.: Harper, 1954, 400p.

Schaer, H. *Religions and the Cure of Souls in Jung's Psychology*. London: Routledge & Kegan Paul, 1951, 226p.

Seger, I. *Durkheim and His Critics on the Sociology of Religion*. N.Y.: Bureau of Applied Social Research, Columbia Univ., 1957.

Sumner, W. G. Religion and the Mores. *Amer. J. Sociol.*, 60/3, 1955, p.19–33. Also in 15/5, 1910, p.577–95.

Tawney, R. H. *Religion and the Rise of Capitalism: A Historical Study*. N.Y.: New American Library, 1963, 280p.

Taylor, S. Some Implications of the Contribution of Emile Durkheim to Religious Thought. *Philos. Phenom. Res.*, 24, 1963–64, p.125–34.

Tonnies, F. *Community and Society* (Trans. C. P. Loomis). N.Y.: Harper & Row, 1957.

Wach, J. The Role of Religion in the Social Philosophy of Alexis de Tocqueville. *J. Hist. Ideas*, 7/1, 1946, p.74–90.

Wolff, K. H. (ed.) *Essays on Sociology and Philosophy With Appraisals of Durkheim's Life and Thought*. N.Y.: Harper, 463p.

Yinger, J. M. On Anomie. *J. Sci. Stud. Rel.*, 3/2, 1964, p.158–73.

Sigmund Freud

Aron, W. Notes on Sigmund Freud's Ancestry and Jewish Contacts. *Yivo Ann. Jew. Soc. Sci.*, 11, 1956–67, p.280–95.

Bakan, D. Moses in the Thought of Freud. *Commentary*, 26, 1958, p.322–31.

Bakan, D. *Sigmund Freud and the Jewish Mystical Tradition*. Princeton, New Jersey: Van Nostrand, 1958, 326p.

Bartemeir, L. H. Psychoanalysis and Religion. *Bull. Menninger Clin.*, 29/5, 1965, p.237–44.

Burchard, E. M. L. Mystical and Scientific Aspects of the Psychoanalytic Theories of Freud, Adler, and Jung. *Amer. J. Psychoth.*, 14, 1960, p.289–307.

Drever, J. Sigmund Freud, 1856–1939: A Critical Appreciation. *Brit. J. Educ. Psychol.*, 10/1, 1940, p.1–7.

Eichhoff, A. R. The Psychodynamics of Freud's Criticism of Religion. *Past. Psychol.*, 11/104, 1960, p.35–8.

Feldman, A. B. Freudian Theology. *Psychoanalysis*, 1/3, 1952, p.31–52; 1/4, 1953, p.37–53.

Fine, R. *Freud: A Critical Re-evaluation of His Theories*. N.Y.: David McKay Co., 1962, 307p.

Freud, S. If Moses Was an Egyptian. *Int. J. Psychoanal.*, 20, 1939, p.1–32.

Freud, S. *Collected Papers* (Trans. J. Riviere). London: Hogarth Press and Institute of Psychoanalysis, 1948–50, 5 vols.

Freud, S. *Character and Culture: Psychoanalysis Applied to Anthropology, Mythology, Folklore, Literature, and Culture in General* (Ed. P. Reiff). N.Y.: Collier Books, 1963, 10 vols.

Freud, S. *Moses and Monotheism*. N.Y.: Vintage Books, Random House, 1955.

Freud, S. *On Creativity and the Unconscious: Papers on the Psychology of Art, Literature, Love, Religion* (Ed. B. Nelson). N.Y.: Harper and Brothers, 1958.

Fromm, E. *Sigmund Freud's Mission: An Analysis of His Personality and Influences*. N.Y.: Harper and Brothers, 1959, 120p.

Guirdham, A. *Christ and Freud*. London: Allen and Unwin, 1959.

Hyatt, J. P. Freud on Moses and the Genesis of Monotheism. *J. Bib. Rel.*, 8, 1940, p.85–8.

Klauber, J. The Present Status of Freud's Views on Religion. *Psyche*, 16/1, 1962, p.50–7.

Klausner, S. Images of Man: An Empirical Enquiry. *J. Sci. Stud. Rel.*, 1/1, 1961, p.61–73.

Kroeber, A. L. Totem and Taboo in Retrospect. *Amer. J. Sociol.*, 45, 1939, p.446–51.

Lehrman, N. S. Moses, Monotheism, and Marital Fidelity. *J. Rel. Health*, 3/1, 1963, p.70–89.

Masih, Y. Metapsychology of James and Freud. *J. Bihar Univ.*, 1, 1956, p.61–9.

McLean, H. V. A Few Comments on "Moses and Monotheism." *Psychoanal. Quart.*, 9, 1940, p.207–13.

Mead, M. An Ethnologist's Footnote to "Totem and Taboo." *Psychoanal. R.*, 17, 1930, p.297–304.

Meadow, A. and Vetter, H. L. Freudian Theory and the Judaic Value System. *Int. J. Soc. Psychiat.*, 5/3, 1959, p.197–207.

Moxon, C. Freud's Denial of Religion. *Brit. J. Med. Psychol.*, 11, 1931, p.151–7.

Murphy, M. B. Freud and Nietzsche on Religion. *Insight*, 3/1, 1964, p.19–34.

Philp, H. L. *Freud and Religious Belief*. N.Y.: Pitman, 1956, 415p.

Racker, H. On Freud's Position Towards Religion. *Amer. Imago*, 13/2, 1956, p.97–121.

Rieff, P. The Meaning of History and Religion in Freud's Thought. *J. Rel.*, 31/2, 1951, p.114–31.

Rieff, P. *Freud: The Mind of the Moralist.* N.Y.: Viking Press, 1959, 397p.

Tourney, G. Freud and the Greeks: A Study of the Influence of Classical Greek Mythology and Philosophy upon the Development of Freudian Thought. *J. Hist. Behav. Sci.*, 1/1, 1965, p.67–85.

Ernst Troeltsch

Adams, J. L. Ernst Troeltsch as an Analyst of Religion. *J. Sci. Stud. Rel.*, 1/1, 1961, p.98–109.

Bainton, R. H. Ernst Troeltsch: Thirty Years Later. *Theol. Today*, 8/1, 1951, p.70–96.

Berger, P. L. Sectarianism and Religious Sociation. *Amer. J. Sociol.*, 64/1, 1958, p.41–4.

Johnson, G. B., Jr. A Critical Appraisal of the Church-Sect Typology. *Amer. Sociol. R.*, 22, 1957, p.88–92.

Johnson, G. B., Jr. On Church and Sect. *Amer. Sociol. R.*, 28/4, 1963, p.539–49.

Johnson, R. A. Troeltsch on Christianity and Relativism. *J. Sci. Stud. Rel.*, 1/2, 1962, p.220–3.

Miller, D. E. Troeltsch's Critique of Karl Marx. *J. Sci. Stud. Rel.*, 1/1, 1961, p.117–21.

Troeltsch, E. *The Social Teachings of the Christian Churches.* N.Y.: Macmillan, 1950, 2 vols.

Max Weber

Alatas, S. S. The Weber Thesis and South East Asia. *Archiv. Sociol. Rel.*, 8/15, 1963, p.21–34.

Bellah, R. N. Reflections on the Protestant Ethic Analogy in Asia. *J. Soc. Issues*, 19/1, 1963, p.52–60.

Bendix, R. *Max Weber: An Intellectual Portrait.* N.Y.: Doubleday, 1960, 480p

Best, E. E. Max Weber and the Christian Criticism of Life. *Theol. Today*, 16, 1959, p.203–14.

Birnbaum, N. Conflicting Interpretation of the Rise of Capitalism: Marx and Weber. *Brit. J. Sociol.*, 4, 1953, p.125–41.

Gordon-Walker, P. C. Capitalism and the Reformation. *Econ. Hist. R.*, 8/1, 1937, p.1–19.

Greeley, A. M. The Protestant Ethic: Time for a Moratorium. *Sociol. Anal.*, 25/1, 1964, p.20–33.

Hertz, K. H. Max Weber and American Puritanism. *J. Sci. Stud. Rel.*, 1/2, 1962, p.189–97.

Johnsen, C. T. The Protestant Ethic and the Spirit of Capitalism in Norway. *Amer. Sociol. R.*, 12/6, 1947, p.676–86.

Kennedy, R. E., Jr. The Protestant Ethic and the Parsis. *Amer. J. Sociol.*, 68/1, 1962, p.11–20.

Kolko, G. Max Weber on America: Theory and Evidence. *Hist. Theory*, 1/3, 1961, p.243–60.

Kosa, J. and Rachiele, L. D. The Spirit of Capitalism, Traditionalism and Religiousness: A Re-examination of Weber's Concepts. *Sociol. Quart.*, 4/3, 1963, p.243–69.

Lopes, J. R. Max Weber. *Sociologica*, 18/1, 1956, p.51–69.

Means, R. L. American Protestantism and Max Weber's Protestant Ethic. *Rel. Educ.*, 60/2, 1965, p.90–8.

Means, R. L. Weber's Thesis of the Protestant Ethic: The Ambiguities of Received Doctrine. *J. Rel.*, 45/1, 1965, p.1–11.

Nelson, B. Max Weber's Sociology of Religion. *Amer. Sociol. R.*, 30/4, 1965, p.595–9.

Parsons, T. Christianity and Modern Industrial Society. In E. H. Tiryakian (ed.)—*Sociological Theory, Values and Socio-Cultural Change.* N.Y.: Free Press of Glencoe, 1963, p.33–70.

Paul, R. S. Weber and Calvinism: The Effects of a "Calling." *Canadian J. Theol.*, 11/1, 1965, p.25–41.

Robertson, H. M. *Aspects of the Rise of Economic Individualism: A Criticism of Max Weber and His School.* N.Y.: Kelley & Millman, 1959.

Salman, D. H. Psychology and Sociology in Weber's Theories. *Soc. Compass*, 10/6, 1963, p.536–9.

Salmon, J. H. M. Religion and Economic Motivation: Some French Insights on an Old Controversy. *J. Rel. Hist.*, 2/2, 1963, p.181–203.

Salomon, A. Max Weber's Sociology. *Soc. Res.*, 2, 1935, p.60–73.

Scheler, M. The Thomistic Ethic and the Spirit of Capitalism (Trans. G. Neuwirth). *Sociol. Anal.*, 25/1, 1964, p.4–19.

Schniper, L. Max Weber on the Sociological Basis of the Jewish Religion. *Jew. J. Sociol.*, 1/2, 1959, p.250–60.

Stark, W. Capitalism, Calvinism and the Rise of Modern Science. *Sociol. R.*, 43/5, 1951, p.95–104.

Stark, W. Max Weber's Sociology of Religious Belief. *Sociol. Anal.*, 25/1, 1964, p.41–9.

Steeman, T. M. Max Weber's Sociology of Religion. *Sociol. Anal.*, 25/1, 1964, p.50–8.

Thorner, I. Ascetic Protestantism and the Development of Science and Technology. *Amer. J. Sociol.*, 58/1, 1952, p.25–33.

Turksma, L. Protestant Ethic and Rational Capitalism:

A Contribution to a Never Ending Discussion. *Soc. Compass*, 9/5–6, 1962, p.445–73.

Van der Sprenkel, O. B.   Max Weber on China. *Hist. Theory*, 3/3, 1964, p.348–70.

Wax, R. and Wax, M.   The Vikings and the Rise of Capitalism. *Amer. J. Sociol.*, 61/1, 1955, p.1–10.

Weber, M.   *From Max Weber: Essays in Sociology* (Trans. and Eds. H. H. Gerth and C. W. Mills). N.Y.: Oxford Univ. Press, 1946.

Weber, M.   *The Sociology of Religion* (Trans. E. Fischoff). Boston: Beacon Press, 1963.

Wood, H. G.   Puritanism and Capitalism. *Congreg. Quart.*, 29, 1951, p.104–14.

See Also:

Benedict, R.   7b3
Brodbeck, A. J.   4g1
Chiang, A. C.   4b
Durkheim, E.   5a3
Dynes, R. R.   4j3
Fanfani, A.   8a2
Faris, E.   8a2
Fischoff, E.   8a2
Frazer, J. G.   3, 8a5

Freud, S.   3 (2)
Godstein, B.   7b3
Goldenweiser, A. A.   1
Green, R. W.   5b3
Gross, L.   4d
Hason, N. M.   4b
Hudson, W.   3a1
James, W.   7b3 (2), 8a2
Jonassen, C. T.   7b3
Jung, C. G.   1e (2)
Lowie, R.   8a3
Malinowski, B.   4e
Marx, K.   8a2
Matthijssen, A. J. M.   7b2
Pitcher, A.   4d
Powers, R. H.   4d
Radcliffe-Brown, A. R.   3f, 4, 8a3
Samuelsson, K.   4b
Selsam, H.   4b
Simmel, G.   8a2
Troeltsch, E.   6, 7
Tylor, E. B.   8a3
Wach, J.   7a1, 8a1, 8a2, 8a5
Wachs, M.   4b
Weber, M.   2h2, 3e, 4b
Zenter, H.   4c

8b.   Readers

Bier, W. C. and Schneiders, A. A.   *Selected Papers From the American Catholic Psychological Association Meetings of 1957, 1958, 1959.* Fordham Univ., Amer. Cath. Psychol. Assoc., 1960, 168p.

Browne, L.   *The Worlds Great Scriptures.* N.Y.: Macmillan Co., 1946.

Campbell, J. (ed.)   *Papers from the Eranos Yearbooks* (Trans. M. Ralph and R. F. C. Hull). N.Y.: Pantheon Books, 1954–64, 5 vols.

DeLaguan, F. (ed.)   *Selected Papers from the American Anthropologist, 1888–1920.* Evanston, Illinois: Row, Peterson, 1960, 930p.

Diamond, S. (ed.)   *Culture in History: Essays in Honour of Paul Radin.* N.Y.: Columbia Univ. Press, 1960, 1014p.

Green, R. W. (ed.)   *Protestantism and Capitalism: The Weber Thesis and its Critics.* Boston: D. C. Heath & Co., 1959.

Jeffery, A. (ed.)   *A Reader on Islam: Passages from Standard Arabic Writings Illustrative of the Beliefs and Practices of Muslims.* Gravenhage: Mouton, 1962, 678p.

Johnson, F. E. (ed.)   *Religion in the World Order.* N.Y.: Harper Brothers, 1944.

Jurji, E. J. (ed.)   *Great Religions of the Modern World.* Princeton: Princeton Univ. Press, 1946.

Leroi-Gourhan, *et al.* (eds.)   *VIe Congrés International des Sciences Anthropologiques et Ethnologiques, Paris, 30 juillet—6 aout 1960 (Actes), Tome II, Ethnologie (deuxieme volume).* Paris: Musee de l'Homme, 1964, 666p.

Leslie, C. (ed.)   *Anthropology of Folk Religion.* N.Y.: Vintage Books, 1960.

Lessa, W. A. and Vogt, E. (eds.)   *A Reader in Comparative Religion.* Evanston: Row, Peterson Co., 1958.

Monson, C. H., Jr. (ed.)   *Philosophy, Religion and Science: An Introduction to Philosophy.* N.Y.: Scribners, 1963, 557p.

Schneider, L. (ed.)   *Religion, Culture and Society: A Reader in the Sociology of Religion.* N.Y.: John Wiley & Sons, 1964.

Stiernotte, A. P. (ed.)   *Mysticism and the Modern Mind.* N.Y.: Liberal Arts Press, 1959.

Tsunoda, R., *et al.* (eds.)   *Sources of Japanese Tradition.* N.Y.: Columbia Univ. Press, 1964, 2 vols.

Vidyarthi, L. P. (ed.)   *Aspects of Religion in Indian Society.* London: Luzac, 1964, 420p.

Von Grunebaum, G. E. (ed.) *Unity and Variety in Muslim Civilization*. Chicago: Univ. of Chicago Press, 1955.

Wallace, A. F. C. (ed.) *Men and Cultures: Selected Papers, 5th International Congress of Anthropological and Ethnological Sciences, Philadelphia, 1956*. Phila.: Univ. of Pennsylvania Press, 1960, 810p.

See Also:

Barry, C. J.   4a

Clark, E. T.   2a1
Freemantle, A.   4
Giles, E.   7a1
Godin, A.   4h
Halvorson, L. W.   4
Harper, E. B.   2
Miller, P.   4a1
Odegard, P.   4a
Smart, N.   1c
Yinger, J. M.   8a2

9.   Bibliographies of Religion and Encyclopedias and Dictionaries

Adler, C., *et al.* (eds.)   *The Jewish Encyclopedia*.   N.Y.: Ktay Publishers, 1964, 12 vols.

Albert, E. M. and Kluckhohn, C.   *A Selected Bibliography on Values, Ethics, and Esthetics in the Behavioral Sciences and Philosophy, 1920–1958*.   Glencoe: The Free Press of Glencoe, 1959, 342p.

American Universities Field Staff.   *A Select Bibliography: Asia, Africa, Eastern Europe, Latin America*.   N.Y.: American Universities Field Staff, 1960.

Andrews, T.   *The Eastern Orthodox Church: A Bibliography*.   N.Y.: Greek Archdiocese of North and South America, National Youth Office, Office of Public Relations, 1953, 32p.

Attwater, D. (ed.)   *The Catholic Encyclopaedic Dictionary*.   London: Cassell and Co., 1949, 552p.

Bibliography of Publications About Jews in America in Five Chicago Libraries: A Tercentenary Publication.   Chicago: Jewish Historical Association of Chicago in Co-operation With the Chicago Tercentenary Committee, 1955, 144p.

Bleeker, C. J. and Alich, S.   *International Bibliography of the History of Religions*, 1960–61.   Leiden: E. J. Brill, 1964, 104p.; see other issues.

Borton, H., *et al.*   *A Selected List of Books and Articles on Japan in English, French and German*.   Cambridge, Massachusetts: Harvard Univ. Press, 1954, p.134–50.

Braham, R. L. and Haver, M. M.   *Jews in the Communist World: A Bibliography 1945–1962*.   N.Y.: Pro Arte Publishers, 1963, 125p.

Buck, C. F.   The Older Person, the Family and Church: Selected References.   *Fam. Life Coord.*, 8/4, 1960, p.71–6.

Bulletin Bibliographique.   *Archiv. Sociol. Rel.*, 10/20, 1965, p.133–211: see other issues.

Burstein, S. R.   Some Modern Books on Witchcraft.   *Folk Lore* (London), 72, 1961, p.520–35.

Cammack, F. M. and Saito, S.   *Pacific Island Bibliography*.   N.Y.: Scarecrow Press, 1962, 421p.

Carrier, H. and Pin, E.   *Sociologie du Christianisme: Bibliographie International*.   Rome: Presses de'l Université Gregorienne, 1964, 314p.

Celnik, M. and Celnik, E. (Compilers)   *A Bibliography on Judaism and Jewish Christian Relations*.   N.Y.: B'nai Brith, 1965, 72p.

Chan, W. T.   *An Outline and Annotated Bibliography of Chinese Philosophy*.   New Haven: Yale Univ. Press, 1959, 127p.

Christian Periodical Index, 1956–1960: A Subject Index to Selected Periodical Literature.   Buffalo, N.Y.: Christian Librarians Fellowship, 1961, 63p.

Collins, J.   Annual Survey of Philosophy, 1964.   *Crosscurrents*, 15/2, 1965, p.213–36; see other issues.

Collison, R. L.   *Bibliographies, Subject and National: A Guide to Their Contents, Arrangement and Use*.   N.Y.: Hafner Publishing Co., 1962, p.13–20.

Coltrera, J. T.   Psychoanalysis and Existentialism.   *J. Amer. Psychoanal. Assoc.*, 10/1, 1962, p.166–215.

Council on Graduate Studies in Religion.   *Doctoral Dissertations in the Field of Religion, 1940–1952: Their Titles, Location, Fields and Short Precis of Contents*.   N.Y.: Columbia Univ. Press, 1954, 194p.

Creswell, K. A. C.   *A Bibliography of the Architecture, Arts and Crafts of Islam to 1st January, 1960*.   Cairo: American University at Cairo Press, 1961.

deBary, W. T. and Embree, A. T. (eds.)   *A Guide to Oriental Classics*.   N.Y.: Columbia Univ. Press, 1964, 199p.

DeGroot, A. T.   *Check List of Faith and Order Commission Official, Numbered Publications: Series I, 1910–1948; Series II, 1948 to Date (1962)*.   Geneva: Faith and Order Commission, World Council of Churches, 1963.

Dictionary Catalogue of the Cincinnati Library of the Hebrew Union College. Jewish Institute of Religion, Klau Library, Cincinnati.   Boston: G. K. Hall, 1964, 32 vols.

Diehl, K. S.   *Religions, Mythologies, Folklores: An Annotated Bibliography*.   New Brunswick, New Jersey: Scarecrow, Press, 1962, 573p.

Downs, R. B.   *American Library Resources: A Biblio-*

graphical Guide, Supplement 1950–1961. Chicago: American Library Association, 1962, p.34–42; see earlier issue, 1951, p.69–86.

Durnbaugh, D. F. and Shultz, L. W. A Brethren Bibliography, 1713–1963: Two Hundred Fifty Years of Brethren Literature. Elgin, Illinois: Brethren Journal Association, 1964, 177p.

Ellis, J. T. A Guide to American Catholic History. Milwaukee: Bruce Publishing Co., 1959, 147p.

Evans, I., et al. (ed.) The New Library of Catholic Knowledge. N.Y.: Hawthorn Books, 1963, 1964, 2 vols.

Ferm, V. (ed.) Encyclopedia of Morals. N.Y.: Philosophical Library, 1956, 682p.

Forlong, J. G. R. Faiths of Man: Encyclopaedia of Religions. N.Y.: University Books, 1964, 3 vols.

Frumkin, R. M. Death and Bereavement: A Bibliography. J. Hum. Relat., 13/1, 1965, p.118–41.

Funk and Wagnall's Standard Dictionary of Folklore, Mythology and Legend. N.Y.: Funk and Wagnall, 1949, 2 vols.

Gaynor, F. (ed.) Dictionary of Mysticism. N.Y.: Philosophical Library, 1953, 208p.

Gibson, G. D. A Bibliography of Anthropological Bibliographies. Curr. Anthropol., 1, 1960, p.61–75.

Guiraun, F., et al. (ed.) Larousse Encyclopedia of Mythology. N.Y.: Prometheus Press, 1959, 842p.

Hair, P. E. H. Christianity in Medieval Nubia and the Sudan: A Bibliographical Note. Bull. Society Afr. Church Hist., 1/3, 1964, p.67–73.

Handy, R. T. Survey of Recent Literature: American Church History. Church Hist., 27/2, 1958, p.161–5.

Hastings, J. (ed.) Encyclopedia of Religion and Ethics. N.Y.: Scribners, 1951, 3 vols.

Hay, S. M. and Case, M. H. (eds.) Southeast Asian History: A Bibliographic Guide. N.Y.: F. A. Praeger, 1962, 138p.

Holzmann, D., et al. Japanese Religion and Philosophy. Ann Arbor: Univ. of Michigan Center for Japanese Studies, 1959, 192p.

Hostetler, J. A. An Annotated Bibliography on the Amish: An Annotated Bibliography on Source Materials Pertaining to the Old Order Amish Mennonites. Scottdale, Pennsylvania: Mennonite Publishing House, 1951.

Howard, R. C. Bibliography of Asian Studies, 1963. J. Asian Stud., 23/5, 1964, p.1–354; see other issues.

The Information Centre of Asian Studies. A Selected List of Books on Japan in Western Languages (1945–1960). Tokyo: Sobunsha Co., 1964.

International Bibliography of Sociology of Religion. Soc. Compass, 12/4–5, 1965, p.326–31; see other issues.

Jobes, G. Dictionary of Mythology, Folklore and Symbols. N.Y.: Scarecrow Press, 1961, 1,759p., 2 vols.

Judah, J. S. and Ziegler, L. J. Index to Religious Periodical Literature: An Author and Subject Index to Periodical Literature, 1949–1952. Chicago: American Theological Library Association, 1953; see other issues.

Kaganoff, N. M. Judaica Americana. Amer. Jew. Hist. Quart., 55/2, 1965, p.235–44; 54/4, p.450–9; see other issues.

Kanitkar, J. M., et al. A Bibliography of Indology. Calcutta: National Library, 1960, 290p.

Kapsner, O. L. A Benedictine Bibliography. Collegeville, Minnesota: St. John's Abbey Press, 1962, 2 vols.

Kapsner, O. L. Catholic Subject Headings: A List Designed for Use With Library of Congress Subject Headings on the Sears List of Subject Headings. Collegeville, Minnesota: St. John's Abbey Press, 1963, 488p.

Kiell, N. (ed.) Psychoanalysis, Psychology and Literature: A Bibliography. Wisconsin: Univ. of Wisconsin Press, 1963, 225p.

Kolarz, W. (ed.) Books on Communism. N.Y.: Oxford Univ. Press, 1964.

Lebar, F. M., et al. Ethnic Groups of Mainland Southeast Asia. New Haven, Connecticut: Human Relations Area Files, 1964, 288p.

Le Bras, G. Sociology of Religions: A Trend Report and Bibliography. Curr. Sociol., 5/1, 1956, p.5–78.

Leeson, I. Bibliography of Cargo Cults and Other Nativistic Movements in the South Pacific. South Pacific Commission Paper, Sydney, Australia, 1952.

Library of Congress, Division of Bibliography. List of Books on the Russian Orthodox Church. Washington: Library of Congress, 1920.

Liebman, S. B. (ed.) A Guide to Jewish References in the Mexican Colonial Era, 1521–1821. Phila: Univ. of Pennsylvania Press, 1964, 134p.

Little, L. C. Toward Understanding the Church and the Clergy: Contributions of Selected Doctoral Dissertations. Pittsburgh: Univ. of Pittsburgh Press, 1963.

Loetscher, L. A. (ed.) Twentieth Century Encyclopedia of Religious Knowledge: An Extension of the New Schaff–Herzog Encyclopedia of Religious Knowledge. Grand Rapids, Michigan: Baker Book House, 1955, 2 vols.

Loewenthal, R. Russian Materials on Islam and Islamic Institutions: A Selective Bibliography. Washington:

Dept. of State, External Research Staff, Office of Intelligence Research, 1958, 34p.

Logasa, H. *McKinley Bibliographies, Volume III: World Culture a Selected Annotated Bibliography.* Phila.: McKinley Publishing Co., 1963.

Lyons, J. An Annotated Bibliography on Phenomenology and Existentialism. *Psychol. Rep.*, 5/4, 1959, p.613–31.

McDill, T. H. Books in Pastoral Psychology: 1964. *Past. Psychol.*, 15/150, 1965, p.60–70; see other issues.

Meissner, W. W. *Annotated Bibliography in Religion and Psychology.* N.Y.: Academy of Religion and Mental Health, 1961.

Menges, R. J. and Dittes, J. E. *Psychological Studies of Clergymen: Abstracts of Research.* Camden, New Jersey: Thomas Nelson & Sons, 1965, 208p.

Methodist Periodical Index. Nashville: Abingdon, 1960 and since.

Murdock, G. P. *Ethnographic Bibliography of North America.* New Haven, Connecticut: Human Relations Area Files, 1960, 393p; see other bibliographies by same publisher.

New York Public Library Reference Department. *Dictionary Catalog of the Jewish Collection.* Boston: G. H. Hill, 1960, 11 vols.

Periodical Literature. *Cath. Hist. R.*, 50/4, 1965, 681–93; see other issues.

Pike, E. R. *Encyclopedia of Religion and Religions.* London: Allen & Unwin, 1951, 406p.

Pittman, D. J. Bibliographic Appendix: The Sociology of Religion. In J. B. Gittler (ed.)—*Review of Sociology: Analysis of a Decade.* N.Y.: John Wiley and Sons, 1957, p.546–58.

Radford, E. and Hole, C. *Encyclopaedia of Superstitions.* London: Hutchinson, 1961, 384p.

Reader's Guide to Books on Religion. London: Library Association, 1952, 63p.

Richmond, W. E. Annual Bibliography 1964. *Abstracts Folklore Stud.*, 3/3, 1965, p.109–93; see other issues.

Robbins, R. H. *The Encyclopedia of Witchcraft and Demonology.* N.Y.: Crown Publishers, 1959, 571p.

Robinson, M. S. and Wilson, K. *The Encyclopaedia of Myths and Legends of all Nations.* London: Ward, 1962, 244p.

Runes, D. D. *Concise Dictionary of Judaism.* N.Y.: Philosophical Library, 1959, 237p.

St. Joseph's Seminary. *Catholic Encyclopedia For School and Home.* N.Y.: McGraw-Hill, 1965, 12 vols.

Sen Gupta, S. and Parmar, S. Bibliography of Folklore of India and Pakistan. *Folklore*, 6/7, 1965, p.301–17; 6/8, p.344–52; 6/9, p.377–89; see other issues.

The Shelf List of the Union Theological Seminary Library, New York. Boston: G. K. Hall, 10 vols.

Shunami, S. *Bibliography of Jewish Bibliographies.* Jerusalem: Magnes Press of the Hebrew Univ., 1965, 992p.

Silberman, B. *Japan and Korea: A Critical Bibliography.* Tucson, Arizona: Univ. of Arizona Press, 1962, p.29–39.

Spence, L. *An Encyclopedia of Occultism.* New Hyde Park, N.Y.: University, 1960, 440p.

A Theological Book List. London: Theological Education Fund, 1963, 41p.

Uhrich, H. B. and Schmitt, C. H. (eds.) *Index to Religious Periodical Literature: An Author and Subject Index to Periodical Literature Including Author Index of Book Reviews.* Princeton: Princeton Theological Seminary (American Theological Library Association), 1963.

United Nations Educational, Scientific and Cultural Organization. Middle East Science Cooperation Office—*Middle East Social Science Bibliography: Books and Articles of the Social Sciences Published in Arab Countries of the Middle East in 1955–1960.* Cairo, Unesco, 1961, 152p.

Vismans, T. A. and Brinkhoff, L. *Critical Bibliography of Liturgical Literature* (Trans. R. W. Fitzpatrick and C. Howell). Nijmegen: Bestelcentrale der V. Sk. B. Pub., 1960, 1961, 2 vols.

Von Furer-Haimendorf, E. *An Anthropological Bibliography of South Asia.* The Hague: Mouton, 1958, 748p.

Winchell, C. M. *Guide to Reference Books.* Chicago: American Library Association, 1951; see also Supplements, 1950–52; 1953–55; 1956–58 etc.

Wood, E. *Zen Dictionary.* N.Y.: Philosophical Library, 1962, 165p.

Zaehner, R. C. (ed.) *The Concise Encyclopaedia of Living Faiths.* London: Hutchinson, 1959, 431p.

See Also:

Journals Consulted and Abbreviations[1]

Abstracts of Folklore Studies . . . . Abstracts Folklore Stud.

Academia Sinica Institute of Ethnology Bulletin . . . . Bull. Inst. Ethnol. Acad. Sinica

Acta Americana . . . . Acta Americana

Acta Ethnographica Academiae Scientiarum Hungaricae . . . . Acta Ethnog. Acad. Scient. Hung.

Acta Sociologica . . . . Acta Sociol.

°Administrative Science Quarterly . . . . Admin. Sci. Quart.

Africa . . . . Africa

Africa South . . . . Afr. South

Africa Today . . . . Afr. Today

African Notes and News . . . . Afr. Notes News

African Studies . . . . Afr. Stud.

Alba Regia . . . . Alba Regia

Alcoholism Research . . . . Alcoholism Res.

America . . . . America

America Indigena . . . . Amer. Indig.

American Anthropological Association Memoirs . . . . Amer. Anthropol. Assoc. Mem.

American Anthropologist . . . . Amer. Anthropol.

American Antiquity . . . . Amer. Antiq.

American Catholic Historical Society of Philadelphia Records . . . . Amer. Cath. Hist. Society Phila. Rec.

American Catholic Quarterly Review . . . . Amer. Cath. Quart. R.

°American Catholic Sociological Review (Sociological Analysis) . . . . Amer. Cath. Sociol. R. (Sociol. Anal.)

American Ecclesiastical Review . . . . Amer. Eccles. R.

American Ethnology Bureau . . . . Amer. Ethnol. Bur.

American Historical Review . . . . Amer. Hist. R.

American Imago . . . . Amer. Imago

°American Journal of Economics and Sociology . . . . Amer. J. Econ. Sociol.

American Journal of International Law . . . . Amer. J. Int. Law

American Journal of Mental Deficiency . . . . Amer. J. Ment. Defic.

American Journal of Nursing . . . . Amer. J. Nursing

°American Journal of Orthopsychiatry . . . . Amer. J. Orthopsychiat.

American Journal of Psychiatry . . . . Amer. J. Psychiat.

American Journal of Psychoanalysis . . . . Amer. J. Psychoanal.

American Journal of Psychotherapy . . . . Amer. J. Psychoth.

°American Journal of Sociology . . . . Amer. J. Sociol.

American Journal of Theology . . . . Amer. J. Theol.

American Mercury . . . . Amer. Mercury

°American Political Science Review . . . . Amer. Polit. Sci. R.

American Psychoanalytic Association . . . . Amer. Psychoanal. Assoc.

American Psychologist . . . . Amer. Psychol.

American Quarterly . . . . Amer. Quart.

American Scandinavian Review . . . . Amer. Scand. R.

American Scholar . . . . Amer. Scholar

American Slavic and East European Review . . . . Amer. Slavic E. Europ. R.

°American Sociological Review . . . . Amer. Sociol. R.

The Americas . . . . Americas

Anglican Theological Review . . . . Anglic. Theol. R.

Annales Universitatis Mariae Curie-Sklodowska . . . . Ann. Univ. M. Curie-Sklodowska

°Annals of the American Academy of Political and Social Science . . . . Ann. Amer. Acad. Polit. Soc. Sci.

[1]The journals marked with an asterisk (°) are those journals which the authors have surveyed completely, from their initial publication dates through December 1965.

Annals of the Association of American Geographers . . . .
Ann. Assoc. Amer. Geog.

Annals of the Bhandarkar Oriental Institute . . . .
Ann. Bhandarkar Orient. Inst.

Annals of the New York Academy of Science . . . . Ann.
New York Acad. Sci.

Annals of Psychotherapy . . . . Ann. Psychother.

Année Sociologique . . . . Ann. Sociol.

Anthropologica . . . . Anthropologica

Anthropological Linguistics . . . . Anthropol. Ling.

Anthropological Papers of the University of Alaska . . . .
Anthropol Pap. Univ. Alaska

Anthropological Quarterly . . . . Anthropol. Quart.

Anthropological Records of the University of California
. . . . Anthropol. Rec. Univ. Calif.

Anthropos . . . . Anthropos

Antioch Review . . . . Antioch R.

Artibus Asiae . . . . Artibus Asiae

Archiv für Reformationsgeschichte . . . . Archiv Reform.

Archiv für Volkerkunde . . . . Archiv Volkerk.

Archives of European Sociology . . . . Archiv. Europ.
Sociol.

Archives für Religionspsychologie . . . . Archiv. Rel.
Psychol.

°Archives de Sociologie des Religions . . . . Archiv.
Sociol. Rel.

Archivo per l'Antropologia e la Etnologia . . . . Archiv.
Antropol. Etnol.

Arctic Anthropology . . . . Arctic Anthropol.

Aryan Pathology . . . . Aryan Path.

Asia . . . . Asia

Asia Major . . . . Asia Major

Asian Review . . . . Asian R.

Asian Survey . . . . Asian Surv.

Asiatic Studies . . . . Asiat. Stud.

Asiatische Forschungen . . . . Asiat. Forsch.

°Australian and New Zealand Journal of Sociology . . . .
Australian New Zealand J. Sociol.

Australian Journal of Psychology . . . . Australian J. of
Psychol.

Australian Outlook . . . . Australian Outlook

Australian Quarterly . . . . Australian Quart.

Australian Territories . . . . Australian Terr.

Ave Maria . . . . Ave Maria

Belleten . . . . Belleten

Berkeley Publications in Social Institutions . . . .
Berkeley Pub. Soc. Instit.

Bijdragen tot de Taal-, Land-en Volkenkunde . . . .
Bijdrag. Taal-Land-Volkenk.

Black Orpheus . . . . Black Orpheus

Blackfriars . . . . Blackfriars

British Journal of Clinical Psychology . . . . Brit. J. Clin.
Psychol.

British Journal of Educational Psychology . . . . Brit. J.
Educ. Psychol.

British Journal of Medical Psychology . . . . Brit. J.
Med. Psychol.

British Journal of Psychology . . . . Brit. J. Psychol.

°British Journal of Sociology . . . . Brit. J. Sociol.

Bulletin of the Atomic Scientists . . . . Bull. Atomic Sci.

Bulletin of the Bureau of American Ethnology . . . .
Bull. Bur. Amer. Ethnol.

Bulletin of the Institute for the Study of the U.S.S.R.
. . . . Bull. Inst. Study U.S.S.R.

Bulletin of the Institute of Traditional Culture . . . .
Bull. Inst. Trad. Cult.

Bulletin of the Japan Society . . . . Bull. Japan Society

Bulletin de l'Institut Français d'Afrique Noire . . . .
Bull. Inst. Francais Afrique Noire

Bulletin of the Maritime Psychological Association . . . .
Bull. Maritime Psychol. Assoc.

Bulletin of the Menninger Clinic . . . . Bull. Menninger Clin.

Bulletin of the National Catholic Educational Association
. . . . Bull. Nat. Cath. Educ. Assoc.

Bulletin of the Philadelphia Association for Psychoanalysis
. . . . Bull. Phila. Assoc. Psychoanal.

Bulletin of the Ramakrisna Mission Institute of Culture
. . . . Bull. Ramakrisna Mission Inst. Cult.

Bulletin of the School of Oriental and African Studies
. . . . Bull. School Orient. Afr. Stud.

Bulletin of the Society of African Church History . . . .
Bull. Society Afr. Church Hist.

Bulletin of the Tribal Research Institute (Chindivara,
India) . . . . Bull. Tribal Res. Inst.

Cahiers d'Etudes Africaines . . . . Cah. Et. Afr.

Cahiers Economiques et Sociale . . . . Cah. Econ. Soc.

Calcutta Review . . . . Calcutta R.

°Canadian Journal of Economics and Political Science
. . . . Canad. J. Econ. Polit. Sci.

Canadian Journal of Psychology . . . . Canad. J. Psychol.

Canadian Journal of Theology . . . . Canad. J. Theol.

°Canadian Review of Sociology and Anthropology . . . .
Canad. R. Sociol. Anthropol.

Caribbean Studies. . . . Caribbean Stud.

Catholic Charities Review . . . . Cath. Charit. R.

Catholic Counselor . . . . Cath. Counselor

Catholic Educational Review . . . . Cath. Educ. R.

Catholic Educator . . . . Cath. Educator

Catholic Historical Review . . . . Cath. Hist. R.

Catholic Mind . . . . Cath. Mind

Catholic School Journal . . . . Cath. School J.

The Catholic University Law Review . . . . Cath. Univ.
Law R.

The Catholic World . . . . Cath. World

Caucasian Review . . . . Caucasian R.

Central Asian Review . . . . Cent. Asian R.

Central Asiatic Journal . . . . Cent. Asiat. J.

Ceylon Journal of Historical and Social Studies . . . .
Ceylon J. Hist. Soc. Stud.

Ceylon Today . . . . Ceylon Today

Character and Personality . . . . Charac. Person.

Character Potential . . . . Charac. Potent.

Child Development . . . . Child Devel.

Child Study . . . . Child Study

Child Welfare . . . . Child Wel.

°The China Quarterly . . . . China Quart.

China Reconstructs . . . . China Reconstructs

Chinese Culture . . . . Chinese Cult.

Christendom . . . . Christendom

Christian Century . . . . Christ. Cent.

Christian Register . . . . Christ. Reg.

Christian Scholar . . . . Christ. Scholar

Christianity and Crisis . . . . Christ. Crisis

Christianity Today . . . . Christ. Today

Christus Rex . . . . Christus Rex

Church History . . . . Church Hist.

Church Quarterly Review . . . . Church Quart. R.

Church and State . . . . Church State

City Church . . . . City Church

°Civilisations . . . . Civilisations

Clergy Review . . . . Clergy R.

Co-Existence . . . . Co-Existence

Columbia University Contributions to Anthropology
. . . . Columbia Univ. Contr. Anthropol.

Commentary . . . . Commentary

Commonwealth . . . . Commonwealth

Communio Viatorum . . . . Communio Viatorum

°Comparative Education Review . . . . Comp. Educ. R.

°Comparative Literature Studies . . . . Comp. Lit. Stud.

°Comparative Studies in Society and History . . . .
Comp. Stud. Society Hist.

Confluence . . . . Confluence

Congregational Quarterly . . . . Congreg. Quart.

Contemporary Japan . . . . Contemp. Japan

Contemporary Religions in Japan . . . . Contemp. Rel.
Japan

Contemporary Review . . . . Contemp. R.

Contemporary Russia . . . . Contemp. Russia

Continuum . . . . Continuum

Contributions to Indian Sociology . . . . Contrib. Ind.
Sociol.

Controversy . . . . Controversy

Corona . . . . Corona

Correspondance d'Orient: Études . . . . Correspond.
d'Orient: Études

Crane Review . . . . Crane R.

Cross Currents . . . . Cross Currents

°Current Anthropology . . . . Curr. Anthropol.

Current History . . . . Curr. Hist.

Current Religious Thought . . . . Curr. Rel. Thought

°Current Sociology . . . . Curr. Sociol.

°Daedalus . . . . Daedalus

°Demography . . . . Demography

Diogenes . . . . Diogenes

Discovery . . . . Discovery

Diseases of the Nervous System . . . . Dis. Nerv. Syst.

Dublin Review . . . . Dublin R.

East Europe . . . . E. Europe

Eastern Anthropologist . . . . East. Anthropol.

Ecclesiastical Record . . . . Eccles. Rec.

Economic Development and Cultural Change . . . .
Econ. Develop. Cult. Change

Economic History Review . . . . Econ. Hist. R.

Ecumenical Review . . . . Ecumen. R.

Educational and Psychological Measurement . . . .
Educ. Psychol. Meas.

El Palacio . . . . El Palacio

Encounter . . . . Encounter

Eranos Jahrbuch . . . . Eranos Jahrbuch

Ethnohistory . . . . Ethnohistory

°Ethnology . . . . Ethnology

Ethnos . . . . Ethnos

Ethos . . . . Ethos

Eugenics Quarterly . . . . Eugenics Quart.

Eugenics Review . . . . Eugenics R.

European Journal of Sociology . . . . Eur. J. Sociol.

Existential Inquiry . . . . Exist. Inq.

Family . . . . Family

Family Life Coordinator . . . . Fam. Life Coord.

°Family Process . . . . Fam. Proc.

Far Eastern Economic Review (Journal of Asian Studies) . . . . Far East. Econ. R. (J. Asian Stud.)

Far Eastern Quarterly . . . . Far East. Quart.

Federal Probation . . . . Fed. Probation

Fellowship . . . . Fellowship

Folk Lore (London) . . . . Folk Lore (London)

Folklore (Carcassonne) . . . . Folklore

Folklore Studies . . . . Folkl. Stud.

Foreign Affairs . . . . For. Aff.

Foundations . . . . Foundations

France-Asie . . . . France-Asie

Free University Quarterly . . . . Free Univ. Quart.

Genetic Psychology Monographs . . . . Genet. Psychol. Monogr.

Genus . . . . Genus

Geographical Magazine . . . . Geogr. Mag.

Geographical Review . . . . Geogr. R.

George Washington Law Review . . . . George Washington Law R.

Geriatrics . . . . Geriatrics

Gerontologist . . . . Gerontologist

Greek Orthodox Theological Review . . . . Greek Orth. Theol. R.

The Hanover Forum . . . . Hanover Forum

Harvard Business Review . . . . Harvard Bus. R.

Harvard Education Review . . . . Harvard Educ. R.

Harvard Journal of Asiatic Studies . . . . Harvard J. Asiat. Stud.

Harvard Slavic Studies . . . . Harvard Slavic Stud.

Harvard Theological Journal . . . . Harvard Theol. J.

Harvard Theological Review . . . . Harvard Theol. R.

Hebrew Medical Journal . . . . Hebrew Med. J.

Hibbert Journal . . . . Hibbert J.

Hispanic American Historical Review . . . . Hisp. Amer. Hist. R.

Historica Judaica . . . . Hist. Judaica

Historical Studies of Australia and New Zealand . . . . Hist. Stud. Australia and New Zealand

°History of Education Quarterly . . . . Hist. Educ. Quart.

°History of Religions . . . . Hist. Rel.

°History and Theory . . . . Hist Theory

The Homiletic and Pastoral Review . . . . Homil. Pastoral R.

Hospital Progress . . . . Hosp. Progr.

Human Biology . . . . Hum. Biol.

Humanist . . . . Humanist

°Human Organization . . . . Human Org.

Human Problems in British Central Africa . . . . Human Prob. Brit. Centr. Afr.

°Human Relations . . . . Hum. Relat.

In the Dispersion . . . . In Dispersion

India Quarterly . . . . India Quart.

Indian Culture . . . . Ind. Cult.

Indian Folklore . . . . Ind. Folklore

Indian Historical Quarterly . . . . Ind. Hist. Quart.

Indian Journal of Adult Education . . . . Ind. J. Adult Educ.

Indian Journal of Economics . . . . Ind. J. Econ.

Indian Journal of Social Work . . . . Ind. J. Soc. Work

Indian Review . . . . Ind. R.

Indo-Asian Culture . . . . Indo-Asian Cult.

Indo. Iranica . . . . Indo-Iranica

Industrial and Labor Relations Review . . . . Indust. Lab. Relat. R.

Insight . . . . Insight

Inter-American Quarterly . . . . Inter-Amer. Quart.

International Affairs . . . . Int. Aff.

International Archives of Ethnography . . . . Int. Archiv. Ethnogr.

International and Comparative Law Quarterly . . . . Int. Comp. Law Quart.

International Journal . . . . Int. J.

International Journal of Clinical and Experimental Hypnosis . . . . Int. J. Clin. Exp. Hypnosis

International Journal of Comparative Sociology . . . . Int. J. Comp. Sociol.

International Journal of Ethics . . . . Int. J. Ethics

International Journal of Group Psychotherapy . . . . Int. J. Group Psychother.

International Journal of Opinion and Attitude Research . . . . Int. J. Opin. Att. Res.

International Journal of Psycho-Analysis . . . . Int. J. Psychoanal.

International Journal of Religious Education . . . . Int. J. Rel. Educ.

International Journal of Social Psychiatry . . . . Int. J. Soc. Psychiat.

International Migration Digest . . . . Int. Migration Digest

International Philosophical Quarterly . . . . Int. Philosoph. Quart.

International Review of Education . . . . Int. R. Educ.

International Review of Missions . . . . Int. R. Missions

International Review of Social History . . . . Int. R. Soc. Hist.

°International Social Science Bulletin(now, International Social Science Journal) . . . . Int. Soc. Sci. Bull. (Int. Soc. Sci. J.)

°International Social Work . . . . Int. Soc. Work

Internationale Spectator . . . . Int. Spec.

Interpretation . . . . Interpretation

Islamic Culture . . . . Islamic Cult.

Islamic Literature . . . . Islamic Lit.

Islamic Quarterly . . . . Islamic Quart.

Islamic Research . . . . Islamic Res.

Islamic Review . . . . Islamic R.

Islamic Studies (Karachi) . . . . Islamic Stud. (Karachi)

Japan Christian Quarterly . . . . Japan Christ. Quart.

Japan Quarterly . . . . Japan Quart.

Japanese Sociological Review . . . . Jap. Sociol. R.

Jewish Digest . . . . Jew. Digest

Jewish Education . . . . Jew. Educ.

°Jewish Journal of Sociology . . . . Jew. J. Sociol.

Jewish Quarterly Review . . . . Jew. Quart. R.

Jewish Social Service Quarterly . . . . Jew. Soc. Serv. Quart.

Jewish Social Studies . . . . Jew. Soc. Stud.

Jewish Social Work Forum . . . Jew. Soc. Work Forum

Journal of Abnormal and Social Psychology . . . . J. Abnorm. Soc. Psychol.

Journal of African Administration . . . . J. Afr. Adm.

Journal of African History . . . . J. Afr. Hist.

Journal of African Law . . . . J. Afr. Law

Journal of American Folklore . . . . J. Amer. Folklore

Journal of the American Medical Association . . . . J. Amer. Med. Assoc.

Journal of the American Oriental Society . . . . J. Amer. Orient. Society

°Journal of the American Psychoanalytic Association . . . . J. Amer. Psychoanal. Assoc.

Journal of the American Statistical Association . . . . J. Amer. Stat. Assoc.

Journal of the Anthropological Society of Bombay . . . . J. Anthropol. Society Bombay

°Journal of Applied Sociology (Sociology and Social Research) . . . . J. Appl. Sociol. (Sociol. Soc. Res.)

Journal of the Asiatic Society Letters . . . . J. Asiat. Society Letters

Journal of the Asiatic Society of Pakistan . . . . J. Asiat. Society Pakistan

Journal of Bible and Religion . . . . J. Bib. Rel.

Journal of Biblical Literature . . . . J. Bibl. Lit.

Journal of the Bihar Research Society . . . . J. Bihar Res. Society

Journal of Bihar University . . . . J. Bihar Univ.

Journal of Central European Affairs . . . J. Centr. Europ. Aff.

Journal of the Christian Medical Association of India . . . . J. Christ. Med. Assoc. India

A Journal of Church and State . . . . J. Church State

°Journal of Conflict Resolution . . . . J. Conf. Resol.

Journal of Consulting Psychology . . . . J. Consult. Psychol.

Journal of Counseling Psychology . . . . J. Counseling Psychol.

Journal of Criminal Law and Crimonology . . . . J. Crim. Law Crimin.

Journal of the Economic and Social History of the Orient . . . . J. Econ. Soc. Hist. Orient

Journal of Ecumenical Studies . . . . J. Ecumen. Stud.

°Journal of Educational Sociology (Sociology of Education) . . . . J. Educ. Sociol. (Sociol. Educ.)

Journal of Family Law . . . . J. Fam. Law

Journal of the Folklore Institute (Hague) . . . . J. Folklore Inst.

Journal of General Psychology . . . . J. Gen. Psychol.

Journal of Genetic Psychology . . . . J. Genet. Psychol.

Journal of the Gypsy Lore Society . . . . J. Gypsy Lore Society

°Journal of Health and Human Behavior . . . . J. Health Hum. Behavior

The Journal of Higher Education . . . . J. High. Educ.

Journal of the Historical Society of Nigeria . . . . J. Hist. Society Nigeria

Journal of the History of the Behavioral Sciences . . . . J. Hist. Behav. Sci.

Journal of the History of Ideas . . . . J. Hist. Ideas

°Journal of Human Relations . . . . J. Hum. Relat.

Journal of Indian History . . . . J. Ind. Hist.

Journal of Individual Psychology . . . . J. Individual Psychol.

°Journal of Intergroup Relations . . . . J. Integr. Relat.

Journal of Jewish Communal Service . . . . J. Jew. Commun. Serv.

Journal of Jewish Studies . . . . J. Jew. Stud.

Journal of Maharaja Sayajiro . . . . J. Maharaja Sayajiro

Journal of the Malayan Branch of the Royal Asiatic Society . . . . J. Malayan Branch Roy. Asiat. Society

Journal of Medical Education . . . . J. Med. Educ.

Journal of Mental Science . . . . J. Ment. Sci.

Journal of Modern African Studies . . . . J. Mod. Afr. Stud.

Journal of Modern History . . . . J. Mod. Hist.

Journal of Near Eastern Studies . . . . J. Near East. Stud.

Journal of Negro History . . . . J. Negro Hist.

Journal of Nervous and Mental Disease . . . . J. Nervous Ment. Disease

Journal of Obstetrics and Gynaecology of the British Empire . . . . J. Obstet. Gynaec. Brit. Emp.

Journal of Oriental Studies . . . . J. Orient. Stud.

Journal of the Pakistan Historical Society . . . . J. Pakistan Hist. Society

Journal of Parapsychology . . . . J. Parapsychol.

Journal of Pastoral Care . . . . J. Past. Care

°Journal of Personality and Social Psychology . . . . J. Person. Soc. Psychol.

°Journal of Philosophy, Psychology and the Scientific Method (Journal of Philosophy) . . . . J. Philos. Psychol. Scientific Meth. (J. Philos.)

Journal of Political Economy . . . . J. Polit. Econ.

°Journal of Politics . . . . J. Polit.

Journal of the Polynesian Society . . . . J. Polynes. Society

Journal of the Presbyterian Historical Society . . . . J. Presb. Hist. Society

Journal of Projective Techniques . . . . J. Proj. Tech.

Journal of Psychiatric Social Work . . . . J. Psychiat. Soc. Work

Journal of Psychological Studies . . . . J. Psychol. Stud.

Journal of Psychology . . . . J. Psychol.

Journal of Religion . . . . J. Rel.

°Journal of Religion and Health . . . . J. Rel. Health

Journal of Religious History . . . . J. Rel. Hist.

Journal of Roman Studies . . . . J. Roman Stud.

Journal of the Royal African Society . . . . J. Roy. African Society

Journal of the Royal Anthropological Institute of Great Britain and Ireland . . . . J. Roy. Anthropol Inst.

Journal of the Royal Asiatic Society of Great Britain and Ireland . . . . J. Roy. Asiat. Society

Journal of the Royal Asiatic Society of Ceylon . . . . J. Roy. Asiat. Society (Ceylon)

°Journal for the Scientific Study of Religion . . . . J. Sci. Stud. Rel.

Journal of the Siam Society . . . . J. Siam Society

°Journal of Social Issues . . . . J. Soc. Issues

°Journal of Social Psychology . . . . J. Soc. Psychol.

Journal of Social Research . . . . J. Soc. Res.

Journal of Southeast Asian History . . . . J. Southe. Asian Hist.

Journal of Southern History . . . . J. South. Hist.

Journal of Southwest Asian History . . . . J. Southw. Asian Hist.

Journal of Theological Studies . . . . J. Theol. Stud.

Journal of Theology . . . . J. Theol.

Journal of the University of Bombay . . . . J. Univ. Bombay

Journal of the University of Poona . . . . J. Univ. Poona

Journal of World History . . . . J. World Hist.

Journalism Quarterly . . . . Journalism Quart.

Judaism . . . . Judaism

Kroeber Anthropological Society Papers . . . . Kroeber Anthropol. Society Pap.

Kush, Journal of the London Antiquaries Service . . . . Kush

°Kyklos . . . . Kyklos

Latitude . . . . Latitude

Liberty . . . . Liberty

London Quarterly and Holborn Review . . . . London Quart. Holborn R.

London Quarterly Review . . . . Lond. Quart. R.

Lumen Vitae . . . . Lumen Vitae

Lutheran Quarterly . . . . Luth. Quart.

Lutheran Social Welfare Quarterly . . . . Luth. Soc. Welf. Quart.

Maha Bodhi . . . . Maha Bodhi

Main Currents in Modern Thought . . . . Main Curr. Mod. Thought

Man . . . . Man

Man in India . . . . Man India

Mankind . . . . Mankind

Marquette Law Review . . . . Marquette Law R.

°Marriage and Family Living (Journal of Marriage and the Family) . . . . Marr. Fam. Liv. (J. Marr. Fam.)

Maryland Medical Journal . . . . Maryland Med. J.

Meddelelser om Grønland . . . . Medd. Grønland

Medical Economics . . . . Med. Econ.

Medical History . . . . Med. Hist.

Medieval Studies . . . . Medieval Stud.

Medievalia et Humanistica . . . . Medievalia Humanistica

Memoirs de l'Institute Francais d'Afrique Noire . . . . Mem. Inst. Fran. Afr. Noire

Menninger Quarterly . . . . Menninger Quart.

Mennonite Quarterly Review . . . . Menn. Quart. R.

Mental Hygiene . . . . Ment. Hyg.

°Merrill-Palmer Quarterly . . . . Merr.-Palm. Quart.

Michigan Law Review . . . . Michigan Law R.

Middle American Research Institute Publications . . . . Mid. Amer. Res. Inst. Publ.

Middle East Journal . . . . Mid. East J.

Middle East Studies . . . . Mid. East Stud.

Middle Eastern Affairs . . . . Mid. East. Aff.

Middle Way . . . . Middle Way

Midstream . . . . Midstream

Midwest Folklore . . . . Midwest Folkl.

°Midwest Journal of Political Science . . . . Midwest J. Polit. Sci.

Migration News . . . . Migration News

Milbank Memorial Fund Quarterly . . . . Milbank Memor. Fund Quart.

Mississippi Valley Historical Review . . . . Miss. Valley Hist. R.

Modern Law Review . . . . Mod. Law R.

Modern Review . . . . Mod. R.

Monumenta Serica . . . . Monum. Serica

Muséon . . . . Muséon

Moslem World (Muslim World) . . . . Moslem World (Muslim World)

Nada (Salisbury, Southern Rhodesia) . . . . Nada

National and English Review . . . . Nat. Eng. R.

National Museum of Canada Bulletin . . . . Nat. Mus. Canada Bull.

Nebraska History . . . . Nebraska Hist.

Neue Zeitschrift für Missionswissenschaft . . . . Neue Z. Miss. Wiss.

New England Quarterly . . . . New England Quart.

New Lanka (Columbo) . . . . New Lanka

New Outlook . . . . New Outlook

New World Antiquity . . . . New World Antiq.

New York Folklore Quarterly . . . . New York Fokl. Quart.

New York State Museum Bulletin . . . . New York State Mus. Bull.

Nigeria . . . . Nigeria

Northwest Missouri State Teachers College Studies . . . . Northw. Missouri State Teachers Coll. Stud.

Notes on Islam . . . . Notes Islam

°Numen . . . . Numen

Nyasaland Journal . . . . Nyasaland J.

Oceania . . . . Oceania

Odú . . . . Odú

Oriens Extremus . . . . Oriens Extremus

Orissa Historical Research Journal . . . . Orissa His. Res. J.

Oxford Slavonic Papers . . . . Oxford Slav. Pap.

Pacific Affairs . . . . Pac. Aff.

°Pacific Sociological Review . . . . Pac. Sociol. R.

Pacific Spectator . . . . Pac. Spect.

Pakistan Horizon . . . . Pakistan Hor.

Palacio . . . . Palacio

Pan America . . . . Pan Amer.

The Papers of the Bibliographical Society of America . . . . Pap. Biblio. Society Amer.

Papers of the Michigan Academy of Science, Arts, and Letters . . . Pap. Michigan Acad. Sci. Arts Letters

Papers of the Peabody Museum of Archeology and Ethnology . . . . Pap. Peabody Mus. Archeol. Ethnol.

Parliamentary Affairs . . . . Parliamentary Aff.

Partisan Review . . . . Partisan R.

Past and Present . . . . Past Present

Pastoral Psychology . . . . Past. Psychol.

Personnel and Guidance Journal . . . . Personnel Guid. J.

Philippine Sociological Review . . . . Philippine Sociol. R.

Philosophy East and West . . . . Philos. East West

Philosophy and Phenomenological Research . . . Philosoph. Phenom. Res.

°Phylon . . . . Phylon

Plain View . . . . Plain View

Plains Anthropologist . . . . Plains Anthropol.

Polish Sociological Bulletin . . . . Polish Sociol. Bull.

Political Quarterly . . . . Polit. Quart.

Political Science . . . . Polit. Sci.

Political Science Quarterly . . . . Polit. Sci. Quart.

°Political Studies . . . . Polit. Stud.

Politico . . . . Politico

Popular Medicine . . . . Pop. Med.

Population Studies . . . . Popul. Stud.

Practical Anthropology . . . . Pract. Anthropol.

Présence Africaine (Dakar) . . . . Présence Afr. (Dakar)

Primitive Man . . . . Primitive Man

Proceedings of the American Academy for Jewish Research . . . . Proc. Amer. Acad. Jew. Res.

Proceedings of the American Philosophical Society . . . . Proc. Amer. Philos. Society

Proceedings of the International Congress of Americanists . . . . Proc. Int. Cong. Amer.

Proceedings of the West Virginia Academy of Science . . . . Proc. W. Va. Acad. Sci.

Psyche . . . . Psyche

Psychiatric Quarterly . . . . Psychiat. Quart.

Psychiatry . . . . Psychiatry

Psychoanalysis . . . . Psychoanalysis

Psychoanalysis and Psychoanalytic Review . . . . Psychoanal. Psychoanal. R.

Psychoanalytic Quarterly . . . . Psychoanal. Quart.

Psychoanalytic Review . . . . Psychoanal. R.

Psychoanalytic Study of the Child . . . . Psychoanal. Stud. Child

Psychologia . . . . Psychologia

Psychological Monographs . . . . Psychol. Monographs

Psychological News Letter, New York University . . . . Psychol. News.

Psychological Reports . . . . Psychol. Rep.

Public Law . . . . Pub. Law

°Public Opinion Quarterly . . . . Pub. Opin. Quart.

Publications of the American Sociological Society . . . . Publ. Amer. Sociol. Society

Quarterly Journal of the Mythic Society . . . . Quart. J. Mythic Society

Quarterly Journal of Studies on Alcohol . . . . Quart. J. Stud. Alcohol

Quarterly Review . . . . Quart. R.

Quarterly Review of Psychiatry and Neurology . . . . Quart. R. Psychiat. Neurol.

Queen's Quarterly . . . . Queen's Quart.

Race . . . . Race

Recherches Sociographiques . . . . Rech. Sociog.

Reformed Review . . . . Reformed R.

Rehabilitation Literature . . . . Rehab. Lit.

Religion East and West . . . . Rel. East West

Religion in Life . . . . Rel. Life

Religion in the Making . . . . Rel. Making

Religious Education . . . . Rel. Educ.

°Religious Studies . . . . Rel. Stud.

Reports of the Bureau of American Ethnology . . . . Rep. Bur. Amer. Ethnol.

Research Group in European Migration Problems . . . . Res. Group Europ. Mig. Prob.

Review and Expositor . . . . R. Exp.

Review of Politics . . . . R. Polit.

Review of Religion . . . . R. Rel.

Review for Religious . . . . R. for Rel.

°Review of Religious Research . . . . R. Rel. Res.

°Revue Francaise de Sociologie . . . . R. Franc. Sociol.

Revue Internationale D'Ethnopsychologie Normale et Pathologique . . . . R. Int. D'Ethnopsychol. Norm. Pathol.

Revue de Internationale Sociologie . . . . R. Int. Sociol.

The Rhodes-Livingstone Journal . . . . Rhodes-Livingstone J.

Rocznik Orientalistyczny . . . . Rocznik Oriental.

Royal African Society Journal (African Affairs) . . . . Roy. Afr. Society J. (Afr. Aff.)

Royal Central Asian Journal . . . . Roy. Cent. Asian J.

°Rural Sociology . . . . Rural Sociol.

Sarawak Museum Journal . . . . Sarawak Mus. J.

School Review . . . . School R.

School and Society . . . . School Society

Science . . . . Science

Scientific American . . . . Sci. Amer.

Science Monthly . . . . Sci. Monthly

Sierra Leone Bulletin of Religion . . . . Sierra Leone Bull. Rel.

Silliman Journal . . . . Silliman J.

Sino-Indian Studies . . . . Sino-Ind. Stud.

Slavonic Review . . . . Slavonic R.

Smithsonian Institute Annual Report . . . . Smithsonian Inst. Ann. Rep.

Smithsonian Institute Bureau of Ethnology . . . . Smithsonian Inst. Bur. Ethnol.

Social Action . . . . Soc. Action

Social Casework . . . . Soc. Casework

°Social Compass . . . . Soc. Compass

°Social and Economic Studies . . . . Soc. Econ. Stud.

°Social Forces . . . . Soc. Forces

Social Order . . . . Soc. Order

°Social Problems . . . . Soc. Problems

Social Process . . . . Soc. Process

Social Process in Hawaii . . . . Soc. Proc. Hawaii

°Social Research . . . . Soc. Res.

Social Science . . . . Soc. Sci.

°Social Work . . . . Soc. Work

°Sociologia Neerlandica . . . . Sociol. Neerlandica

Sociologia Religiosa . . . . Sociol. Religiosa

Sociologica . . . . Sociologica

Sociological Bulletin (Bombay) . . . . Sociol. Bull. (Bombay)

Sociological Inquiry . . . . Sociol. Inq.

°Sociological Quarterly . . . . Sociol. Quart.

°Sociological Review . . . . Sociol. R.

Sociologisch Bulletin . . . . Sociol. Bull.

Sociologus . . . . Sociologus

°Sociometry . . . . Sociometry

South African Journal of Science . . . . S. Afr. J. Sci.

South Atlantic Quarterly . . . . S. Atlantic Quart.

South East Asia Journal of Theology . . . . South E. Asia J. Theol.

South Pacific . . . . S. Pacific

Southern Folklore Quarterly . . . . S. Folklore Quart.

Southwestern Journal of Anthropology . . . . Southw. J. Anthropol.

Southwestern Journal of Theology . . . . Southw. J. Theol.

Southwestern Lore . . . . Southw. Lore

°The Southwestern Political and Social Science Quarterly (Southwestern Social Science Quarterly) . . . . Southw. Polit. Soc. Sci. Quart. (Southw. Soc. Sci. Quart.)

Soviet Anthropology and Archeology . . . . Soviet Anthropol. Archeol.

Soviet Sociology . . . . Soviet Sociol.

Soviet Studies . . . . Soviet Stud.

Speculum . . . . Speculum

Studia Islamica . . . . Stud. Islam.

Studia Patristica . . . . Studia Patristica

Studies . . . . Studies

Studies in Higher Education . . . . Stud. High. Educ.

Studies in Psychology and Psychiatry . . . . Stud. Psychol. Psychiat.

Studies in Romanticism . . . . Stud. Romanticism

Studium Generale . . . . Stud. Gen.

Sudan Notes . . . . Sudan Notes

Survey Graphic . . . . Survey Graphic

Swiss Review of World Affairs . . . . Swiss R. World Aff.

Tamil Culture . . . . Tamil Cult.

Tanganyika Notes Record . . . . Tanganyika Notes Rec.

Te Ao Hou . . . . Te Ao Hou

Tenri Journal of Religion . . . . Tenri J. Rel.

Thailand Today . . . . Thailand Today

Theology Today . . . . Theol. Today

Theory and Society . . . . Theory Society

Thomist . . . . Thomist

Thought . . . . Thought

Timehri . . . . Timehri

T'oung Pao . . . . T'oung Pao

Trans-Action . . . . Trans-Action

Transaction of New York Academy of Science . . . . Trans. New York Acad. Sci.

Tropical and Geographical Medicine . . . . Trop. Geog. Med.

Turku Institute of Sociology . . . . Turku Instit. Sociol.

Twentieth Century . . . . Twent. Cent.

Uganda Journal . . . . Uganda J.

Ukrainian Quarterly . . . . Ukrainian Q.

Union Seminary Quarterly Review . . . . Union Sem. Quart. R.

United Asia . . . . United Asia

University of California Publications in American Archaeology and Ethnology . . . . Univ. Calif. Public. Amer. Archaeol. Ethnol.

University of Colorado Studies, Series in Anthropology . . . . Univ. Colorado Stud., Series Anthropol.

Vanyajati . . . . Vanyajati

Virginia Quarterly Review . . . . Virginia Quart. R.

Visva-Bharati Quarterly . . . . Visva-Bharati Quart.

Welt des Islams . . . . Welt Islams

West African Review . . . . West Afr. R.

°Western Political Quarterly . . . . West. Polit. Quart.

Western Reserve Law Review . . . . West. Reserve Law R.

World Affairs Quarterly . . . . World Aff. Quart.

World Dominion . . . . World Domin.

World Politics . . . . World Polit.

World Today . . . . World Today

Yale Divinity News . . . . Yale Div. News

Yale Review . . . . Yale R.

Yale University Publications in Anthropology . . . . Yale Univ. Pub. Anthropol.

Yearbook of World Affairs . . . . Yearbook World Aff.

Yivo Annual of Jewish Social Science . . . . Yivo Ann. Jew. Soc. Sci.

Zeitschrift Für Ethnologie . . . . Z. Ethnol.

Index

236

241

Meliton, M., 117
Meller, N., 140
Menczer, B., (ed.), 60
Mendelsohn, E., 75
Mendelsohn, I. (ed.), 41
Mendelson, E. M., 30, 60, 67
Menes, A., 182
Meng, H., 166
Menges, R. J. and Dittes, J. E., 208
Mental Health Aspects . . . , 162
Merkelbach, R., 97
Merriam, A. P. and D'Azevedo, W. L., 96
Merrill, G., 49
Merton, R. K., 3
Mervin, W. C. and Jones, F. P. (eds.), 139
Merzbach, A., 78
Messenger, J., 179
Messenger, J. C., Jr., 80, 119, 151
Messing, S. D., 129
Methodist Periodical Index, 208
Metraux, A., 37(2), 151, 154, 171, 197
Metzger, C. H., 134
Meuser, F. W., 44
Meyendorff J., 22
Meyer, A. E., 8
Meyer, C. S., 156
Meyer, D., 60
Meyer, P., 67(3)
Meyerowitz, E. L. R., 69
Michael, F., 71
Michaelson, R., 101
Michalson, C. (ed.), 5
Michaud, P., 147
Michelet, J., 179
Michonneau, G., 151
Middlemore, M., 141
Middleton, J., 34(3), 179
Middleton, R. and Putney, S., 80
Middleton, W. C., 171
Middleton, W. C. and Fay, P. J., 176
Midgley, L. C., 80
Miegge, M., 117
Mihanovich, C. S., 107
Mihanovich, C. S. and Janson E. W., 178
Millard, W. J., 97
Miller, A. W., 151
Miller, B. D., 162
Miller, D. E., 203
Miller, D. H., 55
Miller, H. M., 113
Miller, J. Q., 117
Miller, K., 89, 92
Miller, N., 158
Miller, P., 44
Miller, P. and Johnson, T. H. (eds.), 44
Miller, P., *et al.*, 133
Miller, R. C. (ed.), 143
Miller, R. J., 76, 143
Miller, R. M., 76, 110, 113
Miller, R. R., 110
Miller, W. L., 60(2)
Millet, J. H., 147
Millican, C. N., 76
Millman, H , 57
Millroth, B., 34
Mills, L. O., 145
Minen, J. R., 141

Minihan, J., 197
Mintz, J. S., 76
Mintz, S. W. and Wolf, E. R., 78
Mischel, F., 127, 151
Mischel, W. and Mischel, F., 104
Misha, V., 76
Misiak, H., 129
Misiak, H. and Stuadt, V. M., 8
Misra, S. C., 51
Mission and Service, 136
Mitchell, F. W., 101
Mitchell, R. C., 154
Mitchell, W. E., 82
Mitra, S. K., 30
Miyakawa, T. S., 147
Mizami, K. A., 60
Mizzi, F. P., 67
Moberg, D. O., 57, 104, 111, 140, 187, 197, 200
Mode, P. G., 117
Modern Environment and Religion, 156
Moehlman, C. H., 71
Moellering, R. L., 134
Mohan, R. P. (ed.), 76
Mohler, M., 151
Moir, J. S., 67
Mol, J. J., 107, 133
Mollat, G., 46
Molnar, A., 18
Moloney, J. C., 104, 129
Momigliano, A. (ed.), 123
Monahan, T. R. and Kephart, W. M., 84
Monet, D., 24
Monier-Williams, M., 25
Monro, D. H., 191
Monroe, P., 76
Monson, C. H., Jr. (ed.), 204
Montgomery, W. W., 27
Moody, J. N., 181
Moody, J. N. (ed.), 67
Moody, J. N., *et al.* (eds.), 46
Moody, J. N. and Lawler, J. G. (eds.), 174
Mooney, J., 55
Moore, C. A., 5
Moore, D. H., 197
Moore, E. A., 73
Moore, E. H. and Mammer, C., 158
Moore, O. K., 195
Moore, S., 104
Moore, T. V., 129
Moos, F., 151
Mootsi, L. and Mkele, N., 123
Moraczewski, A., 3
Moraes, G. M., 42
Morall, J. B., 61
Moray, V. E., 82
More, P. and Cross, F. L., 44
Moreau, J. L., 97
Moreton, F. E., 176
Morgan, B., 76
Morgan, E. S., 174
Morgan, K. W. (ed.), 25, 27, 52
Morgenstern, J., 191
Morner, M., 61
Morris, J. F., 80
Morris, J. S., 69
Morris, R. E., 151
Morris, W. D., 147

Redfield, R., 151
Reed, H A., 68, 151(2)
Reese, T. R., 45
Regamey, C., 200
Reggs, M. D., 83
Reich, N., 76
Reichard, G. A., 35, 54
Reichelt, G. M., 115
Reid, I. DeA., 154
Reifenberg, A., 96
Reik, T., 49(2), 105, 169, 192(2)
Reimers, D. M., 133
Reinders, R. C., 133
Reines, C. W., 94, 178
Reis, R. H. and Hoene, R., 83
Reischaver, A. R., 136
Reiser, O. L. and Davies B., 3
Reisman, L., 89
Reiss, P. J., 86
Religion and the Intellectuals . . . , 186
The Religions, Conference, 39
Religious Organizations Engaged . . . , 8
Religious Psychology, Thought . . . , 197
Renou, L. (ed.), 25
Repke, A., 10
Report of the Committee . . . , 10
Rescher, N., 5
Resnik, R. B., 86
Retting, S. and Pasamanick, B., 80(2)
Reumann, J., 41
Reuss, C., 83, 197
Reyburn, W. D., 83, 97, 120, 192
Reynoldine, M. (ed.), 21
Reynolds, B., 38
Reynolds, B. C., 129
Reynolds, R., 135
Rhodes, A. L., 178
Rhodes, H. T. F., 141
Riad, M., 69
Ribeiro, R., 162
Rice, C. S. and Steinmetz, R. C., 19
Rice, D. T., 96
Rice, M. H., 178
Rich, M., 118
Richards, A. I. (ed.), 69
Richards, G. W., 47
Richardson, A., 3
Richardson, H. E., 30(2)
Richardson, W. J. (ed.), 136
Richmond, W. E., 208
Rieff, P., 203(2)
Riesman, D., 188
Rieterman, C., 131
Riga, P. J., 70
Rightmyer, N. W., 45
Riley, C. L. and Hogood, J., 151
Riley, H. J., 8
Riley, O. L., 184
Rim, Y. and Kurwell, Z. E., 178
Ring, G. C., 15
Ringer, B. B. and Glock, C. Y., 178
Riordan, J., 35
Rischin, M., 89
Rivkin, E., 115
Robb, J. H., 122
Robbins, R., 151
Robbins, R. H., 208

Robbins, W. J., 54
Roberts, B. H. and Myers, J. K., 129
Roberts, D. E., 8
Roberts, H. L., 61
Roberts, H. W., 162, 166
Roberts, R. G., 162
Roberts, T. E., 19
Robertson, A. 188
Robertson, D. B., 61
Robertson, H. M., 203
Robinson, D. F., 138
Robinson, G. K., 192
Robinson, J. and Friedman, P., 49
Robinson, M. E., 162
Robinson, M. P., 192
Robiinson, M. S. and Wilson K., 208
Robinson, S. B., 94
Rocher, L. and Rocher, R., 50
Rochlin, S. A., 51
Rock, J. F., 37
Rodehaver, M. and Smith, L. M., 159
Rodinson, M., 197
Roediger, V. M., 54
Roff, W. R., 51
Roger, L. and Hollingshead A., 130
Rogers, A. K., 5
Roggendorf, J., 15
Rogier, A., *et al.* (eds.), 47
Roheim, G., 41, 42, 54, 130, 195
Rohner, K., 162
Rokeach, M., 154, 178(3)
Rolo, C. (ed.), 8
Romano, O. I. V., 127
Rommetveit, R., 107
Rooney, E., 84
Root, R., 133
Rose, A. M., 73
Rose, B. W., 200
Rose, E., 56
Rose, P. I., 115
Rose, R., 171
Rosen, B. C., 140
Rosenberg, L., 87
Rosenberg, M., 127
Rosenberg, S. E., 89
Rosenbloom, J. R., 127
Rosenblum, A. L., 178
Rosenfeld, H., 83
Rosenmayr, L., 197
Rosenthal, C. S., 112
Rosenthal, E., 131, 182
Rosenthal, E. I., 61(2), 68
Rosenthal, F., 27, 51(2), 118
Rosenthal, H. M., 58
Rosenthal, T. and Siegel, B. J., 2
Rosenstiel, A., 10
Rosenwaike, I., 87, 89
Roshwald, M., 68
Rosmarin, T. W., 102
Ross, A., 35, 89
Ross, E., 147
Ross, E. A., 145
Ross, E. J., 10(2), 178, 197(2)
Ross, F. H., 115, 200
Ross, M. G., 171
Ross, N., 8
Ross, N. W.(ed.), 30

Whitley, C. F., 155
Whitley, O. R., 152, 188
Whitlock, G. E., 167
Whitman, L. B., 198
Whittaker, M. L., 130
Whitten, N. E., 179
Wiarda, H. J., 69
Wichmann, A. A., 77, 132
Wickham, E. R., 90
Widdrington, P. E. T., 48
Widengren, G., 36, 49
Wieder, N., 116
Wieman, H. N., 135
Wienpahl, P., 30
Wiesinger, R., 78
Wilber, D. N., 28
Wilbur, E. M., 31, 56
Wild, J., 5
Wilder, A. N., 155, 175
Wilder, E. W., 127(2)
Wile, I. S., 9
Wilhelm, H., 69
Wilkowski, S., 69
Wilks, I., 95
Willems, E., 182
Willetts, R. F., 54
Williams, B. C., 5
Williams, C. R., 152
Williams, C. W. S., 56
Williams, E., 147
Williams, F. E., 56
Williams, G. H., 45, 101
Williams, J. A. (ed.), 28
Williams, J. P., 172, 193, 198, 200
Williams, J. R., 5
Williams, M., 21
Willaims, M. J., 21, 58, 193
Williams, M. O., Jr., 163
Williams, P. (ed.), 31
Williams, R. H. B., 54
Williams R. M., Jr., 58, 120
Williams, R. M., Jr., et al., 133
Williams, T. J. and Campbell, A. W., 163
Williamson, H. A., 138
Williamson, H. R., 139
Williamson, R. deV., 179
Williamson, S. G. and Dickson, K. A. (eds.), 147
Willms, A. M., 19
Willner, A. R. and Willner, D., 155
Willner, D. and Kohls, M., 49
Willoughby, R. R., 172
Wills, G., 62
Wilson, B. R., 19, 200
Wilson, C. L., 168
Wilson, C. R. and Brown, J. E., 167
Wilson, D. R., 193
Wilson, E., 24, 118
Wilson, F. G., 179
Wilson, G. R., 177
Wilson, H. H., 25
Wilson, J. B., 31
Wilson, M., 70
Wilson, M. H., 38, 147
Wilson, N. H., 69
Wilson, R. C., 113
Wilson, W. C., 179
Wilson, W. D., 155

Wilson, W. E., 45
Wilson, W. H., 152
Winchell, C. M., 208
Windell, G. G., 62
Winder, R. B., 69
Wing-Sou Lou, D., 54
Winkeler, H., 181
Winnett, A. R., 84
Winsberg, M. D., 24
Winslow, C E. A., 179
Winstedt, R. O., 159
Winter, G., 81, 92(2), 188
Wirth, L., 90
Wise, C. A., 163(2)
Wise, C. A. (ed.), 163
Wise, J. E., 100
Wishlade, R. L., 19
Witherington, H. C., 188
Withey, R. A., Jr., 101
Wittfogel, K. and Goldfrank, E. S., 54
Wiznitzer, A., 49
Wolch, C., 165
Wolcott, L., 163
Wolf, A. J., 9
Wolf, C. U., 28
Wolf, E. R., 147, 184, 200
Wolff, K. H., 172
Wolff, K. H. (ed.), 202
Wolff, M. S., 105
Wolin, S. S., 62(2), 69
Wolseley, R. E., 97
Wolters, G., 91
Wonderly, W. L., 138, 152
Wonderly, W. L. and Nida, E. A., 97, 136
Wood, E., 109, 208
Wood, H. G., 157, 204
Wood, J. E., et al., 72
Wood, L. F., 83
Wood, R. W., 107
Woodard, W. P., 69, 72
Woodhouse, A. S. P., 62(2)
Woodhouse, A. S. P. (ed.), 62
Woodruff, D., 69
Woods, F. J., 2, 11
Woodward, L. H and Kluge, W., 9
Woolcott, P., Jr., 193
Woolston, H. B., 125
Workman, H. B., 124
World Council of Churches, 118, 198
World of Islam, 28
Worsley, P. M., 36(2), 185
Worthy, W., 28
Wright, A. F., 30, 52
Wright, A. F. (ed.), 36
Wright, C., 56
Wright, E. D., 130
Wright, J. C., 130
Wright, L. B., 97
Wright, R. R., Jr., 12
Wrigley, C. C., 148
Wrijhof, P. H., 198
Wrong, D. H., 122
Wu, C. C., 83
Wu-Chi, L., 36
Wulff, I., 159
Wyckoff, D. C., 100
Wylie, T., 52